2018/19

THE GUIDE TO

EDUCATIONAL GRANTS

15th edition

Rachel Cain & Ian Pembridge

Additional research by Mairéad Bailie,
Denise Lillya, María Alejandra Puerta Reyes,
Jennifer Reynolds & Judith Turner

directory of social change

Published by the Directory of Social Change (Registered Charity no. 800517 in England and Wales)

Head office: Resource For London, 352 Holloway Road, London N7 6PA

Northern office: Suite 103, 1 Old Hall Street, Liverpool L3 9HG

Tel: 020 7697 4200

Visit www.dsc.org.uk to find out more about our books, subscription funding websites and training events. You can also sign up for e-newsletters so that you're always the first to hear about what's new.

The publisher welcomes suggestions and comments that will help to inform and improve future versions of this and all of our titles. Please give us your feedback by emailing publications@dsc.org.uk.

It should be understood that this publication is intended for guidance only and is not a substitute for professional or legal advice. No responsibility for loss occasioned as a result of any person acting or refraining from acting can be accepted by the authors or publisher.

First published 1988
Second edition 1992
Third edition 1994
Fourth edition 1996
Fifth edition 1998
Sixth edition 2000
Seventh edition 2002
Eighth edition 2004
Ninth edition 2006
Tenth edition 2009
Eleventh edition 2011
Twelfth edition 2013
Thirteenth edition 2014
Fourteenth edition 2016
Fifteenth edition 2018

ISBN 978–1-78482–044-2

British Library Cataloguing in Publication Data
A catalogue record for this book is available from the British Library

Cover and text design by Kate Griffith
Typeset by Marlinzo Services, Frome
Printed and bound by Page Bros, Norwich

Contents

Foreword

Previous forewords of this book have reflected upon themes such as the changing nature of education policy and increased costs for students. Despite major progress, it is still these issues that affect education today. In 2018, we will see the creation of a new Office for Students (OfS) to replace the existing funding body. Furthermore, as Brexit negotiations progress, the implications for students will emerge more clearly. Despite an undergraduate tuition fee freeze in 2018, there is little certainty over the toxic fee debate, which continues to mask the bigger access issue – the ever-increasing cost of living.

Nationwide, the application cycle for 2018 has seen significant decline in the number of undergraduate university applicants, with mature students and carers being affected the most. The lack of appropriate funding and flexible courses are among the defining factors behind this change. Likewise, despite the introduction of a postgraduate loan to relieve the burden of fees, covering living costs remains challenging. As job prospects appear increasingly uncertain and loan repayment terms for tuition fees are set significantly above market rates, many now question the value of a degree.

As the job market changes, however, the importance of education has never been so great. Despite challenges, the past decade has seen a considerable increase in the number of students accessing higher education from disadvantaged backgrounds in particular. For students from all backgrounds, universities do offer enormous support with budgeting, study skills and wellbeing advice. More importantly, and as *The Guide to Educational Grants* shows, a significant amount of funding is readily available. Whether you are an adviser or prospective student, this accessible and comprehensive book is exactly what you need to guide you through the available support to ensure you can access the best possible funding. For their recognition of education as a public good across society, the generosity of the donors must be commended; as must the work of DSC for so effectively collating grant information for this book.

Alexander Tayler, General Secretary, University of Manchester Students' Union

Introduction

Note: All annual reports and accounts are available on the Charity Commission for England and Wales website.

Welcome to the fifteenth edition of *The Guide to Educational Grants*. The main objective of this guide is to provide information on grant-making charities which offer financial support for individuals who are in education or training. This edition contains over 1,100 grant-making charities with a total of £55.9 million available in grants to individuals for educational purposes, and over 100 grant-makers new to this edition. Many of the organisations included in this guide also give grants to individuals in need for welfare purposes. These are detailed further in the guide's sister publication *The Guide to Grants for Individuals in Need*, also published in 2018 by the Directory of Social Change (DSC).

Further and vocational education

During 2017, government-allocated funding for further education remained relatively stable. The November budget announced that no further cuts would be made – colleges would receive extra funding in preparation for T-levels, and schools and colleges would enjoy £600 per student opting to study A-level maths (HM Treasury, 2017). However, students choosing to take an apprenticeship route are finding their education at risk, due to funding cuts in other sectors – including a cut of up to 89% for schemes supporting small businesses offering apprenticeships (Makoff, 2017). Complex restrictions, difficulty accessing funds and a lack of flexibility in spending, have led to employers being put off creating apprenticeship posts. This means that there has been a significant drop (59%) in young people taking up apprenticeships from April to July 2017 (Butler, 2017).

Furthermore, those choosing to take up an apprenticeship are continuing to face financial hardship during their studies, with two in five apprentices spending more money than they earn on the cost of completing their apprenticeship, on top of an 8% gap in apprentice wages between men and women (Bulman, 2017; Young Women's Trust, 2016). In addition to this, numbers of adult learners in further education have been decreasing by an average of 11% per year (Department for Education, 2017). A lack of incentive for employers to provide apprenticeships, potential learners being priced out of education and a decline in adult learners, are all having a huge impact on the country's skills market (City and Guilds, N.D.), something that could get worse after Brexit. Despite apprenticeships being a major government policy since the coalition government (2010 to 2015), there is a long way to go in terms of policy reform and funding allocation before apprenticeships can be marketed as a serious alternative to university, and something that could successfully fill the skills gap.

Higher education

In December 2017, UCAS revealed that 13.8% of disadvantaged 18-year-olds entered higher education, an increase of 0.2% from the previous year (UCAS, 2017).

However, entries from more advantaged groups also rose to 53.1%, leaving the ratio between the two groups largely unchanged. Similarly, they found that the rate of university entries for pupils who receive free school meals was 17% – compared to 34% admissions of students who do not (Adams, 2017). These statistics show a large and continuing gap in university entry rates between advantaged and disadvantaged groups in what should be an area of universal and equal opportunity. In October 2017, in a move to sway more young people from disadvantaged backgrounds into higher education, the government announced they would raise the repayment threshold for university fees to those earning a minimum of £25,000 (Belfield et al., 2017). However, this is little incentive to students from low-income backgrounds who, as of 2016, have had to accrue more debt because of the abolition of maintenance grants – which were replaced by more loans (BBC, 2016). There has also been an assault on health and medical courses such as physiotherapy and nursing, with the decision to axe NHS bursaries, meaning potential applicants must fund their study using the student loans system (Department of Health, 2017). This reform is putting many potential students off studying these vital courses – UCAS figures show that nursing applications declined by 23% compared to last year (UCAS, 2017). These figures will have a knock-on effect and will greatly harm the health profession, one that is likely to see a further fall in workers post-Brexit.

Refugees

While conducting our research for the guide we noted several charities commenting on the lack of education provision for refugees. According to research by Refugee Action (2017) government funding for English for Speakers of Other Languages (ESOL) courses has fallen from around £212 million in 2008/09 to £95 million in 2015. A recent poll by the same organisation which surveyed 71 ESOL providers showed that 45% of people are waiting at least six months or more to start English lessons. The Ruth Hayman Trust offers this synopsis of the situation in its 2015/16 annual report:

'For only a relatively short time in England were ESOL classes provided under the same conditions as adult literacy and numeracy so that learners did not have to pay fees. The Trust has also had to take into account the very different policies towards ESOL provision across the four nations of the UK, with no fees being charged in Scotland and some learners in England being asked for up to £350 for a term's course. As a result of the recent reduction in Treasury funding for ESOL the Trust is being asked to support learners in provision run by voluntary schemes – a reversion to what we did in earlier decades.

UK Governments have also at times made special arrangements for specific groups of learners. Currently there is a commitment to accepting 20,000 refugees from Syria by 2020 and this is to be accompanied by a £10 million funding package to boost English tuition. Whilst this has been welcomed, the programme again underestimates the time needed to acquire the language.

More importantly, it ignores the many other groups who need support. Last year Syrians were by no means the largest group of refugees the Trust supported and our beneficiaries came from 44 countries.'

Ruth Hayman Trust, 2016

Brexit

After the vote to leave the EU in June 2016 there was a lot of uncertainty regarding the status of EU students studying in the UK as well as EU-funded programmes such as Erasmus+ and Horizon 2020. However, a clearer picture is now developing of what will happen in the period before the UK leaves the EU in March 2019. In a statement in April 2017 Jo Johnson, Minister of State for Universities, Science, Research and Innovation confirmed that EU students will continue to remain eligible for undergraduate, master's, postgraduate and advanced learner financial support in the academic year 2018 to 2019. EU nationals will also remain eligible to apply for Research Council PhD studentships at UK institutions for 2018 to 2019 to help cover costs for the duration of their study.

Erasmus+ offers people from education, sports, training and youth organisations opportunities to study, work, volunteer, teach and train abroad. It started life as Erasmus in 1987 and in the 30 years it has been running, an estimated 600,000 people from the UK have taken part (Erasmus, 2018). The prime minister has stated that the UK will continue participation in the Erasmus+ programme up until the end of the current budget plan in 2020 (BBC, 2017).

The aim of the Horizon 2020 programme is to improve Europe's competitiveness in research and innovation. Since the programme started in 2014, the UK has been the second most successful country in terms of funding received and the number of projects it has participated in (Mason, 2017). The UK government states on its website (2017):

'UK government has committed to underwriting payment of Horizon 2020 awards while the UK remains a member of the EU. It will underwrite payment of such awards, even when specific projects continue beyond the UK's departure from the EU. This includes awards where the application is submitted before the exit and is subsequently approved after exit.'

The fate of these funding programmes and EU students' access to UK educational institutions after 2018/19 is less clear and will likely depend on the outcome of the UK's wider negotiations with the EU.

These examples show the very complex and changing environment that grant-makers supporting individuals have to work in. Challenges such as government cuts and changes in policy remain, but new ones such as refugee education and Brexit have emerged. The way grant-makers have adapted to these challenges is one of the issues explored in further detail in the additional analysis available to download from the DSC website.

INTRODUCTION

Acknowledgements

We would like to offer a special thank you to Alexander Tayler for his contribution to this introduction.

We are extremely grateful to the many charity trustees, staff and volunteers who have provided up-to-date details for inclusion in this guide, and others who have helped. To name them all individually would be impossible.

How to give feedback to us

The research for this guide was undertaken as carefully and thoroughly as we were able, but there will still be relevant charities that we have missed and some of the information may be incomplete or will become out of date. If you come across omissions or mistakes in this guide please let us know by emailing DSC's Research Team (research@dsc.org.uk) so that we can rectify them for the future.

References

Adams, R., 'Poorest school-leavers half as likely to attend university as their peers' [web article], The Guardian, www.theguardian.com/education/2017/dec/14/poorest-school-leavers-half-as-likely-to-attend-university-as-their-peers, 14 December 2017, accessed December 2017.

BBC, 'Student grants replaced by loans' [web article], BBC, www.bbc.co.uk/news/education-36940172, 1 August 2016, accessed December 2017.

BBC, 'Brexit: UK in Erasmus student scheme until at least 2020' [web article], BBC, www.bbc.co.uk/news/uk-politics-42360849, 14 December 2017, accessed January 2018.

Belfield, C., Britton, J., and van der Erve, L., *Higher Education finance reform: raising the repayment threshold to £25,000 and freezing the fee cap at £9,250* [PDF], The Institute of Fiscal Studies, 2017, www.ifs.org.uk/uploads/publications/bns/BN217.pdf, accessed December 2017.

Bulman, M., 'Two in five apprentices spending more to complete apprenticeship than they earn, finds study' [web article], The Independent, www.independent.co.uk/news/uk/home-news/apprentices-two-in-five-spending-more-complete-apprenticeship-earn-young-womens-trust-a8032096.html, 2 November 2017, accessed December 2017.

Butler, S., 'Calls for change to apprenticeships after numbers fall by 59%' [web article], The Guardian, www.theguardian.com/education/2017/nov/23/rethink-apprenticeship-scheme-employers-and-unions-urge, 23 November 2017, accessed December 2017.

City and Guilds, 'Skill Shortage Nation' [web page], City and Guilds, 2017, www.cityandguilds.com/skills-shortage-nation, accessed December 2017.

Department for Education, *Further Education and Skills in England March 2017* [PDF], UK Government, June 2017 revision, www.gov.uk/government/uploads/system/uploads/attachment_data/file/618924/SFR13–2017-June-revision.pdf, accessed December 2017.

Department of Health, 'NHS Bursary Reform' [web page], UK Government, 2017, www.gov.uk/government/publications/nhs-bursary-reform/nhs-bursary-reform, accessed December 2017.

Erasmus, '30 Years of Erasmus+' [web page], Erasmus+, www.erasmusplus.org.uk/30-years-of-erasmus, accessed December 2017.

Gov.uk, 'Government confirms funding for EU students for 2018 to 2019' [press release], UK Government, www.gov.uk/government/news/government-confirms-funding-for-eu-students-for-2018-to-2019, 21 April 2017, accessed January 2018.

HM Treasury, *Autumn Budget 2017* [PDF], UK Government, 22 November 2017, www.gov.uk/government/uploads/system/uploads/attachment_data/file/661480/autumn_budget_2017_web.pdf, accessed December 2017.

Makoff, A., 'Funding cuts put two-thirds of apprenticeships at risk' [web article], People Management, www.peoplemanagement.co.uk/news/articles/funding-cuts-put-two-thirds-apprenticeships-at-risk, 2 May 2017, accessed December 2017.

Mason, P., 'Horizon 2020: universities need clarity on UK participation in EU research and innovation programme' [web article], Universities UK, www.universitiesuk.ac.uk/blog/Pages/Horizon-2020-universities-need-clarity-on-UK-participation-in-EU-research-and-innovation-programm.aspx, 7 November 2017, accessed January 2018.

Refugee Action, 'New research: English language provision not 'fit for purpose' as refugees wait up to three years to start lessons' [press release], Refugee Action, www.refugee-action.org.uk/6179–2/, 6 October 2017, accessed January 2018.

Ruth Hayman Trust, *The Ruth Hayman Trust Annual Report 2015–16* [PDF], Ruth Hayman Trust, 2017, www.ruthhaymantrust.org.uk/s/Ruth-Hayman-Trust-Annual-Report-2015–16.pdf, p. 6, accessed December 2017.

UCAS, *Deadline Applicant Statistics: January* [PDF], UCAS, 2017, www.ucas.com/file/92646/download?token=FFC9R2rP, accessed December 2017.

UCAS, 'English and Scottish 18 year olds from disadvantaged backgrounds more likely to enter higher education than ever before' [web article], UCAS, www.ucas.com/corporate/news-and-key-documents/news/english-and-scottish-18-year-olds-disadvantaged-backgrounds-more-likely-enter-higher-education-ever, 14 December 2017, accessed December 2017.

Young Women's Trust, *Making apprenticeships work for young women* [PDF], Young Women's Trust, www.youngwomenstrust.org/assets/0000/2906/Making_Apprenticeships_Work_for_Young_Women.pdf, 2016, accessed December 2017.

Grant-making charities: their processes and effectiveness

The Directory of Social Change has a vision of an independent voluntary sector at the heart of social change. Based upon this vision and our experience of researching this publication for over 25 years, we would like to suggest some ways in which charities that give grants to individuals could seek to encourage greater fairness and more effective practices in grant-making. We suggest that they do the following:

- Seek to collaborate with others that have similar objectives. By sharing knowledge and best practice, organisations can contribute towards improving the wider grant-making landscape.
- Do as much as possible to decrease the amount of ineligible applications they receive. This is a joint responsibility with applicants, who should make sure that they read criteria carefully and should not apply to charities for funding for which they are not eligible. However, grant-makers should facilitate this by ensuring that eligibility criteria and applications guidelines are transparent and easily available. Our research suggests that a growing number of charities choose to move towards electronic application forms and also sometimes consider a two-stage application process. Many willingly offer help and guidance with filling in the application form.
- Ensure, where they are local, that they are very well known within their area of benefit by writing to local Citizens Advice, local authorities, schools and other educational establishments and community centres. As made clear by the comments of the charity trustees during our research, an effective measure of raising the organisation's profile remains word of mouth, particularly with smaller charities. Ideally charities should aim to ensure that needs can be met as rapidly as possible, for example by empowering the clerk or a small number of trustees to make small emergency grants. If trustees can only meet twice a year to consider applications these should cover the peak times: in May to June when people are running out of money at the end of the academic year, or looking ahead to funding courses beginning in September; and November to December when people who have started their courses have a much clearer picture of how much money they need.
- Form clear policies on who they can support and what they can provide, targeting those most in need. A small number of charities in this guide are restricted to making grants to inhabitants of relatively wealthy areas and appear to have great difficulty finding individuals in need of financial support. In these cases, it would be appropriate for the trustees of these charities to consider applying to the Charity Commission for amendments to their governing document. The majority, however, receive a high volume of applications and cannot support all of them.

About this guide

What charities are included?

We have included in this guide grant-making charities that give or have the potential to give:

- At least £500 a year in educational grants (most give considerably more)
- Grants based upon need rather than academic performance
- Funding for levels of education from primary school to first degree level: there may be some that will also support pre-school education or postgraduate degrees ('education' is defined in its loosest sense, and therefore includes all types of vocational education and training, extra-curricular activities and personal or professional development)
- Grants to students of more than one educational establishment

We have not included those that (except where they appear to be particularly relevant to people in need):

- Give grants that are solely for postgraduate study
- Provide awards or scholarships for academic excellence

About 30% of the charities in this guide also give grants to individuals in need for the relief of poverty and hardship. These, along with many others, are included in the guide's sister publication *The Guide to Grants for Individuals in Need*. The charities in this guide often aditionally support educational charities, youth organisations, community groups and educational establishments. However, the information given relates only to that which is relevant for individuals. *The Directory of Grant Making Trusts*, also published by DSC, contains funding sources for organisations.

How charities are ordered

The grant-making charities in this guide are listed in five sections. The majority of grant-makers featured in the first four sections operate nationally, with criteria defined by something other than the geographical area of the applicant, although there are a few exceptions.

The five sections are:

- Charities by need (for example, general educational needs, further and higher education, illness and disability, independent and boarding schools)
- Subjects
- Occupation or parent's occupation
- Livery companies, orders and membership organisations
- Local charities (grant-makers which support individuals living in specific geographical areas – see page 127 for details about how to use this section)

What are grants given for?

Generally the charities in this guide offer one-off grants for a specific purpose or recurrent support for the duration of the individual's course or project. In some instances support may be given for a specific number of years or, in some rare instances, throughout the individual's education. The majority of the support given is intended to be supplementary and applicants will often need to secure money from different sources. However, small costs of necessities or sometimes even bigger projects may be covered in full. A handful of the grant-makers listed may offer low-interest or interest-free loans as well.

Grant-makers in this guide can give supplementary help with small grants for:

▶ Uniforms and other school clothing, sport kits, specialist outfits for professionals and clothes for a job interview
▶ Books, training materials, equipment, tools and specialist instruments
▶ Small-scale fees associated with the course or training, such as exam, registration or workshop fees
▶ Living expenses and maintenance costs or accommodation
▶ Travel costs both in the UK and overseas, including for overseas study, educational trips, voluntary and gap year experience, field studies or research purposes
▶ Course, school or training fees, particularly those for professional, technical or vocational courses and qualifications
▶ Extra-curricular activities aimed at the physical and social development of the individual, including sports, outdoor activities, music (including the purchase or the loan of musical instruments), arts and so on

▶ Specialist equipment related to disability that cannot be funded from statutory sources
▶ Childcare costs, particularly for mature students
▶ Expenses associated with apprenticeships or entering a trade or profession (this can sometimes include business start-up costs)
▶ Vouchers, such as for the local school uniform shop

Supporting information and advice

This guide also contains supporting information and advice on:

▶ Statutory grants and student support (see page 323)
▶ Types of schools in the UK and their funding (see page 327)
▶ Alternative routes to employment: apprenticeships (see page 331)
▶ Company sponsorships (see page 333)
▶ Funding for gap years and overseas voluntary work (see page 335)
▶ Contacts and sources of further information (see page 339)

How to use this guide

Below is a typical charity entry, showing the format we have used to present the information on each of the charities.

On the following page is a flowchart. We recommend that you follow the order indicated in the flowchart to look at each section of the guide and find charities that are relevant to you. You can also use the information in the sections 'About this guide' and 'How to make an application' to help inform your applications.

The Fictitious Charity

£24,000 (120 grants)

Correspondent: Ms I M Helpful, Charity Administrator, 7 Pleasant Road, London SN0 0ZZ (020 7123 4567; email: admin@fictitious.org.uk; website: www.fictitious.org.uk).

CC Number: 112234

Eligibility

Children or young people up to 25 years of age who are in need. Preference is given to children of single-parent families and/or those who come from a disadvantaged family background.

Types of grants

Small one-off grants of up to £250 for a wide range of needs, including school uniforms, books, equipment and educational trips in the UK and abroad. Grants are also available for childcare costs.

Annual grant total

In 2014 the charity had an income of £25,000 and a total expenditure of £27,000. Grants awarded to 120 individuals totalled £24,000.

Exclusions

No grants are given for private school or university fees.

Applications

Applications can be made using a form available from the correspondent. They can be submitted directly by the individual, or by the parent or guardian for those under 18. Applications are considered in January, April, July and October.

Other information

The charity also gives relief-in-need grants to individuals.

Award and no. of grants

This shows the total (or estimated) amount given in grants during the financial year in question. Where further information was available, we have also included the total number of grants made.

Correspondent

This shows the name and contact details of the charity's correspondent. In many cases, this correspondent is the same contact listed on the Charity Commission's online register. However, in cases where we could find a more appropriate correspondent on a charity's website, their name has been included here instead.

Charity Commission number

This is the number given to a charity upon registration with the Charity Commission. A small number of the grant-makers detailed in this guide are not registered charities and so do not have a Charity Commission number.

Eligibility

This states who is eligible to apply for a grant. For example, criteria can be based on place of residence, age, subject studied or occupation.

Types of grants

Specifies whether the charity gives one-off or recurrent grants, the size of grants given and for which items or costs grants are actually given. This section will also indicate if the charity runs various schemes.

Annual grant total

This section shows the total amount of money given in grants to individuals in the last financial year for which there were figures available. Other financial information may be given, where relevant.

Exclusions

This field gives information, where available, on what the charity will not fund.

Applications

Information on how to apply, who should make the application (i.e. the individual or a third party) and when to submit your request.

Other information

This section contains other helpful or interesting information about the charity.

How to identify sources of help: a quick reference flowchart

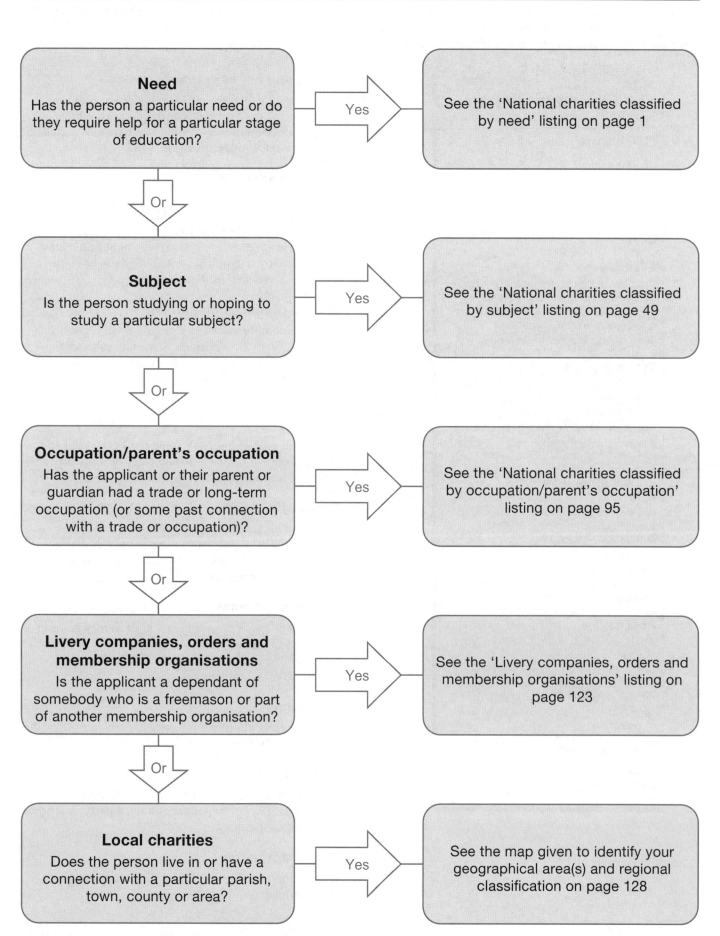

Need
Has the person a particular need or do they require help for a particular stage of education?

Yes → See the 'National charities classified by need' listing on page 1

Or

Subject
Is the person studying or hoping to study a particular subject?

Yes → See the 'National charities classified by subject' listing on page 49

Or

Occupation/parent's occupation
Has the applicant or their parent or guardian had a trade or long-term occupation (or some past connection with a trade or occupation)?

Yes → See the 'National charities classified by occupation/parent's occupation' listing on page 95

Or

Livery companies, orders and membership organisations
Is the applicant a dependant of somebody who is a freemason or part of another membership organisation?

Yes → See the 'Livery companies, orders and membership organisations' listing on page 123

Or

Local charities
Does the person live in or have a connection with a particular parish, town, county or area?

Yes → See the map given to identify your geographical area(s) and regional classification on page 128

How to make an application

This section gives you some information on how to make an application, with additional tips from funders' perspectives.

1. Exhaust other sources of funds

All sources of statutory funding should have been applied for and/or received before applying to a charity. Applications, therefore, should include details of these sources and any refusals. Where statutory funding has been received but is inadequate, an explanation that this is the case should be made. A supporting reference from a relevant agency may also be helpful.

If the applicant attends an educational establishment it should also have been approached to see if there are any funds that may give financial support or if a reduction in fees is available.

> 'The best way to get help for individual funding is to start by helping yourself – try every avenue to raise as much of the money yourself before and while you approach others for a contribution to your cause. If they can see how determined you are and how hard you've worked already, they'll naturally feel motivated to help you find the remainder.'
>
> BBC Performing Arts Fund

Other possible sources of funding and advice are listed on page 339.

2. Use the flowchart on page x to identify potential sources of funding

Do this once you have found a grant-maker that may be relevant to you.

3. Check eligibility criteria

Submitting ineligible applications is the biggest mistake that applicants make. A charity cannot fund you if you are not eligible and you merely waste both your own and the charity's time and resources by applying. If you are in any doubt, contact the grant-maker for clarification. Please remember that many charities are run by volunteers and their time is particularly valuable.

> 'Always read carefully a charity's criteria for eligibility. We, for example, are only allowed to help the children of actors, but three quarters of the applications I receive do not match this basic requirement. You are wasting your time and hopes by applying to a trust which clearly is not allowed to help you.'
>
> TACT

4. Follow the application procedures precisely

Wherever they are available, we have included application procedures in the entries; applicants should take great care to follow these. If there is an application form, use it! Please read any guidelines thoroughly and take note of deadlines. Some charities can consider applications throughout the year whereas others may meet monthly, quarterly or just once a year. Very urgent applications can sometimes be considered between the main meetings. Make sure that the appropriate person submits the application – this could be the individual, their parent or guardian or a professional such as a social worker.

Evidence from our research shows that the majority of organisations welcome initial contact before a full application is made, so if you are unsure about anything, get in touch with them.

5. Give details of any extenuating or unforeseen circumstances

Potential applicants should think carefully about any circumstances which put them at a disadvantage from other families or students, such as coming from a low-income background, being in receipt of state benefits, being a single parent, having a health problem or disability and so on. Where relevant, try to show how the circumstances you are now in could not have been foreseen (for example, illness, family difficulties, loss of job and so on). Charities are often more willing to help if financial difficulties are a result of unforeseen circumstances rather than a lack of forward planning. The funding in this guide is aimed at those facing the largest number of barriers to education or training.

6. Give clear, honest details about your circumstances, including any savings, capital or compensation

Most trustees will consider the applicant's savings when they are awarding a grant, although sometimes this does not need to affect the trustees' calculations. In circumstances where you are certain that your savings are not relevant to grant calculations, you should explain this in the application.

> 'Be open and honest about your circumstances. We have to ensure that we have all the information we need to put your case forward. If essential details emerge at a later date, this can affect your application. Be honest about how much you want to apply for and don't ask for the most expensive item. If you show that you've done your research, then that helps us too.'
>
> Fashion and Textile Children's Trust

7. Tailor the application to suit the particular charity

For example, if an application is being made to a trade charity on behalf of a child whose parent had lengthy service in that particular trade, then a detailed description (and, where possible, supporting documentation) of the parent's service would be highly relevant.

8. Ask for a suitable amount

Ask for an amount that the organisation is able to give. If a charity only makes small grants, try asking for help with books, travel, childcare expenses and similar costs, and apply for fees elsewhere.

9. Mention applications to other charities

Explain that other charities are being approached, when this is the case, and state that any surplus money raised will be returned.

10. Offer to supply references

For example, from a teacher, college tutor, support worker and/or another independent person. If the individual has relevant disabilities or medical needs then a report from a GP would be necessary.

11. Be honest and realistic, not moralising and emotional

Some applicants try to morally bribe trustees into supporting the application, or launch into tirades against the current political regime. It is best to confine your application to clear and simple statements of fact.

12. Be clear, concise and provide sufficient detail

Give as much relevant information as possible, in the most precise way. For example, 'Place of birth' on an application form is sometimes answered with 'Great Britain', but if the charity only gives grants in Liverpool, 'Great Britain' is not a detailed enough answer and the application will be delayed pending further information. Make sure that you write clearly and do not use jargon so that your application is easily understood.

13. Say thank you

Charitable organisations generally like to be kept informed of how their grants have made a difference. It is also important to keep in touch if you are in need of recurrent funding. Feedback also helps charities in their future grant giving.

> 'Don't consider the moment the grant appears in your bank account as the end of your relationship with the grant-maker – try to provide updates on the work the grant has helped you to undertake, including photos, videos and other resources.'
>
> Royal Geographical Society

Remember to thank grant-makers for their support and let them know how their funding has helped you and others.

The next section covers notes on the application form template.

Using the application form template for financial assistance

Following on from this is a general purpose application form. It has been compiled with the help of the Gaddum Centre. It can be photocopied and used whenever convenient and should enable applicants (and agencies or persons applying on behalf of individuals) to state clearly the basic information required by most grant-makers.

Alternatively, applicants can use it as a checklist of points to include in the letter. Applicants using this form should note the following things in particular:

1 It is worth sending a short letter setting out the request in brief, even when using this application form.

2 Because this form is designed to be useful to a wide range of people in need, not all the information asked for in the form will be relevant to every application. For example, not all applicants are in receipt of state benefits, nor do all applicants have HP commitments. In such cases, applicants should write N/A (not applicable) in the box or on the line in question.

3 If, similarly, you do not have answers for all the questions at the time of applying (for example, if you have applied to other charities and are still waiting for a reply) you should write 'Pending' under the question: 'Have you written to any other charities? What was the outcome of the application?'

4 The first page is relevant to all applications, but the second page is only relevant to people applying for school or college fees. If you are applying for clothing or books for a schoolchild, then it may be worth filling in only the first page of the form and submitting a covering letter outlining the reasons for the application.

5 Filling out the weekly income and expenditure parts of the form can be worrying or even distressing. Expenditure when itemised in this way is usually far higher than people expect. It is probably worth filling out this form with the help of a professional.

6 You should always keep a copy of the completed form in case the trust has a specific query.

7 This form should not be used where the trust has its own form, which must be completed.

Application form template

Purpose for which grant is sought	Amount sought from this application £
Applicant (name)	Occupation/School
Address Telephone no.	
Date of birth	Age	Place of birth
Nationality	Religion (if any)

☐ Single   ☐ Married   ☐ Divorced   ☐ Partnered   ☐ Separated   ☐ Widow/er

Family details: Name	Age	Occupation/School
Parents/ Partner	. . . . . .	. . . .
Brothers/Sisters/ Children	. . . . . .	. . . .
. . . .	. . . . . .	. . . .
. . . .	. . . . . .	. . . .
Others (specify)	. . . . . .	. . . .

Income (weekly)	£	p	**Expenditure** (weekly – *excluding course fees*)	£	p
Father's/husband's wage	. . . . . .		Rent/mortgage	. . . . . .	
Mother's/wife's wage	. . . . . .		Council tax	. . . . . .	
Partner's wage	. . . . . .		Water rate	. . . . . .	
Income Support	. . . . . .		Electricity	. . . . . .	
Jobseeker's Allowance	. . . . . .		Gas	. . . . . .	
Employment and Support Allowance	. . . . . .		Other fuel	. . . . . .	
Pension Credit	. . . . . .		Insurance	. . . . . .	
Working Tax Credit	. . . . . .		Fares/travel	. . . . . .	
Child Tax Credit	. . . . . .		Household expenses (food, laundry etc.)	. . . . . .	
Child Benefit	. . . . . .		Clothing	. . . . . .	
Housing Benefit	. . . . . .		School dinners	. . . . . .	
Attendance Allowance	. . . . . .		Childcare fees	. . . . . .	
Disability Living Allowance	. . . . . .		HP commitments	. . . . . .	
Universal Credit	. . . . . .		Telephone	. . . . . .	
Personal Independence Payments	. . . . . .		TV rental	. . . . . .	
Maintenance payments	. . . . . .		TV licence	. . . . . .	
Pensions	. . . . . .		Other expenditure (specify)		
Other income (specify)	. . . . . .		. . . .	. . . . . .	
. . . .	. . . . . .		. . . .	. . . . . .	
. . . .	. . . . . .		. . . .	. . . . . .	
. . . .	. . . . . .		. . . .		

Total weekly income £ ☐   **Total weekly expenditure** £ ☐

Name of school/college/university:

Address

Course:

Is the course ☐ full-time? ☐ part-time?

Date of starting course: | Date of finishing course:

Name of local education authority:

Have you applied for a grant? ☐ YES ☐ NO

What was the outcome of the application?

Give details of any other grants or scholarships awarded: | Have you applied to your school/college/university for help? ☐ YES ☐ NO

What was the outcome of the application?

Have you applied to any other charities? ☐ YES ☐ NO

What was the outcome of the application? | Have you applied for any loans? ☐ YES ☐ NO

What was the outcome of the application?

How much are your school/college fees?

£

Have they been paid in full? ☐ YES ☐ NO

If NO, please give details: | Other costs (e.g. books, clothing, equipment, travel etc.):

How much money do you need to complete the course? £

Examinations passed and other qualifications | **Previous employment** (with dates)

Any other relevant information (please continue on separate sheet if necessary)

Signature: | **Date:**

About the Directory of Social Change

The Directory of Social Change (DSC) has a vision of an independent voluntary sector at the heart of social change. We believe that the activities of independent charities, voluntary organisations and community groups are fundamental to achieve social change. We exist to help these organisations in acheiving their goals.

We do this by:

▶ Providing practical tools that organisations and activists need, including online and printed publications, training courses and conferences on a huge range of topics
▶ Acting as a 'concerned citizen' in public policy debates, often on behalf of smaller charities, voluntary organisations and community groups
▶ Leading campaigns and stimulating debate on key policy issues that affect those groups
▶ Carrying out research and providing information to influence policymakers, as well as offering bespoke research for the voluntary sector

DSC is the leading provider of information and training for the voluntary sector and publishes an extensive range of guides and handbooks covering subjects such as fundraising, management, communication, finance and law. Our subscription-based websites contain a wealth of information on funding from grant-making charities, companies and government sources. We run more than 300 training courses each year, including bespoke in-house training provided at the client's location. DSC conferences and fairs, which take place throughout the year, also provide training on a wide range of topics and offer a welcome opportunity for networking.

For details of all our activities, and to order publications and book courses, go to www.dsc.org.uk, call 020 7697 4200 or email cs@dsc.org.uk.

National and general sources of help

The entries in this first section are arranged in three groups: 1) classified by need, 2) classified by subject, and 3) classified by occupation of parent or applicant. Charities appear in full in the section that is most relevant (usually the section which occurs first) and are then cross-referenced.

This breakdown is designed to be the easiest way to identify charities which might be of relevance and as such we have attempted to make the terms as specific as possible. There is some crossover between sections; for instance, mature university students could identify charities in the 'Adult education and training' and 'Further and higher education' sections, with various other categories possibly being relevant depending on personal circumstances.

There are a number of grant-makers which do not fall into any specific category; these appear in the 'General' section.

Charities are arranged alphabetically within each category. We always caution against using these lists alone as a guide to sources of money. Read each main entry carefully as there will usually be other criteria that must be met; for example, someone who is blind should not simply apply to all the charities in the 'sensory impairment' section. See the advice in the 'How to make an application' section on page xi for more information on how to apply.

NATIONAL AND GENERAL SOURCES OF HELP

National charities classified by need

General educational needs

Al-Mizan Charitable Trust

£19,500 (90 grants)

Correspondent: The Grants Officer, PO Box 2488, Watford WD18 1YL (email: admin@almizantrust.org.uk; website: www.almizantrust.org.uk)

CC number: 1135752

Eligibility

The existing criteria for eligibility is: British citizens, those granted indefinite leave to remain in the UK and asylum seekers who are living in a condition of social or economic deprivation. Preference is given to the following groups:

▶ Orphans (a child who has lost either both parents or one parent who was the main bread-winner in the family)
▶ Children and young people under the age of 19 (particularly those in care or who are carers themselves)
▶ Individuals who have disabilities, are incapacitated or terminally ill (particularly those who have severe mental health issues)
▶ Single parents (particularly divorcees and widows/widowers with children)
▶ Estranged or isolated senior citizens
▶ Individuals with severe medical conditions or their families
▶ People who have offended, reformed drug addicts or alcoholics
▶ Victims of domestic violence and/or physical or sexual abuse
▶ Victims of crime, anti-social behaviour and/or terrorism

Prisoner Training Fund: Serving prisoners, including foreign nationals, in custody of HMPS at any one of the following prisons in the North West: HMP Manchester; HMP Styal; HMP Forest Bank; HMP Wymott; HMP Kirkham; HMP Lancaster Farms; and HMP Hindley.

Applicants must have demonstrated good behaviour and/or have taken part in a regular programme of academic/vocational learning, work or skills development workshops, and must have successfully acquired match-funding and/or made a personal contribution towards their training costs.

The trust prioritises the following groups:

▶ Individuals who are unable to read or write to an adequate standard
▶ Foreign nationals
▶ Individuals with a physical, mental or learning disability

Types of grants

As stated, the trustees are reviewing their grant-making policy but previously they have awarded mainly one-off grants, which have ranged from £34 to a maximum £500, with an average grant being £232. Interest-free loans can also be given. Grants are awarded with the aims of: providing access to education and/or vocational skills; increasing employability; and encouraging excellence in education, sport and/or the arts. They are also made to help relieve and to break the cycle of poverty for individuals and families.

Prisoner Training Fund: the trust runs a specialist grants programme to help support the training and rehabilitation of prisoners in the UK. Grants for up to £200 are available for prisoners and detainees who are looking to access funding for vocational courses and/or books in prison that will assist their personal development and/or rehabilitation.

Annual grant total

In 2015/16 the trust had assets of £140,000 and an income of £102,000. Grants totalled £39,000 but we were unable to determine how much was given to social welfare and how much to education. We have estimated that £19,500 was awarded in educational grants.

Exclusions

Currently, the trust cannot help with: general appeals; applications from organisations or formal groups (except when assisting an individual or family); applicants who are not claiming all benefits for which they are eligible; applicants who have received funding from the trust in the last 12 months; applications for items or costs that have already been paid for; expenses relating to the practise or promotion of religion; debts, including rent and council tax arrears; fines or criminal penalties; university tuition fees; gap year projects; immigration costs; funeral expenses; gifts (including birthdays or festivals); holidays (however, the trust will consider funding trips for children and/or young people which 'enrich learning opportunities or very occasionally where a short vacation may serve a medical or social need'); international travel; applications for more than £500 (the trust will consider match-funding requests if the rest of the required amount is raised from other sources); products/services which conflict with the ethos and values of the trust.

Prisoner Training Fund:

▶ Individuals who have served less than six months
▶ Individuals who have been awarded a grant from the trust within the last 12 months
▶ Individuals who are on remand or serving a sentence for offences related to terrorism

▶ Applications for training which will not have been completed by the end of the individual's sentence (applications for training beginning after the individual's release from prison should be made to the general fund)

▶ Applications which support a second undergraduate course or postgraduate study

Applications

At the time of writing (August 2017) the website stated: 'We are now closed for applications. This is while we review our Grants Policy and implement a new online grant application system.'

Note that, in order to reduce administrative costs, the trust does not accept enquiries by telephone.

Other information

The 2015/16 annual report provides this account of the charity's grants policy:

Our flexible Grants Policy meant that this support ranges from helping people access education and employment to escape the vicious cycle of poverty to simply putting food on the table for the families that cannot afford it. Our seasonal fundraising appeals, such as the Ramadan Food Parcels, Winter Warmer Packs, and Mother & Baby Kits, also provided items to poor families across the UK. These three appeals were run in partnership with grassroots organisations to ensure the packs reached those who genuinely needed them.

The trust has an informative website.

Black Family Charitable Trust

£10,000

Correspondent: Dr Thomas Black, Black Family Charitable Trust, PO Box 232, Petersfield, Hampshire GU32 9DQ (email: enquires@bfct.org.uk; website: www.bfct.org.uk)

CC number: 1134661

Eligibility

Schoolchildren, further and higher education students who are in need. The trust's website states that the trust 'primarily aims to help young people to access high quality education, focusing its support particularly on those who would otherwise be denied appropriate education due to a lack of financial resources'.

Types of grants

Bursaries for education for schoolchildren, and students in further or higher education. Research projects can also be supported.

Annual grant total

In 2015/16 the trust had an income of £5,400 and a total expenditure of

£42,000. We estimate the total amount awarded in bursaries to students was £10,000.

Applications

Apply in writing to the correspondent.

Other information

Grants are also awarded to assist with the relief of poverty, building schools and providing facilities, and preventing and relieving sickness abroad.

The Brenley Trust

£30,000

Correspondent: Patrick Riley, 17 Princes Drive, Oxshott, Leatherhead KT22 0UL (01372 841801; email: patrick.riley@ btinternet.com)

CC number: 1151128

Eligibility

People in financial hardship.

Types of grants

Grants are awarded for general educational purposes; the 2016/17 annual report states 'The trust does not adopt a rigid approach in...grant making. Grants are awarded as the trustees see fit.'

Annual grant total

In 2016/17 the trust held assets of £11 million and had an income of £10 million, made from a large endowment to the trust. We estimate the total amount awarded in grants to individuals for education was £30,000.

Applications

Apply in writing to the correspondent.

Other information

The trust also provides grants to organisations (£777,000 in 2016/17) and to individuals for welfare purposes. The trust operates in the UK and in South Africa.

The Alan Brentnall Charitable Trust

£20,000

Correspondent: Roger Lander, Spinney Corner, Green Lane, Aspley Guise, Milton Keynes, Bedfordshire MK17 8EN (01908 582958)

CC number: 1153950

Eligibility

People in education who are in need. The trust imposes no geographical restrictions.

Types of grants

Grants are made to help individuals with their education.

Annual grant total

In 2015/16 the trust held assets of £1.3 million and had an income of £46,000. We estimate a total of £20,000 was awarded in educational grants to individuals.

Applications

Applications may be made in writing to the correspondent.

Other information

The trust also makes grants to organisations and individuals for the relief of poverty, financial hardship and sickness. There is also medical aid provision for victims of war or natural disaster.

M. R. Cannon 1998 Charitable Trust
See entry on page 289

The Chizel Educational Trust

£13,800

Correspondent: Geoffrey Bond, Trustee, Burgage Manor, Southwell, Nottingham NG25 0EP (01636 081 685)

CC number: 1091574

Eligibility

People under the age of 25 throughout the UK who are in need of financial assistance.

Types of grants

Bursaries, maintenance allowances and grants towards equipment, clothing, instruments, books and travel in the UK or abroad. Grants can be made to people entering a trade. The trust states that due to present level of funds only small grants are available.

Annual grant total

In 2016/17 the trust had an income of £15,700 and a total expenditure of £27,700. The charity had no further accounts available to view. Therefore, we estimate that the trust gave around £13,800 in grants to individuals for educational purposes.

The trust also awards grants to organisations.

Applications

Applications should be made in writing to the correspondent. They must be submitted in May or November for consideration in June and December, respectively. An sae must be enclosed.

Other information

Financial assistance is also provided towards the maintenance of Ackworth School Yorkshire and the Inverness Royal Academy Mollie Stephens Trust.

The Coats Foundation Trust

£35,000

Correspondent: Roslyn Cooper, Coats plc, 107 West Regent Street, Glasgow G2 2BA (0141 207 6835; email: andrea. mccutcheon@coats.com; website: www. coatspensions.co.uk/about-us/coats-foundation-trust)

CC number: 268735

Eligibility

Those wishing to pursue education but are facing financial hardship.

Types of grants

One-off grants according to need, for general educational purposes.

Annual grant total

In 2015/16 the charity had an income of £1,200 and a total expenditure of £111,000. We estimate the total amount awarded in grants for education was around £35,000.

Applications

Applications can be made using the application form, which is available to download from the website along with a financial statement, which must also be completed. Any other relevant information that may help the trustees when considering the applicant's case should be included.

Other information

The trust also makes grants to individuals for welfare purposes.

Family Action

£65,000

Correspondent: The Grants Service, 24 Angel Gate, City Road, London EC1V 2PT (020 7254 6251 (Wednesday and Thursday only between 2 pm and 4 pm); email: grants.enquiry@family-action.org.uk; website: www.family-action.org.uk)

CC number: 264713

Eligibility

Family Action helps people 'experiencing poverty, disadvantage and social isolation across England'. Educational support is given to individuals over the age of 14 who wish to enter further education, undertake training/retraining and otherwise pursue their career. Applicants must be studying at an organisation affiliated to Family Action's Educational Grants Service, attending a further education course (including pre-access and access), living on low income (primarily in receipt of benefits) and have a right of residency in the UK (EU students included).

Preference is given to people undertaking 'commercial' subjects (for example IT, bookkeeping or accounting).

Types of grants

Educational grants are normally in the region of £200 to £300 and can be made towards costs associated with a course of study, for example clothing and/or equipment required for the course, travel, examination costs or computers/laptops.

Annual grant total

In 2015/16 the charity had assets of £12.2 million and an income of £21.5 million. A total of 1,770 grants were made to individuals totalling £740,000. Educational grants to individuals totalled £65,000.

Exclusions

Course fees; costs already incurred; items provided by the college for the course; childcare; study outside the UK; higher education courses; postgraduate study or personal expenditure not directly associated with study such as food, clothing or household bills.

Applications

Applications must be submitted online by authorised members of college staff (usually student welfare advisors or equivalent) from affiliated organisations.

Other information

Family Action provides a range of advice and support services across the country – see the 'Find us' facility on the website to find your local office. Support is given to help in the areas of some of the most complex issues, including financial hardship, mental health problems, social isolation, learning disabilities, domestic abuse, or substance misuse and alcohol problems. It is aimed to improve the lives of children and families, help through the early years of child development and ensure adult mental health and well-being.

George Heim Memorial Trust

£500

Correspondent: Paul Heim, Trustee, Wearne Wyche, Picts Hill, Langport TA10 9AA (01458 252097)

CC number: 1069659

Eligibility

People under the age of 30 who are in education or training. Our research suggests that further/higher education students are particularly supported.

Types of grants

Grants range up to £1,000 and are given to 'encourage [beneficiaries] in education'.

Annual grant total

In 2015/16 the trust had an income of £1,400 and a total expenditure of £570. We have estimated that the annual total amount of grants awarded was around £500.

Applications

Applications may be made in writing to the correspondent.

The Leverhulme Trust

£2,016 (80,000 grants)

Correspondent: Prof. Gordon Marshall, Director, The Leverhulme Trust, 1 Pemberton Row, London EC4A 3BG (020 7042 9888; email: grants@ leverhulme.ac.uk; website: www. leverhulme.ac.uk)

CC number: 1159154

Eligibility

Researchers at every career stage. The trust prioritises 'work of outstanding scholarship', focusing on the following criteria: originality; importance; significance; merit. Further detail is given on the website.

Types of grants

The trust has a wide range of grant schemes which include:

- Research assistance on projects (including leadership awards, fellowships and project grants)
- International travel scholarships
- Research leave to pursue projects
- Postdoctoral research (including awards, early career fellowships and study abroad)
- Emeritus fellowships
- Arts scholarships
- Visiting professorships
- Major research initiatives

Information about each of the trust's grant schemes, including eligibility and what the grant can be used for, is given on its website.

Annual grant total

In 2016 the trust had assets of £2.6 million and an income of £86,500. There were 619 grants made altogether (out of a total 4,186 applications), which amounted to £80,000, broken down as follows:

Responsive Mode Projects	£39,000
Research Awards Advisory Committee	£16,300
Research Leadership	£12,400
Major Research Fellowships	£4,600
Academy Fellowships/Scholarships	£3,100
Prizes	£3,000
Visiting Professors	£1,500
Artists in Residence	£300

Exclusions

According to its website, the trust does not fund the following kinds of research:

- Studies of disease, illness and disabilities in humans and animals, or research that is intended to inform clinical practice or the development of medical applications
- Policy-driven research where the principal objective is to assemble an evidence base for immediate policy initiatives
- Research where advocacy is an explicit component
- Research aimed principally at an immediate commercial application
- Proposals in which the balance between assembling a data bank or database and the related subsequent research is heavily inclined to the former

The following costs are also ineligible:

- Core funding or overheads for research organisations
- Individual items of equipment over £1,000
- Sites, buildings or other capital expenditure
- Support for the organisation of conferences or workshops
- Contributions to appeals
- Endowments
- A shortfall from a withdrawal/ deficiency of public funding
- Student tuition fees unless associated with an application for one of the trust's grants (see details on the website)

Refer to the website for exclusions from each specific grant scheme.

Applications

Information about each of the grant schemes, including how to apply and deadlines, is given on the trust's website. The website also lists the contact details of the relevant individuals to contact for information on particular schemes.

Other information

Although the trust does not provide funding for postgraduate and undergraduate study, its sister charity, Leverhulme Trade Charities Trust (CC number: 1159171), does offer support for individuals whose parent or spouse is a commercial traveller, grocer or chemist.

P. and M. Lovell Charitable Trust

£6,000 (20 grants)

Correspondent: The Trustees, c/o KPMG LLP, 69 Queen Square, Bristol BS1 4BE (0117 905 4000)

CC number: 274846

Eligibility

People in education who are in need.

Types of grants

One-off grants, typically for £300.

Annual grant total

In 2015/16 the trust held assets of £2.3 million and had an income of £129,500. Grants totalled £6,000 and were awarded to 20 individuals, with a further £42,500 awarded to 82 charitable organisations.

Applications

Apply in writing to the correspondent.

One Me

£520 (two grants)

Correspondent: The Trustees, Welton House, Lime Kiln Way, Lincoln LN2 4WH (01522 574100; email: administrator@one-me.org.uk)

CC number: 1159762

Eligibility

Young people between the ages of 16 and 25.

Types of grants

Funding is awarded for a wide range of purposes with the aim of allowing people to achieve their potential through education, training and employment. Grants of between £100 and £1,000 may be given to enable access to training, support for further education, extra-curricular activities, or starting up a business.

Annual grant total

In 2015/16 the charity had assets of £2,600 and an income of £35,000. Grants were made to two individuals totalling £520.

Applications

Applications can be made using the form on the charity's website, submitted online, or a form can be downloaded from the website and submitted by post. Applications by those under the age of 18 must be signed by a parent or guardian. Subject to requests for additional information, the charity aims to consider applications and communicate a decision within 28 working days.

Other information

This charity was established in January 2015; the financial information reflects a 15-month period ending 31 March 2016, taken from the first set of accounts available on the Charity Commission's record.

The Osborne Charitable Trust

£2,200

Correspondent: John Eaton, Trustee, 57 Osborne Villas, Hove, East Sussex BN3 2RA (01273 732500; email: john@ eaton207.fsnet.co.uk)

CC number: 326363

Eligibility

People in need who are undertaking education in the UK and overseas.

Types of grants

Awards are made to schoolchildren for equipment/instruments, and to people with special educational needs towards fees and equipment/instruments.

Annual grant total

In 2015/16 the trust had an income of £8,000 and a total expenditure of £9,800. We estimate that around £2,200 was given in grants to individuals for educational purposes.

Applications

Our research suggests that the trust does not respond to unsolicited applications.

Other information

The trust can also make grants to individuals for social welfare purposes and supports organisations (especially children's charities).

The Praebendo Charitable Foundation

Correspondent: Helen Leech, Trustee, The Redoubt, Second Drift, Wothorpe, Stamford PE9 3JH

CC number: 1137426

Eligibility

People under the age of 30 in England, Wales and Scotland, with a possible preference for those living in Stamford, Lincolnshire.

Types of grants

Scholarships, maintenance allowances or grants can be awarded to those in higher or further education. The foundation can also support the provision of education (including the study of music or other arts), travel to further such education, or those who are preparing to enter an occupation, trade or profession after leaving education.

Annual grant total

In 2015/16 the foundation had assets of £288,000 and an income of £44,000. Charitable activities expenditure by the foundation amounted to £374,500, which we have taken to represent grants made. The annual report for the year explains that 13 grants were made, including 'direct financial assistance for relief of financial hardship' and support, totalling £45,000, to two local organisations. We were unable to determine the amount distributed to individuals, neither in total nor for educational purposes specifically.

Applications

Apply in writing to the correspondent.

Other information

The foundation makes a small number of awards to organisations and individuals each year.

The Prince's Trust

£1 million (6,737 grants)

Correspondent: Sarah Haidry, Secretary, Prince's Trust House, 6–9 Eldon Street, London EC2M 7LS (0800 842842; email: info@princes-trust.org.uk; website: www. princes-trust.org.uk)

CC number: 1079675, SC041198

Eligibility

Young people between the ages 13 and 30 who have struggled at school, are not in education or training, are in or leaving care, are long-term unemployed, have been in trouble with the law, are facing issues such as homelessness or mental health issues, or are otherwise disadvantaged.

Types of grants

The Prince's Trust aims to change the lives of young people, helping them to develop confidence, learn new skills and get practical and financial support. A wide range of support is offered, including:

- Development awards – cash grants of between up to £500 that are available to assist young people aged 14 to 25 to access education, training or employment. Examples of what can be funded include tools and equipment, course fees, interview clothes, transport or childcare costs
- Enterprise programme – assists young people aged between 18 and 30 to start their own business through the provision of financial and mentoring support. The focus of the programme is on supporting young people to choose and achieve the outcome which is best for them. It also helps those who believe they are ready to start a business to plan and test their ideas thoroughly, improving the quality of their propositions and therefore increasing their chances of success

There are also a number of programmes to help individuals into work, education or training, or to build the skills and confidence of those aged 11 to 25, including work experience programmes;

personal development programmes; mentoring; courses to help individuals discover new talents; and courses to boost confidence and skills.

For up-to-date and more detailed information on the current programmes and support available, refer to the trust's website.

Annual grant total

In 2016/17 the trust had assets of £54 million and an income of £70.9 million. More than £1 million was distributed in grants to individuals, consisting of:

Development awards	3,906	£544,000
Enterprise programme grants	16,823	£485,000

Exclusions

Development awards cannot be given for:

- Living expenses
- Retrospective costs
- Gap year or overseas projects
- Community projects
- Medical treatment
- Fees for courses higher than Level 3 (e.g. NVQ Level 4, HNC, HND, degree or postgraduate courses)
- Business start-up (see the Enterprise programme instead)

For restrictions from other programmes, and further information, refer to the website.

Applications

An initial enquiry form should be completed online on the trust's website. The trust aims to respond within five working days. Alternatively, you can contact the trust by phone on 0800 842842, or text 'Call Me' to 07983 385418 to discuss an application.

Other information

The Prince's Trust also runs many programmes which provide young people with personal development, training and opportunities to help them move into work. Details of these can be found on the trust's website.

Professionals Aid Council

£16,500 (46 grants)

Correspondent: Finola McNicholl, Chief Executive, 10 St Christopher's Place, London W1U 1HZ (020 7935 0641; email: admin@professionalsaid.org.uk; website: www.professionalsaid.org.uk)

CC number: 207292

Eligibility

The dependants of people who are graduates or have worked in a professional occupation requiring that level of education, or those who have a

first degree themselves, studying in the UK.

With regard to assistance for college or university students, the charity states the following information on its website:

We may be able to assist you if you are studying in the UK and are:

- a UK citizen or have indefinite leave to remain
- an EU or overseas student undertaking studies in the UK
- a medical, dental or veterinary student in the final two years of your course

Types of grants

Grants are given for: children's education – modest grants to assist with the costs of uniforms, (in some circumstances) school travel expenses, and other school-related costs (books, stationery etc.); college and university students – grants, usually in the range of £300 to £500, are given for (in some circumstances) course-related travel expenses (e.g. work or research placements) and other related course expenses (stationery, books, thesis production etc.).

Annual grant total

In 2016 the charity had assets of £5.3 million and an income of £118,000. There were 46 educational grants made totalling £16,500.

Exclusions

The charity does not assist with: extra tutorial fees; study abroad; ordination or conversion courses; intercalated years or medical elective periods; or IELTS, ORE or PLAB tests for overseas doctors.

Applications

Initial enquiries can be made using the form on the website or by writing to the charity's Administration Department. Grants are means-tested.

Other information

The organisation also offers advice and assistance. Grants are also made for welfare purposes.

Scarr-Hall Memorial Trust

£4,000

Correspondent: Ruth Scarr-Hall, Trustee, Amhuinnsuidhe Castle, Amhuinnsuidhe, Harris HS3 3AS

CC number: 328105

Eligibility

People in education and training throughout the UK.

Types of grants

Small, one-off grants.

Annual grant total

In 2015/16 the trust had an income of £16,100 and a total expenditure of £9,200. We estimate the annual total amount of grants awarded to individuals to be around £4,000.

Applications

Apply in writing to the correspondent providing an sae and stating all the relevant individual circumstances, reasons why the grant is needed and how much is required.

Other information

Grants may also be made to organisations.

The Stanley Stein Deceased Charitable Trust

£100,000

Correspondent: Brian Berg, 14 Linden Lea, London N2 0RG (email: michael. lawson@williamsturges.co.uk)

CC number: 1048873

Eligibility

People under the age of 21, or over the age of 75, who are in need. The charity awards grants to applicants across the UK.

Types of grants

One-off and recurrent grants are given according to need towards general educational costs.

Annual grant total

In 2015/16 the charity had an income of £5,000 and a total expenditure of £204,000. We estimate that around £100,000 was awarded to grants for educational purposes.

Applications

Application forms can be requested from the correspondent.

Other information

The charity also awards to individuals for welfare purposes.

The Talisman Charitable Trust

£17,000 (29 grants)

Correspondent: Philip Denman, Lower Ground Floor Office, 354 Kennington Road, London SE11 4LD (020 7820 0254; email: talismancharity@gmail.com; website: www.talismancharity.org)

CC number: 207173

Eligibility

People in the UK living in poverty (under the Charity Commission's definition) who wish to continue education but do not have the means.

Types of grants

One-off and recurrent grants are given according to need, to assist with payments of books, equipment, uniforms, instruments, fees, research etc.

Annual grant total

In 2016/17 the charity had assets of £14.4 million and an income of £218,500. The charity awarded £17,000 in educational grants to 29 individuals.

Exclusions

The trust cannot accept applications made by recorded delivery or 'signed-for' services.

Applications

Applications should be made on behalf of an individual by a local authority, charitable organisation, or a social or professional worker. Complete the application letter on letter-headed paper. As a minimum, applications should include the following:

- Full name and address of the beneficiary
- Overview of financial situation
- A brief history of the case
- Explanation of what is needed and to what extent being in poverty is involved
- Estimate of funds needed and payee details (the charity usually prefers to pay the organisation supporting the grant so they can oversee grant spending)
- A list of other charities approached, if any

Where possible, include:

- Medical documentation
- Quotes for building work
- School acceptance letter or transcript
- Information on other assistance received

Other information

The trust also provides grants to individuals for welfare purposes. Occasionally, it may support other organisations with similar aims.

Mrs R. P. Tindall's Charitable Trust

£3,900

Correspondent: Giles Fletcher, Trustee, Appletree House, Wishford Road, Middle Woodford, Salisbury SP4 6NG (01722 782329)

CC number: 250558

Eligibility

People in education, particularly clergy and their dependants.

Types of grants

Small grants appear to be made for educational purposes, with some focus on the Christian Church.

Annual grant total

In 2016 the trust had assets of £3.3 million and an income of £101,500. Grants were made to 35 individuals, of which £3,900 was in for educational purposes, and £1,100 was given in support of the Christian Church. A further £110,000 was given in grants to 42 organisations.

Applications

Apply in writing to the correspondent.

The Zobel Charitable Trust

£35,000

Correspondent: Stephen Scott, Trustee, Tenison House, Tweedy Road, Bromley, Kent BR1 3NF (020 8464 4242 (ext. 402))

CC number: 1094186

Eligibility

People in education in the UK, particularly in the Christian field.

Types of grants

Small, one-off grants according to need.

Annual grant total

In 2015/16 the trust had an income of £285,000 and a total expenditure of £67,500. We estimate that about £35,000 was given in grants to individuals.

Exclusions

Grants are not made for school, university or postgraduate fees.

Applications

Our research indicates that this trust does its own research and does not always respond to unsolicited applications.

Other information

Grants are also made to organisations.

Business start-up

The Oli Bennett Charitable Trust

£400

Correspondent: Joy Bennett, Camelot, Penn Street, Amersham HP7 0PY (01494 717702; email: info@olibennett.org.uk; website: www.olibennett.org.uk)

CC number: 1090861

Eligibility

Young people between 18 and 30 and are UK residents. Support is for new or emerging businesses, rather than expansion of larger businesses.

Types of grants

Grants not in excess of £2,000 for people starting up their own businesses.

Annual grant total

In 2016 the trust had an income of £9,100 and a total expenditure of £460. We estimate the total amount awarded in grants was £400.

Exclusions

No grants are given for training courses.

Applications

Application forms are available on the trust's website. Applications are considered every three months. A business plan is required to assess the viability of the idea.

Other information

The trust was set up in memory of Oli Bennett, who died in the September 11 2001 attacks in New York.

The Prince's Trust
See entry on page 7

Carers

Carers Trust

£35,000

Correspondent: Grants Team, 32–36 Loman Street, London SE1 0EH (email: info@carers.org; website: www. carers.org)

CC number: 1145181

Eligibility

Unpaid carers in the UK, especially those who live near a Princess Royal Trust for Carers Centre.

Types of grants

One-off grants are awarded, usually of up to £300. Funding is given to provide support to carers towards equipment, essential items, personal and skills development or other educational activities.

Annual grant total

In 2015/16 the charity had assets of £4.8 million and an income of £6 million. We estimate the amount awarded in educational grants to be £35,000.

Applications

Applications should be made via your local Carers Service centre. Direct applications are not considered.

Other information

The trust was formed by the merger of The Princess Royal Trust for Carers and Crossroads Care in April 2012 and acts as a resource body, providing advice, information and support for carers. Carers who are in need of support can contact the online support team by emailing support@carers.org. The support team is available over the Christmas and New Year period.

Children and young people

The Athlone Trust

£25,500

Correspondent: David King-Farlow, 36 Nassau Road, London SW13 9QE (07496 653542; fax: 020 7972 9722; email: athlonetrust@outlook.com; website: www.athlonetrust.com)

CC number: 277065

Eligibility

Adopted children under the age of 18 who are in need.

Types of grants

According to our research, the trust can give grants for school fees (including private education). The trust marks that support is increasingly given to families with children who have serious disabilities such as Asperger's Syndrome or Attention Deficit Hyperactivity Disorder (ADHD). In exceptional circumstances one-off grants could be provided to help with the cost of educational essentials for schoolchildren.

Annual grant total

In 2016 the trust had an income of £27,000 and awarded educational grants totalling £25,500.

Exclusions

People at college or university are not supported.

Applications

Apply in writing to the correspondent. Applications should be submitted by the applicant's parent/guardian and are considered twice per year, usually in May and November.

Other information

The trust may consider assisting people who are 19 years old providing they are still at school.

John Collings Educational Trust

£16,300

Correspondent: Anthony Herman, Trustee, 11 Church Road, Tunbridge Wells, Kent TN1 1JA (01892 526344)

CC number: 287474

Eligibility

Children, normally up to the age of 14, who are in need.

Types of grants

Support towards general educational needs, including books, fees, equipment/ instruments and other essentials for schoolchildren.

Annual grant total

In 2015/16 the charity had an income of £46,500 and a total expenditure of £34,500. Throughout the year, the charity awarded a total of £32,500 in grants. We estimate that £16,300 of this amount was given to individuals for educational purposes.

Exclusions

Grants are not available to people at college or university.

Applications

Apply in writing to the correspondent. Previously the trust has noted that its income is accounted for and new applicants are unlikely to benefit.

Other information

Grants can also be made to organisations.

The EAC Educational Trust

£36,500 (28 grants)

Correspondent: Daniel Valentine, Trustee, Sherwood, The Street, Brook, Ashford, Kent TN25 5PG (01580 713055)

CC number: 292391

Eligibility

Children and young people, normally between the ages of 8 and 16, from single-parent families, poor families and, particularly, sons and daughters of the Church of England clergymen.

Types of grants

According to our research, grants are almost exclusively given for school fees, including boarding. The trust has a close link with one particular school which specialises in educating the families of clergy but other applications are also accepted, especially for the education of children in choir schools or other establishments with musical or dramatic emphasis. Individual grants almost never exceed one-third of the pupil's annual fees.

Annual grant total

In 2016/17 the charity had an income of £105,500 and a total expenditure of £107,500. Throughout the year the charity gave around £36,500 in grants to 28 individuals.

Applications

Apply in writing to the correspondent. Applications are normally considered in spring.

Other information

The main objectives of the charity are the relief of poverty and advancement of education for the benefit of the public and particularly among the families of clergy of the Church of England, single parent families or other poor families.

The French Huguenot Church of London Charitable Trust

£79,000 (53 grants)

Correspondent: Duncan McGowan, Clerk to the Trustees, Haysmacintyre, 26 Red Lion Square, London WC1R 4AG (020 7969 5500; email: dmcgowan@ haysmacintyre.com)

CC number: 249017

Eligibility

People under the age of 25. Support is given in the following priority: people who/whose parents are members of the Church; people of French Protestant descent; other people as trustees think fit (see the type of grants section for preferences).

Types of grants

Annual allowances, bursaries and emergency or project grants to school pupils, further/higher education students, people in training or those entering a trade/starting work. Preference is given to French Protestant children attending French schools in London, choristers at schools of the Choir Schools' Association, girls at schools of the Girls' Day School Trust and United Learning, and boys in selected independent day schools (list can be received upon request from the trust).

Support can be given for various educational needs, including outfits, necessities, equipment and instruments, books, study of music or other arts, also home/overseas projects. Special allowances for people of French Protestant descent are given in modest one-off payments towards books.

Annual grant total

In 2016 the trust had assets of £11.8 million and an income of £325,500. The trust awarded a total of £79,000 in grants to individuals. Grants were distributed in the following categories:

Ancestry grants	£500
Bursaries	£63,500
Consistorial grants	£10,000
Project grants	£5,000

During the year, 51 pupils at various colleges, boys' and girls' day schools and choir schools received special allowances, bursaries and emergency grants and two young people were assisted with grants totalling £250 for overseas projects.

Applications

Applications for grants and bursaries from members of the Church and French Protestant children attending schools in London should be made to the Secretary of the Consistory, 8–9 Soho Square, London W1V 5DD.

Requests for special allowances to people of French Protestant descent and for project grants should be addressed to the correspondent.

Applications from choristers and pupils at the selected schools should be addressed to the educational institution concerned, mentioning the applicant's connection (if any) with the French Protestant Church.

Other information

In addition to the educational fund there also are church and hardship funds mostly supporting organisations.

In 2016 grants totalling £21,000 were made to nine organisations providing assistance mainly to young people with disabilities or who are experiencing hardship.

The William Gibbs Trust

£7,750

Correspondent: Antonia Johnson, Trustee, 40 Bathwick Hill, Bath BA2 6LD

CC number: 282957

Eligibility

Children and young people in education who are of British nationality.

Types of grants

One-off and recurrent grants are given towards general educational needs.

Annual grant total

In 2016 the trust had an income of £9,100 and a total expenditure of £15,700. We estimate that the trust awarded around £7,800 to individuals for educational purposes.

The trust also awards grants to organisations.

Applications

The trust has previously stated it does not respond to unsolicited applications as the funds are already allocated. Any enquiries should be made in writing.

Other information

Grants are also given to organisations for educational purposes.

The Journal Children's Fund (in conjunction with the Royal Antediluvian Order of Buffaloes)

£19,000

Correspondent: The Secretary, R. A. O. B. Grand Lodge of England, Grove House, Skipton Road, Harrogate HG1 4LA (01423 502438; email: hq@ raobgle.org.uk; website: www.raobgle. org.uk)

CC number: 529575

Eligibility

Orphaned or needy children of deceased members of the Royal Antediluvian Order of Buffaloes Grand Lodge of England.

Types of grants

Help with the cost of books, clothing and other essentials for schoolchildren. Grants may also be available for those at college or university who are eligible.

Annual grant total

In 2016/17 the fund had assets of £444,500 an income of £37,000. Grants were made to individuals for education totalling £19,000.

Applications

Initial enquiries regarding assistance can only be made through the individual's branch of attendance.

The Lloyd Foundation

£116,500 (60 grants)

Correspondent: Margaret Keyte, Secretary, 1 Churchill Close, Breaston, Derbyshire DE72 3UD (01332 873772; email: keytelloyd@btintenet.com)

CC number: 314203

Eligibility

Children (aged between 5 and 25 years old) of British citizens ordinarily living/working overseas.

Assistance is also available to 'teaching members of staff of schools outside the UK conducted in accordance with British educational principles and practice' and to people in need who 'for at least five years or at the time of its closure was a member of the staff of the former English School, Cairo'.

Types of grants

The foundation may offer scholarships, bursaries, maintenance allowances to school pupils and further/higher education students 'to obtain British type education either overseas or in the UK whilst family is living/working overseas'. Our research suggests that grants can be given towards general educational purposes, such as fees, books, equipment/instruments, living expenses, travel costs, study of music or the arts. According to our research, grants are primarily given to attend the nearest English-medium schools and where no such school exists, help can be given towards fees for a school in the UK.

Annual grant total

In 2015/16 the foundation had assets of £3.6 million, an income of £171,500 and grants totalling £116,500 were awarded to 60 beneficiaries. A further 114 applications and enquiries for awards were not eligible for funding from the foundation.

Applications

To enquire about making an application contact the foundation's secretary – either in writing at the given address, or by telephone or email.

The McAlpine Educational Endowments Ltd

£90,000

Correspondent: Gillian Bush, Secretary, Eaton Court, Maylands Avenue, Hemel Hempstead, Hertfordshire HP2 7TR (email: g.bush@srm.com)

CC number: 313156

Eligibility

Children and young people in need who could benefit from education at 'preparatory, public or other independent school, and at any technical college or university', according to the Charity Commission's record.

Types of grants

According to our research, grants are mainly towards the cost of independent school fees for children attending schools selected by the trustees and are awarded to those who, for reasons of financial hardship, would otherwise have to leave the school.

From the 2015/16 annual report: 'support is given for an academic year by year basis, but can be renewed for subsequent years subject to a satisfactory school report for the academic year and the availability of funds'.

Annual grant total

In 2015/16 the charity had assets of £135,000 and an income of £79,500. It made grants totalling almost £90,000.

Exclusions

Our previous research has suggested that grants for pupils at specialist schools (such as ballet or music schools, or schools for children with learning difficulties) are not normally considered.

Applications

Apply in writing to the correspondent. The 2015/16 annual report states that the charity 'carries out its objectives by receiving applications from individuals or parents in connection with mainstream education'. Applications should normally be made through the selected schools, the list of which is available from the correspondent. Applications are considered during the summer before the new academic year. Note, that because of the long-term nature of the charity's commitments, very few new grants can be considered each year.

Victoria Shardlow's Children's Trust

£4,500

Correspondent: Liz Clifford, Charities Administrator, 9 Menin Way, Farnham GU9 8DY (email: victoriashardlowtrust@googlemail.com)

Eligibility

Children or young people up to the age of 18 who are coping with difficult circumstances and are disadvantaged in being able to participate and benefit from formal or non-formal education.

Types of grants

Small, one-off grants are awarded towards equipment, fees (excluding for independent schools), transportation costs and educational trips in the UK or abroad. The maximum available grant is £3,000.

Annual grant total

In previous years, the trust has awarded grants totalling around £4,500.

Exclusions

Grants are not given for university fees, gap year activities, independent school fees or for personal computers.

Applications

Application forms can be obtained from the correspondent and should be submitted either directly by the individual or by the parent/guardian. Applications are considered in January, April, July and October.

Other information

Support can be given to small registered groups providing educational opportunities for disadvantaged children. The trust has also informed us that larger amounts are given to organisations.

This trust is very small and therefore is not registered with the Charity Commission. The correspondent has confirmed that the trust's beneficial area is not restricted and, in practice, applications can be made from anywhere in the world.

Dr Meena Sharma Memorial Foundation
See entry on page 18

Thornton-Smith and Plevins Trust

£224,500 (94 grants)

Correspondent: Heather Cox, Grants Secretary, 298 Icknield Way, Luton, Bedfordshire LU23 2JS (01582 611675; email: thornton.smithypt@ntlworld.com; website: www.educational-grants.org/find-charity/thornton-smith-plevins)

CC number: 1137196

Eligibility

Currently the trust mostly supports young people aged 16 to 19 who are in distressed circumstances.

Support may also be given to people under the age of 25 who are in need, including people undertaking work practice or apprenticeships in any trade or profession and young people in preparatory, secondary, higher or further education. Assistance is also given to individuals of the professional or business classes who have fallen into poverty and are unable to make adequate provision for their retirement or old age.

Types of grants

Support is given in grants and loans towards school fees and associated costs or in scholarships to travel overseas for educational purposes. Grants are means-tested and are paid per term, subject to reasonable progress. Preference is given to short-term applications primarily in relation to A-levels.

Annual grant total

In 2015/16 the trust held assets of £12.2 million and had an income of £357,500. Grants were made to 94 individuals totalling £224,500 and consisted of £222,500 in individual grants and loans to assist with school fees and expenses and £2,200 given in scholarships for educational travel abroad (Kew Scholarship). The average grant was £2,365.

Exclusions

Our research suggests that grants are not normally given for first degree courses. Support will not be given in circumstances where parents were not in a position to fund the fees when entering the child for the school.

Applications

Apply in writing to the correspondent. Applications should include details of candidates' education and their parents' financial situation. If the applicant is considered eligible further inquiries are made. Applications are normally considered twice a year.

Other information

This trust was formerly the Thornton-Smith Young People's Trust which has been combined with the Wilfred Maurice Plevin's Trust, Thornton-Smith Plevins Common Investment Fund and The Thornton-Smith Trust for efficiency.

To be assisted by The Wilfred Maurice Plevins fund, beneficiaries must also be aged ten or over and be the children of a professional. Beneficiaries older than 25 may only receive assistance from The Thornton-Smith fund.

The T. A. K. Turton Charitable Trust

£14,000

Correspondent: R. Fullerton, Trustee, 47 Lynwood Road, London W5 1JQ (020 8998 1006)

CC number: 268472

Eligibility

Young people with a good academic record (e.g. good GCSE results or equivalent) who are in their final years at school (A-levels or other university entrance qualifications). The trust usually supports three pupils in the UK and three in South Africa who are in need.

Types of grants

Support is given to cover a proportion of school fees for a two-year period, normally leading to A-levels or equivalent university entrance qualifications. Applications are only accepted from schools which have awarded the candidate a bursary of at least 25% of the fees.

Annual grant total

In 2016 the trust had an income of £16,800 and a total expenditure of £15,600. We estimate that grants totalled around £14,000.

Applications

Applications should be made in writing to the correspondent, through the school where the applicant wishes to study.

Other information

Our previous research suggests that since grants are normally given for a two-year period, new applications from UK students can now only be considered every two years.

Further and higher education

The Benlian Trust

£44,000 (34 grants)

Correspondent: Maral Ovanessoff, 15 Elm Crescent, Ealing, London W5 3JW (020 8567 1210; email: benliantrust@gmail.com)

CC number: 277253

Eligibility

Children of Armenian fathers. Applicants must be members of the Armenian Church studying at universities and colleges in the UK.

Types of grants

Scholarships to Armenian people in higher education. Grants are given towards the cost of fees and/or living expenses. Priority is given to undergraduates.

Annual grant total

In 2015/16 the trust had assets of £2.7 million and an income of £108,500. The total amount awarded in charitable grants was £88,000 – 25 individuals were awarded a total of £44,000 and £30,500 was distributed between nine organisations.

Applications

Apply in writing to the correspondent via post or email. Completed applications should be returned before 30 April. Two academic referees and one social referee are required.

Other information

The trust provides grants for educational and charitable purposes connected with the cultural life of Armenians in London, as well as for the maintenance of Armenian House. The trust also provides grants for the furtherance of medical research at Westminster Hospital and Middlesex Hospital. Armenian hospitals in Istanbul and France are also supported.

The Mihran and Azniv Essefian Charitable Trust

See entry on page 31

The Follett Trust

£14,300

Correspondent: Jamie Westcott, Administrator, The Follett Office, Broadlands House, Primett Road, Stevenage, Hertfordshire SG1 3EE (01438 810400; email: folletttrust@ thefollettoffice.com)

CC number: 328638

Eligibility

Students in higher education. Our previous research indicates that some priority may be given to the arts and medical/health concerns.

Types of grants

One-off and recurrent scholarships and grants according to need.

Annual grant total

In 2015/16 the trust had assets of £43,500 and an income of £170,000. Throughout the year the trust expended a total of £159,500 on charitable activities. Of this amount, £14,300 was awarded to individuals for educational purposes.

Applications

The majority of successful applications come from people known to the trustees or in which the trustees have a particular interest. The trust has stated in the past that it does not accept unsolicited applications.

Gilchrist Educational Trust

£24,500 (34 grants)

Correspondent: Val Considine Acis, Secretary, 20 Fern Road, Storrington, Pulborough, West Sussex RH20 4LW (01903 746723; email: gilchrist.et@ blueyonder.co.uk; website: www. gilchristgrants.org.uk)

CC number: 313877

Eligibility

Full-time students at a UK university who either 'have made proper provision to fund a degree or higher education course but find themselves facing unexpected financial difficulties'. Or 'those who, as part of a degree course, are required to spend a short period studying in another country'.

Types of grants

Both study and travel grants are usually of around £500. Four book prizes are also available to students achieving high grades at Birkbeck College, London University's Department of Extra-Mural Studies.

Annual grant total

In 2016/17 the trust had assets of over £2 million and an income of £88,500. The trust awarded a total of £74,500 in grants during 2016/17.

Of this amount, £24,500 was given to individuals for educational purposes. Grants were distributed as adult study grants (15 grants awarded) and travel grants (29 grants awarded).

Exclusions

According to the trust's website, support is not given to the following:

- part-time students
- people seeking funds to enable them to take up a place on a course
- students seeking help in meeting the cost of maintaining dependants
- students who have, as part of a course, to spend all or most of an academic year studying in another country
- those wishing to go abroad under the auspices of independent travel, exploratory or educational projects

Applications

Applicants must contact the grants officer on gilchrist.et@gmail.com or write to: 4 St Michaels Gate, Shrewsbury SY1 2HL.

Other information

The trust also offers the biennial Gilchrist Fieldwork Award of £15,000. This competitive award is offered in even-numbered years and is open to small teams of qualified academics and researchers in established posts in university departments or research establishments, most of British nationality, wishing to undertake a field season of over six weeks.

Throughout 2016/17 the trust supported 17 organisations and 13 expeditions.

Helena Kennedy Foundation

£138,500 (97 grants)

Correspondent: Shahida Aslam, Operations Manager, Room 243A, University House, University of East London, Water Lane, Stratford E15 4LZ (020 8223 2027; email: enquiries@hkf. org.uk; website: www.hkf.org.uk)

CC number: 1074025

Eligibility

Socially, economically or otherwise disadvantaged students attending a publicly funded further education institution in the UK who are progressing to university education. Applicants must be intending to undertake a higher diploma or undergraduate degree for the first time. Students taking a gap year will also be considered, as will students studying part-time or distance learning degrees. The foundation's Article 26 scheme also supports people who have fled persecution and sought asylum in the UK and who wish to study in higher education.

Types of grants

Main bursary scheme

The main bursary scheme provides a bursary of £1,500 over instalments during the student's time in higher education. The foundation also provides successful applicants with: a named contact at the foundation to provide support and advice; access to free training sessions on a range of skills; work-shadowing opportunities; volunteering opportunities.

Article 26

The Article 26 project aims to promote and improve access to higher education for students who have fled persecution and sought asylum in the UK. Bursaries are available through a number of higher education institutions, which are listed on the website. There are a range of undergraduate and postgraduate opportunities and each university has its own eligibility criteria.

Other bursaries

The foundation also provides bursaries to students at specific further education or Sixth Form colleges, which are listed on the website. DISCOVER bursaries of £1,000 each are also provided to students in the first year of a two-year level three study programme at certain further education institutions, also listed on the website.

Annual grant total

In 2015/16 the foundation had assets of £550,000 and an income of £214,500. A total of £138,500 was awarded in bursaries, of which £15,800 was through the Article 26 programme and £3,500 through the DISCOVER bursaries programme. The number of new students receiving a bursary during the year was 97.

Exclusions

Funding is not available to:

- People who have already undertaken a higher education course
- Postgraduate students
- Students at private institutions
- Previous bursary recipients
- Students at international institutions

Applications

Applications can be made using the form on the foundation's website, where further guidance is also provided. Applications generally open in January and close in April, for awards to be made in September. Applicants will need to demonstrate severe financial hardship and barriers to accessing higher education and all applications must be supported by the applicant's educational institution.

Other information

The foundation also provides mentoring, information, one to one advice, specialist and practical support, skills training and work experience opportunities.

The Leathersellers' Company Charitable Fund

£178,000 (82 grants)

Correspondent: David Santa-Olalla, Clerk, The Leathersellers' Company, 7 St Helen's Place, London EC3A 6AB (020 7330 1444; fax: 020 7330 1454; email: enquiries@leathersellers.co.uk; website: www.leathersellers.co.uk)

CC number: 278072

Eligibility

Higher education students on a full-time degree course at any UK university. Applicants must have an unconditional offer for, or be enrolled on, a full-time course. Preference may be given to students from the Greater London area and to those studying engineering or subjects related to the leather trade, including fashion students working with leather.

Types of grants

Grants of up to £4,000 a year, for up to four years, are given to support higher education.

Annual grant total

In 2015/16 the fund had assets of almost £57.9 million and an income of £1.7 million. During the year 82 individual grants were made to students totalling £178,000. A further £1.8 million was given in 264 grants to organisations.

Exclusions

Funding is not given for one-year professional conversion courses.

Applications

Applications should be made using the online form on the Leathersellers' Company website. Guidance on what to include, deadlines for applications (usually around July for the next academic year) and other information is given on the website.

Other information

The fund also gives grants to organisations for both education and a wide range of welfare causes.

Both successful and unsuccessful applicants are informed in due course and the fund requests not to be contacted with queries regarding the outcome of the application, unless your contact address has changed.

The Sidney Perry Foundation

£147,500 (123 grants)

Correspondent: Lauriann Owens, Secretary, PO Box 889, Oxford OX1 9PT (website: www.the-sidney-perry-foundation.co.uk)

CC number: 313758

Eligibility

The foundation's primary aim is to assist students undertaking their first degree. Applicants must be under the age of 35 when the course starts. Eligible foreign students studying in Britain can also apply. Students undertaking medicine as their second degree and therefore not qualifying for any support are welcomed to apply (see particular exclusions relating to the medicine degree). There may be some preference for those training for careers in natural or applied sciences.

Types of grants

One-off and recurrent grants from £300 onwards with an average award of around £900. The maximum general award is of £1,000, or £1,500 for 'super grants'. In 2016 grants ranged from £500 to £1,300. The foundation's website notes that 'grants are considered to be supplemental and to go part of the way to bridge a gap with the applicant finding the bulk of funding elsewhere'. Applications with a shortfall of more than £3,000 will not be considered. Grants are usually towards books and equipment/instruments.

Annual grant total

In 2016 the foundation had assets of £4.7 million and an income of £197,000. There were 123 awards made during the year (out of 500 applications), totalling £147,500 altogether. This included: 4 'super grants'; 13 grants to promising young musicians with the Philharmonia Orchestra/Martin Musical Scholarship Fund (totalling £20,000 altogether); vocal awards to three students on the Guildhall School of Music and Drama (totalling £15,000); awards to two students for Open University courses towards professional status in engineering (£3,500).

Exclusions

According to its website, the foundation is unable to assist:

- The first year of a (three or four year) first degree, save for veterinary, medicine and in exceptional circumstances
- Medical students during their first year if medicine is their second degree
- Medical students during elective periods and intercalated courses

- Second degree courses where the grade in the first is lower than a 2:1, save in exceptional circumstances
- Second degree courses or other postgraduate study unrelated to the first unless they are a necessary part of professional training (e.g. medicine or dentistry)
- Expeditions or courses overseas, emergency funding or clearance of existing debts
- Students over the age of 35 when their course of study commences, save in the most exceptional circumstances
- A-Level and GCSE examinations
- Students on access, ESOL, HNC, HND, BTEC, GNVQ and NVQ levels 1–4 and foundation courses
- Those with LEA/SAAS funding, except in exceptional circumstances
- Open University courses (except engineering, which is supported)

Distance learning, correspondence, part-time and short-term courses may only be considered in some circumstances.

Applications

Applications can be made using the application on the foundation's website, and should be submitted by post, enclosing: the completed form; proof of college/university offer; personal statement; names and addresses of two referees (one of which must be an academic reference); an up-to-date, signed, original academic reference, on official paper; a statement by an independent person recommending the applicant for a grant; a self-addressed, stamped envelope. Applicants will be notified of the outcome by post and no further correspondence will be undertaken following a refusal. Applications should usually be submitted by January – refer to the website for more information.

Other information

The foundation is generally unable to deal with student debt or financial problems needing a speedy resolution.

Reuben Foundation

£1.3 million

Correspondent: Patrick O'Driscoll, 4th Floor, Millbank Tower, 21–24 Millbank, London SW1P 4QP (020 7802 5014; fax: 020 7802 5002; email: contact@reubenfoundation.com; website: www.reubenfoundation.com)

CC number: 1094130

Eligibility

Students of Oxford or Cambridge University studying for, or about to study for, a postgraduate degree.

Types of grants

Scholarships are awarded to postgraduate students attending Oxford or Cambridge University, to cover course fees and associated learning costs such as training or equipment.

Annual grant total

In 2016 the charity had assets of £87.8 million and an income of £5 million. The foundation awarded £1.3 million in educational scholarships.

Applications

The foundation has partnerships with University of Oxford and University of Cambridge in order to identify applicants. Interested pupils enrolled at any of these schools should make enquiries at the school and not to the foundation.

Other information

The main purpose of the foundation is to provide grants to charities, organisations, and projects which closely align with the foundation's objectives to advance education and health. The charity also makes grants to individuals, to cover health care and medical costs.

Sloane Robinson Foundation

£440,500

Correspondent: Michael Wilcox, Trustee, Old Coach House, Sunnyside, Bergh Apton, Norwich NR15 1DD (01508 480100; email: info@wilcoxlewis. co.uk)

CC number: 1068286

Eligibility

Overseas students wishing to study at British universities and British students wishing to study overseas.

At an undergraduate level emphasis is placed on liberal arts, orthodox sciences (but not religion), social sciences and languages. At postgraduate level no restrictions apply. With regard to overseas studies emphasis should be placed on the subjects in which the country offers better courses.

Types of grants

Grants and scholarships according to need.

Annual grant total

In 2015/16 the foundation held assets of almost £14.5 million and had an income of £491,500. Grants made during the year totalled £440,500 of which £316,500 was made to institutions for bursaries and £124,000 to individual pupils of Latymer School.

Applications

The foundation states in its annual report for 2015/16 that it is 'continuing to develop long-term relationships with a number of academic institutions, with the ultimate goal of establishing scholarships and bursary schemes'. Our

research suggests that applications should be made directly through educational establishments. The trustees meet at least twice a year.

Note that 'only successful applicants are notified, in order to avoid increased administrative costs for the foundation'.

Thornton-Smith and Plevins Trust

See entry on page 12

The Unite Foundation

£1.2 million (179 grants)

Correspondent: Helen Arber, Foundation Manager, South Quay House, Temple Back, Bristol BS1 6FL (0117 302 7073; email: info@ unitefoundation.co.uk; website: www. unitefoundation.co.uk)

CC number: 1147344

Eligibility

Students aged 25 or under who are a care leaver or estranged from their family, and are starting their first undergraduate degree at one of the foundation's partner universities (listed on the its website).

Types of grants

The scholarship provides free accommodation for three years in a Unite Students property (including household bills, Wi-Fi and site maintenance). A 'welcome pack' containing essential items such as bedding, towels and kitchen equipment is also provided. The foundation may also be able to provide additional support through working with their donors and supporters – such as paid internships, employability coaching or mentoring.

Annual grant total

In 2016 the foundation had assets of £5.9 million and an income of £6.4 million. During the year, scholarships were awarded to a further 44 students, bringing the total number of students supported altogether in the year to 179. Student bursaries totalled £385,500 (for living costs – see 'other information') and student rent payments totalled £828,500.

Exclusions

Only students with UK home university fee status are eligible.

Students on the following years of study are not eligible for support:

- Foundation year
- Years involving study credits towards a master's (whether as a postgraduate qualification or as part of an integrated Bachelor's degree)

- Resit years
- Repeat years arising from changing courses

Applications

Applications are accepted between January and May for the following academic year, and should be made using the form provided on the foundation's website.

Other information

This is the corporate charity of Unite Group plc, which provides student accommodation.

There are 28 partner universities working with the foundation, which are listed on its website.

The foundation used to provide living allowances to students in addition to accommodation; however, this was discontinued as the foundation is now focusing on providing more scholarships at a larger number of universities (although those previously receiving the allowance will continue to do so until graduation).

W Wing Yip and Brothers Foundation

£70,000 (35 grants)

Correspondent: Robert Brittain, Trustee, W. Wing Yip plc, The Wing Yip Centre, 375 Nechells Park Road, Birmingham B7 5NT (0121 327 6618; email: robert. brittain@wingyip.com)

CC number: 326999

Eligibility

Undergraduate students from the UK and China.

Types of grants

Grants can be made to contribute towards fees and living expenses while studying.

Annual grant total

In 2015/16 the foundation held assets of almost £1.2 million and had an income of £85,000. Bursaries totalling £70,000 were awarded to 35 students with a further £57,500 awarded to universities and charities.

Applications

Apply in writing to the correspondent.

Other information

The 2015/16 annual reports notes the following:

The Foundation provides scholarships for three Chinese students from Universities in China to study at Churchill College, Cambridge. The students are selected by the University. Scholarships have also been provided for two students at Aston University, Birmingham who study there, the students being nominated by the University.

S. C. Witting Trust

£2,500

Correspondent: Christopher Gregory, S. C. Witting Trust, Friends House, 173 Euston Road, London NW1 2BJ (020 7663 1082; email: friendstrusts@ quaker.org.uk)

CC number: 237698

Eligibility

University students.

Types of grants

One-off grants of up to £200 are made to students for the provision of books and equipment.

Annual grant total

The correspondent has informed us that there is a budget of £2,500 for educational grants.

Exclusions

The trust does not supply loans, and grants are not made towards debts, tuition fees, or living expenses.

Applications

Applications should be made in writing to the correspondent, including a short case history, reasons for need, and the amount being requested. Applications need to include proof of attendance at university, and a letter of support from a tutor.

Applications are considered monthly. Unsuccessful applications will not be acknowledged unless an sae is enclosed.

Other information

Grants are also made to individuals under 16, and over 60, for welfare and relief-in-need purposes.

Gender

Diamond Education Grant (DEG)

£8,000

Correspondent: Administrator, 2nd Floor, Beckwith House, 1 Wellington Road North, Stockport, Cheshire SK4 1AF (0161 480 7686; email: hq@ soroptimistgbi.prestel.co.uk; website: sigbi.org/our-charities/deg)

CC number: 1139668

Eligibility

Women who are permanently resident in one of the countries of the Federation of Soroptimist International Great Britain and Ireland who wish to refurbish their skills after an employment break or acquire new ones to re-enter the employment market and improve their opportunities of employment/ promotion.

Types of grants

Grants towards course fees, books or equipment. Grants are normally paid for one year but may be extended in exceptional circumstances.

Annual grant total

In 2015/16 the charity had an income of £13,300 and a total expenditure of £8,200. We estimate that the charity gave around £8,000 in grants to individuals.

Exclusions

Living expenses cannot be supported.

Applications

Apply in writing to the correspondent.

Other information

Grants are only paid over after the successful applicants have started their courses.

Edinburgh Association of University Women – President's Fund

£22,500

Correspondent: Alison MacLachlan, Trustee, 6/5 Craigleith Avenue South, Edinburgh EH4 3LQ

OSCR number: SC004501

Eligibility

Women in their final year of study for a degree (postgraduate or undergraduate) at UK universities who face unexpected financial hardship.

Types of grants

One-off modest grants, usually between £150 and £500. Awards are intended to help with costs of books, equipment and maintenance/living expenses. Applicants receive only one award which is intended to help them to complete the current study.

Annual grant total

In 2016 the fund had an income of £18,100 and a total expenditure of £23,000. We estimate that the fund gave around £22,500 in grants to individuals

Exclusions

Grants are not given to begin a new course, towards diplomas, certificates, access courses, childcare, one-year undergraduate and one-year postgraduate degrees or for study or work overseas (outside the UK).

Applications

Application forms can be requested by writing to the correspondent. Requests must be submitted directly by the applicant (not third parties). Two academic references are required. The trustees usually meet in October, January and April.

Other information

The fund has previously stated that 'applications which disregard the exclusions will not be acknowledged'.

The Girls of The Realm Guild (Women's Careers Foundation)

£15,200

Correspondent: Beth Hayward, Secretary, 2 Watch Oak, Blackham, Tunbridge Wells, Kent TN3 9TP (01892 740602)

CC number: 313159

Eligibility

Women over the age of 21 who are UK citizens and are seeking assistance to begin or continue studies for a career. Younger applicants (over the age of 16) may be supported for music or dance studies.

Types of grants

One-off grants and loans to help with any costs relating to education or training, preferably leading to a career.

Annual grant total

In 2015 the foundation had an income of £9,300 and a total expenditure of £15,500. At the time of writing (November 2017) the charity had no accounts available to view.

We estimate that the foundation awarded around £15,200 in grants to women for educational purposes.

Exclusions

Grants are not generally given for PhD or postgraduate studies, particularly if the subject indicates a complete change of direction.

Applications

Application forms and further guidelines can be requested from the correspondent.

Other information

Note that this charity is small and has limited resources.

The Marillier Trust

£66,500

Correspondent: William Stisted, Trustee, 38 Southgate, Chichester, West Sussex PO19 1DP (01243 787899; email: ws@andersonrowntree.co.uk)

CC number: 1100693

Eligibility

Boys between the ages of 5 and 13.

Types of grants

Grants are given for education other than formal teaching in class. The trust will support educational and recreational opportunities, residential trips, after-school activities and so on. Loans are also made to individuals.

Annual grant total

In 2015/16 the trust had an income of £18,000 and a total expenditure of £665,500. Due to its low income, the latest accounts were not available on the Charity Commission and but previous grants to individuals represented around 10% of the total expenditure. We have therefore estimated that around £66,500 was awarded to individuals.

Applications

Apply in writing to the correspondent.

Other information

The trust mainly makes grants to educational organisations or those working with young people.

The Hilda Martindale Educational Trust

£23,000 (15–20 grants)

Correspondent: Administrator, c/o The Registry, Royal Holloway, University of London, Egham TW20 0EX (01788 434455; fax: 01784 437520; email: hildamartindaletrust@rhul.ac.uk; website: www.royalholloway.ac.uk/aboutus/governancematters/thehildamartindaletrust.aspx)

Eligibility

Women over the age of 21 who are British nationals and pursuing a profession or career requiring vocational training in the areas where women are underrepresented. The website states that generally women are underrepresented in STEM subjects and architecture, but that other fields will be considered if the applicant can demonstrate that women are underrepresented.

Courses/training must be a full academic year in length and preferably start in September/October. Priority is given to undergraduates in their final year of study.

Types of grants

A small number of one-off grants in the range of £200 to £3,000 are offered for training courses and are normally paid in three instalments, in October, January and April. Awards can be used for fees, books, equipment, living expenses, childcare and so on.

A limited number of awards can also be given towards the costs of any graduate training (MSc/MA and PhD) in an area which is underrepresented by women (e.g. science, technology, engineering, architecture and some branches of medicine such as surgery), and leadership roles in all fields at a UK institution approved by the trustees.

Annual grant total

The trust generally awards 15 to 20 women each year totalling £20,000 to £25,000.

Exclusions

Assistance is not given for:

- Short courses
- Access courses
- Courses attended abroad
- Elective studies
- Intercalated BSc years during a UK medical, dental, veterinary or nursing course
- Wholly academic courses
- Academic research
- Special projects in the UK or abroad
- First year undergraduates
- People holding grants from research councils, British Academy and other public sources
- Retrospective awards

Funding can only be given to women who cannot access any other funding. Medical, dental, or veterinary students will only be considered if they are pursuing an area within that field where women are underrepresented.

Applications

Application forms are available from the Council of Royal Holloway website. Applications open in August and should be submitted, together with two references and a personal statement, by February for the courses taking place in the following academic year. Submissions can be made by email or via post, providing an sae. The trustees normally meet in April to consider awards.

Other information

The trust only invites applications from the candidates who exactly suit its eligibility criteria. The correspondent has requested us to direct potential applicants to the Council of Royal Holloway website where the application forms and detailed guidelines can be found and are regularly updated.

The Muirhead Trust

£6,000

Correspondent: Administrator, c/o Franchi Law LLP, Queens House, 19 St Vincent Place, Glasgow G1 2DT (website: www.themuirheadtrust.org.uk)

OSCR number: SC016524

Eligibility

Female students of Scottish origin and almost exclusively those who are studying in Scotland. Support is available to students of medicine, veterinary science, pharmacy, nursing, dentistry, science and engineering.

Types of grants

Grants of around £2,000 to £3,000 are available for two years, after which the student is eligible for a statutory grant for the further three years.

Annual grant total

In 2016/17 the trust had an income of £7,400 and a total expenditure of £6,400. We have estimated that grants to individuals totalled £6,000.

Exclusions

Biomedical or forensic science students are outside the remit of the trust.

Applications

Applications should be submitted together with a CV and an academic transcript. The deadline for applications is 31 August annually.

The NFL Trust

£127,500 (33 grants)

Correspondent: Margot Chaundler, Secretary, 9 Muncaster Road, London SW11 6NY (020 7223 7133; email: nfltrust@mail.com; website: www.nfltrust.org.uk)

CC number: 1112422

Eligibility

Girls between the ages of 11 and 18 who are attending schools and colleges in the UK (primarily fee-charging institutions). Support is given in line with 'Christian principles'.

Types of grants

Recurrent bursaries (up to the end of course, usually by the age of 18) towards day education. Awards are subject to means-testing and annual financial review. Individual needs of the child and the parents' commitment are also taken into account when considering grants.

Annual grant total

In 2015/16 the trust had assets of £5 million and an income of £71,500. During the year bursaries were given to 33 pupils totalling £127,500. The annual report explains that, of these, ten were new bursaries, all for students with difficult family circumstances or medical conditions. There was also a grant of £780 awarded from the Diana Matthews Trust Fund to pay for the singing lessons of a bursary holder.

Applications

Application forms and further details can be requested from the correspondent. The trust's website states that applications should be made in the summer around 18 months ahead of the academic year in which the bursary is needed.

Other information

The trustees of The NFL Trust also administer the designated funds of a small Diana Matthews Trust Fund. The funds are used to provide educational extras for girls in need, whether or not they benefit from the NFL bursary.

Dr Meena Sharma Memorial Foundation

£5,500

Correspondent: Dr B. K. Sharma, 14 Magdalene Road, Walsall, West Midlands WS1 3TA (01922 629842; email: gwalior@onetel.com)

CC number: 1108375

Eligibility

Children and women in the UK and India, especially those who have disabilities, are disadvantaged or underprivileged. Teachers, other educational professionals and medical personnel or medical students may also be supported.

Types of grants

Awards may include scholarships, travel grants and other educational costs. Support can be given to teachers, other educational professionals and medical personnel or medical students to assist their training and professional development.

Annual grant total

In 2015/16 the foundation had an income of £24,00 and a total expenditure of £23,000. We estimate that about £5,500 was given in educational support to individuals.

Applications

Eligible candidates should apply in writing to the correspondent via post, providing an sae. Requests should give full contact details (including email address) and reasons for seeking a grant. Applications can be made at any time. Only successful applicants are informed.

Other information

Grants are also made to organisations, especially in India, and individuals may be supported for welfare needs.

Yorkshire Ladies' Council of Education (Incorporated)

£21,500

Correspondent: Phillida Richardson, Administrator, Ground Floor Office, Forest Hill, 11 Park Crescent, Leeds LS8 1DH (0113 269 1471; email: info@ylce.org; website: www.ylce.org.uk)

CC number: 529714

Eligibility

British women over the age of 21 who are in need of financial assistance towards their education at a British educational institution and who do not qualify for local authority support.

Types of grants

Grants in the range of £100 to £500 (average grant £200 to £300) are given for the course fees only. The award is available for one year but can be renewed for up to three years.

Annual grant total

In 2015/16 the charity held assets of £599,000 and had an income of £32,500. A total of £30,000 was spent in charitable activities, of which £21,500 was awarded in scholarships and educational grants.

Exclusions

Members, and the dependants of members, of Yorkshire Ladies' Council of Education are not eligible for support.

Applications

Application forms can be found on the charity's website together with detailed guidelines. A completed form and an sae should be submitted directly by the individual by 1 January, March, June or September for consideration later in the month. The awards committee meets four times a year. Grants are made to institutions on the individual's behalf.

Other information

The charity also provides grants to local community bodies and institutions.

Illness and disability

Able Kidz

£21,000

Correspondent: Cathryn Walton, Trustee, 43 Bedford Street, London WC2E 2HA (0845 123 3997; email: info@ablekidz.com; website: www.ablekidz.com)

CC number: 1114955

Eligibility

Children and young people under 18 who live in the UK. Applications are not means-tested. Applications from schools and other educational establishments are welcomed.

Types of grants

One-off and recurrent grants according to each child's requirements. Grants are typically made for specialist educational equipment and extra tuition.

Annual grant total

In 2015/16 the charity had an income of £28,500 and a total expenditure of £29,000. A total of £21,000 was awarded in grants.

Applications

Apply in writing to the correspondent. Applications should include a letter which details:

▶ A summary of the child's circumstances
▶ What the child requires, and how Able Kidz might help with requirements
▶ An outline of the costs involved

A supporting letter from an educational or medical professional is also required.

Ataxia UK

£3,000

Correspondent: Stephanie Marley, Ground Floor, Lincoln House, 1–3 Brixton Road, London SW9 6DE (020 7582 1444; email: office@ataxia.org.uk; website: www.ataxia.org.uk)

CC number: 1102391

Eligibility

The Mark Dower Trust grant is available to young people (between the ages of 16 and 30) who have ataxia and are working towards living independently.

Types of grants

The Mark Dower Trust

A grant of up to £3,000 is available to support young people 'in their quest for independent living through enabling them to develop skills or hobbies or to pursue educational goals', according to the website. The grant can be used for purposes such as participation in training or development of a skill, hobby or creative activity, or purchase of equipment which will enable this.

Further information is given on the Mark Dower Trust website: www. markdowertrust.org.uk.

Annual grant total
In 2015/16 the charity had assets of £453,500 and an income of £1 million. Grants from the Mark Dower Trust usually total £3,000.

Applications
An application form is available to download from the charity's website, along with guidance on what to include, and should be submitted between 30 November and 31 January of the following year.

Other information
The charity administers the Mark Dower Trust grant.

It also previously provided the Jerry Farr Travel Fellowship, which offered up to £3,500 for individuals with ataxia to undertake travel abroad, broadening their horizons. It appears from the website that the final grant from this scheme was made in 2017.

Ataxia UK also acts as third party to applications made to two other grants schemes: The Headley Trust, which provides grants towards equipment for use at home; and the Florence Nightingale Aid in Sickness Trust, which provides grants towards equipment and also respite breaks.

Barnwood Trust
See entry on page 301

The British Kidney Patient Association

£19,000

Correspondent: Fiona Armitage, 3 The Windmills, St Mary's Close, Turk Street, Alton GU34 1EF (01420 541424; fax: 01420 89438; email: info@britishkidney-pa.co.uk; website: www.britishkidney-pa.co.uk)

CC number: 270288

Eligibility
Dialysis patients and their families who are on low incomes. Also, other patients, including transplant patients and those receiving conservative care, if their health and health and quality of life is being seriously affected by their renal condition.

Types of grants
Grants to help with, where appropriate, the cost of university or college fees, or the cost of books, equipment, accommodation or other expenses involved with educational and job opportunities.

Annual grant total
In 2016 the association had assets of £33.9 million and an income of £1.8 million. Grants through Patient Aid amounted to £802,500, with grants for educational purposes amounting to £19,000. The rest was given to patients for social welfare purposes.

Exclusions
Grants are not made: to reimburse patients for bills already paid; for telephone bills, court fines, home improvements, the repayment of credit cards or loans, medical equipment, or council tax payments; or to help with the costs of getting ongoing dialysis.

Applications
Application forms, along with guidelines, are available to download from the association's website. The form must be submitted by a renal social worker or a member of the patient's renal team, who must sign the form and attach a detailed social report on the hospital's headed paper.

Other information
The association makes grants to hospitals and, as part of its work, supports the Ronald McDonald Houses at children's hospitals in Liverpool (Alder Hey), Birmingham, Bristol, London (Evelina Children's Hospital), Manchester and Glasgow (Royal Hospital for Sick Children, Yorkhill), which provide support for the families of young renal patients attending the units at these hospitals.

It also funds non-laboratory research and provides support services, information and advice to kidney patients, among other projects.

In 2016 the association directly helped 1,367 patients with financial aid of whom 565 were approaching them for the first time.

CLIC Sargent (formerly Sargent Cancer Care for Children)

£414,500

Correspondent: Kevin O'Brien, Horatio House, 77–85 Fulham Place, London W6 8JA (020 8752 2878; email: info@clicsargent.org.uk; website: www.clicsargent.org.uk)

CC number: 1107328

Eligibility
Young people aged 16 to 24 who are eligible for free NHS treatment and have been diagnosed with cancer in the last 12 months.

Types of grants
The educational expenditure is part of the 'Don't Just Survive, Thrive' objective of the charity and funding is given to pay for specialist cancer nurses to visit patients in school, to provide equipment and support, and to make the transition from diagnosis back into education smoother.

Annual grant total
In 2016/17 the charity had assets of £17.1 million and an income of £24.8 million. We estimate that educational spending by the charity was £414,500.

Applications
Applications for grants can be found online. Before issuing the grant, CLIC Sargent will need to verify your details through a clinician or nurse.

Crohn's and Colitis UK

£37,500

Correspondent: Julia Devereux, Support Grants Assistant, PO Box 334, St Albans AL1 2WA (0800 011 4701 or 0300 222 5700; email: support.grants@crohnsandcolitis.org.uk; website: www.crohnsandcolitis.org.uk)

CC number: 1117148, SC038632

Eligibility
People affected by Inflammatory Bowel Disease (IBD) who are aged 15 or older, have been resident in the UK for at least six months and are undertaking an educational or vocational training course.

Types of grants
Grants of up to £1,000 are made towards any educational or training needs, including tuition fees, books, equipment, retraining courses, additional costs of university/college en-suite, and travel passes. Grants are also given for special education needs, retraining purposes or other items and services arising as a consequence of having IBD.

Annual grant total
In 2016 the charity held assets of £3.6 million and had an income of almost £5 million. During the year 236 grants were awarded for both welfare and educational purposes and totalled £75,000. As a breakdown was not provided, we have estimated that grants to individuals for education totalled £37,500.

Applications

Application forms are available to download from the charity's website, along with guidance notes. The form has two extra sections, one of which should be completed by a doctor to confirm the individual's illness and one to be filled in by a social worker (or health visitor, district nurse, Citizens Advice advisor, or another 'professional person'). Full guidance, restrictions and deadlines are available online.

Other information

Grants are also made for welfare purposes and to institutions for research. Occasionally local grants are made to hospitals. The main role of the association is to provide information and advice to people living with IBD.

The Fletchers Trust

£8,900 (16 grants)

Correspondent: Michael Holden, Honorary Almoner, Worshipful Company of Fletchers, 99 High Street, Linton, Cambridgeshire CB21 4JT (01329 288489; email: michaelholden@ hotmail.com; website: www.fletchers.org. uk/charity.html)

CC number: 258035

Eligibility

Individuals with any kind of disability participating in the sport of archery. Both experienced archers and those new to the sport are welcome to apply.

Types of grants

Grants are made for equipment such as arrows, bows, stabilisers, wheelchairs and other equipment to enable individuals to participate in the sport of archery.

Annual grant total

In 2015/16 the trust had assets of £177,500 and an income of £35,000. The trust made grants to 16 archers, totalling £8,900. Grants were also made to organisations totalling £22,500.

Applications

Application forms are available to download from the trust's website and must be accompanied by a letter from a coach.

Other information

The trust also works with relevant organisations to widen access to the sport and support those with potential.

Hylton House and Specialist Support Fund

£2,500

Correspondent: County Durham Community Foundation, Victoria House, Whitfield Court, St John's Road, Meadowfield Industrial Estate, Durham DH7 8XL (0191 378 6340; fax: 0191 378 2409; email: info@cdcf.org.uk; website: www.cdcf.org.uk)

CC number: 1047625–2

Eligibility

People in the North East (County Durham, Darlington, Gateshead, South Shields, Sunderland and Cleveland) with cerebral palsy and related neurological conditions. Applicants, or their families, must also be on low income, and have exhausted all other avenues of funding.

Types of grants

Grants of up to £1,000 are available to meet the costs of education and training. Funding can be used for specialist communication aids, travel, and for alternative versions of educational resources, for example large-print materials.

Annual grant total

In 2016/17 grants for education and training totalled £2,500.

Applications

Applications can be made online under the Hyland House page on the website. Applications are invited from social and professional workers, on behalf of a client, and must include details of the client's current situation at home, medical condition, and what the funds will be used for.

Other information

The charity also makes grants for welfare purposes, such as domestic equipment and respite for carers.

The fund is managed by the County Durham Community Foundation (CC number: 1047625).

The Joseph Levy Memorial Fund

£44,000 (85 grants)

Correspondent: Maria Zava, Administrator, 1st Floor, 1 Bell Street, London NW1 5BY (020 7616 1207; email: education@jlef.org.uk; website: www.jlef.org.uk)

CC number: 1079049

Eligibility

Children and young adults up to the age of 25 who have cystic fibrosis.

Types of grants

Grants are available to help individuals develop their career through further/ higher education or professional qualifications. Support is given for tuition fees, examination fees, living costs and similar expenses to progress the applicant's career.

Annual grant total

In 2015/16 the fund had an income of £20,000. During the year 85 grants were made to individuals for educational purposes and totalled £44,000.

Applications

Applications can be made using a form available on the charity's website, or from the correspondent. The deadline for applications is 30 March and awards are decided in mid-June.

Other information

The fund is administered by the Cystic Fibrosis Trust.

The Dan Maskell Tennis Trust
See entry on page 85

Meningitis Now (formerly known as Meningitis Trust)

£71,500

Correspondent: Dr Tom Nutt, Chief Executive Officer, Fern House, Bath Road, Stroud GL5 3TJ (01453 768000; fax: 01453 768001; email: info@ meningitisnow.org; website: www. meningitisnow.org)

CC number: 803016, SC037790

Eligibility

People in need who have meningitis or who have disabilities as a result of meningitis and reside in the UK.

Types of grants

Funding is given as part of the charity's service to help people to rebuild their lives following meningitis. Support can be given for counselling and creative and complementary therapy services, as well as unexpected expenditure, such as specialist equipment and computer software, re-education and special training or tuition (e.g. sign language or driving lessons).

Annual grant total

In 2016/17 the charity had assets of £939,500 and an income of £3.2 million. The amount of grants given to individuals totalled £143,000. We estimate that educational grants amounted to around £71,500.

Exclusions

Our previous research has found that support may not be given for the following: services or items which should normally be supplied by a statutory body e.g. NHS or local authority; home adaptations on rented property; holidays; payment of domestic bills; arrears e.g. mortgage payments; bedding, furniture or clothing; domestic appliances; or swimming pools.

Applications

More information on eligibility criteria and how to apply for support can be obtained by calling the Meningitis Helpline (0808 801 0388) or by emailing helpline@meningitisnow.org.

Other information

Meningitis Now was formed following the merger of Meningitis Trust and Meningitis UK. The charity provides a wide range of information, advice and support for people affected by meningitis, as well as promoting meningitis awareness and education to the general public.

The MFPA Trust Fund for the Training of Handicapped Children in the Arts

£11,500

Correspondent: Tom Yendell, 88 London Road, Holybourne, Alton, Hampshire GU34 4EL (01420 88755; email: tom@flatspaces.co.uk; website: www.uniqueartawards.uk)

CC number: 328151

Eligibility

Children with physical or mental disabilities between the ages of 5 and 18 living in the UK.

Types of grants

One-off and recurrent grants towards participation in arts, crafts, painting, music, drama and so on. Awards can be given, for example, towards books, educational outings, equipment and materials or school fees. The maximum grant available is £6,000.

Annual grant total

In 2015/16 the fund had an income of £292,000, and a total expenditure of £50,000. Grants awarded totalled £36,500 of which £11,500 was awarded to children.

Applications

Apply in writing to the correspondent. Applications can be made directly by the individual or through a third party such as their school, college or educational welfare agency. They are considered throughout the year. Candidates should also enclose a letter explaining their needs and a doctor's letter confirming their disability.

Other information

The trust also gives grants to organisations.

It also recently launched the Unique Art Awards to celebrate five artistic mediums and encourage people under 21 to unleash their creativity.

The Adam Millichip Foundation

£10,500

Correspondent: Stuart Millichip, Trustee, 17 Boraston Drive, Burford, Tenbury Wells WR15 8AG (07866 424286; email: apply@ adammillichipfoundation.org; website: adammillichipfoundation.org)

CC number: 1138721

Eligibility

People with disabilities in the UK who wish to participate in sports.

Types of grants

Grants have been awarded to enable access to a range of different sports, through equipment, facilities and lessons. Examples of previous grants include riding lessons, specialist bikes, ski lessons and swimming lessons.

Annual grant total

In 2015/16 the foundation had an income of £14,900 and a total expenditure of £11,400. We estimate that grants totalled around £10,500.

Exclusions

Our research suggests that grants cannot be awarded for competitive purposes.

Applications

There is a six-stage application process which begins on the website. Applications are processed on a first-come-first-served basis and can take up to two months once all the information has been gathered.

Other information

This foundation was established in memory of Adam Millichip.

Richard Overall Trust

£9,000

Correspondent: The Trustees, New Barn Cottage, Honey Lane, Selborne, Alton GU34 3BY (01420 511175; email: therichardoveralltrust@gmail.com)

CC number: 1088640

Eligibility

Young people with disabilities participating in physical education.

Types of grants

Grants are made to support participation in physical education. Examples of what may be funded include: specialist equipment; training; sports clothing; transport; and support for attending or participating in sporting events.

Annual grant total

In 2015/16 the trust had an income of £10,900 and a total expenditure of £17,800. We estimate that grants given to individuals totalled around £9,000.

Applications

Application forms are available from the trust's website and should be accompanied by an assessment letter from a professional such as a teacher, physiotherapist or occupational therapist.

Other information

Grants may also be given to groups or organisations.

Sam Pilcher Trust

£3,000

Correspondent: Colin Pilcher, Springhill Barn, Upper Slaughter, Cheltenham GL54 2JH (01451 824378; email: sam. pilchertrust@btinternet.com; website: www.sampilchertrust.org.uk)

CC number: 1151779

Eligibility

Children who are suffering from cancer.

Types of grants

One-off grants for educational equipment, such as iPads, computers, books, and other learning materials.

Annual grant total

In 2016 the trust had an income of £15,000 and a total expenditure of £18,000. We estimate that the trust awarded £3,000 in grants for educational equipment.

Applications

Applications should be made in writing to the correspondent, detailing the situation and how the equipment would help a child with cancer continue their education.

Other information

The trust was established after 11-year-old Sam Pilcher died from leukaemia. Before his death, Sam took part in many fundraising activities to help other children with cancer.

The majority of the trust's donations go to hospitals, for example it helped to set up a dedicated Teenage Cancer Unit, and also supported the refurbishment of the activity rooms at Bristol Royal Children's Hospital and Gloucester Royal Children's Hospital.

The trust also provides grants to families of children with cancer, to help ease financial need. The trust has helped families to purchase equipment to help at home, white goods, and respite holidays.

Reach Charity Ltd

£7,800

Correspondent: Joanna Dixon, c/o Tavistock Enterprise Hub, Pearl Assurance House, 2 Brook Street, Tavistock PL19 0BN (0845 130 6225 or 020 3478 0100; email: reach@reach.org.uk; website: reach.org.uk/apply-reach-bursary)

CC number: 1134544

Eligibility
Children and young people under the age of 25 who have upper limb differences and who have been a member of Reach for at least one year.

Types of grants
One-off grants to help with education and training. Grants can also be made for car adaptations and driving lessons.

Annual grant total
In 2015/16 the charity held assets of £142,000 and had an income of £209,500. The amount of grants given to individuals totalled £7,800.

Applications
Application forms can be downloaded from the charity's website and submitted by email or post. The charity is happy to discuss potential applications and aims to give a decision within four weeks. References from an appropriate third party are required.

Other information
The charity also runs events, conferences and offers support for people with upper limb differences and their families.

A Smile For A Child

£89,000 (41 grants)

Correspondent: Christopher Read, 17 Sugarhill Crescent, Newton Aycliffe, County Durham DL5 4FH (07904448296; email: asmileforachild@btinternet.com; website: www.asmileforachild.org)

CC number: 1123357

Eligibility
Children in the UK who are disadvantaged or have a disability and wish to participate in sports.

Types of grants
Grants range from £25 to £8,000 and are available for mobility support, specialist wheelchairs and other specialist sports equipment as well as covering the costs of lessons.

Annual grant total
In 2015/16 the charity held assets of £55,500 and had an income of £139,000. Grants to 41 individuals totalled £89,000, with a further £70,500 awarded to organisations to help them buy equipment or provide services for children with disabilities.

Applications
An application form is available on the charity's website and should be returned to the correspondent.

The Snow Sports Foundation

£42,500 (388 grants)

Correspondent: Amanda Masterman, Treasurer, 11 East Street, Hemel Hempstead, Hertsfordshire HP2 5BN (01442 213324; email: amanda@snowsportsfoundation.org.uk; website: www.snowsportsfoundation.org.uk)

CC number: 1158955

Eligibility
People of any age who need additional support for daily living due to a sensory, neurological, developmental disability or an acquired brain injury and wish to take up snow sports. You must be able to stand and walk unaided. The foundation is unlikely to consider applications from people who are not in receipt of any benefits.

The additional needs that the foundation supports, but not limited to, are:
- Acquired brain injury
- Asperger's Syndrome
- Attention Deficit Disorder
- Attention Deficit Hyperactivity Disorder
- Autism/Autistic Spectrum Disorder
- Diabetes
- Down's Syndrome
- Dyslexia
- Dyspraxia
- Epilepsy
- Hearing impairment
- Rehabilitation challenges
- Stroke and brain injury
- Visual impairment

Types of grants
Grants are made for an assessment/taster session, followed by ten one-to-one sessions. This may be extended if funds are available.

Annual grant total
In 2016/17 the foundation held assets of £192,000 and had an income of £101,500. Grants totalled £42,500 and benefitted 388 students.

Applications
Application forms can be completed online on the foundation's website, or downloaded and returned to the correspondent. Applications can be submitted by individuals, small groups (e.g. Day Care Centre, DENS, disability support groups), schools and colleges. If your application is successful, the foundation will advise you on how to book the lessons.

Snowdon Trust

£147,000 (87 grants)

Correspondent: Paul Alexander, Chief Executive Officer, Unit 18, Oakhurst Business Park, Wilberforce Way, Southwater, Horsham, West Sussex RH13 9RT (01403 732899; email: info@snowdontrust.org.uk; website: www.snowdontrust.org)

CC number: 282754

Eligibility
Students with physical or sensory disabilities who are in or about to enter post-16 education or training in the UK and, because of their disability, have financial needs which are not covered by statutory funding.

Types of grants
Bursaries for up to two years are available to people in further/higher education and those training towards employment. Support is aimed to cover additional costs incurred due to the disability which cannot be met in full from statutory sources, such as human support (e.g. sign language interpreters or people to take notes); computer equipment or specialist software; adapted or additional accommodation; travel costs; wheelchairs and other mobility equipment; or other similar expenses.

Grants are normally between £250 and £3,000.

Annual grant total
In 2015/16 the trust had assets of £1.3 million and an income of £403,000. Grants were made to 87 students totalling £147,000.

Exclusions
The trust does not normally cover expenses for tuition fees or standard living, accommodation and childcare costs, but can occasionally help with tuition fees if the need is justifiably and

directly related to the applicant's disability. Retrospective awards are not made.

Applications

Application forms and guidelines can be completed online or downloaded from the trust's website. Applicants are required to provide academic and personal references and supporting documentation such as medical information of disability if applicable.

Applications are accepted from 1 February and the deadlines for applications are 31 May and 31 August each year, with decisions made around July and October respectively.

Other information

The trust was formerly known as The Snowdon Award Scheme.

In 2015 the trust removed a previously-stated age preference for students between 17 and 25, reflecting the fact that the trust supports a significant number of applications from those retraining following later onset of disability, or those undertaking postgraduate study.

This trust also provides mentoring support and advice to beneficiaries and occasionally undertakes research.

Snowdon Scholarships are also available to fund masters programmes at certain institutions, which are administered by the universities themselves – refer to the website for more information.

Student Disability Assistance Fund (SDAF)

£12,000

Correspondent: Patricia Esswood, Administrative Secretary, University of Nottingham Health Centre, Cripps Health Centre, University Park, Nottingham NG7 2QW (07982 040005; website: www.studenthealthassociation. co.uk)

CC number: 253984

Eligibility

Students over the age of 18 on a higher education course in the UK who are affected by disability or illness. Candidates are expected to apply for Disabled Students Allowance (DSA) before applying to the fund. Priority is given to individuals who are not eligible for funding from the local authorities and those who do not qualify for DSA. Students on both full-time and part-time courses at both undergraduate and postgraduate levels, as well as Open University courses, are eligible.

Types of grants

One-off grants of up to £500 towards educational aids made necessary by the student's illness or disability. For example, support could be given for special computer equipment and software, additional books, photocopying, extra travel costs for those with mobility problems, cost of note-takers or signers and other special equipment.

Annual grant total

In 2015/16 the fund had an income of £14,700 and a total expenditure of £12,900. We estimate the total amount of grants awarded to be around £12,000.

Exclusions

Funding is not given for general educational expenses incurred by all students (e.g. fees, living costs or compulsory textbooks) or for medical treatment or equipment, unless it is specific to study problems. Funding is only given to recipients of DSA in exceptional circumstances.

Applications

Eligible applicants are asked to apply on an online form on the fund's website. Supporting evidence has to be posted to the correspondent (a full list of required documentation can be found on the website). The deadlines for applications are normally 1 March, 1 June and 1 November each year, and it can take around one month to finalise awards. Incomplete applications are not accepted. Note that the fund cannot respond to telephone enquiries.

Other information

The fund is now also known as the Student Health Association Fund; it was formerly known as BASHE (The British Association of Health Services in Higher Education). It can also offer guidance, advice and information.

Sensory impairment

The Christina Aitchison Trust

£500

Correspondent: Revd Roger Massingberd-Mundy, Trustee, The Old Post Office, The Street, West Raynham, Fakenham NR21 7AD

CC number: 1041578

Eligibility

Young people under the age of 25. Support can particularly be provided to people who are blind or suffering from any ophthalmic disease or disability. Some preference may be given to individuals in the north east or south west of England.

Types of grants

One-off or recurrent grants for up to £300 are made to support young people in educational activities, including arts and music. Awards are made in the form of books, equipment, fees, bursaries and fellowships.

Annual grant total

In 2016/17 the trust had an income of £1,800 and a total expenditure of £2,400. We estimate that educational grants to individuals totalled around £500.

Applications

Application forms are available from the correspondent and should generally be submitted in March or September for consideration in April or November.

Other information

Relief-in-need grants are also given to assist people who have an ophthalmic disease or who are terminally ill and to organisations.

The Amber Trust

£88,000 (178 grants)

Correspondent: Julia Walport, Trustee, 64A Princes Way, London SW19 6JF (020 8788 9755; email: contact@ ambertrust.org; website: www. ambertrust.org)

CC number: 1050503

Eligibility

Children and young people up to and including the age of 18 who are blind or partially sighted and have a talent or love for music.

Types of grants

One-off and recurrent grants for up to one year are awarded to fund three terms (maximum 36 lessons) of music lessons and/or music therapy sessions. Funding is also available to cover the cost of one-off events such as concerts or musical activities, the purchase of musical instruments, and specialist computer software (such as Sibelius).

Annual grant total

In 2015/16 the trust had assets of £232,000, income of £180,500 and a total expenditure of £107,000. During the year, 178 grants were made, totalling £88,000.

Exclusions

The trust will not make retrospective grants. In some instances the charity will not be able to fund the full costs and the balance will have to be raised from other sources, but the applicants are welcome to use the trust's pledge to encourage other funding.

Applications

Application forms can be found on the trust's website. Applications should be completed by the child's parents or carers, but can be assisted or prepared by a support worker or teacher. Completed forms should be sent to the correspondent.

Applications for the purchase of instruments or software should include prices and supplier details. Applications for lessons or music therapy sessions must include full details of the teacher's or therapist's qualifications, experience and DBS clearance.

The trustees meet three times a year, in March, July and November. Applications should be received by the end of February, June and October, respectively. All eligible applications will be acknowledged in writing. A separate second or subsequent application for can also be found on the website.

Other information

If parents have not found a suitable music teacher or therapist for their child, they are encouraged to get in touch with RNIB's Music Advisory Service providing information and advice on music education at all levels.

Elizabeth Eagle-Bott Memorial Fund

£14,000

Correspondent: Music Advisory Service, RNIB, 105 Judd Street, London WC1H 9NE (email: mas@rnib.org.uk; website: www.rnib.org.uk)

CC number: 226227

Eligibility

Musicians, normally aged 18 and over, who are blind or partially sighted. Candidates must be registered as sight impaired or seriously sight impaired (partially sighted or blind) and be UK citizens.

Types of grants

Previously grants have been awarded for the purchase of instruments, vocal tuition, music course fees, transcriber and reader costs, the purchase or development of accessible and assistive music technology, costs associated with staging concerts and so on.

The Elizabeth Eagle-Bott Memorial Fund, in Phase Three running from 2015 to 2020, grants three types of awards A, B and C.

A. Major awards for individuals, of up to £10,000 per bid, to blind or partially sighted UK citizens aged 18 and over, to support their music-making. These are awarded annually.

B. Major awards, of up to £15,000 per bid, for those working on behalf of the music-making of blind or partially sighted UK musicians. These are awarded annually.

C. Minor awards for individuals, of up to £500 per bid, to blind or partially sighted UK citizens aged 18 and over, to support their music-making. These are awarded quarterly.

Annual grant total

In 2015/16 the fund had an income of £28,000 and a total expenditure of £28,000. We estimate that around £14,000 was given to individuals.

Applications

Application forms are available from the correspondent. To request an application form or to discuss your bid email mas@rnib.org.uk.

All bids will be considered by an expert Panel, with their decisions approved by RNIB. The closing time for applications for awards A and B is noon on 31 March each year.

The closing time for applications for award C are:

- 31 March for awards valid between 1 June and 31 August
- 31 July for awards valid between 1 September and 30 November
- 31 October for awards valid between 1 December and end of February
- 31 January for awards valid between 1 March and 31 May

During phase three, from 2015 to 2020, any one person may receive up to two major and two minor awards (A and C) and any one group or person may receive up to three major awards (B). Awards A and B run from 1 June to 31 July thirteen months on, in the year awarded.

Other information

The fund was set up by Miss Elizabeth Eagle-Bott whose great interest was music. She learnt to play the organ in her sixties. She then played for her parish church for twenty years. Her particular desire to assist young musicians who are visually impaired arose from her attending an organ recital given by a student, who was blind, at the Royal College of Music. The first phase of this award, 2000 to 2009, allocated almost £100,000 to young classical musicians with a particular focus on preparing them for paid employment in the music business.

The fund is administered by RNIB. We have used financial information relating to the fund only. Grants may also be given to support organisations and individuals assisting blind or partially sighted musicians in their music-making.

Gardner's Trust for the Blind

£21,500

Correspondent: Angela Stewart, 117 Charterhouse Street, London EC1M 6AA (020 7253 3757)

CC number: 207233

Eligibility

Registered blind or partially sighted people who live in the UK.

Types of grants

Grants are mainly for computer equipment and course fees.

Annual grant total

In 2015/16 the trust had assets of £3.7 million and an income of £97,500. Educational grants to individuals totalled £21,500.

Exclusions

Loans are not given.

Applications

Apply in writing to the correspondent. Applications can be submitted either directly by the individual or by a third party, but they must also be supported by a third party who can confirm that the applicant has a disability and that the grant is needed.

The Anne Herd Memorial Trust

£500

Correspondent: The Trustees of The Anne Herd Memorial Trust, 27 Bank Street, Dundee DD1 1RP

OSCR number: SC014198

Eligibility

People who are blind or partially sighted who live in Broughty Ferry. Applicants from the City of Dundee, region of Tayside or those who have connections with these areas and reside in Scotland will also be considered.

Types of grants

Grants are given for educational equipment such as computers and books. Grants are usually at least £50.

Annual grant total

In 2015/16 the trust had a total income of £112,500, of which £72,500 was derived from the sale of investments, and a total expenditure of £97,500, of which £68,500 was attributed to the purchase of investments. Grants totalled £2,000. We estimate that educational grants to individuals totalled £500.

Applications

Applications can be made in writing to the correspondent. They can be submitted directly by the individual in March/April for consideration in June.

The Society for the Education of the Deaf

£24,000 (126 grants)

Correspondent: Nancy Ward, Administrator, c/o Alexander Sloan, Chartered Accountants, 38 Cadogan Street, Glasgow G2 7HF (0141 204 8989; email: nancy.ward@alexandersloan.co.uk; website: www.gsedd.org.uk)

OSCR number: SC003804

Eligibility

Scottish individuals who are deaf and/or speech impaired.

Types of grants

Grants are mainly awarded towards British sign language courses or similar activities and educational courses that will improve applicants' ability to communicate with others.

Annual grant total

In 2015/16 the society held assets of £1 million and had an income of £35,500. Grants awarded to 126 individuals totalled £24,000.

Exclusions

Grants are not given for taster or introductory courses. Grant applications will only be considered from individuals and not course organisers or businesses.

Applications

Application forms can be completed online on the society's website or printed off and sent to the correspondent. Applications can be submitted directly by the individual or through a third party and are normally assessed within three to eight weeks.

Webster and Davidson Mortification for the Blind

£2,900 (three grants)

Correspondent: G. Fulton or N. Barclay, Trust Administrators, Thorntons Law LLP, Whitehall House, 33 Yeaman Shore, Dundee DD1 4BJ (01382 229111; fax: 01382 202288; email: gfulton@ thorntons-law.co.uk; website: www. thorntons-law.co.uk/for-you/wills,- trusts-and-succession/charitable-trusts)

OSCR number: SC004920

Eligibility

Blind or partially sighted people who are undertaking musical education. Applicants must be resident, or normally resident, in Britain, and preference is given to those in Scotland.

Types of grants

Grants are given to support the learning and appreciation of music. Generally, but not exclusively, grants are given at secondary school level or to further/ higher education students. Grants are generally for one year, but may be renewed at the discretion of the trustees.

Annual grant total

In 2016 the charity had an income of £29,500 and a total expenditure of £25,000. Grants to three individuals totalled £2,900 and were given for: bagpipes; coaching sessions; and university fees. A further two grants were given to organisations, totalling £2,000.

Exclusions

The bursary is not intended to take the place of or supplement Scottish Students' Allowances or other awards derived from public funds.

Applications

Application forms, guidance notes and referee report forms (also available in Braille) can be obtained from the correspondent or can be downloaded from the Thorntons Law LLP website. Applications should be submitted by 31 March.

Other information

Grants are also given to organisations working with visually impaired people to provide funding for educational visits to places of historical or other interest. Organisations from Dundee, Tayside or Scotland are preferred.

Special educational needs

Dyslexia Institute Ltd (Dyslexia Action)

£147,000

Correspondent: Anne Frater, Company Secretary, Dyslexia Action House, 10 High Street, Egham, Surrey TW20 9EA (01784 222300; email: getinvolved@dyslexiaaction.org.uk; website: www.dyslexiaaction.org.uk)

CC number: 268502, SC039177

Eligibility

People in the UK who have dyslexia or literacy difficulties and are from low-income families.

Types of grants

A small number of grants are made from the Learning Fund for subsidised assessment and specific periods of tuition based on educational needs related to dyslexia and literacy difficulties. Grants for one term's tuition are for approximately £400, totalling £2,400 for six terms. A contribution from the individual or their family is required at a minimum of £5 per week. The fund is solely reliant on fundraising activities, therefore the amount of grants given is restricted and varies each year.

The majority of bursary-funded pupils attend the nationwide centres of Dyslexia Action for one and a half or two hours of multi-sensory tuition each week during the academic year.

Annual grant total

In 2015 the charity had assets of £907,000 and an income of £6.4 million. Throughout the year the charity awarded around £147,000 in grants to individuals from its Learning Fund.

Exclusions

Applicants from families where joint annual income is in excess of £22,000 will not be considered without evidence of exceptional circumstances.

Applications

Apply by contacting the Dyslexia Action Centre at which the applicant wishes to have tuition. Applications are considered three times a year (one meeting each academic term). Applicants for tuition grants should indicate family income and severity of dyslexia – a full educational psychologist's assessment is normally required.

Note that while a grant is awarded to an individual, the payment of fees for tuition is made directly to the Dyslexia Action centre where the tuition will take place.

Other information

The charity also organises training events, conferences, fundraising events, provides guidance, advice and supports schools across England working with children with dyslexia and literacy difficulties who are on free school meals and live in deprived communities.

Independent and boarding schools

The BMTA Trust Ltd

£152,000 (108 grants)

Correspondent: L. J. Dolphin, Wild Wood, Fairfield Road, Shawford, Winchester SO21 2DA (01962 715025; email: bmtatrust@yahoo.co.uk)

CC number: 273978

Eligibility

Children between the ages of 13 and 15 who are already attending an independent school with a preference for those whose families are connected with the motor industry. Children in exceptional circumstances of social need are occasionally supported to begin attending an independent or boarding school. The trustees 'aim to consider, primarily, cases brought about by unforeseen disaster rather than giving assistance to fund over-ambitious plans'.

Types of grants

Short-term educational grants are given to enable children to complete their current stage of schooling when families have suffered unforeseen financial difficulties.

Assistance may be given up to GCSE level and further education is only funded in exceptional circumstances.

Annual grant total

In 2015/16 the trust held assets of £5 million and had an income of £237,500. A total of £152,000 was awarded in educational grants to 108 individuals.

Applications

Apply by contacting the correspondent via email, letter or phone.

Other information

The trust also provides grants to individuals for welfare purposes, and to other charitable organisations. In 2015/16 the trust awarded £20,500 to 15 individuals for non-educational purposes. No grants were made to organisations.

Buttle UK – School Fees Programme

£1.2 million (917 grants)

Correspondent: Alan Knowles, 15 Greycoat Place, London SW1P 1SB (020 7828 7311; email: info@buttleuk. org; website: www.buttleuk.org)

CC number: 313007

Eligibility

Children aged between 11 and 18 who are either: adopted; cared for by grandparents, relatives or friends; from single parent families; or with two carers.

Types of grants

Grants of up to £4,500 to pay for school fees. Day school fees are no longer provided for.

Annual grant total

In 2016/17 the trust held assets of £57.5 million and had an income of £4.5 million. A total of £1.2 million was awarded in grants for school fees.

Exclusions

The trust cannot assist:

▶ A school that has been chosen for a particular type of education, such as sport or drama
▶ Young people under the care of the local authority, or where there is any other clear statutory responsibility
▶ Where there is a reasonable possibility the needs of the young person can be met through the state day system, possibly through a change of school
▶ Where the sole grounds of the application are that the child or young person has a learning or developmental difficulty for which special facilities may be available at a fee-paying school
▶ Young people without settled immigration status in the UK
▶ Young people who normally reside outside the UK

Applications

An enquiry form is available for completion on the trust's website – if you are found to be eligible, the trust will send you a full application form.

Other information

The trust also runs a small grants programme helping individuals in need.

The Emmott Foundation Ltd

£346,500

Correspondent: Julie and Paul Spillane, Education Officers, 136 Browns Lane, Stanton-on-the-Wolds, Nottinghamshire NG12 5BN (0115 937 6526; email: emmottfoundation@btinternet.com; website: emmottfoundation.org)

CC number: 209033

Eligibility

Students aged 16 to 18 in fee-paying schools (including state boarding schools) who have high academic achievements (a majority of actual or predicted A*s or As at GCSE).

From the 2015/16 trustees' annual report:

Accordingly grants are primarily intended for children whose parents or guardians can no longer meet their considered financial commitments for education in either state or independent sixth forms as a result of a family crisis such as death, severe illness, accident, divorce, desertion or loss of employment. Consequently support is often given to children of families where the household income is very low. Consideration will also be given to cases where there is a major educational or pastoral problem, including the impact of parental drug and/or alcohol abuse, domestic violence and bullying.

Awards may be granted to students with lower grades in circumstances of exceptional need or where there is a major educational, social or pastoral problem, including domestic violence, bullying, or parental drug/alcohol abuse.

Note: Grants are made only where the school is willing to make a significant contribution towards the fees.

Types of grants

Grants are for Sixth Form students only. Their purpose is to enable pupils to enter or remain in the Sixth Form in their present school. The grants help only with basic fees, not with incidental expenses (music lessons, travel, books, expeditions and so on). Grants are usually of between £500 and £1,500 per term, paid directly to the school at the start of each Sixth Form term.

Annual grant total

In 2015/16 the foundation held assets of £10.6 million and had an income of £440,500. Direct individual fee assistance totalled £346,500. Annual scholarships of £2,000 each were awarded to three Sixth Form pupils by the Arkwright Scholarship Trust for Design Technology.

Exclusions

Students in other age groups than those specified above are not considered.

Applications

Apply initially in writing to the correspondent. Application forms will be sent to eligible applicants. The trustees meet in March, June and November to consider applications. Enquiries and applications should be made to the Education Officers.

Fishmongers' Company's Charitable Trust

£26,500

Correspondent: Peter Woodward, Trustee, Fishmongers' Hall, London Bridge, London EC4R 9EL (020 7626 3531; fax: 020 7929 1389; email: ct@fishhall.org.uk; website: www.fishhall.org.uk/Education–Grants)

CC number: 263690

Eligibility
Children and young people under the age of 19 who are in need of a sum of money to complete schooling.

Types of grants
Small, one-off grants to assist in cases of short-term need; scholarships.

Annual grant total
In 2016 the trust had assets of £30.6 million and an income of £797,500. Grants to individuals for educational purposes totalled £26,500. Of this, £25,500 was awarded in Elizabeth Garrett Anderson Scholarships to help female medical students at the Royal Free Hospital School of Medicine.

Applications
Application forms can be requested from the correspondent. They can be submitted directly by the individual or by a parent/guardian for those under the age of 18. The trustees usually meet in March, June/July and October/November.

Other information
The trust also gives to organisations for welfare, medical, environment and heritage causes. The largest recipient of the trust's funding is Gresham's School in Norfolk, but a number of other schools are also supported.

IAPS Charitable Trust

£32,500 (35+ grants)

Correspondent: Richard Flower, Secretary, 11 Waterloo Place, Leamington Spa, Warwickshire CV32 5LA (01926 887833; email: rwf@iaps.uk; website: iaps.uk/about/our-charities)

CC number: 1143241

Eligibility
Children in early, primary or middle school years (i.e. up to the age of 13), both in the UK and overseas. Support is also given to children of members or deceased members of the teaching profession to continue their education in independent senior schools, where their families' financial circumstances have changed.

Children between the ages of 8 and 14 are supported to attend residential music courses in the UK (principally supported courses are the National Schools Symphony Orchestras (NSSO and Young NSSO), the National Preparatory School Orchestras (NPSO) and the Junior Eton Choral Courses (JECC)).

Types of grants
General grants
Grants are available to support the education of children up to the age of 13.

Bursaries
The trust provides bursaries of up to £2,500 per year per pupil. According to the website, priority is given where 'pupils have already started their education in independent schools and whose families' financial circumstances have changed'. Applicants must have the support of their school, or intended school, and all awards are subject to an annual needs assessment review.

Music
Music bursaries are awarded from the Harrison Memorial Fund to children aged between 8 and 14 years, providing the financial support they need to attend residential music courses in the UK.

Schools Access Scheme
The trust supports the scheme, which enables children to attend a prep school in cases where their families would not normally have the resources for them to do so.

Annual grant total
In 2016/17 the trust had assets of £1.6 million and an income of £171,000. Grants totalled £61,000, of which £20,000 was distributed to organisations. Individuals were awarded grants amounting to £41,000.

The trustees' report states 'The restricted funds were used to make Bursary fund education grants of £8,500; Benevolent fund hardship grants of £8,584; Harrison Memorial fund music grants totalling £3,150; and School Access Scheme grants of £21,010.' Based on this information, we believe educational grants to individuals amounted to around £32,500.

Exclusions
Support is not given where public funding is available. Gap year students are not assisted.

Applications
For more information about general grants, contact the correspondent. Application forms for bursaries and music grants are available to download from the website, where the details of relevant contacts who can provide further information can also be found. Application forms and guidance notes for the Schools Access Scheme are also available from the website, but must be made through an IAPS member school.

Other information
In 2012 the IAPS Benevolent Fund and the IAPS Bursary Trust, and in 2013 the IAPS Orchestra Trust, merged with the trust allowing to extend its work.

The trust is also known as 'itrust'.

Reedham Children's Trust

£416,000 (111 grants)

Correspondent: Sarah Smart, Chief Executive, 23 Old Lodge Lane, Purley, Surrey CR8 4DJ (020 8660 1461; email: info@reedham-trust.org.uk; website: www.reedhamchildrenstrust.org.uk)

CC number: 312433

Eligibility
Children (typically aged 11 to 16, although each case is assessed individually) who are in need of boarding school care, due to difficult circumstances such as: the death, disability or absence of one or both of their parents, or other domestic or personal circumstances.

The trust states that it focuses on social need for boarding, not on educational need or academic ability, but closely monitors the progress (both academic and social) of the children assisted.

Types of grants
Boarding grants for children who are in need of care. The trust may also be able to provide assistance with travel and small items of equipment in some circumstances.

Annual grant total
In 2015/16 the trust had assets of £8.2 million and an income of £360,500. Grants were awarded totalling £416,000 in support of 111 children (of which 24 were new recipients) at 39 schools in the UK.

Exclusions
The trust will not give support in cases where the local authority should bear the responsibility (for example where a care order is in place).

Children below the age of 11 are supported only in exceptional circumstances and funding after GCSEs can only be continued following a review of the home situation.

Applications
Application forms can be downloaded from the trust's website. Eligible applicants should contact the trust via email or phone for further guidance on

the application process. The trust will need confirmation from a professional that boarding is in the interests of the applicant. Deadlines for applications are posted on the website.

From the charity's website:

Due to high demand and for the foreseeable future, we are only able to consider cases where children live within a 60-mile radius of our office here in Purley, Surrey. If you live outside the area please telephone the office on 020 8660 1461 to discuss your case prior to completing any of our forms.

Other information

The trust has a restricted North East Fund to support children in that specific area.

Royal National Children's Foundation

£1.3 million (373 grants)

Correspondent: Jane Pocock, Case Worker, Sandy Lane, Cobham, Surrey KT11 2ES (01932 868622; fax: 01932 866420; email: admin@rncf.org.uk; website: www.rncf.org.uk)

CC number: 310916

Eligibility

Children between the ages of 7 and 18 who have one or no active parents, whose development is compromised by adverse home or school circumstances (e.g. those who have suffered trauma, neglect or are at risk in some way) and whose family cannot meet the costs of boarding education unaided.

Types of grants

The foundation provides support towards state and independent boarding school fees. Some pupils in independent day school are also assisted (normally younger children aged 7 to 13). Emphasis is on boarding need rather than on educational need. The foundation aims to support children until they leave secondary school.

Annual grant total

In 2015/16 the foundation had assets of £23.3 million and an income of £1.5 million. A total of almost £1.3 million was spent in support to 373 children.

Exclusions

Support cannot be given on the sole basis of financial difficulties, educational preferences or special needs.

Applications

Eligible applicants should make initial contact with the foundation via phone or email. Potential beneficiaries are often referred by parents, guardians, or relevant professionals such as medical professionals, community workers and

schools. A home visit will take place and a full review of the case will be put to the selection committee for consideration. Informal enquiries prior to the application are also welcomed.

Other information

The Royal Wanstead Children's Foundation and Joint Educational Trust have merged to form Royal National Children's Foundation, retaining the registered charity number of the former.

Miscellaneous

The Buchanan Society

£3,800

Correspondent: Ian Buchanan, 16 Ribblesdale, East Kilbride G74 4QN (01355 243437; email: Contact form on website; website: www.buchanansociety. com)

OSCR number: SC013679

Eligibility

People with any of the following surnames: Buchanan, McAuslan (any spelling), McWattie or Risk.

Types of grants

Bursaries of around £1,000 are given to students who are in severe financial difficulties. One-off grants can also be given for general educational purposes.

Annual grant total

In 2016 the society had assets of £1.6 million and an income of £54,000. Educational grants to individuals totalled £3,800.

Applications

Application forms are available to download from the charity's website or can be requested from the correspondent.

Other information

The Buchanan Society is the oldest Clan Society in Scotland having been founded in 1725. Grant-making is its sole function.

Fenton Trust

£24,000

Correspondent: Fiona MacGillivray, Correspondent, Family Action, 501–505 Kingsland Road, London E8 4AU (020 7241 7609; email: grants. enquiry@family-action.org.uk; website: www.family-action.org.uk)

CC number: 247552

Eligibility

Any dependant of a member of professional class undergoing a course of education or training or 'poor and deserving members of the professional or middle classes and their dependants'.

Types of grants

Grants are normally of about £200 to £300 and can be given to assist with general educational costs.

Annual grant total

In 2015/16 the trust had a total expenditure of £25,000. We estimate that around £25,000 was awarded in grants to individuals.

Exclusions

Grants are not available for private school fees, loan repayments, childcare costs, living expenses or to postgraduate students.

Applications

The trust is administered by Family Action. Enquiries should be directed to the correspondent.

Other information

Our research suggests that the grant is paid to the governing body not the individual.

The Vegetarian Charity

£11,000

Correspondent: Susan Lenihan, 56 Parliament Street, Chippenham SN14 0DE (01249 443521; email: grantssecretary@vegetariancharity.org.uk; website: www.vegetariancharity.org.uk)

CC number: 294767

Eligibility

Vegetarians and vegans up to the age of 26 who are in need.

Types of grants

One-off and recurrent grants can be made for educational purposes, for example to meet the costs of books, equipment, or course fees.

Annual grant total

In 2015/16 the charity had assets of £1.1 million and an income of £53,000. We estimate that the charity awarded £11,000 in grants for education.

Exclusions

The website states: 'In the current economic climate postgraduate applications are only considered in exceptionally difficult personal circumstances.'

Applications

Application forms can be found online and should be completed and returned to the Grants Secretary, preferably via email. The application form asks for details of personal income, expenditure, and debts to assess financial eligibility.

Parents should complete the application on behalf of a child who is under 16.

Other information

Grants are also made to support individuals in need, and to organisations running projects for vegetarians and vegans under the age of 26.

The Matthews Wrightson Charity Trust

£1,500 (three grants)

Correspondent: Jon Mills, 46 Foreland Road, Bembridge, Isle of Wight PO355XW (email: office@ matthewswrightson.org.uk; website: matthewswrightson.org.uk)

CC number: 262109

Eligibility

Applicants must be UK-registered charities, or individuals currently living in the UK preparing to volunteer in the UK or overseas

Particular regard is given to those working with young people, people with disabilities and underprivileged people. Individuals undertaking charitable projects (trainee doctors with medical elective expenses) or undertaking volunteering work overseas are also invited to apply.

Types of grants

The typical grant is for £500, however there is potential to get access to a grant of £1,000. The trustees will not commit to offer long-term funding. Only one grant can be awarded per year to each individual/organisation.

Annual grant total

In 2016 the charity had an income of £64,500 and a total expenditure of £75,000. Three grants to individuals were awarded amounting to £1,500.

Exclusions

Grants towards the personal education of an applicant, or gap year students are not applicable.

Applications

Applications must be made online to one of the trustees. Applicants must choose the area of their charitable work and select the relevant trustee in order to access the appropriate application form. Applications should be made to one trustee only – do not apply to multiple trustees.

Students from the Royal College of Art wanting to apply for a hardship grant must apply through the college.

Grants are awarded four times a year, and payments are normally made in March, July, October and December.

Overseas students

The Anglo-Czech Educational Fund

£64,000 (one grant)

Correspondent: Paul Sheils, Trustee, Moon Beever Solicitors, Bedford House, 21 A. John Street, London WC1N 2BF (02074007770; email: info@moonbeever. com)

CC number: 1110348

Eligibility

Students from the Czech Republic who wish to study primarily in the UK, USA and European countries.

Types of grants

Educational grants and loans.

Annual grant total

In 2015/16 the trust had assets of £1.3 million, an income of £34,500 and a total expenditure of £81,000. A total of £64,000 was donated to Karlova Univerzita in Prague to distribute as grants.

Applications

Apply in writing to the correspondent.

Armenian General Benevolent Union London Trust

£47,500 (33 grants)

Correspondent: Camilio Azzouz, Kent House, 14–17 Market Place, London W1W 8AJ (website: www.agbu.org.uk)

CC number: 282070

Eligibility

University students of Armenian descent studying full-time at accredited UK educational institutions. Both undergraduate and postgraduate programmes are eligible. Preference can be given for courses in Armenian studies or subjects which may benefit the Armenian community.

There are specific programmes available for students studying performing arts.

Types of grants

Scholarships generally range from £1,000 to £3,000 and are awarded annually for up to three years. Support is both need- and merit-based and is normally intended to cover educational fees or to

contribute to essentials, books or maintenance. The trust offers both grants and interest-free loans.

Students studying performing arts have the opportunity to apply for funding to study in the US. For undergraduates, see the AGBU Performing Arts Fellowship. For postgraduates (master's and above), see the US Graduate Fellowship programme.

Annual grant total

In 2015/16 the charity had an income of £202,500 and a total expenditure of £125,000. A total of £47,500 was awarded in scholarships to 33 beneficiaries.

Exclusions

Citizens of Armenia studying in Armenia are not eligible for the scholarship. The trust does not offer travel grants, support for conferences, semesters of study abroad, non-degree courses, research studies and similar short-term educational or professional experience.

Applications

Applications can be made online on the AGBU Scholarship program website. There is a convenient eligibility checking programme. There are various scholarships and fellowships with different deadline dates, check the website carefully before submitting an application.

Other information

Support is also given for the relief of poverty among Armenians, and for the promotion of Armenian history, culture, literature, language and religion. In 2015/16 aid to Armenia and other charitable causes totalled £72,000 – £60,000 was awarded to the Syria Relief Programme; £5,000 to the Armenian Church Trust; £4,000 to K Tahta Armenian School; £2,000 to career development; and £1,000 to Shakespeare Festival.

The Armenian Relief Society of Great Britain Trust

£650

Correspondent: The Trustees, 19 Somervell Road, Middlesex HA2 8TY

CC number: 327389

Eligibility

Poor, sick or bereaved Armenians, worldwide.

Types of grants

One-off and recurrent grants of £150 are available to promote the study and research into the history and culture of Armenians or to pay fees or educational costs.

Annual grant total

In 2016 the charity had assets of £84,000 and income of £31,000. The total amount awarded for educational support was £650. Support is mainly given to organisations.

Applications

Apply in writing to the correspondent.

Other information

This charity mainly provides support to other charitable organisations to assist with welfare support.

The Bestway Foundation

£183,000 (51 grants)

Correspondent: M. Y. Sheikh, Trustee, Bestway Foundation, Abbey Road, London NW10 7BW (020 8453 1234; fax: 020 8453 8219; email: zulfikaur. wajid-hasan@bestway.co.uk; website: www.bestwaygroup.co.uk/page/Bestway-Foundation.html)

CC number: 297178

Eligibility

Higher education students who are of Indian, Pakistani, Bangladeshi or Sri Lankan origin.

Types of grants

One-off and recurrent scholarships, grants and loans towards tuition fees. Payments are normally made directly to academic institutions.

Annual grant total

In 2015/16 the foundation held assets of £6.3 million and had an income of £252,000. The total amount awarded in grants was £183,000, awarded to 41 individuals.

Applications

Apply in writing to the correspondent. Considerations are usually made in January.

Other information

Grants are also made to organisations in the UK and overseas (ten grants totalling £254,000 were made during the year).

The British Institute for the Study of Iraq (Gertrude Bell Memorial)

£28,500 (15 grants)

Correspondent: Lauren Mulvee, 10 Carlton House Terrace, London SW1Y 5AH (020 7969 5274; email: bisi@britac.ac.uk; website: www.bisi.ac.uk)

CC number: 1135395

Eligibility

People undertaking research, projects, conferences or development events on Iraq, and Iraqi scholars visiting the UK for a study. The charity can support scholars in areas relating to Iraq and neighbouring countries in anthropology, archaeology, geography, history, language and related disciplines within the arts, humanities and social sciences.

Types of grants

Grants are available for research projects, to cultural heritage professionals of Iraq for retraining and re-equipment, also for educational events that develop the understanding of Iraq's society, history and culture.

Research and conference grants are awarded to people in the field of humanities and social sciences. Assistance is available for direct educational expenses (such as equipment, travel costs, consultancy fees) and can be of up to £4,000. Applicants must be employed by, or have an official connection with, a UK higher education institution.

Pilot project grants are given to support up to one year of preliminary research on Iraq, the arts, humanities or social sciences that has a potential to turn into a long-term project. The award can reach up to £8,000. Application criteria are the same as for regular research grants.

Outreach grants, usually of up to £500, can be awarded for various public engagement events and projects (such as lectures or study days) relating to Iraq. Applicants should normally be UK residents.

Visiting Iraqi Scholarships are offered each year to two Iraqi scholars and cultural heritage professionals for research, training and collaborative projects in the UK, particularly those who already work in partnership with UK institutions/academies. These awards are available for institutional fees (excluding tuition fees), living and travel expenses and emergency travel insurance.

Annual grant total

In 2015/16 the charity had assets of £2.6 million and an income of £105,500. A total of £28,500 was awarded in grants to 15 people for research, projects, and outreach.

Exclusions

Visiting Iraqi Scholarships do not cover salary expenses, tuition fees or routine medical expenses. Research grants cannot be offered for institutional overheads, salary costs, PhD studentships or living costs.

Applications

Application forms for different schemes can be found on the charity's website or requested from the correspondent. The deadlines are: 1 October for Outreach grants (applications must be emailed providing two references) and 1 February for Research, Pilot Project, and Visiting Scholarship grants (applications must be made both by email and post).

Other information

The charity also organises public events, lectures, study days, conferences, as well as publishing books and a journal.

The British Institute of Archaeology at Ankara (British Institute at Ankara)
See entry on page 91

Canadian Centennial Scholarship Fund (UK)

£43,500 (14 grants)

Correspondent: The Trustees, Canadian Centennial Scholarship Fund, c/o Canadian Women's Club, Canada House, Trafalgar Square, London SW1Y 5BJ (020 7228 0698; email: info@canadianscholarshipfund.co.uk; website: www.canadianscholarshipfund.co.uk)

CC number: 313966

Eligibility

Canadian citizens who are in need of financial assistance for a postgraduate study in the United Kingdom. Applicants should have at least one term remaining when applying.

Types of grants

The fund offers scholarships ranging from £2,000 to £5,000 which can be used towards fees, travel expenses, books, maintenance and living expenses.

Annual grant total

In 2015/16 the charity held assets of £92,000 and had an income of £31,000. The total amount awarded in grants was £43,500.

Exclusions

Applicants undertaking a one-year programme are not accepted.

Applications

Application forms and guidelines are available to download from the charity's website, and completed applications should be emailed to scholarship@canadianscholarshipfund.co.uk.

The deadline for applications is usually the beginning of March. Applicants have been unsuccessful if they do not receive a response from the charity by mid-May.

Sir Ernest Cassel Educational Trust (The Cassel Trust)

£12,000

Correspondent: Kathryn Hodges, 5 Grimston Park Mews, Grimston Park, Grimston, Tadcaster LS24 9DB (01937 834730; email: casseltrust@btinternet. com; website: www.casseltrust.co.uk)

CC number: 313820

Eligibility

Overseas students from the Commonwealth countries studying in the UK who are in the final year of their studies and are experiencing unforeseen financial difficulties.

Types of grants

The trust offers grants to individuals in the following two categories:

- Mountbatten Memorial Grants – for overseas students from the Commonwealth countries who are facing financial difficulties in their final year at a UK university to help them finish the course by contributing towards living expenses only
- Postdoctoral Travel Grants – awards of up to £1,000 to assist with the travel costs of postdoctoral students who are at university in the UK undertaking research overseas in the humanities and other fields

Annual grant total

In 2016/17 the trust held assets of £1.7 million and had an income of £65,500. The total amount awarded to individuals was £12,000.

Exclusions

Grants are not intended to cover or contribute to the course fees. The trust will not provide retrospective grants, repayment of debts or support to overseas students who are UK-registered for fees purposes. Students on a one-year course are unlikely to be supported.

Applications

The grants for individuals are managed by the Churches Together in Britain and Ireland (CTBI) Hardship Fund but are open to all students regardless of faith or religion. Applications should include:

- A CV and information about your intended career after your course
- Details about your course or research and an estimate of its completion

- Your current financial position and the nature of the unforeseen circumstances causing the difficulty
- Any awards already received or outstanding applications
- A letter of support from your academic supervisor

Applications should be sent to Mr Robert Anderson at hardship@ctbi.org. uk or by post to:

The Acting Grants Secretary, CTBI Hardship Fund, 121 George Street, Edinburgh EH2 4YN

Email correspondence is preferred.

Other information

The trust also provides grants to registered UK charities which provide educational projects in financially developing countries, as well as charities involved in higher and adult education in the UK.

Peter Alan Dickson Foundation

£110

Correspondent: Conchita Garcia, Correspondent, Robins Roost, Thruxton, Andover SP11 8NL (email: conchita@ thefsi.org or info@padfoundation.org; website: www.tarncourt.com/the-pad-foundation)

CC number: 1129310

Eligibility

The foundation's education fund provides financial support to individuals who cannot pursue education or develop their skills and abilities because of poverty or other circumstances. The focus specifically, but not exclusively, is placed on people in financially developing countries.

Preference may be given to applications in the areas of marine biology or the food and beverage industry but all applications will be given full consideration.

Types of grants

Individual bursaries to help with tuition fees and related educational expenses. Grants can range from £250 to £1,000.

Annual grant total

In 2015/16 the foundation had an income of £12,000 and a total expenditure of £220. The foundation's expenditure has been much higher in previous years. We estimate that the amount awarded to individuals to be around £110.

The foundation had no accounts available to view due to its low income.

Exclusions

The foundation will not:

- Give support where central/local/ national government should be responsible for the provision of assistance
- Provide for people in independent education sector
- Offer retrospective funding

Applications

Application forms are available on the foundation's website together with full guidelines.

Other information

The foundation also assists charitable organisations, families and communities in relation to educational causes, youth support and development, and disaster or poverty relief.

The Mihran and Azniv Essefian Charitable Trust

£25,000 (six grants)

Correspondent: Maral Ovanessoff, Administrator, 15 Elm Crescent, Ealing, London W5 3JW (020 8567 1210; email: benliantrust@gmail.com)

CC number: 275074

Eligibility

University students of Armenian origin studying in Armenia or Armenian students in the UK.

Types of grants

Scholarships to university students.

Annual grant total

In 2015/16 the trust held assets of £1.67 million and had an income of £54,500. The amount of grants given to individuals totalled £75,000, of which £25,000 was awarded to six British-Armenian students and the rest was distributed among 518 students in Armenia. A further £27,000 was awarded to organisations and institutions promoting educational, cultural and charitable activities of the Armenian community during the year.

Applications

Apply in writing to the correspondent. The deadline for applications is usually the end of April each year.

The Miles Morland Foundation

See entry on page 63

Schilizzi Foundation in Memory of Eleutherios and Helena Veniselos (The Schilizzi Foundation)

£69,000

Correspondent: A. Cruise, Secretary, Rowan, Turweston, Brackley, Northamptonshire NN13 5JX (01295 710356; email: admin@ schilizzifoundation.org.uk or schilizzifoundation@gmail.com; website: www.schilizzifoundation.org.uk)

CC number: 314128

Eligibility

Greek nationals pursuing an undergraduate degree course (normally for three years) or vocational training in Great Britain who can demonstrate need and financial hardship. Priority is given to students in their final year of study but postgraduates and other students will be considered too.

Children of Greek nationals resident in Great Britain could also be eligible for support to further their education in the language, history, literature and institutions of Greece.

Types of grants

The foundation's website notes that its present policy is to 'provide financial assistance in two main areas: hardship grants for students currently at British universities and further education scholarships awarded in conjunction with King's College London'.

Hardship grants are awarded for tuition fees, cost of books or living expenses. Support can also be given for expenditure outside Great Britain provided it has been incurred in pursuance of education.

Education scholarships for further education in Great Britain can be one-off or recurrent and are awarded to selected students, therefore direct applications will not be considered.

Annual grant total

In 2015/16 the foundation held assets of £2.4 million and an income of £70,500. Grants totalled £69,000 and were distributed as follows; scholarship grants £37,000 and special awards £32,000. A one-off grant of £30,000 was also made to King's College London to assist in re-endowing the Koraes Chair of Modern Greek and Byzantine History, Language and Literature.

Applications

Application forms for hardship grants can be requested from the secretary at the following address: The Secretary, The Schilizzi Foundation, Rowan, Turweston, Brackley, Northamptonshire NN13 5JX. Applications should be then submitted through the student counsellor/adviser at the candidate's college.

The Sino-British Fellowship Trust
See entry on page 44

The Charles Wallace India Trust

£268,000 (60 grants)

Correspondent: Richard Alford, Secretary, 36 Lancaster Avenue, London SE27 9DZ (020 8670 2825; email: cwit@ in.britishcouncil.org; website: www. wallace-trusts.org.uk)

CC number: 283338

Eligibility

Students, scholars and professionals of Indian nationality and citizenship (generally between the ages of 25 and 38) studying in the UK in the field of arts, heritage, conservation or humanities. Applicants should normally be resident in India and intend to return to there at the end of their study. Certain short-term awards are available for people aged between 25 and 45.

Types of grants

Grants and scholarships towards educational courses, research or professional development in the fields of the visual and performing arts, heritage, conservation and humanities. Most awards are given at a postgraduate level to supplement other sources of funding or constitute completion of study awards for those whose scholarships have run out.

A limited number of postdoctoral or post-professional research grants are awarded. Support includes fully-funded awards, visiting fellowships in agreed subjects at specific institutions, grants for research and professional visits, grants for doctoral study and grants to attend the Scottish Universities Summer School or specialist training.

Annual grant total

In 2015/16 the trust held assets of £6.38 million and had an income of £286,000. A total of £268,000 was awarded in grants and scholarships.

Exclusions

Studies relating to economic development or leading to professional legal, business or administrative qualifications are not normally considered.

Applications

Apply in writing to the correspondent. Applications can be found on the British Council website together with respective deadlines. Applicants are required to identify what benefit an award will bring not only to them personally but also to the people of India.

Other information

There are separate, smaller Charles Wallace Trusts for Bangladesh, Burma and Pakistan. All of the trusts are registered charities in the UK with separate and independent boards of trustees.

Note: The British Council facilitates and advises on the visas but the cost must be borne by the applicant. Further enquiries can also be addressed to the British Council in New Delhi at: cwit@in. britishcouncil.org.

W Wing Yip and Brothers Foundation
See entry on page 15

World Friendship

£14,500

Correspondent: Applications Secretary, 15 Dudlow Lane, Liverpool L18 0HH (0151 722 9700; email: worldfriendship@ hotmail.co.uk; website: www. worldfriendship.merseyside.org)

CC number: 513643

Eligibility

International students studying at universities in the diocese of Liverpool. Priority is given to students from outside the European Union and those in their final years of study. Eligibility is not restricted by faith.

Types of grants

One-off grants of about £500 towards relieving unexpected hardships which have arisen since the beginning of the course and which would prevent individuals from completing their studies.

Annual grant total

In 2015/16 the charity had an income of £18,200 and a total expenditure of £15,700. We estimate that grants given to individuals totalled around £14,500.

Exclusions

Grants are not given to those whose place of study is outside the diocese of Liverpool. Students from an EU country, those who are intending to stay in the UK at the end of their course, or applicants from overseas who are not yet studying in Liverpool are not usually supported.

Applications

Application forms should be sought from student support offices at relevant institutions (listed on the charity's website) or can be requested from the Applications Secretary (email: su05@liv.ac.uk).

Personal development and extra-curricular activities

The Michael Barnard Charitable Trust

£6,200

Correspondent: Michael Barnard, Trustee, Brown Heath Park, Gregory Lane, Durley, Southampton SO32 2BS (07977 403 704)

CC number: 1157878

Eligibility

People who are in need due to their social or economic circumstances, natural disasters or because of crime, injustice or violence.

Types of grants

Grants are made to train and educate young people particularly, but not exclusively, through leisure-time activities such as music, art and sport, including through the provision of facilities, tuition and sponsorship. Grants are also made to support the education or training of individuals to become self-sufficient or obtain employability skills.

Annual grant total

In 2015/16 the trust had assets of £1.96 million and an income of £43,500. Grants were made totalling £28,000, of which £12,400 was awarded to individuals. We estimate that the amount given to individuals for educational purposes totalled around £6,200.

Applications

Apply in writing to the correspondent.

Jim Bishop Memorial Fund

£2,000

Correspondent: Roger Miller, c/o Young Explorers Trust, 6 Manor Road, Burnham-on-Sea, Somerset TA8 2AS (01278 784658; email: ted@theyet.org.uk; website: www.theyet.org)

Eligibility

People under 19 who wish to participate in any adventure activity.

Types of grants

Grants of between £50 and £150. Recent grants have been given to enable participation in expeditions abroad, at sea and in the UK.

Annual grant total

Grants from the Jim Bishop Memorial Fund generally total around £2,000 and are awarded to individuals for educational purposes.

Exclusions

University expeditions will not be supported.

Applications

Application forms are available from the correspondent or to download from the Young Explorers' Trust website. Applications should include an sae and be submitted by the end of March of the year you wish to undertake an expedition.

Other information

Jim Bishop was an outstanding young engineer, scientist and explorer who was tragically killed while on an international expedition to the Karakorum. He was originally inspired by mountains and adventure as a teenager and he always regarded this initial experience as an important factor in his subsequent life. He always endeavoured to encourage this taste for adventure in the young and the Jim Bishop Awards were established by his family and friends to help further these ideals.

The fund is administered by the Young Explorers' Trust.

The Alec Dickson Trust

£17,800

Correspondent: Emily Evans, Trustee, 18–24 Lower Clapton Road, Hackney, London E5 0PD (020 7643 1360; email: alecdickson@gmail.com; website: www.alecdicksontrust.org.uk)

CC number: 1076900

Eligibility

Young people under 30 years of age who are involved in volunteering or community service in the UK.

Types of grants

The trust's mission is to support young people who are able to demonstrate that through volunteering or community service they can enhance the lives of others, particularly those marginalised by society. The trust particularly welcomes applications from innovative projects in the spirit of Alec Dickson.

Annual grant total

In 2015/16 the trust had no income and a total expenditure of £18,000. We estimate that the trust gave around £17,800 in grants to individuals.

Exclusions

The fund does not support overseas trips or gap year projects. Normally uniforms, equipment or training for personal benefit (e.g. university course fees, training fees, laptop for an individual) or direct expenditure for a fundraising event (such as venue hire) are not supported.

Applications

Application forms are available to download from the website. Completed application forms must be returned via email to: alecdicksontrust@gmail.com

Trustees review applications and decide which to fund on a quarterly basis.

The Duveen Trust

£13,100

Correspondent: Alan Kaye, Trustee, 1 Beauchamp Court, Victors Way, Bernet, Hertfordshire EN5 5TZ (020 8216 2520; email: administrator@ theduveentrust.org.uk; website: www. theduveentrust.org.uk)

CC number: 326823

Eligibility

Individuals aged up to 25 who are in financial need and wish to get involved with projects which require initiative and which give something back to the community. Educational assistance is given to enable individuals to work in community projects specialising in the social education of young people.

Types of grants

One-off grants of £100 to £500.

Annual grant total

In 2015/16 the trust had an income of £16,200 and a total expenditure of £13,300. We estimate that the trust gave around £13,100 in grants to individuals for educational purposes.

The trust also awards grants to organisations.

Exclusions

Grants are unlikely to be made to support formal education, except for courses leading to qualifications in youth and community work.

Applications

Application forms are available from the website for those who fit the criteria. Payments of grants are generally made through the organisation or agency organising the programme.

Other information

The trust has a grant potential of around £15,000 for distribution each year.

The Kearns Foundation

£5,000

Correspondent: James Kearns, 21 Garrett Court, Gertrude Road, Norwich NR3 4SD (01603 408713; email: contact@kearnsfoundation.org.uk; website: www.kearnsfoundation.org.uk)

CC number: 1156557

Eligibility

Young people, aged 11 to 21.

Types of grants

Small grants, between £50 and £250, to access training and development courses to learn skills which can be passed on to others in the community, and to support international exchanges or study visits that promote co-operation and build personal development.

Annual grant total

In 2015/16 the foundation had an income of £6,000 and a total expenditure of £11,000. We estimate that the foundation awarded £5,000 in grants for education.

Applications

Applications can be made online using the portal.

Other information

The foundation also makes grants to community organisations to recruit volunteers.

The Pain Trust (The Pain Adventure Trust)

£32,500

Correspondent: Secretary to the Trustees, 14a Rolle Street, Exmouth, Devon EX8 1NJ (email: admin@pain-trust.org.uk; website: www.pain-trust.org.uk)

CC number: 276670

Eligibility

Boys and young men, aged between 10 and 21 years (on the day of the expedition or activity, not the date of application), living in the East Devon area or within eight miles of Exmouth Town Hall, excluding the area to the west of the estuary of the River Exe.

Types of grants

One-off grants towards travel and adventure to further physical development, character building, leadership training or fostering a team spirit. Examples on the trust's website include trekking in the foothills of the Himalayas, assisting communities in deprived areas of the world, Antarctic exploration or challenges 'closer to home'.

Annual grant total

In 2015/16 the trust had an income of £52,500 and a total expenditure of £41,000. The annual report and accounts for the year were not available to view at the time of writing (November 2017). We estimate, based on previous years' information, that grants totalled around £32,500.

Exclusions

The trustees cannot/will not fund: activities which could be considered to be a part of the National Curriculum (including activity week at both primary and secondary schools); competitive sport (i.e. a sporting activity with recognised rules, regulations and leagues) or the pursuit of excellence in sport; top-up payments; retrospective applications; applications which fail to meet the trust's safety criteria; activities the trustees consider to be the responsibility of statutory authorities; the purchase of equipment.

Applications

Application forms are available from the trust's website. The trust invites potential applicants to contact the correspondent to discuss their application or for further guidance. Applications must be submitted at least 16 days before a meeting, the dates of which can be found on the website. Applications must be accompanied by a detailed itinerary with costs and demonstrate adequate evidence of background research into the proposed expedition. Repeat applications can be considered as long as they fulfil the objectives for funding.

Other information

The following important information is taken from the website:

> All activities supported by the Pain Adventure Trust must conform with current safety legislation and, wherever possible, should be supervised by a qualified leader. Details of the elements

must be outlined in the application. Certain core activities must be overseen by nationally recognised qualified instructors, with an appropriate instructor to pupil ratio. All applicants under the age of 16 must be under the supervision of an adult during the course of their expedition or activity.

The Torch Trophy Trust
See entry on page 85

Religion

Charities of Susanna Cole and Others

£3,500

Correspondent: Tony Pegler, Central England Quakers Office, Friends Meeting House, 40 Bull Street, Birmingham B4 6AF (0121 682 7575)

CC number: 204531

Eligibility

Quakers in need who live in the West Midlands, with preference for Worcester.

Types of grants

One-off and recurrent grants for education, retraining, and starting a business.

Annual grant total

In 2016 the charity had an income of £16,000 and a total expenditure of £8,500. We estimate that the amount awarded in grants for educational purposes was £3,500.

Applications

Applications should be made in writing to the correspondent, detailing personal need and what the grant will be used for.

Other information

Grants are made for both welfare and educational purposes.

Christianity

Catenian Association Bursary Fund Ltd

£117,000 (980 grants)

Correspondent: Bernard Noakes, The Catenian Association Ltd, 1 Park House, Station Square, Coventry CV1 2FL (024 7622 4533; email: gill.board@ thecatenians.com; website: www. thecatenians.com/bursary)

CC number: 1081143

Eligibility

Young Catholics (between the ages of 16 and 24) who want to work on projects around the world to assist local communities. Grants are also made to young people working as helpers on diocesan and HCPT pilgrimages.

Types of grants

Bursaries to help with the expenses related to undertaking overseas projects which 'have a clear benefit for others as well as widening the individual's life experience'. Awards may cover travel costs, medical expenses, essential clothing, personal subsistence and other needs. Any activity must have clear Christian ethos.

Most recently funding for any diocesan or ordinary workers on pilgrimages to Lourdes was worth £45 and for HCPT workers – £75.

Annual grant total

In 2015/16 the charity had assets of £438,000 and an income of £143,000. The amount of grants given to individuals totalled £117,000.

Exclusions

The guidance notes state:

> Awards are not made for medical electives, projects that are part of an educational course or for gap years. However an award may be made for a specific project undertaken during the year between School and University, or during the time between University and employment.

Funding is not given retrospectively.

Applications

Application forms for both overseas projects and pilgrimages, as well as guidance notes, are available online on the association's website. Two references are required. Applications should be submitted to the correspondent via email (do not send the form as a PDF file) at least three weeks before the trustees' meeting – for the dates of upcoming meetings see the application form – and no less than two months before the project/expedition is due to start. All receipts are acknowledged by email.

Note: Individuals applying as young workers who are joining official pilgrimages to Lourdes are not required to submit the form online as signatures are required from their parish priest/ chaplain and group leader/Diocesan Pilgrimage Director.

Daily Prayer Union Charitable Trust Ltd

£23,000

Correspondent: C. Palmer, Administrator, 12 Weymouth Street, London W1W 5BY (email: dputrust@ hotmail.co.uk)

CC number: 284857

Eligibility

Christians undertaking religious training or education.

Types of grants

Grants to support Christian training and education.

Annual grant total

In 2015/16 the trust had assets of £45,000 and an income of £49,500. During the year the trust awarded grants to individuals totalling around £23,000 for religious educational purposes.

The trust also gives grants to organisations.

Applications

Apply in writing to the correspondent.

Other information

Grants were also made to Monkton Combe School, Jesus Lane Trust and Crosslinks.

The Duchess of Leeds Foundation for Boys and Girls

£33,000 (14 grants)

Correspondent: John Sinfield, Administrator, 19 Kenton Road, Harrow, Middlesex HA1 2BW (020 8422 1950)

CC number: 313103

Eligibility

Roman Catholic children attending Catholic schools who are resident in England, Wales or the Channel Islands and who are either orphaned/fatherless or whose fathers do not support them sufficiently. Our research suggests that help is concentrated on secondary education and children in primary school are helped only in exceptional circumstances.

Types of grants

One-off awards and recurrent grants in the range of around £300 to £400 per term. According to our research, support is normally given towards the cost of school fees. Grants may continue until the end of an A-level course.

Annual grant total

In 2016 the foundation held assets of £711,500 and had an income of £44,500. Grants were made to 14 students and totalled £33,000.

Applications

Apply in writing to the correspondent directly by individual or their parents/ guardians. The deadline for applications is normally the end of January.

Milton Mount Foundation

£92,000 (12 grants)

Correspondent: Revd Erna Stevenson, Secretary, 11 Copse Close, Slough, Berkshire SL1 5DT (01753 748713; email: miltonmountfoundation@gmail. com)

CC number: 306981

Eligibility

The children of ministers of the United Reformed Church, the Congregational Federation, the Evangelical Fellowship of Congregational Churches and the Unaffiliated Congregational Churches. The female children of members of these churches can also be supported.

Types of grants

Bursaries and grants are available to children aged 11 to 18 towards school fees and other educational needs, including school uniforms and necessities.

Most support is given in bursaries towards independent boarding and day school fees for children aged 11 or over, which the trust aims to maintain throughout a child's time in secondary education, although this cannot be guaranteed. Grants may also be awarded for the cost of school uniforms for children starting secondary education. The website also states that 'grants may be awarded to any women taking up further education for the first time'. In 2017 the foundation began awarding grants to those commencing a first degree course.

Grants are means-tested and higher awards are given to those with a low family income.

Annual grant total

In 2015/16 the foundation had assets of £3.5 million and an income of £131,000. Annual bursaries to individuals totalled £92,000 and were broken down as follows:

Bursaries – boys' schools	£40,000
Bursaries – other schools (girls)	£36,000
Bursaries – Bournemouth Collegiate School (girls)	£13,500
Outfitting and other allowances (boys)	£1,100
Single grants	£250
Single grants	£200

Applications

Apply in writing to the secretary, providing information about family income. Applications should be submitted by 10 May to be considered for the following academic year.

The Mylne Trust

£44,000

Correspondent: Robin Twining, Secretary, PO Box 530, Farnham GU9 1BP (email: admin@mylnetrust.org.uk; website: www.mylnetrust.org.uk)

CC number: 208074

Eligibility

Members of the Protestant faith who have been engaged in evangelistic work, including missionaries and retired missionaries, and Christian workers whose finances are inadequate. Married ordinands with children are also supported when all other sources of funding have failed to cover their needs.

Types of grants

Grants are given towards educational training at theological colleges, for the cost of books and living expenses to undergraduates and overseas students.

Annual grant total

In 2016/17 the trust had assets of £2.1 million and an income of £55,500. Grants totalled £87,500. We estimate that grants for educational purposes amounted to £44,000.

Exclusions

The trust cannot support individuals who are not of a Protestant denomination.

Applications

The trust notes the following helpful information on its website:

> The trust has reviewed and, in 2013, changed its policy and procedure for making grants. Most grants are now being handled with partners already in Christian mission work. (Applications based on earlier procedures, using the old application forms, will no longer be considered by the trust.)

Worldwide except Africa

> In principle, the only grant applications that will be considered by direct application to the trust are those from candidates for mission work who are studying or planning to study within the UK. Such applicants are invited to contact the Clerk to the Mylne Trust at admin@mylnetrust.org.uk requesting a current application form.

Africa

> There are special arrangements for applicants who are based in Africa.

We would advise potential applicants to at first visit the website for more information.

North of Scotland Quaker Trust

£2,000

Correspondent: The Trustees, Quaker Meeting House, 98 Crown Street, Aberdeen AB11 6HJ

OSCR number: SC000784

Eligibility

People who are associated with the Religious Society of Friends in the North of Scotland Monthly Meeting area and their dependants.

Types of grants

Grants are given to schoolchildren and to people studying in further or higher education for books, equipment, instruments and educational outings. Grants for travel and conferences are also available.

Annual grant total

In 2016 the trust had an income of £17,900 and a total expenditure of £9,800. Grants are made to individuals and organisations. We estimate that grants given to individuals for educational purposes totalled around £2,000.

Exclusions

No grants are given to people studying above first degree level.

Applications

Apply in writing to the correspondent.

Other information

Grants are also given for welfare purposes.

The Podde Trust

£5,500

Correspondent: Peter Godfrey, Trustee, 68 Green Lane, Hucclecote, Gloucester GL3 3QX (01452 613563; email: thepodde@gmail.com)

CC number: 1016322

Eligibility

Individuals involved in Christian work in the UK and overseas.

Types of grants

One-off and recurrent grants.

Annual grant total

In 2016/17 the trust had assets of £9,400 and an income of £49,000. There were 27 grants to individuals totalling £11,200. The purposes for which awards were given were not specified. We estimate grants for educational purposes to have totalled around £5,500.

Applications

Applications may be made in writing to the correspondent.

Note: the trust has previously stated that it has very limited resources, and those it does have are mostly already committed. Requests from new applicants, therefore, have very little chance of success.

Other information

Organisations involved in Christian work in the UK and abroad are also supported (£30,000 was given to organisations in 2016/17). The trust awards grants for charitable purposes, including the advancement of religion, of education and the relief of poverty.

Saint George's Trust (FSJ (UK) TA SSJE)

£14,000

Correspondent: Linden Sheffield, Administration Officer, 11 Mayhew Crescent, High Wycombe HP13 6BX (01494 446636 or 07739 012459; email: lindensheffield@fsje.org.uk; website: www.fsje.org.uk/St-Georges-Home.html)

CC number: 253524

Eligibility

Members of the Church of England – Anglican clergy, seminarians and students.

Types of grants

Small, one-off grants of up to £350 are made towards specific projects in the UK or abroad. Support can be given to:

- Clergy undertaking a recognised study during their sabbaticals towards travel and accommodation costs
- Seminarians in Anglican theological colleges or on ministerial courses for the costs of pastoral placements that are part of formation (three members of a college/course may apply each year)
- Students between the ages 18 and 25 towards work on a Christian mission and service (usually as a gap year activity)

Annual grant total

In 2015 the trust had an income of £15,500 and a total expenditure of £14,900. We estimate the total amount of grants awarded to be around £14,000.

Exclusions

The trust will not provide any long-term financial support and cannot contribute towards restoration projects or education fees.

Applications

Applications should be initiated via the eligibility checker on the website. The trustees set a yearly budget from which grants can be awarded until the limit is reached. Applicants are therefore encouraged to apply early in the financial year.

Other information
In 2006 the administration of the trusts was transferred to The Fellowship of Saint John (UK) Trust Association.

Judaism

The Anglo Jewish Association

£90,500

Correspondent: Jonathan Walker, Trustee, 75 Maygrove Road, West Hampstead, London NW6 2EG (020 7449 0909; email: info@anglojewish.org.uk; website: www.anglojewish.org.uk)

CC number: 256946

Eligibility
British undergraduate and postgraduate Jewish students in need who are studying a full-time course at a recognised UK university or further education college. Part-time courses are not eligible for funding.

Types of grants
Scholarships available in amounts up to £1,500 per year. Payments are made on a one-off basis but can be reapplied for in future years. A year in industry can be provided for, only if it is unpaid and a mandatory part of the course.

Annual grant total
In 2015/16 the trust had £1.8 million in assets, a total income of £97,000 and a total expenditure of £94,000. Donations of £90,500 were made to Jewish students, including funding for two commissioned research projects.

Applications
In the first instance, potential applicants should email admin@ujs.org.uk.

Other information
The association also administers grants to Israeli postgraduate (master's or PhD) students in the UK through their Karten Scholarship Programme.

Finnart House School Trust

£194,000

Correspondent: Sophie Reindorp, Correspondent, The Charities Advisory, Radius Works, Back Lane, London NW3 1HL (07804 854905; email: info@finnart.org; website: www.finnart.org)

CC number: 220917

Eligibility
Finnart Scholarships applicants must be:
- Jewish and able to provide proof of this (applicants must have Jewish parents, a Jewish mother or evidence of conversion by a Rabbinic authority)
- Attending a college/university course at a recognised UK institution which ends in a recognised qualification (a degree or diploma)
- Under the age of 21 at the time of starting the course
- Going directly from Sixth Form to university without taking a 'gap' year
- Eligible for UK home fees
- In financial need (scholarships are means-tested – an applicant's family income will usually be below the national average and there may be several dependants). Applicants are required to provide information on family income and savings

Types of grants
Finnart Scholarships range between £1,000 and £3,000 per year for courses between three and seven years in length. Bursaries are distributed through a number of secondary schools.

Annual grant total
In 2015/16 the trust had assets of £5 million and an income of £138,500. Throughout the year the charity awarded around £194,500 in grants to educational purposes.

The charity also gives grants to organisations.

Exclusions
Only members of the Jewish faith can be supported. Funding is not given for study abroad or to international students.

Applications
Bursaries are awarded via schools. Scholarship applications are made by the individual on an application pack, which is available to download from the website. Applications should usually be completed and returned to the trust by the end of April.

Other information
The trust also gives grants to individuals for welfare purposes.

Gur Trust

£17,000

Correspondent: The Trustees, 206 High Road, London N15 4NP (020 8801 6038)

CC number: 283423

Eligibility
People connected to the Jewish Orthodox faith in the UK.

Types of grants
One-off and recurrent grants for education and personal development. The trust aims to support education in and the religion of Orthodox Jewish faith.

Annual grant total
In 2015/16 the trust had assets of £1.4 million and an income of £44,000. We estimate that educational grants to individuals totalled £17,000.

Applications
Applications may be made in writing to the correspondent. Our previous research notes the trust stating that 'all calls for help are carefully considered and help is given according to circumstances and funds then available'.

Other information
The trust also makes grants to organisations, Talmudical colleges and may provide some relief in need for individuals.

The Jewish Widows and Students Aid Trust

£55,000 (22 grants)

Correspondent: Alan Philipp, Trustee, 5 Raeburn Close, London NW11 6UG (email: alan@gapbooks.com)

CC number: 210022

Eligibility
Jewish students from the UK, Ireland, Israel, France and the British Commonwealth who are aged 16 to 30 years old.

Types of grants
The trust offers interest-free loans ranging from £1,000 to £1,500 mainly for course fees, although living expenses, books, travel or similar necessities can also be supported. Awards are made on the basis of academic excellence and need. On occasion, grants can also be given to UK schoolchildren over the age of ten.

Annual grant total
In 2016/17 the trust held assets of £844,000 and had an income of £56,000. Grants were made to 22 students and totalled £55,000.

Applications
Apply in writing to the correspondent including a CV and confirmation of acceptance at an educational establishment.

Other information

Grants are also given to widows with young children.

Allan and Gerta Rank Educational Trust Fund
See entry on page 169

Specific circum-stances

Crisis

£93,000 (61 grants)

Correspondent: Keith Felton, 66 Commercial Street, London E1 6LT (03006 361967; fax: 03006 362012; email: enquires@crisis.org.uk; website: www. crisis.org.uk)

CC number: 1082947

Eligibility

People over 18 who are homeless in the UK.

Types of grants

Grants to assist people with the costs of courses or equipment to get started in the world of work.

Annual grant total

In 2015/16 the charity had assets of £15.6 million and an income of £29.5 million. Throughout the year, the charity awarded £93,000 in grants to individuals through the 'Crisis changing lives' scheme.

Applications

Applicants must be engaged with Crisis for three months before submitting an application, via a Crisis staff member – contact Crisis for more information.

Other information

Crisis is a national charity for single homeless people that delivers education, employment, housing and health services and campaigns for change.

The Prisoners of Conscience Appeal Fund

£45,000

Correspondent: Lynn Carter, PO Box 61044, London SE1 1UP (020 7407 6644; email: info@prisonersofconscience.org; website: www.prisonersofconscience.org)

CC number: 213766

Eligibility

Prisoners of conscience and/or their families, who have suffered persecution for their conscientiously-held beliefs. The fund's website states: 'A degree of personal persecution has to be established.'

Applicants for bursaries must also have previously completed an undergraduate degree (not necessarily in the UK) and must be able to provide evidence of the postgraduate or conversion course at the time of application.

Types of grants

Mainly one-off grants of about £350 each for travel, resources, equipment, some vocational conversion courses (such as PLAB and IELTS) and re-qualification costs.

Bursary grants are also made for tuition fees for postgraduate study and professional conversion courses. The website states that funding will be made available for one year; funding for subsequent years can be re-applied for.

Annual grant total

In 2016 the charity had assets of £144,000 and an income of £336,500. We estimate that the charity awarded £45,000 in educational grants, including funding for postgraduate bursaries.

Exclusions

No support is given to people who have used or advocated violence or supported a violent organisation. A person who is seeking asylum or has been a victim of civil war is not sufficient grounds in itself for funding. Funding cannot be given retrospectively.

Applications

Applications are not considered directly from individuals but rather from approved referral organisations that apply on behalf of individuals. The fund advises the following on its website:

> You can ask your solicitor to make an application or you can contact the many local Citizens Advice Bureaux who may apply to us on your behalf. If you are in touch with any other refugee organisations or official bodies, you could also ask them to make an application. If you do not know of any organisation who might be able to assist you, please contact us grantsofficer@ prisonersofconscience.org and we will try to help.

Referral agencies must register with the fund's online system in order to apply for a grant. See the website or contact the correspondent for more information.

Other information

The fund was initially established in 1962 as the relief arm of Amnesty International, but is now a charity in its own right. It is the only agency in the UK making grants specifically to prisoners of conscience – individuals who have been persecuted for their conscientiously-held beliefs, provided that they have not used or advocated violence. Grant recipients include political prisoners, human rights defenders, lawyers, environmental activists, teachers and academics who come from many different countries such as Burma, Zimbabwe, Sri Lanka, Tibet, Iran, Cameroon and Eritrea.

The charity's aim is to raise and distribute money to help them and/or their families rehabilitate themselves during and after their ordeal. Financial grants cover general hardship relief, furniture, medicines, travel costs, family reunion costs, education, requalification and resettlement costs and medical treatment and counselling after torture.

The Unite Foundation
See entry on page 15

Warwickshire Corporate Parents' Association

£9,200 (25 grants)

Correspondent: John Scouller, Trustee, 10 Stoneleigh Avenue, Coventry CV5 6BZ (024 7671 1688; email: virtualschool@warwickshire.gov.uk)

CC number: 1151383

Eligibility

Grants for apprenticeships, extracurricular lessons and activities for young people in care and unaccompanied asylum-seeking children in Warwickshire.

Types of grants

Grants of up to £600 are available for extra lessons and tuition, clothing, equipment and travel for work experience.

Annual grant total

In 2015 the charity held assets of £120,000 and had an income of £70,000. During the year 25 grants were awarded to individuals and totalled £9,200. The typical award was around £400.

Applications

Apply in writing to the correspondent.

Other information

The charity also provides one-to-one tuition, a mentoring and befriending service and offers work experience and apprenticeships.

People who have offended

The Longford Trust

£60,000

Correspondent: Magdalen Evans, Scholarship Manager, 42 Callcott Road, London NW6 7EA (020 7625 1097; email: info@longfordtrust.org; website: www.longfordtrust.org)

CC number: 1164701

Eligibility

People who have offended or those awaiting release in the near future whose sentence was or is still being served in a UK prison who cannot afford education. Applicants must have identified a specific course they want to study at degree level offered by an institute of higher education (including Open University) and have obtained a provisional offer of a place (eligibility remains open for up to five years after release). The chosen course should improve the applicant's career chances and advance the rehabilitation process.

Types of grants

Scholarships are given to enable individuals to continue their rehabilitation through education at a UK university or equivalent institute.

A small number of awards are made under the Patrick Pakenham Awards Scheme to those who want to study law and under the Nat Billington Awards Scheme for those who want to study computer science.

Both awards are worth up to £5,000 per annum. The Longford Scholarship is extendable for up to three years on receipt of suitable reports of academic progress. Grants are intended to cover both the cost of tuition fees on higher education courses and offer a contribution to living expenses, books and other course materials.

Annual grant total

In 2015/16 the trust held assets of £184,000 and had an income of £176,000. Grants to individuals through the scholarship programmes totalled £60,000 and an additional £27,000 was awarded to universities.

Exclusions

Grants are not made for postgraduate study. Applicants should be ineligible for student loans or other financial support.

Applications

Application forms can be made online on the trust's website or can be downloaded, printed off and posted to the correspondent. Applications for courses beginning in September must be made by 1 June in that year.

Other information

In 2016 the trust transferred all its assets to a CIO and re-registered with a new Charity Commission number. Its objects and activities have not changed.

NIACRO

Correspondent: Olwen Lyner, NIACRO, Amelia House, 4–8 Amelia Street, Belfast BT2 7GS (028 9032 0157; email: gareth@niacro.co.uk; website: www.niacro.co.uk)

CC number: NIC101599

Eligibility

Prisoners, people who have offended and their immediate relatives in Northern Ireland in need of support. People in detention seeking access to education, training and/or employment who cannot obtain help from other sources may be supported financially.

A number of projects are available to children and young people at risk of (re)offending.

Types of grants

The vast majority of support is available through specific advice services, although some grants can be provided to individuals referred to the organisation. Support is given to help individuals access academic qualifications and vocational training which will advance their integration back into society and the job market. One-off and recurrent grants are given according to need and can be given towards degrees, vocational qualifications, NVQs, HGV driving licenses or other training and associated needs.

Annual grant total

In 2016/17 the association had an income of £2.6 million and a total programme expenditure of £2.6 million (on 'Children and Young People', 'Adults in the Community' and 'People in Prison and their Families'). We have been unable to determine the amount given in grants to individuals for educational purposes for this financial year. Note that the overall expenditure is not representative of grant-giving.

Exclusions

Grants are not normally given for computer hardware, capital equipment or set-up costs of small business initiatives.

Applications

Individuals in need of support should contact the correspondent to find out more about the support available and the application procedure.

Other information

The organisation's main activities are providing support, advice and guidance to prisoners, people who have offended and their relatives. A number of projects are undertaken in partnership with other bodies.

There also are regional offices.

Prisoners' Education Trust

£526,000

Correspondent: John Lister, Advice Manager, Prisoners' Education Trust, The Foundry, 17 Oval Way, London SE11 5RR (020 3752 5680; fax: 020 8648 7762; email: info@prisonerseducation.org.uk; website: www.prisonerseducation.org.uk)

CC number: 1084718

Eligibility

Individuals over the age of 18 who are serving a custodial sentence in the UK and still have at least six months of their sentence to serve.

Types of grants

Grants are made from the Access to Learning programme to pay for: distance learning courses; beginning study with the Open University; and art/creative hobby materials. Priority is given to subjects and qualifications that cannot usually be found in prison education provision. Courses are available at a range of different levels, including GCSEs and IGCSEs, A-levels and Open University courses, as well as other vocational qualifications – the Distance Learning Curriculum is distributed to prisons, this is available to download from the trust's website, or copies can be requested from the Advice Manager. Grants of up to £60 are available for creative arts materials.

Annual grant total

In 2015/16 the trust had assets of £1 million and an income of £1.3 million. A total of £526,000 was awarded in grants in the following categories:

General education courses and arts/ hobby material	£431,500
Open University courses	£94,500

Exclusions

Applications for retrospective funding are not accepted.

Applications

Apply in writing to the correspondent by sending a completed application form (which can be downloaded from the trust's website or obtained from prison education departments) and a 200 to 300-word letter stating why the applicant would like to do the course and how it will benefit them. An endorsement by a prison education manager is also required. Applications are considered every month and the outcome is communicated to all applicants. Further detailed guidance is given in the trust's Distance Learning Curriculum or funding guidelines.

Any questions about learning in prison, or requests for copies of the trust's curriculum, can be directed to the Advice Manager, John Lister. He can be contacted on: 020 3752 5680 or by post: FREEPOST Prisoners' Education Trust.

Other information

The organisation also provides advice about distance learning courses and how they relate to employment paths and possibilities. It supports learners in prisons, trains people to act as peer learning mentors and commissions research, projects, reports and conferences to help in evaluating and advancing prison education. It has an alumni network for those who have studied a course funded by PET to share experience, support and advice, as well as support the trust's work.

Note that applications are welcomed from any prison in the UK, Isle of Man and the Channel Islands.

Sacro Trust

£1,900

Correspondent: The Trust Fund Administrator, 29 Albany Street, Edinburgh EH1 3QN (0131 624 7270; website: www.sacro.org.uk)

OSCR number: SC023031

Eligibility

People living in Scotland who are subject to a license/court order or who have been released from prison in the last two years, and their families.

Types of grants

Grants are usually to a maximum of £300 for fees, books and equipment, or other needs helping the individual pursue education during the process of rehabilitation.

Annual grant total

In 2016/17 the trust had an income of £33,500 and a total expenditure of £46,000. The trust awarded £1,900 in grants for education.

Exclusions

Grants are not made where financial help from other sources is available.

Applications

Applications can only be accepted if they are made through a local authority, voluntary sector worker, health visitor or so on. The forms may be obtained from

the correspondent and are considered every two months. Payments cannot be made directly to an individual, rather to the organisation making the application. Other sources of funding should be sought before applying to the trust.

Other information

The trust also provides grants for household appliances and welfare for individuals in need.

The Sheriffs' and Recorders' Fund

£45,000

Correspondent: Lady Tessa Brewer, 16 Cowley Street, London SW1P 3LZ (020 7222 5481; email: secretary@srfund. net; website: www.srfund.org.uk)

CC number: 221927

Eligibility

People who have offended and recently come out of prison, in the Greater Metropolitan London area.

Types of grants

One-off grants for vocational education training, including cover for the costs of tools, equipment, exam fees, and clothing.

Annual grant total

In 2015/16 the charity had assets of £1.5 million and an income of £405,000. The charity awarded £45,000 in grants for educational purposes.

Applications

Application forms can be requested from the correspondent. Where possible, they should be supported by a probation officer, or a social/professional worker.

Other information

Grants are also available to individuals for welfare purposes, and to other prisoner rehabilitation organisations to 'break the cycle of reoffending'.

Refugees and asylum seekers

Ruth Hayman Trust

£30,000 (165 grants)

Correspondent: Administrator, PO Box 17685, London N6 6WD (email: info@ruthhaymantrust.org.uk; website: www.ruthhaymantrust.org.uk)

CC number: 287268

Eligibility

Adults (aged over 16) in state-funded education or training who have come to settle in the UK and who speak English as their second or other language.

Applicants must be resident in the UK as citizens of the UK/EU, spouses of citizens or as asylum seekers/refugees.

Types of grants

One-off and recurrent grants of up to £500 (on average £150) are available to help with the cost of fees (registration, course, exam), joining the professional bodies (if it is essential for the course), disclosure and barring service fees. Depending on the finances available, the trust could also assist with the cost of equipment and instruments. Grants towards travel costs are also made to people with disabilities who can provide a statement from the doctor. The trust also suggests that for a limited period the £500 maximum could be increased for those on courses at level 3 and above or for membership of professional associations where fees are very high. Cheques are usually paid to the educational institution directly.

There is an additional annual Rose Grant Special Award of £500 available to 'applicants who can show exceptional academic achievement, an outstanding commitment to the community or human rights as well as financial need'.

Annual grant total

In 2015/16 the trust held assets of £24,000 and had an income of £33,000. Grants totalling £29,000 were awarded to 165 individuals with a further ten students receiving book tokens totalling £1,100. The trust also gave away 34 dictionaries to students.

Exclusions

Grants cannot be given towards travel costs (except for people with a disability), childcare, living expenses, postgraduate education (unless it leads directly to employment) or private education courses (unless the course is only available in specialist private training).

People studying as overseas students are not supported and individuals on distance learning courses can only be supported if they are unable to travel to the place of education.

Applications

Application forms can be found on the trust's website or requested from the correspondent. Grants are awarded about five times a year and applications should be submitted in February, late April, late June, early September or late November. Candidates are required to provide an academic reference.

Applications for the Rose Grant Special Award should be made on the same form providing evidence that the candidate satisfies the additional requirements.

The trust reminds that it is crucial to fill in the application form in full (do not forget to demonstrate financial need, state your first language, include a reference and specify what the support is needed for). Further application guidelines can be found on the website; read them carefully to avoid your application being rejected on technical grounds.

The Walter and Liesel Schwab Charitable Trust (also known as Schwab and Westheimer Trust)

£149,500

Correspondent: Paola Churchill, PO Box 12327, Colchester CO6 4XE (07711 386 974; email: info@swtrust.org. uk; website: swtrust.org.uk)

CC number: 1091870

Eligibility
Young refugees and asylum seekers who want to access education or who have made exceptional effort and achievements within their schools and colleges. Applicants must have claimed asylum in the UK or have been recognised as a refugee by the Home Office.

Types of grants
The trust has two grant-making programmes:

Schwab educational grants
Grants of up to £2,000 to help young refugees and asylum seekers with their studies where no other funding is available. These range from helping with transport, books or computers, to paying contributions towards fees.

Westheimer Scholarships
Scholarships of up to £10,000 to £20,000 per year are awarded to exceptional candidates studying a first degree or professional qualification in the field of health and social care.

Annual grant total
In 2015/16 the trust had assets of £1.7 million and an income of £81,500. The amount of grants given to individuals totalled £149,500.

Exclusions
Refugees and asylum seekers who are aged over 28 years old are not normally awarded grants.

Applications
Applications can be made using the online form on the trust's website.

Other information
The trust has developed close working partnerships with the Helena Kennedy Foundation and Refugee Support

Network, who also support refugees and asylum seekers seeking access to education.

Study, work and voluntary work overseas

The British Council

Correspondent: Alison Coutts, Secretary, 10 Spring Gardens, London SW1A 2BN (email: trustees@ britishcouncil.org; website: www. britishcouncil.org)

CC number: 209131

Eligibility
See your programme area of interest for eligibility criteria.

Types of grants
Bursaries, scholarships and grants are available through external partners. Some schemes are fully funded, others are part funded.

Annual grant total
The charity provides bursaries and scholarships to people wishing to study, work, or volunteer through connected partners such as Erasmus. The amount of funding awarded is different for each programme – see the website for further details.

Applications
Applications are made online through the British Council website.

Other information
The British Council also offers the opportunity to learn English and become IELTS qualified to people living in countries abroad.

The Cross Trust
See entry on page 134

English-Speaking Union of the Commonwealth

£167,000

Correspondent: Education Department, Dartmouth House, 37 Charles Street, London W1J 5ED (020 7529 1550; email: education@esu.org; website: www.esu. org)

CC number: 273136

Eligibility
People involved in teaching the English language overseas and other education-related or cross-cultural projects. There are scholarships relating to the clergy, library professionals, literary translators, scientists, young musicians, teachers and students of various subjects.

Types of grants
The union administers a number of grant and scholarship awards for students and professionals, often in the form of travel scholarships. For details of individual funds, applicants are advised to refer to the union's website.

Annual grant total
In 2015/16 the charity held assets of £37.5 million and had an income of £3.87 million. Grants and awards totalled £167,000.

Applications
Applications vary for the different scholarships; applicants should refer to the website for more information.

Some schemes require applicants to attend an interview/audition.

Other information
The organisation offers training, initiates youth and academic exchanges and organises educational programmes, conferences, meetings and cultural activities.

The Nottingham Roosevelt Memorial Travelling Scholarship Fund

£6,000

Correspondent: Russell Blenkinsop, Trustee, 8 The Corner, Lowdham, Nottingham NG14 7AE (07767 797335; website: www.rooseveltscholarship.org)

CC number: 512941

Eligibility
People between the ages of 21 and 30 (cut-off date is 1 August of the current year) who work and/or live in the city or county of Nottingham and are primarily engaged in trade, commerce or 'the professions'.

Types of grants
A scholarship to enable an individual to visit the USA for a period between one and three months. Scholars are expected to fulfil an ambassadorial role while travelling widely throughout the USA and learning about the American way of life. The value of each scholarship can be between £1,500 and £3,000, plus a return flight to New York.

Annual grant total

In 2016 the fund had an income of £18,500 and a total expenditure of £7,300. We have estimated that grants totalled around £6,000.

Applications

Detailed guidelines, application forms and submission deadlines can be found on the fund's website. Applications are usually invited in spring and the fund prefers to receive them via email. Shortlisted candidates are required to attend interviews.

Other information

Applicants do not need to have any formal qualifications. Further queries can be submitted online on the fund's website.

The Sir Philip Reckitt Educational Trust Fund

£24,500 (282 grants)

Correspondent: John Lane, Trustee, Rollits LLP, Forsyth House, Alpha Court, Monks Cross, York YO32 9WN (01904 625790; email: andy.cook@rollits.com; website: www.spret.org)

CC number: 529777

Eligibility

People in full-time education who live in Kingston upon Hull, East Riding of Yorkshire, or the county of Norfolk.

Types of grants

Contributions towards the costs of travel, residence and attendances at conferences, lectures and educational courses, held nationally or internationally, for individuals and groups of individuals.

Annual grant total

In 2016 the trust held assets of over £1 million and had an income of £38,000. Educational grants to individuals in Norwich and Norfolk totalled £18,500 with a further £5,800 awarded to individuals in Hull and the East Riding of Yorkshire.

Exclusions

Awards will not normally be made to people under the age of 14 on the date of travel. Repeat applications for identical activities are not normally considered.

Applications

An application form can be completed and submitted online or can be downloaded and posted to the appropriate address after completion. A reference from the head of the institution of study, an employer or other suitable referee is required.

Note: Applications should be received by the trust more than six weeks before the intended departure date. Those submitted later are not normally considered. Successful applicants must complete a report to be returned to the trustees within three months of the end of the project or period of study.

Other information

Contacts:

Kingston upon Hull and East Riding of Yorkshire – The Trustees, Sir Philip Reckitt Educational Trust, Rollits, Wilberforce Court, High Street, Hull HU1 1YJ (email: christine.atherton@rollits.com).

Norfolk – The Trustees, Sir Philip Reckitt Educational Trust, c/o Mrs J. Pickering, 99 Yarmouth Road, Ellingham, Bungay NR35 2PH (email: spretrust@googlemail.com).

The Rotary Foundation Scholarships

Correspondent: Administrator, Rotary International in Great Britain & Ireland, Kinwarton Road, Alcester, Warwickshire B49 6PB (01789 765411; fax: 01789 764916; email: info@ribi.org; website: www.ribi.org)

Eligibility

Scholarships to further international understanding for secondary school students, graduates, undergraduates, teachers and professional journalists.

Individuals must be members of the Rotary Club.

Types of grants

Global Grant Scholarships overseas are available to graduates and are given towards achieving sustainable high-impact outcomes in the areas of peace and conflict prevention/resolution, disease prevention and treatment, water and sanitation, maternal and child health, basic education and literacy, economic and community development.

District Grant Scholarships are available for small-scale projects locally or abroad. Clubs and districts create their own scholarships funded through district grants.

The purpose of the scholarships is to further international understanding and friendly relations among people of different countries, rather than to enable beneficiaries to achieve any particular qualification.

Annual grant total

We were unable to determine a grant total for scholarships.

Applications

Applications can only be made through a rotary club in the district where the applicant lives, studies or works. Applications can be done through the grant application tool found in the 'My Rotary' section of each district's webpage. Applications are normally considered throughout the year but the foundation encourages making enquiries well in advance to the planned activity. It is recommended that before applying, the project and application should be discussed with the officer in the relevant district office.

The Erik Sutherland Gap Year Trust

£6,000

Correspondent: Viki Sutherland, Erik's Gap Year Trust, Torren, Glencoe, Argyll, Scotland PH49 4HX (01855 811207; fax: 01855 811338; email: info@eriks-gap year-trust.com; website: www.eriks-gap year-trust.com)

OSCR number: SC028293

Eligibility

School leavers living in the UK.

Types of grants

Grants, loans, donations, gifts or pensions are given to young people who wish to take a gap year or take part in voluntary work overseas before entering university or college. The trust primarily gives partial funding in instances where the young person has a shortfall in funds; however the charity may take on the whole cost of a year out in exceptional cases. The trust aims to help one or more school leavers each year.

Annual grant total

In 2015/16 the trust had an income of £630 and an unusually high total expenditure of £6,300. We estimate that grants given to individuals totalled around £6,000.

Applications

An application form is available to download from the website.

Study/work

Sir Ernest Cassel Educational Trust (The Cassel Trust)

See entry on page 31

Charles and Julia Henry Fund

£153,500 (four grants)

Correspondent: Dr. Jon Sudholt, c/o University of Cambridge, International Strategy Office, The Old Schools, Trinity Lane, Cambridge CB2 1TT ((3)33659; email: secretary@henry.fund.cam.ac.uk; website: www.henry.fund.cam.ac.uk)

CC number: 1155582

Eligibility

Undergraduates who have completed at least two years of higher education study; or graduates who are in their first year of postgraduate study and who finished their undergraduate degree within the last year.

Types of grants

Grants are made to four students (two from the UK, two from America) to study for one academic year at Harvard, Yale, Oxford, or Cambridge. Grants cover tuition fees, travel expenses, living costs, and accommodation for the year.

Annual grant total

In 2015/16 the fund had assets of £7.2 million and an income of £219,500. A total of £153,500 was awarded in educational grants.

Applications

Applications can be made in writing to the correspondent. You must demonstrate:

- High academic attainment
- Full engagement in the broader intellectual life of your university
- Participation and achievement in non-academic activities
- Evidence of character and intellectual ability

Also include a scheme of research to be carried out at your host university.

Other information

The charity also recommends candidates for fellowships at the Graduate School of Princeton University.

The Winston Churchill Memorial Trust

£794,500

Correspondent: Julia Weston, Chief Executive, Winston Churchill Memorial Trust, 29 Great Smith Street, London SW1P 3BL (020 7999 1660; fax: 020 7799 1667; email: office@wcmt.org.uk; website: www.wcmt.org.uk)

CC number: 313952

Eligibility

British citizens resident in the UK who are over 18. Preference is given to individuals who are unlikely to obtain funding from other sources.

Types of grants

Grants are made to people for a specific project which involves travelling overseas (normally for four to eight weeks) in order to bring back knowledge and best practice for the benefit of others in their professions, communities and the UK as a whole. Support can cover return travel, daily living, insurance, travel within the countries being visited and occasionally assistance with home expenses. Categories are drawn from the following fields:

- Crafts and makers
- Designers
- Education
- The arts
- Older people
- Early years prevention and intervention
- Environment and sustainable living
- Medicine, health and patient care
- Prison and penal reform
- Science technology and innovation
- Young people

Annual grant total

In 2015/16 the charity had assets of £41 million and an income of £3.1 million. Grants awarded for education totalled £794,500.

Exclusions

Awards are not made for attendance of courses, academic studies, student grants, gap year projects, electives, degree placements, internships and postgraduate studies (unless real and wider benefits to others in the UK can be clearly demonstrated). Projects involving less than four weeks of travel are not eligible. Existing fellows may not re-apply.

Applications

Applications can be made online on the trust's website. Applications open in May of each year and should be submitted by the end of September. Shortlisted candidates will be asked to attend an interview in January or early February.

Other information

The charity also awards bursaries of up to £2,000 per year to students at Churchill College, Cambridge, who are studying science, maths, or the arts. The charity's financial reports state this makes up about 5% of their charitable expenditure.

CoScan Trust Fund

£1,500 (Around 15 grants)

Correspondent: Tony Bray, 14 Ridge Avenue, Marple, Cheshire SK6 7HJ (07778 648082; email: tony.bray@coscan. org.uk; website: www.coscan.org.uk)

Eligibility

British people between the ages of 15 and 25 who are undertaking a project of a broadly educational nature involving travel between the UK and Scandinavia and within Scandinavia. Only short visits will be considered.

Types of grants

One-off grants between £75 and £150 to visit a Scandinavian country. Previous grant recipients have included young people looking for vocational experience, attending summer camps/courses, university students, young farmers, members of youth orchestras and scouts or guides.

Annual grant total

Our research suggests that previously approximately 15 grants have been awarded annually through the travel awards scheme.

Exclusions

Due to limited funds, large-scale projects cannot be supported.

Applications

Application forms can be downloaded from the website. Applications are considered once a year and should be submitted by March at the latest for consideration in April/May.

Other information

Applicants do not necessarily have to be members of an affiliated society, although a recommendation from one may be helpful.

The Worshipful Company of Cutlers General Charitable Fund – Captain F. G. Boot Scholarships

£6,000 (five grants)

Correspondent: Rupert Meacher, Clerk, The Worshipful Company of Cutlers, Cutlers' Hall, 4 Warwick Lane, London EC4M 7BR (020 7248 1866; fax: 020 7248 8426; email: clerk@cutlerslondon. co.uk; website: www.cutlerslondon.co. uk)

CC number: 283096

Eligibility

Students between the ages of 17 and 25 travelling abroad for at least six months to develop a second language and learn about other cultures. Applicants should either be awaiting entry to further education or be studying abroad as a part of their university degree.

Types of grants

At least five scholarships are awarded each year. Grants can range between £500 and £1,200 depending on the individual's circumstances.

Annual grant total

In 2015/16 the charity had assets of £2.3 million and an income of £129,500. Throughout the year the fund awarded £6,000 in scholarships to five individuals.

Exclusions

Grants are not available to Project Trust applicants.

Applications

Application forms can be downloaded from the charity's website. Application forms, completed in handwriting, should be accompanied by two references and posted to the charity before 12 June. Shortlisted applicants will be invited for an interview.

Other information

The charity also: provides a number of specific awards to students at nominated universities/schools/colleges; gives recurrent grants to charitable organisations; offers an annual Surgical Prize to a scientist developing the design or application of surgical instruments or surgical techniques.

The trustees approved an overall sum of £98,500 in grants throughout the year.

The Peter Kirk Memorial Fund

Correspondent: Leah Gilliatt, 358A Old Ford Road, London E3 5TA (email: mail@kirkfund.org.uk; website: www. kirkfund.org.uk)

CC number: 1049139

Eligibility

Citizens of any European country aged between 18 and 26 years, (under some circumstances an older candidate up to age 29 might be considered). Applicants must have been in full-time education at some time during the 12 months preceding the application.

Types of grants

Scholarships worth £2,000 to undertake research in European countries.

Annual grant total

In 2016/17 the charity had assets of £548,500 and an income of £26,500. No scholarships were awarded in 2016 due to changes in the timetable for interviewing.

Exclusions

Peter Kirk Scholarships are awarded for independent study projects. Scholarships cannot be used to pay for course work which is required as part of an academic qualification but applicants sometimes find it possible to undertake an independent project alongside studies abroad. Contact mail@kirkfund.org.uk if uncertain of your position.

Applications

Application forms can be downloaded from the website and should be submitted by email. Applicants must provide a summary of the proposed investigation. Applications must be submitted by 1 March, with selection/interviews normally completed by April (check the website for the most up-to-date deadlines). Interviews take place in London at the applicant's expense.

The Leverhulme Trust
See entry on page 5

The Mount Everest Foundation
See entry on page 63

The Sino-British Fellowship Trust

£390,000 (31 grants)

Correspondent: Anne Ely, Flat 23, Bede House, Manor Fields, London SW15 3LT (020 8788 6252)

CC number: 313669

Eligibility

Students and academic staff at universities, higher education institutions and vocational training institutions in Britain or China, focusing on senior academics and postgraduate students.

Types of grants

Grants are awarded to enable students and academic staff in Britain to undertake study or research in China, or participate in academic or professional conferences, courses, placements and similar events in China. Grants are awarded for students and staff in China to do the same in Britain. Grants are also given to enable students and staff to take part in joint programmes, courses and exchanges between Britain and China, as well as between China and

Hong Kong. Support can also be given to promote the study of Chinese languages, as well as to fund experienced British GP trainers to raise the standard of primary healthcare in China.

Annual grant total

In 2016 the trust had assets of £17.1 million and an income of £556,000. There were ten grants made directly to individuals, as well as 13 grants to UK institutions and eight grants to overseas institutions, which totalled £390,000 altogether, and were broken down as follows:

Grants to Chinese academics for study visits to Great Britain	£232,500
Grants to British academics for study visits to China	£78,000
Joint UK/China academic programmes and exchanges between Hong Kong and other parts of China	£70,500
Promotion of Chinese language studies	£8,700

Applications

Application forms are available from the trust or through the relevant institution.

The Trans-Antarctic Association

£12,000

Correspondent: Dr J. A. Smith, Grants Secretary, c/o British Antarctic Survey, High Cross, Madingley Road, Cambridge CB3 0ET (01223 728222; email: taagrants@bas.ac.uk; website: www. transantarctic.org.uk)

CC number: 205773

Eligibility

Citizens of the UK, Australia and New Zealand seeking to further knowledge or exploration of the Antarctic region.

Types of grants

Grants are given to support expeditions to Antarctica, including travel and equipment costs, and research and publication expenses. Awards are normally up to £1,500.

Annual grant total

In 2016 the association had an income of £12,500 and a total expenditure of £12,400. We estimate that grants totalled around £12,000.

Exclusions

Grants cannot be made for: salaries; subsistence or living expenses; retrospective applications.

People who are not nationals of the countries named above are not normally supported.

Applications

Applications must be made using the form on the association's website – hard copies are no longer accepted. The closing date for UK citizens is 31 January.

Other information

The total of funds available for distribution in any one year typically ranges between £10,000 and £15,000. One third of available funds are awarded to New Zealand nationals, with the remainder being awarded to nationals from Australia, South Africa and the United Kingdom.

Volunteering

Reg Gilbert International Youth Friendship Trust (GIFT)

£7,000

Correspondent: Pamela Lindsay Brewster, 23 Linnet Way, Frome BA112UY (01373 465225; email: yorkie77pam@aol.com; website: giftfriendshiptrust.org.uk)

CC number: 327307

Eligibility

UK citizens aged between 16 and 25 who are visiting a developing country on a project lasting at least six weeks. Applicants must live and volunteer within an indigenous community in the host country, preferably in a 'homestay' environment. Candidates need to demonstrate their own fundraising initiatives, research and preparation for the visit. Normally candidates have to be vetted and accepted by an approved overseas project agency, but independent travellers may be considered provided a comprehensive and verifiable breakdown of their travel arrangements is submitted.

Types of grants

Grants of up to £500 are given to travellers who can demonstrate need and have already started preparation for the project.

Annual grant total

In 2015/16 the trust had an income of £6,000 and a total expenditure of £7,200. We estimate that grants given to individuals totalled around £7,000.

Exclusions

Grants are not available for proposals leading to academic or vocational qualifications.

Applications

Application forms can be downloaded from the trust's website after the eligibility criteria has been read and understood. An independent academic or professional reference is required together with the application.

Other information

The charity is an autonomous trust under the supervision of the Rotary Club of Frome.

Hazel's Footprints Trust

£9,200 (14 grants)

Correspondent: The Trustees, Legerwood, Earlston, Berwickshire TD4 6AS (01896 849677; fax: 01896 849677; email: info@hazelsfootprints.org; website: www.hazelsfootprints.org)

OSCR number: SC036069

Eligibility

People of any age from the UK and Europe who want to take part in voluntary projects abroad. Proposed projects must have an educational focus and should last no less than six months (the preferred duration is a year).

Types of grants

'Footprinter' grants to people who want to take part in voluntary work abroad but are struggling to cover the whole cost themselves.

Annual grant total

In 2015/16 the trust had assets of £520,000 and an income of £35,000. During the year a total of £9,200 was awarded to 14 'footprinters' volunteering in 12 different countries. A further £37,000 was awarded in grants to organisations.

Applications

Application forms can be downloaded from the trust's website. The trustees meet in May and October to consider applications and all applicants are notified of the outcome. Candidates may be invited for an interview.

The website provides the following information: 'Partly on a first-come, first-served basis. We will give two or three awards for those setting off in January (applications by late September). A larger number of volunteer grants are awarded for summer departures (applications required by mid-March).'

Other information

The trust also makes grants to UK charities running educational projects in other countries.

The Jack Petchey Foundation

£158,000 (661 grants)

Correspondent: Hannah Cilia, Head of Grants Team, Dockmaster's House, 1 Hertsmere Road, London E14 8JJ (020 8252 8000; email: mail@jackpetcheyfoundation.org.uk; website: www.jackpetcheyfoundation.org.uk)

CC number: 1076886

Eligibility

Young people aged 11 to 25 who live in London or Essex. The project must involve voluntary work with a recognised UK-based organisation, for example educational organisations, youth groups, registered charities, or organisations experienced in planning volunteering programmes that are registered or based in the UK.

Types of grants

Grants can be made for up to £400 per person and the foundation will fund up to 50% of the cost of the project.

Annual grant total

In 2016 the foundation held assets of £10,700 and had an income of £7.5 million. Grants given to individuals totalled £158,000, with a further £6.58 million awarded to organisations working with disadvantaged young people in London and Essex.

Exclusions

The foundation cannot fund the following:

- Applications made on the behalf of a group of young people
- Individuals who have previously received an Individual Grant for Volunteering
- Applications where you are delivering the project by yourself and not with a UK-based organisation
- Applications where you are delivering the project with an organisation based or registered outside the UK
- Individual training or education courses
- Specialist equipment, clothing or items required for a specific event
- Attendance at local, national or international competitions (i.e. sports or dance)
- Personal holidays or student exchange programmes
- Projects that are established only for the purposes of promoting a specific political or religious belief

Applications

Applications can be made through the foundation's website, where helpful guidance notes and FAQs can also be found. Although the application is to be completed by the person requesting support, it must also be endorsed by a responsible adult who is not a relation and who is not directly involved in the project itself. Applicants are expected to raise 50% of the costs themselves, and submit a report after the project has taken place.

The foundation advises that you should apply at least three months (but not more than nine months) before the project's start date. Applications typically take up to eight weeks to process but may take longer.

The Roger and Miriam Pilkington Trust

£6,300 (15 grants)

Correspondent: Jane Fagan, Administrator, c/o Brabners, Chaffe Street, Horton House, Exchange Flags, Liverpool L2 3YL (0151 600 3000; email: jane.fagan@brabners.com)

CC number: 261804

Eligibility

The trustees' report from 2015/16 states that grants are given to 'enterprising young people, particularly those who are undertaking imaginative projects abroad which could be said to broaden horizons, to give them experiences which they might not otherwise have, to increase their awareness of other cultures and ways of living'. Grants are awarded to those between the ages of 16 and 25.

Types of grants

One-off grants only, usually of around £500. Due to a great demand, grants are spread across a wide selection of projects.

Annual grant total

In 2015/16 the trust had assets of £837,000 and an income of £29,000. Grants to 15 individuals totalled £6,300.

Exclusions

The trustees do not offer support where it should be provided by the education authorities. Long-term funding is not available.

Applications

Applications should be submitted in writing to the correspondent. Applications can be made directly by individuals at any time for consideration in March and August. All grants are contingent on the applicant raising a significant proportion of the funds through their own efforts.

Other information

The trust is currently running a grant scheme in seven schools or colleges in the UK and Jersey, with applicants being selected by the staff and approved by the trustees.

Virgin Atlantic Be The Change Volunteer Trip Scholarship

£13,400 (30 grants)

Correspondent: Alison Herr, 7–11 St John's Hill, London SW11 1TR (020 7978 5225; email: ukyouth@we.org; website: www.we.org/tripscholarship)

CC number: 1138645

Eligibility

Volunteering travel scholarships are available to UK students between the ages of 12 and 18 (at the application deadline) who have 'demonstrated a commitment to global issues or community volunteerism'.

The website states:

> Applicants will be selected based on personal interest, merit, and demonstrated commitment to raising awareness in their local community. The ideal candidates are young people who are already working to improve their local or global community, and who will use this experience to motivate and inspire others to take action.

Types of grants

Each summer 30 scholarships are given to travel to one of the WE Village communities in India, experience the local culture and way of life, volunteer on a building project and participate in workshops exploring global issues.

Annual grant total

In 2015/16 the charity's 'Scholarship Fund' had an income of £71,500 and a total expenditure of £46,500. Scholarships totalled £13,400.

Exclusions

The scholarship will not cover 'certain incidentals, including passport, visa, vaccinations, insurance, travelling costs to a London airport and spending money'. The website notes: 'We will work with students to help them fundraise for these costs, should this become a barrier to travel.'

Applications

Application forms can be accessed online and are usually due to be submitted by March/April (see the website for exact dates). Students can nominate themselves or can be nominated by a third party such as a teacher, family member or someone from their local community.

Other information

Scholarships are provided by the Virgin Atlantic Foundation in partnership with Free The Children UK, which is also known as WE Charity (CC number: 1138645).

Vocational training and apprentice-ships

ABTA LifeLine (The ABTA Benevolent Fund) Bursary

Correspondent: The Trustees, 30 Park Street, London SE1 9EQ (020 3117 0500; email: lifeline@abtalifeline.org.uk; website: www.abtalifeline.org.uk)

CC number: 295819

Eligibility

Anyone who is currently working for an ABTA (Association of British Travel Agents) Member and is unable to consider further or higher education without support.

The website states:

> ABTA LifeLine are especially interested in people who work in small or medium sized companies (fewer than 250 employees) front line travel agents or individuals who feel that in order to reach their full potential they currently lack an appropriate qualification.

Types of grants

The bursary is offered to 'an individual in [the] travel community who does not have the means to further their education and develop their career potential within the industry'. The maximum grant available is £2,000 a year for a maximum of three years and is aimed to help with the course fees for a relevant vocational or professional qualification. The candidate must demonstrate their commitment and progression in order to receive funding for years two and three.

Successful applicants will also be allocated a senior mentor from the travel industry to offer support and enable the bursary recipients to attend key industry events and 'may be invited to spend a day with an ABTA Member company, Midcounties Cooperative or Kuoni, to gain experience of a different organisation'.

Annual grant total

In 2016 the charity held assets of £573,000 and had an income of £160,500. No grants were awarded for education.

Applications

Application forms are available from the correspondent or can be downloaded from the website.

Other information

The bursary was established in 2014 in partnership with Travel Weekly in memory of Colin Heal.

The charity mainly provides social welfare support. In 2016 grants to individuals totalled £50,000.

The William Barry Trust

£215,000

Correspondent: Keiko Iwaki, Trustee, Flat 56, Avenue Close, Avenue Road, London NW8 6DA (email: williambarrytrust@gmail.com)

CC number: 272551

Eligibility

People in vocational studies and training, such as hospitality, hotel management, technical crafts, or artistic occupations (singing, dancing, acting etc.).

Types of grants

Grants are available on a one-off and recurrent basis, to assist with education and training fees for courses, workshops, exhibitions, lectures, seminars, and other educational activities.

Annual grant total

In 2015/16 the trust held assets of £6.7 million and had an income of £225,500. The total amount donated in grants to individuals was £215,000.

Exclusions

Grants are not available for career development or postgraduate degrees.

Applications

Applications are available on the trust's website. Candidates are required to include an introductory letter explaining:

- Why you are applying for your particular course
- What you hope to achieve, and how the trust might help you with this
- How you intend to fund any remaining costs

Other information

The trust also supports organisations and has limitations on individual grants.

The City and Guilds of London Institute

£250,000

Correspondent: David Miller, City and Guilds of London Institute, 1 Giltspur Street, London EC1A 9DD (020 7294 3444; fax: 020 7294 2400; email: david.

miller@cityandguilds.com; website: www. cityandguilds.com/qualifications-and-apprenticeships/support/bursaries)

CC number: 312832

Eligibility

To be eligible, you must: be age 16 or over; be currently studying, or wanting to study, a City and Guilds or ILM qualification; be a resident of, and studying in, the UK; and have genuine financial need.

Types of grants

Educational bursaries of up to £10,000 per individual are available for course and exam fees, living costs, books/equipment, travel costs, childcare and other needs. Around 100 awards are made each year.

Annual grant total

In 2015/16 the charity had assets of £78.4 million and an income of £137.3 million. The total amount awarded in bursaries was £250,000.

Exclusions

Retrospective payments, grants for career development or deferred loans taken out with a college or bank are not covered.

Applications

Applications can be made online on the website. There are two application rounds each year, in the Spring and Autumn. Shortlisted applicants will be required to attend an interview. See the website for a full guide to the bursary applications.

Other information

The institute primarily exists to provide qualifications, awards, assessments and support across a range of occupations in industry, commerce and the public services.

Henry Dixon's Foundation for Apprenticing – administered by Drapers' Charitable Fund

£7,700 (33 grants)

Correspondent: Andrew Mellows, Charities Administrator, The Drapers' Company, Drapers' Hall, Throgmorton Avenue, London EC2N 2DQ (020 7588 5001; fax: 020 7628 1988; email: charities@thedrapers.co.uk; website: www.thedrapers.co.uk)

CC number: 251403

Eligibility

Apprentices, students, schoolchildren, school leavers and people in vocational training under the age of 25. Particular

regard may be given to those studying in the fields of technical textiles and art or design, with preference for inner city London.

Types of grants

One-off grants are made towards vocational training initiatives and apprenticeships, as well as activities in sports, arts and music, including support towards books, clothing, equipment/instruments, fees, travel costs and other educational needs.

Annual grant total

In 2015/16 the charity had assets of £60.2 million and an income of £8.2 million. Throughout the year the charity awarded £7,700 in grants to individuals.

Applications

Grants are normally made through educational institutions; therefore applications should be made to the university or college rather than the foundation.

Other information

The foundation's funds have been transferred to the Drapers' Charitable Fund and are administrated as a restricted fund. Previously the charity was registered under the number 314292.

Go Make it Happen: A Project In Memory of Sam Harding

£6,500

Correspondent: Keith Harding, Administrator, 72 New Caledonian Wharf, 6 Odessa Street, London SE16 7TW (020 3592 7921, 07790 622381 (mob); email: keithhard@hotmail.co.uk; website: www.gomakeithappen.co.uk)

CC number: 1145369

Eligibility

People between the ages of 18 and 30 who want to build a career in the tourism and travel industry. The charity has a particular, but not exclusive, focus on young people who have not necessarily followed a 'conventional' academic route and wants to help them 'achieve things in their lives that they would not otherwise be able to achieve'.

Types of grants

Funding is available for training courses, travel expenses and other educational opportunities in the UK and overseas. Some examples include: support for volunteering and internships, language learning, and skills-based qualifications.

Annual grant total

In 2015/16 the charity had an income of £5,900 and a total expenditure of £6,700. We estimate that the charity awarded around £6,500 in grants to individuals for educational purposes.

Applications

Applications can be made online on the charity's website. The charity will normally make contact within two weeks and may arrange for an interview.

Other information

The charity also provides information and advice on opportunities for working overseas and in travel or tourism generally (both in the UK and abroad).

It also campaigns for cycling safety and driver awareness in memory of Sam's tragic death.

The Prince's Trust
See entry on page 7

The Thomas Wall Trust

£34,000 (32 grants)

Correspondent: Deborah French, Chief Accountant, Skinners' Hall, 8 Dowgate Hill, London EC4R 2SP (020 7236 5629; email: information@thomaswalltrust.org. uk; website: www.thomaswalltrust.org. uk)

CC number: 206121

Eligibility

People who are over the age of 16 who have been resident in the UK for at least three years prior to the beginning of the course to be attended and who are facing financial difficulties stopping them from entering education or employment. Applicants should not have any qualifications for work and be unable to fund their courses through any other means (e.g. statutory grants or loans). The courses should be below degree level and lead to employment.

Types of grants

Small, one-off grants (generally of up to £1,000) to overcome financial barriers to work or education. Awards are given towards fees, equipment and other expenses related to vocational, skill-based or technical study and professional training. Interest-free loans can also be made. Both full-time and part-time courses are considered for support.

Annual grant total

In 2015/16 the trust held assets of £3.77 million and had an income of £119,000. Grants to individuals totalled £34,000 with a further £29,000 awarded to organisations.

Exclusions

Grants are not given:

- For undergraduate and postgraduate degree courses or PhD students
- Towards higher education courses that qualify for Student Loan Company funding
- To people earning above £26,000 per year
- To individuals with family income above the average salary (£26,000 per year)
- To people who are considered 'employable' or 'qualified to work'
- For travel, study or work overseas
- For elective periods or intercalated courses
- Towards business start-up costs
- For GCSEs or A-levels
- To schoolchildren

Applications

The application form can be completed online once the applicant has registered with the trust and completed an eligibility quiz. Further information on parental income is required from all applicants under the age of 25 (including those who no longer live with their parent/s).

National charities classified by subject

Formal sciences

The Lillingstone Trust

£18,300 (21 grants)

Correspondent: Julie Powell, Trustee, Bridge House, Brookside, Lillingstone Lovell, Buckingham MK18 5BD (email: julie.powell@lillingstonetrust.co.uk)

CC number: 1151686

Eligibility

Individuals attending schools in North Buckinghamshire, Northampton and South Northamptonshire, who are from low-income backgrounds and are continuing into higher education. Preference is given to those studying subjects relating to science, technology, engineering or mathematics, at research-based universities.

Types of grants

Scholarships of up to £4,000 are awarded, with payments spread over the three years of the degree course (with £1,500 in the first year). There is also some funding available to assist with the costs of travel to university interviews.

Annual grant total

In 2016 the trust had assets of £220,500 and an income of £94,500. Grants to individuals during the year totalled £18,300 and were awarded to 13 existing scholars and eight new scholars.

A further £25,000 was given in grants to two organisations.

Applications

Application forms are available to download from the trust's website and should be returned by post to the correspondent by the end of November. Applicants will be informed of the outcome of their application by the end of December.

For assistance towards travel costs for interviews, you should have a discussion with your school's head of sixth form.

Other information

The trust also supports a community laboratory in a science centre at a local school.

At the time of writing (October 2017), the website states that the trust is also 'currently in discussion with Nottingham University concerning possible funding for STEM scholarships for women'.

The Ogden Trust

See entry on page 64

Humanities

The Broncel Trust

£19,000

Correspondent: The Trustees, 371 Uxbridge Road, London W3 9RH (020 8992 9997; email: info@akpp.co.uk)

CC number: 1103737

Eligibility

People involved with Polish history, literature, art or social sciences. The trustees are prepared to consider a varied range of requests.

Types of grants

The trust awards scholarships, financial assistance for research and grants for publishing Polish works of literature.

Annual grant total

In 2015/16 the trust had an income of £2,500 and a total expenditure of £41,500. We have estimated that grants to individuals totalled £19,000 during the year.

Applications

Apply in writing to the correspondent.

Other information

Grants are made to both organisations and individuals. Occasional financial support can be provided for libraries, museums and exhibitions.

Council for British Research in the Levant

£130,500 (28 grants)

Correspondent: Administrator, 10 Carlton House Terrace, London SW1Y 5AH (020 7969 5296; fax: 020 7969 5401; email: cbrl@britac.ac.uk; website: www.cbrl.org.uk)

CC number: 1073015

Eligibility

British citizens or those ordinarily resident in the UK, Isle of Man or the Channel Islands carrying out research in arts, humanities, social and related sciences in connection with the countries of the Levant (Cyprus, Israel, Jordan, Lebanon, Palestine, Syria and adjacent territories).

Types of grants

The charity administers a range of support for scholars, currently:

- Arabic Language Training – grants to cover the cost of full tuition, air travel and accommodation to members of academic staff at a UK university, or academic staff (faculty) with a UK PhD and CBRL membership participating in the CBRL Academic Arabic Programme;
- Visiting Research Fellowships and Scholarships – for scholars in university posts, early career postdoctoral candidates and students conducting PhD/DPhil research to spend a period of time at CBRL's overseas institutes to conduct primary

research, develop contacts, give lectures and write up project results/publications derived from a thesis/research;

▸ Pilot Study Awards – up to £7,500 to enable postdoctoral scholars to undertake initial exploratory work or a feasibility study as a preliminary to making major funding applications to a research council, the British Academy or another body;

▸ Travel Grants – up to £800 to cover costs of travel and subsistence of students, academics and researchers undertaking reconnaissance tours or smaller research projects in the countries of the Levant;

▸ Conference and Outreach Funding – lectures, seminars, workshops and conferences in London, Amman, and Jerusalem, as well as occasional meetings elsewhere, mostly initiated by the CBRL (formal applications for support towards conferences, exhibitions, or other forms of outreach are also encouraged)

Awards range from £700 to around £12,000.

Annual grant total

In 2015/16 the charity had assets of £339,000 and an income of £908,000. Throughout the year 28 individuals received grants totalling almost £130,500.

Exclusions

Grants are not normally made towards maintenance, fees, group tours, books or equipment. Grants can no longer be used to support students, except where these grants directly benefit UK humanities and social sciences research (e.g. by building capacity in areas of strategic importance to the UK).

Applications

Separate application forms for each of the awards, together with extensive guidance notes and conditions are available on the charity's website. Also see the website for application deadlines as these vary.

Other information

This charity has a website which should be referred to by any interested applicants.

A report is required to be submitted after the completion of the research, which is then made publicly available.

English-Speaking Union of the Commonwealth
See entry on page 41

The Hellenic Foundation

£13,500

Correspondent: The Trustees, 150 Aldersgate Street, London EC1A 4AB (020 7251 5100)

CC number: 326301

Eligibility

Students studying the culture, tradition and heritage of Greece, particularly in subjects involving education, research, music, theatre productions, exhibitions and concerts.

Types of grants

One-off and recurrent grants for projects involving education, research, music and dance, books and library facilities and university symposia.

Annual grant total

In 2015 the foundation had an income of £24,500 and a total expenditure of £14,400. We estimate that grants totalled £13,500.

Applications

Apply in writing to the correspondent.

Il Circolo Italian Cultural Association Ltd

£5,800

Correspondent: Lady Belinda Aylmer, Secretary, 16 Edgarley Terrace, London SW6 6QF (020 7731 1939; email: grants@ilcircolo.org.uk; website: www.ilcircolo.org.uk)

CC number: 1108894

Eligibility

Students who have been accepted onto a course at a British higher education institution, either at undergraduate or postgraduate level, pursuing studies, training or research relating to Italian culture (humanities, arts and crafts, sciences and performing arts).

Types of grants

Scholarships for students who wish to further their education in the field of Italian and related studies.

Annual grant total

In 2015 the association held assets of £69,500 and had an income of £67,000. Grants to students totalled £5,800 with a further £20,000 awarded to two organisations.

Applications

Apply in writing to the correspondent. Selected candidates will be interviewed, usually in May.

Arts

The Artistic Endeavours Trust

£19,500 (16 grants)

Correspondent: Richard Midgley, Trustee, MHA Macintyre Hudson LLP, New Bridge Street House, 30–34 New Bridge Street, London EC4V 6BJ (020 7429 4100; email: james.midgley@mhllp.co.uk)

CC number: 1044926

Eligibility

Students undertaking education in the arts and other creative subjects, or entering artistic professions.

Types of grants

Grants to graduates and undergraduate students for fees, clothing, equipment, books, and travel, as well as living expenses to those who are unable to secure employment for a period not exceeding two years.

Annual grant total

In 2015/16 the trust held assets of £43,500 and had an income of £43,500. A total of £19,500 was awarded in grants.

Applications

Apply in writing to the correspondent by post or email.

The Lionel Bart Foundation

£20,000

Correspondent: John Cohen, Trustee, Clintons, 55 Drury Lane, London WC2B 5SQ (02073796080; email: jc@clintons.co.uk)

CC number: 1086343

Eligibility

Undergraduate and postgraduate students who are aiming to become actors, composers, lyricists, book writers, playwrights, designers, choreographers, directors and anyone who wishes to make the theatre their career.

Types of grants

Up to £2,000 per student.

Annual grant total

In 2015/16 the foundation had assets of £17,000 and an income of £37,000. The total amount awarded in grants to individuals was £20,000.

Applications

Applicants must apply in writing to the correspondent. Two candidates are also chosen from the Royal Central School of Speech and Drama. All applications must demonstrate financial need, commitment to the course, and how the funds will be used.

The Carne Trust

£64,000 (30 grants)

Correspondent: Karen Toth, Kleinwort Hambros Trust Company LTD, 5th Floor, 8 St James's Square, London SW1Y 4JU (020 3207 7014; email: karen.wall@kleinwortbenson.com; website: www.carnetrust.org)

CC number: 1115903

Eligibility

Young people studying music and theatre in selected institutions who are in need.

Types of grants

Grants are given according to need, and can be used for equipment, tuition, performance fees, and early career development.

Annual grant total

In 2016 the trust held assets of £809,000 and had an income of £219,000. A total of £64,000 was awarded in grants to individuals.

Applications

Unsolicited applications are not accepted. The website states: 'Working closely with major drama schools and music academies, The Carne Trust provides scholarships to individuals selected by those institutions, both on the basis of talent and financial need.'

Other information

The trust also makes awards to organisations and companies in the support of performances and programmes to do with performing arts. In 2016 the trust awarded £253,000 to organisations.

The Costume Society

£11,000

Correspondent: Jill Salen, Hon. Secretary, Rose Cottage, Crofft Y. Genau, St Fagans, Cardiff CF5 6DU (029 2056 8622; email: awards@costumesociety.org.uk or info@costumesociety.org.uk; website: www.costumesociety.org.uk)

CC number: 262401

Eligibility

Students in history and theory of design (fashion and textiles), dress, costume, theatre wardrobe and related fields. Support is given to students engaged in further and higher education, including postgraduate courses and also to researchers and trainee museum curators.

Types of grants

The society offers the following awards:

- **Museum Placement Award** – up to £1,000 to student volunteers to undertake a placement (full or part-time for a minimum of two months) in a public museum in the UK
- **Conference Student Bursary** – covers costs of two student attendees at the Costume Society's annual three-day conference (excluding transport to and from the event). It is open to UK full-time and part-time students at a graduate and postgraduate level engaged in research directed towards the presentation of a dissertation or thesis
- **The Patterns of Fashion Award** – an award of £500 open to students in costume and fashion-related education courses who 'produced a reconstructed garment from a pattern in one of the Janet Arnold *Patterns of Fashion* books that reflect the high standards presented in the books'
- **The Yarwood Award** – up to £500 plus one-years' membership available to master's students 'engaged in high quality research into the history of dress and/or textiles with expenditure relating to the completion of their dissertation'. The award is intended to cover specific expenses, such as 'travel to a library, archive or collection, subsistence while away and archive reproduction fees' not the overall cost of the degree

Annual grant total

In 2016 the society had assets of £359,500 and an income of £59,500. Charitable grants from the society totalled £11,000 through the following award schemes: Costume Conservation Award (£9,600); Museum Placement Award (£150); Patterns of Fashion Awards (£800); Yarwood Award (£500).

Applications

Application procedures and deadlines are different for each of the awards. Detailed eligibility and application guidelines are available on the society's website and are also published in *Costume*, the annual journal of the society. Applicants are encouraged to approach the society with initial enquiries.

Other information

The society's aims are the promotion of the study and preservation of historic and contemporary dress.

Craft Pottery Charitable Trust

£1,600

Correspondent: John Higgins, Trust Secretary, Taplands Farm Cottage, Webbs Green, Soberton, Southampton SO32 3PY (023 9263 2686; email: JohnHigginsceramics@gmail.com; website: www.cpaceramics.co.uk/craft-potters-charitable-trust)

CC number: 1004767

Eligibility

People involved in the field of ceramics. Applicants must be British citizens or have permanent resident status, as defined by UK Visas and Immigration, and meet the definition of a professional artist.

Types of grants

The trust offers awards through the Annual Grant Scheme. According to the guidance notes, awards of up to £1,000 can be used:

> For a period of independent research and creation of a body of work, the development of prototypes, participation in artists' residencies and specialised professional development activities (such as workshops or specialised training), as well as production of work for confirmed public exhibitions in the UK and/or abroad.

In the past, bursaries of £500 were also made to new graduate makers to undertake individual postgraduate projects.

Support may be used towards training, travel, conference attendance, preparation of books or films and other projects relevant to the education of the public in craft pottery.

Annual grant total

In 2016 the trust had an income of £3,600 and a total expenditure of £1,800. Throughout the year, we estimate that the charity gave around £1,600 in grants to individuals for educational purposes.

Applications

Application forms and further guidelines can be obtained from the correspondent via email or by post including an sae. Further information is also given on the trust's website.

The Thomas Devlin Fund

See entry on page 131

The Ann Driver Trust

£23,500 (ten grants)

Correspondent: Penny Neary, Administrator, 10 Stratford Place, London W1C 1BA (07939 556574; email: secretary@anndrivertrust.org)

CC number: 801898

Eligibility

Young people wishing to pursue an education in the arts, particularly music.

Types of grants

Scholarships and bursaries for the advancement of education in the arts, principally music.

Annual grant total

In 2015/16 the trust had assets of £27,000 and an income of £27,500. Throughout the year the trust awarded £23,500 in bursaries and scholarships.

Applications

Application forms should be requested by the principal or head of department at the applicant's place of study.

Other information

The 2015/16 trustees' annual report states:

The principal activity of the trust has continued to be the distribution of scholarships and bursaries for the advancement of education in the arts, principally music. The trustees confirm that they have referred to the guidance contained in the Charity Commission's general guidance on public benefit when reviewing the Trust's aims and objectives and in planning future activities and setting the grant making policy for the year. They have continued their successful programme of raising the profile of the charity through its website. This enables all those talented in music and the arts to identify the aims and objects of the charity.

The Elmley Foundation

£24,500

Correspondent: John de la Cour, Chief Executive, West Aish, Morchard Bishop, Crediton EX17 6RX (01363 877433; email: foundation@elmley.org.uk; website: www.elmley.org.uk)

CC number: 1004043

Eligibility

Students born and schooled in Herefordshire and Worcestershire taking up places on nationally recognised specialist arts courses. Preference will be given to postgraduates and to young people offered exceptional opportunities such as membership of the National Youth Orchestra or the National Youth Theatre.

Types of grants

Grants of between £300 and £2,500 although the foundation's website states that it 'rarely makes grants over £2,000 to unsolicited applications'. Grants are to help students take up places on courses, especially postgraduate courses.

Annual grant total

In 2015/16 the foundation held assets of £3.7 million and had an income of £334,500. Grants to students during the year and totalled £24,500. Grants are also made to organisations and individual artists and totalled £203,000 during the year.

Applications

The foundation requests that you contact the correspondent prior to making an application. Applications should be submitted in writing, explaining the costs and why it is needed. An application form is provided on the website, but there is no obligation to use it, although it may help structure your application. There are no deadlines and the foundation can usually provide an answer within two months.

The Fenton Arts Trust

£1,400

Correspondent: Shelley Baxter, Trust Manager and Administrator, PO Box 68825, London SE23 9DG (website: www.fentonartstrust.org.uk)

CC number: 294629

Eligibility

People who are making, or who aspire to make, a worthwhile contribution to the artistic and cultural life of the UK. Grants are made towards the creative arts, principally painting and drama. Students should have British nationality and be aged under 35.

Types of grants

Scholarships and bursaries to charitable bodies and to individuals or organisations that support work or performance by those early in their careers.

Annual grant total

In 2015/16 the trust had assets of £4 million and an income of £142,000. All grants payable were to institutions with the exception of one made to an individual totalling £1,400.

Applications

Applications for scholarships and bursaries can come from any institution which provides study opportunities and wishes to offer its students the scholarships and bursaries.

Applications for other grants can be made in writing directly by the individual to the administrator. Requests should include a fully budgeted proposal with the amount requested and information regarding other sponsors to the project.

Applications should preferably be sent nine months to a year in advance.

The trustees meet to discuss applications three times a year.

Other information

The trust also provides grants to organisations.

The Derek Hill Foundation

£17,000 (17 grants)

Correspondent: The Trustees, c/o Rathbone Trust Company Ltd, 8 Finsbury Circus, London EC2M 7AZ

CC number: 801590

Eligibility

People studying or working in the arts in the UK.

Types of grants

Bursaries for the arts, ranging from £100 to £3,000. Grants can also be made to cover travel costs.

Annual grant total

In 2015/16 the foundation held assets of £1.5 million and had an income of £47,000. Grants totalling £17,000 were made to 17 individuals and ranged from £100 to £3,000, including one scholarship to the British School at Rome

Applications

Apply in writing to the correspondent.

National Youth Arts Trust (NYAT)

£9,000

Correspondent: Ruth O'Briend, c/o The Furniture Practice, 31 Pear Tree Street, London EC1V 3AG (07891835589; email: admin@nationalyouthartstrust.com; website: www.nationalyouthartstrust.com)

CC number: 1152367

Eligibility

Applicants must be UK citizens, enrolled in full or part-time education and eligible for Pupil Premium
- Dance Bursary – must be for dance classes taught by an Imperial Society of Teachers of Dance teacher, a Council for Dance Education and Training (CDET) School, or an Arts Council funded Dance Company
- Music Bursary – the trust will only accept applications from secondary

school age individuals for singing. All other beginners must be under 12 years of age

- Access Bursary – individuals must be between 17 and 25 years old, and funding must be for auditions to Drama UK or Conservatoire for Dance and Drama accredited schools. Applications for first-time auditions will not be accepted

Types of grants

The trust offers scholarships, bursaries and other support in the fields of music, drama and dance. Assistance can be given towards training, tuition, necessities, clothing, instruments, travel costs, exam fees, auditions and related expenses. It aims to build and maintain partnerships with schools and local arts institutions and to mentor young people towards higher education.

- Dance Bursary – up to £1,000 to access professional dance training, specialist dance clothing, and travel costs
- Music Bursary – up to £1,000 to access professional music lessons (instrumental and singing)
- Access Bursary – up to £200 to cover fees and expenses for auditions at accredited drama schools and conservatoires

Annual grant total

In 2016/17 the trust had an income of £111,500, and a total expenditure of £62,000. Grants awarded to individuals totalled £9,000; 4 Music bursaries, 6 Dance bursaries, and three access bursaries.

Exclusions

The trust does not fund retrospectively.

Applications

Application forms can be downloaded from the trust's website and be submitted either by email or post. Applications must include:

- A letter of recommendation by a referee who can attest to the applicant's talent and commitment to the art form (signed, stamped, and on school letterhead paper)
- A letter from the senior management team of the applicant's school confirming the individual is currently in receipt of Pupil Premium (if applicable), otherwise the applicant must provide evidence that they receive benefits
- A copy of a bill or council tax letter or any Home Office documents in support of your residency status (if applicable)
- A copy of the applicant's passport
- A copy of a letter of enrolment to a dance or music school

- A copy of a letter of invitation to audition at an accredited drama school
- A copy of an academic transcript/ certificate or CV showing proficiency in the art form
- An optional video of no more than five minutes of the individual's performing arts practice (only webpage links, no CDs)

Other information

The trust is working with partner charities and organisations to help fund apprenticeships in theatre, television and film for care leavers. The current key partner is the Drive Forward Foundation.

Rhona Reid Charitable Trust
See entry on page 81

The Society for Theatre Research

£5,000 (13 grants)

Correspondent: Chair of the Research Awards Sub-Committee, c/o Theatres Trust, 22 Charing Cross Road, London WC2H 0QL (email: awards@str.org.uk; website: www.str.org.uk)

CC number: 266186

Eligibility

People involved with research into 'one or more of the history, historiography, art, and practice of the British theatre (including music-hall, opera, dance, and associated skills and crafts of performance)', according to the society's website. Applicants should be aged 18 or over. There are no restrictions on status, nationality, or the location of the research.

Applications from academic staff, postgraduate students, theatre professionals and private researchers are all equally eligible.

Types of grants

Annual theatre research awards ranging between £100 and £1,000. Awards can be given towards the completion of work already in progress, for training in research techniques for established projects and towards publication of completed work. Grants may also be given towards fees to attend conferences relating to society's purpose.

Annual grant total

In 2015/16 the society had assets of £676,500 and an income of almost £51,000. The society made 13 research awards to individuals totalling £4,500, with a further £500 given through the society's Craig Fund.

Exclusions

Grants are never given for course fees or towards general subsistence costs. Exclusively literary, textual or dramatic topics not relating to the theatre are not eligible.

Applications

Application forms are provided on the society's website, along with further information about the awards available, deadlines and guidance on what to include in an application.

The application form for the awards is available from around October of each year, closing dates are usually in March, and successful recipients are announced at the society's AGM in May. For precise dates, see the website.

The South Square Trust

£33,000 (27 grants)

Correspondent: Nicola Chrimes, Clerk to the Trustees, PO Box 69, Wadebridge, Cornwall PL27 9BZ (07951 822916; website: www.southsquaretrust.org.uk)

CC number: 278960

Eligibility

Students over the age of 18 years who are studying full-time practical degree courses in the fine and applied arts (especially those related to gold, silver and metalwork), music, drama and dance.

Preference is given to students who have been educated mainly in the UK, those in their third year of an undergraduate level or postgraduate students.

Types of grants

The trust assists students directly and also provides scholarships and bursaries to a number of schools/colleges. Individual awards can be given towards fees or for living expenses.

Annual grant total

In 2015/16 the trust had assets of £4.4 million and an income of £178,000. Grants to 27 individuals totalled £33,000.

Exclusions

Grants are not given for:

- People under 18
- Part-time or short courses
- Expeditions or travel outside the UK
- Courses outside the UK
- Film, architecture and interior design courses
- Foundation courses and research degrees
- Purchase of equipment
- Private lessons

Applications

Application forms can be completed online on the trust's website. Individual applications are invited from 1 January to 30 April each year. Two references (preferably from the applicant's current tutors) and a photograph are required. If the applicant is on an arts-related course, photographs of their work must also be provided.

Initial enquiries by telephone are also welcomed.

Other information

In 2015/16 bursaries and scholarships to 50 schools and colleges totalled £151,000. The trustees have set up scholarship awards with a number of colleges and institutions. A full list of these can be obtained from the Clerk to the Trustees.

Split Infinitive Trust

£32,500

Correspondent: Heather Stoney, Trustee, PO BOX 409, Scarborough YO11 9AJ (email: splitinfin@ haydonning.co.uk; website: www. splitinfinitivetrust.co.uk)

CC number: 1110380

Eligibility

People in arts education and artists requiring funding for a specific project. Performance arts courses (such as music, drama or dance) are favoured, although other arts areas may be considered. Before applying, applicants are asked to check with the correspondent to confirm the eligibility of their course.

Types of grants

Grants are given for needs associated with arts education and specific arts projects. Awards can be between £250 and £750.

Annual grant total

In 2015/16 the trust held assets of £58,000 and had an income of £30,500. The trust received 186 applications and made grants totalling £42,000 to 126 successful applicants. The amount given to individuals totalled £32,230.

Training	£29,500
Productions	£1,100
Social	£830
Education	£800

Exclusions

Projects outside the UK will not be supported.

The trust's website notes the following: 'repeat grants are rare and although previous recipients are welcome to re-apply, the fact of a previous grant is no guarantee of a future one'.

Applications

Application forms are available on the trust's website and should be completed electronically, although handwritten and posted copies will also be accepted. Remember that supporting evidence – a covering letter, an acceptance letter from the course of study (for students) or evidence of the project/commission and/or a CV (for non-students) – must be attached.

The trustees meet every three months, normally in March, June, September and December, but this can vary.

The Talbot House Trust

£10,000

Correspondent: Jayne Day, The Trust Partnership LLP, 6 Trull Farm Buildings, Trull, Tetbury GL8 8SQ (01285 841900; email: info@thetrustpartnership.com)

CC number: 1010214

Eligibility

Students aged 16 to 25 living in the UK who come from a household with low income and are undertaking courses in the UK in performing arts, such as drama, dance and music.

Types of grants

One-off grants to students in further/higher education to help with the cost with the costs of fees. In exceptional circumstances a contribution towards equipment and instruments or maintenance and living costs will be considered. The grants are intended to be supplementary only and applicants will be expected to raise funds through their own efforts.

Annual grant total

In 2015/16 the trust had an income of £10,200 and a total expenditure of £11,000. We estimate the total of grants awarded to be around £10,000.

Exclusions

Postgraduate students are not supported.

Applications

Application forms are available from the correspondent. Applications must be received by March for consideration in May. Applicants should involve detail of any financial hardship and any other reason why special consideration should be given to their application.

Sydney Dean Whitehead's Charitable Trust

£42,000 (23 grants)

Correspondent: The Trustees, Moore Stephens, Chartered Accountants, 30 Gay Street, Bath BA1 2PA (01225 486100; email: mark.burnett@ moorestephens.com)

CC number: 207714

Eligibility

Children under the age of 18 who have special artistic talents, especially in music, dance or ballet, and whose parents are on a low income or are unable to help them develop these talents. Preference will be given to applicants who demonstrate efforts of raising funds themselves.

Types of grants

Grants are given mainly towards school fees, but support may also be given to help fund one-off purchases (e.g. musical instruments).

Annual grant total

In 2015/16 the trust held assets of almost £1.3 million and had an income of £48,000. Grants were awarded to 22 individuals in the UK and one child in Kenya and totalled £42,000. The trust also supports small local charities and grants to these totalled £2,700 during the year.

Applications

Application forms can be obtained from the correspondent providing an sae. They can be submitted directly by the individual. The trustees meet once a year, in June.

The Marie Duffy Foundation

£290

Correspondent: Michael Pask, Trustee, 4A Flaghead Road, Poole, Dorset BH13 7JL (01202 701173; email: enquiries@marie-duffy-foundation.com; website: www.marie-duffy-foundation.com)

CC number: 1145892

Eligibility

People over the age of 12 who are passionate about excellence in dance, music, composition or choreography of Irish Dance.

Types of grants

The foundation provides 'financial assistance to aspiring dancers, musicians and choreographers so they may fulfil their dreams in the world of Irish Dance'.

Awards may include support towards fees, seminars, bursaries, projects, competitions and so on. The website notes that 'applications can be made for funding Irish Dance-related projects which exhibit creativity, flair and entrepreneurship in the promotion of Irish Dance skills, performance, scholarship or business acumen'.

Annual grant total

In 2015/16 the foundation had an income of £5,100 and a total expenditure of £770. We estimate that the charity awarded around £290 to individuals for educational purposes.

The foundation also awards grants to organisations.

Applications

Application forms are available on the foundation's website. They should be submitted by 31 December.

Lisa Ullmann Travelling Scholarship Fund

£7,400

Correspondent: Emma McFarland, Secretary, c/o Charlton Associates, 16 Berkeley Mews, Cheltenham, Gloucestershire GL50 1DY (email: secretary@lutsf.org.uk; website: www. lutsf.org.uk)

CC number: 297684

Eligibility

UK residents (for at least five years) over the age of 18 working in the field of movement and dance (choreographers, performers, lecturers/teachers, writers, therapists, administrators, producers and related professionals) who wish to travel in the UK or abroad to advance their professional development.

Types of grants

Grants are available for travel expenses, generally in the range of £600, but occasionally larger. Travel must originate and end in the UK. Where necessary, the trust may also fund the travel costs of a carer for applicants with disabilities. The fund's website states:

> Innovative programmes of professional development which clearly relate to your professional work and interests will have a greater chance of success. We prefer to fund plans which are more individually tailored; build on the applicant's previous experience and which demonstrate significant benefits in terms of the applicant's artistic and/or career development.

Annual grant total

According to the website, the grant total for 2017/18 was £7,400 and grants were made to ten individuals.

Exclusions

The fund will not support:

- Courses or conferences
- Subsistence
- Undergraduate courses
- Travel to or from institutions for full-time or long courses (lasting a year or more, including most degree, diploma, certificate and postgraduate courses)
- Individuals who have received a scholarship within the last five years
- Gap year travel
- Degree placements and fieldwork
- Joint or group applications (although applications from individuals as part of a larger project team may be considered)
- Projects where a proportion of the time away is used for leisure or paid work
- Travel insurance, visas or additional baggage costs
- Travel between home and departure point (apart from in the case of applicants with disabilities)

Master's degrees are only considered when the applicant has a professional track record of at least two years.

Applications

Application forms and guidelines are available on the foundation's website between November and January. All applicants are informed of the outcome of their application by the end of March.

The John Thaw Foundation

£66,000

Correspondent: The Trustees, PO Box 477, Amyand Park Road, Twickenham TW1 9LF

CC number: 1090668

Eligibility

People wishing to pursue a career in theatre and performing arts. Preference is given to individuals who are underprivileged and disadvantaged.

Types of grants

The foundation provides scholarships and bursaries of around £3,000 towards fees through specifically chosen training programmes at established schools or youth groups.

Annual grant total

In 2015/16 the foundation held assets of £80,000 and had an income of £66,000. A total of £66,000 was awarded to individuals.

Applications

The foundation does not accept unsolicited applications. Awards are made through the named bursary programmes of specific institutions and submissions made by individuals are not considered by the trustees.

Other information

The foundation works with a number of partner bodies and can also support educational organisations.

Benney Arts Foundation

£750

Correspondent: Paul Benney, Trustee, Somerset House, Strand, London WC2R 1LA (07973 373 220; email: info@ benneyartsfoundation.org)

CC number: 1154043

Eligibility

Young artists over the age of 18 who have financial difficulties and would not have sufficient funds to continue their education with an established artist.

Types of grants

Applicants are paired with an established artist to apprentice under, and can be awarded bursaries of up to £15,000 dependent on financial means and the period of apprenticeship.

Annual grant total

In 2015/16 the foundation had no income and a total expenditure of £840. We estimate that the total amount awarded in grants was £750.

Applications

Application forms are available to download on the website. Applications must include copies of educational transcripts, financial information, and a reference. The correspondence address is available on the application.

The Company of Arts Scholars Charitable Trust

£2,300

Correspondent: Georgina Gough, The Furniture Makers Co., 12 Austin Friars, London EC2N 2HE (020 3894 5642; email: georginaegough@hotmail.com; website: www.artsscholars.org)

CC number: 1121954

Eligibility

Applicants for the Arts Scholar Research Award and Geoffrey Bond Travel Award should be university students in the UK, studying art or architecture.

Sixth form students wishing to undertake placement at a heritage site should be attendees of one of the following schools:

- City of London Academy (Southwark)
- William Morris Sixth Form (Hammersmith)

- The Charter School (Southwark)
- Bacon's College (Southwark)

Types of grants
Grants are available to undertake research as part of a university course.

Annual grant total
In 2016/17 the charity had assets of £3.5 million and an income of £106,000. A total of £2,300 was awarded in grants, broken down as follows:

Art Scholars Research Awards: £1,000; Geoffrey Bond Travel Award: £500; Other grants: £750.

Applications
Applicants wishing to apply for the Arts Scholar Research Award should make themselves known to the charity and application details will be provided.

Applicants for the Geoffrey Bond Travel Award should make an application to Tara Draper-Stumm (tara@heritageoflondon.com).

Sixth form students wishing to undertake a placement at a heritage site should discuss this with their school (see eligibility for included schools).

All university applicants should be aware that if successful, a copy of the final dissertation should also be send to the charity.

The Tom Acton Memorial Trust

£1,800

Correspondent: Alan Gage, Trustee, Hamilton House, Cobblers Green, Felsted, Dunmow CM6 3LX (01371 820382; email: applications@tomacton. org; website: tomactonorg.wordpress.com/home)

CC number: 1088069

Eligibility
People in musical education who are under the age of 25 who were born in, educated in, or reside in Essex.

Types of grants
Financial assistance is available towards the costs of musical education fees, the purchase or loan of an instrument, travel expenses in respect of musical education or performance, and music-related physical and psychological health needs. Grants can reach up to a maximum of £800 and are awarded according to need.

Annual grant total
In 2015/16 the trust had an income of £300 and a total expenditure of £2,100. Based on previous years, we estimate the grant total to be £1,800.

Applications
Applicants must be born in, educated in, or live in Essex and below the age of 25

on 31 May. Applicants must also have reached an advanced standard of musical education.

Application forms can be requested from the correspondent or downloaded from the website. Completed application forms must be accompanied by a reference from a music teacher, and must be returned to the trust by post or email by 31 May. Successful applicants will be invited to audition, to take place in July.

The Australian Music Foundation in London

£25,000

Correspondent: Dr Marcus Cox, 51 Musgrove Road, London SE14 5PP (07778 313 479; email: info@ australianmusicfoundation.org; website: australianmusicfoundation.org)

CC number: 270784

Eligibility
Instrumentalists up to the age of 26 and singers, conductors, accompanists, repetiteurs and composers under the age of 30.

Candidates must be Australian citizens.

Candidates who have been offered a place of postgraduate study, or are part-way through postgraduate study will be considered.

Candidates who are part-way through undergraduate study can be supported.

Candidates must be studying at an institution in the UK, the USA, or Europe.

Types of grants
Awards are made to contribute towards:
- Tuition fees for both full-time and part-time study at an institution with an outstanding international reputation
- Maintenance costs during full-time study at an overseas institution with outstanding international reputation
- Private tuition
- Language courses
- Purchase of musical instruments
- Travel costs

Applicants are required to produce evidence that the award has been used for the purpose of which it was given. Funds are paid in Australian dollars into an Australian bank account.

Annual grant total
In 2015/16 the foundation had income of £35,000 and a total expenditure of £29,000. We estimate that the total amount awarded in grants was £25,000.

Exclusions
Candidates who have not yet started their undergraduate course or who are in

their first year of undergraduate study are not eligible.

Applications
Applications are completed in two stages:
- Candidates must first complete the application form (available to download from the website) and submit it online together with audition videos. There is a £10 administration fee for this submission. Applications must be sent by early May
- Successful candidates will be invited to perform at the live finals in London in early October. Candidates who are unable to attend the finals will be considered based on the strength of their new and original video material

Candidates should also have two referees, who are required to be distinguished members of the music profession. Written references should be sent via email to the Administrator.

Other information
The foundation is keen to hear from jazz musicians considering tertiary education in the UK, the USA or Europe as they are in the process of creating a new jazz fund.

Awards for Young Musicians

£90,000 (184 grants)

Correspondent: Hester Cockcroft, PO Box 2754, Bristol BS4 9DA (0117 904 9906; email: enquiries@a-y-m.org.uk; website: www.a-y-m.org.uk)

CC number: 1070994

Eligibility
Musicians aged 5 to 17 who are in financial need and have exceptional musical potential. Applicants must include a performance video with the application so the board can assess the level of talent or potential. Any musical genre is accepted.

The grants are means-tested; the website states that household incomes over £40,000 are likely to be ineligible.

Types of grants
Up to £2,000 can be awarded, however the average grant is around £500.

Annual grant total
In 2016 the charity had assets of £300,000 and an income of £427,500. A total of £90,000 was awarded as musical grants to individuals.

Exclusions
No support is given for singers, beginner musicians, or university study.

Applications

Applications can be made online through www.aym-awards.fluidreview. com. Each funding round has a different beginning and deadline date – sign up for the newsletter or check the website to see if funding is open.

Other information

The charity also funds other organisations that nurture musical talent and provides resources for music teachers on how to stop musical potential.

Josephine Baker Trust

£30,000

Correspondent: David Munro, Trustee, Grange Cottage, Frensham, Farnham, Surrey GU10 3DS (01252 792485; email: munrodj@aol.com)

CC number: 1086222

Eligibility

People studying vocal music and young singers at the beginning of their career.

Types of grants

Grants are available to pay for all or part of candidate's performance fees at concerts.

Annual grant total

In 2015/16 the trust had assets of £127,000 and an income of £146,000. The total amount awarded in grants to individuals was £30,000.

Applications

Applications should be sent in writing to the correspondent. The trust also selects students from the Royal College of Music and Royal Academy of Music. All applicants are required to audition.

The Philip Bates Trust

£3,500

Correspondent: The Trustees, 24 Elmfield Road, Castle Bromwich B36 0HL (0121 747 5705; email: info@ philipbatestrust.org.uk; website: www. philipbatestrust.org.uk)

CC number: 1094937

Eligibility

People under 25 pursuing creative and artistic achievement. Preference is given to musicians and applicants in the West Midlands.

Types of grants

One-off, and in exceptional circumstances recurrent, grants of between £100 and £250 and musical instrument loans. There are also four prizes for composition awarded each year.

Annual grant total

In 2016 the trust had an income of £9,500 and a total expenditure of £8,000. We estimate that grants awarded to individuals for educational purposes totalled around £3,500.

Exclusions

Grants to individuals will not be made to more than one sibling per family.

Applications

Applications should be made in writing, summarising the activities for which a grant is needed and the requirements of the applicant, and submitted by post. The guidelines (which can be downloaded from the trust's website) set out points which should be included in the application. The trustees meet three times each year, in February, June and October, and applications should be submitted by the end of the previous month (i.e. in January, May or September, respectively). Where possible, trustees prefer to receive a personal request from the applicant rather than from a parent, guardian or other person on their behalf. Due to the large number of applications received, the trust can only notify those who are successful.

Other information

Grants are also made to charitable organisations in support of projects or workshops which aim to develop creative and artistic interests and skills in young people.

The Nicholas Boas Charitable Trust

£23,000 (37 grants)

Correspondent: Bob Boas, 22 Mansfield Street, London W1G 9NR (020 7436 0344; email: boas22m@btinternet.com; website: www.nicholasboastrust.org.uk)

CC number: 1073359

Eligibility

Applicants must either be studying architecture or beginning their music career.

Types of grants

Small grants for musicians at the beginning of their career for activities such as masterclasses, travel to auditions, recordings, and commissioning new work.

Travel grants are awarded to architecture students from The AA or Cambridge University to attend the British School at Rome.

Annual grant total

In 2015/16 the trust held assets of £388,000 and had an income of £38,000. A total of £23,000 was awarded in grants to 37 individuals.

Exclusions

The trust does not pay for tuition fees.

Applications

An application form can be requested from the correspondent via email.

Other information

The trust also awards grants to musical organisations and festivals such as the English National Opera, English Music Festival and IMA Prussia Cove. In 2015/16 around £23,000 was donated to organisations.

The Choir Schools Association Bursary Trust Ltd

£208,000 (94 grants)

Correspondent: Susan Rees, 39 Grange Close, Winchester, Hampshire SO23 9RS (01962 853508; email: admin@ choirschools.org.uk; website: www. choirschools.org.uk)

CC number: 1120639

Eligibility

Pupils or proposed pupils between the ages of 7 and 13 at a member school of the Choir Schools' Association.

Ex-choristers over the age of 13 may also be supported from the money donated by the School Fees Insurance Agency.

Types of grants

Grants of up to £1,500 are available to pay the fees of choristers attending member schools of the Choir Schools' Association, or to students studying dance or music at affiliated schools. Applications are means-tested. The grant is paid directly to the institution on behalf of the applicant.

Annual grant total

In 2015/16 the trust had assets of £1.6 million and an income of £370,000. A total of £208,000 was awarded in educational grants.

Applications

Applicants should contact the head of the choir or arts school concerned. Applications should normally be submitted by 15 March, 31 August and 15 December for consideration in May, October and February respectively.

EMI Music Sound Foundation

£144,500

Correspondent: Janie Orr, Chief Executive, Beaumont House, Avonmore Road, Kensington, London W14 8TS (020 7550 7898; email: emimusicsoundfoundation@umusic.com; website: www. emimusicsoundfoundation.com)

CC number: 1104027

Eligibility

Young people in the UK who are undertaking music education. Applicants must have been resident in the UK for a minimum of three years and: be a British citizen; be a national of a member state of the European Economic Area; have been granted leave to enter or remain in the UK for an indefinite period; or hold a certificate of right of abode in the UK.

Note: Individuals resident in the UK for the purpose of education or attending a course of study are not eligible.

Types of grants

Grants, usually of up to £2,000, towards the purchase of instruments and music equipment in primary, secondary and tertiary education.

The foundation also operates a bursary scheme of £5,000 for students at selected musical colleges and institutes. These are: Birmingham Conservatoire; Brighton and Bristol Institute of Modern Music (BIMM); Centre for Young Musicians; English National Opera (ENO); International World Music Centre; Limerick; National Children's Orchestra; Royal Academy of Music; London; Royal Conservatoire of Scotland; Royal Welsh College of Music and Drama; and Tech Music Schools (London).

Annual grant total

In 2015/16 the foundation held assets of £7.5 million and had an income of £306,500. Grants to individuals totalled £144,500 and an additional £55,000 was awarded in bursaries.

Exclusions

Grants are not provided to/for:

- Applicants based outside the UK and Ireland
- Applications for tuition fees and living expenses (other than through the bursary scheme)
- Applications over £2,000
- Private instrumental lessons

Applications

Application forms for instrument/ equipment grants can be downloaded from the foundation's website or requested from the correspondent. They should be submitted by individuals or their school via post, together with all the relevant documentation and references a month before the trustees' meeting. The meetings are held twice a year, normally in October and March (for exact dates consult the website). Candidates are invited to approach the foundation with queries prior to application.

Applications for bursaries should be made through the individual's educational establishment.

Other information

The foundation also gives grants to a number of secondary schools to fund music education. In 2015/16 £354,500 was also awarded to institutions. During the year 554 individual and school applications were approved.

The Gerald Finzi Trust

£8,600 (five grants)

Correspondent: Administrator, The Finzi Trust, PO Box 137, Stour Row, Shaftesbury, Dorset SP7 0WX (email: admin@geraldfinzi.org; website: www. geraldfinzi.org)

CC number: 313047

Eligibility

Musicians and music students between the ages of 18 and 80. Formal training, qualifications or previous professional experience are not prerequisite.

Types of grants

The trust offers grants for the purchase of musical instruments and scholarships for projects in the UK and overseas which 'might show a creative initiative or could involve engaging in some practical experience, education or research, perhaps giving a personal change of direction'. The projects would ideally last between three to eight weeks. If a project involves travel, then the trust can meet these expenses along with the cost of accommodation, subsistence and equipment for the period involved. Scholarships awarded in recent years have covered studies in Estonia, Finland, France, Germany, India, Ireland, Italy, South America, Sweden, the UK and the USA.

In the past, grants awarded have ranged from £2,000 to £5,000.

Annual grant total

In 2016/17 the trust had assets of £914,500 and an income of £876,000. Throughout the year the trust awarded a total of £39,500 in grants to both organisations and individuals.

Grants to individuals for educational purposes totalled £8,600. In total, five individuals were supported through scholarship awards and grants to purchase musical instruments.

Exclusions

Grants are not given for attendance of courses, to support academic degree qualifications or for fees or living expenses.

The trust will not ordinarily make a further award to an individual who has previously been awarded either a Finzi Scholarship or a Churchill Finzi Fellowship.

Applications

Application forms can be found on the trust's website or requested from the correspondent providing an sae. Completed applications should be emailed to admin@geraldfinzi.org or posted to The Finzi Trust, PO Box 137, Shaftesbury SP7 0WX.

Applications should include an outline of the proposal and an estimate of the costs involved. They are considered twice a year; deadlines for submission are 20 February and 1 September. Candidates who are successful with their initial application are invited for an interview which is normally held in January, in London.

The Michael James Music Trust

£15,000

Correspondent: Edward Monds, Trustee, 4 Blind Lane, Wimborne BH21 1NJ (01202 887681; email: office@merlins. org.uk; website: www.wimborneminster. org.uk/116/michael-james-music-trust. html)

CC number: 283943

Eligibility

Individuals engaged in any musical education, particularly in a Christian context. Priority is given to choral scholars and organists.

Types of grants

One-off and recurrent grants are given towards tuition fees and expenses.

Annual grant total

In 2016/17 the trust had an income of £24,500 and a total expenditure of £35,000. We estimate that grants totalled about £15,000.

Exclusions

Grants are not given for the purchase of instruments or equipment.

Applications

Applicants should first contact the correspondent to enquire about making an application.

Other information

Grants are also made to churches, universities and schools.

The Kathleen Trust

£89,000 (54 grants)

Correspondent: Edward Perks, Trustee, Currey & Co., 21 Buckingham Gate, London SW1E 6LS (020 7828 4091)

CC number: 1064516

Eligibility

Young musicians of outstanding ability who are in need.

Types of grants

According to our previous research, the trust offers loans in the form of musical instruments and sometimes bursaries to attend music courses, ranging between £500 and £3,000.

Annual grant total

In 2015/16 the trust had assets of almost £1.2 million and an income of £26,000. Grants were made to 54 individuals totalling £89,000, with a further £10,000 given in one grant to an organisation.

Applications

Apply in writing to the correspondent.

The Macfarlane Walker Trust

£16,500 (nine grants)

Correspondent: Sophie Walker, Administrator, 4 Shooters Hill Road, London SE3 7BD (020 8858 4701; email: sophiewalker@mac.com)

CC number: 227890

Eligibility

Music students over 18 who are in need, with a preference for those who live in Cheltenham and Gloucestershire.

Types of grants

One-off grants ranging from £300 to £4,800, for the purchase of musical instruments for music students.

Annual grant total

In 2016/17 the trust held assets of £657,000 and had an income of £38,000. Grants to nine individuals totalled £16,500.

Exclusions

The trust does not provide financial assistance towards tuition fees or gap year trips. Large charities, animal charities, foreign charities or major building projects are not supported.

Applications

Apply in writing to the correspondent. Applications should be made directly by the individual, giving the reason for

applying and an outline of the project with a financial forecast. Our previous research suggests an sae and references from an academic referee must accompany the initial application.

Other information

The charity also supports various projects in the fields of music, drama and fine arts. The trust assists in the provision of educational facilities, particularly for scientific research. Grants awarded to organisations totalled £26,000.

The Music Libraries Trust

£1,000

Correspondent: Edith Speller, Secretary to the Trustees, c/o Jerwood Library of the Performing Arts, Trinity Laban Conservatoire of Music and Dance, King Charles Court, Old Royal Naval College, Greenwich, London SE10 9JF (020 8305 4422; email: secretary@ musiclibrariestrust.org; website: www. musiclibrariestrust.org)

CC number: 284334

Eligibility

Music librarians in the UK and Ireland involved in education or training and people carrying out research into music librarianship, music bibliography, musicology and related disciplines.

Types of grants

Bursaries between £200 and £300 are available for students and library staff to attend courses offered by IAML (UK and Ireland). Full and partial bursaries are available (including travel expenses).

The trust also awards grants (between £100 and £5,000) for research projects related to music libraries and music bibliography. Second grants will be considered in exceptional cases.

Annual grant total

In 2015/16 the trust had an income of £2,200 and a total expenditure of £2,500. We estimate that grants given to individuals totalled around £1,000.

Exclusions

The trust will not provide funding for general undergraduate and postgraduate studies.

Applications

Application forms can be found online. Applicants should provide full details of the project, state other sources of funding considered and give a full analysis of anticipated expenses. The trust welcomes informal discussions by email. The trustees meet at least three times a year. Applicants should provide

a referee who must email or write to the Bursaries Secretary independently.

Other information

Support is also given to organisations. In addition to regular funding, the trust also offers bursaries and a memorial prize.

E.T. Bryant Memorial Prize

The award (£250 in 2014) is made in conjunction with IAML (UK and Ireland) 'to a student of Library and Information Science or to a librarian in the first five years of the profession for a significant contribution to the literature of music librarianship'.

Worshipful Company of Musicians Charitable Fund

£164,000

Correspondent: Hugh Lloyd, Clerk, The Worshipful Company of Musicians, 1 Speed Highwalk, Barbican, London EC2Y 8DX (020 7496 8980; email: clerk@wcom.org.uk; website: www. wcom.org.uk)

CC number: 310040

Eligibility

Musicians and music students (including those working in/studying performance, composition, musicology and music technology).

Types of grants

There are a number of different scholarships and bursaries funded through schools, conservatoires and other academic institutions, as well as awards and prizes for outstanding musicians. Support is given towards purposes such as auditions, interviews, competitions, concerts, courses, training, study and commissions. All award winners can compete for the Prince's Prize, which offers £10,000 from the company. Details of the awards given by the charity are on its website.

Annual grant total

In 2016 the charity had assets of £5.5 million and an income of £382,000. Grants to individuals for prizes, awards and medals totalled £69,500. A further £94,000 was given in bursaries, scholarships and training fees through educational institutions. There were also grants totalling £14,900 to other organisations, as well as £29,000 for outreach projects in schools.

Applications

Refer to the website for information on specific awards and how to apply.

Other information

The charity also carries out outreach work with children and young people in London, particularly focusing on those from disadvantaged backgrounds.

The website states that many award winners become members of the Musicians' Company.

The Royal College of Organists

£22,000 (23 grants)

Correspondent: Philip Meaden, Chief Executive, PO Box 7328, New Milton, Hampshire BH25 9DU (020 3865 6998; email: admin@rco.org.uk; website: www. rco.org.uk)

CC number: 312847

Eligibility

People studying to play the organ, particularly those working towards RCO diplomas. Most awards are given to members or student members of the Royal College of Organists.

Types of grants

The college offers various scholarships and awards, which are listed in detail on its website. Awards are broken down into the following categories: Group A – short courses and general tuition support; Group B – undergraduate or postgraduate study; awards and bursaries at particular institutions; special awards; travelling scholarships.

Annual grant total

In 2015/16 the college had assets of £2.56 million and an income of £664,500. Scholarships and prizes totalled £22,000. Awards and bursaries were broken down in the annual report as follows:

Bursary type	No. of individuals
Group A	13
Dr John Birch Scholarship	4
Group B	3
Named awards	3

Applications

Refer to the college's website for details of awards available, how to apply and deadlines.

The Rushworth Trust

See entry on page 251

The RVW Trust

£20,000 (five grants)

Correspondent: Hannah Vlcek, 13 Calico Row, Plantation Wharf, London SW11 3YH (02072233385; email: info@rvwtrust.org.uk; website: www.rvwtrust.org.uk)

CC number: 1066977

Eligibility

The applicant must have been accepted on a taught master's course in composition at a British university.

Types of grants

Up to five grants for postgraduate study in composition are made annually of £4,000 each.

Annual grant total

In 2016 the trust had an income of £440,500 and a spending of £289,500. During the year the trust awarded 139 grants totalling £220,000, of which five grants, totalling £20,000, were towards postgraduate study.

Exclusions

The trust does not make grants for:

- Courses in TV/film composition
- Courses teaching only electro-acoustic composition
- Performance courses
- PhDs and other research degrees
- Courses outside the UK

Applications

Application forms for postgraduate study can be found online and are considered once a year, in May.

Other information

The trust also assists organisations in order to promote public knowledge and appreciation of 20th and 21st century British music.

The trust also provides assistance for the recording of music, concerts, performances and other events.

The Stringwise Trust

£1,000

Correspondent: Michael Max, Trustee, 71 Queen Victoria Street, London EC4V 4BE (020784414000)

CC number: 1048917

Eligibility

People who play stringed instruments, particularly children and aspiring teachers.

Types of grants

Bursaries and scholarships to enable attendance at any training courses or experiential events.

Annual grant total

In 2016 the trust had an income of £160 and a total expenditure of £1,300. We estimate that grants totalled around £1,000.

Applications

Applications may be made in writing to the correspondent.

The Tillett Trust

£19,800

Correspondent: Katie Avey, Administrator, The Tillett Trust, Neopardy, Crediton, Devon EX17 5EP (01363 777844; fax: 0845 070 4969; email: infor@thetilletttrust.org.uk; website: www.thetilletttrust.org.uk)

CC number: 257329

Eligibility

Young classical musicians at the start of their professional solo careers.

Types of grants

One-off grants of between £250 and £1,000 to assist young musicians undertaking performance-related projects designed to further their careers. Grants can be given towards short performance courses, specialist coaching prior to performance of new repertoire, and travel costs to participate in international competitions.

Annual grant total

In 2015/16 the trust held assets of £518,000 and had an income of £71,000. The amount of grants given to individuals totalled £19,800, with most grants awarded through the Young Artists' Platform.

Exclusions

No grants are given for new instruments, full-time undergraduate courses, commissioning of new works or commercial readings.

Applications

Applicants for one-off grants should send a covering document outlining the nature of their project, a CV, a budget and two references. Further guidance is available on the trust's website.

Other information

Also available each year are two to five postgraduate bursaries for an outstanding student about to enter their second/subsequent year of study. Applicants must be nominated by a main British conservatoire. In 2015/16 bursaries represented £4,500 of the grant total.

The Wessex Young Musicians Trust

£5,000

Correspondent: Sandrey Date, Trustee, 7 Southbourne Coast Road, Bournemouth BH6 4BE (01202 423429; email: sandreydate@yahoo.co.uk)

CC number: 1100905

Eligibility

Young musicians who live in Dorset and Hampshire, particularly, but not exclusively, the participants and supporters of the Centre for Wessex Young Musicians.

Types of grants

Grants towards equipment and facilities, and loans, scholarships, bursaries and prizes, not usually provided by the statutory authorities.

Annual grant total

In 2016/17 the trust had an income of £8,700 and a total expenditure of £10,300. We have estimated that grants to individuals totalled £5,000 during the year. The trust also provides support for organisations.

Applications

Apply in writing to the correspondent.

Miss E. B. Wrightson's Charitable Settlement

£23,500 (40 grants)

Correspondent: N. Hickman, Administrator, Swangles Farm, Cold Christmas Lane, Thundridge, Ware SG12 7SP (email: info@wrightsontrust. co.uk; website: wrightsontrust.co.uk)

CC number: 1002147

Eligibility

Young musicians, usually between the ages of 8 and 18, who are in financial hardship.

Types of grants

One-off and recurrent grants ranging from £100 to £800 are given for instruments, lessons, choir/orchestra fees, Saturday conservatoires, travel costs and similar expenses. Recurrent grants would not normally be renewed more than three times per person. The charity prefers to make payments directly to the teachers/instrument dealers/conservatoires and so on.

Annual grant total

In 2015/16 the charity had assets of £986,000 and an income of £28,000. Throughout the year the charity awarded almost £23,500 in grants to 40 individuals.

Exclusions

People over the age of 21, undergraduates and postgraduates are not normally supported. Assistance cannot be given for tuition fees.

Applications

Application forms can be downloaded from the website and returned to info@wrightsontrust.co.uk, making sure that the candidate's name is in the subject section of the email.

Application forms must contain:

- Letters of support from two tutors/teachers
- A brief music CV for those over 12
- Reasons for applying
- A list of other grant-giving bodies you are applying to
- Any other supporting matter as scanned attached documents

If you would rather post the documents, three copies of the application form must be sent and two of each of the references to the correspondent.

Other information

The charity also supports organisations, makes grants to assist young children in their personal development and runs a boat, Lady Elsa.

History

The Catherine Mackichan Trust

£2,400

Correspondent: David Mackichan, Treasurer, 2 Hutton Avenue, Houston PA6 7JS (email: david.mackichan@sky.com; website: www.mackichantrust.co.uk)

OSCR number: SC020459

Eligibility

Grants are available to the students of history, particularly (but not exclusively) Celtic and/or West Highland history or medieval history. People who are researching various aspects of Scottish history, including archaeology, genealogy and language studies are equally eligible. Further information about what the trust prefers to fund is given on its website.

The website also states: 'Applicants will receive particular consideration if they demonstrate that they are unable to obtain funding via normal channels, or if their work is an extension of a topic previously funded through one of these channels.'

Types of grants

Grants range from £200 to £500 but in exceptional circumstances greater amounts can be awarded. Support can be given for specific costs of research e.g.

the costs of travel for site visits, excavations, access to specialist services such as radiocarbon dating, and documentation or publication.

Assistance is available to postgraduate students, individuals without formal attachment to any institute of education, local history societies, amateur historians or school groups.

Annual grant total

In 2015/16 the trust had an income of £2,300 and a total expenditure of £2,700. We have estimated that around £2,400 was distributed in grants to individuals.

Exclusions

Grants are given to people whose education or research should be funded by the statutory sources. Support is not provided for university undergraduate or postgraduate fees or living expenses while studying for a degree.

Applications

Application forms can be requested from the correspondent at the email address shown. They should be submitted between January and 16 April and are usually considered before the end of June. The trust's website mentions that 'it is desirable, but not essential, that the names and addresses of two referees accompany each application'.

Other information

Grants are also given to schools, groups and local history societies for local history and archaeological purposes.

Society of Antiquaries of London

See entry on page 76

Languages

Interdoceo

£564,000

Correspondent: Thomas Dawid, 1 Princeton Mews, 167–169 London Road, Kingston Upon Thames, Surrey KT2 6PT (email: info@interdoceo.org; website: www.interdoceo.org/index.php)

CC number: 1163436

Eligibility

The charity's website states:

Requirements & Applying:

- Young individuals aged over 18 with less than two years of professional experience in teaching their own language
- Having English, French or German as a first language, or having completed secondary education in any of these languages

▶ When an undergraduate degree is required to join one of the programs, it must have been obtained in the four years previous to the start of the grant
▶ The minimum stay in Spain will be 5 months

Types of grants

The charity's website states:

The application period to request a grant or scholarship is permanently open for:

▶ Students interested in pursuing a postgraduate degree in Spain oriented towards learning and teaching foreign languages
▶ Those interested in receiving training to then teach foreign languages
▶ Teaching internships in Spain being the language implemented the teacher's mother tongue, varying on the level or training received

Types of programs for which you can apply:

▶ **Postgraduate:** Aimed at graduates. Degrees and previous studies should preferably be: a degree related to teaching, to their own language, or to any other degree with a sufficiently in-depth training that will allow them to teach foreign languages (Tefl or equivalent training)
▶ **Graduate:** Aimed at graduates from any degree
▶ **Speakers:** Aimed at young people aged between 18 and 24. Minimum amount of training required: A levels or equivalent

Annual grant total

In 2015/16 the charity had assets of £8,300 and an income of £659,000. The amount of grants given to individuals totalled £564,000.

Applications

Contact the charity using the form on the website.

The Norwich Jubilee Esperanto Foundation (NOJEF)

£6,500

Correspondent: Clare Hunter, c/o Esperanto-Asocio de Britio, Esperanto House, Station Road, Barlaston, Stoke-on-Trent ST12 9DE (email: clare.hunter@esperanto.org.uk; website: www.nojef.org)

CC number: 313190

Eligibility

People under the age of 25 who either are British or live in the UK and demonstrate efficiency in the study of Esperanto.

Research funding is only given upon condition that a copy of research will be available (in English or Esperanto) for the Butler Library. Greater grants will be given for research which is in the public domain, for proposals at higher academic level and depending on the extent of attention on Esperanto in the proposal.

Types of grants

The foundation provides two different grants:

▶ Travel grants: grants to cover travel, entrance fee and accommodation for individuals attending Esperanto-related events
▶ Research grants: Support towards research with a maximum grant of £1,000 for a PhD thesis. Non-Esperantists are welcome to request funding

Annual grant total

In 2016/17 the foundation had an income of £23,200 and a total expenditure of £7,100. We estimate that the total amount of grants awarded was around £6,500.

Exclusions

Financial support cannot be made retrospectively.

Applications

Applications for travel grants should be made by sending a letter in Esperanto to the Secretary, Tim Owen (email: secretary@nojef.org), giving some details of the travel plans and likely costs. New applicants are also asked to introduce themselves and give details of a referee who can confirm the applicant's efforts in learning Esperanto and give an insight into their character.

Applications for research funding should be made by sending a letter to the Secretary at tim.owen@nojef.org with the research proposal including any anticipated costs.

Other information

Further grants for different events will only be considered if the reports are delivered within reasonable time and at respectable length.

John Speak Foundation Foreign Languages Scholarships Trust Fund (John Speak Trust)

£16,000

Correspondent: Sandy Needham, Bradford Chamber, Devere House, Vicar Lane, Bradford BD1 5AH (01274 230090; email: john.speak@wnychamber.co.uk; website: www.johnspeaktrust.co.uk)

CC number: 529115

Eligibility

British-born citizens over the age of 18, wishing to advance their abilities in foreign languages while residing overseas, with the aim of advancing British trade or services abroad. Applicants must study at a recognised college or university, or obtain suitable voluntary employment.

A good basic knowledge (at least GCSE or equivalent) of the foreign language is essential. While abroad, candidates will be required to live within the local community rather than with English speakers, volunteer for a business firm in the country or, alternatively, attend a school/university/training course and provide short monthly reports in both English and the foreign language to the trust.

Types of grants

Grant recipients will receive monthly payments for the period of their stay (normally between three months and a full academic year), subject to receipt of monthly reports. Usually, support is given to cover living expenses and sometimes towards travel costs. Awards are aimed at people who are intending to follow a career connected with the export trade of the UK, so applicants should usually be (or should stand a reasonable chance of becoming) a representative who will travel abroad to secure business for the UK.

Annual grant total

In 2015/16 the trust an income of £14,300 and a total expenditure of £17,800. We estimate that around £16,000 was awarded in grants.

Applications

Applications can be made online on a form available on the trust's website. There are two deadlines – 30 April and 31 October – for consideration in June and November respectively. Potential applicants are invited for an interview with the trustees and will be expected to read, translate and converse in their chosen language. References from a current/prospective employer or the principal/head of languages of the applicant's school may be required.

Literature

The Miles Morland Foundation

£145,000 (eight grants)

Correspondent: Miles Morland, 2nd Floor, Jubilee House, 2 Jubilee Place, London SW3 3TQ (020 7349 5030; email: mmf@blakman.com)

CC number: 1150755

Eligibility
African writers either in the UK or overseas.

Types of grants
Scholarships of up to £27,000 paid in equal monthly instalments over a year and a half.

Annual grant total
In 2015/16 the foundation held assets of £307,000 and had an income of £1.25 million. During the year the foundation awarded eight scholarships totalling £145,000, of which £18,000 each was awarded to four fiction writers and £27,000 each was awarded to two non-fiction writers. A further £644,000 was awarded to 58 organisations.

Applications
Apply in writing to the correspondent.

Natural sciences

The Lillingstone Trust
See entry on page 49

Biology

Botanical Society of Britain and Ireland

£12,000 (40 grants)

Correspondent: Dr Clive Lovatt, 57 Walton Road, Bristol BS11 9TA (07725 862 957; email: enquiries@bsbi.org)

CC number: 1152954

Eligibility
People studying botany.

Types of grants

Training grants
Grants of up to £250 are given to aspiring botanists wishing to go on short training courses. The website states that applicants typically include recent graduates who are 'looking to start a career in botany or take part in interest-led botanical recording'. It is not necessary to be a member of the society to apply; however, members are given preference when there is competition for grants.

Plant study grants
Grants of up to £1,000 are awarded to undergraduate and postgraduate botany students.

Conference grants
Students can apply for bursaries to help with the costs of conferences.

Research grants
Small grants are awarded to support research in Britain and Ireland which enhances the knowledge of flora. According to the website, these grants are designed for PhD students, academic researchers and amateur researchers for work which 'should be capable of resulting in a scientific publication'.

Annual grant total
In 2016/17 the charity had assets of £1 million and an income of £359,500. Grants totalled £12,000 and were distributed to 40 individuals in two categories: training and education (£8,300) and scientific work (£3,700).

Applications
See the website for application information, including dates of opening rounds, for the various types of grants.

Earth sciences

The Institute of Materials, Minerals and Mining (IOM3)

£46,000

Correspondent: Dr Graham Woodrow, Deputy Chief Executive, The Institute of Materials, Minerals and Mining, The Boilerhouse, Springfield Business Park, Caunt Road, Grantham, Lincolnshire NG31 7FZ (01476 513880; email: graham.woodrow@iom3.org or for travel grants alison@willis@iom3.org; website: www.iom3.org)

CC number: 269275

Eligibility
People studying minerals, mining and metallurgy disciplines. Preference is given to current and former members of the institution and their dependants. Membership is a requirement for some grants and some awards are restricted to people under the age of 35 – refer to specific awards for more details.

Types of grants
The institute offers support through one-off and recurrent grants, bursaries, scholarships and various awards. Travel grants are available to members (usually up to the age of 35) to travel long distances to conferences (usually abroad), preferably to present papers.

Annual grant total
In 2016 the institute had assets of £19.7 million, an income of £3.5 million and spent over £3 million in charitable activities. Grants, scholarships, awards and prizes from the restricted funds totalled £46,000.

Applications
Applications can be downloaded from the institute's website and should be returned via email or in hard copy. **Note:** Different grants and awards may have different deadlines, eligibility requirements and correspondents. Candidates are advised to see the website for specific details.

Other information
The institute's website has detailed information on all grants available as well as the assistance from other bodies. There are a variety of prizes and awards offered.

The Mount Everest Foundation

£42,000 (23 grants)

Correspondent: Glyn Hughes, Hon. Secretary, 73 Church Street, Chesham HP5 1HY (01494 792073; email: glynhughes@waitrose.com)

CC number: 208206

Eligibility
Support is given for education and research across a wide range of subjects including geography, glaciology, and the effects of altitude.

Types of grants
Expedition grants of between £900 and £3,250 to explore mountain regions. Expeditions should be able to show that a large proportion of the estimated budget will be raised elsewhere, and that personal contributions are of a sufficient size.

Annual grant total
In 2015/16 the foundation held assets of almost £1.45 million and had an income of £52,500. During the year, 23 expeditions were awarded grants totalling £42,000.

Exclusions
The foundation does not normally support scientific work that is part of an individual's undergraduate degree course and cannot make grants for an expedition that has already returned home.

Applications

Full application details and guidance can be found on the foundation's website. When completing the application form, details of any type of commercial assistance (e.g. a support trek, paying clients, sponsorship etc.) must be fully declared, and the foundation expects members to raise a large proportion of the budget elsewhere. Expedition members may be asked to attend an interview with the screening committee in London. completed application forms must be submitted by 30 September and 31 January in order for these interviews to be arranged.

Other information

The following is taken from the application guidelines that can be found on the foundation's website:

> It is important that you comply with the current regulations of the countries you propose to visit. These may include the payment of peak fees, the insurance and equipping of porters, the employment of a Liaison Officer, and the deposit of environmental, customs and rescue bonds. It is a condition of MEF support that all political requirements are satisfied. Where appropriate you should also advise the Foreign and Commonwealth Office of your intentions.

Physics

The Ogden Trust

£623,500 (90 grants)

Correspondent: Clare Harvey, Chief Executive, Unit 3c, The Phoenix Brewery, 13 Bramley Road, London W10 6SP (020 8634 7470; email: office@ogdentrust.com; website: ogdentrust.com)

CC number: 1037570

Eligibility

Undergraduate students of 'outstanding scientific ability' wishing to study physics (including Natural Sciences) at university. Scholarships are only awarded to those already associated with the trust, with a parental income of less than £50,000 (or £60,000 in some circumstances), and who meet the academic requirements – refer to the trust's website for further information.

Types of grants

Means-tested scholarships are offered to students studying physics or natural sciences at university. Grants of up to £1,500 per annum are given for up to four years of undergraduate study, payable in two instalments of £750, in October and February each year.

Annual grant total

In 2015/16 the trust had assets of £52 million and an income of £233,500. Bursaries and scholarships totalled £623,500, of which £363,000 was awarded in 63 undergraduate scholarships and £260,500 in 27 sixth form bursaries (scheme now discontinued).

Grants awarded to organisations totalled £2.4 million altogether (including teaching fellowships, prizes to schools and colleges, school science partnerships and other awards).

Exclusions

Postgraduate degrees are not supported (except PGCE physics students).

Applications

Undergraduate Science scholarship applications can be made using the form on the trust's website. Applications should be accompanied by an academic reference and supporting documentation.

Other information

The trust also runs a number of programmes aimed at encouraging engagement in maths and science, particularly physics, ranging from partnerships with schools, initiatives to promote teaching physics and university outreach work. Further information can be found on the trust's website.

The trust previously also offered sixth form science scholarships; the final cohort was selected in 2016.

Professional and applied sciences

Air Pilots Trust

£121,500

Correspondent: Paul Tacon, Trustee, Cobham House, 9 Warwick Court, Gray's Inn, London WC1R 5DJ (020 7404 4032; email: office@airpilots.org; website: www.airpilots.org)

CC number: 313606

Eligibility

British, Irish or Commonwealth citizens who are or intend to be engaged professionally as air pilots or navigators in commercial aviation.

Types of grants

Grants and scholarships to assist education and training in aviation.

Annual grant total

In 2015/16 the trust had assets of £617,500, an income of £154,500, expenditure of £141,500 and a grant total of £130,500. Of this amount, £121,500 was given as scholarships and bursaries. The table shows the full breakdown of awards:

Scholarships	101,000
Academic bursaries	£9,000
Sponsorships/grants	£7,560
Tymms Lecture	£6,630
Flying bursaries	£2,380
P B Saul Prize (restricted)	£2,000
Other scholarship expenses	£1,580
Trophies and awards	£370

Applications

Enquiries for application forms can be made in writing to the available postal or email address.

Other information

The trust makes awards to contribute to the establishment and maintenance of a technical library and information centre on matters connected with aviation. The trust also promotes the study and research into problems with aviation and flight, both within and beyond the atmosphere.

The Leadership Trust Foundation

£10,000

Correspondent: Ann Topping, The Leadership Trust, Penyard House, Weston Under Penyard, Ross-on-Wye, Herefordshire HR9 7YH (01989 767667; email: enquiries@leadership.org.uk; website: www.leadershiptrust.co/leadership-trust-foundation)

CC number: 1063916

Eligibility

Individuals from the charitable sector.

Types of grants

Bursaries for training in leadership development.

Annual grant total

In 2016 the foundation held assets of £520,000 and had an income of £100,000. Grants to individuals totalled £10,000.

Applications

Apply in writing to the correspondent, who will then send an application form to relevant applicants. Completed forms are considered quarterly.

Architecture and design

The Nicholas Boas Charitable Trust

See entry on page 57

Design History Society

£18,300

Correspondent: Michaela Young, Administrator, Design History Society, 70 Cowcross Street, London EC1M 6EJ (020 7490 4712; email: designhistorysociety@gmail.com)

Eligibility

People engaged with the subject of design history.

Types of grants

A variety of grants, awards and prizes are available to support students, researchers, educators, designers, critics, curators and others involved with design history. See the website for details of the types of funding available.

Annual grant total

In 2015/16 the charity had assets of £129,000 and an income of £136,500. Grants and awards amounted to at least £18,300 and were awarded as follows:

Student travel award	£5,500
Research publication grant	£4,800
DHS research and conference grant	£4,600
Strategic research grant	£980
Research grant	£860
Research exhibition grant	£820
Student essay prize	£800

A further £34,500 was expended on 'Conference expenses including student bursary places'; however, we were not able to determine the proportion of this amount attributed to bursaries.

Applications

Application forms, along with guidance notes and full eligibility information, are available from the website.

Business and finance

Company of Actuaries Charitable Trust Fund

£15,800 (21 grants)

Correspondent: Patrick O'Keeffe, Administrator, Broomyhurst, Shobley, Ringwood, Hampshire BH24 3HT (01425 472810; email: almoner@ actuariescompany.co.uk; website: www. actuariescompany.co.uk)

CC number: 280702

Eligibility

Further and higher education students progressing towards actuarial qualifications.

Types of grants

Bursaries are available to those in their final year of an Actuarial Science degree at a UK university to help with course and exam fees.

Annual grant total

In 2015/16 the trust had £379,500 in assets and an income of £15,000. The trust gave 21 bursaries totalling £15,800.

Applications

Application forms are available on the website or from the trust. Applications are mainly considered in October, but also in January, April and July. Applicants must provide details of their financial situation, demonstrate serious intentions of joining the Institute and Faculty of Actuaries, and be making good progress on their course and examinations.

Other information

The trust also gives prizes to university and Institute and Faculty of Actuaries students, as well as donations to organisations and other charities.

The AIA Education and Benevolent Trust

£2,000

Correspondent: Tim Pinkey, Director of Professional Standards, Staithes 3, The Watermark, Metro Riverside, Tyne and Wear NE11 9SN (0191 493 0272; fax: 0191 493 0278; email: trust.fund@ aiaworldwide.com; website: www. aiaworldwide.com)

CC number: 1118333

Eligibility

Those wishing to undergo training and education in accountancy.

Types of grants

Grants for training and education in accountancy.

Annual grant total

In 2015 the trust had an income of £2,300 and a total expenditure of £5,000. We estimate that educational grants totalled around £2,000. Funding is also awarded to fellows and associates of the institute, and their close dependants, for social welfare purposes.

Applications

Apply in writing to the correspondent using the form available from the trust's website. Applications are received on an ongoing basis.

Anderson Barrowcliff Bursary

£4,500

Correspondent: Hugh McGouran, Tees Valley Community Foundation, Wallace House, Falcon Court, Preston Farm Industrial Estate, Stockton-on-Tees TS18 3TX (01642 260860; email: info@ teesvalleyfoundation.org; website: www. teesvalleyfoundation.org)

CC number: 1111222

Eligibility

Students from Tees Valley on a full-time undergraduate degree in accountancy, maths or business studies at a UK university. Decisions are made based on A-level results, UCAS personal statement and financial circumstances.

Types of grants

Bursary of £4,500 over three years.

Annual grant total

Payments of around £500 per term over three years.

Applications

Application forms are available on the Tees Valley Community Foundation website, when the application round opens.

Other information

This fund is administrated by the Tees Valley Community Foundation.

The successful applicant will have to take part in a six to eight-week placement with the Anderson Barrowcliff during the summer vacation.

The Institute of Actuaries Research and Education Fund

£3,500

Correspondent: David Burch, Institute and Faculty of Actuaries, 7th Floor, Holborn Gate, 326–330 High Holborn, London WC1V 7PP (020 7632 2194; email: david.burch@actuaries.org.uk; website: www.actuaries.org.uk)

CC number: 274717

Eligibility

Actuarial students at any educational establishment approved by the actuarial profession.

Types of grants

Awards, scholarships and grants for professional training and research in actuarial science.

Annual grant total

In 2015/16 the fund had an income of £5,700 and a total expenditure of £3,800. We estimate that grants totalled around £3,500.

Applications

Applications may be made in writing to the correspondent.

Construction

Alan Baxter Foundation

£6,000

Correspondent: Petra Dokubo, Alan Baxter LTD, 75 Cowcross Street, London, EC1M6EL (020 7250 1555; email: aba@alanbaxter.co.uk)

CC number: 1107996

Eligibility

People involved in study or research of the built and natural environment.

Types of grants

Grants are available according to need for general educational costs, research and projects.

Annual grant total

In 2015/16 the trust had an income of £9,000 and a total expenditure of £32,500. Based on previous years, we estimate that the total amount awarded in grants was £6,000.

Applications

Applications may be made in writing to the correspondent.

Other information

Grants are also made to various organisations supporting education and research relating to the built and natural environment. The foundation also organises educational activities to publicise research and other information on the topic.

Scottish Building Federation Edinburgh and District Charitable Trust

£9,000

Correspondent: Jennifer Law, Charity Accounts Manager, Exchange Place 3, Semple Street, Edinburgh EH3 8BL (0131 473 3500; email: jennifer.law@scott-moncrief.com; website: www.scott-moncrieff.com/services/charities/charitable-trusts/scottish-building-federation-edinburgh)

OSCR number: SCO29604

Eligibility

Students studying skills relating to the building industry at the following universities and colleges: Heriot-Watt University; Napier University; West Lothian College; and Edinburgh College.

Types of grants

Scholarships for study, research and travel associated with the building industry and grants for course expenses such as books, equipment and travel.

Annual grant total

In 2016 the charity had assets of £1.5 million and an income of £47,000. Educational grants to individuals totalled £14,000 and were broken down as follows:

Scholarships and bursaries	£9,000
Academic prizes	£5,000
Charitable aid (welfare cases)	£2,700

Applications

Applications can be made by completing the form, which is available to download from the Scott-Moncrieff website, and forwarding it to the appropriate university or college department. Representatives of the trust liaise with universities and colleges to arrange applications and interviews and to decide which applications should be funded.

Education

Hockerill Educational Foundation

£58,000 (126 grants)

Correspondent: Derek Humphrey, Secretary, 3 The Swallows, Harlow, Essex CM17 0AR (01279 420855; email: info@hockerillfoundation.org.uk; website: www.hockerillfoundation.org.uk)

CC number: 311018

Eligibility

The foundation awards grants for causes related to religious education, which are usually given under the following categories:
- Students and teaching assistants taking teaching qualifications, or first degrees leading to teaching
- Teachers, teaching assistants and others in an educational capacity seeking professional development through full-time or part-time courses
- Those undertaking research related to the practice of religious education in schools or further education
- Students taking other first degree courses, or courses in further education
- Others involved in teaching and leading in voluntary, non-statutory

education, including those concerned with adult and Christian education

Grants are also made for gap year projects with an educational focus to those whose home or place of study is in the dioceses of Chelmsford and St Albans.

Types of grants

Grants of £500 to £1,000 are available for students for help with fees, books, living expenses and travel. Priority is given to those training to be teachers, with priority given to those teaching religious education. If funds are available, other students with financial difficulties will be funded.

Annual grant total

In 2015/16 the foundation had assets of £6.6 million and an income of £298,000. Grants to individuals totalled £58,000 and a further £214,000 was awarded to religious organisations.

Exclusions

The foundation does not support the following:
- Teachers who intend to move out of the profession
- Those training for ordination or mission, or clergy who wish to improve their own qualifications, unless they are also involved in teaching in schools
- Those taking courses in counselling, therapy, or social work
- Training for other professions, such as accountancy, business, law, or medicine
- Courses or visits abroad, including gap year courses
- Primary or secondary schoolchildren
- Those training to teach English as an additional language

Applications

Application forms are available from the foundation's website www.hockerillfoundation.org.uk to be returned by 31 March.

The foundation's website states: 'If you have not finalised your course until later in the summer you can still apply in April and May, and these applications will be considered in June.'

Other information

The charity states that the majority of annual funding is committed to long-term projects or activities in education, but funding is also given to other projects, namely:
- Training and support for the Church of England's educational work, particularly in the dioceses of Chelmsford and St Albans;
- Research, development and support grants to organisations in the field of religious education

The charity also supports conferences for new RE teachers and a 'Prize for Innovation in the Teaching of RE'.

Engineering

Charities Administered by The Worshipful Company of Founders

£26,000

Correspondent: Andrew Bell, The Founders Co., Founders Hall, 1 Cloth Fair, London EC1A 7JQ (020 7796 4800; email: office@foundersco.org.uk; website: www.foundersco.org.uk)

CC number: 222905

Eligibility

You must be a student or prospective student in material sciences, material engineering or other related course, or metallurgy.

Types of grants

Grants are available for travel costs, partial payment of tuition fees, to undertake research projects, to provide metallurgy apprenticeships, and for costs associated with the course e.g. books and equipment.

Annual grant total

In 2015/16 the charity held assets of £1.5 million and had an income of £37,000. A total of £26,000 was awarded in educational grants to individuals.

Applications

Apply in writing to the correspondent.

The Coachmakers and Coach Harness Makers Charitable Trust 1977

£14,000 (17 grants)

Correspondent: Commander Mark Leaning, The Old Barn, Church Lane, Glentham, Market Rasen, Lincolnshire LN8 2EL (email: clerk@coachmakers.co.uk; website: www.coachmakers.co.uk)

CC number: 286521

Eligibility

People studying/working in the aerospace, automotive and coach-making or associated industries.

Types of grants

Grants are available to individuals in technical education and training, including apprenticeships. Awards are usually given towards general educational needs, research, study/travel overseas and maintenance expenses.

Bursaries are given for individuals studying motor vehicle design at The Royal College of Art and students of aerospace sciences at Cranfield University.

There is also a 'flying scholarship for an individual who, in competition, has shown aptitude and determination to become a pilot' and an annual Award to Industry made 'to promote excellence in design, technical development and commercial significance'.

Annual grant total

In 2015/16 the charity had assets of £1.9 million and an income of £181,000. The total amount awarded in grants to individuals was £14,000.

Exclusions

The trust's website states that 'awards are as substantial as possible, but bursaries are allocated on an annual basis and, because funds cannot always be guaranteed, the Livery cannot accept commitments to individuals for long-term educational courses'.

Applications

Apply in writing to the correspondent. Applications should normally be submitted in December and October for consideration in January and November respectively.

Other information

The charity also makes awards to organisations; in 2015/16 a total of £52,500 was donated.

The Worshipful Company of Engineers Charitable Trust Fund
See entry on page 123

ICE Benevolent Fund

£2,000 (two grants)

Correspondent: Lindsay Howell, Caseworker, 5 Mill Hill Close, Haywards Heath, West Sussex RH16 1NY (01444 417979 or 0800 587 3428 (free 24-hour helpline); email: info@icebenfund.com; website: www.icebenfund.com)

CC number: 1126595

Eligibility

Student members of Institution of Civil Engineers (ICE), who have disabilities or are otherwise disadvantaged and undertaking an ICE accredited course at a UK university. Applicants should have been members for a year or more. Applications can only be considered from students whose course fees for the year have been paid.

Although the charity cannot provide a strict definition of 'disadvantaged', the following groups of students are identified (see the Eligibility Criteria and Guidance document on the website) as being in particular need of help:

- Students with dependants, especially lone parents
- Students aged 25 and over with extra financial commitments
- Students who were previously in Local Authority care
- Students estranged from their parents
- Students repeating a year due to reasons beyond their control
- Second, third and final year students who have lost their initial source of funding
- Students who are permanent residents in the UK but are unable to apply for loans to support their studies because of their UK residence status

Students with disabilities are defined as those with a recognised and diagnosed disability.

Types of grants

Grants of up to £1,000 per term are made towards living costs, travel, equipment or course materials.

Annual grant total

In 2016 the charity had assets of £17 million and an income of £1.4 million. Grants to beneficiaries amounted to £579,000. A breakdown of grants distributed was not available in the annual report and accounts, however it is stated that the charity awarded funding to two individuals who applied through the scheme for disadvantaged students. Based on this information and the maximum grant available through the scheme, we estimate that educational grants totalled around £2,000.

Exclusions

A grant cannot be made unless the student is in receipt of all other financial assistance available. Students are also expected to take on part-time and holiday employment, unless there is a reason why this isn't possible.

The Eligibility and Criteria document also states that grant support will not usually be given to students who:

- Have not yet started their university course
- Have yet to be offered a university place
- Have mismanaged their finances and simply run out of money
- Are studying for post-graduate degrees
- Are not studying for a civil engineering degree accredited by ICE
- [Are] in their first year of study (unless there are exceptional circumstances)
- Do not have funding for their fees in place

Grants are not usually given to pay for course or examination fees, to clear old debts, for social activities, or for the purchase or hire of non-essential equipment and materials.

Applications

Application forms are available from the website or the correspondent, along with full guidance and eligibility criteria. They can be submitted at any time during the academic year and *must* be accompanied supporting documents, including a reference or letter of support from your head of department, or their nominee. Applicants are usually visited by a representative of the charity.

Other information

The charity runs a 24-hour helpline (0800 587 3428), which offers support and advice on a wide range of issues, including counselling, stress management, relationship problems, financial troubles, parenting, illness and well-being and work life. Face-to-face support can also be arranged. There is also the 'Back to Work' scheme, which provides advice and coaching for people who have been out of work for at least three months.

The Institution of Engineering and Technology (IET)

£382,000 (125 grants)

Correspondent: Andrew Wilson, Correspondent, The Institution of Engineering and Technology, 2 Savoy Place, London WC2R 0BL (020 7344 5415; email: governance@theiet.org; website: www.theiet.org)

CC number: 211014, SC038698

Eligibility

The following list of regulations applies as a general rule to all scholarships and prizes (however, candidates should refer to the website to ensure they fit the specific criteria of different awards):

- Students must be studying or about to study (in the next academic session) on an IET-accredited degree course at a UK university (for a list of accredited programmes see the website)
- Each candidate should be supported by the head of the educational or training establishment, the course tutor, the university head of department or by a chartered member of the IET (for some awards it is necessary to become a member)
- A candidate who is shortlisted for an award may be required to attend an interview at the IET
- The scholarship will be paid in instalments, as determined by the IET (it will be withdrawn and any unpaid instalments withheld if the holder leaves the course)

- Successful candidates must not hold any other IET scholarship or grant at the same time
- Applicants should demonstrate passion to engineering and/or high academic achievements

Types of grants

The IET offers a range of scholarships, prizes and travel awards. These include undergraduate and postgraduate scholarships, travel grants to members of the IET (for study tour, work in the industry, to attend a conference), apprenticeship and technician awards and various prizes for achievement and innovation.

The Diamond Jubilee Scholarship Fund also offers £1,000 for each year of the degree to students applying for IET accredited courses in Computing, Electrical, Electronic and Manufacturing Engineering. Around 100 scholarships are available each year.

For further information on the awards currently available, refer to the IET website.

Annual grant total

In 2016 the charity had assets of £156 million and an income of £58.4 million. During the year, 125 scholarships, awards and prizes were awarded to individuals, totalling £382,000. A further seven grants were made to individuals for welfare purposes, amounting to £7,000. There was also one grant of £440,000 to an organisation.

Exclusions

There may be certain conditions attached to separate awards e.g. undergraduate grants are not intended to cover placement years and IET postgraduate scholarships are not currently given for MSc degrees (but awards from specific funds may offer support). Applicants are advised to read the guidelines for specific awards carefully.

Applications

Further details and application forms are available from the IET website. The deadlines vary for different awards.

Other information

The institution also administers a number of restricted funds to assist training and education in engineering and electrical engineering.

The institution's website contains extensive information on all awards available.

The Benevolent Fund of the Institution of Mechanical Engineers (IMechE) – known as Support Network

Correspondent: Maureen Hayes, Casework & Welfare Officer, 1 Birdcage Walk, Westminster, London SW1H 9JJ (020 7304 6816; email: supportnetwork@imeche.org; website: www.imeche.org/support-network)

CC number: 209465

Eligibility

Students who are financially disadvantaged or who have disabilities or long-term health conditions, who are, or are dependants of, IMechE members. Applicants must be studying for a mechanical engineering-related undergraduate degree, master's degree course, PhD, or course at another level. IMechE members, and their dependants, who are on a mechanical engineering apprenticeship can also be supported.

The website states that the charity prioritises applicants who:

- Are in the final year or stage of their programme
- Have a disability
- Have left Local Authority care
- Are estranged from their parents
- Are aged 25 or over and have extra financial commitments
- Have children under the age of 18, particularly if they are a single parent
- Are a carer or have financial dependants
- Are managing significant debts accrued before their course started
- Due to reasons beyond their control, are repeating a year of study
- Do not have access to other sources of funding

Types of grants

Student Grants of up to £1,515 are given for living costs, travel, accommodation, course materials, software, books etc. Grants are also made towards disability-related costs, additional disability needs and ongoing health-related needs. Final year students or those with additional financial needs, such as children under the age of 18, can apply for extra funding.

Members who are on a mechanical engineering apprenticeship can apply for Apprentice Grants to help with: financial need, particularly if it was unexpected; the costs of equipment vital to an apprenticeship; costs related to disability or additional disability needs; assistance for mature apprentices (aged over 24); and adverse changes in circumstances.

Annual grant total

In 2016 the charity had assets of £25.9 million and an income of £1.3 million. Grants for the relief of poverty totalled £293,500, which we have taken to include amounts awarded for educational purposes to members in need. A breakdown of grants allocated was not included in the annual report and accounts.

Exclusions

Grants cannot be made to those who have not yet been offered a university place or started their course, or those who have mismanaged their finances and run out of money. Grants cannot be given for tuition fees, although support towards industrial placements can be given.

Applications

Applications can be made throughout the year, but applicants must have started their course before they apply. Students should at first contact their education provider's student services department to check that they are in receipt of all statutory support available and if there are any university funds from which they can seek assistance. Following this, the charity can be contacted to confirm eligibility and to request an application form, which can then be completed and returned to the charity. Application forms for Apprenticeship Grants can be requested from the charity by email.

Other information

Support Network provides information, advice and financial, emotional and practical support to eligible individuals who are in need. The charity has partnered with Law Express to provide its members with a telephone helpline to help with a broad range of everyday problems (helpline: 01275 376029 – 8am to 8pm, Monday to Friday; and 9am to 12pm, Saturday to Sunday). Full information on all of the support available can be found on its very informative website or from the charity itself by email or telephone.

The ISTRUCTE (Institution of Structural Engineers) Educational Trust

£9,900

Correspondent: Darren Byrne, Trustee, 47–58 Bastwick Street, London EC1V 3PS (020 7201 9138; email: edtrust@istructe.org; website: www.istructe.org/education-and-careers/educational-trust)

CC number: 1001625

Eligibility

Structural engineers, students and pupils considering career in the field.

Types of grants

The trust awards bursaries, scholarships, travel grants, prizes encouraging young people to enter structural engineering career and supporting their development. According to the website, the following are available:

Pai Lin Li Travel Award

Grants of between £1,000 and £3,000 to members of the institution to spend between four and six weeks in another country, studying 'current practice or trends related to the use of any construction material in the field of structural engineering'. The trust is particularly keen to support study of innovative materials and construction techniques. Those who receive an award will also present a lecture on their work.

Young Structural Engineers International Design Competition

This competition is run every three years and is aimed to promote collaboration between young professionals (under the age of 30), with the chief representative for each team being a member of the institution. Individuals or teams of up to four people can enter and there are three cash prizes available: The John Barrett Prize, awarding £5,000 for the overall winners; the Drury Medal awards £2,500 to the best entry from an individual or team under the age of 25; the Undergraduate Prize awards £2,000 to the best entry by an undergraduate individual or team. Refer to the website for further information.

Other awards and prizes

Other awards, given in partnership with other organisations, include:

- Maths Inspiration – a programme of lecture shows for 15 to 17-year-olds
- TeamBuild – a construction industry competition for teams of university students to collaborate on a multi-disciplinary challenge
- The Engineering Architecture Prize – a biennial essay competition for sixth form students
- A bursary with the charity Starfish Zambia

Annual grant total

In 2016 the trust had assets of £76.8 million and an income of £70. Grants awarded for educational purposes totalled £16,200 and were broken down as follows:

Pai Lin Travel Awards	£5,400
Maths inspiration	£5,000
2016 TeamBuild Competition	£3,000
Other grants and prizes	£1,500
Young Structural Engineer of the Year Award 2016	£1,300

Applications

The application procedure varies for different awards – see the website for details and deadlines or contact the correspondent for more information on each.

Other information

Both individuals and organisations are supported. The trust can provide schools with teaching materials and also participates in various educational projects and partnerships with institutions.

The Educational Trust is a charity connected to and receiving donations from the Institution of Structural Engineers.

Mining Institute of Scotland Trust

£1,500

Correspondent: Keith Donaldson, Hon. Secretary/Treasurer, 14/9 Burnbrae Drive, Edinburgh EH12 8AS (0131 629 7861; website: www.mining-scotland.org/trust.htm)

OSCR number: SC024974

Eligibility

Former members of the Mining Institute of Scotland and their dependants; members or former members of The Institute of Materials, Minerals and Mining living in Scotland or who worked in connection with Scottish mining matters for at least five consecutive years and their dependants.

Types of grants

The trust's webpage describes the three components of its educational fund:

- Norman Henderson Prize – Each year, the trustees can purchase a medal for presentation to the author of any paper considered by them to be of 'outstanding merit'
- Sam Mavor Travelling Scholarship – Bursaries or prizes can be awarded to an MIS student or students to allow them to visit places, works or mines in any such place of special interest to them as may be determined by the trustees
- Cunningham Scholarship – Scholarships for education in the science of mining, insight into contemporary mining methods, or visiting/studying mines anywhere in the world may be provided

Annual grant total

In 2016 the trust had assets of £873,000 and an income of £32,500. We estimate that educational grants to individuals totalled around £1,500.

Applications

Applications for assistance can be made in writing to the correspondent.

Other information

Organisations are also supported.

The Mott MacDonald Charitable Trust

£101,500 (19 grants)

Correspondent: Steve Wise, Administrator, Mott MacDonald House, 8–10 Sydenham Road, Croydon CR0 2EE (020 8774 2090; email: carole.teacher@mottmac.com; website: mottmac.com/article/5901/mott-macdonald-charitable-trust)

CC number: 275040

Eligibility

People undertaking higher education in the fields of civil, structural, mechanical, electrical and allied engineering (disciplines directly related to the work of Mott MacDonald company).

Types of grants

Undergraduate bursaries (generally on an annual basis) and recurring scholarships mainly to master's students (or occasionally PhD). The amount of money available to any person is a maximum of £12,000. Awards are given to cover the course fees.

Annual grant total

In 2015 the trust had assets of £227,000 and an income of £66,000. During the year, 19 scholarships totalling £101,500 were made.

Exclusions

Funding is not given retrospectively.

Applications

Apply in writing to the correspondent. Applications should be submitted by 30 March for courses starting later in that year. The trustees meet in May. Candidates should have obtained a conditional offer of acceptance and provide details of fees. Each application is acknowledged and if the consideration is taken further the trust will ask for some more clarification.

Applicants employed by Mott MacDonald need to supply two employer references and those that do not work in the company need to supply two academic or one academic and one employer references.

Other information

The trust also awarded £6,000 in research and development (2015).

South Wales Institute of Engineers Educational Trust

£10,400 (25 grants)

Correspondent: Megan Hardy, Secretary, Suite 2, Bay Chambers, West Bute Street, Cardiff CF10 5BB (01792 879409; email: megan.hardy@swieet2007.org.uk; website: www.swieet2007.org.uk)

CC number: 1013538

Eligibility

People entering and practising engineering in Wales – school pupils deciding on their career, undergraduate students on engineering courses, graduates starting work in engineering industry, apprentices and equivalent.

Types of grants

One-off and recurrent grants are given according to need, generally from £100 to £1,000. The trust has funded engineering education from pre-GCSE level through to postgraduate/professional qualifications.

Annual grant total

In 2015/16 the trust held assets of £935,500 and had an income of £28,000. Grants were made to 24 individuals and totalled £10,400, and a further £20,000 was awarded to organisations.

Applications

The trust's office should be contacted directly to find out the details of the current year's awards/prizes and to discuss an application.

UK Electronics Skills Foundation

£15,000

Correspondent: Stew Edmonson (CEO), Suite 41, Geddes House, Kirkton North, Livingston, West Lothian EH54 6GU (email: info@ukesf.org; website: www.ukesf.org)

OSCR number: SC043940

Eligibility

Individuals must:

- Be registered at a UKESF partner university on an IET accredited BEng or MEng degree which has significant amount of Electronics or Electronic Engineering
- Be a UK or EU student with a permanent right to work in the UK after graduation
- Have not previously withdrawn from a UKESF scholarship (an individual may be able to re-apply is the scholarship was permanent due to exceptional circumstances)

- Not hold any sponsorship/scholarship funded by a single commercial organisation

For more information on eligibility criteria, individuals are invited to email the foundation.

Types of grants

The charity offers scholarships to electronics undergraduate students at partner universities. The duration of the scholarship varies between the sponsoring companies but generally lasts from the year the individual has applied until their graduation. The scholarship includes:

- Annual bursary of £1,000 per annum
- Paid summer work placements, and a paid-for place at a residential UKESF Scholar Workshop
- Mentorship and networking opportunities with leading employers in the industry
- Pre-loaded £200 Blackwell's gift card in first year of the scholarship

The charity also supports final year female students to attend the WES Student Conference

Annual grant total

In 2015/16 the foundation had assets of £470 and an income of £415,500. We estimate that grants given to individuals totalled around £15,000.

Other information

The UKESF Scholar Workshops are four-day residential courses for scholars in order to network and build professional relationships.

The Institution of Works and Highways Management (Bernard Butler) Trust

£23,000

Correspondent: Geoff Porter, Trustee, 27 Ashley Park, Ashley Heath, Ringwood BH24 2HA (01425 837790; email: info@bernardbutlertrust.org; website: www.bernardbutlertrust.org)

CC number: 1063735

Eligibility

People studying or working in the fields of engineering who are in need.

Types of grants

Grants, of at least £1,000, can be one-off or recurrent. Assistance can be given to college/university students (including mature and postgraduate), people in vocational training or individuals who wish to undertake courses to improve their skills and professional qualifications. Support is available towards various course-related costs (including fees, necessities, books), travel and accommodation costs to attend seminars/conferences/meetings, childcare or costs of dependants, and any other project or expenses which will enable individuals to advance their education.

Annual grant total

In 2016/17 the trust had an income of £9,000 and a total expenditure of £30,000. Due to the trust's low income, its accounts for this year were not available to view on the Charity Commission. Based on past expenditure we have estimated that £23,000 was awarded in grants to individuals.

Applications

Application forms are available from the trust's website or can be requested from the correspondent. They can be submitted at any time. The remit of support available is very wide and the trust welcomes informal enquires to discuss applications.

Other information

Grants can also be made to organisations.

Environment and agriculture

The Douglas Bomford Trust

£24,000 (15+ grants)

Correspondent: Dr Paul Miller, 46 Howard Close, Haynes, Bedford MK45 3QH (01234 381342; fax: 01234 751319; email: enquiries@dbt.org.uk; website: www.dbt.org.uk)

CC number: 1121785

Eligibility

People involved in the education, research and practice of agricultural engineering and mechanisation who are aiming to become professional engineers or scientists and intend to work applying their expertise to agricultural and land-related problems. Priority is given to individuals who work in areas of particular national or technical importance and those who can receive part of the costs from other sources. Some connection with the UK is required, either through nationality, residency, or place of learning/registration.

Types of grants

The trust can offer: travel scholarships for educational tours overseas, conferences and for presenting papers at international conferences; scholarships to undergraduate students; support towards postgraduate study and research; discretionary awards in cases of

hardship; and various prizes to students showing high academic achievements or to the authors of papers published in allied journals.

Annual grant total

In 2015/16 the trust held assets of £4.1 million and had an income of £153,000. A total of £24,000 was awarded in educational grants to individuals, in the following categories:

Travel grants	£8,000
Studentships	£7,500
Discretionary awards	£4,000
Research	£2,000
Other awards	£1,800

Applications

There are different grant schemes for travel awards, undergraduate students, postgraduate research and other awards. Application details for each of them can be found on the trust's website.

Other information

The trust also awards grants to organisations (in 2015/16 a total of £81,000 was awarded to organisations for purposes such as PhD research, other postgraduate research, and student competitions).

The Farmers' Company Charitable Fund

£16,100

Correspondent: Graham Edward Bamford Fih Mi, 24 Herons Place, Isleworth TW7 7BE (020 8326 2945; email: clerk@farmerslivery.org.uk)

CC number: 258712

Eligibility

Young people in agriculture and associated industries who wish to study to improve their knowledge and skills.

Types of grants

Grants in the form of scholarships, bursaries, £500 awards for training purposes, travel overseas and gifts in-kind.

Annual grant total

In 2015/16 the charity had assets of £4.3 million and an income of £270,500. Throughout the year the charity gave around £16,100 in grants to individuals.

The charity also awards grants to organisations.

Applications

Application forms for various funds can be found on the charity's website.

Other information

The individual funds which are available to apply for are:
- The Henman Trust Fund
- The Attfield Brooks Apprentices Fund
- The Jubilee Fund

- Recognition of Achievement in Education Award
- Support for Community Education

Details of the areas which these funds support can be found on the charity's website.

Forest Industries Education and Provident Fund

See entry on page 105

See entry on page 105

The Gamekeepers Welfare Trust

£1,250

Correspondent: Helen Benson, Chief Executive and Charity Manager, Keepers Cottage, Tanfield Lodge, West Tanfield, Ripon, North Yorkshire HG4 5LE (01677 470180 (helpline) or 01677 47010; email: enquiries@thegamekeeperswelfaretrust. com or gamekeeperwtrust@btinternet. com; website: thegamekeeperswelfaretrust.com)

CC number: 1008924

Eligibility

Young people in need who wish to make gamekeeping their career. People over 24 will not be considered unless there are extenuating circumstances.

Types of grants

One-off and recurrent grants are given according to need.

Annual grant total

In 2016 the trust had assets of £139,500 and an income of £32,000. Throughout the year the charity awarded almost £19,500 in grants to 55 individuals. Of this amount, £1,250 was given for educational purposes.

The trust awarded £18,200 in grants to individuals for social welfare.

Applications

Apply on a form available from the correspondent or through the website, along with guidelines. Applications can be made at any time.

The Dick Harrison Trust

£3,000

Correspondent: Robert Addison, Secretary, Hexham Auction Mart Ltd, Mart Offices, Tyne Green, Hexham NE46 3SG (07702 737560 or 01434 605444; email: raddison@hexhammart. co.uk; website: www.dickharrisontrust. org.uk)

CC number: 702365

Eligibility

Further and higher education, mature and postgraduate students training in livestock auctioneering and/or rural estate management who were born in Cumbria, Northumberland or Scotland, or who are (or whose parents or guardians are) at the time of the award living in any of these places.

Types of grants

One-off grants towards fees, books, equipment/instruments, maintenance/living expenses and study or travel in the UK and abroad.

Annual grant total

In 2015/16 the trust had an income of £1,900 and a total expenditure of £3,300. We estimate that around £3,000 was given in grants.

Applications

Application forms can be downloaded from the trust's website or requested from the correspondent. Applicants are required to provide references and to attend an interview. The deadline for applications is 31 August.

The Elwyn Jones Memorial Trust Fund

£1,500

Correspondent: Rebecca Price, Wales Young Farmers Clubs, Royal Welsh Showground, Llanelwedd, Builth Wells, Powys LD2 3NJ (01982 553502; email: information@yfc-wales.org.uk)

CC number: 260862

Eligibility

Individuals who want to travel abroad in order to study agriculture.

Types of grants

Grants for travel abroad to study agriculture.

Annual grant total

In 2015/16 the charity had an income of £790 and a total expenditure of £1,700. We estimate that grants given to individuals totalled £1,500.

Applications

Apply in writing to the correspondent.

The Alice McCosh Trust

£2,300

Correspondent: Grace Carswell, Trust Secretary, 49 Cluny Street, Lewes, Sussex BN7 1LN (email: info@ thealicemccoshtrust.org.uk; website: www.thealicemccoshtrust.org.uk)

OSCR number: SC035938

Eligibility

People of any age undertaking work or study related to natural history and/or the environment. Preference will be given to individuals from (or work relating to) Scotland, England and Turkey.

Types of grants

One-off grants in the range of £600 to £1,000, to cover, for example, the cost of a school field trip or project, an expedition as part of a research project or the development of new teaching materials for schools or institutes of higher education.

Annual grant total

In 2015/16 the trust had an income of £3,800 and a total expenditure of £2,600. We estimate that grants totalled around £2,300.

Exclusions

Projects which involve joining an existing commercial organisation on a pre-paid tour or expedition will not be considered.

Applications

Applications can be made on a form available from the website along with guidelines. They should be emailed to the correspondent between 1 October and 30 November each year. Applications received at other times, or sent by post, will not be considered. Applications should be concise (no more than four typed pages) and include two referee statements.

The Merlin Trust

£17,500 (26 grants)

Correspondent: Sarah Carlton, Trust Secretary, Alpine Department, RHS Garden Wisley, Wisley Lane, Woking, Surrey GU23 6QB (email: info@merlin-trust.org.uk; website: www.merlin-trust.org.uk)

CC number: 803441

Eligibility

People between the ages of 18 and 35 or in their first five years of a career in horticulture. Horticulturists of British or Irish nationality resident in Britain or Ireland only. Foreign nationals may apply but must be studying in a British or Irish horticultural training establishment.

Types of grants

Grants towards visiting gardens in different parts of the country or abroad, or travelling to see wild plants in their native habitats. Any suitable project, large or small, will be carefully considered.

Applicants will be considered for two annual £500 prizes awarded by the trustees: the Christopher Brickell Prize for the best written report and the Valerie Finnis VMH Prize for the report demonstrating photographic excellence.

Annual grant total

In 2015/16 the trust held assets of £594,500 and had an income of £32,000. Grants to 26 individuals totalled £17,500, and two of them received an additional £500 prize.

Exclusions

Grants are not given towards postgraduate study or to fund highly technical laboratory-based research.

Applications

Application forms are available to download from the website. The form should be completed and emailed to the secretary along with a one-page description of your project and a CV. A signed copy of the form should also be posted to the secretary. The trust welcomes telephone enquiries. A written report must be presented within three months of the project being completed.

The NFU Mutual Charitable Trust Centenary Award

£22,000 (two grants)

Correspondent: James Creechan, Company Secretary, Tiddington Road, Stratford upon Avon, Warwickshire CV37 7BJ (email: centenary_award@nfumutual.co.uk; website: www.nfumutual.co.uk/news-and-stories/the-nfu-mutual-charitable-trust-centenary-award)

CC number: 1073064

Eligibility

Postgraduate students in agriculture. Students should have gained/be expecting a 2:1 or above in agriculture or a closely related degree and have been accepted/provisionally accepted on a master's or PhD course in agriculture in the UK. Successful applicants will show excellent academic achievements and commitment to the future of agriculture.

The following three topic areas have been specifically identified:

- Sustainable agriculture and climate change
- International agriculture development
- The application of science and innovative technology to the agricultural industry

Types of grants

Annual bursaries to pay up to 75% of course fees for selected postgraduate students in agriculture (master's or PhD).

Annual grant total

In 2016 awards were made to two individuals totalling £22,000. The award came from the restricted fund which represents the funds available under The NFU Mutual Charitable Trust Centenary Award Scheme.

Applications

Application forms together with further details can be requested by emailing the correspondent. Full details of application deadlines can be found on the scheme's website.

Other information

According to the website, 'the Centenary Award is a long-term scheme, run by NFU Mutual Charitable Trust, and was launched in 2010 to celebrate the 100th birthday of NFU Mutual'.

Note that we use the figures for the restricted fund. Charitable activities of The NFU Mutual Charitable Trust are of greater extent and are aimed at organisations. The trust receives most of its income from NFU Mutual.

Nuffield Farming Scholarship Trust

£161,000 (18 grants)

Correspondent: Mike Vacher, Director, Southill Farmhouse, Staple Fitzpaine, Taunton, Somerset TA3 5SH (01460 234012; email: director@nuffieldscholar. org; website: www.nuffieldscholar.org)

CC number: 1098519

Eligibility

UK residents between the ages of 22 and 45 who have been working for at least two years in farming, food, horticulture rural and associated industries in the UK or are in a position to influence those industries. Applicants should be able to demonstrate a passion for the industry, be well-established in their career and be three years post-tertiary education.

Types of grants

Awards are given to around 20 individuals each year, to facilitate opportunities to research topics in farming, food, horticulture or rural industries. Scholarships allow individuals to travel anywhere in the world, for at least eight weeks, to further their knowledge and understanding.

Around £7,000 can be given towards travel and subsistence; travel and expenses for the pre-study briefing and the Contemporary Scholars Conference are also covered, bringing the total award to around £12,000. According to the website scholars are expected to present a written report to the Nuffield

Farming Conference and to 'use all other means at [their] disposal to spread the knowledge [they] have gained within [their] industry and beyond'.

Annual grant total

In 2015/16 the trust had assets of £1.2 million and an income of £418,000. Scholarships were awarded to 18 individuals, totalling £161,000.

Exclusions

Funding cannot be given for academic courses, gap year or research projects and to people in full-time education.

Applications

Applications can be made using the form on the trust's website. Applications open on 1 January and close on 31 July, with shortlisting for interviews taking place in September. Final decisions are made in October.

Other information

A number of other specific awards are offered, such as The Young Nuffield (Bob Matson) Award for young entrepreneurs, the Frank Arden Memorial Award to UK residents working in the fields of food, farming or forestry, and various special interest awards. Further details can be found on the trust's website.

The John Oldacre Foundation

£202,500 (nine grants)

Correspondent: Henry Shouler, Trustee, Hazleton House, Hazleton, Cheltenham, Gloucestershire GL54 4EB (01451 860752; email: h.shouler@btinternet. com)

CC number: 284960

Eligibility

Undergraduate and postgraduate students who are carrying out research in the agricultural sciences which is meaningful to the UK agricultural industry. The research must be published.

Types of grants

One-off and recurrent grants are given according to need towards structured research in the UK and overseas. Previously funded research has included projects on pig welfare, drought effect on rape, UK food security, potato diseases, soil fertility, wheat vulnerability to environmental stress and sustainable crops.

Annual grant total

In 2015/16 the foundation had assets of £11 million and an income of £157,500. During the year nine awards were made totalling £202,500

Applications

Apply in writing to the correspondent. Applications are usually considered twice a year.

Other information

Grants are made through organisations and educational establishments, not to individuals directly.

The Henry Plumb Foundation

£35,500

Correspondent: John Thorley, Bat's Loft, The Sheep Centre, Malvern, Worcestershire WR13 6PH (01684 899255; email: info@ thehenryplumbfoundation.org.uk; website: www.thehenryplumbfoundation. org.uk)

CC number: 1151449

Eligibility

Young people aged 18 to 35 with interests, business ideas or study plans that will lead to a careers in the agricultural or food industry.

Types of grants

Funding of £500 to £3,000 for business start-ups, internships, overseas exchanges and courses/events.

Annual grant total

In 2015/16 the foundation had assets of £288,500 and an income of £86,500. Grants to individuals totalled £35,500.

Applications

Application forms are available to download from the foundation's website.

The Royal Bath and West of England Society

£4,500 (eight grants)

Correspondent: Paul Hooper, Company Secretary, The Bath and West Showground, Shepton Mallett, Somerset BA4 6QN (01749 822200; email: paul. hooper@bathandwest.co.uk; website: www.bathandwestsociety.com)

CC number: 1039397

Eligibility

People under the age of 25 studying any aspect of agriculture, horticulture, forestry, veterinary, conservation or any form of food production or marketing. Applicants must be from Somerset, Dorset, Devon, Wiltshire and Gloucestershire or be intending to live in the South West on completion of their studies to contribute to the local economy during their career.

Artists between the ages of 21 and 30 working on artwork on the theme of rural life in the UK are also supported.

Types of grants

Scholarships and grants for personal development and projects in furtherance of agriculture and rural economy. In the past, money has been used to assist funding in many different areas from assisting youngsters through agricultural college and veterinary schools.

An art scholarship is awarded bi-annually and, in addition to prize money, the selected artist has the unique opportunity to exhibit a selection of their work at the show.

Annual grant total

In 2016 the society had assets of over £6 million and an income of £3.8 million. Grants were made to eight individuals and totalled £4,500. The art scholarship was not awarded during the year.

Applications

Application forms can be requested from the correspondent. They are normally considered twice a year, in spring and autumn.

To apply for the Art Scholarship, contact Josie Weller. Consult the website for further details.

Other information

The society aims to promote agriculture, rural economy, manufacture, commerce, arts and crafts through conferences, seminars, study tours, open days, exhibitions and other initiatives to individuals and rural businesses.

The Royal Horticultural Society (RHS)

£120,000 (93 grants)

Correspondent: RHS Bursaries Manager, 80 Vincent Square, London SW1P 2PE (01483 479719; email: bursaries@rhs.org.uk; website: www.rhs.org.uk/education-learning/bursaries-grants)

CC number: 222879, SC038262

Eligibility

Professional and student gardeners/horticulturalists, plant and soil scientists, botanists, arboriculturalists, landscapers, botanical artists and related professionals. While priority is given to professional horticulturists and students, applications are also considered from serious amateur gardeners. Eligible proposals must be closely identified with horticulture.

Types of grants

Grants can be awarded for horticultural projects, expeditions, study tours, voluntary work placements, conferences, educational and training courses, artwork, taxonomy, research and other purposes with clear horticultural relevance. Grants can be used towards the costs of travel, accommodation, food, essential equipment, administration, publication and other costs.

There are a number of different funds and bursaries administered by the RHS; the committee selects the most appropriate fund for each application. For further information on the funds available, refer to the RHS website.

Annual grant total

In 2015/16 the society had assets of £129.7 million and an income of £76.5 million. The annual report states that a total of just over £120,000 was awarded in 93 bursaries during the year.

Exclusions

Funding is not awarded for:

- Salaries
- Household expenses (e.g. utility bills)
- Infrastructure (e.g. poly-tunnels, pergolas or buildings)
- Commercial enterprises
- Courses which lead to a qualification or accreditation
- Costs related to undertaking a course (e.g. purchase of books or materials)

Applications

Application forms can be obtained from the society's website. Completed forms should be submitted by email by 31 March, 30 June, 30 September or 15 December, unless otherwise indicated on the website.

Other information

Organisations, charities and gardens open to the public may also be supported.

The Royal Horticultural Society administers a number of bursary funds, established and maintained through generous bequests and donations, to support professional and student gardeners/horticulturalists.

Scottish Power Foundation

Correspondent: The Trustees, 320 St Vincent Street, Glasgow G2 5AD (website: www.scottishpower.com/pages/scottishpower_foundation_scholarships.aspx)

OSCR number: SC043862

Eligibility

Students from the UK, USA, Brazil, Mexico and Spain studying postgraduate courses at universities in the UK, Spain and the USA, in areas related to renewables, energy efficiency, biodiversity, clean technologies, emissions management, energy storage, electric vehicles and smart grids, cybersecurity and big data management and information and computer technology. See the foundation's website for a list of applicable universities.

Types of grants

Scholarships for master's studies.

Annual grant total

In 2016 the foundation had assets of £126,000 and an income of £800,500. We were unable to determine the value of grants to individuals.

Applications

Details of the application process and application deadlines can be found on the foundation's website.

Studley College Trust

£105,500 (100 grants)

Correspondent: Christine Copeman, Trust Secretary, Kernow House, Lower Boddington, Daventry, Northamptonshire NN11 6YB (01327 260165; email: studleyct@btinternet.com; website: www.studleytrust.co.uk)

CC number: 528787

Eligibility

British or Irish nationals aged 18 to 30 (except cases of genuine career change) enrolled on a college/university course connected with UK land-based activities (agriculture, horticulture, forestry, fish farming, agri-food technology, agricultural or horticultural marketing, arboriculture, game keeping and estate skills and agricultural engineering) whose progress is obstructed by lack of funds. Practical experience and/or a strong rural background are required, as is a satisfactory performance throughout the course.

The trust looks to support students in their early qualifications.

Types of grants

One-off and recurrent (up to three years) grants towards: course fees; examination and external test fees; books and study materials; transport; protective clothing; accommodation; food and course study trips (between £500 and £2,000).

The trust also provides scholarships through the Professional Gardeners' Guild, Nuffield Farming Scholarships Trust and Tresco Abbey Gardens, as well as bursaries for studying at certain colleges – refer to the website for more information.

Annual grant total

In 2015/16 the trust had assets of £2.7 million and an income of £147,000.

A total of around £105,500 was paid in 100 grants and bursaries to students.

Exclusions

Grants are not usually given for:

- Master's degree courses or PhDs
- Courses in the following subjects: veterinary science; animal behaviour; food science; farriery; floristry; animal care; environmental studies; countryside and land management; equine management; landscape architecture
- Hire purchase payments
- Overdraft and loan repayments
- Long-term housing costs
- Students on industrial placements more than six weeks in length

Applications

Partner colleges

The trust has made partnerships with eight land-based colleges (listed on the trust's website) and students at these institutions should apply through their student support office.

Sponsored scholarships

Applications for sponsored scholarships should be made through the appropriate organisations, details of which can be found on the website.

Students at other institutions and traineeships and travel scholarships

Applications from students at universities/colleges not listed on the trust's website, as well as applications for travelling scholarships or traineeships, can be submitted directly to the trust. Application forms can be requested on the website or from the correspondent. The trustees consider applications in July and October and the deadlines are 1 June and 1 October, respectively.

Any queries can be directed to the Trust Secretary.

The Water Conservation Trust

£54,000

Correspondent: Administrator, HQS Wellington, Temple Stairs, Victoria Embankment, London WC2R 2PN (0118 983 3689; email: waterloo@aol.com)

CC number: 1007648

Eligibility

People who are working or studying in the fields of water or environment conservation and industry, and their dependants.

Types of grants

The trust offers one-off grants to individuals and runs a bursary programme for postgraduate studies and research in environment/water at nine UK universities.

Annual grant total

In 2015/16 the trust had assets of £532,500 and an income of £142,500. Grants to individuals for educational purposes totalled £54,000 and can be broken down as follows:

University bursaries and dissertation support	£52,000
Grants to individuals	£1,700
Pupil prizes	£200

Applications

When funds are available, applicants for scholarships are invited through the water and environmental press. Applications should then be made via specific universities.

Unsolicited applications are not invited.

Other information

The trust also awards grants to environmental organisations, promotes environmental education in schools and the community and supports activities with an environmental focus for people with disabilities.

Heritage and conservation

Aradin Charitable Trust

£17,000

Correspondent: Dr Amal Marogy PhD, 10 Pembroke Street, Cambridge CB2 3QY (01223301920; email: info@aradin.org.uk; website: www.aradin.org.uk)

CC number: 1153576

Eligibility

People studying and researching ancient languages and Middle Eastern heritage.

Types of grants

One-off and recurrent grants for research into the study and preservation of ancient languages, minority Middle Eastern community inclusion, and heritage protection. Grants can cover project costs, travel costs, additional learning materials etc.

Annual grant total

In 2015/16 the charity had an income of £22,000 and a total expenditure of £21,000. The trust awarded a total of £17,000 in grants for education.

Applications

Applications can be made on the trust's website by visiting the 'What We Do' page. There are three educational options to choose from:

1 **Support scholarship:** this funding stream supports research fellowships, student exchange, mentoring and collaborative courses in the study and revival of ancient languages
2 **Protect and preserve languages:** training and grants for learning and research for Middle Eastern language scholars
3 **Promote collaboration:** supporting collaboration projects by multi-disciplinary teams and networks, particularly between academia and minority Middle Eastern communities, to help save languages and heritage.

Other information

The trust also provides support to empower Christian communities in Iraq, Egypt, Israel and Lebanon, spotting talent from minority communities, and giving them support to flourish. It also provides grants to preserve and protect neglected heritage, particularly churches, houses, manuscripts and artefacts that receive no further funding.

The Zibby Garnett Travelling Fellowship

£9,000

Correspondent: Martin Williams, Trustee, 20 Rutland Terrance, Stamford, Lincolnshire PE9 2QD (01636 636288; email: info@zibbygarnett.org; website: www.zibbygarnett.org)

CC number: 1081403

Eligibility

Students, craft apprentices or young professionals working in the fields of historic and decorative crafts, architectural conservation, historic landscape and gardens, traditional building skills, sculpture, artefacts and similar or associated areas, who wish to travel abroad for educational purposes or research.

Types of grants

Grants and bursaries in the range of £300 to £3,000 are given to allow individuals to travel overseas for practical study and conservation work. According to the website, the trustees are looking for 'imaginative and unusual ideas likely to broaden the applicant's understanding of their subject and widen their horizons'. Preference will be given to projects which are not part of the academic curriculum, but rather the applicant's own initiative. The awards are not restricted to British nationals but overseas students should plan projects outside their country of origin.

Annual grant total

In 2015/16 the charity had an income of £4,200 and a total expenditure of £9,200. We estimate that the charity gave around £9,000 in grants to individuals.

Exclusions

Grants are not given retrospectively, for placements in the UK, for conferences/ formal courses or holidays. Support is intended for practical work in conservation, not new work.

Applications

Application forms can be found on the charity's website. Applications are considered once a year and the submission deadline can be found on the website (usually around February/ March). Applicants who are successful with their initial application are invited for an interview (usually in March) which is held in London and in Lincoln/ Newark.

Anna Plowden Trust

£85,000 (43 grants)

Correspondent: Francis Plowden, Trustee, 4 Highbury Road, London SW19 7PR (020 8879 9841; email: info@ annaplowdentrust.org.uk; website: www. annaplowdentrust.org.uk)

CC number: 1072236

Eligibility

People who want to train for a qualification in conservation of movable heritage and professionals who are looking to develop their skills in conservation.

Types of grants

The trust offers conservation bursaries to individuals (usually graduates) seeking to obtain qualifications to enter conservation profession and awards Continuing Professional Development (CPD) grants covering up to 50% of the costs for short, mid-career skills development opportunities.

Annual grant total

In 2015/16 the trust had assets of £545,000 and an income of £70,500. A total of £85,000 was awarded in grants. During the year the trust awarded 32 bursaries and 11 conservators received CPD grants.

Exclusions

Courses on the conservation of non-moveable heritage are not eligible (e.g. building or natural environment conservation).

Applications

Application forms, further guidelines, eligibility criteria and deadlines are available from the trust's website. Applications for funding are also invited through advertisements in national conservation journals.

Society of Antiquaries of London

£84,000 (24 grants)

Correspondent: John Lewis, General Secretary, Burlington House, Piccadilly, London W1J 0BE (020 7479 7080; email: admin@sal.org.uk; website: www.sal.org. uk/grants)

CC number: 207237

Eligibility

People in higher education (including postgraduates), early career researchers and scholars studying archaeological, antiquarian, architectural subjects, art history, documentary and other research projects focusing on material cultural heritage.

Types of grants

The society offers a number of research and travel grants in the range of £500 to £5,000. Awards are given on an annual basis with a potential renewal up to two years.

A number of specific awards named after various benefactors are offered in addition to the general grants. See the website for the details of these individual funds.

Annual grant total

In 2015/16 the society had assets of £15.37 million and an income of £1.77 million. A total of £82,500 was awarded for research grants to 21 individuals and a further £1,500 was awarded to three individuals as travel grants.

Exclusions

Research and travel grants are not made for work contributing to an undergraduate or postgraduate degree.

Some of the awards are not available to students.

Applications

Applications can be made online or downloaded from the society's website. Applications should not exceed four A4 pages and, together with a reference, should be submitted by 15 January for consideration in March. Applicants will be notified of a decision by 31 March.

Other information

The society also awards William and Jane Morris Fund (Church Conservation Grant Awards) grants to churches, chapels and other places of worship in the United Kingdom.

Hospitality

The Geoffrey Harrison Foundation

£13,100

Correspondent: Richard Harrison, Secretary, Oxford House, Oxford Road, Thame, Oxfordshire OX9 2AH (email: enquiries@geoffreyharrisonfoundation. org.uk; website: www. geoffreyharrisonfoundation.org.uk)

CC number: 1142242

Eligibility

People in education or training in the hotel, restaurant and hospitality industries. Currently, support is mainly aimed at Year 10 and 11 students attending the Junior Chefs Academy courses at selected institutions, and individual students in the 16 to 18 age group at Westminster Kingsway College and the University of West London, who show exceptional talent and would benefit from specific support.

Types of grants

Grants to support education and training connected with the catering and hospitality industries.

Annual grant total

In 2015/16 the foundation held assets of £118,500 and had an income of £59,000. Student support totalled £13,100.

Applications

Apply in writing to the correspondent.

Other information

The main activity of the foundation is to contribute to the Saturday Morning Junior Chefs Academy courses held at University of West London, Ealing and the Westminster Kingsway College, Victoria. In 2015/16 the amount spent on the courses totalled £44,000.

The foundation is a sponsor of the Chair in Hospitality Management at the University of West London, which involves a commitment of £20,000 per annum over four years. There are two years remaining on this agreement.

The Savoy Educational Trust

£1,400 (five grants)

Correspondent: Margaret Georgiou, Savoy Educational Trust, Room 160, 90 Long Acre, London WC2E 9RZ (020 7849 3001; fax: 020 7269 9694; email: info@savoyeducationaltrust.org.uk; website: www.savoyeducationaltrust.org. uk)

CC number: 1161014

Eligibility

Individuals undertaking a hospitality-related course and those training for management within the hospitality industry.

Candidates applying for a scholarship must hold a degree in hotel management or similar and have at least four years of experience. Candidates who have attained their positions in the hospitality industry through a company scheme can apply as long as they show aptitude and an attitude for promotion.

Types of grants

Grants of up to £500 are available towards college fees, clothing and uniforms, books, equipment, instruments and tools, as well as for educational outings in the UK and study or travel abroad.

There is also a scholarship scheme run in partnership with the Worshipful Company of Innholders which gives around £3,000 per scholarship towards training for management in the hospitality sector.

Annual grant total

In 2015/16 the trust had an income of £54.2 million and spending of £679,000. Grants awarded totalled £945,000, of which £1,400 was towards five grants for individuals.

The trust also awarded 18 scholarships from the Professional Development Programme.

Exclusions

Funding is not available for students studying a non-hospitality-related course, or those studying hospitality at a private institution.

Applications

Initially in writing to the correspondent. Eligible applicants will then be provided an application form. Grants are normally considered in March, July, September and December.

Other information

Grants are also made to educational institutions and associations connected with the hospitality industry.

The trust also awards a number of prizes in leading industry competitions.

Media, journalism and communication

The Richard Beeston Bursary Trust

£24,000 (four grants)

Correspondent: Natasha Fairweather, Trustee, 75 Faroe Road, London W14 0EL (07957131731; email: richardbeestonbursary@gmail.com; website: www.richardbeestonbursary.com)

CC number: 1158897

Eligibility

Aspiring UK-based foreign correspondents, who are under the age of 30 and have at least two years of journalistic experience.

There is also an award for a young journalist based in Israel, Lebanon or the Palestinian territories.

Types of grants

An award of £6,000 is provided for an aspiring foreign correspondent to spend six weeks abroad, researching and reporting on a foreign news story, in association with the Times newspaper.

The trust also provides another £6,000 award for a young journalist based in Israel, Lebanon or the Palestinian territories to undertake a six-week fellowship on the foreign desk at the Times in London.

Annual grant total

In 2015/16 the trust had assets of £61,500 and an income of £89,000. Grants to individuals during the year totalled £24,000. It appears that this information covers the first two years of the trust's awards – it usually awards two bursaries of £6,000 each year.

Applications

The website states that applications should include: 'a detailed outline of the proposed destination of travel and the broad nature of the story which you are intending to report on'; a brief CV; five samples of published press journalism; a journalistic referee and a scan of your passport. Further information is given on the website, along with the deadline date (usually in October).

The Journalism Diversity Fund

£164,000

Correspondent: Joanne Butcher, National Council for the Training of Journalists, New Granary, Station Road, Newport, Saffron Wealden, Essex CB11 3PL (01799 544014; email: joanne.butcher@nctj.com; website: www.nctj.com)

CC number: 1026685

Eligibility

Applicants must meet all of the following criteria which have been taken from the fund's website:

- Provide proof they have secured a place on an NCTJ-accredited course
- Must come from a socially or ethnically diverse background
- Be a British citizen residing in the UK
- Must be able to demonstrate a genuine commitment and potential to be a successful journalist through a range of journalism-related work experience (due to the high standard of applicants, experience on a student newspaper is not sufficient)
- Must not be in receipt of any other bursary award

Types of grants

Bursaries are available to people from socially and ethnically diverse backgrounds to cover the costs of National Council for the Training of Journalists accredited journalism courses and examination fees.

Annual grant total

In 2015/16 the fund spent £164,000 on bursaries.

Applications

Application forms and guidelines are available from the fund's website. Visit the schedule section for this year's deadlines.

Royal Television Society

£75,000 (25 grants)

Correspondent: Anne Dawson, Kildare House, 3 Dorset Rise, London EC4Y 8EN (020 7822 2810; email: bursaries@rts.org.uk; website: rts.org.uk/education-training/rts-bursaries)

CC number: 313728

Eligibility

UK students studying full-time accredited undergraduate degree courses in television production, broadcast journalism or technology (computer and engineering). A full list of eligible universities and courses can be found on the society's website. The charity will **only** consider applicants who:

- Are from households with an annual income below £25,000 for a Production and Broadcast Journalism Bursary/£35,000 for a Technology Bursary
- Are new to higher education
- Are full-time and 'home' students (not applying from abroad or another EU country)
- Have accepted an offer as their firm choice to study full-time on one of the Creative Skillset or Broadcast Journalism Training Council accredited undergraduate programmes (for TV Production and Broadcast Journalism bursaries) or one of the undergraduate programmes listed by the society (for Technology Undergraduate bursaries)
- Meet the application deadline

Types of grants

The society offers two bursary schemes for undergraduates – a Television Production and Broadcast Journalism Bursary and a Technology Bursary. Grants are awarded towards living costs, paid in yearly instalments of £1,000, for undergraduates on specified relevant courses. Successful applicants will also receive a free student membership of the Royal Television Society while studying and one year's free full membership after graduation, affiliate membership of the Hospital Club while studying, as well as mentoring and placement opportunities. Full guidance notes and FAQs are available on the RTS website. Broadcast Journalism applicants will also automatically be considered for the Steve Hewlett Scholarship.

Annual grant total

In 2015 the society had assets of £6.3 million and an income of £2.9 million. Bursaries are generally made to 25 students each year, totalling £75,000.

Exclusions

The society's website provides an exhaustive list of eligible institutions and courses. Students enrolling on any other course that is not listed on the website are not eligible to apply.

Applications

Application forms can be found on the society's website. All applications have to be sent electronically and must be accompanied by a copy of the applicant's UCAS personal statement. Applicants must also include a link to an example of their work or attach a file. Further guidelines on completing the application form and the shortlisting criteria are on the website. Note that the application criteria and deadlines are subject to change and it is best to consult the society's website for any updates before applying.

Note the following request by the society: 'Please do not leave [the application] until the last minute, as IT systems are likely to be busy, and it may take some time to upload your application.'

The society may contact the applicant to arrange a short telephone interview.

Other information

The society receives approximately 200 applications annually.

The Stationers' Foundation

£185,000 (36 grants)

Correspondent: Pamela Butler, Administrator, Stationers' Hall, Stationers' Hall Court, Ave Maria Lane EC4M 7DD (020 7246 0990; email: foundation@stationers.org; website: www.stationers.org)

CC number: 1120963

Eligibility

UK residents under the age of 25 who are in need and studying courses relating to the communications and content industries – a list of eligible areas is given on the foundation's website. Preference is given to those intending to enter into these industries after completing their course. Children of members of the company may also be supported.

Types of grants

The foundation offers support through a number of different schemes:

- **Postgraduate bursary scheme** – postgraduate students under the age of 25 (students between 25 and 30 should contact the relevant course director and the foundation's administrator) who hold an offer on one of the specific courses listed on the website, supporting progression in or entry into the communications and content industries. There are 12 bursaries of £6,000 awarded each year, alongside mentoring from a member of the Stationers' Company. Upon completion of the course, students are awarded freedom of the company
- **Major awards** – around £2,000 for young people under the age of 25 who wish to study a course or educational project associated with printing, bookbinding, paper conservation, stationery, papermaking, publishing, book selling or newspaper production
- **Francis Mathew Stationers' Company Scholarships** – travel scholarships for those aged between 18 and 35 in the industries supported by the foundation
- **Prize and scholarship fund** – for the children of members of the company studying or carrying out research at a university, as well as prizes for those studying in the communication and content industries

For further information on these and any other funds available, refer to the foundation's website.

Annual grant total

In 2015/16 the foundation had assets of £4.5 million and an income of £480,000. It appears that around £185,000 was awarded in educational grants, including £84,500 for educational projects, £70,000 for postgraduate bursaries and £30,500 for 'general awards'.

Exclusions

People over the age of 25 are only supported in exceptional circumstances.

Applications

Application forms are available from the foundation's website along with detailed guidance notes and deadlines, specific to each award. Any queries should be addressed to the foundation's administrator.

Other information

The foundation also supports a number of specific schools, organises and sponsors Shine School Media Awards, funds three Saturday Supplementary Schools for disadvantaged children in London, holds a welfare fund to support to people within the industry and administers a library for the use of people involved in historical studies related to printing, publishing, bookselling, bookbinding, newspaper making and similar trades. Grants are also made to charities connected with the City of London.

George Viner Memorial Fund Trust

£28,500

Correspondent: Lorna Jones, Fund Administrator, National Union of Journalists, Headland House, 72 Acton Street, London WC1X 9NB (020 7843 3700; email: georgeviner@nuj.org.uk; website: www.nuj.org.uk/rights/george-viner-memorial-fund)

CC number: 328142

Eligibility

Students from black and Asian backgrounds who have received a formal offer of a place on a National Union of Journalists recognised media course in the fields of print, broadcasting, online or photo journalism but have not yet commenced their studies. Applicants must be UK or Irish citizens who intend to continue their education or start a career within the British/Irish media industry.

Types of grants

Grants are given for tuition fees, travel expenses, accommodation, books, equipment and other necessities. Mentoring and career guidance are also provided. Payments are made directly to institutions.

Annual grant total

In 2015/16 the fund had an income of £24,500 and a total expenditure of £29,000. Based on previous years' grant expenditure, we have estimated grants totalled £28,500.

Exclusions

Individuals who have already received a student loan/sponsorship and previous recipients of an award from the fund are not supported.

Applications

Application forms can be obtained from the fund's website once the funding round opens, which happens at the end of May. The deadline for applications is in August. It is crucial to include the estimated costs for the course, including fees, travel, accommodation, books and other equipment. Note that handwritten applications or late submissions are not accepted.

Yr Ymddiriedolaeth Ddarlledu Gymreig (The Welsh Broadcasting Trust)

£15,500

Correspondent: Mali Parry-Jones, Islwyn, Lon Terfyn, Morfa Nefyn, Pwllheli, Gwynedd, North Wales LL53 6AP (01758 720132; email: gwybod@ydg.org.uk; website: ymddiried.cymru/home)

CC number: 700780

Eligibility

Applicants must satisfy at least one of the following criteria:

- Applicant was born in Wales
- Applicant is a Welsh Speaker
- Applicant has lived in Wales full-time for at least two years prior to the application

Types of grants

The trust supports participation in appropriate training or career development courses related to television, radio and new media. The courses can be short, part-time, or full-time (including postgraduate courses), The trust also supports travel costs to festivals or recognized media marketing events

Annual grant total

In 2016 the trust had an income of £15,000 and a total expenditure of £32,000. We estimate that around £15,500 was awarded in individual grants.

Exclusions

The trust does not fund first degrees, production costs, off-work time to develop an idea, or performing arts courses.

Applications

Application forms are available from trust's website or can be requested from the correspondent.

There are three official closing dates every year: 1 March, 1 July, and 1 November.

Other information

Grants are also made to training bodies or companies which offer specific training/educational programmes.

Medicine

Ted Adams Trust Ltd

£11,600

Correspondent: Rosie Stables, Administrator, 208 High Street, Guildford, Surrey GU1 3JB (email: tedadamstrust@live.co.uk; website: www. tedadamstrust.org.uk)

CC number: 1104538

Eligibility

Students of nursing/midwifery, whether pre or post-registration, working or attending courses in the Guildford area. Individuals or nursing service managers are also eligible to apply for funding towards the course fees or associated costs to further their professional education and development. The trust is 'particularly keen to fund individuals where the outcomes of their course/ study will enhance patient care in the local area.'

Types of grants

The trust will fund in-house training events and lectures, the cost of courses leading to specialist qualifications, and attendance at conference and study days. Grants are also available to fund course fees and other costs, to enable nurses and midwives to further their professional education.

Annual grant total

In 2015/16 the trust had assets of £169,500, an income of £133,500 and a total expenditure of £131,000. A total of £11,600 was made payable in grants.

Exclusions

The trust does not offer support towards living expenses, childcare or debts.

Applications

From the trust's website:

> Applications are available from the website and are to be returned to the trust's administrator. If funding is confirmed, the applicant will be informed of when the funds will become available and the address for forwarding the invoice of the agreed amount. Confirmation of attendance may also be requested. Funds are usually paid through electronic transfer.

The Worshipful Society of Apothecaries General Charity Ltd

£35,000 (35 grants)

Correspondent: The Trustees, Apothecaries Hall, Black Friars Lane, London EC4V 6EJ (020 7236 1189; email: clerk@apothecaries.org; website: www.apothecaries.org)

CC number: 284450

Eligibility

Candidates must be final-year medical and pharmaceutical students who are in need. Undergraduates taking courses in history of medicine and the ethics and philosophy of healthcare can also be supported.

Types of grants

Grants of £1,000 provided on a one-time basis to final year medical and pharmacy students in the UK.

Annual grant total

In 2015/16 the charity held £1.8 million in assets and had an income of £97,000. A total of £35,000 was awarded in grants to 35 medical and pharmacy students.

Applications

Every year, the trustees write to the deans of all 33 medical schools, and to the charity Pharmacist Support, seeking the nomination of one undergraduate to receive financial assistance to be submitted by 30 June. Recommendations are considered in July and the grants are disbursed in August. Additional meetings can also be held as required.

Other information

The charity also supports a student at the Guildhall School of Music and Drama and provides awards at the London medical schools, Christ's Hospital School and the City of London Academy (Southwark).

Donations to City of London medical charities and other institutions totalled £8,600 in 2015/16.

BMA Charities Trust Fund

£182,000

Correspondent: Marian Flint, Principal Officer, BMA House, Tavistock Square, London WC1H 9JP (020 7383 6142; email: info.bmacharities@bma.org.uk; website: www.bma.org.uk/about-us/who-we-are/bma-charities)

CC number: 219102

Eligibility

Medical students who are taking medicine as a second degree at a UK medical school; asylum-seeking or refugee doctors struggling to meet the cost of PLAB exams and GMC registration.

Types of grants

One-off and recurrent grants of up to £2,500 are given towards fees, books, and living costs.

Annual grant total

In 2016 the fund had assets of £5 million and an income of £309,000. The fund awarded £182,000 in grants to second degree medical students.

Exclusions

No grants are made to students who benefit from the NHS bursary scheme or from student loans.

Applications

Application forms can be requested by email or telephone (the charity requests that no attachments are in the email as they will not be opened). For refugee and asylum-seeking doctors, applications are open throughout the year. For second degree medical students, application packs are available from November to mid-January.

Other information

The BMA Charities Trust Fund also awards grants to medical students, unemployed doctors, and working doctors in financial hardship, for well-being purposes.

The BMA also administers the Dain Fund (CC number: 313108) which provides funds for education to children of doctors.

British Society for Antimicrobial Chemotherapy

£137,500 (13 grants)

Correspondent: Tracey Guise, 53 Regent Place, Hockley, Birmingham B1 3NJ (0121 236 1988; email: tguise@bsac.org. uk; website: www.bsac.org.uk)

CC number: 1093118

Eligibility

Postgraduate and undergraduate students and members of the society involved in research and training in antimicrobial chemotherapy.

See the relevant grant-making programme for specific eligibility guidelines.

Types of grants

The following grants are currently available:

▷ **Research grants:** up to £50,000. Priority areas include diagnostics; antimicrobial stewardship; virology;

antibiotic adjuvants; and molecular mechanisms of antimicrobial resistance
▷ **Project grants:** up to £15,000. Priority areas are the same as research grants
▷ **Education grants:** up to £50,000. Priority areas include: improving undergraduate and postgraduate teaching; development and delivery of initiatives to increase public understanding about antibiotics; and development and assessment of educational interventions
▷ **Postgraduate studentships:** early career research opportunities for postgraduates
▷ **Terry Hennessy Microbiology Fellowship:** a travel grant up to £1,500 for a researcher of infectious diseases to present a paper at ASM Microbe Meeting USA
▷ **Travel grants:** up to £1,000 for travel to ECCMID and ASM Microbe meetings
▷ **Vacation scholarship:** up to £270 per week for ten weeks for undergraduate research experience
▷ **Overseas scholarship:** a grant of £1,250 per month for six months to overseas students to work in the UK

Annual grant total

In 2015/16 the charity had assets of £7 million and an income of £196,000. The total amount awarded in research grants was £137,500.

Applications

Each programme has specific application forms, guidance notes and deadlines. See the society's website for full details for each programme and note that changes are likely to have been made.

The society also warns that the awards are very competitive, subject to a stringent peer review process and require two to three independent referees.

Other information

The society makes large grants to institutions to fund research and liaises with organisations across the globe in promoting medical research.

The Elizabeth Casson Trust

£90,000

Correspondent: Pamela Anderson, 6 Langdale Court, Witney OX28 6FG (email: ec.trust@btinternet.com; website: www.elizabethcasson.org.uk)

CC number: 227166

Eligibility

Training and practising occupational therapists.

Types of grants

Funding is available to cover the costs of: courses and conferences; bespoke research; scholarships; and postdoctoral career development.

Annual grant total

In 2015/16 the trust held assets of £7.7 million and had an income of £243,000. The total amount awarded to individuals was £90,000.

Applications

Application forms are available to complete online.

For applications for grants under £2,000, you will need to include a current copy of your CV and a letter from your line manager or academic supervisor.

For applications for grants over £2,000, you will need to include a current copy of your CV, a letter from your line manager or academic supervisor, a CDP statement, and a personal statement (maximum 500 words).

Other information

In 2015/16 the trust committed to a grant of £250,000 to Oxford Brookes University, payable over five years, to support the development of a sustainable research stream focused on occupational therapy.

The Chartered Society of Physiotherapy Charitable Trust

£80,000 (77 grants)

Correspondent: Stuart De Boos, Administrator, 14 Bedford Row, London WC1R 4ED (020 7306 6646; email: debooss@csp.org.uk; website: www.csp. org.uk/charitabletrust)

CC number: 279882

Eligibility

Qualified, associate and student members of the society.

Types of grants

Grants can be given for fees of academically accredited research courses, UK and overseas presentations, overseas development projects, research visits, master's research dissemination and student elective placements.

Annual grant total

In 2016 the trust had assets of £4.8 million and a total income of £957,500. During the year, the trust awarded grants to 77 individuals totalling £80,000 towards education and research activities.

The trust also awards grants to organisations.

Applications

Applications for educational awards should be submitted using the CSP ePortfolio, which can be accessed on the society's website. The deadlines for applications for different awards vary – for the most up-to-date information see the website.

Other information

Awards can also be made for experienced researchers and those only starting their research career. Research funding comprises Physiotherapy Research Foundation (PRF) awards, paediatric research funding and a special care of older people research award. For specific details and latest available awards in this category, see the website.

During the year, grants totalling £180,000 were awarded to the Physiotherapy Research Foundation.

The Nightingale Fund

£16,200 (28 grants)

Correspondent: Rebecca Stanford, Honorary Secretary, Half Thatch, Deers Green, Clavering, Saffron Walden, Essex CB11 4PX (01799 550668; email: rlstanford@thenightingalefund.org.uk; website: www.thenightingalefund.org.uk)

CC number: 205911

Eligibility

Nurses, midwives and community public health nurses who are registered with the Nursing and Midwifery Council and healthcare assistants in the UK.

Types of grants

Grants are given for course fees only. Support is given towards further education and training to allow individuals to improve and develop their nursing practice.

Annual grant total

In 2015/16 the fund held assets of £620,000 and had an income of £25,500. Grants totalled £16,200 and ranged from £250 to £1,000. The trustees met three times during the year, interviewing 32 candidates by telephone before awarding 28 grants.

Applications

Application forms can be downloaded from the fund's website and should be emailed to the correspondent together with a current CV. Grants are considered three times a year, in March, July and November. The deadline for applications is stated on the website. Applicants are required to attend an interview either in person or by telephone.

The Queen's Nursing Institute

£10,200 (25 grants)

Correspondent: Joanne Moorby, Welfare and Grants Officer, 1A Henrietta Place, London W1G 0LZ (020 7549 1405; email: joanne.moorby@qni.org.uk; website: www.qni.org.uk)

CC number: 213128

Eligibility

Working and retired nurses, midwives and health visitors undertaking post-qualification and community nursing courses.

Eligible training includes: specialist community practitioner qualifications; specialist community public health nursing courses; advanced nurse practitioner qualifications; or other community nursing courses.

Types of grants

Grants of up to £500 towards education and training to improve nursing skills. The institute's website notes that only 'accredited education courses and modules promoting excellence in community nursing' can be considered for funding.

Annual grant total

In 2016 the institute held assets of £10.5 million and had an income of nearly £949,000. Educational grants totalled £10,200, awarded to 25 individuals.

Applications

Application forms are accessible on the institute's website. You will need a copy of your latest bank statement and a utility bill too. Initial contact may also be made to Joanne Moorby (020 7549 1405; joanne.moorby@qni.org.uk) to discuss the application. Requests can be made at any time.

Other information

Welfare support is also given to nurses. The institute undertakes campaigning, lobbying and various projects. Organisations are also assisted.

The RCN Foundation
See entry on page 111

Rhona Reid Charitable Trust

£9,000

Correspondent: Kerry Clayton, c/o Rathbone Taxation Services, Port of Liverpool Buildings, Pier Head, Liverpool L3 1NW (0151 236 6666; email: elaine.wilson@rathbones.com)

CC number: 1047380

Eligibility

People involved in the study and advancement of medicine (especially ophthalmology), music and the arts.

Types of grants

One-off and recurrent grants are given according to need for necessities and activities which would support excellence in the chosen field.

Annual grant total

In 2015/16 the trust had an income of £13,400 and a total expenditure of £18,300. We have estimated that grants totalled £9,000. Grants are also made to organisations and people who are blind, visually impaired or have another disability.

Applications

Apply in writing to the correspondent. Applications are considered in March and September.

Royal Medical Benevolent Fund (RMBF)
See entry on page 112

Sandra Charitable Trust

£70,000 (94 grants)

Correspondent: Martin Pollock, Secretary to the Trustees, c/o Moore Stephens LLP, 150 Aldersgate Street, London EC1A 4AB (020 7334 9191)

CC number: 327492

Eligibility

Nurses and nursing students who are in financial need. Postgraduate, overseas and part-time students can all be supported.

Types of grants

One-off and recurrent grants are given according to need, for courses, equipment and other necessities.

Annual grant total

In 2015/16 the trust held assets of £20.47 million and had an income of £726,000. Grants to 94 individuals totalled £70,000. The trust also makes grants to organisations and a total of £641,000 was awarded during the year.

Applications

Application forms can be requested from the correspondent. Previously the trust has stated that its funds are largely committed. The trustees meet on a frequent basis to consider applications.

The Swann-Morton Foundation

£13,800

Correspondent: Mr M. I. Hirst, Swann-Morton Ltd, Owlerton Green, Sheffield S6 2BJ (0114 234 4231)

CC number: 271925

Eligibility

People studying or working in the fields of surgery and medicine.

Types of grants

One-off and recurrent grants are given according to need to students of medicine and surgery for electives, general educational expenses and research projects.

Annual grant total

In 2015/16 the foundation had assets of £101,000 and an income of £61,000. A total of £13,800 was given in 'student grants and electives'.

Applications

Apply in writing to the correspondent. The annual report for 2015/16 states: 'Applicants are invited to submit a summary of their proposals in a specific format. The applications are reviewed against specific criteria and research objectives which are set by the trustees.'

Other information

The foundation welcomes applications from individual students, charities and hospitals. Support can also be given to current or former employees of W R Swann and Co. Ltd.

Nautical subjects

The Corporation of Trinity House, London

£5,500

Correspondent: Graham Hockley, Secretary, Trinity House, Tower Hill, London EC3N 4DH (020 7481 6914; email: graham.hockley@thls.org; website: www.trinityhouse.co.uk)

CC number: 211869

Eligibility

Candidates must be between 16 and 18 and a half years old with five GCSE at grade C or better and must also have passed the Department of Transport medical examination. Applicants must also be British and permanently resident in the British Isles. Applicants must be applying to become an officer in the Merchant Navy.

Types of grants

The Trinity House Merchant Navy Scholarship Scheme provides financial support for young people seeking careers as officers in the Merchant Navy. The website states: 'Cadets undertake a three or four year programme split between nautical college and time at sea in a variety of British-managed vessels. Cadets can train as either Deck or Engineer Officers or pursue a Marine Cadetship encompassing both disciplines.'

Annual grant total

The charity's significant assets are no reflection of the money available for grant-making which is a very small part of its activities.

In 2016/17 the corporation had assets of £263 million and an income of more than £9 million. Grants were made to 28 retired seafarers in financial need at a rate of £728 per year. This totalled around £20,000. A further £11,700 was awarded in grants to individuals, some of which was distributed for welfare purposes. We estimate that grants for educational purposes totalled around £5,500.

The vast majority of the charity's grants expenditure was distributed to organisations throughout the year.

Applications

Details of the scholarship scheme are available upon application in writing to the correspondent.

Other information

The following information is taken from the corporation's website: 'The safety of shipping, and the well being of seafarers, have been our prime concerns ever since Trinity House was granted a Royal Charter by Henry VIII in 1514.'

Today there are three distinct functions:
- The General Lighthouse Authority (GLA) for England, Wales, the Channel Islands and Gibraltar. The remit is to provide Aids to Navigation to assist the safe passage of a huge variety of vessels through some of the busiest sea-lanes in the world
- A charitable organisation dedicated to the safety, welfare and training of mariners
- A Deep Sea Pilotage Authority providing expert navigators for ships trading in Northern European waters.

The Honourable Company of Master Mariners and Howard Leopold Davis Charity

£22,000

Correspondent: Honourable Company of Master Mariners, HQS Wellington, Temple Stairs, Victoria Embankment, London WC2R 2PN (020 7836 8179; email: info@hcmm.org.uk; website: www.hcmm.org.uk/activities/charitable-giving)

CC number: 1127213

Eligibility

People who are serving in the Merchant Navy, those intending to serve, and also individuals who have an interest in seamanship or sail training.

Types of grants

Grants are made for general educational costs for those with an interest in seamanship, sailing, and a career in the Merchant Navy.

Annual grant total

In 2016 the charity had assets of £4.1 million and an income of £103,000. Grants to individuals for educational purposes totalled £22,000.

Applications

In the first instance, members of the Honourable Company of Master Mariners should send their application to the charity's address.

Other information

This charity is an amalgamation of four separate funds: the Education Fund, the Benevolent Fund, the London Maritime Institution and the Howard Leopold Davis Fund.

The charity makes awards for welfare purposes for Master Mariners, Navigating Officers, and their families and dependants. The charity also makes grants to seafaring organisations.

Reardon Smith Nautical Trust

£85,000

Correspondent: Sarah Fox, FoxSE Consultancy, 4 Bessemer Road, Cardiff CF11 8BA (029 2089 0383; email: sarah@foxseconsultancy.co.uk)

CC number: 1153623

Eligibility

Residents of Wales up to the age of 25 studying recognised nautical or maritime courses in the UK or abroad. These should relate to shipping, maritime law and commerce, navigation, sailing, oceanography and marine related environmental issues, in particular those which give the individual first hand practical experience of being at sea. Preference is given to residents of city and county of Cardiff.

Types of grants

Grants, scholarships, exhibitions and bursaries towards general educational expenses.

Annual grant total

In 2016/17 the trust held assets of £3.35 million and had an income of £137,000. Grants to individuals are made through institutions (£81,000) or directly to the individual (£4,000).

Applications

Applications should be made through a relevant educational establishment or sail training provider. Grants are paid through sail training providers, these include Island Trust, Tall Ships Youth Trust and Challenge Wales.

Sailors' Society

£106,000

Correspondent: Welfare Fund Manager, Sailors' Society, Seafarer House, 74 St Annes Road, Southampton, Hampshire SO19 9FF (023 8051 5950; email: enquiries@sailors-society.org; website: www.sailors-society.org)

CC number: 237778

Eligibility

Students or nautical cadets preparing for a career at sea in the Merchant Navy (of any country) and enrolled at a recognised college or academy of nautical education. Seafarers who have already entered the profession and have been accepted on a course of study by an accredited institution to further their qualifications.

Types of grants

The society offers maritime scholarships in the UK, Greece, Poland and the Ukraine to help students who are otherwise unable to pursue a career at sea. The society also has a nautical grant scheme which enables trainee seafarers or seafarers who need to upgrade their qualifications.

Annual grant total

In 2016 the society had assets of £16.4 million and an income of £3.7 million. Educational grants to individuals totalled £106,000.

Applications

In the first instance, contact the correspondent via email.

Other information

The society maintains a network of chaplains at the various key ports around the world, who carry out ship visiting routines and minister to seafarers. It also provides centres and clubs for seafarers and associated maritime workers at strategic seaports.

The Shipwrights Charitable Fund

£37,000 (17 grants)

Correspondent: Lt Col Richard Cole-Mackintosh, Clerk, Worshipful Company of Shipwrights, Ironmongers Hall, 1 Shaftesbury Place, Barbican, London EC2Y 8AA (020 7606 2376; email: clerk@shipwrights.co.uk; website: www.shipwrights.co.uk)

CC number: 262043

Eligibility

People studying modern and traditional timber ship and boat building, naval architecture or marine engineering. Preference is given to those under the age of 25.

Types of grants

Grants typically range from a minimum of £200 for tools and up to a maximum of £1,600 for help with fees or living expenses. Bursaries of £2,000 are available for students at Strathclyde, Newcastle and Southampton Universities.

Annual grant total

In 2015/16 the fund held assets of £6.2 million and had an income of £2.6 million. Grants to 15 individuals through the Billmeir Award programme totalled £25,000. Grants ranged from between £750 and £2,500. A further £12,000 was allocated to support six students at Strathclyde, Newcastle and Southampton Universities.

Applications

Application forms can be completed online and potential applicants will need to provide the names of two referees. The grants committee meets three times a year in February, June and November. Further details can be found on the charity's website.

Other information

The fund is a part of the Worshipful Company of Shipwrights' charitable programme. Grants to individuals are awarded through the Billmeir fund, but the company mainly awards grants to organisations (£193,500 in 2015/16) as well as supporting schools and apprenticeships.

Public services

Institution of Fire Engineers

£10,000

Correspondent: Sarah Simpson, IFE House, 64–66 Cygnet Court, Timothy's Bridge Road, Stratford-upon-Avon, Warwickshire CV37 9NW (01789261463; fax: 01789 296426; email: frstt@ife.org. uk; website: www.ife.org.uk)

OSCR number: SC012694

Eligibility

Grants are available for fire professionals, members of fire research organisations and the fire engineering profession or students of these areas in the UK. Applicants must be endorsed by an academic body, professional association or public agency.

Applicants must prove through their qualifications that they will benefit from further study and their capacity to produce a piece of work worth publishing that would benefit others in the fire profession.

Types of grants

The Fire Service Research and Training Trust (FSRTT) provides funds to support applicants undertaking training or studies in fire-related programmes for the benefit of fire-related research. The grant is intended to cover/assist towards the cost of completing an educational course or scholarship including costs of travel. Other expenses are considered on their merits.

Annual grant total

In 2016 the charity had an income of £1.1 million and spending of £1 million. During the year, charitable activities totalled £1 million. Previous research has shown that grants to individuals normally amount to £10,000.

Applications

Application forms can be downloaded from the charity's website and posted to the correspondent. Applications should include an outline of the project plan, which must include mention of possible risks to the project or the delivery of the outcomes.

Successful applicants will be expected to produce a written paper on aspects of their work, findings and conclusions.

Other information

The institute makes grants on behalf of the Fire Service Research and Training Trust.

Social work

Social Workers' Educational Trust

£16,000

Correspondent: Catherine Poulter, Secretary, Social Workers' Educational Trust, The British Association of Social Workers, Wellesley House, 37 Waterloo Street, Birmingham B2 5PP (01269 824454; email: swet@basw.co.uk or policyadmin@basw.co.uk; website: www.basw.co.uk/financial-support/social-workers-educational-trust)

CC number: 313789

Eligibility

Qualified social workers, with at least two years of post-qualifying experience, who work or are looking for work in the UK, and are undertaking post-qualifying training to improve their knowledge and skills for social work practice. Membership of the British Association of Social Workers (BASW) will be taken into account.

Types of grants

One-off and recurrent grants of up to £500 for fees, travel costs, childcare and books. Grants for courses of more than one year are made on an annual basis and are dependent on the recipient's successful completion of the year's training and the trust's level of funds. Part-funding of fees or expenses may also be considered should the additional funding be available from another source.

Annual grant total

In 2015/16 the trust had an income of £24,600 and a total expenditure of £17,000. We have estimated that grants to individuals totalled £16,000.

The trust's website notes that the trust's income usually allows it to make about 50 grants of up to £500 each year.

Exclusions

The trust cannot assist those undertaking initial social work training or qualifications. Successful applicants may not re-apply within three years of the completion of a supported training course or project.

Applications

Application forms are available from the correspondent or can be downloaded from the website along with guidelines. Applications can be submitted at any time and are normally considered in February, July and October.

Other information

The trust also manages funds bequeathed or subscribed in memory of colleagues. The trust's website states: 'These funds provide more substantial scholarships which are awarded annually through competition.' Enquiries for these larger annual scholarships should be made to the Hon. Secretary.

Sports

Athletics for the Young

£15,000

Correspondent: Alan Barlow, Trustee, 12 Redcar Close, Hazel Grove, Stockport SK7 4SQ (0161 483 9330; email: runalan55@hotmail.com; website: www.englandathletics.org)

CC number: 1004448

Eligibility

Young people under the age of 23 who are in full-time education, active in athletics and eligible to compete for England.

Types of grants

One-off educational grants (usually between £50 and £200) towards athletic pursuits, including equipment and travel expenses.

Annual grant total

In 2015/16 the charity had an income of £110 and a total expenditure of £23,500. The total amount given to individuals was £15,000.

Exclusions

People already receiving funding from other sources are not normally supported.

Applications

Application forms can be downloaded from the England Athletics website and should be returned via post. The deadline for applications is mid-February. Note that applications should be handwritten and provide a reference.

Other information

Grants can also be made to organisations supporting young athletes.

The Dickie Bird Foundation

£4,800

Correspondent: W. Edward Cowley, Flat 3, The Tower, The Tower Drive, Pool in Wharfedale, Otley, West Yorkshire LS21 1NQ (07503641457; website: www.thedickiebirdfoundation.org)

CC number: 1104646

Eligibility

Disadvantaged young people age 16 and under who are participating, or wish to participate, in sport.

Types of grants

Small, one-off grants, usually up to the value of £1,000, are available to pay for sporting equipment for disadvantaged young people.

Annual grant total

In 2016/17 the foundation had an income of £4,900 and a total expenditure of £5,200. We estimate that a total of £4,800 was awarded in grants.

Exclusions

Grants cannot be given for:

- Professional fees of any kind, including club membership, or club fees
- Travel outside the UK
- Scholarships, summer/winter/training camps
- Equipment that is available for use elsewhere
- Overnight accommodation

Applications

Application forms are available from the foundation's website, to be completed in black ink, and sent to:

Grants Officer, The Dickie Bird Foundation, 23B Rawson Street, Low Moor, Bradford BD12 8PH.

The application also requires two referees. Other guidelines are available to view on the application form.

The Monica Elwes Shipway Sporting Foundation

£2,100

Correspondent: Simon Goldring, Trustee, c/o Trowers & Hamlins LLP, 3 Bunhill Row, London EC1Y 8YZ (020 7423 8000; email: sgoldring@trowers.com)

CC number: 1054362

Eligibility

Children and young people in full-time education engaged in sporting activities who have limited resources.

Types of grants

One-off grants of up to £300 towards clothing, equipment and fees in relation to sport activities.

Annual grant total

In 2015/16 the foundation had an income of £400 and a total expenditure of £4,300. We estimate that the charity awarded around £2,100 to individuals for educational purposes.

The charity also awards grants to organisations.

Exclusions

General university fees are not supported. Help is not available to individuals with sufficient resources.

Applications

Applications may be made in writing to the correspondent. They are considered throughout the year.

The Brian Johnston Memorial Trust

£14,000 (27 grants)

Correspondent: Richard Anstey, c/o The Lord's Taverners, Brian Johnston Memorial Trust, 10 Buckingham Place, London SW1E 6HX (020 7821 2828; email: raganstey@btinternet.com; website: www.lordstaverners.org)

CC number: 1045946

Eligibility

Young promising cricketers who are in need of financial assistance to further their personal and cricketing development.

Types of grants

Scholarships are available for young cricketers at county academy and university level, towards travel, equipment and coaching.

Annual grant total

In 2015/16 the trust had assets of £5,400 and an income of £72,000. Brian Johnston Scholarships totalled £14,000 and were awarded to 27 individuals. In addition, grants for the Brian Johnston Memorial Trust/England and Wales Cricket Board (BJMT/ECB) Elite Spin programme totalled £16,400 and grants supporting participation of people who are visually impaired or blind totalled £18,700.

Applications

For further information, contact Richard Anstey (raganstey@btinternet.com). Applications are considered on an annual basis by the awards committee.

Other information

The trust is also known as The Johnners Trust.

As well as awarding individual scholarships, the trust runs the BJMT/ECB Elite Spin Bowling Programme and provides grants to cricket associations to assist participation of people who are visually impaired and blind.

The Dan Maskell Tennis Trust

£25,000

Correspondent: Gilly English, Executive Director, c/o Sport Wins, PO Box 238, Tadworth KT20 5WT (01737 831707; email: danmaskell@sportwins.co.uk; website: www.danmaskelltennistrust.org.uk)

CC number: 1133589

Eligibility

UK citizens resident in the UK who have disabilities (including mobility, hearing and visual impairments and those with learning disabilities) and are playing tennis or wish to engage in this sport.

Types of grants

Individuals may apply for their own sports wheelchair – two types are currently available, as detailed in the guidance notes on the trust's website. Applicants are required to raise a deposit (£400 or £925, depending on the type of chair).

Individuals may also apply for specific items or needs, such as tennis rackets, equipment bags, coaching lessons with the Lawn Tennis Association (LTA) licensed coach or course fees for official LTA development or coaching courses.

The maximum grant for individuals is £500.

Annual grant total

In 2016 the trust had assets of £573,500 and an income of £78,000. During the year the trust made 88 grants to individuals and groups totalling almost £58,500, in the following categories:

Monetary grants for individuals	30
Individual tennis wheelchairs	21
Monetary grants for groups	22
Tennis wheelchairs for groups	9
Tennis equipment bags	6

The exact amount granted to individuals was not specified in the accounts. We have estimated that grants to individuals totalled around £25,000.

Applications

Application forms are available on the trust's website, along with guidance notes. The trustees meet at least three times a year and deadlines are posted on the trust's website. Completed application forms can be returned by post or emailed to the correspondent.

Other information

Groups, clubs and specific projects can also receive support for one or more wheelchairs designed for general use at grassroots level, as well as help with equipment, facilities and programmes or projects. A deposit of £250 is required. Tennis equipment bags, containing rackets, balls, mini nets and coaching aids (such as cones and throw-down marker lines) are also available and will be delivered directly by the trusts. The maximum grant for groups or projects is £1,500.

The 2016 annual report states: 'The trust works closely with The Tennis Foundation in liaising on grant applications and supporting the Foundation's disability programmes where appropriate.'

The Torch Trophy Trust

£11,500

Correspondent: Hayley Morris, Administrative Volunteer, 4th Floor, Burwood House, 14–16 Caxton Street, London SW1H 0QT (020 7976 3900; email: hayley.morris@torchtrophytrust.org; website: www.torchtrophytrust.org)

CC number: 306115

Eligibility

Volunteers working for any organisation involved in sports or outdoor activities within local communities who want to improve their skills and whose governing body is keen to help out but is unable to provide the necessary funding.

Types of grants

Bursaries from £100 to £500 to take courses to qualify as club coaches or officials/administrators. The award will not cover more than 50% of the total costs involved, although exceptional circumstances may be considered.

Annual grant total

In 2016 the trust had an income of £14,400 and a total expenditure of £24,500. We have estimated that awards to individuals totalled around £11,500 as grants are also awarded to organisations.

Applications

Application forms can be requested from the correspondent or found on the trust's website. A supporting letter from the relevant governing body must be included. For submission deadlines and further details see the trust's website.

Other information

The trust also presents annual Trophy Torch Awards to the most outstanding nominated volunteers in the UK.

Religion

The All Saints Educational Trust

£174,000

Correspondent: The Trustees, Knightrider House, 2 Knightrider Court, London EC4V 5AR (020 7248 8380; email: aset@aset.org.uk; website: www. aset.org.uk)

CC number: 312934

Eligibility

Applicants must be studying a course which includes Qualified Teacher Status, with preference given to those studying religious studies or home economics (including food technology and consumer sciences). Preference is also given to those studying for a first degree, and second degrees or postgraduate courses are also considered.

Applicants must demonstrate that they have explored options for funding through university, local authority or central government (including loans).

Applicants will preferably have a religious commitment to the Church of England, however other Christian and non-Christian applicants will be considered.

Types of grants

Most grants total a few hundred pounds, however where the need is established much larger sums can be given. Grants are designed to cover tuition fees and day-to-day expenses.

Annual grant total

In 2015/16 the charity held £17 million in assets and had an income of £717,000. A total of £174,000 was awarded in scholarships and bursaries to individuals.

Applications

Those interested should initially complete an eligibility questionnaire, which is available on the website, and send it to the trust by email or post. If the applicant meets the eligibility criteria, the trust will send them a full application pack, to include three referees and to be sent back by post.

Eligibility checks and requests for full applications must be received by the beginning of February each year. Completed full applications must be received by the beginning of March each year. The awards committee considers UK/EU applications in April, and overseas applications in May.

The Andrew Anderson Trust

£35,500

Correspondent: Andrew Robertson Anderson, Trustee, 1 Cote House Lane, Bristol BS9 3UW (0117 962 1588)

CC number: 212170

Eligibility

People studying theology.

Types of grants

One-off and recurrent grants are given according to need.

Annual grant total

In 2015/16 the trust had assets of £12 million and an income of £496,500. The vast majority of grants (£411,000) were awarded to organisations. The amount of grants given to individuals totalled £71,000 and we estimate that those for educational purposes amounted to around £35,500.

Applications

The trust has previously stated that it rarely gives to people who are not known to the trustees or who have been personally recommended by people known to the trustees. Unsolicited applications are therefore unlikely to be successful.

The Duncan Trust

£3,000

Correspondent: Administrator, c/o Thorntons Law LLP, Brothockbank House, Arbroath, Angus DD11 1NE (01241 872683; fax: 01241 871541)

OSCR number: SC015311

Eligibility

Students who are training or intend to train for the Ministry of the Church of Scotland on either a regular or modified course. Preference is given to individuals within the Presbytery of Angus and Mearns.

Types of grants

Bursaries and scholarships.

Annual grant total

In 2015/16 the trust had an income of £82,000 and a total expenditure of £73,000. Throughout the year the trust awarded around £3,000 in grants to individuals.

Applications

Apply in writing to the correspondent.

The Elland Society

£7,000

Correspondent: Revd Colin Judd, Trustee, 57 Grosvenor Road, Shipley BD18 4RB (01274 584775; email: elland@saltsvillage.co.uk; website: www. ellandsocietygrants.co.uk)

CC number: 243053

Eligibility

Grants are made to ordinands who are 'Evangelical in conviction and outlook' and can prove genuine financial need. Candidates must be in the course of their theological training, be it residential or non-residential, which has been approved by the diocese.

Priority for grants is given to ordinands sponsored by dioceses in the Province of York, or who intend to serve their title in that province.

Types of grants

One-off grants and general cash contributions according to need are given to those who have already started training at residential or non-residential theological college. Previously, grants have been awarded for clothing/ footwear, household items, living expenses, travel expenses, study overseas, books and educational equipment. Our research suggests that grants rarely exceed £500 per person.

Annual grant total

In 2015/16 the charity had an income of £6,500 and a total expenditure of £7,200. We estimate that the charity gave around £7,000 in grants to individuals for educational purposes.

Exclusions

Grants are not provided for items already included in the main church grant.

Applications

Application forms can be downloaded from the society's website or requested from the correspondent.

Other information

The charity prefers communication by email.

Lady Hewley's Charity

£50,000

Correspondent: Neil Blake, Military House, 24 Castle Street, Chester CH1 2DS

CC number: 230043

Eligibility

Young men or women preparing for United Reformed and Baptist Church ministries. Preference will be given to students who were born in the north of England.

Types of grants

One-off grants according to need.

Annual grant total

In 2015/16 the charity had assets of £16.9 million and an income of over £1 million. Grants to individuals totalled £146,000, of which £50,000 was given in student grants.

Exclusions

No grants will be given where local authority funds are available.

Applications

Applications for grants are invited through contact with respective churches at both local church, regional and province levels. Individual applications are considered twice a year and grants are made according to an individual's personal and financial circumstances.

Hockerill Educational Foundation

See entry on page 66

The Leaders of Worship and Preachers Trust

£21,000

Correspondent: Amelia Gosal, 77 Mortlake Road, Richmond TW9 4AA (020 8878 0701; fax: 01923 296899; email: lwptoffice@lwpt.org.uk; website: www.lwpt.org.uk)

CC number: 1107967

Eligibility

Individuals who wish to pursue their vocation in ministry, including individuals who are 'in the early stages of exploring their calling to preach'. Applicants should be committed Christians and active members of a church.

Types of grants

Grants can be made to assist with fees or materials for any recognised course or conference that enables the applicant to explore or develop their preaching skills. This can include 'gap year' style courses and those to continue professional development. Grants can vary in size but are generally in the region of £500.

Annual grant total

In 2015/16 the charity had assets of £273,000 and an income of £486,000. The total amount awarded in vocational grants was £21,000.

Exclusions

Grants are not made to assist with accommodation or subsistence.

Applicants are normally awarded only one grant within a twelve-month period.

Applications

An application form is available to download from the website along with guidance notes. Information about the applicant's financial circumstances will be requested by the trust in order to determine the need for support. Applicants must have the support of a member of their church staff, who will be asked for a reference confirming the individual's interest and potential ability in preaching, their Christian faith and their character.

Applications must be submitted by 30 June for a grant in September or by 30 October for a grant in January. In exceptional circumstances, requests for applications to be considered outside these timeframes may be accepted.

Other information

The trust notes on its website: 'It is important to note before making an application, that your church may be able to offer you financial support.'

The charity also runs a separate grant scheme for individuals suffering financial hardship.

Powis Exhibition Fund

£11,000

Correspondent: John Richfield, 39 Cathedral Road, Cardiff CF11 9XF (029 2034 8200)

CC number: 525770

Eligibility

People who are training as ordinands of the Church in Wales. Applicants must be born or be resident in Wales and speak Welsh.

Types of grants

Grants are available only for the period of study at university or a theological college.

Annual grant total

In 2017 the fund had an income of £12,600 and had a total expenditure of £11,800. We have estimated that grants to individuals for educational purposes totalled £11,000

Applications

Application forms are available from the correspondent or from individual dioceses.

Sola Trust

£362,000 (124 grants)

Correspondent: Simon Pilcher, Trustee, Green End Barn, Wood End Green, Henham, Bishop's Stortford CM22 6AY

(01279 850819; email: admin@solatrust. org.uk; website: www.solatrust.org.uk)

CC number: 1062739

Eligibility

Individuals training for full-time Christian work, either at a theological college or at a church, as well as to those already involved in full-time ministry.

Types of grants

Grants are usually one-off or up to one year and intended to be supplementary only. Support is available towards books, other necessities, conferences, training courses, retreats and other expenses. Additionally, the charity aims to relieve the financial hardship of those involved in Christian ministry.

Annual grant total

In 2015/16 the trust had assets of £132,000 and an income of £482,500. The amount of grants given to individuals totalled £365,000 (including £3,000 for relief of poverty) and were distributed as follows:

Theological and ministry training grants	108	£309,500
Other ministry grants	9	£34,000
PhD studies	5	£18,500
Relief of poverty	2	£3,000

Grants were also made to 42 organisations totalling £263,000, consisting of theological and ministry training, church plants grants and other ministry purposes.

Exclusions

The trust's 2015/16 annual report states that it 'aims to avoid being the sole source of funding for any applicant and will generally not extend promises of financing beyond one year'.

Applications

Apply in writing to the correspondent. According to the website, applications should include: 'what you are applying for funding for; Christian background; age, education, Christian ministry and other work (e.g. non-church paid employment); hopes, ambitions and plans; an annual budget – accounting for any spouse, children or other dependents'. References are also required. Further detail is given on the trust's website. Where appropriate, grants may be routed through a church or equivalent body that is providing training to individuals. The trustees meet several times a year to consider applications.

Other information

The trustees' annual report from 2015/16 states that:

> The charity also seeks to facilitate the strategic placement of trained gospel workers – working in new geographical areas (areas of the country where there is little or no biblical ministry at present) and

in new types of ministry (for example youth or women's ministry).

The Spalding Trusts

£64,500

Correspondent: Tessa Rodgers, Secretary, PO Box 85, Stowmarket IP14 3NY (website: www.spaldingtrust. org.uk)

CC number: 209066

Eligibility
People undertaking research projects into world religions, particularly comparative studies, who are in need of financial support. Projects must primarily have a religious focus rather than sociological or anthropological.

Types of grants
Awards of up to £2,000 for the comparative study of the major religions. Support is available for research projects, publications, occasionally travel costs, conferences and related expenses. Applications may not necessarily be academically orientated, provided they have sufficient practical and beneficial aspect. Recurrent grants extending over one year are only considered in exceptional circumstances.

Annual grant total
In 2016 the trust held assets of £2.3 million and had an income of £79,000. Grants totalled £64,500.

Exclusions
Grants are not given retrospectively and will rarely be provided towards expenses related to the first degree.

Applications
Apply in writing to the correspondent providing:

▶ An outline of the proposal/course
▶ A copy of the applicant's CV, specifying their own religious commitment, if any
▶ Details of the budget and of other possible sources of funding that have been applied for (this should be done using a copy of the financial statement available on the trust's website)
▶ Preferably two academic references
▶ Daytime and evening phone numbers and email address

Applications should be submitted by post. Further application guidelines are available on the trust's website. The trustees meet once a year to decide on major proposals but smaller grants are considered on a monthly basis (it may take up to three months to reach a decision).

Other information
The trust also makes grants to institutions, such as libraries, colleges, other educational establishments.

A subsidiary of the trust, the Ellen Rebe Spalding Memorial Fund, makes grants to disadvantaged women and children.

The Foundation of St Matthias

£72,000 (48 grants)

Correspondent: Karine Prescott, Clerk to the Trustees, Hillside House, First Floor, 1500 Parkway North, Newbrick Road, Stoke Gifford, Bristol BS34 8YU (0117 906 0100; email: stmatthiastrust@ bristoldiocese.org; website: www. stmatthiastrust.org.uk)

CC number: 311696

Eligibility
Further and higher education students, including mature students and occasionally postgraduates, who are studying in accordance with the doctrine of the Church of England. This includes:

▶ People who are, or intend to become, engaged in social welfare work as social workers, community workers, youth workers, teachers or supervisors of pre-school groups, etc.
▶ People who are intending to become ministers of the Church of England or of a church in communion therewith

Preference is given to applicants from the dioceses of Bath and Wells, Bristol and Gloucester, although applicants from elsewhere are considered.

Types of grants
One-off grants can be given for books, fees, maintenance/living expenses, childcare and for some study or travel abroad. Overseas courses may be supported only if the visit is integral to the course or research. PhD scholarships are also available.

Annual grant total
In 2016 the foundation held assets of nearly £7 million and had an income of £254,500. The amount of grants given to individuals totalled £72,000, of which 33 grants were of less than £1,000 and 14 were of £1,000 or more. Scholarship grants of £1,000 or more were awarded to four PhD students.

Exclusions
No retrospective grants.

Applications
Applicants should telephone in the first instance to discuss their applications with the correspondent. Applications must be made on a form available from the foundation's website. They should be submitted by 31 May for consideration in July or 30 September for consideration in November.

Other information
The foundation advises applicants to apply to as many sources of funding as possible as funding is not guaranteed and often, the charity cannot offer the full amount requested. There is a link to other religious education trusts on its website.

The foundation is not able to cover the costs of fees, maintenance or travel etc. of students from overseas, but small contributions may be offered should evidence be supplied that substantial funding is available from other sources.

The Stewardship Trust Ripon

£8,500

Correspondent: Anne Metcalfe, Trustee, Hutton Hill, Hutton Bank, Ripon HG4 5DT (email: stewardship.ripon@ gmail.com)

CC number: 224447

Eligibility
People connected with Christian causes and studies.

Types of grants
One-off and recurrent grants for people training in Christian ministry, engaged in studies of Christianity or working for Christian causes.

Annual grant total
In 2016/17 the trust had an income of £24,500 and a total expenditure of £44,000. Most of the trust's support goes to organisations. In previous years the total of grants to individuals has reached up to around £8,500.

Applications
Apply in writing to the correspondent. Our research has suggested that the trust's funds are usually fully committed and new applications are only considered if there is significant need.

Other information
The trust also supports various churches, societies and the Christian Institute.

Thornton Fund

£7,500

Correspondent: Dr Jane Williams, 93 Fitzjohn Avenue, Barnet EN5 2HR (020 8440 2211; email: djanewilliams@ dsl.pipex.com)

CC number: 226803

Eligibility
Students training for Unitarian ministry.

Types of grants

Grants to help with books, equipment, instruments, living expenses, study exchange and study or travel abroad.

Annual grant total

In 2016 the charity had an income of £21,000 and a total expenditure of £18,500. The amount awarded in grants for ministry training was £7,500.

Applications

Applications should be made in writing to the correspondent, with the support of a minister. Applications are considered throughout the year.

Other information

The fund also provides grants to ministers in financial need, and occasionally makes project grants to the assembly of Unitarian and Free Christian Churches.

Women's Continuing Ministerial Education Trust

£45,000

Correspondent: Administrator, Archbishops' Council, Church House, Great Smith Street, London SW1P 3AZ (020 7898 1000; email: webmaster@ churchofengland.org; website: www. ministrydevelopment.org.uk/wcmet)

CC number: 1093320

Eligibility

Women (ordained or not) who are licensed into a nationally recognised ministry in the Church of England or the Scottish Episcopal Church (with the exception of readers). Religious sisters and retired clergy who are involved in active ministry can also apply.

Types of grants

Grants are given for continuing ministerial education. Support is given towards general educational needs, conferences, educational fees (where possible, any costs of fees will be awarded). Grants are intended to supplement funds available from the applicant's diocese.

Accommodation, travel costs or childcare are not normally covered, but anticipated costs of those needs should be included in the budget.

Due to limited funds, the trust focuses on applications for courses/projects that clearly relate to assisting the minister in their work and professional development.

Annual grant total

In 2016 the trust had no income and a total expenditure of £48,500. Generally about £45,000 is given a year.

Exclusions

The trust does not normally fund courses in Initial Ministerial Education (IME) 4–7 and retreats/sabbaticals.

Applications

Application forms can be accessed from the website. Applications must be endorsed by the Diocesan CME Officer or Dean of the Women's Ministry. Grants are normally considered quarterly, in February, May, July and October and the deadline for applications is in the preceding month. Candidates are informed about the outcome of their application in the following month.

Skilled crafts

The Worshipful Company of Framework Knitters Education Charity

£22,500 (12 grants)

Correspondent: Capt. Shaun Mackaness, Clerk, The Grange, Walton Road, Kimcote, Lutterworth LE17 5RU (01455 203152; email: clerk@frameworkknitters. co.uk; website: www.frameworkknitters. co.uk/student-bursaries)

CC number: 292630

Eligibility

Students in further and higher education about to enter the final year of a diploma or first degree, on a postgraduate course, or registered for a research degree, are eligible to apply. Students of design, management, marketing, science and technology relevant to the knitting/knitwear industries are eligible for consideration. Applicants are normally British citizens and resident in the United Kingdom.

Types of grants

Bursaries of £1,000 or £2,500 for exceptional projects and research that benefits the British knitting/knitwear industries.

Annual grant total

In 2015/16 the charity held assets of £963,500 and had an income of £56,000. Grants were made to 12 individuals and totalled £22,500.

Applications

Application forms and information are sent to heads of departments or tutors and students' unions at the start of each academic year, with a closing date for the receipt of completed applications around mid-October. The project or research should benefit the British knitting/knitwear industries and applicants should include a CV and an outline of the project.

Other information

During 2015/16 the committee visited 15 universities and colleges, interviewed 35 candidates and gave 12 bursaries and awards. The annual report states that:

> A grant was made to a National Theatre apprentice in the costume design and make up department to enable him to further his experience in his chosen field. A grant was also given to Cockpit Arts to enable a student to gain valuable experience and mentoring in a commercial environment.

The Gunmakers' Company Charitable Trust

£26,500 (four grants)

Correspondent: John Peter Allen, Secretary, Proof House, 48–50 Commercial Road, London E1 1LP (02074812695; email: clerk@ gunmakers.org.uk; website: www. gunmakers.org.uk)

CC number: 1100227

Eligibility

Individuals wishing to undertake an apprenticeship in the gun trade.

Types of grants

Bursaries of £5,000 per year are provided to support apprenticeships for up to three years. Those receiving grants are also mentored by a trustee and visited in their workplace to monitor progress. The trust aims to provide at least five bursaries each year.

Annual grant total

In 2015/16 the trust had assets of £363,500 and an income of £51,500. Bursaries totalling £26,500 were awarded during the year, to continue supporting four individuals in their training.

Applications

Apply in writing to the correspondent. The trustees meet at least twice a year to consider applications.

The Leathersellers' Company Charitable Fund

See entry on page 14

The Doctor Dorothy Jordan Lloyd Memorial Fund

£10,000

Correspondent: Dr Kerry Senior, UK Leather Federation, Leather Trade House, Kings Park Road, Northampton NN3 6JD (01604 679955; email: info@uklf.org)

CC number: 313933

Eligibility

People under the age of 40 working in the leather industry, studying or doing a research on related subjects, and scientist developing the leather production technology. Grants are available to both UK and overseas students (who are required to be fluent in English and intend to return to work in their home country).

Types of grants

Grants are available for travel overseas to study the leather science and technology or work on related projects. The support is not intended for students in full/part-time courses rather to encourage short and focused visits.

Annual grant total

In 2015/16 the fund had an income of £5,500 and a total expenditure of £11,200. We have estimated the total amount of grants awarded to be around £10,000.

Exclusions

Our research suggests that the fellowship may not be offered to an applicant resident in, or a citizen of, a country which restricts free trade in hides, skins or leather.

Applications

Apply in writing to the correspondent.

Norton Folgate Trust

£198,000 (58 grants)

Correspondent: Vivienne Pocock, Craft and Charities Administrator, Carpenter's Company, Carpenter's Hall, 1 Throgmorton Avenue, London EC2N 2JJ (020 7588 7001 or 020 7382 1667; email: info@carpentersco.com or vivienne@carpentersco.com; website: www.carpentersco.com/education/educational-grants)

CC number: 230990

Eligibility

Students, mainly in secondary or tertiary education, at an institution in the UK who are studying the craft of carpentry, fine woodwork, stonemasonry, historic building conservation or other building craft-related courses.

Types of grants

Grants ranging from £500 to £10,000 can be given to help with school, college or university fees or to supplement existing grants. Support may be available to school pupils towards general educational necessities but most grants are distributed to secondary or tertiary education students, particularly to individuals at the Building Crafts College in Stratford, East London. Some funds may be given towards woodcraft tools.

Annual grant total

In 2015/16 the trust had assets of £7 million and an income of £288,000. Grants totalling £236,000 were made to 66 individuals, of which it appears £198,000 was for educational purposes and £37,500 for social welfare. Grants were broken down as follows:

Craft education	43	£139,000
Other education	15	£59,000
Liverymen, Freemen, retirees and their dependants	8	£37,500
Total	**66**	**£236,000**

Exclusions

Grants are not made retrospectively.

Applications

Application forms are available on the trust's website and have to be submitted by June for the academic year beginning in September. Applicants will be notified of a decision in August.

Students at the Building Crafts College should apply in writing to the following address before May (applicants will be notified of a decision in June): The Bursar, Building Crafts College, Kennard Road, Stratford, London E15 1AH.

People applying for grants for woodcraft tools should use the online application form.

Other information

A few grants are made to individual members of the company for welfare purposes, particularly to older members.

The Printing Charity

£90,000 (76 grants)

Correspondent: James Povey, Trustee, First Floor, Underwood House, 235 Three Bridges Road, Crawley, West Sussex RH10 1LS (01293 542820; email: support@theprintingcharity.org.uk; website: www.theprintingcharity.org.uk)

CC number: 208882

Eligibility

People who have worked for at least three years in the printing profession, graphic arts or allied trades who are in need. A list of eligible trades can be found on the charity's website.

Types of grants

Training grants are given to help with costs associated with:

- Occupational training and related expenses such as travel, buying computers and course books
- Access to training
- Redundancy support
- Apprenticeships
- Learning support/college top-up fees

For more information on educational support given by the charity, see the website.

Annual grant total

In 2016 the charity held assets of £37.7 million and had an income of £1.8 million. Educational bursaries totalled £90,000. The website states that 76 people were supported during the year.

The charity also continued its work through the Future Proposals scheme and its partnership with The Prince's Trust which is aimed at assisting younger people with education and employment. Grants are also given for welfare needs and a great part of the overall charitable expenditure is spent in the provision of specifically sheltered accommodation for older people.

Applications

Application forms and guidelines are available from the charity's website. Further information on the application process can also be received by contacting the correspondent. Assistance is means-tested so applicants should be prepared to make a full declaration of their finances, including state benefits and funding from other charitable sources. Applications can be made by individuals directly or through a welfare agency. The charity advises potential applicants to contact them before submitting an application.

Other information

The Print Futures Awards

In conjunction with partners (British Printing Industries Federation – BPIF, The John Crosfield Foundation, St Bride Foundation and Unite the Union GPM Sector) the charity supports The Print Futures Awards to assist people between the ages of 16 and 30 with costs associated with a relevant training course in printing, publishing or graphic arts. Cash grants of up to £1,500 are awarded.

Individuals between the ages of 16 and 30 who live in the UK may apply to the awards if they: already work in printing, publishing or graphic arts; or intend to study or are already studying for a career in printing, publishing or graphic arts. See the charity's website for more information.

Queen Elizabeth Scholarship Trust Ltd

See entry on page 120

See entry on page 120

Social sciences

The Airey Neave Trust

£50,000

Correspondent: Sophie Butler, PO Box 111, Leominster HR6 6BP (email: aireyneavetrust@gmail.com; website: www.aireyneavetrust.org.uk)

CC number: 297269

Eligibility

People engaged in research projects looking into 'issues related to personal freedom under democratic law against the threat of political violence'. Fellowships must be taken up in the year they are offered.

Types of grants

Fellowships of one or two years are available to cover or contribute to the researcher's salary from his or her regular institution, or to cover the cost of replacement staff, while the fellow is released of their normal duties for the duration of the fellowship.

Annual grant total

In 2015/16 the trust had an income of £21,000 and a total expenditure of £57,000. The total amount given in grants was £50,000.

Exclusions

Financial assistance to refugees is no longer provided.

Applications

Applications should be sent to the trust's email and must include an up to date CV, including ambitions and interests. Candidates should also supply a 500-word summary of the planned research, and a more detailed proposal 'suitable for an expert referee's judgement'. Names and addresses of two referees, including one academic, must also be provided. Shortlisted candidates will be invited to attend an interview with a selection panel.

Applications should be sent by 31 October annually with interviews taking place the following May.

Other information

The trust has stopped funding for refugees in order to focus all of its funds on research grants.

The Barry Amiel and Norman Melburn Trust

£80,500

Correspondent: Millie Burton, Administrator, 34 Claverdale Road, London SW2 2DP (07949716043; email: millie.burton@outlook.com; website: www.amielandmelburn.org.uk)

CC number: 281239

Eligibility

Groups and individuals working to advance public education in the philosophy of Marxism, the history of socialism, and the working class movement.

Types of grants

Grants to individuals and organisations are available for a range of archiving, research, printing, publishing and conference costs.

Previously funded projects have included: the organisation of lectures, discussions, seminars and workshops; research, written work and publications; and the maintenance of libraries and archive material.

There is also funding for one fellowship per year to undertake research outlined by the trust.

Annual grant total

In 2015/16 the trust had assets of £2.5 million, an income of £19,100 and a total expenditure of £102,000. The total amount given in grants was £80,500 and funding was awarded as follows:

- Conferences and seminars – £50,000
- Publications and pamphlets – £11,300
- Annual fellowship – £6,800
- Research and archiving – £9,100
- Annual lecture – £3,500

Exclusions

The trust does not award funds: to subsidise the continuation or running of university/college courses; to cover transport costs to or from conferences; or to subsidise fees/maintenance for undergraduate/postgraduate students.

Applications

Application forms are available to download from the website and must be returned in hard copy via post, and uploaded to the online form. Applications are considered in January and July. Funding bids for £6,000 or more are only considered in January.

The British Institute of Archaeology at Ankara

£92,000 (21 grants)

Correspondent: Simon Bell, 55C Talbot Road, London N6 4QX (020 7969 5204; fax: 020 7969 5401; email: biaa@britac.ac.uk; website: www.biaa.ac.uk)

CC number: 313940

Eligibility

British undergraduates and postgraduates studying the Turkish and Black Sea littoral in academic disciplines within the arts, humanities and social sciences, particularly the archaeology of Turkey. Applicants must be based at a UK university or academic institution.

Scholars from Turkey and the countries surrounding the Black Sea who are studying in the UK can also be supported.

Types of grants

Various grants are available, ranging from £2,000 for a fieldwork trip, to fully funded PhD opportunities and postdoctoral research posts.

Annual grant total

In 2015/16 the institute held assets of £357,000 and had an income of £666,500. A total of 18 research grants and three scholarship funds were awarded to individuals totalling £92,000.

Applications

There are a number of different funding opportunities available, including: project funding; research positions with the British Institute at Ankara (BIAA); academic purpose trips to Turkey; and facilitation support to non-BIAA funded projects. Applications can be made online – refer to the relevant programme for funding calls and deadlines.

Other information

The institute also supports institutions where research is being carried out. In 2015/16 the institute awarded £61,000 to institutions to top up and support individual research grants.

Marc Fitch Fund

£44,000

Correspondent: Christopher Catling, Flat 9, 13 Tavistock Place, LONDON WC1H 9SH (020 7387 6580; email: admin@marcfitchfund.org.uk; website: marcfitchfund.org.uk)

CC number: 313303

Eligibility

Individuals publishing scholarly work in the fields of British and Irish national, regional and local history, archaeology, antiquarian studies, historical geography, the history of art and architecture, heraldry, genealogy and surname studies, archival research, artefact conservation and the broad fields of the heritage, conservation and the historic environment.

Types of grants

Publication grants, research grants, special project grants and journal digitisation – see the website for details.

Annual grant total

In 2016/17 the fund had assets of £7 million and an income of £256,500. Throughout the year the fund awarded £44,000 in grants to individuals for educational purposes.

Exclusions

The following information can be found on the charity's website:

Cut-off date: the fund does not contribute to works principally concerned with recent history (post-1945). **Revised works:** the fund does not support new or revised editions of works already published. **Disciplinary criteria:** the fund does not contribute to scientific and technical research, only work in the humanities and social sciences; fieldwork is also not funded, only the publication of the results of such work.

Applications

Prospective applicants should submit a brief outline of their project by email. If the proposal meets the fund's criteria, the relevant application forms will be provided.

Gilbert Murray Trust – International Studies Committee

£3,500

Correspondent: Richard Alston, Classics Department, Royal Holloway University of London, Egham Hill, Surrey TW20 0EX (07786543925; email: r.alston@rhul.ac.uk; website: www.gilbertmurraytrust.org.uk)

CC number: 212244

Eligibility

People under the age of 25 who are studying, or have studied, international relations (including international law, security, peace, development studies, global governance) at an institution of higher education in the UK. Applicants above the age of 25 could be considered if there are specific reasons for a delay in their education, such as ill health or financial problems.

Types of grants

Grants of up to £1,000 are available towards a specific project relevant to the work and purposes of the United Nations (for example, research-related visits to a specific country/headquarters of an international organisation, or a short course at an institution abroad) which will directly contribute towards the applicant's studies.

Annual grant total

In 2015/16 the charity had an income of £6,500 and a total expenditure of £7,500. The charity also supports organisations. We estimate that around £3,500 was granted to individuals

Exclusions

Grants are not intended to support international affairs students with general educational expenses and needs.

Applications

Applications should be submitted to Dr Peter Wilson. Applications should include a brief CV, a short statement of career intentions, a detailed description of the project with associated costs and sources of additional funding (if required), a reference letter by someone suitable to judge the suitability of the applicant, and reasons for delayed education (if required).

Applications and all the relevant information should be provided in five copies.

Other information

The charity's Classical Committee also offers recurring support and awards for various projects and initiatives which seek to promote the studies of ancient Greek civilisation, culture and language.

Organisations can also be supported.

Society of Antiquaries of London
See entry on page 76

Trades Union Congress Educational Trust
See entry on page 125

Cultural studies

The British Institute for the Study of Iraq (Gertrude Bell Memorial)
See entry on page 30

Turath Scholarship Fund

£5,000

Correspondent: Dr Imran Satia, Trustee, 4 West Park Road, Blackburn BB2 6DG (07825346320; email: scholarship@turath.co.uk; website: www.turath.co.uk/front/turath-scholarship-fund)

CC number: 1138153

Eligibility

To be eligible for a grant you must: be a UK citizen; be between the ages of 18 and 24; preferably hold a degree from a good UK university with at least a 2:1 grading; be committed to studying your chosen discipline for a prolonged period of time; and demonstrate some teaching experience.

Types of grants

Grants are available to individuals hoping to study any aspect of the Islamic Sciences outside their university degree. Grants can be used to pay for training or tuition including fees and travel. After completing the proposed study, individuals are expected to produce a report and go on to teach other in their communities.

Annual grant total

In 2016/17 the fund had both an income and a total expenditure of £10,000. We estimate that around £5,000 was given in grants to individuals.

Applications

Application forms are available from the website and should be returned by email. Shortlisted candidates will have a discussion with the trustees and advisors about their proposal, and will be asked to provide references.

Successful candidates will be informed of the decision one month after the deadline.

Geography

Royal Geographical Society (with the Institute of British Geographers)

£89,000

Correspondent: Grants Office, 1 Kensington Gore, London SW7 2AR (020 7591 3073; email: grants@rgs.org; website: www.rgs.org)

CC number: 208791

Eligibility

People over the age of 16 who are carrying out geographical research and projects. Teachers, undergraduate and postgraduate students, scientists, and non-academics (e.g. independent travellers) are all eligible.

The society has previously stated that its grants programme aims to promote geographical research and a wider understanding of the world and therefore applicants are not required to have a geography degree, work in a geography department or define themselves as a geographer, but must share the society's interest in the world, people and environment.

Note: Some grants are only open to fellows of the society.

Types of grants

The society administers a large number of grants each with separate eligibility criteria and application processes. The awards are broken down into the following categories: Established Researchers; Early Career Researchers; Postgraduate; Undergraduate; Expeditions, Fieldwork and Independent Travel; Teaching. For full details of each award see the society's website.

Support can be given for work both in the UK and overseas in the range of £250 to £30,000.

Annual grant total

In 2016 the society had assets of £17.5 million, an income of £6.5 million and made grants totalling £216,000. Out of that sum, £89,000 was awarded to individuals and consisted of support for Expeditions and Fieldwork (£76,000); Research (£12,000); and Education and Teaching (£1,000).

Exclusions

Grants are not made retrospectively or given for fees/living costs associated with degrees.

Applications

All grant details, guidelines, application forms and specific deadlines can be obtained from the society's website. Generally, the application process takes between three and four months. All candidates are informed about the outcome of their application.

Other information

The society also supports institutions and offers information, advice, resources and training to support anyone planning a fieldwork or scientific expedition.

National charities classified by occupation/parent's occupation

Armed forces

ABF The Soldiers' Charity

£836,000 (1,125 grants)

Correspondent: The Welfare Team, Mountbarrow House, 6–20 Elizabeth Street, London SW1W 9RB (020 7901 8900; fax: 020 7901 8901; email: info@soldierscharity.org; website: www.soldierscharity.org)

CC number: 211645

Eligibility

Members and ex-members of the British Regular Army and the Reserve Army (TA) and their dependants who are in need. Serving TA soldiers must have completed at least one year's satisfactory service, and former TA soldiers should have completed at least three years' satisfactory service.

Types of grants

Funding is given:

- To training colleges helping to retrain soldiers with disabilities and training course fees and essential equipment for individual soldiers
- To support ex-soldiers taking higher education courses to start on new careers after leaving the army
- To help the children of soldiers who have died or have been severely disabled while serving with continuing education

Annual grant total

In 2015/16 the charity had assets of £62.6 million and an income of £22.8 million. Grants totalled £6.6 million, of which £3.4 million was awarded to individuals. The charity's website states that it awards around 4,500 grants to individuals in each year. In this financial year, grants to individuals were given in the form of routine grants totalling £3.3 million, and from the Quick Reaction Fund (QRF) totalling £24,000. There were no grants made for specialist employment consultants (2015: £632,000). It has not been possible to determine how much of the total awarded in individual grants was for education and training. We have estimated a split of 75/25 in favour of social welfare, giving educational awards a total of £836,000.

Exclusions

Grants for legal fees and non-priority debt are not considered.

Applications

The fund does not deal directly with individual cases. Soldiers who are still serving should contact their regimental or corps association, which will then approach the fund on their behalf. Former soldiers should first contact SSAFA Forces Help or The Royal British Legion. Applications are considered at any time, but all are reviewed annually in July.

Enquiries may be made directly to the fund to determine the appropriate corps or regimental association.

Other information

As well as also making grants to individuals for social welfare purposes, ABF makes grants to other charities working to support service and ex-service people. According to the annual report, in 2015/16 there was a focus on the following areas: care for the elderly, mental health and respite care, homelessness, supported housing, education and training for employment and welfare support to the Army Family.

Help for Heroes

£756,500

Correspondent: Grants team, Unit 14 Parker's Close, Downton Business Park, Downton, Salisbury, Wiltshire SP5 3RB (01980 844354; email: grants@helpforheroes.org.uk; website: www.helpforheroes.org.uk)

CC number: 1120920, SC044984

Eligibility

Current and former members of the Armed Forces who have suffered a life-changing injury or illness while serving, or as a result of their service, and their dependants.

Types of grants

Grants towards equipment, facilities or services to assist individuals' rehabilitation. Individuals are supported through the Quick Reaction Fund (QRF). Assistance can be given towards academic and (re)training courses, vocational or employment opportunities and associated needs, such as educational necessities or specialist equipment. In urgent cases, QRF support is aimed to be provided within 72 hours.

Annual grant total

In 2015/16 the charity had assets of £115.9 million and an income of £36.5 million. The annual report for the year provides the following information about the Quick Reaction Fund: 'Between 1 October 2015 and 30 September 2016 we have supported 1,182 cases totalling in excess of £1.44m and in September granted our 10,000th award to individuals.' We estimate that educational grants to individuals totalled around £756,500.

Applications

Candidates are encouraged to contact the team to discuss their needs and the application procedure.

Other information

Help for Heroes provides a wide range of support services, including the H4H Career Recovery service to help individuals with their new futures outside the armed forces. For more information on this or the other services available, visit the website.

Individuals and their families or carers are also welcome to visit one of the 'Support Hubs' to receive further advice and support on a range of welfare issues. For more details and contact information of the recovery centres see the website.

The charity works with the armed forces and other military charities. Funding is also given to individuals for general welfare needs and organisations working for the benefit of members of the armed forces.

Lloyd's Patriotic Fund

£7,500

Correspondent: The Secretary, Lloyd's Patriotic Fund, Lloyd's, One Lime Street, London EC3M 7HA (020 7327 6144; email: communityaffairs@lloyds.com; website: www.lloyds.com/lpf)

CC number: 210173

Eligibility

Children of officers and ex-officers of the Royal Navy, the Army, Royal Marines and Royal Air Force. Preference may be given to schoolchildren with serious family difficulties where the child has to be educated away from home and to people with special educational needs.

Types of grants

Bursaries ranging from around £800 to £1,500 per year are given for school fees.

Annual grant total

In 2015/16 the fund had assets of £3 million and an income of £398,500. Educational grants in the form of bursaries and scholarships totalled £7,500.

Applications

Grants are awarded through The Royal Navy and Royal Marines Children's Fund and The Royal Naval Scholarship Fund. All applications should be made through these organisations.

Other information

The fund works with SSAFA Forces Help and other partners through which funds are administered. Various military organisations are supported, with a particular focus on those helping people who have disabilities or individuals facing poverty, illness and hardship.

Poppyscotland (The Earl Haig Fund Scotland)

Correspondent: Welfare Services, New Haig House, Logie Green Road, Edinburgh EH7 4HQ (0131 557 2782; fax: 0131 557 5819; email: enquiries@poppyscotland.org.uk; website: www.poppyscotland.org.uk)

OSCR number: SC014096

Eligibility

Armed forces veterans in Scotland and their families, who are unemployed or who have a low household income (of less than £22,000 per year). Service leavers who are within 13 weeks of discharge can also apply for support.

Full eligibility criteria are available from the CivvyStreet website (civvystreet.org).

Types of grants

Employment Support Grants of up to £2,000 are given to support vocational training taking place over a period of up to eight weeks. There must be a strong likelihood that the training will lead to a long-term job.

Annual grant total

In 2015/16 the charity had assets of £9.86 million and an income of £4.7 million. We were unable to determine a specific figure for Employment Support Grants based on the information in the annual report and accounts as these appear to be distributed via The Royal British Legion's CivvyStreet programme.

Applications

Applications can be made directly through The Royal British Legion's employability programme CivvyStreet (civvystreet.org). Further information about Employment Support Grants can be obtained from Poppyscotland by calling 0131 550 1568 or emailing GetHelp@poppyscotland.org.uk.

Other information

In 2006 the Earl Haig Fund Scotland launched a new identity – 'Poppyscotland' – and is now generally known by this name.

Poppyscotland offers a wide range of support and advice services for beneficiaries, including in the areas of employment, housing and mental and physical health. It also provides for the general welfare of veterans through its welfare centres in Ayrshire and Inverness, tailored welfare grants and by working with other organisations.

Information on how to access support is available on the website or by contacting Poppyscotland directly by telephone (0131 550 1557) or email (GetHelp@poppyscotland.org.uk). Specialist advice for veterans is also available from the Armed Services Advice Project (ASAP) which is part-funded by Poppyscotland and delivered by Citizens Advice Scotland; to access specialist advice call (0808 800 1007) or visit the ASAP website (adviceasap.org.uk).

The Royal British Legion

Correspondent: Welfare Services, 199 Borough High Street, London SE1 1AA (helpline: 0808 802 8080 (8am-8pm, 7 days a week); email: info@britishlegion.org.uk; website: www.britishlegion.org.uk)

CC number: 219279

Eligibility

Ex-service people and their dependants. The website states that to be eligible you must be:
▶ Of working age
▶ Living in England, Wales, Northern Ireland or Scotland
▶ Undertaking the activities in the UK, and
▶ Unemployed or under-employed and actively seeking work (normally on Jobseeker's Allowance or income-related Employment Support Allowance)

Types of grants

Grants are available to people who are unemployed or under-employed to help them find long-term employment. The website states that grants can be used to:

- Fund skills development courses
- Pay for costs associated with attendance on a course
- Pay for costs associated with a job offer, including work-related clothing; hand tools; equipment; and travel costs

Annual grant total

In 2015/16 the charity had assets of £295.7 million and an income of £151.3 million. We were unable to determine the value of educational grants.

Exclusions

Grants are not made to support higher education courses and courses which do not improve vocational skills.

Applications

Applications can be made through the charity's CivvyStreet website, www. civvystreet.com.

The Royal British Legion Women's Section President's Award Scheme

Correspondent: Welfare Team, The Royal British Legion, 199 Borough High Street, London SE1 1AA (020 3207 2183; email: wswelfare@britishlegion.org.uk; website: www.rblws.org.uk/how-we-help/president-s-award-scheme)

CC number: 219279

Eligibility

Serving or ex-Service personnel, their spouses and dependants who are in need. This includes widows and divorced spouses/partners who have not re-married and are not in another cohabitating relationship.

Dependent children applying for scholarships must be under the age of 21.

Types of grants

The scheme offers:

- Educational scholarships – awards of £1,500 per year (or for a term) for a first degree course towards fees, books, travel costs, living/maintenance expenses and other course-related needs
- Educational grants – of up to £500 towards educational courses or retraining (people training for a new career can receive small grants towards course costs, books and travel expenses)

Annual grant total

In 2015/16 the fund held assets of over £5 million and had an income of £1 million. Total expenditure for the year was £1.3 million but we were unable to establish a grant total. Previous research has indicated that the annual grant total is around £30,000.

Exclusions

Scholarships are not given for postgraduate studies. This scheme is available to non-commissioned ranks only.

Applications

Initial enquiries should be made to the correspondent by telephone or in writing. Applicants will be visited by a welfare team officer who will submit an application form and financial statements. Applications are considered and approved by a grants committee three times a year, generally in January, July and September, the website notes that applications should be returned by the 15th of the month before. Full guidelines, definitions and eligibility criteria can be found online.

Other information

Grants are made through the Women's Section, which is an autonomous organisation within The Royal British Legion, concentrating on the needs of widows and ex-servicewomen and dependent children of ex-Service personnel. It works in close association with the Legion but has its own funds and its own local welfare visitors.

This scheme also helps with the costs of a welfare break. The Royal British Legion and the Women's Section have many grants available for welfare purposes and the charity's website also notes that where it is unable to assist, the welfare team will signpost the applicants to other agencies that may be able to help.

The Royal Caledonian Education Trust

£119,000

Correspondent: Karen Stock, Grants Officer, 121 George Street, Edinburgh EH2 4YN (0131 240 2224; email: grants@rcet.org.uk; website: www.rcet.org.uk)

CC number: 310952

Eligibility

Children of Scottish people who have served or are serving in the armed forces. Priority is given to families who are facing financial difficulties, health problems and other difficult circumstances, as well as individuals who have left school who might be prevented from continuing their studies without financial support. Support may also be given to the children of Scottish people in financial need living in London who are not entitled to parochial relief.

Types of grants

Grants are made for a range of educational purposes, across primary, secondary, tertiary and further education. Examples include: school uniforms; sports equipment; tuition fees for music and arts courses; residential school trips in the UK; school stationery; books; living expenses for a first degree course; and essential course materials or specialist equipment.

The trust also offers advice, guidance and referrals to other sources of support.

Annual grant total

In 2015/16 the trust had assets of £4.6 million and an income of £286,000. The amount of grants given to individuals totalled £119,000.

Exclusions

The trust will not provide funding where the need should be met by the statutory provisions.

Applications

Application forms are available from the trust's website (or can be requested from the correspondent). The grants committee meets in January, March, June and October to consider the applications. The trust's grant policy is also available to download on the website. Any queries can be directed to the Grants Officer: grants@rcet.org.uk.

Other information

In addition to making grants to individuals, the trust also works through its education programme with schools, local authorities, armed forces charities and military communities to support the armed forces children, teachers and families in the school environment, especially in relation to children's emotional well-being. In 2015/16 £119,000 was spent through the education programme.

Army

The Black Watch Association

£16,000

Correspondent: The Trustees, Balhousie Castle, Hay Street, Perth PH1 5HR (01738 623214; email: bwassociation@btconnect.com; website: theblackwatch.co.uk/regimental-association)

OSCR number: SC016423

Eligibility

Serving and retired Black Watch soldiers, their wives, widows and children.

Types of grants

One-off grants, usually ranging from £250 to £500. Grants can be made to schoolchildren, people starting work and students in further/higher education for equipment/instruments, fees, books and maintenance/living expenses.

Annual grant total

In 2016 the charity had assets of £3 million and an income of £288,500. Throughout the year the charity awarded a total of £32,000 in grants to individuals. We estimate that £16,000 of this amount went to individuals for educational purposes.

The charity also awarded £21,500 to organisations.

Exclusions

Our research suggests that no grants are given towards council tax arrears, loans or large debts.

Applications

The website states: 'Financial assistance is given when a report, prepared by SSAFA Forces Help, indicates a genuine need. Any grant given is authorised by an experienced Welfare Committee (who meet monthly) and is then paid to SSAFA Forces Help who administer the expenditure.' The contact details of local SSAFA branches can be found on the SSAFA website (www.ssafa.org.uk). Alternatively, SSAFA's Forcesline telephone service can be contacted from the UK by calling 0800 731 4880.

Royal Artillery Charitable Fund

£31,000

Correspondent: Lt Col Vere Nicoll, Artillery House, Royal Artillery Barracks, Larkhill, Salisbury, Wiltshire SP4 8QT (01980 845698; email: rarhq-racf-raa-gensec@mod.uk; website: www.theraa.co.uk/about/ra-charitable-fund)

CC number: 210202

Eligibility

Current or former members of the Royal Artillery and their dependants who are in need.

Types of grants

The charity makes one-off and recurrent grants to assist with most costs associated with education, for example by providing grants for school fees, school trips, uniforms, and equipment.

Annual grant total

In 2016 the charity had assets of £30.6 million and an income of £1.5 million. We estimate that around £31,000 was awarded in grants for education.

Exclusions

Grants are not given towards income tax, loans, credit card debts, telephone

bills, legal fees or private medical treatment.

Applications

To begin the application process, or for initial enquiries, email rarhq-racf-welfaremailbox@mod.uk.

Other information

Grants are mostly awarded to individuals for relief-in-need purposes.

The fund is the sole corporate trustee of the Royal Artillery Charitable Fund (Permanent Endowment), the Royal Artillery Benevolent Fund, the Royal Artillery Association and the Kelly Holdsworth Artillery Trust.

Royal Air Force

The Royal Air Force Benevolent Fund

£252,000

Correspondent: Welfare Team, 67 Portland Place, London W1B 1AR (0800 169 2942; email: info@rafbf.org.uk; website: www.rafbf.org)

CC number: 1081009

Eligibility

The children (aged 8 to 18) of officers and airmen who have died or were severely disabled while serving in the Royal Air Force. Additionally, help may be considered in those circumstances where the parent dies or becomes severely disabled after leaving the Royal Air Force. Ex-Service personnel who are retraining or in need of educational qualifications so they may enter the job market.

Types of grants

Grants to enable the education and retraining of ex-Service personnel or for their dependants.

Annual grant total

In 2016 the charity held assets of £108.3 million and had an income of £23.3 million. We estimate educational grants amounted to around £252,000.

Exclusions

No grants are given for private medical costs or for legal fees.

Applications

Requests for assistance can be made by contacting the charity. There is an online contact form on the website. Alternatively, assistance can also be obtained through RAFA and SSAFA. The charity runs a free helpline which potential applicants are welcome to call for advice and support on the application process. Applications are considered on a continuous basis.

Other information

The charity provides advice and assistance on a range of issues including benefits, debt advice and relationships. It also can support its beneficiaries with residential and respite care and housing. See the website for more information on the services, support and financial assistance available.

Royal Navy and Marines

Greenwich Hospital

Correspondent: K. Evers, Greenwich Hospital, 1 Farringdon Street, London EC4M 7LG (020 7396 0150; email: enquiries@grenhosp.org.uk; website: www.grenhosp.org.uk)

Eligibility

For bursaries to attend the Royal Hospital School in priority order:
- Children of serving officers and ratings of the Royal Navy, Royal Marines and UK Merchant Navy
- Children of retired officers and ratings of the Royal Navy, Royal Marines and UK Merchant Navy
- Children of certain other seafaring professions

A minimum of three years qualifying seafaring service is required. Note that eligibility does not guarantee that a bursary or a discount will be awarded.

Types of grants

The charity provides bursaries to attend the Royal Hospital School. The awards are only available upon entry and will not be made retrospectively. Some discounts can also be offered to eligible seafarers who are successful in the January entrance examination and at the interview.

The charity also offers funding for tertiary education to first generation Royal Navy seafarers leaving the Royal Hospital School after A-levels.

Annual grant total

Our research indicates that generally around £3,000 is awarded in bursaries.

Applications

Initial application forms can be found on the charity's website or can be requested from the admissions officer. Applications should be submitted before the closing date in December and not before 5 April in the year preceding entry to the school. Awards are usually awarded by January.

Further details are available on the website.

Other information

The charity also provides awards in partnership with other universities:

- University Undergraduate Awards – three annual bursaries of up to £3,000 for a maximum of three years available to former members of the Royal Navy or Royal Marines or the children of current or former members of the Royal Navy or Royal Marines. Applicants must be studying for an undergraduate degree at University of Greenwich, University of Portsmouth, or Newcastle University
- Bursaries to study at the Trinity Laban Conservatoire of Music and Dance – to the children of current or former members of the Royal Navy or Royal Marines for a maximum of four years

The Royal Naval Benevolent Trust

£77,500

Correspondent: The Grants Administrator, Castaway House, 311 Twyford Avenue, Portsmouth PO2 8RN (023 9269 0112; email: rnbt@rnbt.org.uk; website: www.rnbt.org.uk)

CC number: 206243

Eligibility

Members of 'The RNBT Family': serving and former Royal Navy ratings and Royal Marines other ranks, and their dependants, who are in need.

Types of grants

Educational grants are available to schoolchildren and people wishing to get back into employment.

Annual grant total

In 2016/17 the trust had assets of £43.5 million and an income of £5.6 million. Educational grants to individuals totalled £77,500.

Applications

Contact your local Royal Marines or Royal Navy Welfare or local branch of SSAFA or The Royal British Legion. They will arrange a caseworker to visit you to complete an application form.

The Royal Navy and Royal Marines Children's Fund

£443,500

Correspondent: Monique Bateman, Director, Castaway House, 311 Twyford Avenue, Stamshaw, Portsmouth PO2 8RN (023 9263 9534; email: caseworkers@rnrmchildrensfund.org.uk; website: www.rnrmchildrensfund.org)

CC number: 1160182

Eligibility

Dependants of serving and ex-serving members of the Royal Navy, the Royal Marines, the Queen Alexandra's Royal Naval Service or the former Women's Royal Naval Service, who are under the age of 25 and are in need.

Types of grants

One-off and recurrent grants are made to schoolchildren, college students, undergraduates and vocational students where there is a special need. Grants are given towards school fees, the costs of extra tuition and school uniforms, for example.

Annual grant total

In 2016/17 the charity had assets of £10.5 million and an income of £1.2 million. Educational grants totalled at least £443,500. Grants to individuals were broken down as follows:

School fees	£386,000
Clothing and equipment	£243,000
Childminding and respite	£161,500
Children's travel	£64,000
Extra tuition fees	£57,500
Other charitable expenditure	£270

Applications

Apply using a form available from the correspondent or to download from the website. Applications can be submitted directly by the individual or through the individual's school/college, SSAFA, Naval Personal, social services or other third party. The charity can be contacted by telephone and can provide, where possible, assistance with the form's completion. Applications can be made at any time.

The Royal Navy Officer's Charity

£10,000

Correspondent: The Director, 70 Porchester Terrace, Bayswater, London W2 3TP (020 7402 5231; email: rnoc@arno.org.uk; website: www.arno.org.uk)

CC number: 207405

Eligibility

Serving and retired officers of the Naval Service (RN, RM and QARNNS), their spouses, former spouses and dependants who are in need of financial support.

Types of grants

Awards from the RN Scholarship Fund are of up to £500 per term and given for private school fees.

Annual grant total

In 2016 the charity had assets of £15 million and an income of £539,500 million. Grants to individuals totalled £327,500, the vast majority of which was given for social welfare purposes. Scholarships totalled £10,000.

Applications

Contact the Director for further information.

The WRNS Benevolent Trust

£3,100

Correspondent: Roger Collings, Grants Administrator, Castaway House, 311 Twyford Avenue, Portsmouth, Hampshire PO2 8RN (023 9265 5301; fax: 023 9267 9040; email: grantsadmin@wrnsbt.org.uk; website: www.wrnsbt.org.uk)

CC number: 206529

Eligibility

Ex-Wrens and female serving members of the Royal Navy (officers and ratings) who joined the service between 3 September 1939 and 1 November 1993 who are in need.

Types of grants

This charity is essentially a relief-in-need charity which offers grants for educational purposes. These are usually given to former Wrens who are mature students to help with training courses, study costs, computers, books etc.

Annual grant total

In 2016 the trust had assets of £4 million and an income of £454,500. Grants awarded amounted to £276,000, of which £3,100 was awarded for educational purposes.

Exclusions

People who deserted from the service are not eligible.

Applications

Applications can be made directly to the correspondent. Applications can be made directly by the individual or, with their consent, by a relation or friend.

Other information

The trust states the following on its informative website:

> One of our biggest problems is raising awareness; it is surprising how many former Wrens do not even know of our existence. If you ever hear of a former Wren who you think may be having difficulties, do please tell her about us or approach us on her behalf. Many are too proud to ask for help, but we always stress that we are their special charity and one which they may have contributed to

during their time in the Women's Royal Naval Service.

Arts and culture

Equity Charitable Trust

£100,500 (48 grants)

Correspondent: Kaethe Cherney, Plouviez House, 19–20 Hatton Place, London EC1N 8RU (020 7831 1926; email: kaethe@equitycharitabletrust. uk; website: www.equitycharitabletrust. org.uk)

CC number: 328103

Eligibility

Professional performers who have 10 years' adult professional work and are eligible for an Equity card.

Types of grants

Grants to enable retraining or education at recognised colleges or training centres on courses which must lead to a recognised qualification. Grants can be given to assist with some or all of the course costs (depending on the applicant's circumstances) and, in some cases, the trust has assisted simply with the purchase of books or essential materials.

Annual grant total

In 2015/16 the trust had assets of £10.8 million and an income of £419,500. Education and training grants to 48 individuals totalled £100,500. Grants to 108 individuals for welfare purposes totalled £102,000.

Exclusions

The trust cannot help amateur performers, musicians or drama students. Courses for the improvement of performance skills are not eligible for funding, and assistance with short courses, courses overseas or summer schools is not usually considered.

Applications

Applications can be made using a form, which is available to download from the website or on request by emailing kaethe@equitycharitabletrust.org.uk or by calling 020 7831 1926. As part of the application, a CV showing the applicant's experience and evidence of their current financial position are required. The application form should be returned to the trust accompanied by any supporting documents. The trust will make contact with the applicant if there are any questions about their application and, if the application is accepted, it will be considered at the next trustees' meeting.

Other information

The trust also assists professional performers who are suffering hardship through welfare and benevolence grants. As part of the application process for these grants, beneficiaries are able to speak with an experienced money advisor who can help to find other sources of funding, including state benefits.

The Derek Hill Foundation
See entry on page 52

The R. C. Sherriff Rosebriars Trust

£5,000

Correspondent: Peter Allen, Director, Charity House, 5 Quintet, Churchfield Road, Walton on Thames, Surrey KT12 2TZ (01932 229996; email: arts@ rcsherrifftrust.org.uk; website: www. rcsherrifftrust.org.uk)

CC number: 272527

Eligibility

Amateur and professional artists (composers, craftspeople, curators, designers, directors, film-makers, musicians, performers, producers, promoters, theatre technicians, visual artists, writers etc.) in the borough of Elmbridge.

The trust's grant-making guidelines specify that 'managers, education officers, fundraisers, marketing staff, press officers and workshop leaders may apply for individual grants towards training and personal development only'.

Types of grants

Grants and bursaries, usually of up to £500 a year for up to three years, to assist with:

- Professional development and training (including travel grants), such as short courses in specific skills, work placements with other artists or specified periods of travel and/or study
- Research and development for arts projects
- Publication, production or exhibition of a specific piece of work
- Capital items (e.g. equipment)

Applicants are expected to raise around 50% of their total required budget from other sources, apart from in the case of Underwriting Grants, where an event is expected to 'break even' (see the guidelines on the website for more information).

Annual grant total

In 2015 the trust had assets of £3.9 million and an income of £192,500. There were 26 grants to organisations and individuals, which totalled £44,500; we estimate that around £5,000 was given in grants to individuals.

Exclusions

Grants are not given for:

- Arts activities or events taking place outside Elmbridge (except in the case of attendance at training courses/ development opportunities for individuals)
- Activities that are not arts-related
- Fundraising events, e.g. special performances in aid of a local charity
- Activities that provide no potential benefit to the public a
- Activities which have already taken place
- Goods or services that have been bought or ordered before receiving an offer letter
- Commercial ventures which could recoup their costs from profits
- Costs already covered by other sources of funding
- Ongoing overheads
- Higher education courses, long-term vocational training (for example, drama school) or ongoing training programmes (such as piano lessons or regular dance classes)

If successful, applicants can apply once a year for a maximum of three consecutive years, after which they must wait at least one complete financial year (January – December) before applying again.

Applications

Initial contact should be made with the correspondent prior to formal application to ensure that the project meets the eligibility criteria. Application forms are available to download from the trust's website. The trustees meet quarterly to consider applications. Deadlines typically fall in January, April, July and October. Specific dates can be found on the charity's website. The guidelines on the website provide further information on making an application.

Other information

Grants are also made to arts organisations and for various arts projects. Part of the trust's expenditure is allocated for the publication of a magazine *Art Focus* and for organising and managing arts initiatives.

Further guidance, information and advice can also be obtained via phone.

Acting

The Actors' Children's Trust (TACT)

£199,000

Correspondent: Robert Ashby, General Secretary, 58 Bloomsbury Street, London WC1B 3QT (020 7636 7868; email: robert@tactactors.org; website: www.tactactors.org)

CC number: 206809

Eligibility

Children of professional actors. Eligible acting jobs include characters with speaking roles, whether on stage, TV or film, in role play, TIE, corporates or commercials. Grants are usually given to families where the household income is less than £40,000.

Types of grants

The trust provides the following types of support:

- Grants to cover 'school extras' such as music lessons, sports clubs, lunches and uniform
- Grants to support children with special educational needs, disability or long-term illness
- Grants to support young adults at college and in apprenticeship schemes
- Grants for coaching and tuition in the sport and performing arts for talented young people
- Termly grants of £300 to young people at sixth form or studying a 16+ BTEC or similar at college
- Termly awards of £400 to young people at university or on an apprenticeships or training scheme

Annual grant total

In 2016/17 the trust had assets of £88,000 and an income of £356,000. The amount of grants given to individuals totalled £398,500. We estimate that educational grants totalled around £199,000.

Exclusions

The trust is not able to fund presenters or people who have mainly played extra roles. Grants are not usually given for private school fees.

Applications

Details of how to apply for each type of grant are available on the trust's website.

Dance

Dancers' Career Development

Correspondent: Jennifer Curry, Executive Director, Plouviez House, 19–20 Hatton Place, London EC1N 8RU (020 7831 1449; email: admin@thedcd.org.uk)

CC number: 1168958

Eligibility

Professional dancers of any artistic background wishing to make a transition to a new career. Only those who have been a professional dancer for at least eight years and have worked for a minimum of five years in the UK are eligible. Applications can be made up to ten years after stopping work as a professional dancer. There are different categories:

- Independent dancers – must have earned an income as a dancer for a minimum of 16 weeks each year, on average
- Company dancers – must have spent at least five years as a dancer with one of the partner companies (see list on website)
- Medical grounds – dancers who do not fulfil the criteria for independent or company dancers, but have been forced to retire due to illness or injury may also be eligible for support

Types of grants

Grants to help with retraining for a new career after professional dancing. Grants may be given for: course and training fees; equipment; books and materials; living expenses; travel costs; childcare costs. There are also some bursaries for specific fields of training – refer to the website for current information.

Annual grant total

As the charity was only registered in 2016 August, there were no financial accounts available to view at the time of writing (August 2017).

Applications

Potential applicants should first contact the charity for a one-to-one consultation in person or by telephone. Application forms and guidelines are available to download from the charity's website and should be submitted along with: a dance career CV; a personal statement; an application budget; and information on the course or equipment required. Applications should be submitted at least three months prior to starting training.

Other information

The charity was formerly known as The Independent Dancers Resettlement Trust (CC number: 327747). The charity also offers advice, support, coaching, mentoring and workshops.

Music

The Busenhart Morgan-Evans Foundation

£7,000

Correspondent: Bev Sturdey, 455 Woodham Lane, Woodham, Addlestone, Surrey KT15 3QQ (01932 344806; email: BusenhartME@aol.com)

CC number: 1062453

Eligibility

Young musicians at the start of their professional career.

Types of grants

One-off or recurrent grants towards the cost of equipment, instruments, course fees and also music scholarships.

Annual grant total

In 2015/16 the foundation had an income of £10,500 and a total expenditure of £17,000. The amount awarded in grants was £7,000.

Applications

Applications should be made through the individual's educational institution at any time.

Other information

Organisations are also supported for music, health and local community causes.

Writing

Anglo-Swedish Literary Foundation

£20,000

Correspondent: Ann Nilsen, Embassy of Sweden, 11 Montagu Place, London W1H 2AL (02079176465; website: www.swedenabroad.com/en-GB/Embassies/London/Contact/Anglo-Swedish-Literary-Foundation)

CC number: 230622

Eligibility

Individuals connected to studies of Swedish language and literature, translation work and research. The foundation aims develop the 'cultural intercourse between Sweden and the British Islands through the promotion and diffusion of knowledge and appreciation of Swedish culture in the British Islands'.

Types of grants

Grants are made for translation, research, and writing purposes. A grant is also available for books for students studying Swedish at university.

Annual grant total

In 2015/16 the foundation had an income of £16,500 and a total expenditure of £39,000. We estimate that the total amount awarded in grants to individuals was £20,000.

Applications

Apply in writing to the correspondent. Applicants should outline their project or activity, state funding required and give details of any other funding applied to/secured. Applications must be received by 1 May or 1 November.

Other information

The foundation also awards £2,000 every three years through the Bernard Shaw Translation Prize, for Swedish to English translation of a book which is to be published for the first time by a UK publisher. Awards are also made to SELTA, which is another organisation representing Swedish to English translators.

Business, financial services and insurance

The Bankers Benevolent Fund (The Bank Workers Charity)

£155,500

Correspondent: The Client Advisor, Salisbury House, Finsbury Circus, London EC2M 5QQ (0800 023 4834 (helpline: 9am to 5pm, Monday to Friday); email: info@bwcharity.org.uk; website: www.bwcharity.org.uk)

CC number: 313080

Eligibility

Children of current and former bank employees in the UK, who are in need.

Types of grants

One-off and recurrent grants for fees and other educational expenses.

Annual grant total

In 2015/16 the charity had assets of £46.7 million and an income of £1.9 million. Cash grants, all of which were paid to individuals, totalled £719,500. A breakdown of grants distributed according to purpose was not available; however, in previous years they have been awarded in three categories –

child education, families and retirees. Based on allocations in the most recent year for which a breakdown was available (2013/14), we estimate that educational grants totalled around £155,500.

Exclusions

People who have worked in the insurance or stockbroking industries are generally not eligible for support.

Applications

Contact the charity via its helpline or by using the contact form on the website to find out more about available support.

Other information

The charity provides a wide range of non-financial assistance in the form of information, advice and expert assistance, in areas such as money, mental and physical health, relationships and employment.

The George Drexler Foundation

£89,000

Correspondent: Nicola Extance-Vaughan, Correspondent, 35–43 Lincolns Inn Fields, London WC2A 3PE (020 7869 6086; email: info@georgedrexler.org.uk; website: www.georgedrexler.org.uk)

CC number: 313278

Eligibility

UK citizens who have a direct (personal or family) link with commerce – candidates (or their parents or grandparents) must have worked in or owned a commercial business. Our research suggests that this does not include professional people, such as doctors, lawyers, dentists, architects or accountants. Selected medical schools and schools of music apply by invitation only.

Preference is given to can be given to particularly gifted or talented students who are in need of financial support. Schoolchildren with serious family difficulties so that the child has to be educated away from home and people with special educational needs may also be favoured.

Types of grants

Bursaries of £500 to £1,000 to support a recognised educational course in the UK. Awards can be made to support individuals in full-time undergraduate or postgraduate education. The foundation seeks to 'enrich the educational experiences of younger people' and the trustees bear in mind the founder's expressed desire to benefit medical research and education.

Annual grant total

In 2015/16 the foundation had assets of nearly £6.6 million and an income of £248,500. Educational grants totalled £204,000 consisting of £89,000 given to individuals and £115,000 given to The Royal College of Surgeons of England for educational facilities and tutors.

Exclusions

The foundation will not fund medical electives, volunteering, study abroad or gap year projects.

Applications

The foundation accepts applications between early December and March. Applications must be submitted using an online system on the foundation's website. Outside these dates, appeals are not accepted or processed. Successful and unsuccessful applicants are notified of outcome by letter/email in June.

Alfred Foster Settlement

£11,500 (five grants)

Correspondent: Zedra Trust Company (UK) Ltd, Trustee, ZEDRA UK Trusts, Osborne Court, Gadbrook Park, Rudheath, Northwich CW9 7UE (01606 313118; email: charities@zedra.com)

CC number: 229576

Eligibility

Current and former employees of banks and their dependants who are in need. Applying students should be aged less than 28 years.

Types of grants

One-off grants of £250 to £1,000, for example, to help with university fees, books, travel costs and living expenses while in further education. Support may also be given to help with the education of children, although the general policy is to support people in higher education.

Annual grant total

In 2015/16 the charity had assets of £866,500, an income of £37,000 and awarded over £23,500 in 11 grants. A detailed breakdown was not given; therefore we estimate that about £11,500 was given in educational awards.

Applications

Applications may be made in writing to the correspondent. They can be submitted directly by the individual or through the school/college or educational welfare agency.

Other information

The charity also makes grants to individuals for welfare purposes.

The Ruby and Will George Trust

£57,500

Correspondent: Damien Slattery, 125 Cloverfield, West Allotment, Newcastle upon Tyne NE27 0BE (0191 266 4527; email: admin@rwgt.co.uk; website: www.rwgt.co.uk)

CC number: 264042

Eligibility

The dependants of people in need who have been or who are employed in commerce. A commerce connection can either come directly from you or it can come from one or more of the following:

- Your husband/wife
- Your widow/widower
- Your mother/father
- Your grandmother/grandfather
- Your aunt/uncle

Types of grants

One-off and recurrent grants of up to £2,000 towards maintenance and fees, mainly for those in secondary or further education. Grants relating to fees are usually paid directly to the educational establishment. Occasionally, assistance with maintenance, books and basic travel expenses will be awarded.

Annual grant total

In 2015/16 the trust had assets of £3.5 million and an income of £136,500. A total of 47 grants were made to individuals during the year, amounting to £76,500. The annual report and accounts state that: 'The vast majority of the income generated by the trust's assets is paid out by means of either one-off or continuing grants, these being predominantly made to those in either secondary or further education.' With this in mind, we estimate that grants for educational purposes totalled around £57,500.

Applications

Applications can be made through the trust's website. Applicants will need to provide a brief explanation of their commerce connection and a recent payslip or a letter from your employer.

The Insurance Charities

£500,000

Correspondent: Annali-Joy Thornicroft, 20 Aldermanbury, London EC2V 7HY (020 7606 3763; fax: 020 7600 1170; email: info@theinsurancecharities.org.uk; website: www.theinsurancecharities.org.uk)

CC number: 206860

Eligibility

To be eligible, applicants must:

1) Be a current or past insurance employee:
- With at least five years' work in insurance within the last ten years
- With less than five years' insurance work, but where insurance has made up the majority of your career to date
- With at least five years' experience in insurance immediately prior to retirement
- In receipt of a pension or deferred pension from an insurance employer in respect of at least five years' service

2) Be a dependant of a current or former insurance employee.

3) Be currently or previously employed by insurance service in the UK or Irish insurance industries.

4) Have restricted financial means in terms of income and capital.

5) Have suffered an element of misfortune.

Types of grants

One-off grants are available to current and former insurance employees and their dependants wishing to start or continue education.

Annual grant total

In 2015/16 the charity had assets of £33 million and an income of £3.8 million. We estimate the charity awarded £500,000 in grants for education during the year.

Applications

In the first instance, an initial application form is available to complete and submit online. From this, the charity may request more information or arrange a home visit with a Welfare Advisor. The Advisor will discuss your financial situation with you in detail and may suggest changes to your income and expenditure habits. After this meeting, the Grants Committee will advise you of their decision.

Other information

The charity also makes grants for relief-in-need purposes, and offers a money and support advice service.

The Royal Pinner School Foundation

£414,500 (163 grants)

Correspondent: David Crawford, Company Secretary, 110 Old Brompton Road, South Kensington, London SW7 3RB (020 7373 6168; email: admin@royalpinner.co.uk; website: www.royalpinner.co.uk)

CC number: 1128414

Eligibility

Children of commercial travellers, travelling sales and technical representatives and manufacturer's agents, where the family has experienced adversity or hardship. Preference is given to individuals under the age of 25 and those whose parents are deceased (over a third of the trust's beneficiaries have lost a parent or have a parent with a long-term illness).

Types of grants

Grants are available to individuals at any state, private day or boarding school, college or university. Support is given towards general educational needs, maintenance costs, clothing, equipment, books, travel expenses in the UK and overseas, undertaking activities in arts and music, also assistance to people starting career/entering a profession, trade or calling. In some cases, grants are one-off and only needed for a short-term period; in other cases, support is offered over a long period of time, reviewed on an annual basis. The foundation does not select on an academic basis, and many beneficiaries have special educational needs.

Annual grant total

In 2016/17 the foundation had assets of £5.4 million and an income of £756,500. A total of almost £414,500 was awarded in 171 grants to individuals, broken down as follows:

Children at day and boarding schools	85	£264,500
Students at universities and colleges of further and higher education	49	£91,000
Special education needs, dance, drama, travel and clothing grants	37	£59,000

Exclusions

The foundation does not normally provide loans or support part-time education.

Applications

Apply in writing to the correspondent. The foundation may arrange a home visit as part of the assessment process. The grants committee meets about five times a year.

Other information

Note that no applications can be considered except those applying for the sons and daughters of travelling sales representatives or manufacturer's agents.

The foundation also offers pastoral support through home visits and other contact with the families it supports.

Scottish Chartered Accountants' Benevolent Association

£64,000

Correspondent: Caroline Christie, PO Box 28843, Edinburgh EH14 9BY (07722 932120; email: admin@scaba.org.uk; website: www.icas.com/our-charitable-work/scaba-scottish-chartered-accountants-benevolent-association)

OSCR number: SC008365

Eligibility
The dependants of members of the Institute of Chartered Accountants of Scotland who are in financial need.

Types of grants
One-off grants are given for a variety of needs. Past grants have been given for school fees, maintenance expenses and retraining.

Annual grant total
In 2016 the association had assets of £2.1 million and an income of £139,000. Grants totalled £128,500. We estimate that around £64,000 was made in educational grants to individuals.

Applications
An initial letter or telephone call should be made to the correspondent.

Education and training

The Cutler Trust

£4,500

Correspondent: Carl Hanser, Grants Caseworker, Teacher Support Network, 40A Drayton Park, London N5 1EW (020 7697 2772; email: grantscaseworker@edsupport.org.uk)

CC number: 279271

Eligibility
Young people between the ages of 16 and 25 who are on low income and whose one or both parents are current or former teachers of the Inner or Greater London Area, which includes City of London, Camden, Enfield, Greenwich, Hackney, Hammersmith and Fulham, Islington, Kensington and Chelsea, Lambeth, Lewisham, Southwark, Tower Hamlets, Wandsworth and Westminster. Preference is given to applicants whose one or both parents are deceased.

Types of grants
Small grants or bursaries towards continuing education or undertaking apprenticeships and support for educational necessities, including books, clothing, equipment and tools or instruments to people in training and those entering a profession/trade. Travel expenses are also covered.

Annual grant total
In 2016 the trust had an income of £1,900 and a total expenditure of £4,500. We have estimated that about £4,500 was given in grants to individuals.

Applications
Applications should be made by registering on the Teacher Support website and following the online procedure. Alternatively, a form can be downloaded from the website and emailed however this may delay the process. Candidates are required to provide details of their financial circumstances and evidence of parents' employment in the specified area.

Applications are usually invited from the beginning of July to the end of August, but see the website for the latest updates.

Other information
Teacher Support Network and Recourse award scholarships on behalf of the Cutler Trust.

IAPS Charitable Trust
See entry on page 27

The Lloyd Foundation
See entry on page 11

NASUWT (The Teachers' Union) Benevolent Fund

£132,500

Correspondent: Legal and Casework Team, NASUWT, Hillscourt Education Centre, Rose Hill, Rednal, Birmingham B45 8RS (0121 453 6150 (8.30am - 5.30pm); email: legalandcasework@mail.nasuwt.org.uk; website: www.nasuwt.org.uk)

CC number: 285793

Eligibility
Members, former members and the dependants of members and former members and dependants of deceased members of NASUWT, The Teachers' Union.

Types of grants
Grants of £200 for schoolchildren aged 16 and under and £250 for those 17 and over.

Annual grant total
In 2016 the fund had assets of £2.2 million and an income of £406,500.

A total of £264,500 was given awarded to 647 individuals for both educational and welfare purposes.

We estimate that around £132,500 was given to individuals for educational purposes.

Exclusions
No support is given for private school fees, education courses, repayments of student loans or to assist students with general living expenses.

Applications
All applications must be submitted on behalf of the member by a Benevolence Visitor or another appropriate official of the Union. Applicants must contact their Local Association Secretary to make arrangements for a benevolence visitor to visit and complete the application form. Applicants must also supply information regarding household income and expenditure.

Other information
The fund also supports individuals in the form of interest-free loans and money advice.

Environment and animals

The British Ornithologists' Union

£20,000 (11 grants)

Correspondent: The British Ornithologists' Union, 3 Crowtree Cottages, Straight Drove, Farcet, Peterborough PE7 3DL (01733 844820; email: bou@bou.org.uk; website: www.bou.org.uk)

CC number: 249877

Eligibility
Small Research Grant eligibility
- You must be a British Ornithology Union member
- The applicant must be the principal investigator
- The research must be of high scientific quality, interesting, innovative, and have a potentially high impact
- The project has a clearly justified budget, and is feasible in terms of time and resources allocated
- The amount applied for must make up all or a substantial amount of the funds allocated

Career Development Bursary eligibility
- You must be a British Ornithology Union Early Career Researcher (BOU ECR)

- You must have completed a first or higher degree within the last two years
- The work must not be funded already, however, it may be linked to existing programmes
- The work must take place in a third party institute and be supervised by someone from that institute
- The work must be carried out away from your home institute

Types of grants

There are two types of funding available:

Small Research Grants: awards of up to £2,000 are available to support small projects outright, or to part-fund medium sized projects. The closing date for applications is usually the end of November and the award is made in March the following year. Check the website before applying as these dates may change.

Career Development Bursary: awards of up to £2,500 are available to support short-term research positions for early career ornithologists, usually between a first and higher degree programme, or immediately after completion of a higher degree programme. Applications must be submitted by 30 November each year for award payment in March.

Annual grant total

In 2015/16 the charity had assets of £1.1 million and an income of £196,000. The total amount awarded in grants and bursaries was £20,000 to 11 individuals.

Exclusions

The following are ineligible for funding:

Small Research Grants

- Non-BOU members
- Organisations
- Site-based surveys and species inventories
- Studies of a species at a specific site with no wider scientific aim
- Descriptive studies
- Baseline studies or preliminary studies for setting up long-term monitoring schemes
- Conservation implementation, education, outreach, or awareness raising
- Salaries and course fees
- Attendances at conferences
- Publications
- Projects already commenced before the application deadline

Career Development Grants

- Projects that form part of a degree programme
- Expeditions
- Applicants employed through other funding sources
- Programmes already funded
- Projects within the applicant's home institute

Applications

Small research grants should be applied for via email. Career development bursary application forms are available to download from the website.

British Veterinary Nursing Association

£3,000

Correspondent: The Bursary Administrator, 79 Greenway Business Centre, Harlow Business Park, Harlow, Essex CM19 5QE (01279 408644; email: bvna@bvna.co.uk; website: www.bvna.org.uk/members/bursaries)

Eligibility

People undertaking education and training in veterinary nursing and veterinary nurses seeking to develop their professional skills. Applicants must be members of the association.

Types of grants

The association administers a number of bursary schemes, further details of which can be found on the website. Current schemes include:

- **BVNA Educational Bursary:** up to £500 for veterinary nurses or students towards training and education
- **VN Times Student Bursary:** up to £500 for student veterinary nurses towards training and education
- **The Kennel Club Charitable Trust Bursary:** up to £3,000 towards the costs of veterinary nurse training
- **The Kennel Club Charitable Trust Degree Bursary:** up to £3,000 for one degree student, distributed over three years, towards training costs
- **RCVS Knowledge Grants and Awards:** grants for evidence based veterinary medicine research
- **Petsavers Student Research Projects:** funding for clinical research into conditions that affect small animals that are kept as pets

Annual grant total

In 2016 the charity had assets of £538,500 and an income of £663,000. There are currently six grant-making programmes with funding from £500 to £3,000 available towards educational costs.

Applications

Full details, guidelines, and application forms for the varying programmes are available at the charity's website.

The Dairy Crest and National Farmers' Union Scholarship Fund

£15,000

Correspondent: Catherine Booth, Administrator, Higher Moorlake Cottage, Moorlake, Crediton, Devon EX17 5EL (01363 776623; fax: 01363 774992; email: aba@adelabooth.co.uk)

CC number: 306598

Eligibility

Children of farmers or farm workers, ex-farmers, smallholders and ex-smallholders in Cornwall, Devon, Dorset and Somerset who are studying a dairy-related topic at tertiary level or equivalent and intend to follow a career in this field.

Types of grants

Scholarships in the range from £200 to £2,000 can be provided to people studying dairy-related topics. Support is given for books, fees, equipment, maintenance/living expenses, travel/study costs and research.

Annual grant total

In 2015/16 the charity had an income of £8,900 and a total expenditure of £15,100. The charity distributes £15,000 annually to individuals.

Applications

Application forms can be found on the AgriFood Charities Partnership website at www.afcp.co.uk or requested from the correspondent. Applications should be submitted by 12 August each year. Eligible applicants will be invited for an interview.

Forest Industries Education and Provident Fund

£600

Correspondent: Edward Mills, 5 Beech Court, Birkrigg Park, Ulverston, Cumbria LA12 0UH (07875 248115; email: info@edwardmills.co.uk; website: www.confor.org.uk/resources/education-provident-fund)

CC number: 1061322

Eligibility

Members of the Forestry and Timber Association (or Confor) and their dependants who are in need. Members must have been involved with the association for at least one year.

Types of grants

One-off grants of up to £750 are made towards education, training or professional development in the field of forestry. Support is also given for educational trips and activities (for example, conferences).

Annual grant total

In 2015 the fund had an income of £6,900 and a total expenditure of £1,300. We estimate that educational grants totalled around £600.

Exclusions

Retrospective funding is not given.

Applications

Application forms are available from the fund's website or can be requested from the correspondent.

Other information

Anyone can join Confor who has an interest in trees, woodlands or timber industry. Grants are also made for welfare purposes.

The fund's website also directs beneficiaries to other potential sources of help: The Institute of Chartered Foresters' Educational and Scientific Trust and The Royal Forestry Society.

Gardeners' Royal Benevolent Society (Perennial)

£128,000

Correspondent: Sheila Thomson, Director of Services, 115–117 Kingston Road, Leatherhead, Surrey KT22 7SU (0800 093 8510; email: info@perennial. org.uk; website: www.perennial.org.uk)

CC number: 1155156, SC040180

Eligibility

Horticulturalists or those training to become one, who are experiencing hardship. The dependent children of horticulturalists who are in full-time education. Eligible beneficiaries include employed, self-employed or retired gardeners and horticulturalists.

Types of grants

The charity offers one-off grants and ongoing bursaries for educational activities, training or re-training after a career change. Education is understood in its broad sense and may include training of horticulturalists, professional development needs or child schooling needs, including extra-curricular activities or after-school clubs to allow parents undertake full-time work.

The following support is available:

▶ **The Lioni Training Fund** – helps horticulture students and 'offers a range of training initiatives available to those who are in need of financial support unavailable from any other statutory source'

▶ **'Sons and Daughters' bursaries** – maximum of £1,500 per year to full-time horticultural students under the age of 40 who are themselves children of horticulturalists

▶ **Hardship bursaries** – one-off grants of up to £1,000 to horticultural students experiencing exceptional, unforeseen hardship

▶ Support for long-term career horticulturalists who find themselves in hardship and are looking to regain satisfactory employment within the industry or elsewhere following adverse circumstance, such as an accident or ill health

▶ Grants are also available for general education for the dependent children of horticulturalists. The regional caseworker should be contacted in the first instance

Annual grant total

In 2015/16 the charity had an income of The amount of grants given to individuals totalled £256,000. We therefore estimate that educational grants to individuals totalled around £128,000.

Applications

Applicants are advised to check the website for the application advice relating to separate schemes. Individuals are encouraged to get in touch with the charity to discuss their eligibility and support available.

Other information

The charity's website notes: 'We provide free and confidential advice, support and financial assistance to people of all ages working in, or retired from horticulture.'

RSABI (Royal Scottish Agricultural Benevolent Institution)

£1,000

Correspondent: The Welfare Team, The Rural Centre, West Mains, Newbridge, Midlothian EH28 8LT (0300 111 4166; email: rsabi@rsabi.org.uk; website: www.rsabi.org.uk)

OSCR number: SC009828

Eligibility

People who have been engaged for at least ten years, full-time in a land-based occupation in Scotland, and their dependants. Applicants should be either retired or unable to work, on a low income (RSABI does not include non-means-tested disability benefits when calculating qualifying income) and have limited savings (£12,000 for a single applicant, £16,000 for couples) or be facing a crisis due to ill health, accident or bereavement, for example.

Qualifying occupations include: agriculture, aquaculture, crofting, forestry, fish farming, gamekeeping, horticulture, rural estate work and other jobs that depend on the provision of services directly to these industries.

Types of grants

Occasional, one-off grants towards skills training or accreditation, where it will help address the hardship.

Annual grant total

In 2016/17 the charity had assets of £11 million and an income of £867,000. We estimate the charity awarded around £1,000 in grants for education.

Exclusions

Grants are not made to help with:

▶ Business expenses
▶ Repayment of loans, overdrafts or credit facilities
▶ Setting up any debt arrangement

Applications

Preliminary application forms are available from the correspondent or can be downloaded from the website. They can be submitted directly by the individual or through a third party (such as a social worker or Citizens Advice) and are considered at any time. The charity's website states:

> We will let you know as soon as possible after receiving the Form whether or not we may be able to help you. If we can, one of our Welfare Officers will arrange to visit at a suitable time and will help you to complete our formal Application for Assistance Form and discuss how RSABI may best be able to help.

Candidates are also encouraged to contact the charity to discuss their application.

Other information

The charity mainly awards grants to individuals for welfare purposes on a recurrent basis.

RSABI also offers advice on benefits and support from other organisations; provides guidance through key life events such as redundancy; and offer home visits by welfare officers to provide ongoing support and friendship. The charity also manages a confidential listening and support advice line for Scotland's land based and farming community. Call GATEPOST on 0300 111 4166 Monday to Friday, 9 am to 5 pm.

Hospitality and retail

The Andy Gunn Foundation

£1,500

Correspondent: Wendy Gunn, Greenwood Accountancy, 5–7 Pellew Arcade, Teign Street, Teignmouth TQ14 8EB (01626 776543; email: chairman@andygunnfoundation.co.uk; website: www.andygunnfoundation.co.uk)

CC number: 1162439

Eligibility

People of any age seeking a career in hospitality and related industries in Devon.

Types of grants

Small, one-off grants for training and education, or in work support, for the hospitality industry. Grants can be used towards books, equipment, clothing, travel etc.

Annual grant total

In 2016 the charity had assets of £16,000 and an income of £3,000. The charity awarded £1,500 in training grants for those wishing to enter hospitality.

Applications

Initial applications can be made using the online form or by email.

Other information

The charity was started in memory of Andy Gunn, a young man who was passionate about his role in the hospitality industry. It aims to help others discover their passion and allow them to achieve their goals in the industry.

The Book Trade Charity

£18,200 (29 grants)

Correspondent: David Hicks, Chief Executive, The Foyle Centre, The Retreat, Abbots Road, Kings Langley, Hertfordshire WD4 8LT (01923 263128 or 01329848731; fax: 01923 270732; email: david@btbs.org or info@booktradecharity.org; website: www.booktradecharity.org)

CC number: 1128129

Eligibility

People in need who have worked in the book trade in the UK for at least one year (normally publishing/distribution/book-selling), and their dependants.

Types of grants

Grants are available to help people access and regain employment. This could be support with re-training after redundancy or assistance with an e-learning course. Funding is also provided to support careers guidance.

The charity also supports entry into the book trade by covering interview costs such as travel and accommodation, primarily for people under 30. Support is also provided to younger people undertaking education and training courses which will lead to a career in the industry. Internships in the book trade are also supported.

Annual grant total

In 2016 the charity had assets of £9.6 million and an income of £3.8 million. Educational grants to individuals totalled £18,200.

Applications

Application forms are available to download from the charity's website.

The Fashion and Textile Children's Trust
See entry on page 108

Information and commu-nication

The Chartered Institute of Journalists Orphan Fund

£41,000 (four grants)

Correspondent: Dominic Cooper, Trustee, Institute of Journalists, 2 Dock Offices, Surrey Quays Road, London SE16 2XU (020 7252 1187; email: memberservices@cioj.co.uk)

CC number: 208176

Eligibility

Orphaned children of institute members who are in need, aged between 5 and 22 and in full-time education.

Types of grants

Grants are given to schoolchildren towards the cost of school clothing, books, instruments, educational outings and school fees. Grants are also given to students who are in further or higher education towards the cost of books, help with fees/living expenses and study or travel abroad.

Annual grant total

In 2016 the fund held assets of £2.6 million and had an income of £104,000. The grants to individuals totalled £41,000.

Applications

Application forms can be found on the Chartered Institute of Journalists website, which administer the fund. Applications should be submitted in writing by the child's surviving parent or another third party and are considered quarterly.

The Grace Wyndham Goldie (BBC) Trust Fund

£25,500 (13 grants)

Correspondent: Cheryl Miles, Secretary, BBC, Room M1017, Broadcasting House, Cardiff CF5 2YQ (029 2032 2000; website: www.bbc.co.uk/charityappeals/about/grants/grace-wyndham-goldie)

CC number: 212146

Eligibility

Individuals currently or previously engaged in broadcasting and their dependants.

Types of grants

One-off grants are given to help with educational costs such as school or college fees, travel expenses, school uniforms, books and equipment, living expenses or to supplement existing educational awards.

Annual grant total

In 2016 the charity had assets of £1.5 million and an income of £60,000. The charity made 13 educational grants, totalling £25,500. A further £2,500 was awarded in two grants for welfare purposes.

Exclusions

The charity cannot provide continued support over a number of years.

Applications

Application forms are available to download from the fund's page on the BBC website. Applicants are asked to provide full information about the circumstances supporting their application. All applications are considered in confidence. Completed forms should be returned to: Trustees, Grace Wyndham Goldie (BBC) Trust Fund, BBC Pension and Benefits Centre, Broadcasting House, Cardiff CF5 2YQ.

The Walter Hazell Charitable and Educational Trust Fund

£9,000

Correspondent: Rodney Dunkley, Trustee, 20 Aviemore Gardens, Northampton NN4 9XJ (01604 765925; email: roddunkley@yahoo.co.uk)

CC number: 1059707

Eligibility
Employees and past employees of the printing trade in Buckinghamshire and Berkshire. Spouses, widows, widowers and children and any other financial dependants can also be supported.

Types of grants
One-off and recurrent grants are given to further/higher education students towards the cost of books, necessities, equipment/instruments or other course-related expenses.

Annual grant total
In 2015/16 the fund had an income of £13,900 and an unusually high expenditure of £119,500. Based on expenditure in previous years, we estimate that grants to individuals totalled around £9,000.

Exclusions
According to our research, grants are not made towards the course fees.

Applications
Apply in writing to the correspondent.

Other information
This fund also awards Christmas payments to ex-employee pensioners of BPC Hazells.

The Printing Charity
See entry on page 90

Legal professions

The Barristers' Benevolent Association

£78,000 (15 grants)

Correspondent: Susan Eldridge, 14 Gray's Inn Square, London WC1R 5JP (020 7242 4761; fax: 020 7831 5366; email: susan@the-bba.com; website: www.the-bba.com)

CC number: 1106768

Eligibility
Past or present practising members of the Bar in England and Wales, and their dependants, who are in need.

Types of grants
Grants or loans are given to schoolchildren towards books, educational outings, maintenance or school uniforms or clothing; students in further/higher education for help with books, fees and living expenses. For mature students, grants are made for books, travel, fees or childcare. For people starting work, grants are for books, equipment, clothing and travel. Loans are also made.

Annual grant total
In 2015 the charity had assets of £10.8 million and an income of £813,500. A total of £156,000 was awarded in grants to individuals, £78,000 of this was for educational purposes.

Exclusions
Help is not given to pupils or students of the Bar, and contributions cannot be made towards school fees.

Applications
Application forms are available to download from the website.

The Incorporated Benevolent Association of the Chartered Institute of Patent Attorneys

£19,000

Correspondent: Derek Chandler, 11 Rotherwick Road, London, NW 11 7DG (020 8455 3822)

CC number: 219666

Eligibility
British members and former members of the Chartered Institute of Patent Attorneys, and their dependants.

Types of grants
One-off and recurrent grants or loans according to need to assist with general educational purchases.

Annual grant total
In 2015/16 the charity had assets of £917,000 and an income of £58,000. We estimate the charity awarded £19,000 in grants for education.

Applications
Applications should be sent to the correspondent, detailing financial need and what the grant will be used for. Applications are considered at all times of the year.

Other information
The charity also provides welfare grants for current and former patent attorneys and their dependants.

Manufacturing

The Fashion and Textile Children's Trust

£118,500

Correspondent: Anna Pangbourne, Director, Victoria Charity Centre, 11 Belgrave Road, London SW1V 1RB (0300 123 9002; email: grants@ftct.org.uk; website: www.ftct.org.uk)

CC number: 257136

Eligibility
Children and young people under 18 years old whose parents or full-time carer work or have worked in the UK fashion and textile retailing and manufacturing industry for at least three years (within the last nine years).

Types of grants
Grants are given to support the day-to-day and additional educational needs of children, such as school travel costs, essential study equipment, school uniform, PE kits, learning support, sensory toys and speech therapy. Contributions towards school fees or private tutors can be considered where there is a strong case why the child's needs cannot be met by the state system.*

*The website defines need as 'medical, mental health or complex educational needs'.

Annual grant total
In 2015/16 the trust had assets of £8.25 million and an income of £380,500. Grants were made totalling £174,000, of which £118,500 was awarded to individuals for educational purposes. All educational grants were paid directly to organisations on behalf of individuals.

Exclusions
Funding cannot be given for childcare.

Applications
In the first instance, contact the trust by telephone or by using the online enquiry form to discuss your child's needs. If the trust feels that it may be able to assist, an application form will be sent to you by post or email. Completed forms must be returned to the trust along with photocopies of three more documents:
1. a copy of your P45 or recent payslip;
2. a copy of your P60 or a letter from

your employer confirming the length of your employment; 3. photocopies of a Child Benefit letter or a recent bank statement showing payment into your account. The trust cannot process applications without all of this supporting documentation. Applications for amounts over £750 require additional evidence, detailed on the website.

Other information

Grants are also made for purposes relating to social welfare.

Mariners

The Marine Society and Sea Cadets

£922,000

Correspondent: Mark Hallam, Director of Finance, 202 Lambeth Road, London SE1 7JW (020 7654 7000; email: info@ms-sc.org; website: www.marine-society.org/91-funding)

CC number: 313013/SC037808

Eligibility

Professional seafarers, active or retired, serving in the Royal Navy, the British Merchant Navy or fishing fleets or any other maritime career persons who are serving in the navies, merchant navies or fishing fleets, members of the Sea Cadet Corps, and any other young people considering a maritime career.

Types of grants

The charity administers various grant schemes for scholarships to support professional development and can provide interest-free loans. Full information on the schemes available can be found on the website.

Annual grant total

In 2015/16 the charity had assets of £27.1 million and an income of £15.7 million. Grants were made totalling over £2 million, of which £922,000 was awarded to individuals and £1.1 million to organisations.

The annual accounts for the year state that 'individual grants given are small and not material within the overall total'.

Exclusions

The charity does not make recurrent grants.

Applications

Application forms for the various schemes administered by the society are available from the website.

Other information

Grants are also made to sea cadet units and support can be given to 'nautical or

other schools or training establishments which are charities or to other organisations established for charitable purposes'. Additionally, grants are provided to volunteers to allow upkeep or purchase of uniforms on promotion or for wear and tear during the year.

The Royal Liverpool Seamen's Orphan Institution (RLSOI)

£119,500 (84 grants)

Correspondent: Linda Cotton, Treasurer, Suite 315, Cotton Exchange Building, Old Hall Street, Liverpool L3 9LQ (0151 227 3417 or 07747 607062 (mobile); email: enquiries@rlsoi-uk.org; website: www.rlsoi-uk.org)

CC number: 526379

Eligibility

Children of deceased British merchant seafarers and fishermen. Applicants may be of pre-school age or in full-time education (including further and higher education). Help may also be given to seafarers who are at home caring for their family alone.

Types of grants

Discretionary awards are available to help with education costs and monthly maintenance. Annual clothing grants and support for school fees are available. Grants can be provided throughout the child's education.

Annual grant total

In 2016 the charity held assets of £2.7 million and had an income of £199,000. Grants to 84 individuals totalled £238,500 for both welfare and educational purposes. The breakdown between educational and welfare support was not specified; therefore we estimate that about £119,500 was awarded for educational needs.

Applications

Application forms are available from the correspondent and can be submitted at any time. Each application is considered on its own merits.

Other information

Support is given to both educational and welfare causes. While the proportions given for each cause were not specified, all grants are given to children and young people who are in attendance at school and further or higher education institutions. The charity's website also provides links to other organisations helping seafarers.

In 2013 the charity came to an arrangement with the Royal Merchant Navy Education Foundation whereby they would in future take over the

support of beneficiaries in further education. In 2016 three students have been transferred following the agreement.

Royal Merchant Navy Education Foundation

£233,500 (91 grants)

Correspondent: Cdr Charles Heron-Watson, Secretary, 1A Charnham Lane, Hungerford, Berkshire RG17 0EY (01488 567890; email: office@rmnef.orh.uk; website: www.rmnef.org.uk)

CC number: 1153323

Eligibility

Children in need at any stage of education who have a parent who has served or is serving at of any grade in the British Merchant Navy, and is unable to provide fully for the education, maintenance and upbringing of the child.

The website states:

> The length of sea-service is considered when determining whether a young person is eligible for support and, in all instances, the Trustees will use their discretion[...] In each case, we need to identify a genuine 'need' and this will be based upon factors such as domestic environment, locality, health, finance and education.

Types of grants

Support is available for children and young people at any stage of education – from pre-school, primary school, secondary school, right up to further education, higher education (to professional entry qualification) and career training and apprenticeships (to professional entry qualification).

The website states that support can be given towards some or all of the following: school fees; educational extras; school uniforms; travel between home and school; educational equipment; educational visits; educational books; some university expenses. The foundation states: 'crucially, our view is that each applicant is unique, with unique needs'.

Annual grant total

In 2015/16 the foundation had assets of £13.9 million and an income of £429,500. It made grants totalling £233,500 to support 91 individuals, mostly from secondary school age and above.

Applications

Initial contact should be made with the correspondent via letter or email. Phone enquiries to discuss individual circumstances are also welcomed, and some applicants make contact through and associated charity (see the website for further details). Application forms will then be provided to eligible applicants. Candidates will be paid a home visit and may be required to provide an assessment by a relevant professional. A submission is then put to the trustees for a final decision.

Other information

Previously known as the Royal Merchant Navy School Foundation (CC number: 309047), the assets and liabilities of the foundation were transferred to the Royal Merchant Navy Education Foundation, a charitable incorporated organisation, in 2013.

Foundation also assists beneficiaries over the age of 18 who have previously been supported by the Royal Liverpool Seamen's Orphan's Institution.

Sailors' Children's Society

£10,500

Correspondent: Deanne Thomas, Chief Officer, Francis Reckitt House, Newland, Cottingham Road, Hull HU6 7RJ (01482 342331; email: info@sailorschildren.org. uk; website: www.sailorschildren.org.uk)

CC number: 224505

Eligibility

Seafarers' children (generally under the age of 18 – see 'type of grants' for exceptions) who are in full-time education and the families are in severe financial difficulties. One of the child's parents must have served in the Royal or Merchant Navy or in the fishing fleets, including on ferries, tankers, cruise ships or cargo boats.

Applicants must be in receipt of Housing Benefit or Council Tax Benefit (other than single persons 25% discount or disablement reduction).

Types of grants

One-off grants according to need.

Annual grant total

In 2015/16 the charity had assets of £2.1 million and an income of £601,500. Grants totalled £396,500, the majority of which was given for social welfare purposes. At least £10,500 was given in grants for home computers. We were unable to determine the total of grants for other educational expenditure such as school clothing, school holidays or student support.

Applications

Application forms are available from the correspondent and require details about children, income and expenditure. Copies of relevant certificates, for example, birth certificates and proof of seafaring service should also be provided.

Other information

The charity, which was previously known as Sailors' Families' Society, has an informative website where more details can be found.

Medicine and health

The Birmingham and Three Counties Trust for Nurses

£3,600

Correspondent: David Airston, 16 Haddon Croft, Halesowen B63 1JQ (0121 602 0389; email: p.hyde@hotmail. co.uk)

CC number: 217991

Eligibility

Nurses on any statutory register, who have practiced or practice in the City of Birmingham and the counties of Staffordshire, Warwickshire and Worcestershire.

Types of grants

One-off grants, usually up to £300 per annum, to nurses taking post-registration or enrolment courses (post-basic nurse training or back-to-nursing course). Grants are made towards books, travel and/or fees.

Annual grant total

In 2015/16 the trust had an income of £8,900 and a total expenditure of £14,900. Assistance in previous years has mostly been given for welfare purposes. We estimate that educational grants totalled around £3,600.

Applications

Applications can be made on a form available from the correspondent to be submitted directly by the individual. They are considered at any time.

The Cameron Fund

£113,000

Correspondent: David Harris, Company Secretary, BMA House, Tavistock Square, London WC1H 9HR (020 7388 0796; email: info@cameronfund.org.uk; website: www.cameronfund.org.uk)

CC number: 261993

Eligibility

Current and former registered general practitioners and their dependants.

Types of grants

Grants to GPs' dependent children for travel to school, after-school clubs and similar extra-curricular activities and school uniforms. In certain circumstances, the fund will make a contribution to school fees. Assistance with the cost of private education during an examination year or for a short period before a child joins or re-enters the state system may be provided.

Sons or daughters of an existing or former beneficiary and over eighteen can apply for a grant during a first degree course or a vocational training course.

Annual grant total

In 2016 the fund had assets of £6.2 million and an income of £306,000. We estimate that educational grants to individuals totalled £113,000.

Applications

Application forms can be downloaded from the website or can be requested from the correspondent.

Other information

Grants are also made for welfare purposes. Financial, legal and career advice and counselling are also offered.

The Dain Fund

£22,500 (22 grants)

Correspondent: Marian Flint, Administrator, BMA Charities, BMA House, Tavistock Square, London WC1H 9JP (020 7383 6142; fax: 020 7554 6334; email: info.bmacharities@ bma.org.uk; website: bma.org.uk/about-the-bma/who-we-are/charities)

CC number: 313108

Eligibility

Children of doctors or deceased doctors (not nurses or physiotherapists and so on) in state, private or higher education and whose families have experienced an unexpected change in financial circumstances following crises such as unemployment, family breakdown or serious illness of a parent or guardian. The charity has also undertaken outreach work to support the children of refugee doctors.

Types of grants

Most grants relate to educational expenses such as school uniforms for children in state schools where the family is on a low income. Grants are sometimes made for short-term interventions in which school fees are paid for a few terms either until the child finishes GCSEs or A-levels or the child is found a place in the state education system. Occasionally, grants are made to students in tertiary education.

Annual grant total

In 2016 the fund had assets of £1.75 million and an income of £54,500. Throughout the year the charity awarded almost £22,500 to individuals for educational purposes.

Applications

Application forms are available from the correspondent.

Other information

This fund is designed to help families in an emergency and is not a scholarship charity.

The Florence Nightingale Foundation

£1.2 million

Correspondent: Janet Shallow, 34 Grosvenor Gardens, First Floor Front, London SW1W 0DH (020 7730 3030; website: www.florence-nightingale-foundation.org.uk)

OSCR number: SC044341

Eligibility

Nurses and midwives in the UK.

Types of grants

Scholarships are available for nurses:

- To study elsewhere in the UK and/or overseas to enhance care in the UK
- To develop leadership skills
- To undertake study in research methods

Annual grant total

In 2016 the foundation had assets of £2.4 million and an income of £1.5 million. Educational grants in the form of scholarships totalled £1.2 million.

Applications

Application forms are available to download from the foundation's website.

Forth Valley Medical Benevolent Trust

£5,000

Correspondent: The Correspondent, Meeks Road Surgery, 10 Meeks Road, Falkirk FK2 7ES (01324 619930)

OSCR number: SC000014

Eligibility

People in need who are medical practitioners, or their families or relatives, living in Forth Valley.

Types of grants

Our research indicates that in the past grants have been given for assistance with university fees, normally medical education.

Annual grant total

In 2016/17 the trust had an income of £3,000 and a total expenditure of £10,500. The charity supports both educational and general welfare causes; we estimate that grants for educational purposes totalled around £5,000.

Applications

Applications may be made in writing to the correspondent.

Other information

Welfare needs are also assisted.

Hertfordshire Community Nurses' Charity

£16,200

Correspondent: Louise Landman, Trustee, Lodge Farm, Chapel Lane, Little Hadham, Ware SG11 2AD (0797 0051517; email: louiselandman7@gmail.com; website: hertscommunitynursescharity.co.uk)

CC number: 1158593

Eligibility

Nurses working in the community in Hertfordshire (including nurses working in the following settings: community; practice; school; community – children; community mental health and learning disabilities; hospice; as well as community midwives and health visitors). To be eligible, applicants must have worked in the community in Hertfordshire for at least six months.

Groups of nurses can also apply for a grant to help develop a project or to fund particular equipment which will aid their development and improve quality of care for patients in the area.

Types of grants

Grants are given to enable nurses to undertake professional development. Applicants must be able to demonstrate how the grant will benefit the quality of care to patients. A wide range of courses and levels can be funded, including part-time and full-time degree courses – for example: counselling; palliative care; mental health; learning disabilities; and pain management.

Grants are given for one year only and those undertaking longer courses must re-apply. Applications must relate to just one course or project in a given year. No more than £2,000 will be given to one individual during a year, and a limit of £6,000 is given to any one individual in total.

Annual grant total

In 2015/16 the charity had assets of £877,500 and an income of £65,000. Grants to individuals for educational purposes totalled £16,200. A further £23,500 was given in major grants (for projects) and £10,000 was given in a grant to the Queen's Nursing Institute.

Exclusions

Grants are not given for:

- Nurses working in a hospital setting
- Retrospective funding (i.e. courses or modules already undertaken)
- Subsistence expenses for conference or academic courses (e.g. travel, hotel, food)

Applications

Applications can be made using the form on the charity's website. Applicants will be notified of the outcome of their application within one month of receipt.

Other information

The charity was previously known as Hertfordshire County Nursing Trust (CC number: 207213). It was incorporated in 2014.

The charity occasionally makes major grants of up to £20,000 for projects which will benefit patients in Hertfordshire. The charity may also be able to help nurses with welfare needs – contact the correspondent for more information.

The charity also provides subsidised accommodation for retired nurses who previously worked in the community in Hertfordshire.

Leverhulme Trade Charities Trust
See entry on page 119

The RCN Foundation

£202,000

Correspondent: Grants Manager (Hardship or Educational), 20 Cavendish Square, London W1G 0RN (020 7647 3645; email: rcnfoundation@rcn.org.uk; website: www.rcnfoundation.org.uk)

CC number: 1134606

Eligibility

Registered nurses, midwives, health practitioners, health care assistants and people training for these professions.

Types of grants

Scholarships, bursaries and grants for a range of learning, development and research opportunities.

Annual grant total

In 2016 the charity had assets of £31.6 million and an income of £1.5 million. Educational grants to individuals totalled £202,000.

Applications

There is a list of available bursaries, together with opening and closing dates for applications, listed on the website. Full eligibility criteria and application forms are also available to download.

Other information

Previously known as The Royal College of Nursing Benevolent Fund, the purpose of the foundation is to enable nurses and nursing to improve the health and well-being of the public through:

- Benevolent funding
- Education and training bursaries
- Supporting the development of clinical practice and the improvement of care
- Developing practice to enable people and communities to make positive choices about their own health and well-being
- Promoting research

Royal Medical Benevolent Fund (RMBF)

£223,000 (234 grants)

Correspondent: The Casework Department, 24 King's Road, Wimbledon, London SW19 8QN (020 8540 9194; email: help@rmbf.org; website: www.rmbf.org)

CC number: 207275

Eligibility

Doctors and their dependants, who are on a low income and unable to support themselves due to illness, disability, bereavement or being over state retirement age. Medical students experiencing unforeseen financial hardship, and their dependants. Refugee doctors practising in the UK.

Types of grants

Help provided can range from financial assistance in the form of grants and interest-free loans to a telephone befriending scheme for those who may be isolated and in need of support. Assistance is tailored to the individual's needs. Support includes:

- Regular monthly grants towards day-to-day living costs
- Back-to-work awards for those returning to work following a period of illness (including retraining costs, professional fees and occasionally childcare costs)
- Other awards towards specialist equipment, car and home adaptations
- Top-up for residential care fees, extra care costs
- Secured loans, where the beneficiary has significant equity in property

- Specialist money and debt management advice to renegotiate debts and secure all eligible state benefits
- Support for medical students in exceptional financial hardship
- Support for refugee doctors retraining in the UK

For full details on eligibility for financial help check the financial support section of the charity's helpful website or get in touch with the caseworkers.

Annual grant total

In 2016/17 the charity held assets of £32.9 million and had an income of £992,500. The amount of grants given to individuals totalled £446,000. The breakdown between educational and welfare support was not given; therefore we estimate that about £223,000 was given for educational purposes.

During the year, 18 beneficiaries were supported during their return to work, eight beneficiaries were given help to remain in work and a further 16 beneficiaries were helped with training with the aim of securing employment. Support was also given to 26 medical students to finalise their studies and qualify as doctors.

Exclusions

The following are excluded:

- Private healthcare and medical insurance
- Private education
- Legal fees
- Inland revenue payments
- Debts to relatives or friends

Applications

For an application pack and further information, get in touch with the correspondent via email or phone. Applications can be submitted either directly by the individual or through a third party, for example a social worker, Citizens Advice, other welfare agency, medical colleague or other medical and general charities.

Two references are required (at least one of which should be from a medical practitioner). All applicants are visited before a report is submitted to the Case Committee, which meets on a two month basis (although emergency assistance may be given). The income/capital and expenditure are fully investigated, with similar rules applying as for those receiving Income Support.

Other information

The charity has an informative website where further details can be found. Both educational and welfare needs are assisted.

The Royal Medical Foundation

£74,500 (12 grants)

Correspondent: Helen Jones, Caseworker, RMF Office, Epsom College, College Road, Epsom, Surrey KT17 4JQ (01372 821010; email: rmf-caseworker@epsomcollege.org.uk; website: www.royalmedicalfoundation.org)

CC number: 312046

Eligibility

Dependants under the age of 18 of medical practitioners (GMC registered) past or present, who are in need.

Types of grants

Grants of between are given to schoolchildren and college students towards fees. Preference is given to pupils with family difficulties so that they have to be educated away from home, pupils with special educational needs and medical students.

Annual grant total

In 2015/16 the foundation made 41 grants totalling £146,000. This included educational grants amounting to £74,000 for 13 individuals. Grants were distributed as follows:

Short-term payments or one-off grants where urgent assistance is required	22	£55,000
Financial assistance with educational expenses at Epsom College	2	£37,500
Financial assistance with educational expenses	10	£36,500
Regular payments to medical practitioners and their widows/widowers	5	£16,200
Other grants	2	£650

Applications

There is an online financial assistance request form on the foundation's website. More information is available from the correspondent. Applicants must have applied for any state benefits to which they may be entitled before an application can be considered and will be visited by the caseworker as part of the application process. The foundation's board meets quarterly, in January, April, July and October and applications should be submitted well in advance (specific dates are listed on the website).

Other information

The Royal Medical Foundation is a charity founded by Dr John Propert in 1855 and administered by Act of Parliament. Its original objects were to provide an asylum for qualified medical practitioners and their spouses and to found a school for their sons. Today, the foundation's aims and objectives are to assist registered doctors and their families who are in financial hardship. The foundation is managed by a board of directors drawn from various professions and is located at Epsom College.

Society for Assistance of Medical Families

£35,000

Correspondent: Charlotte Farrar, Lettsom House, 11 Chandos Street, Cavendish Square, London W1G 9EB (01837 83022; email: info@ widowsandorphans.org.uk; website: www.widowsandorphans.org.uk)

CC number: 207473

Eligibility

Grants are available to the following, in order of priority:

1   Dependants of deceased members of the society
2   Members of the society
3   Dependants of current members
4   Medical practitioners who are not part of the society, and their dependants

Types of grants

One-off and recurrent grants are available to help to meet the costs of education for medical students, for example through the provision of equipment or payment of exam fees. Grants are also available to doctors returning to practice for retraining expenses

Annual grant total

In 2016 the charity had assets of £6.6 million and an income of £221,000. We estimate that grants for education totalled £35,000.

Exclusions

Grants are not normally given for second degrees.

Applications

Application forms and income assessment questionnaires are available to download from the charity's website, under the 'Media and Downloads' heading. The trustees meet to consider applications in February, May, August and November. Where possible, either the secretary or a director will visit the applicant.

Other information

Support is also given for welfare needs.

Mining and quarrying

Miners' Welfare National Educational Fund (MWNEF)

£152,500 (128 grants)

Correspondent: Sharon Beckett, Secretary, The Old Rectory, Rectory Drive, Whiston, Rotherham, South Yorkshire S60 4JG (01709 728115; fax: 01709 839164; email: sharon.beckett@ ciswo.org.uk; website: www.ciswo.org/ other-services/education-fund)

CC number: 313246, SC038771

Eligibility

People who are employed in the coal mining industry of Great Britain, or who have been employed in the industry and took up full-time further education within five years of leaving the industry, or people who had to leave employment in the industry due to age or disability. Individuals who are the dependants of such employees or former employees are also eligible, between the ages of 17 and 25, if the employee either completed 20 years of employment in the industry or left due to age or ill health and was not able to obtain further employment. Dependants of those with less than 20 years of employment in the industry may be supported by CISWO (Coal Industry Social Welfare Organisation).

Types of grants

Grants are given towards higher and further education courses. Any full-time courses of education for which statutory higher education student support is available (e.g. from Student Finance England, Student Finance Wales or Student Awards Agency Scotland) can be supported. Some postgraduate courses may be considered where they are related to and taken directly after a first degree or considered essential for an entry into a profession.

Annual grant total

In 2015/16 the fund had assets of £672,500 and an income of £46,000. A total of around £152,500 was awarded in 128 grants.

Applications

Application forms are available from the correspondent. The selection committee meets twice during the academic year to consider applications.

North East Area Miners' Social Welfare Trust Fund

£700

Correspondent: Michael Lally, 4 Bilham Row, Brodsworth, Doncaster DN5 7DN (email: ian.lally@ciswo.org.uk; website: www.ciswo.org.uk)

CC number: 504178

Eligibility

People in need living in Durham, Northumberland and Tyne and Wear who are or have been employed by the coal industry, and their dependants.

Types of grants

One-off grants according to need. The fund aims to improve beneficiaries' health, social well-being and conditions of living.

Annual grant total

In 2015/16 the fund had assets of £3 million and an income of £110,000. We estimate that educational grants to individuals totalled around £700.

Applications

Applications may be made in writing to the correspondent. They can be submitted directly by the individual or through a social worker, Citizens Advice or other welfare agency. Requests are usually considered four times a year.

Other information

The fund also makes grants to mining charities. It also provides group holidays for its beneficiaries and revenue/capital costs relating to the day to day running of the Sam Watson Rest Home. It would appear that most support is given for general welfare needs.

Public and government sector

Conservative and Unionist Agents' Benevolent Association

£10,000

Correspondent: Sally Smith, Conservative Campaign Headquarters, 4 Matthew Parker Street, Westminster, London SW1H 9HQ (020 7984 8172; email: sally.smith@conservatives.com; website: www.conservativeagentscharity. org.uk)

CC number: 216438

Eligibility

Children of deceased Conservative agents only.

Types of grants

One-off and recurrent grants for general educational purposes.

Annual grant total

In 2015/16 the charity had assets of £2.5 million and an income of £105,000. The amount awarded in educational grants was £10,000.

Exclusions

Loans are not given. The charity is not able to provide support to serving or retired Conservative Party staff who are not qualified agents.

Applications

Initial enquiries can be made by post, email or telephone to the correspondent, who will then discuss the possibilities available for the applicant. A member of the Management Committee or a local serving agent will then visit the applicant to discuss their application and their need for support, which is based on an assessment of household income and other circumstances. Every beneficiary is reassessed annually, either in winter or summer.

Other information

The majority of the association's grants are made for welfare purposes.

Emergency services

St George's Police Children Trust (formerly St George's Police Trust)

£650,000

Correspondent: Peter Moore, Northern Police Convalescent Home, St Andrews, Harlow Moor Road, Harrogate HG2 0AD (01423 504448; email: enquiries@thepolicetreatmentcentres.org; website: www.stgeorgespolicechildrentrust.org)
CC number: 1147445/SC043652

Eligibility

All applicants must be children of police officers, who are either serving, unable to work due to injury or illness while on or off duty, retired, or deceased while on or off duty. The grant schemes also have additional eligibility criteria:

 Further Education Grant: applicants must be at least aged 18, and enrolled on a higher education course (university, HNC, HND, NVQ level 4) of up to four years, or to the age of 25, whichever is the lesser

 Ex-gratia Grant: schoolchildren, including school leavers

Types of grants

There are two grant schemes available for educational funding:

 Further Education Grants: £1,500 to be paid in three equal instalments throughout the academic year
 Ex-gratia Grant: funding for trade tools, musical instruments, IT equipment, etc.

If eligible, applicants will receive a £100 registration grant before their application is considered by trustees.

Annual grant total

In 2016 the trust had assets of £12.8 million and an income of £966,000. We estimate that the trust awarded £650,000 in educational grants.

Exclusions

Grants are not awarded for master's or PhD degrees, nor for gap year activities.

Applications

All application forms are available to download from the trust's website. Application forms should be completed by a parent or guardian, and countersigned or validated by a representative of the force Police Federation office, HR/Occupational Health department, or Benevolent Fund.

Applications and all accompanying documents must be sent by post to the trust administrator, for review by the trustees. The trustees meet in February, May, August, and November each year.

Other information

Both educational and general welfare needs can be assisted. The trust also provides one-week respite holidays at the trust's holiday home in Harrogate available to all current and future beneficiaries.

The trust covers the following police forces: British Transport Police; Cheshire Constabulary; Civil Nuclear Constabulary; Cleveland Police; Cumbria Constabulary; Defence Police; Derbyshire Police, Durham Constabulary, Greater Manchester Police, Humberside Police, Lancashire Constabulary, Lincolnshire Police, Merseyside Police, North Wales; North Yorkshire Police; Northumbria Police; Nottinghamshire Police, Police Scotland; South Yorkshire, Staffordshire; West Mercia; West Yorkshire.

The Gurney Fund for Police Orphans

£408,500 (173+ grants)

Correspondent: Christine McNicol, Director, 9 Bath Road, Worthing, West Sussex BN11 3NU (01903 237256; email: gurneyfund@btconnect.com; website: www.gurneyfund.org)
CC number: 261319

Eligibility

Children (under the age of 18) of police officers from 22 subscribing forces in England and Wales, where a parent has died or retired on the grounds of ill health. The list of subscribing forces can be found on the fund's website.

Types of grants

A weekly allowance is provided for children under the age of 18, paid on a quarterly basis to a parent or guardian and reviewed annually; in 2016/17 these allowances ranged between £10 and £100 per week. In addition, funding is available for purposes such as educational trips, musical instruments and tuition, school uniforms, sports kit, driving lessons, course fees and tuition – these additional grants may be awarded to individuals over the age of 18 who are still in full-time education. In 2016/17 these grants ranged between £30 and £2,000. The trustees are willing to consider any application where there is a demonstrable benefit to education or personal development.

The fund also arranges holidays for families and awards Christmas gifts to children.

Annual grant total

In 2016/17 the fund had assets of almost £9.1 million and an income of almost £500,000. Allowances and grants to individuals totalled £408,500 altogether.

During the year, 173 individuals were receiving weekly allowances. There were also 68 grants awarded for additional educational purposes, which totalled £39,500 altogether. Grants were awarded to 46 students in further or higher education, totalling £57,000.

The fund also awarded Christmas gifts amounting to £28,000, as well as spending £44,000 on holidays for beneficiaries.

Exclusions

Grants will not be awarded for skiing trips. The fund does not pay weekly allowances for those in higher education, but can award grants to assist with purposes such as books, equipment and tuition fees.

Applications

Applications can be made through the force's welfare officers, local representatives or the subscribing forces directly. The trustees meet at least four times each year. A copy of the child's birth certificate will have to be provided. Successful candidates will be asked to complete an income and expenditure form and produce receipts if assistance is requested for specific expenditure.

The National Police Fund

£32,000 (24 grants)

Correspondent: Heather Martingell, Claims Manager, Police Dependants, 3 Mount Mews, High Street, Hampton, Middlesex TW12 2SH (020 8941 6907; email: office@pdtrust.org; website: www.pdtrust.org)

CC number: 207608

Eligibility

Dependants of serving, injured, retired or deceased members of police forces in England, Wales and Scotland who are over the age of 16. The annual household income of the candidate's family should be less than £30,000.

Types of grants

One-off grants generally of up to £1,000. Support is given for general needs (such as, accommodation, learning equipment, books and so on) to students on further/higher education courses (at least one year in duration) or vocational training. Occasionally, albeit rarely, awards may be given to mature students or younger children.

Grants can be renewed only upon further recommendation in favour of renewal by the chief officer.

Annual grant total

In 2014/15 the fund had assets of £3.5 million and an income of £115,500. Grants to 24 individuals totalled £32,000.

Exclusions

Grants are not given for A-levels and where support should be obtained from statutory sources.

Applications

Application forms and further information can be requested from the correspondent or obtained from the welfare officer of the police force where the officer is serving or has served. Applications can be made by individuals but must be forwarded by the chief officer. They should be submitted by September. A reference from the student's college or university should be included together with up-to-date weekly expenditure and income of the applicant, details of any benefits received and evidence of academic attainment. The grants committee meet three times a year.

Other information

The fund is administered by the Police Dependants' Trust (registered charity number 251021). Support from this trust can also be given for general welfare needs.

There is also a restricted Mary Holt fund awarding grants in exceptional cases of distress to widows or orphans of policemen below inspector level at retirement or death. Applications have to be forwarded by the chief constable for approval by the board.

The Police Dependants' Trust Ltd

£3,000 (seven grants)

Correspondent: Welfare Team, 3 Mount Mews, High Street, Hampton, Middlesex TW12 2SH (020 8941 6907; email: office@pdtrust.org; website: www.pdtrust.org)

CC number: 1151322

Eligibility

Bursaries for dependants of current or former police officers who are under the age of 25 and undertaking full-time higher education, further education or vocational training.

Types of grants

Bursaries are available for up to £1,000 per year to contribute towards living costs while undertaking full-time higher education, further education or vocational training (up to £1,000 per year).

Note that this is primarily a relief-in-need charity, so most of the grants will be given for welfare rather than educational purposes.

Annual grant total

In 2015/16 the trust held assets of £26.7 million and had an income of £982,000. The amount of grants given to individuals totalled £257,500 of which £3,000 was awarded through seven educational bursaries.

For more information, contact the trust on 020 8941 6907.

Applications

Application forms are available on the trust's helpful website or from the correspondent. They can be submitted at any time but all applicants must first register with the trust. Supporting materials may be required. Applications are generally considered every month and generally applications are received, processed and concluded within 28 days.

Other information

The trust primarily makes grants for welfare purposes. The website notes that the trust 'also administers the National Police Fund, which shares broadly the same eligibility criteria i.e. financial support is provided to the families/dependants of police officers who have been killed or injured on duty, and this support is provided on the basis of need'. The National Police Fund provides grants to:

- Police dependants who are in further education (university degree or vocational qualification)
- Widows and orphans of police officers who were below inspector level at the time of their death or medical retirement
- Police benevolent funds or sports/social clubs
- Police charities and other bodies which assist the police services

The Royal Ulster Constabulary GC – Police Service of Northern Ireland Benevolent Fund
See entry on page 132

Religion

Children of the Clergy Trust

£1,600

Correspondent: The Rev I. Thomson, Trustee, 4 Kierhill Gardens, Westhill, Aberdeenshire AB32 6AX

OSCR number: SC001845

Eligibility

Children of deceased ministers of the Church of Scotland.

Types of grants

One-off or recurrent grants according to need. Our research tells us that grants in previous years have ranged from £500 to £1,000 for any educational need.

Annual grant total

In 2016 the trust had an income of £2,300 and a total expenditure of £3,300. We estimate that the charity awarded around £1,600 in grants for educational purposes, with grants also being given for social welfare.

Applications

Apply in writing to the correspondent. Applications should be submitted directly by the individual and should include information about the applicant's ministerial parent, general family circumstances and other relevant information.

Other information

The trust is also known as Synod of Grampian Children of the Clergy Trust.

Lord Crewe's Charity

£193,000 (131 grants)

Correspondent: Clive Smithers, Clerk Manager, Rivergreen Centre, Aykley Heads, Durham DH1 5TS (0191 383 7398; email: enquiries@ lordcrewescharity.co.uk; website: www. lordcrewescharity.org.uk)

CC number: 1155101

Eligibility

Church of England clergy and their dependants who live in the dioceses of Durham and Newcastle and are in need. Grants may be given more generally to people in need who live in the area of benefit, with preference to people resident in parishes where the charity owns land or has the right of presentation to the benefice.

Types of grants

Grants are given for a whole range of education needs up to and including first degrees.

Annual grant total

In 2016 the charity had assets of £42.5 million and an income of £1.4 million. Throughout the year, 131 educational grants totalling £193,000 were made to members of the clergy in support of the education of their children. (Note that these grants related to two educational years second instalments of grants for 2015/16 and first instalments of grants for 2016/17).

Exclusions

Applicants who are not members of clergy are not supported and the trustees ask not to be contacted by people who do not fit the criteria.

Applications for church buildings and church projects are not assisted (except in the very small number of parishes in which the charity holds property or has rights of presentation.).

Applications

The charity's website states that there is no 'application form or an open application procedure for grants'. 'The charity works directly with its beneficiaries and with a number of partner organisations.' The application round opens in March and continues until July. Grants are considered in the first two weeks of August and the outcome is communicated to the applicant by the end of the month.

Consult the website for the latest updates on awards available.

Other information

The charity awarded £150,000 to Lincoln College who disbursed the amount to individuals through bursaries, scholarships and fellowship awards.

In 2014 the charity became a charitable incorporated organisation and changed its registered charity number (previously 230347). A linked charity, Lord Crewe's Library and Archives Trust (CC number: 1155101–2) has been established to own the libraries and archives collections currently held at Durham Cathedral, Durham University, the North East Religious Learning Resource Centre, and the Northumberland Records Office.

The charity also awards grants to individuals for welfare purposes.

The Glasgow Society of the Sons and Daughters of Ministers of the Church of Scotland – also known as Manse Bairns Network

£12,000 (11 grants)

Correspondent: Jennifer Law, Secretary & Treasurer, Scott-Monicrieff, Exchange Place 3, Semple Street, Edinburgh EH3 9BL (0131 473 3500; email: jennifer. law@scott-moncrieff.com; website: mansebairnsnetwork.org)

OSCR number: SC010281

Eligibility

Children of ministers of the Church of Scotland, with a preference for those children who are training for the ministry or mission work of the Church of Scotland.

Types of grants

Grants are awarded to support the costs of attending university or postgraduate training.

Annual grant total

In 2015/16 the charity had assets of £1.57 million and an income of £60,500. Educational grants totalled £12,000 and were made to 11 individuals. A further £28,000 was awarded to individuals for welfare purposes.

Applications

Application forms are available to download from the charity's associated websites. Applications should be submitted to the correspondent no later than 31 May each year and grants are distributed by early September.

Other information

Further information on the charity is available from its website or from the charities page of Scott Moncrieff, the charity's administrator (www.scott-moncrieff.com/services/charities/charitable-trusts).

Milton Mount Foundation
See entry on page 35

The Silcock Trust

£10,000

Correspondent: Claire Tallis, Trustee, 49 Hereford Road, London W25BB (07880 831473; email: claire.tallis@gmail.com)

CC number: 272587

Eligibility

Mainly children of clergy of the Church of England.

Types of grants

Our previous research has indicated that help is available towards the maintenance costs and fees for schoolchildren.

Annual grant total

In 2016 the trust had an income of £15,900 and a total expenditure of £10,400. We have estimated that grants to individuals totalled £10,000 during the year.

Applications

Apply in writing to the correspondent.

Society for the Benefit of Sons and Daughters of the Clergy of the Church of Scotland

£12,200 (16 grants)

Correspondent: Fiona Watson, Scott-Moncrieff, Exchange Place, 3 Semple Street, Edinburgh EH3 8BL (website: www.scott-moncrieff.com/services/charities/charitable-trusts/society-for-the-benefit-of-sons-and-daughters)

OSCR number: SC008760

Eligibility

Children of ministers of the Church of Scotland aged between 12 and 25. Preference is given to low-income families.

Types of grants

Grants are given towards general educational purposes, and are made for one year only but renewals may be granted following a fresh application. In

2016 grants ranged between £235 and £1,560.

Annual grant total

In 2016 the charity had assets of £1.1 million and an income of £45,000. Grants were made to 16 individuals for educational purposes totalling £12,200. A further six grants were given from the funds for welfare purposes, totalling £11,400.

Applications

Application forms can be downloaded from the Scott-Moncrieff website and should be posted to the correspondent. Applications should provide full details of the family income and need to be submitted by a parent/guardian before 31 May each year. Grants are distributed by early September.

Other information

The society co-operates with the Glasgow Society of Sons and Daughters of Ministers of the Church of Scotland and the Esdaile Trust in the distribution of grants for the benefit of students.

Other limited funds offering support are: the John Lang Macfarlane Fund for unmarried and widowed daughters of ministers (with £6,000 available for distribution each year) and the Robertson Chaplin Fund for unmarried sisters over 40 of ordained ministers, with preference given to older people and those in need of care (£1,000 available annually).

Sons and Friends of the Clergy

£475,000

Correspondent: Jeremy Moodey, 1 Dean Trench Street, Westminster, London SW1P 3HB (020 7799 3696; email: enquiries@clergycharities.org.uk; website: www.clergycharities.org.uk)

CC number: 207736

Eligibility

The charity supports: serving and retired Anglican clergy and their dependants; divorced and separated spouses and civil partners of eligible clergy; widows, widowers and surviving civil partners of eligible clergy; Anglican ordinands training for ministry in the UK.

The relevant clergy must be working in or have been working in: The United Kingdom; The Republic of Ireland; The Diocese of Sodor and Man; The Channel Islands.

Types of grants

Grants are available for university maintenance and school clothing. In exceptional circumstances the trustees may provide help towards school fees where there is a compelling proven educational need for a child to attend an independent school. Grants of up to £350 are also available to ordinands to cover the costs of training.

Annual grant total

In 2016 the charity had assets of £104.2 million and an income of £4.17 million. During the year, 905 grants were awarded to individuals and three to organisations totalling £2.4 million. Grants for educational purposes amounted to £475,000 and were distributed as follows:

General welfare	£1.9 million
University maintenance	£196,500
School fees	£146,500
Ordinand grants	£129,000
Resettlement	£16,500
Bereavement	£6,800
Holidays	£4,200
Other education expenses	£2,100
School clothing	£1,300
Debt	£1,200

Applications

Application forms are available to download from the charity's website.

Other information

The information in this entry is taken from the charity's website:

> The charity now known as the Corporation of the Sons of the Clergy was founded in 1655 by a group of merchants in the City of London and clergymen who were all sons of the cloth. During the Commonwealth, persecution of clergy who had remained loyal to the Crown was widespread and many who had been deprived of their livings by Cromwell were destitute. The charity's foundation dates from a recognition by a body of sons of clergymen that action was required to meet a pressing need among clergy families for charitable help. The charity's present name is often felt to be a misleading one, but it is in fact an accurate description of its founding fathers.

The Wells Clerical Charity

£5,000

Correspondent: The Ven. Nicola Sullivan, Trustee, 6 The Liberty, Wells, Somerset BA5 2SU (01749 670777; email: general@bathwells.anglican.org)

CC number: 248436

Eligibility

People in need under 25 years old who are children of members of clergy of the Church of England serving (or who have retired or died and last served) in the former archdeaconry of Wells as constituted in 1738.

Types of grants

Grants are made to support eligible individuals in preparing for entering any profession or employment by paying travel fees, the costs of clothing/uniform or maintenance costs.

Annual grant total

In 2016 the charity had an income of £8,300 and a total expenditure of £10,500. Grants are made to individuals for both educational and social welfare purposes. We estimate that educational grants totalled £5,000.

Applications

Apply in writing to the correspondent.

Sciences and technology

The Royal Society of Chemistry Chemists' Community Fund

£138,000

Correspondent: Chemists' Community Fund Team, Thomas Graham House, Science Park, Milton Road, Cambridge CB4 0WF (01223 432227; website: www.rsc.org/membership-and-community/chemists-community-fund)

CC number: 207890

Eligibility

People who have been members of the society for the last three years, or ex-members who were in the society for at least ten years, and their dependants, who are in need.

Society members who have at least two years of membership and have completed all planned study (and within 18 months of this study being completed) may apply for a Breathing Space Grant. To be eligible, the individual must be seeking, or have secured, paid employment. Other household and financial circumstances are considered as part of the application.

Types of grants

The charity's annual accounts state: 'To help promote excellence in chemistry, we also fund a number of prizes and awards as well providing grants to fund travel to events and conferences.'

The fund also makes Breathing Space Grants of up to £300 to recent graduates who are seeking their first job.

Annual grant total

In 2016 the charity had assets of £60.7 million and an income of £55.7 million. Grants to individuals for travel, prizes, awards and related events totalled £138,000.

Applications

Individuals should, in the first instance, contact the correspondent to discuss their situation. An application form will then be sent.

Other information

The society also provides advice and guidance services.

Secretarial and adminis-tration

The Worshipful Company of Chartered Secretaries and Administrators Charitable Trust

£6,700

Correspondent: Erica Lee, Secretary, WCCSA Charitable Trust, 3rd Floor, Saddlers Hall, 40 Gutter Lane, London EC2V 6BR (020 7726 2955; email: assistant.clerk@wccsa.org.uk; website: www.wccsa.org.uk/Education.html)

CC number: 288487

Eligibility

Chartered secretaries and administrators studying commercial courses in various universities and the apprentices of the Worshipful Company of Chartered Secretaries and Administrators.

Types of grants

The trust awards prizes of up to £500 for success in the examinations of the Institute of Chartered Secretaries and Administrators (ICSA) and in collaborative courses between ICSA and various universities. Support is also available to apprentices of the Worshipful Company of Chartered Secretaries and Administrators.

Annual grant total

In 2015/16 the trust had assets of £1.6 million and an income of £60,000. Throughout the year the trust awarded a total of £34,000 in grants, 41% of this total was given in educational grants. Of this amount £6,700 was given to individuals in the form of awards and prizes.

The charity also gives grants to organisations.

Applications

Apply in writing to the correspondent. Grants and awards are agreed and approved by the trustees at regular meetings.

Skilled crafts and trades

The Worshipful Company of Butchers' Educational Charity

£12,000

Correspondent: Worshipful Company of Butchers Education Charity, Butchers' Hall, 87–88 Bartholomew Close, London EC1A 7EB (020 7600 4106; fax: 020 7606 4108; email: clerk@butchershall.com; website: www.butchershall.com)

CC number: 297603

Eligibility

People involved in the meat trade who are studying courses related to the trade.

Applicants for the Nuffield Farming Scholarship must be a UK resident between 25 and 45 years who have been in the industry for at least two years and intend to remain involved in the sector.

Types of grants

One-off grants towards further and higher education fees.

The company also provides one Nuffield Farming Scholarship each year to enable someone who is active in the meat and livestock industries to study a topic of their choice, carrying out a tour anywhere in the world to further their knowledge and understanding.

Annual grant total

In 2015/16 the charity had assets of £763,500 and an income of £55,500. The amount awarded in educational grants to individuals was £12,000.

Applications

Apply in writing to the correspondent. Applications should be submitted directly by the individual for consideration monthly.

To apply for the Nuffield Farming Scholarship, email bob@bansback.co.uk.

The GPM Charitable Trust

£6,000

Correspondent: Keith Keys, 43 Spriggs Close, Clapham, Bedford MK41 6GD (07733 262991; email: gpmcharitabletrust@tiscali.co.uk; website: www.gpmtrust.org)

CC number: 227177

Eligibility

Workers, former workers and their dependants in the printing, graphical, papermaking and media industries.

Types of grants

Grants for retraining, skills enhancement, educational requirement especially following redundancy or other reduction in income.

Annual grant total

In 2016/17 the trust had an income of £23,500 and a total expenditure of £12,500. We estimate that educational grants to individuals totalled around £6,000.

Applications

An application form can be downloaded from the website or requested from the correspondent. It must be printed and completed in black ink before being returned to the trust. The dates of application deadlines for subsequent trustee meetings are listed on the website.

The Incorporated Benevolent Fund of the Institution of Gas Engineers and Managers

£400

Correspondent: Lesley Ecob, Correspondent, IGEM House, 28 High Street, Kegworth, Derbyshire DE74 2DA (01509 678167; fax: 01509 678198; email: lesley@igem.org.uk; website: www.igem.org.uk)

CC number: 214010

Eligibility

Present and former members of the institution, and their dependants. Our research suggests that help may also be available to UK and overseas students wishing to study gas engineering.

Types of grants

Grants are given according to need.

Annual grant total

In 2015 the fund had an income £7,900 and a total expenditure of £3,800. In the past, about 20% of the overall expenditure has been given in grants. We estimate that about £400 was given in educational grants to individuals.

Applications

Applications may be made in writing to the correspondent.

Johnson Matthey Public Ltd Company Educational Trust

£20,000

Correspondent: Stephanie Hamilton, Johnson Matthey plc, 25 Farringdon Street, London EC4A 4AB (020 7269 8400; email: group.hr@matthey.com)

CC number: 313576

Eligibility

UK students who have a parent or grandparent employed by Johnson Matthey or associated with the precious metals industry, and who are studying a scientific or technical subject.

Types of grants

Grants are awarded to college students and undergraduates for fees, books, equipment and maintenance/living expenses. The trust also makes awards for research into any scientific academic subject. Our research suggests that grants are usually between £400 and £500.

Annual grant total

In 2015/16 the trust had an income of £2,000 and a total expenditure of £38,500. We estimate that around £20,000 was awarded in grants for education.

Exclusions

Grants are not normally made to students studying second degrees or mature students.

Applications

Apply in writing to the correspondent. If possible, applications should be submitted by the relevant partner or grandparent on behalf of the individual. Applications are normally invited in October, for consideration in December.

Other information

The trust was set up in 1967 to commemorate the 150th anniversary of the founding of the company. It is also concerned with promoting research and establishing professorships, lectureships or other teaching posts.

Leverhulme Trade Charities Trust

£1.7 million (326 grants)

Correspondent: Paul Read, Secretary, 1 Pemberton Row, London EC4A 3BG (020 7042 9885; email: info@leverhulme-trade.org.uk; website: www.leverhulme-trade.org.uk)

CC number: 1159171

Eligibility

Students (undergraduate or postgraduate) at a recognised UK university who are in need and whose parent or spouse has worked as commercial traveller, grocer or pharmacist for at least five years, and is either still currently working in one of these occupations, or has retired within the last ten years.

Individuals are still eligible if their parent/spouse is unemployed (or deceased) but who fell within one of the three categories when the employment ceased (or at the time of death).

Types of grants

One-off or recurrent grants of up to £3,000 a year to full-time undergraduate students and of up to £5,000 a year to postgraduate students. Support is given towards general educational needs, including tuition and examination fees, living expenses, books, equipment, travel costs and accommodation. Awards are paid to the applicant's university.

Annual grant total

In 2016 the trust had assets of £77 million and an income of £2.5 million. The trust made bursaries totalling £1.7 million. Of this, there were 265 undergraduate bursaries (out of 295 applications) totalling £1.36 million and 61 postgraduate bursaries (out of 82 applications) totalling £345,000. There were also five grants made to organisations, totalling £1.6 million.

Exclusions

The trust is not able to fund students at the following universities: BPP University; Leeds College of Art; Middlesex University; Open University.

Applications

Applications for undergraduate funding can be made on the trust's website, where further guidance is also provided. There are two funding rounds each year – one which opens in August and closes in November, and one which opens in January and closes in March (refer to the website for exact dates).

Applications for postgraduate funding are also made online – applications open in August and close in October.

The trust aims to decide on applications within four to six weeks of the closing date. The trust states that if there are a large number of applications, awards may be reduced accordingly.

The Worshipful Company of Plaisterers Charitable Trust

£27,000

Correspondent: Nigel Bamping, Clerk, Plaisterers' Hall, One London Wall, London EC2Y 5JU (020 7796 4333; fax: 020 7796 4334; email: clerk@ plaistererslivery.co.uk; website: plaistererslivery.co.uk/education-training)

CC number: 281035

Eligibility

Individuals who are training or pursuing education within the UK plastering industry.

Types of grants

Bursaries up to £500 can be given to students who are undergoing training or experienced practitioners looking to develop their knowledge within the trade. According to the website, bursaries may be given towards: the costs of travel to attend a course overseas; fees for existing courses (where no other support is available); wage subsidies to enable students to pursue extra-curricular activities; funding to a mentor to support achievement of advanced qualifications; or the costs of enhancing access to training for people with disabilities.

The trust also runs a number of awards programmes, including the Annual Training Awards and the Student of the Year Award. See the website for details of awards available.

Annual grant total

In 2016/17 the trust had assets of £1.95 million and an income of £379,000. Grants totalled £35,000, including £7,800 given to organisations for the promotion of training. Grants to individuals amounted to £27,000, all of which was paid to organisations on behalf of individuals.

Applications

See the website for details of how to apply.

The Worshipful Company of Plumbers' Charitable and Educational Trust

£1,500

Correspondent: The Clerk, Carpenters' Hall, 1 Throgmorton Avenue, London EC2N 2JJ (020 7628 8880; email: clerk@plumberscompany.org.uk; website: www.plumberscompany.org.uk)

CC number: 800043

Eligibility

Applicants must be enrolled on NVQ Level 3 MES (Plumbing) or equivalent.

Types of grants

Bursaries are available to trainee plumbers working towards NVQ Level 3 MES (Plumbing) or equivalent.

Annual grant total

In 2015/16 the trust had assets of £588,500 and an income of £54,000. Educational grants in the form of bursaries totalled £1,500.

Applications

Application forms can be downloaded from the trust's website. Students must have a reference from their lecturer or employer.

Queen Elizabeth Scholarship Trust Ltd

£363,000 (39 grants)

Correspondent: Debbie Pocock, Executive Director, 1 Buckingham Place, London SW1E 6HR (020 7798 1535; email: info@qest.org.uk; website: www.qest.org.uk)

CC number: 1152032

Eligibility

Individuals over the age of 17 who are looking to improve their craft and trade skills. Applicants must be able to demonstrate a high level of skill already and a firm commitment to their craft or trade. A wide variety of craft and trades can be supported, whether contemporary or traditional – refer to the website for examples of what has previously been funded. To be eligible, applicants must be living and working permanently in the UK.

Grants are also awarded to support craft-based apprenticeships for those aged between 16 and 26.

Types of grants

Scholarships of between £1,000 and £18,000 (the average grant is around £7,000) are made to fund further study, training and practical experience for people working in a craft or trade. The trustees prefer to fund training or tuition costs, although living expenses may be considered to a limited extent. Funding may be given for specialist equipment may only be given if it is part of a whole request. Courses outside the UK may be funded, as long as the applicant plans to return to the UK to use their skills in British craft.

Funding of up to £6,000 per year, for up to three years, can also be given for apprenticeships, working within craft companies and with master craftspeople. Funding can be given to part-fund salaries, training costs and materials.

Annual grant total

In 2016 the trust had assets of £5.3 million and an income of £1.2 million. Scholarships were awarded to 25 individuals, totalling £156,500 altogether. There were also 14 apprenticeship awards, which totalled £206,500 altogether.

Exclusions

Funding is not given towards premises, equipment or other business set-up costs.

Applications

Applications for scholarship usually open in December/January and should be made using the application form on the trust's website.

Applications for apprenticeship funding open in June and close in August, when the application form on the website will be available.

Sports

The Professional Footballers' Association Charity

£1.7 million

Correspondent: Education Team, PFA Education Department, 11 Oxford Court, Bishopsgate, Manchester M2 3WQ (0161 236 0575; email: info@thepfa.co.uk)

CC number: 1150458

Eligibility

Current and former members of the Professional Footballers' Association (PFA) looking to study a course which leads to a nationally-recognised qualification or a degree.

Types of grants

Standard grants

Grants towards course fees (usually 50%, up to a maximum of £1,500 per year) are made towards any academic or vocational courses that lead to a nationally-recognised qualification. A range of different educational levels and subjects are supported – examples are listed on the website, but if you are unsure, contact the Education Team for further information. Grants are given towards study costs such as registration fees, tuition fees or exam fees, as well as required books for courses (up to a maximum of £300).

University bursaries

Annual bursaries of £1,250 are available for those undertaking a degree programme at a university in the UK, to assist with living costs. Students at universities outside the UK may also be eligible, as well as those studying for a PGCE or master's degree.

All grants are capped at a lifetime maximum of £5,000 per person.

Annual grant total

In 2015/16 the charity had assets of £46.3 million and an income of £20.6 million. The accounts state that 'PFA Educational and Vocational Grants' totalled £1.7 million.

Exclusions

Grants are not given for:

◗ Retrospective applications
◗ Private tuition or lessons
◗ Multiple applications for courses of a similar nature
◗ Travel/parking expenses
◗ Kit or uniform
◗ Tools and equipment
◗ Postage fees
◗ Training being undertaken on a personal or recreational basis
◗ Medical costs
◗ Accommodation
◗ Membership fees

Grants for language training are only given where the skill is required for job purposes.

Applications

Application forms are available to download from the PFA Charity website and should be submitted by post (faxed or emailed documents are not accepted). Refer to the website for information on when to apply for each type of grant; applications can take four to six weeks to be processed. Applicants who are registered as unemployed may be eligible for a higher rate of support, and should submit their application form along with a letter from their Job Centre. Any queries can be directed to the Education Team at the contact details shown.

Other information

The Professional Footballers' Association Education Fund (CC number: 306097) amalgamated with the Professional Footballers' Association Charity and the assets were transferred in 2014.

National Trainers' Federation Charitable Trust (N. T. F. Charitable Trust)

£9,000

Correspondent: Welfare Officers, Racing Welfare, 20B Park Lane, Newmarket, Suffolk CB8 8QD (0800 630 0443; email: info@racingwelfare.co.uk; website: www. racingwelfare.co.uk)

CC number: 1004308

Eligibility

Individuals who work or have worked in the UK thoroughbred horseracing and breeding industry (at least five years' employment in a seven-year period). Priority is given to applicants employed in racing stables.

Types of grants

Grants are provided for developing workplace skills and retraining within the horseracing industry. Courses previously funded include: equine osteopathy or dentistry; racing secretary and book-keeping courses; LGV driver training; accountancy courses. Applications are means-tested and if the applicant is working full-time, they are expected to contribute 25% towards the cost of the course (although cases are considered on an individual basis, and this can be discussed with a welfare officer).

Annual grant total

In 2015/16 the trust had an income of £19,800 and a total expenditure of £19,500. We estimate that grants given to individuals totalled around £9,000.

Exclusions

Grants are not given to anyone not residing in the UK. Anyone who has been a licensed jockey at any time, must be referred to the Jockeys Employment and Training Scheme. Grants are not given for: legal fees; anything that should be provided on a statutory basis; animal welfare; good/services that have already been paid for; business finance; funeral costs; care home fees; private medical treatment; clearance of non-priority debts; employment equipment; foreign worker repatriation costs; vehicle maintenance or repairs; or remedial repairs to properties.

Applications

The trust invites applicants to contact one of its welfare officers to discuss making an application.

Other information

The trust also supports organisations.

Transport and storage

The Air Pilots Benevolent Fund

£65,000

Correspondent: Captain John Towell, Cobham House, 9 Warwick Court, Gray's Inn, London WC1 R5DJ (01276 47050; email: office@airpilots.org; website: www.airpilots.org)

CC number: 212952

Eligibility

Members of The Honourable Company of Air Pilots and those who have been engaged professionally as air pilots, or air navigators in commercial aviation and their dependants.

People who want to become pilots or wish to gain further qualifications in the aviation industry are supported by The Honourable Company of Air Pilots.

Types of grants

Scholarships and bursaries, including those to flying instructors. Academic bursaries awarded at City University to students in one of the three specific MSc courses. Awards towards the general educational needs of the dependants of aviators.

Annual grant total

In 2015/16 the fund had assets of £721,000 and an income of £71,000. Grants were made totalling £68,500, with one grant of £3,600 awarded directly for an organisation, see below:

PPL Scholarships via Air Pilots Trust	£27,000
Flying Instructor Development Bursary	£10,000
Regular grants	£9,450
Flying Scholarship for Disabled People	£9,000
Ray Jeffs Gliding Scholarships	£4,000
Inner London Schools Gliding	£3,600
City University Bursary via Air Safety Trust	£3,000
Occasional grants	£2,500

Exclusions

The fund cannot give 'grant or loan money for the repayment of debts or long-term expenses such as school fees, prolonged medical care or for obtaining professional pilots' licences and ratings'.

Applications

Application forms are available to download from the fund's website. Further information about the scholarships can be obtained by emailing office@airpilots.org or by telephone 020 7404 4032.

Other information

The charity was previously called The Guild of Air Pilots Benevolent Fund and provides both educational and welfare support.

The fund is administered by The Honourable Company of Air Pilots which is also managing Air Safety Trust and Air Pilots Trust (see a separate entry).

The BMTA Trust Ltd
See entry on page 26

The British Airline Pilots' Association Benevolent Fund (BALPA)

£12,900

Correspondent: Antoinette Girdler, BALPA House, 5 Heathrow Boulevard, 278 Bath Road, West Drayton UB7 0DQ (020 8476 4029; email: tonigirdler@ balpa.org)

CC number: 229957

Eligibility

Dependants of current or retired British commercial airline pilots, flight engineers and winchmen.

Types of grants

Grants are made towards the cost of books, uniforms and associated educational expenses.

Annual grant total

In 2015/16 the fund had assets of £1.6 million and an income of £34,500. Grants totalled £25,800 and interest-free loans were made to the sum of £89,000. We estimate that grants for educational purposes totalled around £12,900.

Exclusions

Grants are not given for school fees.

Applications

Apply in writing to the correspondent to request an application form. Applications are considered quarterly.

The Railway Benefit Fund

£4,000

Correspondent: Jason Tetley, 1st Floor Millennium House, 40 Nantwich Road, Crewe CW2 6AD (0345 241 2885; email: info@railwaybenefitfund.org.uk; website: www.railwaybenefitfund.org.uk)

CC number: 206312

Eligibility

Current and former railway staff, and their dependants, who are in need.

Types of grants

One-off grants to help the parents of dependent children with the costs of clothing and footwear, school projects and the initial costs of beginning higher education.

Annual grant total

In 2016 the charity had assets of £4.1 million and an income of £943,500. Grants to individuals totalled £306,000, the majority of which were made for welfare purposes. In previous years, educational grants have totalled around £4,000.

Applications

Applications are available to download from the website, or can be requested by telephone, via the 'Contact Us' form on the website, or by emailing support@railwaybenefitfund.org.uk.

Other information

This is primarily a welfare charity, and educational grants are part of its wider welfare work.

Livery companies, orders and membership organisations

The Cheshire Freemasons' Charity

£18,000

Correspondent: Christopher Renshaw, 6 Auden Close, Ewloe, Deeside, Clwyd CH5 3TY (01244 534343; email: enquiries@cheshiremasons.co.uk; website: www.cheshiremasons.co.uk)

CC number: 219177

Eligibility
Children of Freemasons in full-time education who reside in Cheshire.

Types of grants
One-off and recurrent grants are available for:

▶ Costs of education and training
▶ Scholarships
▶ Travel grants
▶ Accommodation
▶ Supporting exceptional talent in sport, music and performing arts

Annual grant total
In 2015/16 the charity had assets of £4 million, an income of £193,000 and a total expenditure of £514,000. We estimate the charity awarded £18,000 in grants to individuals for educational purposes.

Applications
In the first instance, potential applicants should contact the charity via telephone or email to help@mcf.org.uk.

Other information
The charity also awards grants to Freemasons and their dependants suffering from financial distress; to non-masonic charities; and the 'Teddies for Loving Care Appeal'.

The Worshipful Company of Engineers Charitable Trust Fund

£22,000

Correspondent: Anthony Willenbruch, Clerk, Wax Chandlers' Hall, 6 Gresham Street, London EC2V 7AD (020 7726 4830; fax: 020 7726 4820; email: clerk@ engineerscompany.org.uk; website: www. engineerstrust.org.uk)

CC number: 289819

Eligibility
Qualified engineers and those training to be chartered engineers, incorporated engineers and engineering technicians. Eligibility criteria differs depending on the award being applied for. See the website for more information.

Types of grants
The trust supports a number of award schemes to encourage excellence in engineering. Grants are also made to support engineers who are facing hardship, particularly while they are in education.

Annual grant total
In 2016 the trust had assets of £1.6 million and an income of £95,000. The annual report for the year stated: 'Monetary prizes to the value of £22,000 (2015: £22,362) were made to 7 individuals and grants to a total value of £50,459 (2015: £34,571) were made to individuals and organisations.'

Applications
Specific application details for different awards can be found on the trust's website. Some schemes require candidates to be nominated by their educational institution.

Other information
The trust supports welfare needs, engineering research and can award grants to organisations in the City of London that further the interest of the history, traditions and customs of the city.

Grand Lodge of Scotland Annuity Benevolent and Charity Funds

£19,400

Correspondent: The Trustees, c/o Freemasons Hall, 96 George Street, Edinburgh EH2 3DH (0131 225 5577; fax: 0131 225 3953; email: curator@ grandlodgescotland.org; website: www.

grandlodgescotland.com/about-masonry/charity)

OSCR number: SC001996

Eligibility

Children of members, living and deceased, of the Grand Lodge of Scotland.

Types of grants

Training grants of up to £450.

Annual grant total

In 2015/16 the charity had assets of £12.3 million and an income of £705,000. Grants were made totalling £118,000, of which £91,000 was awarded in 122 grants to individuals. According to the website, 'some 43 Training Grants were awarded this year at a level of £450 per successful applicant'. Based on this, we estimate that grants for educational purposes totalled around £19,400.

Applications

Apply using a form available from the correspondent or by direct approach to your local lodge. The website explains that cases 'are managed and administered with the assistance of Lodges and Provincial Grand Lodges via [the Grand Lodge's] reporting system'.

Other information

The charity also makes benevolence payments to individuals, as well as grants to organisations, and runs care homes for older people.

Masonic Charitable Foundation

£111,000

Correspondent: Enquiries Team, Freemasons Hall, 60 Great Queen Street, London WC2B 5AZ (0800 035 6090; email: help@mcf.org.uk)

CC number: 1164703

Eligibility

Children and grandchildren of Freemasons under the age of 25. The Freemason does not necessarily need to be a currently subscribing member, but must have joined before the need arose.

Support can only be given to children of Freemasons who are or were a member of a Lodge regulated by the United Grand Lodge of England. This includes England, Wales, the Channel Islands and the Isle of Man as well as members of overseas Lodges which follow the English Constitution.

The website notes the following, 'to demonstrate that any support required is beyond their financial means, those seeking our support must complete an assessment of household income, expenditure, savings and capital'.

Types of grants

Grants are available for IT equipment, course materials, school uniforms and extracurricular activities. Scholarships are also available for further or higher education.

Grants through the TalentAid programme can pay for training or equipment for those with the potential to develop an exceptional talent into a career in music, sport or the performing arts. Further details and criteria can be found on the foundation's website.

Annual grant total

In 2016/17 the foundation held assets of £416.7 million and had an income of £67 million. Grants were made primarily for welfare purposes, but we have estimated that £111,000 was awarded to individuals for educational purposes.

Applications

Before making an application you must contact either your Lodge Almoner or the foundation. If the enquiries team consider you eligible for a grant, a representative will visit you and help you complete the application form. Payments are made directly to the individual or to the supplier providing the equipment or service you require.

If your application is not approved, the foundation can advise you on other organisations and services that may be able to help.

Other information

The foundation makes grants to charitable organisations and hospices. It also provides a counselling helpline and residential homes.

The Provincial Grand Charity

£11,100

Correspondent: Michael de-Villamar Roberts, Ingham & Co., George Stanley House, 2 West Parade Road, Scarborough, North Yorkshire YO12 5ED (01723 500209; email: mdvr@mdvr.karoo.co.uk)

CC number: 517923

Eligibility

Children (including adopted and step-children) of present and deceased masons who live or lived in North Yorkshire and Humberside.

Types of grants

Our research has indicated that grants are given for those at school, college or university towards school clothing, books, school fees and living expenses depending on the parental circumstances.

Annual grant total

In 2015 the charity had assets of £926,000 and an income of £78,500. The amount of grants given to individuals totalled £11,100. A further £52,000 was given in grants to organisations.

Applications

Apply in writing to the correspondent, to be considered at quarterly meetings. Applications must be supported by the relative who is a member of the masons.

The Worshipful Company of Scientific Instrument Makers

£62,500

Correspondent: The Clerk, Glaziers Hall, 9 Montague Close, London SE1 9DD (020 7407 4832; email: theclerk@wcsim.co.uk; website: www.wcsim.co.uk)

CC number: 221332

Eligibility

Schoolchildren, sixth formers, undergraduates and postgraduates with outstanding ability in science and mathematics, and a creative and practical interest in branches of engineering connected with instrumentation and measurement.

Types of grants

The Young Engineers Program supports people to attend national and international events, competitions, prizes and travel support plus apprenticeships. There are also scholarships of £300 for sixth formers.

Postgraduate awards of £2,000 for 'exciting research and design' and a postdoctoral award of £5,000 for up to three years.

Annual grant total

In 2015/16 the charity held assets of £2.9 million and had an income of £98,500. Educational grants, scholarships and fellowships totalled £62,500.

Applications

See the charity's website for details of how to apply to each separate scheme. Students must apply through the university and not directly to the company.

Trades Union Congress Educational Trust

£5,500

Correspondent: Jackie Williams, Secretary, Unionlearn, Congress House, 23–28 Great Russell Street, London WC1B 3LS (020 7467 1278; email: jwilliams@tuc.org.uk; website: www.unionlearn.org.uk/bursaries-tuc-educational-trust)

CC number: 313741

Eligibility

Members of Trades Union Congress affiliated trade unions, to attend courses at selected colleges and universities. Applicants should not be receiving any other grants.

Types of grants

The trust offers scholarships and bursaries to students at selected institutions:

- Keele University bursaries – ten annual bursaries of £250 for Undergraduate Certificate in Industrial Relations (open to anyone with industrial relations experience); also three annual bursaries of £1,000 for part-time postgraduate courses in industrial relations, industrial relations and employment law, industrial relations and HRM or European HRM and industrial relations
- One Year Awards – at Northern College, Coleg Harlech, Hillcroft College, Fircroft College and Newbattle Abbey College for one-year residential courses leading to a diploma in labour studies, history or social studies. These courses are financed by mandatory state grants and the TUC provides three additional bursaries of £925
- Ruskin College bursaries – three annual bursaries of £1,000 (or two payments of £500 if part-time) for an MA in Global Labour and Social Change
- Clive Jenkins European Study Bursary – two bursaries of £800 each to cover travel and subsistence costs for a visit to a European Union country, to study aspects of trade unionism, industrial relations or training and employment

Further information about the grants available is given on the website.

Annual grant total

In 2016 the trust had assets of £1.7 million and an income of £27.7 million. Bursaries during the year totalled £5,500. A further £80,000 was spent on course costs.

Applications

For some awards applications need to be made through an educational institution, for others application forms are available online. See the Unionlearn website for more details on each of the available bursaries.

Local charities

This section lists local charities that award grants to individuals for educational purposes. The information in the entries applies only to educational grants and concentrates on what the charity actually does rather than on what its governing document allows it to do.

Regional classification

We have divided the UK into 12 geographical areas, as numbered on the map on page 128. Scotland, Wales and England have been divided into unitary or local authorities, in some cases grouped in counties or regions. On page 129 you can find the list of unitary or local authorities within each county or area. (Please note: not all of these unitary authorities have a grant-making charity included in this guide.)

Northern Ireland

Unfortunately, the section for Northern Ireland remains limited, as very little information is available at present on charities based there. It is estimated that there are between 7,000 and 12,000 charities operating in Northern Ireland. The Charity Commission for Northern Ireland, therefore, expects the completion of the registration process to take several years. In the meantime, up-to-date information on the progress of registration can be found on the Charity Commission for Northern Ireland's website: www.charity commissionni.org.uk.

The Northern Ireland section has not been subdivided into smaller areas. Within the other sections, charities are ordered as follows:

Scotland

- First, the charities which apply to the whole of Scotland, or at least two areas in Scotland, are listed.
- Second, Scotland is further divided into electoral board areas, and then again into council areas.
- Should an entry apply to at least two council areas, it will appear in the appropriate electoral board section.

Wales

- First, charities which apply to the whole of Wales, or at least two areas of Wales, are listed.
- Second, Wales is sub-divided into four regions. The entries which apply to the whole region, or to at least two local government areas within it, appear first.
- Third, the remaining charities are listed under the relevant local government division.

England

- First, charities which apply to the whole of England, or at least two regions within it, are listed.
- Second, England is divided into nine regions. The entries which apply to the whole region, or to at least two counties within it, appear first.
- Third, the regions are divided into counties.
- The counties are sub-divided into relevant local government areas.

London

- First, the charities which apply to the whole of Greater London, or to at least two boroughs are listed.

- The charities serving London are further sub-divided into the relevant boroughs.

Within each geographical category, the charities are listed alphabetically.

To make sure you identify every relevant local charity, look at the entries in each relevant category in the following order:
1. Unitary or local authority (for England, Scotland and Wales) or borough (for Greater London)
2. County (for England)
3. Region (for England, Wales and, in some cases, Scotland)
4. Country (for England, Northern Ireland, Scotland and Wales)

For example, if you live in Liverpool, first establish which region Merseyside is in by looking at the map on page 128. Then, having established that Merseyside is in region on page 250, North West, look under the 'Geographical areas' list on page 129 and find the page where the entries for Merseyside begin. Firstly, look under the heading for Liverpool to see if there are any relevant charities. Then work back through the charities under Merseyside generally, the charities under North West generally, and then charities listed under England generally.

Having found grant-makers covering your area, please read any other eligibility requirements carefully. While some charities can and do give grants for any need for people in their area of benefit, most have other, more specific criteria which potential applicants must meet in order to be eligible.

Geographical areas

Northern Ireland

Aisling Bursaries

£34,000 (45 grants)

Correspondent: Stephanie Vallely, Secretary, West Belfast Partnership Board, 218–226 Falls Road, Belfast BT12 6AH (028 9080 9202; email: info@wbpb.org; website: belfastmediagroup.com/aislingbursaries/2011-aisling-bursaries/apply-for-an-aisling-bursary)

Eligibility
Students in further or higher education who live in the West Belfast. Applicants must be preparing to study or be currently studying on a full-time or part-time course. People returning to education may also be supported. Our research shows that special consideration is usually given to candidates who have significant barriers preventing them from realising their full potential, for example economic or family circumstances.

Types of grants
Grants of £1,000 and £500 are available, normally for a full-time and part-time bursary respectively, and can be one-off or recurrent.

Annual grant total
In 2016, 45 students received bursaries totalling £34,000.

Exclusions
Grants are not available to students repeating part or all of an academic year unless this has been formally agreed on the basis of medical or personal circumstances. Previous recipients of a full-time bursary cannot re-apply but previous applicants are welcome to.

Applications
Application forms are available from the correspondent or through the Belfast Media Group and West Belfast Partnership websites. The application round usually opens in either May or June.

Other information
Local businesses, companies and individuals in West Belfast are contributing to the funds to make the bursaries available.

The Thomas Devlin Fund

£32,500 (18 grants)

Correspondent: Barbara Woods, Community Foundation for Northern Ireland, Community House, Citylink Business Park, Albert Street, Belfast BT12 4HQ (028 9024 5927; email: bwoods@communityfoundationni.org; website: www.communityfoundationni.org/Grants/Thomas-Devlin-Fund)

Eligibility
Young people in Northern Ireland between the ages of 15 and 19 who are aiming to pursue a career in the arts and require a small amount of financial assistance to undertake an opportunity or training.

Types of grants
Bursaries of up to £1,750 for specific opportunities and activities which will help to develop young people's skills in music and arts.

Annual grant total
In 2016/17 the Thomas Devlin Fund awarded 18 grants totalling £32,500.

The fund is administered by the Community Foundation for Northern Ireland.

Exclusions
Due to high demand, lessons or exam fees are not normally supported and assistance could only be given in exceptional circumstances.

Applications
Application forms can be downloaded from the fund's website and will need to be completed by individuals together with their tutor/teacher. Applicants have to outline how the award would improve their performance and what positive impact it would have on others.

The fund is normally opened in early spring, however the application deadlines are likely to change – consult the website for the latest updates.

Other information
This fund was set up in memory of Belfast teenager Thomas Devlin and has its own website www.thomasdevlin.com. The fund is administered by the Community Foundation for Northern Ireland which also administers a number of funds for organisations. The trustees intend to award grants until 2066.

The Fermanagh Recreational Trust

Correspondent: The Administrator, Fermanagh Recreational Trust, Fermanagh House, Broadmeadow Place, Enniskillen BT74 7HR (02866320 210; email: info@fermanaghtrust.org; website: www.fermanaghtrust.org)

CC number: XR 22580

Eligibility
Individuals based in County Fermanagh.

Types of grants
Grants can be given towards equipment and in educational bursaries for training or other activities which will help individuals to develop their potential, particularly through recreation and sport.

Annual grant total
The total amount of grants awarded was not specified.

Exclusions
Grants are not considered retrospectively.

Applications
Application forms are available to download from the trust's website. They should be submitted by the end of February or August. Two independent references must also be included (this requirement is only waived in exceptional circumstances).

Other information
This fund is administered by the Fermanagh Trust which also administers funds for organisations for a variety of purposes in Fermanagh, particularly involving young people and youth development.

Some of the funds administered by the Fermanagh Trust offer support to individuals, including for voluntary work overseas and bursaries for sport, arts or community service activities. Details of grants available are given on the Fermanagh Trust website.

The Presbyterian Children's Society

£299,500

Correspondent: Dr Paul Gray, Executive Secretary, 5th Floor, Glengall Exchange, 3 Glengall Street, Belfast BT12 5AB (028 9032 3737; email: paulgray1866@gmail. com; website: www. presbyterianchildrenssociety.org)

CC number: NIC101444

Eligibility

Children aged 23 or under who are in full or part-time education, living in Northern Ireland and the Republic of Ireland, usually in single parent families. One parent must be a Presbyterian.

Types of grants

One-off 'exceptional' grants are made to assist with educational expenses. Regular grants are also given to families.

Annual grant total

In 2016 the charity held assets of £11.7 million and had an income of £784,500. Grants to children amounted to £599,500 and were given for both social welfare and educational purposes. We estimate educational grants to have totalled around £299,500.

Applications

Applications are made by Presbyterian clergy; forms are available from the correspondent or to download from the website.

The Royal Ulster Constabulary GC – Police Service of Northern Ireland Benevolent Fund

£185,000

Correspondent: The Administrator, RUCGC-PSNI Benevolent Fund, 77–79 Garnerville Road, Belfast BT4 2NX (028 9076 4200; email: benevolentfund@policefedni.com; website: policebenevolentfund.com)

IR number: XN 48380

Eligibility

Members and former members of the Royal Ulster Constabulary, and their dependants. The main objectives of the charity are to look after serving PSNI officers, widows/widowers, other dependants, injured officers and those with disabilities, pensioners and former members who are not pensionable and parents of deceased officers, all experiencing financial hardship or difficulties. Eligibility relates to financial hardship but 'the bottom line is simply that a case of need must be identified'.

Types of grants

Support can be given in grants and loans to people in education, including schoolchildren, college students, undergraduates, mature students and individuals with special educational needs. Help can be given towards general educational needs. Interest-free loans are also offered.

Annual grant total

In 2016 the fund had assets of £16.4 million and an income of £1.2 million. The amount in grants given to individuals totalled £370,000. We estimate that educational grants to individuals totalled around £185,000.

Applications

Initial contact should be made in writing to the correspondent. Eligible applicants will then be advised further on the application process. Candidates are visited by the representatives of the charity who then present the case to the management committee, which meets on the first Wednesday of each month. Each Regional Board has an appointed Benevolent Fund Representative. Applicants will be required to provide full financial breakdown and quotes where possible.

Other information

Additional help is offered by a number of other organisations, details of which can be found on the Northern Ireland Police Family Assistance website (www. northernirelandpolicefamilyassistance. org.uk).

Scotland

General

The John Maurice Aitken Trust

£47,000

Correspondent: The Trustees, 4th Floor, 221 West George Street, Glasgow G2 2ND (0141 248 1200; email: info@ jmatrust.com; website: jmatrust.com)

OSCR number: SC045343

Eligibility

Young people aged 15 to 25 who are in need and live in Scotland.

Types of grants

One-off grants of £100 to £1,000 to help young people fulfil their potential in cultural, educational and social aspects of their lives or find sustainable long-term employment.

Annual grant total

In 2015/16 the trust had assets of £50,500 and income of £202,000. Educational grants to individuals totalled £47,000.

Applications

Application forms can be downloaded from the trust's website. Applications are awarded quarterly but if your application is urgent contact the trust directly.

The Avenel Trust

£1,900

Correspondent: The Trustees, 77 Comiston Drive, Edinburgh EH10 5QT

OSCR number: SC014280

Eligibility

Children in need under 18 and students of nursery nursing living in Scotland.

Types of grants

One-off grants.

Annual grant total

In 2015/16 the charity had an income of £14,500 and a total expenditure of £12,800. We estimate that educational grants to individuals totalled around £1,900.

Applications

Applications are considered every two months and should be submitted through a tutor or third party such as a social worker, health visitor or teacher. Applicants are encouraged to provide as much information about their family or individual circumstances and needs as possible in their applications. Applications can only be accepted from people currently residing in Scotland.

The Carnegie Trust for the Universities of Scotland

£2.3 million (339 grants)

Correspondent: The Trustees, Andrew Carnegie House, Pittencrief Street, Dunfermline, Fife KY12 8AW (01383 724990; fax: 01383 749799; website: www.carnegie-trust.org)

OSCR number: SC015600

Eligibility

The trust supports undergraduate or postgraduate students and academic staff at the fifteen Scottish universities (Aberdeen, Abertay, Dundee, Edinburgh, Edinburgh Napier, Glasgow, Glasgow Caledonian, Heriot-Watt, Queen Margaret, Robert Gordon, St Andrews, Stirling, Strathclyde, UHI and West of Scotland).

More specific eligibility requirements apply to different categories (very detailed guidelines are available on the trust's website).

Types of grants

The trust offers support through the following awards:

- Fee assistance – help with the tuition fees for a first degree course at a Scottish university to individuals who lack the financial means to attend the course
- Vacation Scholarships – £175 per week to undergraduate degree students at a Scottish university demonstrating exceptional merit to undertake a specific programme of independent research over the summer vacation (two to six weeks in length). Any project should be of direct benefit to the applicant's academic work
- Carnegie-Cameron Bursaries – payment of tuition fees for a one year master's degree course
- Carnegie-Caledonian PhD Scholarships – the value for the 2017/18 year was £16,200. A first-class honours undergraduate degree is a pre-requisite
- St Andrew's Society of New York Scholarships – awarded by the St Andrew's Society for the State of New York. Awards are given to Scottish students towards a year of study in the United States, mainly covering accommodation and travel expenses. Preference is given to individuals who 'have no previous experience of the United States and for whom a period of study there can be expected to be a life-changing experience'
- Research Incentive Grants – from £500 to £7,500 to academics employed by a Scottish university to undertake a short research project. Early career researchers are encouraged and special consideration is given to applicants who are within five years (excluding breaks) of starting their independent academic career;
- Carnegie Centenary Professorship – a maximum of two awards each year of up to £40,000 for a period of three to six months to visiting world class scholars who have been nominated. Professorships are tenable at any of the fifteen Scottish universities;
- Collaborative Research Grants – of up to £50,000 for a joint research project (researchers from more than one Scottish university) lasting one to two years

Annual grant total

In 2015/16 the trust held assets of £74 million and had an income of £2.9 million. A total of £2.3 million was awarded to 339 individuals, broken down into the following categories:

PhD scholarships	£915,000
Collaborative research grants	£416,000
Research incentive grants	£395,500
Carnegie-Cameron bursaries	£361,000
Fee assistance	£153,000
Vacation scholarships	£88,000
Centenary professorships	£67,000

Exclusions

Undergraduates who receive government funding towards the costs of their tuition fees (SAAS support) are not eligible. Courses at the Scottish Higher Education Institute delivered and validated by a university outside Scotland, Open University courses, HNC and HND diploma courses, access courses, accelerated degree courses with a graduate entry, Continuing Professional Development (CPD) courses, university courses below degree level (diploma or certificate courses) and second degrees are not supported towards the tuition fees.

Applications

Some applications may be made online on the trust's website, some may need an academic referral or nomination and Vacation Scholarships **must** be applied for via the university. For specific details of each of the awards see the trust's website. A preliminary telephone call may be helpful.

Other information

Carnegie-Cameron Bursaries are made available to support fees for one-year taught postgraduate degree courses and are awarded through universities.

The Henry Dryerre Scholarship which supports students wishing to undertake a PhD in medical or veterinary physiology is offered every three years. The scheme is administered in the same way as the Carnegie/Caledonian Scholarships. It will next be offered in 2020.

Churchill University Scholarships Trust for Scotland

£24,000

Correspondent: The Trustees, c/o MacRae & Kaur LLP, 6th Floor, Atlantic House, 45 Hope Street, Glasgow G2 6AE

OSCR number: SC013492

Eligibility

Students in Scotland.

Types of grants

Grants are given for one-off educational projects of benefit to the community, for example, medical electives or voluntary work overseas in a student's gap year or holiday.

Annual grant total

In 2015/16 the trust had an income of £19,500 and expenditure of £28,000. We estimate that grants given to individuals totalled £24,000.

Exclusions

Grants are not made for any other educational needs, such as course fees, books or living expenses.

Applications

Apply in writing to the correspondent.

Creative Scotland

£350,000 (50 grants)

Correspondent: Administrator, Waverley Gate, 2–4 Waterloo Place, Edinburgh EH1 3EG (0845 603 6000; email: enquiries@creativescotland.com; website: www.creativescotland.com)

Eligibility

People working at a professional level in the arts, screen and creative industries based in Scotland.

Types of grants

A number of funding programmes are available:

Open Project funding – this fund supports the arts, screen and creative industries, with projects that help them explore, realise and develop their creative potential and widen access to their work. This is open to both individuals and organisations. 'You can apply for funding from £1,000 to £100,000. We will also consider applications up to £150,000.'

Regular funding – supports a range of arts and creative organisations and sustainable environments through which artists and creative people can deepen and deliver their work. Regular funding provides 3-year funding for organisations.

Targeted funding – addresses specific activities and development needs in a sector, specialism, and/or geographic area, and can be shaped in response to sectoral reviews, strategic planning or consultation with external partners.

Annual grant total

From July to September 2017 Creative Scotland awarded almost £350,000 to around 50 individuals through its Open Project Funding and Targeted Funding schemes.

Creative Scotland does not list its awards annually. Awards given on a monthly basis can be found on the website.

Exclusions

Awards are not generally made to students. Most funding is not available to architects/designers, academics, amateur companies, individuals in permanent employment within foundation organisations, flexibly funded organisations or national companies and collections.

For specific exceptions for each of the funds see the guidelines on the website.

Applications

Application forms, guidelines and deadlines for different funding programmes are available from Creative Scotland's website.

Other information

Creative Scotland is a 'public body that supports the arts, screen and creative industries across all parts of Scotland on behalf of everyone who lives, works or visits here'. Funding is distributed from the Scottish government and the National Lottery.

The Cross Trust

£124,000 (35 grants)

Correspondent: Kathleen Carnegie, Secretary, McCash & Hunter LLP, Solicitors, 25 South Methven Street, Perth PH1 5ES (01738 620451; fax: 01738 631155; email: kathleencarnegie@ mccash.co.uk; website: www. thecrosstrust.org.uk)

OSCR number: SC008620

Eligibility

People aged 16 to 30 who are of Scottish birth or parentage proposing 'a study or project that will extend the boundaries of their knowledge of human life'. Applicants must be in genuine financial need.

Types of grants

The trust offers support from £200 to £4,000 through the following:

- Awards for university or college (including music and art schools) students who can demonstrate outstanding academic achievements and who have taken full advantage of support available from local authorities, student loan opportunities and so on. Second degree and postgraduate studies are only considered in exceptional circumstances. Grants are made towards university or college costs, study/travel overseas, study visits and projects. Attendance at conferences, symposia, extra-curricular courses, voluntary work and gap year opportunities can also be considered

▸ Assistance towards projects and expeditions which do not form part of a degree. Candidates are required to provide evidence of efforts to secure funding elsewhere

▸ Awards for vacation studies in the arts (in its broad sense). The awards are designed 'to enable students of the highest academic merit and limited financial circumstances to attend conferences, symposia, workshops or master classes or to visit libraries, museums, galleries, concerts or centres of excellence in direct and demonstrable connection with their studies.' Around 15 to 20 awards can be made each year to people studying at Scottish universities

▸ Awards for medical electives studies abroad (20 awards each year)

▸ The John Fife Travel Award to people (normally under the age of 30, but in exceptional cases up to 40 years old) studying or working in horticulture. The award is generally up to £500 but a maximum of £1,000 can be awarded in exceptional circumstances

Annual grant total

In 2015/16 the trust had assets of £5.2 million and an expenditure of £255,000. Throughout the year the trust awarded a total of £124,000 to individuals.

A total of 35 awards of £2,000 or more were made to individuals across the following disciplines:

Music and musical performance	13
Professional dance/musical theatre	4
Medicine	6
Geography and international studies	4
Art	5
Exercise physiology	1
Arab world studies	1
Educational psychology	1

Exclusions

The trust reminds that 'students who have already received support from the trust for a period of elective study abroad are not eligible for further support'.

Applications

Application forms for each of the awards can be found on the trust's website. Applicants are required to provide full information on their financial circumstances, attach a passport photo, provide an academic reference and details of applications for other funding. Further guidance and closing deadlines for applications for each of the awards can be found on the website.

City of Dundee Educational Trust Scheme

£6,000 (21 grants)

Correspondent: Jeffrey Hope, Administrator, Miller Hendry Solicitors, 13 Ward Road, Dundee DD1 1LU (01382 200000; email: JeffreyHope@ millerhendry.co.uk)

OSCR number: SC015820

Eligibility

Further/higher education students in, or with a strong connection to, Dundee. Priority is given to those who do not receive any statutory awards.

Types of grants

One-off grants ranging from £150 to £300 towards general educational costs.

Annual grant total

In 2016 the trust had assets of £770,000 and an income of £198,500. Throughout the year the trust awarded around £6,000 in 21 grant payments to individuals.

Applications

Application forms can be requested from the correspondent. Applications, together with a CV, should be submitted at least two weeks before the trustees' quarterly meetings. The meetings are held in March, June, September and December.

East Lothian Educational Trust

£29,000

Correspondent: J. Morrison, Administrator, Department of Corporate Resources, John Muir House, Haddington, East Lothian EH41 3HA (01620 827273; email: eleducationaltrust@eastlothian.gov.uk; website: www.eastlothian.gov.uk/info/ 828/activities_and_support_for_young_ people/1496/east_lothian_educational_ trust)

OSCR number: SC010587

Eligibility

People in education or training who live in the area covered by East Lothian Council (former county of East Lothian).

Types of grants

Support is available to people 'undertaking studies, courses or projects of an educational nature, including scholarships abroad and educational travel'. Grants are normally one-off and means-tested. According to our research they range from around £100 to £700 and can be awarded to schoolchildren, further/higher education students

(including mature students and postgraduates), people in training, and individuals with special educational needs. Assistance is available for a wide range of educational needs, including uniforms/clothing, fees, study/travel abroad, books, equipment/instruments, maintenance/living expenses, research, accommodation and excursions.

Annual grant total

In 2015/16 the charity had assets of £1.7 million and an income of £68,000. Throughout the year the charity gave around £29,000 in grants to individuals.

The charity also awarded £18,200 in grants to organisations.

Exclusions

Residents of Musselburgh, Wallyford and Whitecraig are not included. Grants are intended to be supplementary only.

Applications

Application forms can be downloaded from the trust's website or requested from the correspondent. Applicants should provide full costs of the course and associated expenses (such as fees, accommodation, travel, necessities, maintenance, special equipment), as well as give details of their household income. Applications can be submitted directly by the individual or through a parent/guardian. The trustees meet four times a year, usually in February, May, August and November.

Esdaile Trust Scheme 1968

£16,500

Correspondent: Fiona Watson, Administrator, Exchange Place 3, Semple Street, Edinburgh EH3 8BL (0131 473 3500; fax: 0131 473 3535; email: fiona. watson@scott-moncrieff.com; website: www.scott-moncrieff.com/services/ charities/charitable-trusts/esdaile-trust)

OSCR number: SC006938

Eligibility

Daughters of ministers of the Church of Scotland, daughters of missionaries appointed or nominated by the Overseas Council of the Church of Scotland, and daughters of widowed deaconesses. Applicants must be between the ages of 12 and 25. Preference is given to families with a low income.

Types of grants

Annual grants towards general educational costs. In 2015/16 grants ranged from £240 to £1,600.

Annual grant total

In 2015/16 the trust had assets of £948,500 and an income of £28,500. Throughout the year the trustees awarded almost £16,500 in grants to 22 individuals.

Applications

Application forms can be obtained from the trust's website and should be completed by a parent/guardian. Applications should be submitted to the correspondent no later than 31 May each year. Grants are distributed by early September.

Other information

The trust also co-operates with the Society for the Benefit of Sons and Daughters of Ministers of the Church of Scotland and the Glasgow Society of the Sons and Daughters of Ministers of the Church of Scotland in the distribution of student grants. The societies can support both boys and girls.

Fife Educational Trust

£29,500

Correspondent: Education Services, Finance and Procurement, Fife Council, Rothesay House, Glenrothes KY7 5PQ

OSCR number: SC004325

Eligibility

People who have a permanent address within the Fife council area and who attended a secondary or primary school there.

Types of grants

Our previous research suggests support for individuals below postgraduate level is usually restricted to travel grants where this is an integral part of the course of study, but can also be given for music, drama and visual arts.

Annual grant total

In 2015/16 the trust had an income of £74,500 and a total expenditure of £59,500. We estimate that the trust gave around £29,500 in grants to individuals.

Applications

Apply in writing to the correspondent. Applicants must give their permanent address, details of schools they attended within Fife with dates of attendance, and details of other money available. Applications are considered in March.

The Caroline Fitzmaurice Trust

£25,000

Correspondent: The Secretaries, 106 South Street, St Andrews KY16 9QD (01334 468604; email: elcalderwood@pagan.co.uk; website: www. carolinefitzmaurice.org.uk)

OSCR number: SC00518

Eligibility

Girls and young women under the age of 23 who live in the geographical area of the diocese of St Andrews, Dunkeld and Dunblane. The trustees will require successful applicants to make an effort in raising funds elsewhere through their own personal attempts and to subsequently contribute to the community wherever they may settle. Applicants must demonstrate a specific financial need and evidence of high promise.

Types of grants

Grants of between £200 and £5,000 are awarded.

Annual grant total

In 2016/17 the trust had an income of £17,400 and a total expenditure of £25,500. We estimate that the trust gave around £25,000 in grants to individuals.

Exclusions

The application guidelines on the trust's website note that 'the trustees will not approve applications which are based on solely financial need, and will require evidence of high promise. They will fund only a proportion of the total costs.'

Applications

Application forms can be obtained from the correspondent and are considered only once a year, usually in early June. The closing date for applications is 30 April annually. A written report from the applicant's referee is required and applicants who are under the age of 18 at the time of the application are additionally asked to provide full information on parent/s' financial circumstances.

Other information

Successful applicants are required to provide a written report to the trustees as soon as practicable after the end of each period of funding.

James Gillan's Trust

£27,000

Correspondent: The Administrator, R. & R. Urquhart, 121 High Street, Forres, Morayshire IV36 1AB (01309 672216)

OSCR number: SC016739

Eligibility

People training for the ordained ministry in the Church of Scotland who have lived in, or whose parents have lived in, Moray or Nairn for at least three years. There is a preference for those native to the parishes of Dallas, Dyke, Edinkillie, Forres, Kinloss or Rafford.

Types of grants

The trust provides grants, donations, loans, gifts or pensions to individuals. Awards are of up to £1,000.

Annual grant total

In 2015/16 the trust had an income of £23,000 and a total expenditure of £27,400.

We estimate that the trust awarded around £27,000 in grants to individuals for educational purposes.

Applications

Apply in writing to the correspondent.

Glasgow Educational and Marshall Trust

£46,000 (67 grants)

Correspondent: Administrator, Merchants House of Glasgow, 7 West George Street, Glasgow G2 1BA (0141 433 4449; fax: 0141 424 1731; email: enquiries@gemt.org.uk; website: www. gemt.org.uk)

OSCR number: SC012582

Eligibility

People, usually those over 18 years old, who are in need and who have lived in the city of Glasgow (as at the re-organisation in 1975) for a minimum of five years (excluding time spent studying in the city with a home address elsewhere). The trust holds a list of the postcodes which qualify for support and this can be seen on the website.

The trust states that awards to undergraduate students are made only in exceptional circumstances.

Types of grants

One-off and recurrent grants ranging from £195 to £1,500 in 2015/16. Support can be given to mature students, postgraduates, people in further/higher education and vocational training. Travel expenses, school excursions, books, course fees, living expenses, study/travel abroad, equipment/instruments, childcare for mature students can all be funded.

Grants are normally given for courses where a Students Awards Agency for Scotland grant is not available or where such grants do not cover the total costs.

Annual grant total

In 2015/16 the charity had assets of £2.6 million and an income of almost £106,000. During the year, the charity awarded around £46,000 in 67 grants to individuals.

The charity also awarded £10,900 to seven organisations.

Exclusions

Retrospective awards are not made and courses run by privately-owned institutions are not supported.

Applications

Application forms and full guidelines are available on the trust's website and can be submitted directly by the individual together with two written references. The trustees meet on the first Wednesday of March, June, September and December. Applications for grants for university courses which start in September/October must be received by 31 July.

The Glasgow Highland Society

£6,500

Correspondent: The Secretaries, Alexander Sloan C. A, 38 Cadogan Street, Glasgow G2 7HF (0141 354 0354; email: kt@alexandersloan.co.uk; website: www.alexandersloan.co.uk/ghs)

OSCR number: SC015479

Eligibility

Students who have a connection with the Highlands (for example, lived or went to school there) and who are now studying in Glasgow. Grants are normally given for first degrees only, unless postgraduate studies are a natural progression of the degree.

Types of grants

Grants of around £75 help with fees for people at college or university or who are in vocational training (including mature students). Grants may also be given for Gaelic research projects and apprenticeships.

Annual grant total

In 2015 the charity had an income of £5,700 and a total expenditure of £6,900. We estimate that the charity awarded around £6,500 in grants to individuals for educational purposes.

Applications

Apply in writing to the correspondent.

Other information

The correspondent has informed us that the trust may be winding down but a decision has not been made yet. Applications are still being accepted.

Highlands and Islands Educational Trust Scheme

£9,400 (41 grants)

Correspondent: The Trustees, Shepherd and Wedderburn LLP, 1 Exchange Crescent, Conference Square, Edinburgh EH3 8UL

OSCR number: SC014655

Eligibility

Students who live in the local government areas administered by: Highland Council; Argyll and Bute Council; Western Isles Council; Orkney Islands Council; and Shetland Islands Council.

Types of grants

According to the 2015/16 annual report, grants are given for purposes including: bursaries for senior school, further and higher education; grants for those undertaking an apprenticeship or traineeship; travel grants for students; grants and prizes for the study of and proficiency in the Gaelic language; special equipment.

Annual grant total

In 2015/16 the trust had an income of £58,000 and a total expenditure of £59,000. Grants were made to 41 individuals totalling £9,400.

Applications

Apply in writing to the correspondent.

The Lethendy Trust

£4,900 (14 grants)

Correspondent: George Hay, Trust Administrator, Henderson Loggie, The Vision Building, 20 Greenmarket, Dundee DD1 4QB (01382 200055; fax: 01382 221240; email: ghay@hlca.co.uk)

OSCR number: SC003428

Eligibility

Young people with a strong connection to the Tayside or North Fife areas.

Types of grants

Grants of between £150 and £500 are given for young people who are travelling abroad with charitable organisations to carry out charitable activities.

Annual grant total

In 2016/17 the trust had assets of £3 million and an income of £76,500. Grants were awarded to 14 individuals, totalling £4,900. A further £46,500 was awarded in grants to organisations.

Exclusions

Support is not given to individuals for school/college fees. The correspondent has informed us that the trust 'does not currently support purely academic funding requests from individuals nor any requests from individuals for any purpose who do not have a strong connection with Tayside or north Fife'.

Applications

Applications may be made in writing to the correspondent. The trust states that there are regular meetings throughout the year to consider applications.

Other information

The trust also supports local charities.

The Dr Thomas Lyon Bequest

£600

Correspondent: Secretary, The Merchant Company, The Merchant Hall, 22 Hanover Street, Edinburgh EH2 2EP (0131 220 9284; email: info@mcoe.org.uk or gregor.murray@mcoe.org.uk; website: www.mcoe.org.uk)

OSCR number: SC010284

Eligibility

Scottish orphans of members of Her Majesty's Forces and of the Mercantile Marine. Applicants should be between the ages of 5 and 18 and require financial assistance.

Types of grants

Grants ranging from £500 to £1,500 are offered to children in primary and secondary education towards the costs of clothing and school uniforms, books, educational outings and school fees.

Annual grant total

In 2015/16 the charity had an income of £9,000 and a total expenditure of £1,300. We estimate that about £600 was given in grants to individuals.

Applications

Applications may be made in writing to the correspondent. They should state the individual's total income and the regiment/Service of their parent as well as the cause and date of their death.

Other information

The charity also has a competition for young people between 13 and 18 – The Merchant Company of Edinburgh Prize for Initiate, where a top prize of £500 is awarded to the person or group demonstrating initiative and enterprise, business skills, and environmental, community and/or charitable involvement.

Mathew Trust

£2,400 (six grants)

Correspondent: The Trustees, The Vision Building, 20 Greenmarket, Dundee DD1 4QB (01382 200055)

OSCR number: SC016284

Eligibility

People in need who live in the local government areas of the City of Dundee, Angus, Perth and Kinross and Fife.

Types of grants

One-off grants for purposes such as fees, study/travel abroad for college/university students (including mature students), people in vocational or professional training/retraining or adult education, people starting work, people struggling to secure employment, overseas students and people with special educational needs.

Annual grant total

In 2015/16 the trust had assets of £8 million and an income of £297,500. Grants totalling £2,400 were made to six individuals to 'help fund overseas placements to enhance the individual's life skills and knowledge of other cultures', according to the annual report. There were also 17 grants made to organisations for training purposes.

Applications

Apply in writing to the correspondent. Applications can be submitted directly by the individual for consideration by the trustees every two months.

Other information

Grants are also made to organisations.

Maxton Bequest

Correspondent: Jillian Harper, Education and Children's Services, 5th Floor, Rothesay House, Rothesay Place, Glenrothes KY7 5PQ (03451 55 55 55 + Ext 44 41 99; email: jillian.harper@fife. gov.uk; website: www.fifedirect.org.uk)

Eligibility

People above school age who are 'engaged in study at any continuation class, secondary school, further education college or university or engaged in training or serving apprenticeship to any trade or profession'. Applicants must ordinarily reside (or have parents who reside) in Crieff or Kirkcaldy and be in need.

Types of grants

Our research suggests that grants are available for clothing, books, equipment, educational outings in the UK, fees or living expenses.

Annual grant total

We were unable to determine the amount awarded through the fund.

Applications

Application forms and further guidelines can be requested from the correspondent. The exact application deadlines are stated on the website and are usually around October/November.

Other information

The charity's funds form part of the Fife Educational Trust. The fund does not have a registered charity number.

The McGlashan Charitable Trust

£10,000 (44 grants)

Correspondent: Gordon Armour, Administrator, 66 Octavia Terrace, Greenock PA16 7PY (email: gordon. armour66@btinternet.com)

OSCR number: SC020930

Eligibility

Grants are made in a very wide range of subjects to postgraduate students who are aged under 30 and were either born in Scotland or were born elsewhere and are studying in Scotland.

Types of grants

Grants tend to be in the range of £500 to £1,000.

Annual grant total

In 2015/16 the trust had an income of £89,500 and a total expenditure of £109,000. The trust has previously told us that it is fairly small and grants to students vary from year to year, but the total expenditure on postgraduate students tends to be around £10,000 per annum. Grants to organisations during the year totalled £46,000.

Applications

Applications can be made by email to the administrator during April (those arriving earlier or later will be ineligible) and must clearly state a need for financial support. Awards are made during July.

Other information

A few substantial grants are made to major Scottish charities, mainly those active in the arts. These applications may be made at any time of year.

Charities Administered by Scottish Borders Council

£13,900

Correspondent: Administrative Assistant, Council HQ, Newtown St Boswells, Melrose TD6 0SA (01835 824000 ext. 5833; website: www. scotborders.gov.uk/directory/23/ education_trusts)

OSCR number: SC043896

Eligibility

The Scottish Borders Council administers four educational trusts corresponding to the four former counties of Berwickshire, Peeblesshire, Roxburghshire and Selkirkshire. Applicants should either live in these areas or have family resident there.

Types of grants

Small grants can be given for educational outings and travel, adult education, studies of drama, music and visual arts, research, sports, special equipment/ instruments and postgraduate studies. Consult the charity's website for specific details.

Annual grant total

According to the combined accounts for 2015/16, the expenditure of each of the funds was as follows:

Roxburghshire Educational Trust	£9,900
Peeblesshire Educational Trust	£2,500
Selkirkshire Educational Trust	£1,400
Berwickshire Educational Trust	£80

The accounts state that all expenditure is for direct charitable activities. The grant total for the four funds was therefore £13,900.

Applications

Application forms for each of the trusts can be found on the Scottish Borders Council website or requested from the correspondent who can also answer any queries. Applications can be made at any time.

Other information

Awards are made on a first-come, first-served basis. Support can also be given to local clubs.

Scottish International Education Trust

£73,500 (44 grants)

Correspondent: Dr Michael Ewart, Director, Scottish International Education Trust, Turcan Connell, Princes Exchange, 1 Earl Grey Street, Edinburgh EH3 9EE (email: siet@ turcanconnell.com; website: www. scotinted.org.uk)

OSCR number: SC009207

Eligibility

Scottish people (by birth or upbringing) who wish to take their studies or training further in order to start a career. The trust looks for individuals who have 'ability and promise', generally with a good first degree (first-class honours or close to it) or an equivalent. Grants are rarely made to undergraduates and priority is given to postgraduate students, especially if assistance from public funds is not available (for example, if the course is at an overseas institution).

Types of grants

One-off and recurrent grants of up to £2,000 for educational expenses, such as fees, books/equipment, research or travel.

In the past, grants have included those in the areas of: international affairs; history; conservation and restoration; medicine; drama, dance and ballet; music; law; art; film-making and cinematography; and science, engineering and technology.

Annual grant total

In 2015/16 the trust held assets of £1.1 million and had an income of £33,000. During the year, 44 grants were made to individuals and totalled £73,500.

Exclusions

The trust does not normally make grants for:

) Courses leading to qualifications required for entry into a profession (e.g. teaching, legal practice)
) Purchase of musical instruments
) Undergraduate courses or courses below degree level

The website notes: 'Regrettably we cannot accept applications based purely on acute financial need.'

Applications

Applications should be made in writing via post or email to the correspondent including: a CV; details of the course; a statement of aims; the amount sought; two references. Full details of information required can be found on the website. Applications may be submitted at any time and will be assessed when received.

John Watson's Trust
See entry on page 144

Aberdeen and Aberdeenshire

Aberdeen Endowments Trust

£70,000

Correspondent: The Trustees, 19 Albert Street, Aberdeen AB25 1QF (01224 640194; fax: 01224 643918; email: aet1909@btopenworld.com; website: www.aberdeenendowmentstrust.co.uk/ index_1.html)

OSCR number: SC010507

Eligibility

Bursaries for Robert Gordon's College are subject to a review of household income and passing the entrance exam. To apply for other types of grants, applicants must be residents of Aberdeen.

Types of grants

The majority of the trust's grants are made to cover fees at Robert Gordon's College. However, grants can also be made available for:

) Secondary school bursaries – helping households of limited financial means
) Educational travel – to help young people participate in learning activities where they would otherwise be unable to do so
) Education in the Arts – to help people and organisations provide further education in music, drama, dance, and other expressive arts
) Further education – to take up opportunities in college, university, or other further education
) Educational projects – for example in literacy and numeracy, first aid
) Learning and developing skills in modern languages

Annual grant total

At the end of the 2016 financial year, the trust had assets totalling £1.5 million, an income of £1.2 million, and a total expenditure of £1.3 million. A total of £700,000 was awarded in grants, with £630,000 of that sum being used to pay for tuition fees at Robert Gordon's College. The remaining £70,000 was distributed among applicants seeking other educational advancement.

Applications

Application forms can be requested from the trust. The trustees meet around seven times during the year to consider applications. Bursaries for Robert Gordon's College are awarded to cover the first five years of secondary school, and can be extended for a sixth year. Bursaries are reviewed every two years and are subject to satisfactory pupil attendance and attainment.

Aberdeenshire Educational Trust

£39,000

Correspondent: The Trustees, Aberdeenshire Council, Woodhill House, Westburn Road, Aberdeen AB16 5GB (01261 813336; email: trust@ aberdeenshire.gov.uk)

OSCR number: SC028382

Eligibility

Schoolchildren and students of any age who, or whose immediate family, are resident in the former county of Aberdeenshire.

Types of grants

Small grants for students for travel grants to go on school trips. Also, grants to assist individuals in further education. The average amount awarded per person is £200.

Annual grant total

In 2015/16 the charity had assets of £3.3 million and an income of £139,000. A total of £39,000 was awarded in travel grants, prizes, and further education assistance.

Applications

Application forms are available from the correspondent. Grants are considered throughout the year. All applications are means-tested, therefore applicants are required to provide evidence of their income from the last tax year.

Other information

Grants are also made to schools, clubs and educational groups. Annual school prizes and preference grants are also awarded.

Dr John Calder Trust

£2,750

Correspondent: The Administrator, St Machar's Cathedral, 18 The Chanonry, Aberdeen AB24 1RQ

OSCR number: SC004299

Eligibility

People in need who live in the parish of Machar or within the city of Aberdeen. Individuals who are only resident in the area for their education and people from the area studying elsewhere are both eligible.

Types of grants

Grants are usually up to £750 according to our research, and can be given for general educational needs. In exceptional cases, individuals may apply for grants of up to £1,000.

Annual grant total

In 2016/17 the trust had an income of £130,500 and a total expenditure of £129,000. During the year, eight grants for education and welfare were awarded to individuals totalling £5,500. We have estimated that the total awarded for educational purposes was around £2,750.

Applications

Applications may be made in writing to the correspondent.

Other information

A smaller proportion of charitable expenditure is given to individuals for welfare needs. Organisations are also supported.

Huntly Educational Trust 1997

£5,000

Correspondent: The Secretary, 3 The Square, Huntly, Aberdeenshire AB54 8AE (website: gordonschools.aberdeenshire.sch.uk/ finance-grants)

OSCR number: SC026920

Eligibility

Primarily people living in the district of Huntly. Applicants from elsewhere in Scotland may also be supported if there are remaining funds and at the trustees' discretion.

Types of grants

Grants are given towards education and training, including vocational courses. General educational needs can be addressed, including books, equipment, tools, clothing, etc.

Annual grant total

In 2015/16 the trust had an income of £15,500 and a total expenditure of

£10,800. We have estimated that grants to individuals totalled around £5,000.

Applications

Application forms can be requested from the correspondent or downloaded from The Gordon Schools' website. Grants are normally considered at monthly meetings.

Other information

The trust also makes grants to local schools, colleges and other educational establishments.

Ayrshire

Ayrshire Educational Trust

£29,000

Correspondent: The Trustees, East Ayrshire Council, Council Headquarters, London Road, Kilmarnock KA3 7BU (01563 555650; fax: 01563 576269; email: education-admin@east-ayrshire.gov.uk; website: www.east-ayrshire.gov.uk)

OSCR number: SC018195

Eligibility

Individuals who live in the former county of Ayrshire.

Types of grants

Grants are awarded to cover travel, learning a new language, learning a new trade, specialist equipment, school trips and university bursaries. Grants are awarded to candidates in both full and part-time education.

Annual grant total

In 2015/16 the trust had an income of £4,000 and a total expenditure of £33,000. We estimate the total amount awarded in grants to individuals was £29,000.

Exclusions

The trust will not award grants for school uniform or equipment/ instruments.

Applications

Application forms can be requested from the correspondent. Applications are normally considered four times a year and can be submitted directly by individuals.

Other information

The trust seeks to promote formal education through schools and universities, and informal education that takes place in the community.

North Ayrshire

The Spiers Trust

£2,000

Correspondent: Joan Phillips, Community Development Team, Economy and Communities, North Ayrshire Council, 2nd Floor West, Cunninghame House, Irvine KA12 8EE (01294 324475; email: joanphillips@ north-ayrshire.gov.uk; website: www. north-ayrshire.gov.uk)

Eligibility

Children and young people who live in the parishes of Beith, Dalry, Dunlop, Kilbirnie, Lochwinnoch or Neilston and who attend secondary education there. Preference will be given to students from families with financial difficulties.

Types of grants

Grants ranging are available to secondary school and further/higher education students towards the cost of a course or special tuition in any academic, artistic, scientific or technological subject. Grants can be given for purposes including fees, travel costs, uniforms, books, equipment, accommodation and other educational necessities.

Annual grant total

Our research suggests that the trust gives around £2,000 a year in grants.

Applications

Application forms are available to download online or from the correspondent. Guidelines are also provided on the website.

Other information

The trust generates its income from investments and the rent derived from letting the land adjacent to former school grounds for grazing.

South Ayrshire

The C. K. Marr Educational Trust Scheme

£384,500

Correspondent: Alan Stewart, Clerk, 1 Howard Street, Kilmarnock KA1 2BW

OSCR number: SC016730

Eligibility

Students in tertiary education who live in Troon or the Troon electoral wards.

Types of grants

Bursaries, scholarships and educational travel grants to people at college or university, support towards postgraduate research and assistance to individuals with disabilities.

Annual grant total

In 2015/16 the trust had assets of £9.5 million and an income of £524,500. We estimate the amount of grants to individuals totalled £384,500 and were distributed as follows:

Higher Education bursaries	£178,000
Postgraduate scholarships	£64,000
Travel grants	£9,900
Vocational bursaries	£6,000
Prizes	£3,000
Walker Trust bursaries	£1,500

Applications

Apply in writing to the correspondent. Applications can be made either directly by the individual or through a third party, such as a university/college or an educational welfare agency, if applicable.

Other information

The trust also makes grants to organisations and funds the Marr Educational Resources Centre in Troon, which provides free access to computers, internet and other audio-visual equipment.

Central Scotland

Stirling

Stirlingshire Educational Trust

£33,500 (109 grants)

Correspondent: Iain Flett, 68 Port Street, Stirling FK8 2LJ (01786 474956; email: stgedtrust@btconnect.com; website: www.stirlingeducationaltrust. org.uk)

OSCR number: SC007528

Eligibility

People in need who live, or have lived in the past for a period of at least five consecutive years, in Stirlingshire (including Denny/Bonnybridge, Falkirk, Grangemouth, Kilsyth, Polmont, Stirling and environs).

Types of grants

The trust offers:

 Post-graduation scholarships – for research work or advanced/special study for those on a postgraduate course
 Travel scholarships – for travel within the UK or abroad for educational purposes
 Special grants – to mature students (over the age of 21) for obtaining the necessary educational qualifications to

enter university or an institute of further education. Grants may also be given to those undertaking an apprenticeship or practical experience of a profession

Support can be given towards fees, books, travel expenses, equipment/instruments or other educational necessities.

Annual grant total

In 2015/16 the trust had assets of £3.2 million and an income of £129,000. Grants totalling £33,500 were made to 109 individuals. A further £13,600 was given in grants to 41 schools and other organisations.

Applications

Applications can be made online on the trust's website. The trustees meet on the first Wednesday of June, September and March and applications should be submitted at least two weeks in advance of a meeting. An acknowledgement will be sent by email within seven working days of receipt of the application.

Other information

Organisations can also be supported.

Dumfries and Galloway

The Dumfriesshire Educational Trust

£41,000

Correspondent: Janice Thom, Area Committee Administrator, Municipal Chambers, Buccleuch Street, Dumfries DG1 2AD

OSCR number: SC003411

Eligibility

People normally living in Dumfriesshire who have had at least five years of education in Dumfriesshire.

Types of grants

Grants of up to £60, usually recurrent, are given to:

 Schoolchildren towards educational outings
 Students in further/higher education for books, fees/living expenses, study/travel abroad and student exchanges
 Mature students towards books and travel

Annual grant total

In 2015 the trust had assets of £3.7 million and an income of almost £52,500. Throughout the year the trust had a charitable expenditure of £42,500.

The majority of awards were to individuals with a total of £41,000.

Exclusions

Grants are not available for childcare for mature students or foreign students studying in the UK.

Applications

Application forms are available from Joanne Dalgleish, Senior Administrator, Woodbank, 30 Edinburgh Road, Dumfries DG1 1NW (01387 260493; fax: 01387 260453; email: joanne.dalgleish@dumgal.gov.uk); or from schools. They are considered quarterly, usually in March, June, September or December, and closing dates are stated on the form. Applications can be submitted directly by the individual, through the relevant school/college/educational welfare agency or through another third party. The form should be signed by the applicant. For recurrent grants, applicants must re-apply each academic year.

Hart Knowe Trust

£1,700 (two grants)

Correspondent: The Trustees, Hart Knowe, Eskdalemuir, Langholm, Dumfries and Galloway DG13 0QH

OSCR number: SC044303

Eligibility

Individuals in need resident in Dumfries and Galloway.

Types of grants

Grants for general educational needs.

Annual grant total

In 2015/16 the trust had assets of £14,500 and an income of £112,000. Educational grants were made to two individuals totalling £1,700.

Applications

Apply in writing to the correspondent.

The Holywood Trust

£46,000

Correspondent: The Administrator, Hestan House, Crichton Business Park, Bankend Road, Dumfries DG1 4TA (01387 269176; fax: 01387 269175; email: funds@holywood-trust.org.uk; website: www.holywood-trust.org.uk)

OSCR number: SC009942

Eligibility

Applicants should be age 15 to 25 and live in the Dumfries and Galloway regions. However, the trust is flexible and will consider applications from under 15s if there is severe need.

Types of grants

Grants of up to £500 (average £200), and in some exceptional circumstances

£2,500, are available under three categories:

- **Personal challenge:** for activities such as volunteering or studying abroad, or practising sport/music
- **Personal development:** for vocational training, driving lessons, extra qualifications, etc.
- **Student:** general grants for study in and outside the region

Annual grant total

In 2015/16 the trust had assets of £97.1 million and an income of £2.4 million. We estimate the trust awarded around £46,000 in educational grants during the year.

Exclusions

No grants are given towards carpets or accommodation deposits. Retrospective awards are not made.

Applications

Application forms can be downloaded from the website, to be sent back to the correspondent via post in a large-letter envelope. The trust states it is beneficial to include a supporting letter from a third party, e.g. a college tutor.

Other information

The trust also supports individuals for welfare purposes, and provides grants for various organisations across the regions.

John Primrose Trust

£3,800

Correspondent: The Trustees, 1 Newall Terrace, Dumfries DG1 1LN

OSCR number: SC009173

Eligibility

Young people in need who live in Dumfries and Maxwelltown or have a connection with these places by parentage.

Types of grants

Grants may be given to students to help with educational needs or to help people starting work or undertaking apprenticeships.

Annual grant total

In 2016/17 the trust had an income of £16,400 and a total expenditure of £15,900. We estimate that grants given to individuals for educational purposes totalled around £3,800.

Applications

Application forms are available from the correspondent. They are generally considered in June and December.

Other information

The trust awards grants to both individuals and organisations for educational and social welfare purposes.

John Wallace Trust Scheme

£7,500

Correspondent: Joanne Dalgleish, Senior Administrator, Woodbank, 30 Edinburgh Road, Dumfries DG1 1NW (01387 260493; fax: 01387 260453; email: joanne.dalgleish@dumgal.gov.uk; website: www.dumgal.gov.uk/article/16432/John-Wallace-Trust-Scheme)

OSCR number: SC011640

Eligibility

Students living in the upper Nithsdale area of the Dumfries and Galloway region, who are attending/about to enter higher or further education.

Types of grants

The trust provides the following:

- Bursaries for higher and further education to students entering/attending any university or institution of higher or further education, or open university courses
- Agricultural bursaries – to students entering/attending Barony College Parkgate or any other institution specialising in agriculture and allied sciences
- Travel grants for those living in the area to travel in the UK or abroad for an educational purpose

Bursaries can be given for up to five years.

Annual grant total

In 2015/16 the trust had an income of £8,200 and a total expenditure of almost £8,000. We estimate that grants given to individuals totalled around £7,500.

Applications

Application forms for bursaries can be downloaded from the website or obtained from the correspondent or local schools. The closing date for bursary applications is 31 December and students will be informed of their success by the following May.

People applying for travel grants are requested to do so in writing providing a statement of purpose for the journey, places to be visited, anticipated length and costs of the trip.

Other information

The trust also provides money to the Rector of Wallace Hall Academy for distribution of annual Ferguson Prizes to students following courses in agriculture or allied sciences.

Dunbarton-shire and Argyll

Argyll and Bute

Charles and Barbara Tyre Trust

£17,800 (11 grants)

Correspondent: Christine Heads, Clerk to the Governors, William Duncan & Co, Loch Awe House, Barmore Road, Tarbet, Argyll PA29 6TW (01880 820227; email: christine.heads@wdargyll.co.uk; website: www.charlesandbarbaratyretrust.org.uk)

OSCR number: SC031378

Eligibility

Children and young people between the ages of 18 and 25 who live within the former county of Argyll (which includes Kinlochleven but excludes Helensburgh and the Island of Bute), have completed their school education and are of the protestant faith.

Types of grants

Grants are given to improve individuals' qualifications or for retraining. Support can be offered towards further/higher education, Open University courses, training and development courses which are additional to the applicant's existing degree or qualification. Funding can be given for gaining new skills, leadership and initiative development and similar educational activities.

People with physical or mental disabilities (whether temporary or permanent) are also entitled to apply for a 'recreative holiday'.

Annual grant total

In 2016/17 the trust held assets of over £1 million and had an income of £34,500. Grants were awarded to 11 individuals and totalled £17,800.

Applications

Application forms can be downloaded from the trust's website and should be emailed to the correspondent by 31 May annually. Successful applicants will be notified by the end of August. Applications received after the closing date are not considered other than in exceptional circumstances.

Glasgow

James T. Howat Charitable Trust

£7,600 (15 grants)

Correspondent: The Trustees, Harper Macleod LLP, The Ca'd'oro, 45 Gordon Street, Glasgow G1 3PE

OSCR number: SC000201

Eligibility

People who live in Glasgow.

Types of grants

One-off grants can be awarded to schoolchildren and further/higher education students. Mature and overseas students can also be assisted. Support can be given towards books, equipment/instruments, course fees, maintenance expenses or study/travel overseas. Mature students can also get help for childcare costs and people with special educational needs can receive assistance for educational outings/excursions.

Annual grant total

In 2015/16 the trust had assets of £5.45 million and an income of almost £220,000. There were 15 grants made to individuals during the year, which ranged between £300 and £1,000 each and totalled £7,600 altogether. The trust also made grants to organisations totalling £178,000.

Exclusions

Support is not normally given for: medical electives; second or further qualifications; payments of school fees; costs incurred at tertiary educational establishments; individuals who have received a grant in the previous year.

People studying at Glasgow University, Strathclyde University or Royal Scottish Academy of Music and Dance are not likely to be supported, because the trust already makes block payments to the hardship funds of these institutions.

Applications

An application form is available from the trust upon request. The trust's 2015/16 annual report states the following information:

This should be completed as fully as possible to disclose applicants' circumstances and submitted together with a summary, in their own words, extending to not more than a single A4 sheet. If a parent is completing the form on behalf of a child, financial information is required for both parent and child. The possible costs and financial needs should be broken down, evidence of the difference which a grant would make be produced, and details given (with results) of other grants applied for.

The trustees normally meet in March, June, September and December and applications should be submitted by the middle of the month before a meeting. Only successful applications will usually be acknowledged.

Other information

The trust mainly supports organisations.

The Trades House of Glasgow

£27,500

Correspondent: The Clerk, Trades Hall, 85 Glassford Street, Glasgow G1 1HU (0141 553 1605; email: info@tradeshouse.org.uk; website: www.tradeshouse.org.uk)

OSCR number: SC040548

Eligibility

People in need who live in Glasgow. Applicants can be UK citizens, individuals with right to remain status, or asylum seekers with Home Office approval to work in the UK.

Types of grants

Grants are awarded to assist with general educational purposes, up to undergraduate level.

Annual grant total

In 2015/16 the charity had assets of £23.7 million and an income of £1.3 million. The charity awarded £27,500 in educational grants.

Exclusions

The Education Fund is unable to help with the following:

- Payment of school fees incurred by parental choice of school (e.g. private education)
- Contribution towards postgraduate courses, unless a college undergraduate undertakes a higher university degree course
- Course costs
- Living expenses

Applications

Applications can be made online through the 'Education Fund' page. Be aware the fund is subject to application deadlines, however it usually reopens the following month.

Other information

The Trades House of Glasgow also awards grants to individuals for welfare purposes and to organisations (£183,000 and £162,500 in 2016, respectively). The charity also awarded £25,000 to the Scottish TV appeal to assist children in poverty.

Highlands and Na h-Eileanan Siar (Western Isles)

Highland Children's Trust Scheme 1983

£10,000

Correspondent: The Administrator, Saffrey Champness LLP, Kintail House, Beechwood Park, Inverness IV2 3BW (01463 243872; email: info@hctrust.co.uk; website: www.hctrust.co.uk)

OSCR number: SC006008

Eligibility

For all grants, applicants should be under the age of 25 and resident, or have a home address, in the area covered by the Highland Council. If applicants are under 18, a parent or guardian should co-sign the application.

There is some preference to provide grants for orphans.

Types of grants

The trust is currently running three schemes to improve access to education. They are:

The Highland Children's Trust Scheme – grants, loans, and allowances for:

- Accommodation while undergoing full-time education
- Fee payments
- Securing employment and associated costs e.g. to purchase uniforms or for travel
- Business start-ups

Student Scheme: assisting with higher education costs for students suffering financial difficulties.

Expedition Grants: grants for exploration, geographical, geological or other research in an expedition setting; supporting expeditions and overseas study for personal development.

Annual grant total

In 2016/17 the trust had assets of £1.4 million and an income of £50,000. We estimate the charity awarded around £10,000 in grants for educational purposes.

Exclusions

Grants are not given for postgraduate study, to pay off debts, nor to purchase clothing, footwear, food, furniture or cars etc.

Applications

Application forms can be requested in writing from the correspondent, via email, or can be downloaded from the website where there are also guidelines for applying.

Other information

The charity also awards grants for welfare reasons. The trust does not award grants to organisations or local clubs.

Ross and Cromarty Educational Trust

Correspondent: Catriona Maciver, Department of Education and Children's Services, Comhairle Nan Eilean Siar, Sandwick Road, Stornoway HS1 2BW (01851 709546; email: catriona-maciver@cne-siar.gov.uk; website: www.cne-siar.gov.uk/education)

Eligibility

People who live on the Isle of Lewis. The area is quantified by postal codes HS1 and HS2 (sector 0 and sector 9).

Types of grants

Grants in the range of £30 to £200 are available for general educational expenses and various social, cultural and recreational purposes. Schoolchildren can be assisted towards educational outings and excursions; people entering a trade or a vocational occupation towards equipment/instruments and clothing; higher education students (including postgraduates) may be awarded scholarships. Visual arts, drama, music, dance studies and adult education can also be supported. Application guidelines provide a list of specific sections, where assistance can be requested.

Annual grant total

Our previous research has suggested that the trust normally has an income of about £10,000 each year, all of which is distributed for charitable purposes. We estimate the total amount of grants awarded to individuals to be around £5,000.

Applications

Application forms can be found on the Comhairle Nan Eilean Siar website or requested from the correspondent. Applicants should only apply for one specific cause at a time and provide the details of estimated costs of their activities.

Other information

Local schools, educational establishments and other organisations or clubs can be supported towards the cost of special equipment, facilities, sports equipment and so forth.

Since 1975, Comhairle Nan Eilean Siar local government council operates the sections of the Ross and Cromarty Educational Trust Scheme which relate specifically to the Isle of Lewis. These sections are operated in agreement with Highland Council, which is responsible for the capital of the trust fund.

Lothian

John Watson's Trust

£107,000

Correspondent: Anna Bennett, Clerk and Treasurer, The Signet Library, Parliament Square, Edinburgh EH1 1RF (0131 225 0658; email: lcampbell@wssociety.co.uk; website: www.wssociety.co.uk/charities/jwt)

OSCR number: SC014004

Eligibility

Children and young people under the age of 21 who have a physical/learning disability or are socially disadvantaged and live in Scotland. Preference is given to people living in or connected with Edinburgh or the Lothian region.

Orphans, children from a single-parent family or individuals who are burdened with some other special family difficulty, which is not purely financial, can also be supported towards boarding school costs.

Types of grants

Grants in the range of £30 to £2,000 are given towards special tuition, educational trips, computers (especially for people with special educational needs), laptops, books, uniforms, bus passes, and other expenses for further training and education, travel and other activities contributing to education and advancement in life.

School boarding fees may be partially covered but usually in exceptional circumstances, where personal situation makes boarding a necessary option.

Annual grant total

In 2016 the trust held assets of £4.67 million and had an income of £193,000 and a total expenditure of £212,500. Grants to individuals totalled £107,000, of which £37,500 was awarded for boarding school costs.

Grants are also made to organisations and groups working with disadvantaged children or young individuals with physical/learning disabilities. During the year, the trust made grants totalling £51,500 to 71 organisations, primarily for youth activities or equipment and as bursary prizes.

Exclusions

Grants are not available for day school or university fees.

Applications

Application forms and full guidelines can be found on the WS Society's website or requested from the correspondent. They can be submitted directly by the individual, or through a third party, for example, a social worker, Citizens Advice, other welfare agency, if applicable. Applications must include details of the candidate's household income, specify the support required and provide references.

The grants committee meets approximately five or six times each year and the application deadlines are available on the website.

Applications for school trips to outdoor residential centres must be made by the school, not the individual.

East Lothian

The Red House Home Trust

£10,000 (31 grants)

Correspondent: Fiona Watson, Scott-Moncrieff, Exchange Place 3, Semple Street, Edinburgh EH3 8BL (0131 473 3500; email: fiona.watson@scott-moncrieff.com; website: www.scott-moncrieff.com/services/charities/charitable-trusts/red-house-home-trust)

OSCR number: SC015748

Eligibility

Young people under the age of 22 who live in East Lothian and are in need of care, live in deprived circumstances or are adjusting to independent living.

Types of grants

Grants in the range of £150 to £1,000 for general needs relating to education and training.

Annual grant total

In 2015 the trust had an income of £22,000 and a total expenditure of £42,500. The trust's website notes that about £10,000 is available for distribution each year.

Applications

Application forms are available from the Scott Moncrieff website or can be requested from the correspondent. The trustees normally meet three times a year to review applications and award grants.

West Lothian

West Lothian Educational Trust

£10,000

Correspondent: Fiona Watson, Scott-Moncrieff, Exchange Place 3, Semple Street, Edinburgh EH3 8BL (0131 473 3500; fax: 0131 473 3535; email: fiona.watson@scott-moncrieff.com; website: www.scott-moncrieff.com/services/charities/charitable-trusts/west-lothian-educational-trust)

OSCR number: SC015454

Eligibility

People who were born in West Lothian or have lived there for the last two years.

Types of grants

Normally, one-off grants of up to £300 are given; however recurrent grants may be considered for a training course lasting over a year. Financial support is available for undergraduate and postgraduate studies, apprentices, people entering a trade, travel/study costs within and outside Scotland or for educational outings. Adult education, visual arts, music, drama, sports or educational experiments and research can also be supported.

Annual grant total

In 2015/16 the trust has an income of £17,000 and a total expenditure of £20,400. The trust's website states that normally, 'after various prize monies and bursaries have been paid, about £4,500 is available for distribution each year'. We estimate that grants given to individuals totalled around £10,000 altogether.

Applications

Application forms are available from the trust's website or can be requested from the correspondent, and must be received by 1 February, 1 May and 1 September each year.

Other information

Schools and colleges can be supported towards the cost of special equipment, sports facilities and clubs can be supported for activities of an educational nature.

Moray

Banffshire Educational Trust

£10,000 (50 grants)

Correspondent: The Trustees, Education and Social Care, The Moray Council, High Street, Elgin, Moray IV30 1BX

(01343 563374; fax: 01343 563478; email: educationandsocialcare@moray.gov.uk; website: www.moray.gov.uk)

Eligibility

People who live, or whose parents live, in the former county of Banffshire or who attend schools or further education centres there. Applicants' household income should be below £34,000 a year.

Types of grants

The trust awards funds in the forms of:

- Postgraduate scholarships
- Bursaries for higher education (including Open University)
- Grants for second or subsequent degrees
- Grants to assist with entry into higher education (e.g. foundation courses)
- Travel scholarships – for travel outside Scotland
- Travel grants – for travel abroad
- Grants for school trips
- Grants for apprentices and trainees
- Funding for specialist equipment
- Funding for books, equipment, instruments, etc.
- Bursaries for educational experiments and research

Annual grant total

According to our research, grants totalling around £10,000 are made to about 50 individuals each year.

Applications

Separate application forms and detailed guidelines are available on the trust's website or can be requested from the correspondent. Applications should be submitted by 30 September.

Other information

Support is also given to schools, further education centres or youth organisations in Banff to improve and encourage education. Clubs and societies whose activities are of an educational nature are also funded, as well as grants for the promotion of art, music and drama.

Moray and Nairn Educational Trust

£10,000

Correspondent: Education & Social Care, Grants and Bursaries, Council Office, High Street, Elgin IV30 1BX (01343 563374; email: jeananne.goodbrand@moray.gov.uk or educationandsocialcare@moray.gov.uk; website: www.moray.gov.uk/moray_standard/page_43905.html)

OSCR number: SC019017

Eligibility

People who live, or whose parents have lived, in the former combined county of Moray and Nairn for at least five years and schoolchildren/young people attending Moray and Nairn schools or further education centres. Applicants' household income must be below £34,000 a year, plus an allowance for dependent children.

Types of grants

Bursaries are available to students (including mature and postgraduate) in Scottish universities and people pursuing education at a Scottish central institution or training college. Financial support can also be given for study/travel overseas and to school pupils for educational outings and visits. Adult education is also assisted. Grants are normally one-off.

Annual grant total

In 2016/17 the charity had an income of £99,000 and a total expenditure of £10,000. We have estimated that grants to individuals for education purposes totalled £10,000.

Applications

Application forms can be found on the trust's website and should be submitted before 30 September annually. Note that current guidelines and application forms are subject to change – for latest updates you should consult the website.

Other information

Grants can also be made to local schools, further education centres or clubs and organisations operating in the area of benefit, for facilities, special equipment or promotion of adult education.

Renfrewshire

Renfrewshire Educational Trust

£25,000

Correspondent: Sarah White, Renfrewshire Council Corporate Services Department, Cotton Street, Paisley PA1 1TR (0141 840 3499; email: sarah.white@renfrewshire.gov.uk; website: www.renfrewshire.gov.uk)

OSCR number: SC008876

Eligibility

People who live, or have lived for a consecutive period of at least three years in the last ten years, in the Inverclyde, Renfrewshire or East Renfrewshire local authority areas and who, or whose parents, are on a low income.

Funding is available for applicants undertaking higher education, a second degree or who show exceptional promise in vocal or instrumental music, although no grants were made in this category in the last financial year.

Types of grants

Support is given in three categories:

◗ School excursions – grants for educational outings to pupils who receive free school meals

◗ Further and higher education/ performing arts/travel grants – awards ranging from £200 to £400 are given towards the fees of higher education courses to 'exceptional students' in music, drama or visual arts and for travel abroad for educational purposes

◗ Taught masters awards – one grant worth £3,400 is awarded each year to a student on a one year taught master's degree in the UK (the award is paid to the university directly)

Annual grant total

In 2015/16 the trust held assets of £672,000 and had an income of £30,500. Grants totalled £24,000 for school excursions, which represents around 26% of the cost of a school trip per pupil. A further award was made to a first year BA student for £1,000. During the year, no grants were made under the music, drama or arts programme.

Applications

Application forms for each category can be requested from the correspondent. The application deadline for the taught master's degree award is normally 30 June each year, for school excursions in January and for educational/ performing arts/travel grants by the end of January, April, July or October.

Tayside

Angus

Angus Educational Trust

£12,100 (21 grants)

Correspondent: The Trustees, Children and Learning Directorate, Angus Council, Angus House, Orchardbank, Forfar DD8 1AE (03452 777 778; fax: 01307 461848; website: www.angus.gov. uk/media/angus-educational-trust-student-application-form)

OSCR number: SC015826

Eligibility

People in need residing in the Angus council area that are attending or entering undergraduate courses in universities (full and part-time).

Note: Any student entitled to apply for a loan under the Student Loans Scheme must have taken up this option before an application to the trust will be considered.

Types of grants

Awards of £250 and £600 are granted to students on undergraduate university courses as bursaries. The trust also offers travel grants for those studying on higher education courses outside Scotland. Awards are means-tested and are intended to supplement existing grants.

Annual grant total

In 2015/16 the trust held assets of £1 million and had an income of £25,500. A total of £12,100 was awarded to 21 individuals.

Exclusions

Postgraduate studies and students at further education colleges are not supported.

Applications

Application forms can be downloaded from the trust's website or requested from the charity address. Applicants must state full details of their financial situation and enclose a copy of the letter from the awarding authority allocating or rejecting their grant/bursary application. The trustees meet twice a year normally in March and September to consider applications and can take three to four months to come to a decision.

Other information

Grants are also available to various local clubs and groups working to improve educational opportunities and learning in Angus. On some occasions, provisions have also been made to improve the education of deaf children.

Perth and Kinross

The Guildry Incorporation of Perth

£39,500

Correspondent: Lorna Peacock, Secretary, 42 George Street, Perth PH1 5JL (01738 623195; email: secretary@perthguildry.org.uk; website: www.perthguildry.org.uk)

OSCR number: SC008072

Eligibility

Members of the guildry or their children who are attending a full-time course of study at a university or college in the UK. Assistance is also given to non-members who reside in Perth or Guildtown who have a place on a full-time education course in the UK, as well as students who reside outside Perth or Guildtown but attend one of the four local secondary schools in Perth.

Types of grants

Bursaries.

Annual grant total

In 2016/17 the guildry had assets of £6.7 million and an income of £232,500. Grants totalled £107,500, of which £77,000 was given in 89 grants to individuals. Bursaries were awarded totalling £39,500.

Applications

Application forms can be requested from the correspondent. They are considered at the trustees' meetings on the last Tuesday of every month. Applicants are required to write a short covering letter of around 250 words explaining why they require funding and how the grant they receive could help their local community.

Perth and Kinross Educational Trust

£36,000

Correspondent: Administrator, Perth & Kinross Council, Education & Children's Services, Perth PH1 5GD (01738 476311; email: enquiries@pkc.gov.uk; website: www.pkc.gov.uk/article/17411/Perth-and-Kinross-Educational-Trust)

OSCR number: SC012378

Eligibility

Students in further or higher education who were born or attended school in Perth and Kinross. Mature students, postgraduates and people undertaking apprenticeships are all eligible.

Types of grants

Grants of up to £150 can be awarded towards books, fees, living expenses and study/travel abroad.

Annual grant total

In 2015/16 the trust held assets of £847,500 and had an income of £43,000. Grants to individuals totalled £36,000.

Applications

Application forms can be obtained from the Perth and Kinross Council and the application period opens in June. The exact closing date can be found on the application form. Late applications are not considered.

Other information

Organisations may also be supported.

Wales

General

Cambrian Educational Foundation for Deaf Children in Wales

£15,500

Correspondent: Pamela Brown JP, 30 Lon Cedwyn, Sketty, Swansea SA2 0TH (01792 207628; email: pam-brown@homecall.co.uk; website: www.cambrianeducationalfoundationfordeafchildren.org.uk)

CC number: 515848

Eligibility
People who are deaf or have partial hearing aged under 25, who live or whose parents live in Wales. Beneficiaries can be in special classes (units) in any school in Wales, students in further and higher education, and people entering employment.

Types of grants
One-off and (occasionally) annual grants of up to a maximum of £500. Grants have been provided for computers, software, school uniforms, tools/equipment, instruments, books, occasionally for educational outings in the UK and for study or travel abroad, to people starting work and to further and higher education students for books.

Annual grant total
In 2016 the foundation had an income of £18,500 and expenditure of £17,000. We estimate that the total amount awarded in educational grants to individuals was £15,500.

Exclusions
Grants are not given for leisure trips.

Applications
Application forms are available to download from the foundation's website. If the applicant is under the age of 18, the form should be completed by a parent/guardian or another authorised person. Applications should be supported in writing by the applicant's teacher or tutor. They are considered throughout the year.

The Community Foundation In Wales

£41,000 (four grants)

Correspondent: Liza Kellett, St Andrew's House, 24 St Andrew's Crescent, Cardiff CF10 3DD (029 2037 9580; email: mail@cfiw.org.uk; website: www.cfiw.org.uk)

CC number: 1074655

Eligibility
Young people under 25 who live in Wales.

Types of grants
Grants range from small to large under various schemes for equipment, instruments, travel, course/exam fees, bursaries.

Annual grant total
In 2015/16 the foundation had assets of almost £9.4 million and an income of £4.1 million. Throughout the year the foundation gave around £41,000 in grants to four specified individuals in the form of bursaries.

The charity also gives grants to organisations.

Applications
Application details for different schemes are available on the website.

Other information
The Community Foundation in Wales awarded £2.9 million in grants to over 700 organisations and individuals in 2015/16, which was a new high.

The foundation's grants vary in size and purpose according to the donors', clients' and fund-holders wishes. They range in size from £500 to over £150,000, and from a simple community project to investment in a charitable enterprise over multiple years.

The fund has various schemes open for both individuals and organisations throughout the year, see the website for up-to-date details. Schemes available to individuals for educational purposes include:

Cardiff Community Endowment Fund; Flintshire Community Endowment Fund; Powys Community Endowment Fund; Rudbaxton Parish Education Fund; Wales in London Philanthropic Fund.

The Gane Charitable Trust

£9,600

Correspondent: Ken Stradling, Administrator, c/o Bristol Guild of Applied Art, 68–70 Park Street, Bristol BS1 5JY (0117 926 5548)

CC number: 211515

Eligibility
Students of arts and crafts, or design and social welfare. There is a preference for applicants from Bristol and South Wales and those in further education.

Types of grants
Grants are available to help meet the educational costs of college students, vocational students and mature students and their children. Grants are given towards fees, books and equipment/instruments and range from £200 to £500 and are normally one-off.

Annual grant total
In 2016 the trust had assets of £970,000 and an income of £34,000. The trust's charitable expenditure totalled £19,300 and we estimate that £9,600 was given to individuals for educational purposes.

Applications
Application forms are available from the correspondent.

Other information
The trust also makes grants to individuals for social welfare purposes.

The Glamorgan Further Education Trust Fund

£29,000

Correspondent: Naomi Davies, Administrator, 1st Floor Aberafan House, Education Finance, Port Talbot Civic Centre, Port Talbot, West Glamorgan SA13 1PJ (01639 763553; email: n.davies11@npt.gov.uk)

CC number: 525509

Eligibility

Pupils who have for not less than two years attended a county secondary school in the administrative county of Glamorgan or Howells Glamorgan County School in Cardiff.

Grants are intended to benefit those pupils who are attending approved courses not provided for under the normal award scheme, including professional and technical courses.

Types of grants

Grants towards the purchase of outfits, clothing, tools, books or instruments for those leaving school or college to assist their entry into a profession, trade or calling.

Annual grant total

In 2016/17 the trust had an income of £45,500 and a total expenditure of £42,300. The trust made grant payments of around £29,000 to individuals for educational purposes throughout the year.

Exclusions

Applicants are not eligible for assistance if they are in receipt of a central government bursary or a mandatory or discretionary award, or are exempt from the payment of the tuition fee.

Applications

Apply in writing to the correspondent.

The Geoffrey Jones (Penreithin) Scholarship Fund

£7,500

Correspondent: Keith Butler, Trustee, Marchant Harries, 17–19 Cardiff Street, Aberdare CF44 7DP (01685 885500; email: keithbutler@marchantharries.co.uk)

CC number: 501964

Eligibility

Students who have been resident in the parishes or districts of Penderyn, Ystradfellte Vaynor or Taff Fechan Valley, Merthyr Tydfil for at least 12 months.

Types of grants

Assistance with the cost of books, fees, maintenance/living expenses and study/travel abroad is available to students in further or higher education.

Annual grant total

In 2015/16 the fund had an income of £7,000 and a total expenditure of £8,100. We estimate that grants given to individuals totalled around £7,500.

Applications

Apply in writing to the correspondent.

The James Pantyfedwen Foundation (Ymddiriedolaeth James Pantyfedwen)

£253,000 (50 grants)

Correspondent: Gwenan Creunant, Executive Secretary, Pantyfedwen, 9 Market Street, Aberystwyth, Ceredigion SY23 1DL (01970 612806; email: post@jamespantyfedwen.cymru or pantyfedwen@btinternet.com; website: www.jamespantyfedwen.cymru)

CC number: 1069598

Eligibility

Applicants who have been resident in Wales sometime during the three years immediately preceding the date of application (excluding the term-time address as a college/university student). Applicants must also either: have been born in Wales; have a parent/parents who were born in Wales; or have studied at any educational institution in Wales for at least seven years. Currently only applications from postgraduate students are being considered.

Types of grants

One-off and recurrent grants for postgraduate studies, with priority given to those undertaking postgraduate research. Grants are given for tuition fees only and will be given up to a maximum of £7,000.

Annual grant total

In 2015/16 the foundation had assets of £14.7 million and an income of £589,500. Grants totalling £253,000 were made to fifty individuals for educational purposes, including two grants made under the former Undeb Cymru Fydd. Grants were also made to organisations in the following categories: religious buildings (£82,000); Eisteddfodau (£74,000); Urdd Gobaith Cymru (£13,200); registered charities (£8,400); Morlan-Pantyfedwen Lecture (£540).

Exclusions

According to its website, the foundation does not support the following:

- Undergraduate courses (including intercalated degree courses in medical science)
- Courses at institutions which have not been approved by the Department of Education
- Higher degrees where students already have a higher degree (this does not exclude progress from a Master's degree to a PhD)
- Accounting Training Courses
- Private tuition (e.g. for music students)
- PGCE Courses
- Postgraduate training courses in social work
- CPE Course in Law (but Legal Practice courses are permitted)
- Master's courses of more than one year's duration. Where a student is pursuing a two years' Master's course on a full-time basis the Foundation is prepared to consider assistance for the second and final year of study

Support is not given to supplement awards provided by the local authorities and research councils.

Applications

Applications can be made using a form available to download from the foundation's website. Guidelines are also provided on the website, including the deadline for the academic year (usually around June, with forms available from April).

Other information

The foundation also makes grants to organisations, mainly supporting Eisteddfodau and religious buildings.

Mid Wales

Powys

Thomas John Jones Memorial Fund for Scholarships and Exhibitions

£43,500 (32 grants)

Correspondent: David Meredith, Clerk to the Trustees, Cilmery, The Avenue, Brecon, Powys LD3 9BG (01874 623373; email: davidwm@hotmail.co.uk)

CC number: 525281

Eligibility

People under the age of 26 pursuing education and training for a higher post in the engineering industry who have both been resident and attended secondary school in the former county of Breconshire. Preference is given to applicants undertaking courses of advanced technical education.

Postgraduate applicants must have gained an upper second-class degree or above except in exceptional circumstances and applications will only be considered from students who are not in receipt of government grants or similar.

Types of grants

Grants of £1,500 per year for the duration of the course subject to annual review. Engineering PhD scholarship awards of up to £1,500 per year with the potential for an additional £500 for those on full-time courses for up to three years.

Annual grant total

In 2015/16 the fund had assets of £1.7 million, an income of £62,500 and awarded educational grants totalling £43,500 to 32 individuals.

Applications

Apply in writing to the correspondent. The trustees meet at least once a year and as required. Applications should include full details of the nature, location, type (full/part-time) and duration of the study and the qualification aimed at. Usually they must be sent to the correspondent by 31 August annually.

Edmund Jones' Charity

£3,200

Correspondent: Ruth Jefferies, Steeple House, Brecon, Powys LD3 7DJ (01874 638024; email: edmundjonescharity@ gmail.com)

CC number: 525315

Eligibility

People under the age of 25 who live or work within the town of Brecon.

Types of grants

Grants are available to people undertaking apprenticeships and starting work, mainly towards tools; to college students towards equipment; and to university students towards books.

Annual grant total

In 2015 the charity had assets of £440,000 and an income of £35,000. Grants to both individuals and organisations totalled £6,400 and we estimate that grants to individuals totalled around £3,200.

Applications

Apply in writing to the correspondent, giving details of the college/course/ apprenticeship and the anticipated costs, together with the information on any other grants received or applied for. Applications may be submitted by

individuals, or through their parents or college.

Other information

Schools and colleges located in the area of benefit may also be assisted.

Llanidloes Relief-in-Need Charity

£1,300

Correspondent: Elaine Lloyd, Woodcroft, Woodlands Road, Llanidloes, Powys SY18 6HX (01686 413045; email: elainelllloyd@gmail.com)

CC number: 259955

Eligibility

Students who live in the communities of Llanidloes and Llanidloes Without.

Types of grants

Grants can be given to help with the cost of books, living expenses and other essential items for those at college or university.

Annual grant total

In 2016/17 the charity had an income of £130 and a total expenditure of £2,100. We estimate that about £1,300 was given in educational grants.

Exclusions

Support cannot be given to students not living within three miles of the town or to foreign students studying in the area.

Applications

Applications may be made in writing to the correspondent.

Other information

Relief-in-need grants are also given.

Visual Impairment Breconshire (Nam Gweledol Sir Brycheiniog)

£1,000

Correspondent: Michael Knee, Secretary, 3 Beacons View, Mount Street, Brecon, Powys LD3 7LY (01874 624949; email: vibrecon@gmail.com; website: www. visualimpairment.breconshire.powys.org. uk)

CC number: 217377

Eligibility

People who have permanent and uncorrectable eye conditions who live in Breconshire.

Types of grants

One-off grants for equipment, services, training and other needs. The charity also offers an annual bursary (up to

£500) to enable an individual to pursue an educational or sporting activity.

Annual grant total

In 2014/15 the charity had an income of £2,600 and a total expenditure of £3,500. We estimate that educational grants to individuals totalled around £1,000.

Exclusions

In general, the charity will not pay for anything that should be funded by the NHS or a local authority. Nor will it contribute towards the rental of book reading equipment and corresponding library subscriptions, or any equipment for use in care homes and similar institutions where there exists a statutory obligation or requirement to provide for client use.

Applications

Apply in writing to the correspondent. The executive committee meets about six times a year and the annual general meeting is normally held in July.

Other information

The charity also organises audio newsletters and social activities to both individuals and groups. It also makes grants to individuals for social welfare needs.

The 2014/15 accounts were the latest available at the time of writing (November 2017).

North Wales

The Educational Charity of John Matthews

£14,800

Correspondent: P. B. Smith, Administrator, Lyndhurst, 6 Vernon Avenue, Hooton, Ellesmere Port, Cheshire CH66 6AL (0151 327 6103; email: pbsberlian@aol.com; website: www.johnmathewscharity.co.uk)

CC number: 525553

Eligibility

People under the age of 25 who are descendants of the founder of the trust (John Matthews) or are resident in the North Wales areas comprising Chirk, district of Glyndwr, Llanarmon-Yn-Lal, Llandegla, Llangollen Rural, Llantysilio, the borough of Wrexham Maelor and the borough of Oswestry, in Shropshire.

Types of grants

Grants of £250 to £2,000 are awarded to young people 'seeking to build upon their talents and improve their educational and career prospects'. Grants have been given to a wide range of applicants, for example musicians, actors, journalists, tree surgeons, medical students. Support can be provided towards specialist equipment, course fees, books, tools and other necessities.

The charity can support undergraduate, postgraduate, second degree students (particularly on courses with a vocational element), people starting work and individuals undertaking apprenticeships. Those who are not able to get other financial support and can demonstrate exceptional talent and passion are favoured.

Annual grant total

In 2016 the charity had an income of £15,400 and a total expenditure of £15,000. We estimate that the charity gave around £14,800 in grants to individuals throughout the year.

Exclusions

Financial assistance towards ongoing education within the state or private education system can only be considered in exceptional circumstances.

Applications

Application forms and further guidelines can be found on the charity's website. They should be submitted along with a covering letter giving as much information as possible about the course and the applicant's career aspirations as well as financial and personal circumstances (including proof of identity and residence). The trustees usually meet twice a year, in May and November, but considerations can be made more frequently if needed.

People applying as the descendants of the founder will be required to provide extensive supporting documentation.

Other information

The charity welcomes informal contact prior to the application.

From the charity's website:

> John Matthews left his estate in Trust in his Will on 27 October 1630 so that young people should be able to nurture their talents and overcome financial barriers that may stand in their way. Today the charity of John Matthews follows the same ethos and encourages applications from young people seeking to build upon their talents and improve their educational and career prospects.

Conwy

Sir John Henry Morris-Jones Trust Fund

£5,500

Correspondent: Mrs C. Earley, Clerk to the Trustees, The Bay of Colwyn Town Council, Town Hall, 7 Rhiw Road, Colwyn Bay, Conwy LL29 7TE (01492 532248; email: info@colwyn-tc.gov.uk; website: www.colwyn-tc.gov.uk/town-council/grants-available-and-local-trusts)

CC number: 504313

Eligibility

People under the age of 19 who are resident in the area of the former borough of Colwyn Bay, as existing on 31 March 1974 (Colwyn Bay, Llysfaen, Mochdre, Old Colwyn and Rhos-on-Sea). People undertaking full-time education outside the borough but normally resident there are eligible.

Types of grants

One-off scholarships to individuals who demonstrate excellence in one of the following fields: arts, crafts and music; sport; academic and research; commerce and business; science and technology; any other field which would satisfy the trustees.

Annual grant total

In 2015/16 the charity had an income of £6,600 and a total expenditure of £6,200. We have estimated that grants to individuals totalled around £5,500.

Exclusions

Applications for courses at higher or further education levels are not considered.

Applications

Application forms are available on the charity's website or from the correspondent. They should be submitted by 31 March. Applicants are invited for an interview in May.

Denbighshire

Freeman Evans St David's Day Denbigh Charity

£450

Correspondent: Medwyn Jones, Town Clerk, Denbigh Town Council, Town Hall, Crown Square, Denbigh LL16 3TB (01745 815984; email: townclerk@denbightowncouncil.gov.uk)

CC number: 518033

Eligibility

People in need who live in Denbigh and Henllan, particularly those who are older, have disabilities or an illness.

Types of grants

Grants towards tutoring, educational equipment, sports lessons, etc.

Annual grant total

In 2015/16 the charity had assets of £1.4 million and an income of £102,000. Grants were made totalling £58,500. Educational grants totalled £450.

Applications

Applications may be made in writing to the correspondent, either directly by the individual or through a third party, such as a social worker, Citizens Advice or other welfare agency. The trustees meet regularly throughout the year to consider applications.

Other information

Organisations are also supported and assistance is given to individuals for social welfare purposes.

The Robert David Hughes Scholarship Foundation

£17,000

Correspondent: Peter Bowler, Trustee, McLintocks, 46 Hamilton Square, Birkenhead, Wirral CH41 5AR (0151 647 9581)

CC number: 525404

Eligibility

University students who have connections with the community of the former borough of Denbigh. Applicants should either be born in the community of Denbigh or have a parent or parents who have been resident in the area for at least ten years. Full documentary evidence is requested.

Types of grants

One-off and recurrent grants are offered to university students according to need.

Annual grant total

In 2015/16 the foundation had an income of £18,500 and a total expenditure of £18,800. We estimate that grants given to individuals totalled around £17,000.

Exclusions

Students in colleges of further education are not normally supported.

Applications

Apply in writing to the correspondent. Our research suggests that applications should be submitted by end of September for consideration in November. Grants are awarded each term upon receipt of completed certificates of attendance, signed by the principal or registrar of the university.

Gwynedd

Dr Daniel Williams Educational Fund

£44,500 (310 grants)

Correspondent: Dwyryd Williams, Clerk to the Trust, Bryn Golau, Pencefn, Dolgellau, Gwynedd LL40 2YP (01341 423494; email: dwyryd@gmail.com)

CC number: 525756

Eligibility

People under the age of 25 in further/higher education or training. Priority will be given to former pupils of Dr Williams' School, or their descendants, and people who are resident, or whose parents are resident, in the former administrative district of Meirionnydd.

Types of grants

One-off or recurrent grants can be awarded: towards the costs of clothing, uniforms, equipment/instruments, books and other necessities to people entering a trade/starting work; for study/travel overseas; towards the study of music and other arts; for general educational costs to further/higher education students and people in training. Grants usually reach up to a maximum of £500.

Annual grant total

In 2015/16 the charity held assets of £1.2 million, an income of £52,000 and awarded grants to 310 individuals totalling £44,500. The grants were distributed in following categories:

Educational trips	134
College fees or courses	90
Travelling expenses	34
Instrumental, voice or performance tuition	30
Sports training and equipment	6
Miscellaneous costs – vocational equipment, clothing etc.	5
Additional teaching requirements	5
Musical instruments	4
IT equipment and software	2

Applications

Application forms can be requested from the correspondent.

Isle of Anglesey

Owen Lloyd's Educational Foundation

£5,000

Correspondent: Emlyn Evans, Correspondent, Nant Bychan Farm, Moelfre, Gwynedd LL72 8HF (01248 410269)

CC number: 525253

Eligibility

People between the ages of 16 and 25 in further/higher education who live in Penrhoslligwy and neighbouring parishes.

Larger grants may be given to residents of Penrhoslligwy, as this was the original area covered by the trust deed.

Types of grants

Grants are given to help with the cost of books, fees, living expenses, travel costs (but not for study/travel abroad) and tools/equipment. People starting work and apprentices can be supported towards the cost of books, equipment, clothing, travel, etc.

Annual grant total

In 2015/16 the foundation had an income of £10,800 and a total expenditure of £10,900. We have estimated that grants to individuals for educational purposes totalled around £5,000.

Applications

Application forms can be requested from the correspondent. They should include details of the applicant's financial situation. Applications are normally considered in October with grants being awarded in June.

Other information

Grants are also given to organisations and educational establishments.

Wrexham

The Educational Foundation of Dame Dorothy Jeffreys

£2,500

Correspondent: Frieda Leech, Administrator, Holly Chase, Pen Y. Palmant Road, Minera, Wrexham LL11 3YW (01978 754152; email: clerk. wpef@gmail.com)

CC number: 525430

Eligibility

People in need aged between 16 and 25 who live or have attended school in the former borough of Wrexham or the communities of Abenbury, Bersham, Broughton, Bieston, Brymbo, Esclusham Above, Esculsham Below, Gresford, Gwersyllt and Minera.

Types of grants

Grants of £50 minimum. Grants for general education purposes are given to schoolchildren, further/higher education students, people starting work and vocational students. Mature students up to the age of 25 can also receive grants.

Annual grant total

In 2015 the charity had an income of £5,900 and a total expenditure of £2,900. We have estimated that grants to individuals for educational purposes totalled £2,500.

Applications

Application forms are available from the correspondent to be submitted directly by the individual. Applications are usually considered in November/December and should be submitted by 1 October.

Ruabon and District Relief-in-Need Charity

£1,000

Correspondent: James Fenner, 65 Albert Grove, Ruabon, Wrexham LL14 6AF (01978 820102; email: jamesrfenner65@tiscali.co.uk)

CC number: 212817

Eligibility

People in need who live in the county borough of Wrexham, which covers the community council districts of Cefn Mawr, Penycae, Rhosllanerchrugog (including Johnstown) and Ruabon.

Types of grants

Grants are given to schoolchildren towards uniforms/clothing, equipment/instruments and educational visits/excursions.

Annual grant total

In 2016 the charity had an income of £3,100 and a total expenditure of £4,300. We estimate that grants for education totalled approximately £1,000.

Applications

Apply in writing to the correspondent either directly by the individual or a family member, through a third party such as a social worker or teacher, or through an organisation such as Citizens Advice or a school. Applications are considered on an ongoing basis.

The Wrexham (Parochial) Educational Foundation

£37,500

Correspondent: Revd Dr Jason Bray, Clerk, Holly Chase, Pen Y. Palmant Road, Minera, Wrexham LL11 3YW (01978 754152; email: clerk.wpef@gmail.com)

CC number: 525414

Eligibility

People between the ages of 16 and 25 who live in the county borough of

Wrexham and who are former pupils of one of the following: Brymbo and Minera Voluntary Aided Schools, St Giles Voluntary Controlled School and St Joseph's Catholic and Anglican High School.

Types of grants

The foundation provides scholarships, money towards clothing/uniforms, books and equipment/tools, travel expenses in the UK and abroad. Help is offered to students in secondary and further/higher education and people starting an apprenticeship or training.

Annual grant total

In 2016 the foundation held assets of £12.2 million and had an income of £405,000. Grants were made to 63 individuals and totalled £37,500. A further £145,500 was awarded to local schools, churches and charitable organisations.

Applications

Application forms can be requested from the correspondent, preferably by email. Applications can be made by individuals directly.

South East Wales

The Monmouthshire Further Education Trust Fund

£4,200

Correspondent: Grants Team, The Community Foundation in Wales, St Andrews House, 24 St Andrews Crescent, Cardiff CF10 3DD (029 2037 9580; email: mail@cfiw.org.uk; website: www.cfiw.org.uk/eng/grants)

CC number: 1146059

Eligibility

Individuals under the age of 25 who are pursuing further/higher education or training and who reside in the county of Monmouthshire as it existed in 1956 – in particular, the authorities which became Gwent, covering some or part of: Torfaen; Blaenau Gwent; Newport; Monmouthshire. Applicants must also have attended a school in the area for at least two years.

Types of grants

Applicants can apply for grants ranging between £50 and £500, for costs associated with entering into further or higher education (e.g. equipment, materials, travel, course/exam fees), or for costs associated with entering into a

trade or profession (e.g. equipment, materials, training).

Annual grant total

In 2015/16 the fund had an income of £10.500 and a total expenditure of £7,800. According to the 2015/16 accounts for The Community Foundation in Wales, grants from the fund totalled £4,200 during the year.

Exclusions

Awards cannot be made retrospectively.

Applications

Applications can be made on a form available to download from The Community Foundation in Wales' website, where guidance notes are also provided. The trust welcomes informal contact prior to applications being formally made. Applications deadlines are the last day of each month and applicants should be notified of the outcome within four to six weeks. Successful applicants are paid upon proof of enrolment on their stated course.

Other information

The fund is administered by The Community Foundation in Wales (CC number: 1074655).

Cardiff

Cardiff Further Education Trust Fund

£223,000 (663 grants)

Correspondent: N. Griffiths, Cardiff City Council, City Hall, King Edward VII Avenue, Cardiff CF10 3ND

CC number: 525512

Eligibility

Young people in need who are over the age of 16, resident in Cardiff and have attended a secondary school there for at least two years.

Types of grants

The main grant awarded is the Passport to Study Programme, which enables students to continue their education past the age of 16. In 2015/16 grants also covered a trip for 92 students and attendance for four students on special training courses connected with their education.

Annual grant total

In 2015/16 the trust held assets of £20.8 million, and had an income of £132,000. A total of £223,000 was awarded in grants to individuals.

Applications

Apply in writing to the correspondent.

Other information

A contribution of £13,500 was also made to Cardiff and the Vale Sports Association.

Monmouthshire

Llandenny Charities

£1,100

Correspondent: Dr Graham Russell, Trustee, Forge Cottage, Llandenny, Usk, Monmouthshire NP15 1DL (01633 432536; email: gsrussell@btinternet.com)

CC number: 223311

Eligibility

Students in full-time higher education who have been living in the parish of Llandenny for more than one year.

Types of grants

Our research suggests that recurrent grants are available. The charity's record on the Charity Commission's website notes that support is given to 'to certain types of degree students'.

Annual grant total

In 2016 the charity had an income of £2,300 and a total expenditure of £2,400. We estimate that grants for educational purposes totalled around £1,100.

Applications

Applications may be made in writing to the correspondent. They can be made directly by the individual and should be submitted by 15 January for consideration in February.

Other information

Grants are also given to pensioners in need.

Monmouth Charity

£2,200

Correspondent: Andrew Pirie, Trustee, 2 St John Street, Monmouth NP25 3EA (01600 716202)

CC number: 700759

Eligibility

Students who are in further education and live within a ten-mile radius of Monmouth.

Types of grants

One-off grants usually up to a maximum of £500.

Annual grant total

In 2015/16 the charity had an income of £8,800 and a total expenditure of £9,000. Grants are made to individuals and organisations for a wide range of charitable purposes, including for the relief of poverty, disability and education. We estimate that educational grants to individuals totalled £2,200.

Applications

The trust advertises in the local press each September/October and applications should be made in response to this advertisement for consideration in November. Emergency grants can be considered at any time. There is no application form. Applications can be submitted directly by the individual or through a social worker, Citizens Advice or other welfare agency.

The Monmouthshire County Council Welsh Church Act Fund

£2,100

Correspondent: Joy Robson, Head of Finance, Monmouthshire County Council, PO Box 106, Caldicot NP26 9AN (01633 644657; email: davejarrett@monmouthshire.gov.uk; website: www.monmouthshire.gov.uk/welsh-church-fund)

CC number: 507094

Eligibility

People of any age studying at school, university or any other place of study, who live in the boundaries of Monmouthshire County Council and their dependants. Grants are also made to people starting work.

Types of grants

Applications will be considered from individuals for aid towards a specific activity. The normal level of support to individuals is between £50 and £150.

Annual grant total

In 2015/16 the fund had assets of £5.2 million and an income of £226,000. Grants to individuals for the advancement of their education totalled £2,100.

Applications

Application forms can be downloaded from the council's website. Applications are considered seven times a year.

Other information

The fund also makes grants to organisations.

James Powell's Educational Foundation

£4,000

Correspondent: Mr D. T. Hayhurst, Rose Cottage Chapel, Llanvetherine, Abergavenny, Gwent NP7 8PY (01873 821449)

CC number: 525640

Eligibility

People over the age of 16 who live in the ancient parish of Llantilio Crossenny.

Types of grants

Grants can be made for books, equipment/instruments and other essentials, also towards living and maintenance expenses. Students at school, college or university can be supported, as well as people starting work/entering a trade.

Annual grant total

In 2016 the foundation had an income of £3,100 and a total expenditure of £4,700. We estimate the total grants awarded to individuals to be around £4,000.

Applications

Eligible candidates can apply in writing to the correspondent. Applications should be submitted by a parent or guardian, normally by August for consideration in September.

Other information

The foundation awards grants strictly within the area of benefit.

Rhondda Cynon Taff

The Rhondda Trust

£27,000

Correspondent: Chris Bryant, Trustee, Oxford House, Tonypandy, Rhondda CF40 1AU (01443 495151; email: info@rhonddatrust.org.uk; website: www.rhonddatrust.org.uk)

CC number: 1124289

Eligibility

Individuals who live in the Rhondda.

Types of grants

Funding is given towards purposes that will improve the education, training and skills opportunities of people in the area. This may include the purchase or equipment, tools or other items; fees for education and training courses; grants for travel in the UK or abroad for educational purposes; and other educational, skills or employment-related projects. The trust can provide grants of up to £2,500 per annum over three years.

Annual grant total

In 2016/17 the trust had assets of £51,000 and an income of £151,000. Grants awarded to individuals during the year totalled almost £27,000. A further £349,000 was given in grants to organisations. The accounts state that

grants were unusually high compared to previous years.

Exclusions

The 2016/17 annual report states that, due to the high number of applications received:

> We are not able to make awards to people living outside the Rhondda, or to those wholly engaged in areas such as the arts and sports – although we have supported some projects that use the arts and sports to pursue genuine educational opportunities or enhance young people's life chances.

Applications

Application forms can be obtained by calling: 01443 495151 or writing to: Regeneration Resources Team, Development and Regeneration Unit, Level 5 Unit 3, Ty Pennant, Catherine Street, Pontypridd CF37 2TB.

Other information

This trust was established in 2007 when Burberry closed its factory in Treorchy and provided £150,000 to further the education and training opportunities of people in Rhondda.

Grants are also made to charities and voluntary organisations working in the area (up to £15,000 over three years).

Torfaen

The Cwmbran Trust

£2,000

Correspondent: Kenneth Maddox, Secretary, c/o Meritor HVBS (UK) Ltd, Grange Road, Cwmbran, Gwent NP44 3XU (01633 834040; email: cwmbrantrust@meritor.com)

CC number: 505855

Eligibility

People in need living in the town of Cwmbran, Gwent.

Types of grants

The trust gives one-off and recurrent grants for a wide variety of purposes. Previous grants of educational nature have included funding for home-study courses and IT equipment. Grants usually range between £125 and £2,500.

Annual grant total

In 2016 the trust had assets of £2.5 million and an income of £93,500. The amount of grants given to individuals totalled £17,000. Grants are mainly made for welfare purposes and we estimate that grants to individuals for educational purposes, totalled around £2,000.

Applications

Applications may be made in writing to the correspondent. They can be submitted directly by the individual or through a social worker, Citizens Advice, welfare agency or other third party. Applications are usually considered in March, May, July, October and December.

Vale of Glamorgan

The Cowbridge with Llanblethian United Charities

£1,500

Correspondent: Clerk to the Trustees, 66 Broadway, Llanblethian, Cowbridge CF71 7EW (01446 773287; email: h.phillips730@btinternet.com)

CC number: 1014580

Eligibility

People in need who live in the town of Cowbridge with Llanblethian.

Types of grants

Grants are made towards clothing, fees, travel and maintenance for people in further, higher or vocational education.

Annual grant total

In 2015/16 the charity had assets of £709,500 and an income of £26,500. Student grants totalled £1,500.

Applications

Apply in writing to the correspondent. Applications can be submitted directly by the individual or through a school/college or educational welfare agency.

South West Wales

The Roger Edwards Educational Trust (formerly the Monmouthshire Further Education Trust Fund)

£16,000 (16 grants)

Correspondent: R. B. Morse, Trustee, 4 Chepstow Road, Usk NP15 1BL (01291673233; email: rogeredwardstrust@yahoo.co.uk)

CC number: 525638

Eligibility

Further or higher education students who have attended a local comprehensive/secondary school and have lived in the Greater Gwent area, (except Newport) meaning the council

areas of Caerphilly (part), Torfaen, Blaenau Gwent and Monmouthshire.

Types of grants

One-off grants, although students can re-apply in subsequent years, towards books, fees, living costs, travel and equipment.

Annual grant total

In 2015/16 the trust had an income of £64,500 and a total expenditure of £74,800. During the year, the trust awarded grants to 16 individual students totalling £16,000.

The trust also gives grants to organisations.

Exclusions

Full-time students receiving funding from another source are not funded.

Applications

Application forms are available from the correspondent, for consideration throughout the year.

Carmarthenshire

Minnie Morgan's Scholarship

£18,000

Correspondent: Head of Financial Services, c/o Emma Davies, Resources Department, Carmarthenshire County Council, County Hall, Carmarthen SA31 1JP (01267 224172; email: corporateaccountancy@carmarthenshire.gov.uk)

CC number: 504980

Eligibility

People under the age of 25 who have attended any of the secondary schools in Llanelli and who are studying drama or dramatic art at the University of Wales or any school of dramatic art approved by the trustees.

Types of grants

One-off grants, usually around £1,000.

Annual grant total

In 2015/16 the charity had an income of £13,300 and a total expenditure of £18,000. We estimate that grants totalled around £18,000.

Applications

Apply in writing to the correspondent. Applications should be submitted by 31 October each year.

Neath Port Talbot

Elizabeth Jones' Scholarships for Boys and Girls of Aberavon and Margam (Elizabeth Jones' Trust)

£5,500

Correspondent: David Scott, Trustee, 28 Wildbrook, Part Talbot SA13 2UN (01639 887953; email: scott-david11@sky.com)

CC number: 525517

Eligibility

Young people aged between 16 and 25 who or whose parents live in the borough of Port Talbot and who have attended a county or voluntary school in/around the area of benefit for at least two years. Also, students at the Margam College of Further Education.

Types of grants

According to our research, one-off grants ranging from £50 to £400 are available towards general educational costs, including books, equipment/instruments, travel costs and other necessities.

Annual grant total

In 2015/16 the trust had an income of £2,500 and a total expenditure of £6,200. We estimate that grants totalled around £5,500.

Applications

Apply in writing to the correspondent.

Pembrokeshire

The Charity of Doctor Jones

£9,400

Correspondent: Malcolm Crossman, Guinea Hill House, Norgans Hill, Pembroke, Dyfed SA71 5EP (01646 622257; email: mcros94874@aol.com; website: drjonescharity.co.uk)

CC number: 241351

Eligibility

Young people between the ages of 16 and 25 who/whose parents live in Pembroke or the previous Pembroke borough.

Types of grants

Grants are given to further/higher education students, people in training and those undertaking apprenticeships. Support is available towards general costs associated with the course or training, including outfits, tools, equipment, books, travel expenses, maintenance costs and fees.

Annual grant total

In 2016 the charity had an income of £51,000 and a total expenditure of £25,000. The charity awarded £9,400 in grants for education during the year.

Applications

Application forms can be downloaded from the website, or requested from the correspondent, and should be returned by post.

Other information

Our research indicates that the charity advertises locally when grants are available, usually twice a year.

The charity also maintains a number of properties in the area and assists the tenants with maintenance and repairs.

Milford Haven Port Authority Scholarships

£6,000 (four grants)

Correspondent: Administrator, Gorsewood Drive, Milford Haven, Pembrokeshire SA73 3EP (01646 696100; email: communications@mhpa.co.uk; website: www.mhpa.co.uk/scholarship-application)

Eligibility

Undergraduate students at British universities who have completed most of their secondary education in Pembrokeshire or a nearby county.

Types of grants

The charity offers one-off undergraduate scholarships of £1,500 and a placement at the Port of Milford Haven during the summer.

Annual grant total

Four scholarships of £1,500 are awarded every year.

Applications

Application forms can be accessed from the port's website or requested from the correspondent, when the scheme is open. For the scheme opening dates and application deadlines, consult the website. All communication should be marked 'Scholarship Scheme'.

Narberth Educational Charity

£600

Correspondent: Ann Handley, Administrator, Pembrokeshire County Council, County Hall, Freemens Way, Haverfordwest, Dyfed SA61 1TP

(01437776290; email: ann.handley@pembrokeshire.gov.uk)

CC number: 1013669

Eligibility

People who live in the community council areas of Narberth, Llawhaden, Llanddewi Velfrey, Lampeter Velfrey (including Tavernspite and Ludchurch), Templeton, Martletwy (including Lawrenny), Begelly, part of Jeffreyston, Minwere and Reynalton.

Applicants should have lived there for at least two years and be aged under 25.

Types of grants

Grants, normally ranging from £100 to £150, to help those at school and those transferring to a recognised course or further or higher education.

Annual grant total

In 2016/17 the charity had an income of £3,000 and a total expenditure of £1,200. We estimate that grants given to individuals for educational purposes totalled around £600.

Applications

Application forms are available from Student Support, North Wing Reception, Haverfordwest. They should be returned by August for consideration in November.

Other information

The charity also provides financial assistance for local organisations engaged in youth activities and the promotion of education for young people/children living in the catchment area.

East Midlands

General

Thomas Monke

£1,500

Correspondent: Christopher Kitto, Correspondent, 29 Blacksmiths Lane, Newton Solney, Burton on Trent, Staffordshire DE15 0SD (01283 702129; email: chriskitto@btinternet.com)

CC number: 214783

Eligibility
Young people under the age of 25 who live in Austrey, Measham, Shenton and Whitwick.

Types of grants
One-off and recurrent modest grants (up to the maximum of £200) towards the cost of goods, tools, books, fees and travelling expenses for educational purposes, including vocational training.

Annual grant total
In 2016 the charity had an income of £4,000 and a total expenditure of £3,300. We estimate that grants given to individuals for educational purposes totalled around £1,500.

Exclusions
Expeditions, scholarships and university course fees are not funded.

Applications
Application forms are available from the correspondent and should be submitted directly by the individual before 31 March, in time for the trustees' yearly meeting held in April.

Other information
The charity can also support individuals for social welfare purposes and organisations. Educational support is, however, the primary concern.

Derbyshire

Coke's Educational Charity

£2,000

Correspondent: Andrew Cree, Administrator, Damson Lodge, Longford, Ashbourne, Derbyshire DE6 3DT (01335 330074)

CC number: 527028

Eligibility
People under the age of 25 who live in the parishes of Alkmonton, Hollington, Hungry Bently, Longford and Rodsley.

Types of grants
One-off and recurrent grants for general educational purposes. Support is available to people who have completed their secondary education and are entering a university/college or starting a career.

Annual grant total
In 2016 the charity had an income of £3,400 and a total expenditure of £3,900. We estimate that the charity gave around £2,000 in grants to individuals for educational purposes.

The charity also awards grants to organisations.

Applications
Apply in writing to the correspondent.

Other information
Local schools can also be supported towards the purchase of educational materials, items or activities.

Derbyshire Community Foundation

£10,000

Correspondent: Rachael Grime, Unit 2 Heritage Business Centre, Derby Road, Belper, Derbyshire DE56 1SW (01773 525860; email: hello@ foundationderbyshire.org)

CC number: 1039485

Eligibility
John Weston Fund – individuals aged 11 to 25 living in Derbyshire.

Tom Carey Fund – individuals in need living in the Abbey ward of Derby City.

Types of grants
John Weston Fund – The fund will support young people in developing their life skills. As well as funding traditional gap year projects, the fund will also support costs linked to pursuing excellence in sport or music as well as extracurricular educational activities. The age range for applying is 11 to 25 years of age.

Tom Carey Fund – funding is available to allow people to access education and training courses as well as supporting younger people with developing their talents in sport and the performing arts. Grants are available to individuals living in the Abbey Ward only.

Annual grant total
In 2015/16 the foundation had assets of £6.8 million and an income of £454,000. We estimate that educational grants to individuals totalled £10,000.

Applications
Applications can be made online via the foundation's website.

Scargill's Educational Foundation

£6,000

Correspondent: Ellis Pugh, Clerk, Geldards LLP, 1 Pride Place, Pride Park, Derby DE24 8QR (01332 378374; email: ellis.pugh@geldards.com)

CC number: 527012

Eligibility
People under the age of 25 who live in the parishes of West Hallam, Dale Abbey, Mapperley and Stanley (including Stanley Common).

Types of grants
The main beneficiary of the charity is Scargill Church of England Primary School. Priority is also given to three

other schools in the area. After that, help is available for groups and also for individuals for the following purposes:

- Grants for sixth form pupils to help with books, equipment, clothing or travel
- Grants to help with school, college or university fees or to supplement existing grants
- Grants to help with the cost of books and educational outings for schoolchildren
- For the study of music and other arts and for educational travel

Annual grant total

In 2016 the foundation had an income of £237,500 and a total expenditure of £42,500. We estimate that around £6,000 was given in grants to individuals for educational purposes.

Applications

Applications can be made on a form available from the correspondent.

Bolsover

Hardwick Educational Charity

£1,400

Correspondent: Mrs C. E. Hitch, Stainsby Mill Farm, Heath, Chesterfield, Derbyshire S44 5RW (01246 850288)

CC number: 526995

Eligibility

People between the ages of 16 and 26, whose parent(s) live in the civil parish of Ault Hucknall.

Types of grants

Our research suggests that help with the cost of books is given to students in further/higher education and training. People starting work/entering a trade can be assisted towards the cost of books, equipment and instruments.

Annual grant total

In 2015 the charity had an income of £1,700 and a total expenditure of £1,600. We estimate that grants totalled around £1,400.

Exclusions

Grants are not normally available for student exchanges, maintenance or fees.

Applications

Apply in writing to the correspondent.

Derby

Spondon Relief-in-Need Charity

£6,000 (16 grants)

Correspondent: Stephen Williams, 15 Dob Holes Lane, Smalley, Ilkeston DE7 6EN (01332 780496; email: info@ spondonreliefinneedcharity.org; website: www.spondonreliefinneedcharity.org)

CC number: 211317

Eligibility

People who live in the ancient parish of Spondon within the city of Derby.

Types of grants

One-off (and occasionally recurrent, at the discretion of the trustees) grants are available towards the costs of school uniforms and school trips. Support is also given to higher education and sixth form students for the provision of books, equipment, training and fees.

Annual grant total

In 2016 the charity had assets of £753,000 and an income of £27,000. We estimate the amount awarded in grants for educational purposes was £6,000.

Exclusions

No grants are made for the relief of rates and taxes, or any expenses usually covered by statutory sources.

Applications

Application forms are available upon request from the clerk, along with guidance notes. All applications must be returned with a supporting letter from a recognised sponsor, i.e. a social or professional worker. The trustees meet in February, May, September, and November.

Other information

The charity also awards grants to individuals for welfare purposes.

Derbyshire Dales

The Ernest Bailey Charity

£350

Correspondent: Ros Hession, Community Engagement Officer, Community Development Department, Derbyshire Dales District Council, Town Hall, Bank Road, Matlock DE4 3NN (01629 761302; email: grants@ derbyshiredales.gov.uk; website: www. derbyshiredales.gov.uk/community-a-living/funding-and-grants/the-ernest-bailey-charity)

CC number: 518884

Eligibility

People in need who live in Matlock and district (Matlock, Matlock Bath, Bonsall, Cromford, Darley Dale, Northwood and Tinkersley, Rowsley (part) South Darley, Starkholmes and Tansley).

Types of grants

Educational grants are one-off. Awards can be given to students in further/ higher education towards books, fees, living expenses and study or travel abroad. Mature students can apply for costs towards books, travel, fees or childcare. People with special educational needs are considered. Each application is considered on its merits.

Annual grant total

In 2015/16 the charity had an income of £1,500 and a total expenditure of £1,600. The website notes that 'in 2016 a total of a £1,493 was awarded between 14 recipients'. We estimate that educational grants to individuals totalled around £350.

Applications

Application forms are available online or can be requested from the correspondent. They can be submitted online or via post, directly by the individual and/or can be supported by a relevant professional. Most recently the submission deadline was in October. Requests should include costings (total amount required, funds raised and funds promised). Previous beneficiaries may apply again, with account being taken of assistance given in the past.

Other information

Organisations are also supported. Social welfare grants are also given.

Erewash

Risley Educational Foundation

£7,800 (31 grants)

Correspondent: Margaret Giller, Clerk to the Trustees, 27 The Chase, Little Eaton, Derby DE21 5AS (01332 883361; email: mgiller45@gmail.com)

CC number: 702720

Eligibility

People under the age of 25 who live in the parishes of Breaston, Church Wilne, Dale Abbey, Draycott, Hopwell, Risley, Sandiacre or Stanton-by-Dale.

Types of grants

Grants of around £250 are available for further education students, towards the cost of books and equipment/ instruments, for travel for educational purposes, and for the study of music and arts.

Annual grant total

In 2015/16 the foundation had assets of £827,000 and an income of £67,000. The foundation made 31 grants to individuals totalling £7,800. A further £20,000 was given in grants to organisations (schools and Sunday schools).

Applications

Apply in writing to the correspondent. The trustees meet at least four times a year to consider applications.

Other information

The trust also supports local schools, allowing up to 5% of the annual income to be awarded to Church of England Sunday schools and up to 25% to other local schools. The remainder is then allocated for grants to individuals.

High Peak
The Bingham Trust

£10,300

Correspondent: E. Marshall, Secretary, Unit 1, Tongue Lane Industrial Estate, Dew Pond Lane, Buxton SK17 7LN (07966 378 546; email: binghamtrust@aol.com; website: www.binghamtrust.org.uk)

CC number: 287636

Eligibility

People in need who live in and around Buxton, Derbyshire (the SK17 postcode area).

Types of grants

One-off grants, usually up to £1,000, are awarded for educational purposes not available from statutory or parental sources.

Annual grant total

In 2015/16 the trust had assets of £4.3 million and an income of £193,500. Grants totalled £160,500, of which £20,500 was awarded to individuals. We estimate that educational grants to individuals amounted to £10,300, with support also given for social welfare needs.

Exclusions

The trustees cannot consider applications from individuals outside the SK17 postcode area. Grants are not made to repay existing debts or for higher educational purposes (university and college level). In exceptional circumstances, however, funding towards specialised equipment for people in higher education who have disabilities may be considered. No more than one application can be made in any 12-month period.

Applications

Applications can be made using the form available from the website, but will also be considered if sent by letter (the website does note, however, that applications sent by letter can take longer to deal with as the trust may need to request more information). Applications from individuals must always be supported by an agency familiar with the applicant's circumstances, such as social services or a charity or community organisation. Individuals can apply directly but those not applying through an organisation must send a supporting letter with their application.

Applications can be sent by post at the address above, or as an email attachment (with no additional attachments). All applications are acknowledged by post or email. They are usually considered in January, April, July and October/November each year; the date of the next meeting and the closing date for applications are noted on the website. In cases of more complicated applications, the trustees may find it beneficial to arrange a visit if they feel it would help.

Other information

The trust was established through the will of the late Robert Henry Bingham who lived in the Buxton area. Today it supports a broad range of charitable causes that benefit people in the area.

North East Derbyshire
Dronfield Relief in Need Charity

£900

Correspondent: Dr Anthony Bethell, Trustee, Ramshaw Lodge, Crow Lane, Unstone, Dronfield, Derbyshire S18 4AL (01246 413276)

CC number: 219888

Eligibility

People in need who live in the ecclesiastical parishes of Dronfield, Holmesfield and Unstone.

Types of grants

One-off small grants up to a value of £100 can be given, including those for social and physical training.

Annual grant total

In 2016 the charity had an income of £3,500 and a total expenditure of £4,000. We have estimated that £900 was given to individuals for educational purposes.

Applications

Applications may be made in writing to the correspondent although a social worker, doctor, member of the clergy of any denomination, a local councillor, Citizens Advice or other welfare agency. The applicants should ensure they are receiving all practical/financial assistance they are entitled to from statutory sources.

Other information

Grants are also given to local organisations and for social welfare purposes.

The Holmesfield Educational Foundation

£1,500

Correspondent: Geraldine Austen, Greenways, Holmesfield, Dronfield S18 7WB (0114 289 0686)

CC number: 515723

Eligibility

People under the age of 25 who or whose parents live in the parish of Holmesfield.

Types of grants

Awards towards books, clothing, equipment and other educational needs.

Annual grant total

In 2016 the foundation had an income of £4,900 and a total expenditure of £3,200. We estimate that grants given to individuals totalled approximately £1,500.

Applications

Applications can be made in writing to the correspondent.

Other information

Local schools may also be supported, where assistance is not already provided by the local authorities.

South Derbyshire
Hilton Educational Foundation

£3,000

Correspondent: Sue Cornish, Clerk to the Trustees, 6 Willow Brook Close, Hilton, Derby DE65 5JE (01283 734110; email: hiltoneducationalfoundation@gmail.com)

CC number: 527091

Eligibility

Young people under the age of 25 in further or higher education who live, or whose parents live, in the parish of Hilton.

Types of grants

One-off grants, usually of around £100 to £150, are given towards travel, clothing, books and equipment to pupils in secondary school, students in further or higher education or apprenticeships, as well as for those studying music or other arts.

Annual grant total

In 2015/16 the foundation had an income of £11,800 and a total expenditure of £5,600. We estimate that grants given to individuals totalled around £3,000.

Applications

Apply in writing to the correspondent. Applications can be submitted directly by the individual. They should normally be made in March and October and are considered in the same month.

Other information

Grants are also available to schools in the local area.

Leicester-shire

Babington's Charity

£4,500

Correspondent: Helen McCague, Trustee, 14 Main Street, Cossington, Leicester, Leicestershire LE7 4UU (01509 812271)

CC number: 220069

Eligibility

People in need in the parish of Cossington, Leicestershire.

Types of grants

Grants for equipment, clothing, fees, books and other necessities, computer equipment, travel costs or maintenance expenses to people under the age of 25 to help with tertiary education costs, vocational training or entering a trade. One-off or recurrent support towards other educational needs may also be given, according to need. Mature students have been supported for re-training following a redundancy.

Annual grant total

In 2015 the charity had an income of £47,200 and a total expenditure of £49,800, of which £9,000 was awarded to individuals and students for both educational and social welfare needs. We estimate that about £4,500 was given for educational purposes.

Applications

Applications may be made in writing to the correspondent. The trustees meet at least twice a year.

Other information

The charity gives to individuals and organisations for both education and social welfare purposes.

Alderman Newton's Educational Foundation

£116,500

Correspondent: The Clerk to the Governors, Leicester Charity Link, 20A Millstone Lane, Leicester LE1 5JN (0116 222 2200; email: info@charity-link.org; website: anef.org.uk)

CC number: 527881

Eligibility

People in need who are under the age of 25 and live (or whose parents live) in the city of Leicester.

Types of grants

Grants are given to schoolchildren, further/higher education students and people starting work/entering a trade. Support can be offered towards general educational needs, including school uniforms, clothing, books, equipment, instruments, tools, fees, maintenance, educational outings and study or travel overseas.

Annual grant total

In 2015/16 the foundation held assets of £4.2 million and had an income of £168,000. A total of £116,500 was awarded in grants and bursaries to individuals. Grants are also made to schools in Leicester and Leicestershire.

Applications

Application forms are available from the foundation's website or from the correspondent. They must be accompanied by three references and provide information on applicants' and/or their parents' income. Applications can be submitted directly by individuals and are considered regularly throughout the year. Further details can be found on the foundation's website.

Charnwood

The Dawson and Fowler Foundation

£14,600

Correspondent: Lesley Cutler, PO Box 73, Loughborough, Leicestershire LE11 0GA (07765 934117; email: dawsonfowler73@gmail.com; website: www.dawsonfowler.co.uk)

CC number: 527867

Eligibility

Young people between the ages of 11 and 25 who live in the borough of Loughborough (including Hathern).

Types of grants

Grants are available for:

- Pupils in secondary school (years 7 to 11) can apply for a grant to assist with the cost of school uniforms. Applications can be resubmitted every 12 months and are for a maximum value of £100
- Pupils attending a school endowed by the foundation can apply for a scholarship of £1,100 per term. Only one scholarship is available per year
- Students in further/higher/vocational education, and members of Scouts, Girlguides, a sports team, or Duke of Edinburgh Awards can apply for grants to cover the costs of equipment, uniform or other clothes, travel, books, etc.

Annual grant total

In 2016 the foundation had assets of £744,000 and an income of £47,000. The foundation awarded £1,100 in general educational support, and £13,500 in grants for school uniforms.

Exclusions

Grants are not normally given for accommodation, subsistence, day to day travelling costs, tuition, examination fees or childcare costs. Applications from groups of students or classes of pupils cannot be considered.

Applications

Application forms can be requested from the correspondent.

Other information

The foundation also awards grants to local senior schools and academies.

Mountsorrel Educational Fund

£78,500 (98 grants)

Correspondent: Liz Resch, Clerk to the Trustees, 4 Rothley Road, Mountsorrel, Loughborough LE12 7JU (0116 429 9946; email: clerkmef@gmail.com; website: www.mountsorrelunitedcharities.com)

CC number: 527912

Eligibility

People under the age of 25 who have been (or whose parent/guardian has been) resident in the parish of Mountsorrel for at least a year.

Types of grants

The fund's website states: 'a wide range of possible grants are available and the trustees would encourage young people to apply for financial support towards any aspect of their education'. Grants have previously been awarded for purposes such as support with further and higher education; music tuition; educational courses, books and specialist clothing; educational visits and training schemes and apprenticeships.

Annual grant total

In 2016 the fund had assets of £173,500 and an income of around £143,500. Grants to 98 individuals totalled around £78,500, broken down as follows:

Higher education and training	60	£69,500
Other	12	£3,300
A-level college students	16	£3,200
Music	9	£1,400
Christ Church and St Peter's Primary School	1	£900

Exclusions

Support is not normally available where assistance should be provided by the local authorities.

Applications

Application forms for different categories of grants are provided on the fund's website, where deadlines are also posted. Forms should be sent with an sae and relevant documentation to the clerk.

Other information

Together with Mountsorrel Relief in Need Charity (CC number: 217615), the Mountsorrel Educational Fund is administered by Mountsorrel United Charities (CC number: 1027652).

The Thomas Rawlins Educational Foundation

£500

Correspondent: Mrs Bertinat, 21 Haddon Close, Syston, Leicester LE7 1HZ (01509 622800; email: thomasrawlins@bertinat.me.uk; website: www.woodhouseparishcouncil.org.uk)

CC number: 527858

Eligibility

People under the age of 25 living in Barrow-upon-Soar, Quorn, Woodhouse and Woodhouse Eaves only.

Types of grants

Our research shows that grants normally range from £50 up to £250. Support is given to: school pupils to help with books, equipment, school uniform, maintenance or fees; students in further and higher education to help with books, equipment, instruments, study or travel abroad or fees; and people starting work to help with the cost of books, equipment and instruments, travel and clothing.

Annual grant total

In 2016/17 the foundation had an income of £2,400 and a total expenditure of £600. We estimate that grants totalled around £500.

Exclusions

Grants are not available for foreign students studying in the UK.

Applications

Application forms can be requested from the correspondent and should be submitted directly by the individual or their parents/guardians at any time.

Wymeswold Parochial Charities

£1,700

Correspondent: Mrs J. Collington, Correspondent, 94 Brook Street, Wymeswold, Loughborough, Leicestershire LE12 6TU (01509 880538; email: jocollington@sky.com)

CC number: 213241

Eligibility

People in need who have lived in Wymeswold for two years prior to application.

Types of grants

One-off grants are given for educational and relief-in-need purposes.

Annual grant total

In 2015/16 the charity had an income of £5,100 and a total expenditure of £3,800. We estimate that about £1,700 was given to individuals for educational purposes.

Applications

Applications may be made in writing to the correspondent at any time.

Other information

Welfare grants are also made, such as winter cash gifts to pensioners.

Harborough

The Marc Smith Educational Charity

£5,800

Correspondent: Diana Jones, Secretary, 21 Highcroft, Husbands Bosworth, Lutterworth, Leicestershire LE17 6LF (01858 880741; email: dianajones929@gmail.com)

CC number: 1045965

Eligibility

People under the age of 25 who live or have attended school in the ancient parishes of Claybrooke Magna, Claybrooke Parva, Ullesthorpe or Wibtoft, or whose parents live there.

Types of grants

Support is given to people in further education or training and individuals undertaking apprenticeships or starting work. Schoolchildren moving from primary to upper schools can also be supported, usually for clothing.

Annual grant total

In 2016 the charity had an income of £8,400 and a total expenditure of £12,300. We have estimated that grants to individuals totalled £5,800 during the year.

Applications

According to our previous research, applications from pupils should be made in writing to the correspondent and are normally considered in May. Applications from further education students are normally considered in September and should be submitted at a meeting, which applicants are invited to through local advertisements near to the time of the meeting.

Other information

Grants may also be made to local schools for educational projects and to organisations, depending on the income of the charity.

Hinckley and Bosworth

The Dixie Educational Foundation

£20,000

Correspondent: Peter Dungworth, Clerk to the Trustees, 31 Oakmeadow Way, Groby, Leicester LE6 0YN (0116 291 3683; email: pdungworth@hotmail.co.uk)

CC number: 527837

Eligibility

People under the age of 25 who or whose parents/guardians live, or have lived for at least two years, in the civil parishes of Barlestone, Cadeby, Carlton, Market Bosworth, Osbaston, Shenton, Sutton Cheney or in such civil parishes situated in the former rural district of Market Bosworth, as the trustees decide.

Types of grants

One-off grants are available to further education students for general educational costs, including clothing, books, equipment/instruments, educational outings in the UK or study/travel abroad.

The foundation also awards Sir Wolstan Dixie Exhibition scholarship for pupils 'who demonstrate academic excellence in the examination for entry into Year 7 of The Dixie Grammar School'.

Annual grant total

In 2016/17 the foundation had an income of £110,500 and a total expenditure of £112,000. Throughout the year the foundation awarded around £20,000 in grants to individuals for educational purposes.

The charity also gives grants to organisations.

Applications

Apply in writing to the correspondent.

Other information

In 2016/17 £59,500 was awarded to organisations.

Thomas Herbert Smith's Trust Fund

£5,000

Correspondent: Andrew York, 6 Magnolia Close, Leicester LE2 8PS (0116 283 5345; email: andrew_york@ sky.com)

CC number: 701694

Eligibility

People who live in the parish of Groby in Leicestershire.

Types of grants

One-off and recurrent grants, usually ranging from £100 to £500.

Annual grant total

In 2015/16 the fund had an income of £19,500 and a total expenditure of £11,200. Grants are made to individuals and organisations for both social welfare and educational purposes. We estimate that grants given to individuals for educational purposes totalled £5,000.

Applications

Applications can be made using a form available from the correspondent. They can be submitted either directly by the individual, or through a social worker, Citizens Advice or other third party, and are considered throughout the year.

Stoke Golding Boy's Charity

£5,000

Correspondent: Anthony John Smith, The Middle Stores, 2 Church Walks, Stoke Golding, Nuneaton CV13 6HB

CC number: 519728

Eligibility

Young men and boys under the age of 25 who live in Stoke Golding. Our research suggests that some preference may be

given to people with special educational needs.

Types of grants

One-off grants depending on availability and circumstances. Support is given for a wide range of educational needs.

Annual grant total

In 2016 the charity had an income of £6,000 and a total expenditure of £6,000. We estimate that around £5,000 was available for distribution in grants to individuals

Applications

Apply in writing to the correspondent. Applications can be made directly by the individual and normally should be submitted by mid-March for consideration in April.

Leicester

Keyham Educational Foundation

£200

Correspondent: David Witcomb, Trustee, Tanglewood, Snows Lane, Keyham, Leicester LE7 9JS (0116 259 5663)

CC number: 527965

Eligibility

People under the age of 25 who live, or whose parents live, in the parish of Keyham and who are in need.

Types of grants

Small, one-off grants can be given to people in secondary and tertiary education for general educational needs, including books, equipment/instruments, travel, educational outings, study of arts and other educational expenses.

Annual grant total

In 2016 the foundation had an income of £5,000 and a total expenditure of £300. We estimate that grants to individuals totalled around £200.

Applications

Applications may be made in writing to the correspondent. They are normally considered in March and October and can be submitted by the individual or through a third party, such as parent/ guardian. Urgent applications can be considered at other times. If the applicant does not live in Keyham, information about their connection with residents should be provided with the application.

Other information

Village groups participating in educational classes are also supported.

Oadby and Wigston

The Oadby Educational Foundation

£19,800 (140 grants)

Correspondent: Rodney Waterfield, Hon Secretary and Treasurer, 2 Silverton Road, Oadby, Leicester LE2 4NN (0116 271 4507; email: rodatthegnomehouse@ talktalk.net)

CC number: 528000

Eligibility

People under the age of 25 who are in full-time education, who have a home address within the former urban district of Oadby in Leicestershire, and were educated in the parish.

Types of grants

One-off grants, usually in the range of £50 and £200, are made to schoolchildren, college students and undergraduates, including those towards uniforms/clothing, study/travel abroad and equipment/instruments. People of any age can receive one-off grants towards expeditions and voluntary work such as Operation Raleigh or Voluntary Service Overseas.

Annual grant total

In 2016 the foundation had assets of £1.4 million and an income of £49,000. Educational grants to individuals totalled £19,800.

Applications

Applications can be made on a form available from the correspondent. They should be submitted either through the individual's school, college or educational welfare agency, or directly by the individual.

Other information

Grants can also be made for social welfare purposes.

Northamp-tonshire

Arnold's Education Foundation

£4,000

Correspondent: Marina Eaton, Grange Park Court, Roman Way, Grange Park, Northampton NN4 5EA (01604 876697; email: meaton@wilsonbrowne.co.uk)

CC number: 310590

Eligibility

People in need who are under 25 and live in, or were educated for at least one year in, the parishes of Stony Stratford, Nether Heyford, Upper Heyford, Stowe-Nine-Churches, Weedon Bec, and the ancient parish of St Giles. Preference is given to members of the Church of England.

Types of grants

One-off and recurrent grants for the study of music and the arts, as well as social and physical training. Grants are made: for schoolchildren towards the cost of clothing, books, educational outings, maintenance and school fees; towards the cost of books, fees/living expenses, travel exchange and study or travel abroad for students in further or higher education; and towards books, equipment/instruments, clothing and travel for people starting work.

Annual grant total

In 2015/16 the foundation had an income of £33,000 and assets of £116,500. A total of £4,000 was awarded in educational grants.

Applications

Apply in writing to the correspondent.

Other information

The foundation also donated £7,300 in grants to Merton College, Oxford University.

The Charity of Hervey and Elizabeth Ekins

£8,400

Correspondent: Richard Pestell, Trustee, 41 Thorburn Road, Northampton NN3 3DA (01604 408712; email: pestells@btinternet.com)

CC number: 309858

Eligibility

Children and young people who have lived in the borough of Northampton or the parish of Great Doddington for no less than three years, attended a state school for no less than one year, and attended a Church of England church on a regular basis.

Preference will be given to those residing in the ecclesiastical parishes of: St Peter Weston Favell; St Peter and St Paul Abington; and Emmanuel Northampton.

Types of grants

Grants are given to schoolchildren, students in further or higher education and to people starting work towards books, equipment and educational outings in the UK and overseas. Grants are also given for music tuition fees. Preference is given to those entering the ministry of the Church of England.

Annual grant total

In 2015/16 the charity had assets of £1.1 million and an income of £38,500. The amount of grants given to individuals totalled £8,400, of which £5,200 was awarded for further and higher education and £3,200 for music and residential activities. A further £14,700 was given in grants to churches and other charities, for work with children.

Exclusions

Grants are not given for school fees.

Applications

Apply in writing to the correspondent, including details of school and church attended.

Horne Foundation

£118,000 (59 grants)

Correspondent: Ros Harwood, Trustee, PO Box 6165, Newbury RG14 9FY (email: hornefoundation@googlemail.com)

CC number: 283751

Eligibility

Higher education students in need who live in Northamptonshire.

Types of grants

The foundation awards bursaries to higher education students towards course fees, living expenses and other educational costs. Grants of up to of £5,000 are awarded.

Annual grant total

In 2015/16 the foundation had assets of £7.6 million and an income of £160,000. Grants to 59 individuals totalled £118,000. A further £10,000 was given to one organisation.

Applications

Bursaries to schoolchildren are made on the recommendation of schools. If the applicant is at school, they should apply through the headteacher of the school. Students can apply to the foundation directly, in writing. Applications are considered twice a year.

Other information

The foundation also gives support to organisations for educational projects that involve new buildings and through regular smaller donations to local projects in the Northampton and Oxfordshire area.

The trustees' policy is to distribute an amount approximately equal to the investment income received.

The Dorothy Johnson Charitable Trust

£8,000

Correspondent: Ms Z. Silins, Clerk to the Trust, Hybank, 12 Old Road, Walgrave, Northampton NN6 9QW (01604 780662; email: zinaida@zinaidasilins.com)

CC number: 298499

Eligibility

People under 25 who were born and are living, have lived or were educated at some time in Northamptonshire.

Types of grants

One-off and recurrent grants. Grants are made to schoolchildren, college students, undergraduates, vocational students, postgraduates and people with special educational needs, towards clothing/uniforms, fees, study/travel abroad, books, equipment/instruments, maintenance/living expenses and excursions.

Annual grant total

In 2016/17 the trust had an income of £19,700 and a total expenditure of £19,800. We have estimated that grants to individuals totalled £8,000. Grants are also made to educational organisations.

Applications

Apply in writing to the correspondent.

Northamptonshire Community Foundation

£13,400

Correspondent: Victoria Miles, Chief Executive, 18 Albion Place, Northampton NN1 1UD (01604 230033; email: enquiries@ncf.uk.com; website: www.ncf.uk.com)

CC number: 1094646

Eligibility

People who live in Northamptonshire.

Types of grants

The foundation administers a number of different funding schemes – refer to the website for up-to-date information. At the time of writing (August 2017) there was one funding scheme for individuals:

Northamptonshire Champions Fund
Grants are available to 'Northamptonshire's emerging sports stars' to help with the costs of sports-based activities – in particular, people between the ages of 25 and 35 (although those above 35 may be considered) who have a disability. Grants range between £200 and £1,000 in the first year and up to a maximum of £400 in subsequent years and can be given for purposes such

as travel expenses, clothing, equipment and training/coaching. A list of priority and non-priority sports is provided on the website, along with detailed eligibility criteria. Funding can be used to help applicants to remain in education if they are experiencing financial difficulties and to athletes on a low income generally or to athletes with disabilities who require an assistor or carer in order to compete.

Previously, funding from other schemes has been given for purposes such as supporting those engaged in community action, arts and music.

Annual grant total

In 2015/16 the foundation had assets of almost £8 million and an income of £932,500. The amount of grants given to individuals for both educational and welfare purposes totalled almost £63,000 and included: £10,000 from the Northamptonshire Champions Fund; £1,900 from the Henry Martin Centenary Fund (supporting community action, disadvantaged people getting into work, crime prevention and rehabilitation of people who have offended and £1,500 in Arts and Music Fund bursaries.

The foundation also made grants to groups/organisations totalling £988,000.

Exclusions

Refer to the website for exclusions for each scheme.

Applications

Application forms together with detailed guidelines and deadlines can be found on the foundation's website and should be submitted in two copies, one electronically and one by post.

The foundation invites potential applicants to approach its staff members for informal advice or feedback on applications prior to final submission. Applicants should check the website for any changes before applying.

Other information

The foundation manages a number of different funds for both individuals and organisations.

The Wilson Foundation

£10,100 (35 grants)

Correspondent: The Trustees, The Maltings, Tithe Farm, Moulton Road, Holcot, Northamptonshire NN6 9SH (01604 782240; fax: 01604 782241; email: polly@tithefarm.com; website: www. thewilsonfoundation.co.uk)

CC number: 1074414

Eligibility

Young people (normally 10 to 21 years of age) who were born or have lived in Northamptonshire for at least a year, particularly those who are disadvantaged or underprivileged.

Types of grants

Grants are mainly given for school trips, camps, Outward Bound courses or other residential trips, which help to build the individual's character and can make a lasting impact on their life. Grants may also be given for purposes such as arts and sports projects, summer activities or scouting/guiding projects.

Annual grant total

In 2015/16 the foundation had assets of £5.9 million and an income of £113,000. During the year 35 grants were made to individuals, totalling £10,100 altogether. A further £117,000 was given in 33 grants to organisations.

Exclusions

The 2015/16 annual report states: 'A large proportion of the rejected applications are young people requesting financial help with expenses whilst at university or college, over 21 years old or living outside of the county.'

Applications

Application forms can be downloaded from the foundation's website and once completed should be sent to the correspondent. At least one reference must be supplied. The trustees meet at least twice a year.

Daventry

The Chauntry Estate

£2,500

Correspondent: Rita Tank, Walnut Tree Cottage, Main Street, Great Brington, Northampton NN7 4JA (01604 770809; email: ritatank40@yahoo.com)

CC number: 200795

Eligibility

People who live in the parish of Brington. Applicants must have lived in the parish for at least five years.

Types of grants

One-off grants for payment of uniforms for children transferring to secondary schools, books and equipment for students in further/higher education or apprentices, and assistance towards items of school equipment not provided by the local education authority. Grants are also made to mature students.

Annual grant total

In 2015/16 the charity had an income of £11,200 and a total expenditure of £10,000. We estimate that educational grants to individuals totalled £2,500.

Applications

Apply in writing to the correspondent. Ineligible applications are not acknowledged.

The United Charities of East Farndon

£3,500

Correspondent: Nigel Haynes, Newhouse Farm, Harborough Road, East Farndon, Market Harborough LE16 9SG (email: haynestripley@msn.com)

CC number: 200778

Eligibility

People in need who live in East Farndon.

Types of grants

One-off grants of up to £50 for people starting work, schoolchildren and college students. Grants given include those for books, equipment and instruments, as well as to schoolchildren for excursions.

Annual grant total

In 2016 the charity had an income of £6,800 and a total expenditure of £7,700. We estimate that grants given to individuals totalled around £3,500.

Applications

Applications can be made in writing to the correspondent directly by the individual or a family member, for consideration as they are received.

Kettering

Church and Town Allotment Charities and others

£5,000

Correspondent: Anne Ireson, Administrator, Kettering Borough Council, Council Offices, Bowling Green Road, Kettering NN15 7QX (01536 534398; email: anneireson@kettering.gov. uk)

CC number: 207698

Eligibility

People in further/higher education who are over the age of 16 and live in Kettering or Barton Seagrave. Trustees are keen to receive applications from mature students.

Types of grants

Financial support is available towards general educational needs, including books, equipment/instruments and other necessities. People in vocational training, people starting work, mature students and individuals with special educational needs can all be assisted.

Annual grant total

In 2015/16 the charity had an income of £15,000 and a total expenditure of £10,000. We estimate that educational grants to individuals totalled around £5,000.

Applications

Apply in writing to the correspondent. Applications can be made by individuals directly or through their parents/guardians, educational establishment, welfare agency, if applicable. Details of the applicant's financial situation should also be included. The trustees usually meet twice a year, in February and November.

Other information

Support is also given to the Kettering parish church and to local retired people who live alone to help with the cost of fuel in winter.

Northampton

Beckett's and Sergeant's Educational Foundation

£93,000 (160 grants)

Correspondent: Angela Moon, Hewitsons LLP, Elgin House, Billing Road, Northampton NN1 5AU (01604 233233; fax: 01604 627941; email: angelamoon@hewitsons.com)

CC number: 309766

Eligibility

People under the age of 25 who live and are being educated in the borough of Northampton.

The trustees have discretion to award grants to further/higher education students who live in Northampton during holidays but attend an institution elsewhere.

Types of grants

Grants of up to £800 can be given for a wide range of educational and training purposes, including educational trips, books, equipment, study of music or other arts and supplementing existing grants.

Annual grant total

In 2015/16 the foundation had assets of £3.2 million and an income of £231,000. The total amount awarded in grants to individuals was £93,000.

Applications

Application forms can be requested form the correspondent in writing.

Other information

In 2015/16 £20,000 was paid in grants to local schools and organisations.

Blue Coat Educational Charity

£4,000

Correspondent: Richard Pestell, 41 Thorburn Road, Northampton NN3 3DA (01604 408710; email: pestells@btinternet.com)

CC number: 309764

Eligibility

Schoolchildren, students and people entering work who are under the age of 25 and live in the borough of Northampton.

Types of grants

One-off and recurrent grants for general educational purposes, including the costs of clothing, educational outings, books, fees, study/travel abroad or student exchange, equipment/instruments, tools. Grants can reach up to £500 per individual.

Annual grant total

In 2016/17 the charity had an income of £10,700 and a total expenditure of £7,000. We estimate that the amount awarded in grants to individuals was around £4,000.

Exclusions

Grants are not available to mature students or overseas students studying in Britain.

Applications

Apply in writing to the correspondent. Our research suggests that applications are usually considered in February, July and November.

Other information

Grants are also made to the Church of England schools in Northampton.

Sir Thomas White's Northampton Charity

£160,500

Correspondent: Angela Moon, Clerk to the Trustees, Hewitsons LLP, Elgin House, Billing Road, Northampton NN1 5AU (01604 233233; email: info@stwcharitynorthampton.org.uk)

CC number: 201486

Eligibility

People between the ages of 16 and 35 who live in Northampton.

Types of grants

Grants

Grants of up to £1,000 are made to young people aged between 16 and 25 who live in Northampton and have been resident there for the last five years, and are in school or full-time education or vocational training. Examples of what may be funded include musical instruments, sports equipment, books, art materials, tools and other specialist equipment.

Loans

Interest-free loans are given to those aged between 21 and 35, who have been resident in Northampton for at least five years, to advance their education or training or 'help establish them in work, vocation or in life generally', according to the website. Examples of support include funding towards a college course, to help buy a vehicle or adapt a property to start up a business or for the purchase of special equipment. Up to £2,500 may be given for educational purposes and up to £5,000 for business purposes.

Annual grant total

In 2016 the charity had assets of £3.4 million and an income of £301,500. During the year, grants totalling £160,500 were awarded to individuals. A further £109,500 was given in grants to four organisations.

Applications

Applications can be made using the form provided on the charity's website. The relevant subcommittees assess applications four times each year and applicants should be notified within three to four weeks if their application is successful.

Other information

Previously called Sir Thomas White's Loan Fund.

The charity also provides scholarships through the University of Northampton.

South Northamptonshire

Blakesley Parochial Charities

£1,200

Correspondent: Dee Lucas, Bradworthy, Main Street, Woodend, Towcester, Northamptonshire NN12 8RX (01327 860517; email: deelucas@uwclub.net)

CC number: 202949

Eligibility

People over the age of 16 who are in need and live in Blakesley.

Types of grants

One-off and recurrent grants to assist people in post-16 education (college, university), and also people studying for a vocational qualification. Funds can be used towards the cost of books, equipment, trips, and fees.

Annual grant total

In 2016 the charity had an income of £8,000 and a total expenditure of £5,000. We estimate that the amount awarded in educational grants was £1,200.

Applications

Apply in writing to the correspondent.

Other information

The charities also make grants for welfare purposes and to local organisations.

The Brackley United Feoffee Charity

£7,500

Correspondent: Irene Bennett, 24 Broad Lane, Evenley, Brackley NN13 5SF (01280 703904; email: brackleyunitedfeoffee.charity@gmail.com)

CC number: 238067

Eligibility

People under the age of 25 who live in the ecclesiastical parish of Brackley (which consists of the town of Brackley and the village of Halse only).

Types of grants

One-off grants, usually in the range of £100 and £1,000. During the year grants were made for school trips, travel costs, tuition fees and laptops.

Annual grant total

In 2015/16 the charity had assets of £1 million and an income of £258,000. We estimate that educational grants totalled around £7,500.

Applications

Applications can be made in writing to the correspondent either directly by the individual or through the individual's school, college or educational welfare agency. The trustees meet every three to four months.

Other information

The charity awards grants to individuals and organisations for both educational and social welfare purposes.

Litchborough Parochial Charities

£3,300

Correspondent: Maureen Pickford, Trustee, 18 Banbury Road, Litchborough, Towcester NN12 8JF (01327 830110; email: maureen@mojo1904.plus.com)

CC number: 201062

Eligibility

Young people resident in or connected to the ancient parish of Litchborough following a formal programme of study.

Types of grants

One-off and recurring grants to help with course fees.

Annual grant total

In 2015/16 the charity had an income of £7,300 and a total expenditure of £6,800. Grants are made to individuals for both educational and social welfare purposes. We estimate that educational grants to individuals totalled £3,300.

Applications

Apply in writing to the correspondent.

Other information

Grants are also given for widows' pensions and to assist the pensioners with the costs of heating bills.

Middleton Cheney United Charities

£3,500

Correspondent: Linda Harvey, 1 The Avenue, Middleton Cheney, Banbury, Oxfordshire OX17 2PE (01295712650)

CC number: 202511

Eligibility

People who live in Middleton Cheney and are in need.

Types of grants

Our research suggests that one-off grants are available to schoolchildren for equipment/instruments and to students in higher or further education (including mature students) for books and study or travel abroad. Awards are in the range of £100 to £200.

Annual grant total

In 2016 the charity had an income of £9,500 and a total expenditure of £7,500. We estimate that educational support to individuals totalled around £3,500.

Applications

Apply in writing to the correspondent. Applications can be submitted directly by the individual and are considered four times a year.

Other information

Support may also be given to organisations.

Nottinghamshire

Arnold Educational Foundation

£13,800

Correspondent: Brian West, Administrator, 73 Arnot Hill Road, Arnold, Nottingham NG5 6LN (0115 920 6656; email: b.west909@yahoo.co.uk; website: www.stmarysarnold.org.uk/arnold_parochial_charities.html)

CC number: 528191

Eligibility

People under the age of 25 who live in (or whose parents live in) the ancient parish of Arnold (which includes Daybrook and Woodthorpe) and who require financial assistance.

Types of grants

Small awards to specifically help with the purchase of books and equipment for education, or to assist with contributions towards courses and other useful educational outings associated with studies.

Annual grant total

In 2015/16 the trust had an annual income of £16,000 and a total expenditure of £14,500. We estimate that the total amount donated in grants was £13,800.

Applications

Applications can be obtained from the correspondent or downloaded from the website. Receipts for goods purchased must also be included if applying for grants retrospectively.

Bingham United Charities 2006

£600

Correspondent: Susan Lockwood, 23 Douglas Road, Bingham, Nottingham NG13 8EL (01949 875453; email: lockwoodsue79@gmail.com)

CC number: 213913

Eligibility

People in need who live in the parish of Bingham.

Types of grants

Small, one-off grants can be made for school uniforms or travel to and from school. The charity does not give cash grants, preferring to purchase and gift the items to the beneficiary.

Annual grant total

In 2016/17 the charity had an income of £10,000 and a total expenditure of £10,500. We estimate that the amount awarded in grants for education was £600.

Exclusions

School trips, instruments, equipment, books, fees etc. are not funded.

Applications

Applications can be made in writing to the correspondent. Usually, educational grants are made in conjunction with welfare grants.

Other information

The charity mainly supports applicants for welfare purposes. Educational grants are not commonly made.

The Francis Bernard Caunt Education Trust

£40,000

Correspondent: Denise Ryan, 10 Lombard Street, Newark NG24 1XE (01636 703333; email: info@larken.co.uk; website: www.larken.co.uk)

CC number: 1108858

Eligibility

People aged between 16 and 25 who are, or whose parents or guardians are, resident within a 12-mile radius of Newark on Trent Parish Church.

Applicants should have attended or attend Newark schools or colleges or Southwell or Tuxford schools in the previous eight years for at least two years and be intending to study part-time or full-time for at least one year on a recognised academic or vocational course.

Types of grants

Grants, scholarships and loans of £500 to £2,000.

Annual grant total

In 2015/16 the trust held assets of £1.3 million and an income of £55,500. The total amount awarded in grants to individuals was £40,000.

Applications

Application forms are available from the website and should be submitted with a letter of reference from a headteacher, employer or other appropriate person, such as a career adviser.

Nottinghamshire Community Foundation

£250

Correspondent: Nina Dauban, Nottinghamshire Community Foundation, Pine House B, Southwell Road West, Rainworth, Mansfield NG21 0HJ (01623 620202; email: enquiries@nottscf.org.uk; website: www. nottscf.org.uk)

CC number: 1069538

Eligibility

- The Kynan Eldridge Fund: young people under the age of 30 in the Mansfield and Hucknall areas who are using music to help them overcome personal challenges and achieve their full potential
- The Joan Oliver Fund: young people aged 16 to 25 who show talent in the field of fine art
- Dave Hartley Fund: people in the Mansfield and Ashfield area

Types of grants

The charity currently has three funds that offer grants to individuals:

- The Kynan Eldridge Fund: one-off grants of up to £250 which may be used to purchase equipment or for services like musical therapy
- The Joan Oliver Fund: small grants of up to £500 which may be used to pay for art materials, additional training, exhibition space or help towards higher education fees
- Dave Hartley Fund: grants of up to £250 to increase their individual's musical ability and self-esteem. Grants may be used to purchase instruments or supportive musical equipment

Annual grant total

In 2015/16 the foundation had an income of £1 million and a total expenditure of £582,000. Grants from the Hartley and Eldridge funds totalled £250.

Applications

See the foundation's website for details of funds which are currently open and specific guidance on how to make an application.

Other information

The community foundation also makes grants to organisations and voluntary groups.

Bassetlaw

Read's Exhibition Foundation

£3,000

Correspondent: Mr A. Hill, Sandy Acre, Eagle Road, Spalford, Newark NG23 7HA (01522 778250)

CC number: 528238

Eligibility

Children and young people, including university students, who have lived in or attended school in the parish of Tuxford.

Types of grants

Mainly assistance for students in further or higher education. Support is also given towards the cost of education, training, apprenticeships or equipment for those starting work and towards essentials for schoolchildren.

Annual grant total

In 2016/17 the foundation had an income of £3,400 and a total expenditure of £3,300. We have estimated that the total of grants given was around £3,000.

Applications

Apply in writing to the correspondent. The trustees have previously stated that invoices for school equipment must be submitted before any grant is issued. Applications are considered throughout the year.

Mansfield

Faith Clerkson's Exhibition Foundation

£3,500

Correspondent: C. P. McKay, 68 Hillside Road, Beeston, Nottingham NG9 3AY (07771 978622; email: colinp.mckay@btinternet.com)

CC number: 528240

Eligibility

People going to university or entering further education who have lived in the borough of Mansfield or the urban district of Mansfield Woodhouse for at least two years.

Types of grants

Small grants are available to help higher/ further education students with general educational costs, including books, equipment, clothing, travel.

Annual grant total

In 2016/17 the charity had an income of £3,500 and a total expenditure of £4,000. We estimate that around £3,500 was awarded in grants.

Exclusions

According to previous research, grants are not available towards course fees.

Applications

Apply in writing to the correspondent. The trustees normally meet in June and October.

Warsop United Charities

£2,500

Correspondent: Jean Simmons, Trustee, Newquay, Clumber Street, Warsop, Mansfield, Nottinghamshire NG20 0LX

CC number: 224821

Eligibility

People in need who live in the urban district of Warsop (Warsop, Church Warsop, Warsop Vale, Meden Vale, Spion Kop and Skoonholme).

Types of grants

Grants for specific items to people at school, college or university.

Annual grant total

In 2015 the charity had an income of £7,500 and a total expenditure of £10,700. We estimate that grants given to individuals for educational purposes totalled around £2,500.

Applications

Applications may be made in writing to the correspondent. The trustees meet three or four times a year.

Other information

Grants are also made for relief-in-need purposes. Both individuals and organisations can be supported.

Newark and Sherwood

The John and Nellie Brown Farnsfield Trust

£15,000

Correspondent: David Slight, 3 Fernbeck Cottages, Tippings Lane, Farnsfield, Newark NG22 8EP (01623 882349; email: dgcslight@gmail.com)

CC number: 1078367

Eligibility

People in need who live in Farnsfield in Nottinghamshire and the surrounding area.

Types of grants

One-off and recurrent grants are given for the furtherance of education, and can be used for musical and sporting equipment as well.

Annual grant total

In 2016/17 the trust had an income of £32,000 and a total expenditure of £31,000. We estimate the trust awarded around £15,000 in grants towards education during the year.

Applications

Applications should be made in writing to the correspondent.

Other information

The trust also makes grants to individuals for welfare purposes.

Mary Woolhouse

£1,500

Correspondent: Jenny Hamilton, 4 St Wilfreds Close, North Muskham, Newark, Nottinghamshire NG23 6HZ (01636 705300; email: marywoolhousetrust@yahoo.com)

CC number: 528185

Eligibility

People under the age of 25 who, or whose parents, live in the parishes of North Muskham and Bathley.

Types of grants

Our research suggests that one-off grants are given to schoolchildren and college students towards the cost of books and equipment/instruments. The Charity Commission record indicates that support can include 'education in the doctrines of the Church of England' and 'social and physical training'.

Annual grant total

In 2016 the charity had an income of £8,300 and a total expenditure of £3,400. We estimate that grants given to individuals totalled around £1,500.

Applications

Applications can be made in writing to the correspondent. They can be submitted directly by the individual at any time.

Other information

Local schools are also supported, where the need is not addressed by the local authorities.

Nottingham

Audrey Harrison Heron Memorial Fund

£3,000

Correspondent: The Trustees, c/o Natwest Trust Services, 6th Floor, Trinity Quay 2, Avon Street, Bristol BS2 0PT (0345 304 2424; email: nwb.charities@natwest.com)

CC number: 504494

Eligibility

Women and girls under the age of 25, living in the city of Nottingham.

Types of grants

One-off and recurrent grants to help with the cost of books, equipment/instruments, clothing, travel in the UK and overseas, as well as school, college or university fees.

Annual grant total

In 2016/17 the fund had an income of £5,900 and a total expenditure of £3,600. We estimate that grants given to individuals totalled around £3,000.

Applications

Application forms can be requested from the correspondent. Applications can be submitted either directly by the individual or through a third party, such as school/college/educational welfare agency, if applicable. Our research suggests that applications are considered throughout the year.

Other information

Grants may also be awarded to organisations which share the fund's objectives.

Nottingham Gordon Memorial Trust for Boys and Girls

£3,800

Correspondent: Anna Chandler, Charity Administrator, Cumberland Court, 80 Mount Street, Nottingham NG1 6HH (0115 901 5562; email: anna.chandler@freeths.co.uk)

CC number: 212536

Eligibility

Children and young people under the age of 25 who are in need, hardship or distress and live in Nottingham or the area immediately around the city. Preference can be given to individuals who are of the former Nottingham Gordon Memorial Home for Destitute Working Boys.

Types of grants

Grants are given to schoolchildren and further/higher education students. Assistance is awarded towards general education and training needs, books, equipment/instruments, tools, maintenance/living expenses, educational outings in the UK and study/travel abroad and school uniforms or other clothing.

Annual grant total

In 2016 the trust had assets of £1.3 million and an income of £47,000. We estimate that grants given to individuals totalled £3,800.

Applications

Application forms are available from the correspondent. They can be submitted through the individual's school, college, educational welfare agency, a health visitor, social worker, probation officer or similar professional. The 2016 annual report states that: 'Applications for grants made to individuals were received from a variety of different sources such as Social Services, Health Centres, Framework Housing Association and Nottingham Women's Centre, all of which are based in Nottingham.'

Other information

The trust also supports organisations in the Nottingham area (£22,500 in 2016) and provides relief-in-need support for individuals.

Peveril Exhibition Endowment

£6,000

Correspondent: The Clerk to the Trustees, 5 New Road, Burton Lazars, Melton Mowbray, Leicestershire LE14 2UU (01636 813532; email: peverilfund@gmail.com; website: www. peveril.org.uk)

CC number: 528242

Eligibility

Children and young people aged between 11 and 25 who (or whose parents) have lived in Nottingham for at least one year and who are attending, or about to attend, secondary or further education. Preference is given to people who permanently reside in Nottingham rather than on temporary or transitional basis.

Types of grants

One-off and recurrent grants are available to secondary school pupils and further/higher education students. Awards are given for general educational expenses.

Annual grant total

In 2015/16 the charity had an income of £7,400 and a total expenditure of £7,000. We estimate that around £6,000 was given in grants to individuals.

Applications

Application forms can be requested from the correspondent. Academic references or financial details may be requested and taken into account.

Allan and Gerta Rank Educational Trust Fund

£3,000

Correspondent: Nikki Spencer, Trustee, 16 Eyres Gardens, Ilkeston DE7 8JE (0115 849 9216)

CC number: 1091456

Eligibility

Students who are of the Jewish faith and are either living or studying within a 50-mile radius of Nottingham city centre.

Types of grants

One-off and recurrent grants to students undertaking a higher education course at a university or college.

Annual grant total

In 2016/17 the trust had no income and a total expenditure of £3,300. We estimate that educational grants to individuals totalled around £3,000.

Applications

Applications may be made in writing to the correspondent.

Rutland

The Rutland Trust

£3,500

Correspondent: Richard Adams, Clerk, 35 Trent Road, Oakham, Rutland LE15 6HE (01572 756706; email: rjaadams@btinternet.com)

CC number: 517175

Eligibility

People, usually under the age of 35, who are in need and live in Rutland. Applicants may be at any level or stage of their education.

Types of grants

One-off grants, usually ranging between £50 and £400, are made. There are no restrictions on how the grants may be spent. In the past, grants have been made towards music and school trips for needy young people, for European exchange trips, and for young people to take part in educational, missionary and life-experience programmes overseas. Grants may also be spent on books, equipment, fees, bursaries, fellowships and study visits.

Annual grant total

In 2016 the trust had an income of £18,000 and a total expenditure of £14,000. We estimate that grants awarded to individuals for educational purposes totalled around £3,500.

Applications

Our research suggests that an initial telephone call is recommended.

West Midlands

General

Grantham Yorke Trust

£4,500

Correspondent: Christine Norgrove, Clerk to the Trustees, Shakespeare Martineau, 1 Colmore Square, Birmingham B4 6AA (0121 214 0487)

CC number: 228466

Eligibility

People under 25 who were born in what was the old West Midlands Metropolitan County area (meaning Birmingham, Coventry, Dudley, Redditch, Sandwell, Solihull, Tamworth, Walsall or Wolverhampton).

Types of grants

One-off grants are given to:

- Schoolchildren and students for uniforms and other school clothing, books, equipment, instruments, fees, maintenance and living expenses, childcare, educational outings in the UK, study or travel overseas and student exchange
- Students leaving school or further education for equipment and clothing, which will help them enter, or prepare for, their chosen profession or trade
- People starting work for maintenance and living expenses and childcare
- Education focused on preventing unplanned pregnancy, drug, alcohol and gambling abuse, child abuse or young people committing offences

Annual grant total

In 2015/16 the trust had assets of £6.2 million and an income of £245,000. A total of 21 grants were awarded to individuals, for both social welfare and educational needs, amounting to £9,100. We estimate that educational grants to individuals totalled £4,500.

Applications

Applications can be made on a form available from the correspondent. Applications can be submitted either directly by the individual or a relevant third party, or through the individual's school, college or educational welfare agency.

The Anthony and Gwendoline Wylde Memorial Charity

£2,500

Correspondent: Kirsty McEwen, Clerk to the Trustees, c/o Higgs & Sons, 3 Waterfront Business Park, Dudley Road, Brierley Hill, West Midlands DY5 1LX (01384 327322; email: kirsty.mcewen@higgsandsons.co.uk; website: wyldecharity.weebly.com)

CC number: 700239

Eligibility

People in need living in Dudley and Staffordshire, particularly Kinver and Stourbridge. The beneficial area is defined as the DY7, DY8 and DY9 postcodes.

Types of grants

One-off grants, usually up to £750, are given to college students and undergraduates for clothing, fees, books, equipment/instruments, maintenance/living expenses, voluntary work overseas and excursions.

Annual grant total

In 2015/16 the charity had assets of £908,500 and an income of £50,000. Grants were made totalling £37,000 and consisted of awards to 11 organisations amounting to £31,500 and awards to 15 individuals totalling around £5,100. We estimate that grants given to individuals for educational purposes totalled about £2,500.

Exclusions

Applications from areas outside the beneficial area may only be considered in exceptional circumstances. Support is not given for costs that can be met by statutory resources.

Applications

The method of application depends on the type of grant being applied for. Full details of the types of grants available can be found on the website. Applications for grants of up to £750 (small grants), if necessary, can be dealt with quickly by the Small Grants Committee. Applications for amounts greater than £750 (large grants) can only be considered at trustees' meetings, held twice a year. For small educational grants, additional supporting documentation is required – a copy of a confirmation letter or email from the school, college or university, or a copy of the course details showing the student's name. A letter addressed to the applicant is sufficient. The website notes: 'A letter from another person e.g. a teacher, saying the applicant is suitable for a course is not sufficient, it must be from the educational establishment where the course is being taken.' This supporting information must be provided along with the application in order to avoid delays.

Other information

The charity was created by a trust deed dated 6 April 1988, in memory of Anthony and Gwendoline Wylde.

Hereford-shire

Bosbury Educational Foundation

£6,000

Correspondent: Nicola Ruddick, 4 Morton Cottages, Bosbury, Ledbury HR8 1PT (01531 640106; email: nickruddick@yahoo.co.uk)

CC number: 527140

Eligibility

Young people leaving school who live in the parish of Bosbury and have done so for at least three years.

Types of grants

Small grants to assist with the associated costs of higher education, e.g. for items such as books, living expenses and equipment.

Annual grant total

In 2016 the foundation had an income of £22,000 and a total expenditure of £6,500. We estimate the total amount awarded in educational grants was £6,000.

Applications

Apply in writing to the correspondent. Full details of the course should be included. Applications can be submitted directly by the individual and are considered at any time.

Other information

Note: The parish of Bosbury consists of around 500 people. In previous years the foundation has stated that it is being inundated by applications from outside the parish which cannot be considered due to the deeds of the foundation, and these applications will not be acknowledged.

Hereford Municipal Charities

£5,500

Correspondent: Clerk to the Trustees, 147 St Owen Street, Hereford HR1 2JR (01432 354002; email: herefordmunicipal@btconnect.com)

CC number: 218738

Eligibility

People in need who live in the city of Hereford.

Types of grants

One-off grants of up to £200. Grants are given to help with the cost of education and starting work.

Annual grant total

In 2016 the charity had assets of £5 million and an income of £364,000. We estimate that educational grants to individuals totalled around £5,500.

Exclusions

Debts or nursery fees.

Applications

Application forms are available from the correspondent and should be submitted directly by the individual or through a relevant third party. Applications are considered five times a year but can be authorised within meetings if they are very urgent. Applicants are normally interviewed.

Other information

The charity also offers almshouse accommodation. There are two separate funds (eleemosynary and educational) administered by the Grants Committee.

The Hereford Society for Aiding the Industrious

£2,000

Correspondent: Sally Robertson, 18 Venns Close, Bath Street, Hereford HR1 2HH (01432 274014; email: info@hsfai.co.uk)

CC number: 212220

Eligibility

People in all levels of education, of any age, who live in Herefordshire; and are in financial need.

Types of grants

Usually one-off grants for general educational costs, for items such as books, clothing and equipment. The trustees note in the 2015/16 annual report that the majority of applications recently have been made in order to pursue a master's degree.

Annual grant total

In 2015/16 the charity had assets of £909,000 and an income of £109,000. The charity made awards of £2,000 to applicants for educational purposes.

Applications

Applications should be made in writing to the correspondent, detailing financial need and what the funding is for. Previous research has shown that the charity considers applications on a monthly basis.

Other information

The charity's main area of activity is maintaining almshouses. Donations are also given to individuals for welfare purposes, and to Herefordshire charities for specific projects rather than for running costs.

Herefordshire Community Foundation

£6,600

Correspondent: Wilma Gilmour, Secretary, The Fred Bulmer Centre, Wall Street, Hereford HR4 9HP (01432 272550; email: info@herefordshirefoundation.org; website: www.herefordshirefoundation.org)

CC number: 1094935

Eligibility

People under the age of 25 who are in need and live in Herefordshire.

Types of grants

One-off and ongoing grants according to need.

Annual grant total

In 2015/16 the foundation held assets of £3.5 million and had an income of £306,500. The majority of grants are made to organisations however the following funds also make grants to individuals:

▷ The Beckett Bulmer and Richard Bulmer funds are available for people wishing to study the arts, theatre and music and awarded £1,100 during the year

▷ Herefordshire Education Charity supports general educational needs – £500 was awarded to one individual

▷ The Jack Hughes fund supports rural education and training and awarded 33 grants totalling £5,000 during the year

Applications

HCF administers a number of different funds. These all have their specific application processes and criteria. Potential applicants should consult the website or contact the correspondent as funds open and close throughout the year.

The Jarvis Educational Foundation

£4,000

Correspondent: Rachel Jones, Flintsham Court, Titley, Kington HR3 3RG (07929650290)

CC number: 526881

Eligibility

People who are under the age of 25 and live the county of Hereford and Worcester, especially parishes of Staunton-on-Wye, Bredwardine and Letton.

Types of grants

In the past one-off grants ranging from £100 to £1,000 were available:

▷ To individuals at secondary school, university or college where education authority support is not available

▷ To provide outfits, clothing, tools, instruments or books to help people enter a trade, profession or calling on leaving education

▷ To enable such people to travel to pursue their education

Annual grant total

In 2016 the foundation had an income of £30,000 and a spending of £34,500. Grants made to individuals totalled £4,000.

Applications

Normally applications may be made in writing to the correspondent for consideration at any time.

Other information

The foundation also owns land and property, which are used for the purpose of a voluntary school, and have contributed towards the cost of building a new school.

The Norton Canon Parochial Charities

£2,500

Correspondent: Mary Gittins, Ivy Cottage, Norton Canon, Hereford HR4 7BQ (01544 318984)

CC number: 218560

Eligibility

Young people who live in the parish of Norton Canon.

Types of grants

Grants have been given towards books and educational outings for schoolchildren, books, fees/living expenses and study or travel abroad for students in further or higher education and equipment/instruments, books, clothing and travel for people starting work.

Annual grant total

In 2016 the charity had an income of £23,000 and a total expenditure of £11,200. We estimate that educational grants to individuals totalled around £2,500.

Applications

Apply in writing to the correspondent at any time.

Ross Educational Foundation

£1,600

Correspondent: Louise Jarvis, 5 Old Stables, Glewstone, Ross-on-Wye HR9 6AW

CC number: 527229

Eligibility

People under the age of 25 who live (or whose parents live) in the town of Ross Wye and the civil parish of Ross Rural.

Types of grants

Small, one-off and recurrent grants are available to higher education students and people in further education or vocational training. Support is given towards books, equipment and instruments, tools and other necessities or educational travel. People studying music and other arts may also apply.

Annual grant total

In 2016 the foundation had an income of £2,700 and a total expenditure of £1,900. We estimate that grants given to individuals totalled around £1,600.

Exclusions

Our research suggests that accommodation costs and day-to-day travel expenses are not normally considered.

Applications

Applications can be made in writing to the correspondent. Our research suggests that they should normally be submitted in February and August for consideration in April and October, respectively.

Shropshire

The Careswell Foundation

£9,000

Correspondent: Bridget Marshall, 24 The Crescent, Town Walls, Shrewsbury SY1 1TJ (01743 351332; email: terri.gill@lindermyers.co.uk)

CC number: 528393

Eligibility

People under the age of 25 who live in Shropshire, the parish of Bobbington or Staffordshire and have attended any of the following schools: Adam's Grammar School (Newport); Bridgnorth Endowed School; Idsall School (Shifnal); Shrewsbury School; Thomas Adam's School (Wem).

Types of grants

Grants, usually of up to about £150, are available to further/higher education students to assist with general educational expenses, including books, equipment and other necessities.

Annual grant total

In 2015/16 the foundation had an income of £12,000 and a total expenditure of £9,500. We estimate the amount awarded in grants to individuals for education was £9,000.

Applications

Apply in writing to the correspondent. Our research suggests that applications should be submitted by September for consideration in October.

Charity of Charles Clement Walker (The Walker Trust)

£56,500

Correspondent: Edward Hewitt, 2 Breidden Way, Bayston Hill, Shrewsbury SY3 0LN (01743 873866; email: edward.hewitt@btinternet.com)

CC number: 215479

Eligibility

People who live in Shropshire. Applicants should have been resident in the area for at least 12 months prior to application. Preference is given to individuals who are on low incomes or state benefits, people estranged from their families, single parents and young people leaving care.

Types of grants

Grants can be given towards further/higher education and training courses undertaken within or outside the area of benefit, also for gap year projects, music, drama and arts costs and expeditions or travel. Individual grants range from £100 up to about £5,000.

Annual grant total

In 2015/16 the trust held assets of £6.1 million and had an income of £340,500. The amount of grants given to individuals totalled over £52,900, broken down as follows:

Music and drama	£27,000
College course	£15,700
University course	£6,900
Schools and other organisations	£1,600
Health and disability	£1,400
Foreign travel	£350

From the 2013/14 trustees' annual report:

In excess of 45 grants were made to individuals and organisations ranging from £100 to £5,000. Of these 10 were from single-parent families, 16 from families whose only income was benefits and 2 from young people estranged from their families. Eleven were grants for music, drama or art studies, many of which were substantial. Without the Trust's support most of these individuals would have been unable to undertake their courses.

Grants are also made to organisations and totalled £261,000 in 2015/16.

Applications

Apply in writing to the correspondent. Applications are considered four times a year, normally in January, April, July and October. They must reach the correspondent at least one month before help is required. Decisions on urgent cases can be made between meetings.

Other information

The trust's registered name is the Charity of Charles Clement Walker.

Millington's Charity (Millington's Hospital)

£4,200 (four grants)

Correspondent: Richard Gavin Hogg, Caradoc View Cottage, Enchmarsh, Leebotwood, Shropshire SY67JX (01743 360904; email: clerk@millingtons.org.uk)

CC number: 213371

Eligibility

Further/higher education students under the age of 25 who live or have been educated in Shropshire and who, or whose parents/guardians, are members of the Church of England.

Types of grants

One-off grants ranging from £100 to £400 are given to help people in further/higher education (including religious instruction). Support is given towards general educational expenses associated with college or university attendance, including equipment, books, maintenance/living costs, study/travel abroad. Help can also be given for a specific educational project, musical instruments or extra activities within the chosen course.

Annual grant total

In 2016 the charity had assets of £1.1 million and an income of £173,500. Grants to four individuals in further education totalled £4,200.

Exclusions

Grants are not normally given towards fees.

Applications

Application forms can be obtained from the correspondent upon written request. Candidates are required to give details of their parents' income, other funding secured/applied to and provide references. Awards are made at quarterly meetings.

Other information

The charity also provides almshouse accommodation for older and vulnerable people.

The Shropshire Youth Foundation

£5,500

Correspondent: Karen Nixon, The Shirehall, Abbey Foregate, Shrewsbury, Shropshire SY2 6ND (01743 252724; email: karen.nixon@shropshire.gov.uk)

CC number: 522595

Eligibility

People under the age of 25 who live in the county of Shropshire, including Telford and Wrekin.

Types of grants

One-off grants can be provided towards educational leisure activities and opportunities developing physical, mental and spiritual capacities of individuals, such as voluntary work.

Annual grant total

In 2015/16 the foundation had an income of £9,200 and a total expenditure of £12,000. We estimate that grants to individuals totalled around £5,500.

Exclusions

Funding is not given towards educational courses.

Applications

Application forms can be requested from the correspondent. The trustees meet twice a year, usually in January and June.

Other information

The main objective of the foundation is to assist youth clubs and similar organisations with specific projects benefitting local young people.

Shropshire

Bowdler's Educational Foundation

£700

Correspondent: T. Collard, Shropshire Council, Shirehall, Abbey Foregate, Shrewsbury SY2 6ND (01743 252756; email: tim.collard@shropshire.gov.uk)

CC number: 528366

Eligibility

People under the age of 25 who live in the county of Shropshire, with a priority for those living in the Shrewsbury area.

Types of grants

Grants, to a maximum of £100 to £200, for:

- School pupils, to help with books, equipment, clothing or travel
- Help with school, college or university fees or to supplement existing grants
- Help towards the cost of education, training, apprenticeship or equipment for those starting work

Annual grant total

In 2015 the foundation had an income of £2,900 and a total expenditure of £800. We estimate that the amount awarded in educational grants was £700.

Applications

Application forms are available from the correspondent.

The Bridgnorth Parish Charity

£1,500

Correspondent: Elizabeth Smallman, Trustee, 37 Stourbridge Road, Bridgnorth WV15 5AZ (01746 764149)

CC number: 243890

Eligibility

People in need who live in the parish of Bridgnorth, including Oldbury, Quatford and Eardington.

Types of grants

Our research suggests that one-off grants are available according to need, including, for example, towards playgroup fees or school visits.

Annual grant total

In 2015 the charity had an income of £14,300 and a total expenditure of £6,500. Note that the expenditure varies each year and in the past has fluctuated from £0 to £9,400. We estimate that the total of grants awarded to individuals for educational purposes was around £1,500.

Applications

Applications may be made in writing to the correspondent either directly by the individual or through a doctor, nurse, member of the local clergy, social worker, Citizens Advice or other welfare agency.

Other information

The charity also awards grants for social welfare purposes and to organisations.

The Educational Charity of John Matthews

See entry on page 149

The Hodnet Consolidated Eleemosynary Charities

£900

Correspondent: Mrs S. W. France, 26 The Meadow, Hodnet, Market Drayton, Shropshire TF9 3QF (01630 685907; email: wendy547@sky.com)

CC number: 218213

Eligibility

Students in need who live in Hodnet parish.

Types of grants

Grants for books are given to students in further/higher education.

Annual grant total

In 2015 the charity had an income of £4,200 and a total expenditure of £3,700.

Grants are made to individuals and organisations for a range of purposes. We estimate that educational grants to individuals amounted to around £900.

Applications

Applications can be made in writing to the correspondent and are considered throughout the year. They can be submitted directly by the individual or through a social worker, Citizens Advice or other welfare agency.

Other information

This is essentially a relief-in-need charity that also gives money to students for books.

Hopesay Parish Trust

£2,500 (16 grants)

Correspondent: David Evans, Trustee, Park Farm, The Fish, Hopesay, Craven Arms, Shropshire SY7 8HG (01588 660545; email: annedalgliesh@aol.com; website: www.hopesayparish.com/parish%20trust.html)

CC number: 1066894

Eligibility

People under the age of 25 in any level of education who live, or whose parents live, in the parish of Hopesay, Shropshire.

Types of grants

Grants are typically between £25 and £500 and are given for any educational need. Activities supported in recent years include: extracurricular activities for school-age children; books, materials and equipment for university courses; travel costs associated with travel for non-statutory aged students; vocational activities; gap year activities.

Annual grant total

In 2016 the trust had an income of £3,100 and a total expenditure of £2,600. We estimate that educational grants amounted to £2,500.

Exclusions

The grants may not be used for anything that the local authority should provide.

Applications

Application forms are available from the correspondent or can be downloaded from the Hopesay Parish council website.

Other information

The trust gives priority to educational grants. At the trustees' discretion, any surplus income may be applied for other charitable purposes but only within the parish.

Telford and Wrekin

Maxell Educational Trust

£7,000

Correspondent: Ian Jamieson, Oaktree Place, Hortonwood 35, Telford TF1 7FR (01952 522207; email: hr@maxell.eu)

CC number: 702640

Eligibility

Young people aged 9 to 25 years who live, or whose family home is, in Telford, or who attend school or college there. Projects should ideally have an industrial or technological element.

Types of grants

One-off grants for schoolchildren, college students and people with special educational needs, towards books and equipment/instruments.

Annual grant total

In 2015/16 the trust had an income of £5,400 and an unusually high expenditure of £15,000. We estimate that around £7,000 was awarded in grants to individuals for education.

Applications

Apply in writing to the correspondent. Applications are considered throughout the year and should be submitted either by the individual or a parent/guardian, through a third party such as a teacher, or through an organisation such as a school or an educational welfare agency.

Other information

The trust was established in 1989 by Maxell Europe Ltd 'to express the company's appreciation for the support it had received from the local community'.

Grants are also made towards research in electronics and technology in Telford, and may also be made for organisations.

Staffordshire

Lady Dorothy Grey's Foundation

£24,500

Correspondent: Richard Jones, Trustee, Batfield House, Batfield Lane, Enville, Stourbridge, West Midlands DY7 5LF (01746 78350; email: enville.trusts@btopenworld.com)

CC number: 508900

Eligibility

Children and young people under the age of 25 who live in (or whose parents live in) the parishes of Bobbington, Enville or Kinver, with a preference for Enville.

Types of grants

Grants are given towards general educational expenses, including the cost of books, equipment/instruments, fees, maintenance expenses, clothing and uniforms, educational outings or study/travel abroad. Our research suggests that one-off and recurrent grants normally range from £150 to £500 and can be given to schoolchildren or further/higher education students.

Annual grant total

In 2015/16 the foundation had assets of £68,000 and an income of £39,000. A total of £24,500 was awarded in grants to individuals.

Applications

Apply in writing to the correspondent. Applications can be made either directly by individuals or through their parents/guardians. According to our research, applications should be submitted by 31 August for consideration in October.

The Strasser Foundation

£4,000

Correspondent: The Strasser Foundation, c/o Knights Solicitors, The Brampton, Newcastle-under-Lyme, Staffordshire ST5 0QW (01782 627089; email: alfbhjb@gmail.com)

CC number: 511703

Eligibility

Schoolchildren and students in the local area of Stoke-on-Trent and Newcastle-under-Lyme, with a preference for North Staffordshire.

Types of grants

Usually one-off grants for books, equipment and other specific causes or needs for educational purposes.

Annual grant total

In 2016/17 the foundation had an income of £7,000 and a total expenditure of £12,000. We estimate that the total amount awarded in educational grants was around £4,000.

Applications

Applications can be made in writing to the correspondent. Applications cannot be acknowledged unless sent with an sae. The trustees usually meet four times per year.

Other information

The foundation also makes grants to individuals for welfare purposes, and to local organisations assisting the community. All grants are made at the

175

discretion of the trustees and priority areas of funding may change.

Cannock Chase

The Rugeley Educational Endowment

£143,000

Correspondent: Melanie Stokes, Staffordshire County Council, Treasury & Pensions, 2 Staffordshire Place, Tipping Street, Stafford ST16 2DH (01785 276330; email: melanie.stokes@staffordshire.gov.uk)

CC number: 528603

Eligibility

People in need who are under the age of 25 and live in the former urban district of Rugeley as constituted on 31 March 1974. Beneficiaries must have attended any comprehensive school in the area of benefit for at least two years.

Types of grants

One-off grants can be given towards the cost of school and work-related clothing, books, educational outings and projects, educational trips in the UK or abroad, study of music or other arts, sports activities and for equipment/instruments or tools. Support is given to schoolchildren, students in higher or further education and to people preparing to enter a trade/start work.

Annual grant total

In 2015/16 the charity held assets of £1.97 million and had an income of £78,000. The amount of grants given to individuals totalled £143,000.

Applications

Applications should be made through the headteacher of the school attended.

Other information

The charity has specific funds awarding prizes to pupils attending The Fair Oak Comprehensive School in Rugeley.

East Staffordshire

Consolidated Charity of Burton upon Trent

£61,000 (45 grants)

Correspondent: J. P. Southwell, Dains LLP, 1st Floor, Gibraltar House, Crown Square, First Avenue, Burton upon Trent DE14 2WE (01283 527067; fax: 01283 507969; email: clerk@consolidatedcharityburton.org.uk; website: www.consolidatedcharityburton.org.uk)

CC number: 239072

Eligibility

People who live in Burton upon Trent and the neighbouring parishes of Branston, Outwoods and Stretton.

Types of grants

The charity provides educational support in two forms:

- **Bursaries** – each year the charity awards a maximum of 40 bursaries (of £500 per annum for three years) to undergraduate students resident in the area of benefit. The schools and colleges included in the scheme are Abbot Beyne School, Burton College, de Ferrers Specialist Technology College, John Taylor High School, Paget High School and Stapenhill Sixth Form Centre
- **Education and personal development grants** – support is given for a range of purposes including: further education and vocational training; organised opportunities for personal development; sports activities; and arts scholarships. The maximum grant in any one year is £300, although applications may be made by individuals in subsequent years

Annual grant total

In 2016 the charity had assets of £13.5 million and an income of £562,000. The amount awarded in grants and bursaries was £61,000 to 45 individuals.

Exclusions

Grants are not awarded for postgraduate study.

Applications

Application forms can be downloaded to be returned by post, or completed on the charity's website. Applicants are required to provide evidence that they have been accepted onto the course or project for which they are seeking assistance.

Other information

The charity also runs 32 almshouses and supports individuals in financial hardship and organisations working to the benefit of the local area.

The Tutbury General Charities

£1,800

Correspondent: Jeanne Minchin, 66 Redhill Lane, Tutbury, Burton-on-Trent, Staffordshire DE13 9JW (01283 813310)

CC number: 215140

Eligibility

People who are attending further education (college or apprenticeships) and live in the parish of Tutbury.

Types of grants

One-off grants are given, usually in the range of £40 and £80.

Annual grant total

In 2015/16 the charity had an income of £9,300 and a total expenditure of £7,800. We estimate that grants given to individuals totalled around £1,800.

Applications

The charities have application forms, available from the correspondent, which should be returned by 1 October for consideration in November. A letter of acceptance from the place of education is required.

Other information

The clerk has stated that details of the charity are well publicised within the village.

Stafford

The Bradley Trust

£75,000

Correspondent: Stuart Richards, 9 Elm Drive, Bradley, Stafford ST18 9DS (07738980459)

CC number: 528448

Eligibility

Further and higher education students of any age who live in Bradley, Staffordshire.

Types of grants

Grants can range up to £2,000.

Annual grant total

In 2016 the trust had assets of £1.6 million and an income of £40,000. The trust awarded £7,500 in educational grants to individuals.

Applications

Application forms are available from the correspondent. Our research suggests that they are considered once a year in September and should be submitted along with a proof of acceptance/attendance at university in August.

Other information

The trust also aims to promote religion within Bradley. It also maintains the village hall for use by the people of Bradley, who benefit from attending meetings and activities subsidised by the trust.

Stafford Educational Endowment Charity

£7,500

Correspondent: Melanie Stokes, Staffordshire County Council, Treasury & Pensions, 2 Staffordshire Place, Tipping Street, Stafford ST16 2LP (01785 276330; email: melanie.stokes@ staffordshire.gov.uk)

CC number: 517345

Eligibility

Pupils and former pupils of secondary schools in Stafford, who are under 25 years of age and are in need.

Types of grants

Small, one-off grants for books, travel, educational outings, educational equipment and similar expenses incurred by schoolchildren, students and people starting work. There is a preference to award grants for benefits not normally provided for by the local education authority.

Annual grant total

In 2016/17 the charity had an income of £16,700 and a total expenditure of £17,600. We have estimated that grants to individuals totalled £7,500 as grants are also available for local schools and groups.

Exclusions

Grants are unlikely to be given for course fees or the ordinary living costs of students.

Applications

Applications should be made through the headteacher of the secondary school attended by the potential applicant.

Tamworth

The Rawlet Trust

£5,100

Correspondent: Christine Gilbert, 47 Hedging Lane, Wilnecote, Tamworth B77 5EX (01827 288614; email: christine. gilbert@mail.com)

CC number: 221732

Eligibility

Young people under the age of 25 who are in need and live, or have parents living, in Tamworth.

Types of grants

One-off grants ranging between £30 and £200 towards the cost of books, fees, living expenses, student exchange and study or travel abroad. Grants have also been made for equipment, instruments, clothing or travel for people starting work.

Annual grant total

In 2016/17 the trust had assets of £766,000 and an income of £25,500. Educational grants to individuals totalled £5,100.

Applications

Apply using the application form available from the correspondent. Applications should be submitted either directly by the individual or through a third party such as a social worker or Citizens Advice. The clerk or one of the trustees will follow up applications if any further information is needed. The trustees meet in January, April, July and October to consider applications.

Warwick-shire

The Exhall Educational Foundation

£750

Correspondent: Carol Gough, 53 Tewkesbury Drive, Bedworth, Warwickshire CV12 9ST (024 7636 5258; email: cagough@sky.com; website: www. exhalleducationalfoundation.blogspot.co. uk)

CC number: 528663

Eligibility

People under the age of 25 who live, or whose parents live, in the parish of Exhall or Keresley End.

Types of grants

Grants of around £200 for books, music lessons, dance classes, field trips/ expeditions, travel to educational courses and more.

Annual grant total

In 2016 the foundation had an income of £2,400 and a total expenditure of £1,700. We estimate that the foundation awarded around £750 in grants to individuals for educational purposes.

The foundation also awards grants to schools in the area.

Applications

Application forms are available from the foundation's website or can be requested from the correspondent. Applications are considered twice a year, in mid-March and mid-October. They can be submitted by post or by email in advance to the trustees' meeting.

Other information

The area of benefit comprises: Ash Green; Black Bank; Exhall; Goodyers End; Keresley End; Little Bedworth Heath; Neal's Green and Wagon

Overthrow. The trustees encourage potential applicants to get in touch if in doubt about their geographical eligibility.

Rugby

The Bilton Poor's Land and Other Charities

£1,500

Correspondent: Robin Walls, Trustee, 6 Scotts Close, Rugby CV22 7QY (email: biltoncharities@outlook.com)

CC number: 215833

Eligibility

People in need who live in the ancient parish of Bilton (now part of Rugby).

Types of grants

This charity is not primarily an educational charity, concentrating rather on the relief of need; however, some grants are made for books, fees, travel and other educational costs.

Annual grant total

In 2016/17 the charity had an income of £22,500 and a total expenditure of £22,000. At the time of writing (November 2017) the annual report and accounts for the year were not yet available to view at the Charity Commission. In the most recent year for which a grant figure was available (2015/16) awards totalled just over £6,000. Based on this figure, we estimate that grants given to individuals for educational purposes totalled around £1,500, with funding also given to organisations and to individuals for social welfare purposes.

Applications

Applications can be made in writing to the correspondent, by the individual or through a relevant third party such as a minister. The trustees usually meet three times a year.

Stratford-on-Avon

Perkins's Educational Foundation

£21,000

Correspondent: The Clerk to the Governors, c/o Lodders Solicitors LLP, 10 Elm Court, Arden Street, Stratford Upon Avon, Warwickshire CV37 6PA (01789 293259; email: info@ williamperkinscharity.org; website: www. williamperkinscharity.org)

CC number: 528678

Eligibility

People aged 16 to 24 who have been living in Bidford-on-Avon, Broom, Cleeve Prior, Harvington or Salford Priors for at least two years immediately prior to their application.

Types of grants

Grants are mainly given to people entering further/higher education and to individuals undertaking vocational training or apprenticeships. Help is available towards the cost of books, equipment/instruments, clothing, and other necessities as well as fees, living expenses, study or travel abroad.

Annual grant total

In 2016 the foundation held assets of £220,000 and had an income of £67,000. The amount of grants given to individuals totalled £21,000.

Exclusions

Awards are not usually made to students under the age of 18 doing GCSE or A-level courses, or to candidates who have reached the age of 25.

Applications

Application forms can be requested in writing from the correspondent or downloaded from the foundation's website. Applications must be signed by the applicant personally and first-time applicants should provide a statement of recommendation from their headteacher, college principal or employer. Completed forms should be returned to the clerk by 15 October. Late submissions are not accepted.

Shipston-on-Stour Educational Charity

£3,000

Correspondent: Mr D. Squires, Pinnegar House, 49 Telegraph Street, Shipston-on-Stour CV36 4DA (email: ds@pinnegards.com)

CC number: 507400

Eligibility

People under 25 who live, or whose parents live, in the parish of Shipston-on-Stour.

Types of grants

Small, one-off grants are given to students undertaking further and higher education, postgraduate qualifications and apprenticeships. Support can be for uniforms/clothing, books, tools, instruments/equipment, educational outings in the UK or study or travel abroad.

Annual grant total

In 2016 the charity had an income of £3,200 and a total expenditure of £3,300. We estimate that grants totalled £3,000.

Applications

Applications can be made on a form available from correspondent. Our research suggests that they should be submitted directly by the individual by the first week of September for consideration at the end of that month.

Municipal Charities of Stratford-upon-Avon – Relief in Need

£870

Correspondent: Ros Dobson, Charities Administrator, c/o 6 Guild Cottages, Church Street, Stratford-upon-Avon, Warwickshire CV37 6HD (01789 293749; email: municharities@yahoo.co.uk or municharities@btinternet.com; website: www.municipal-charities-stratforduponavon.org.uk)

CC number: 214958

Eligibility

People who are in need and live in the town of Stratford-upon-Avon.

Types of grants

Occasionally, one-off grants of up to £500 are given towards the costs of:

⬩ School uniforms, other school clothing, books, maintenance and school fees for schoolchildren
⬩ Books for students in further and higher education
⬩ Books, equipment and instruments for people starting work

Annual grant total

In 2016 the charity had assets of £116,000 and an income of £59,500. Grants to individuals and organisations totalled £52,500 and included £870 given for educational purposes.

Applications

Application forms are available from the correspondent. They should include details of the course costs and the financial circumstances of the applicant and parent(s) if appropriate. Applications for schoolchildren must be made through the school.

Warwick

Arlidge's Charity

£1,200

Correspondent: Colin Ritchie, Trustee, 10 Inverary Close, Kenilworth, Warwickshire CV8 2NZ (01926 512507; email: cjritchie3@hotmail.co.uk)

CC number: 528758

Eligibility

People under the age of 25 who live in the county of Warwick (preference is given to residents of Kenilworth) and who are, or whose parent/s are, members of the United Reformed Church.

Types of grants

Help to students in further/higher education towards the cost of books, fees and travel. Grants may be recurrent.

Annual grant total

In 2015/16 the charity had an income of £2,500 and total expenditure of £2,500. We estimate that the total amount given in grants was £1,200.

Applications

Apply in writing to the correspondent. Applications should include details of the course to be taken and information of any other funding secured or applied to.

Other information

The charity's Charity Commission record states that a seventh of its income is paid to the minster for Abbey Hill United Reform Church to further religious and other charitable work of the congregation, or in augmentation of his stipend. The residual income is applied to relieving United Reform congregation members in Kenilworth, and/or promoting education to United Reform members in Warwick and Kenilworth who need financial assistance.

The Barford Relief-in-Need Charity

£2,300

Correspondent: Terry Offiler, 14 Dugard Place, Barford, Warwick CV35 8DX (01926 624153)

CC number: 256836

Eligibility

Young people who live in the parish of Barford.

Types of grants

Grants are made to individuals who are attending school, college or university. Occasional financial assistance is provided for specific purposes such as Raleigh International and Outward Bound-type courses.

Annual grant total

In 2016 the charity had an income of £11,100 and a total expenditure of £9,500. Grants are made to individuals and organisations for both social welfare and educational purposes. We estimate that educational grants to individuals totalled £2,300.

Applications

Applications can be made in writing to the correspondent, directly by the individual or a family member. Applications are usually considered in May and October.

Austin Edwards Charity

£2,300

Correspondent: Jackie Newton, 26 Mountford Close, Wellesbourne, Warwick CV35 9QQ (01789 840135; email: jackie.newton114@gmail.com; website: www.warwickcharities.org.uk)

CC number: 225859

Eligibility

People living in the old borough of Warwick (generally the CV34 postcode).

Types of grants

Grants are generally of no more than £300. Our research indicates that support is normally provided to students at college or university (including mature students) or people starting work. Grants are given towards the expenses for clothing, equipment, books, travel, course fees and study/travel overseas.

Annual grant total

In 2015/16 the charity had an income of £10,900 and a total expenditure of £9,300. Grants are made to individuals and organisations for both social welfare and educational purposes. We estimate that educational grants to individuals totalled £2,300.

Exclusions

Grants cannot be provided for follow-on courses, postgraduate courses or additional degrees. The charity's website also reminds that 'where grants are applied for in respect of study courses, the trustees will only consider providing funding for one course per applicant'.

Applications

Apply in writing to the correspondent stating the purpose of the grant and the amount required, as well as details of any other charities approached with the same request. The individual's name and address must be supplied with the application. The trustees usually hold one meeting annually in July but will consider applications throughout the year.

Other information

The charity was named after Mr Austin Edwards who lived and worked in Warwick as a photographic manufacturer in the early years of the twentieth century. As a councillor of the borough of Warwick, he remained deeply interested in Warwickians and Warwick affairs generally. He gave generously to the Corporation of Warwick throughout his life.

William Edwards Educational Charity

£63,000 (103+ grants)

Correspondent: John Hathaway, Clerk to the Trustees, Heath & Blenkinsop Solicitors, 42 Brook Street, Warwick CV34 4BL (01926 492407; email: law@heathandblenkinsop.com)

CC number: 528714

Eligibility

People under the age of 25 who (or whose parents) have lived in the town of Kenilworth, or those who have attended a school in the town.

Types of grants

Grants are given for school uniforms, school trips, other educational needs and in bursaries for postgraduate/undergraduate students and people on vocational courses.

Annual grant total

In 2015/16 the charity had assets of £7.1 million and an income of £247,500. Throughout the year the charity gave almost £63,000 in grants to individuals.

Applications

Apply in writing to the correspondent.

Other information

The trustees' annual report from 2015/16 states:

During the year six full meetings had been held by the Trustees, together with visits to several of the schools within Kenilworth. The Trustees considered one hundred and fourteen applications received by the Charity for assistance from individuals, or on behalf of individuals, under twenty-five years of age (excluding bursary applications). One hundred and three awards were made to assist with school uniforms, school trips and similar needs, the amount being awarded totalling £40,682. The Charity continued its annual bursary scheme. After interviews, one bursary was awarded to the value of £16,150 to assist the postgraduate applicant in respect of tuition fees. In addition during the year payments made in respect of existing bursary awards totalled £32,590, which were awarded in the previous year. The Charity also continued its support of undergraduates. During the year one grant was awarded to the value off £6,000. Also during the year payments made in respect of undergraduate awards totalled £18,000.

Hatton Consolidated Fund (Hatton Charities)

£2,200

Correspondent: Mrs M. H. Sparks, Clerk, Weare Giffard, 32 Shrewley Common, Shrewley, Warwick CV35 7AP (01926 842533; email: bsparks1@talktalk.net)

CC number: 250572

Eligibility

People in need who live in the parishes of Hatton, Beausale and Shrewley. Applications from outside these areas will not be considered.

Types of grants

One-off grants, usually in the range of £50 to £500. Grants have been given to college students, undergraduates, vocational and mature students towards books, clothing, equipment and instruments. People with special educational needs have also been supported. Fees and travel expenses may also be covered.

Annual grant total

In 2015/16 the fund had an income of £10,300 and a total expenditure of £8,900. We estimate that grants awarded to individuals for education totalled around £2,200.

Applications

Applications may be made in writing to the trustees or the correspondent, directly by the individual or a family member. Applications should include details of the course and envisaged expenditure.

Other information

Grants are given to both organisations and individuals for educational and social welfare purposes.

The King Henry VIII Endowed Trust, Warwick

£2,500 (one grant)

Correspondent: Jonathan Wassall, Clerk and Receiver, 12 High Street, Warwick CV34 4AP (01926 495533; email: jwassall@kinghenryviii.org.uk; website: www.kinghenryviii.org.uk)

CC number: 232862

Eligibility

People who live in the former borough of Warwick. The area of benefit is roughly the CV34 postcode but exceptions apply so see the full list of eligible areas within the guidelines or contact the correspondent for clarification.

Types of grants

Grants are available for a wide range of general educational purposes, and are mostly used to cover costs associated with school trips or overseas educational travel, and apprenticeship fees. Grants are intended to be supplementary and applicants are expected to raise additional funds themselves. Payments are normally made upon submission of receipts.

Annual grant total

In 2016 the trust had assets of £31.5 million and an income of £1.1 million. The trust made one grant of £2,500 for educational purposes.

Exclusions

Grants are not made where support should be provided by local or central government. Funding is not given retrospectively.

Applications

Application forms are available from the correspondent or from the trust's website. Applications should include full details of the costs involved and the time schedule of the activity, where relevant. Awards are considered on a quarterly basis, usually in March, June, September and December. The closing dates for applications are the beginning of March/ June and the second half of August/ November. You will normally hear the outcome of your application within a week of the relevant meeting. In urgent cases applications can be 'fast-tracked' (emergency should be specified in the application).

Other information

The income is distributed to the historic Anglican churches in Warwick (50%), Warwick Independent Schools Foundation for allocation in scholarships and bursaries (30%), and to organisations and individuals in the town (20%).

The Leigh Educational Foundation

£38,000

Correspondent: James Johnson, Clerk to the Trustees, 3 Barford Woods, Barford Road, Warwick CV34 6SZ (01926 419300; email: admin@ leigheducationalfoundation.org.uk; website: leigheducationalfoundation.org.uk)

CC number: 701462

Eligibility

People in need who are under the age of 25 and who (or whose parents) are resident in the parishes of Stoneleigh, Ashow, Leek Wootton and Burton

Green. There is a map of the parishes available on the foundation's website.

Types of grants

One-off or recurrent grants according to need, normally ranging from £100 to £1,000. Grants are given to schoolchildren, college students, undergraduates, vocational students and people starting work. Support is offered towards general educational needs, including uniforms/clothing, fees, study/ travel abroad, books, equipment/ instruments and maintenance/living expenses.

Annual grant total

In 2016 the foundation had assets of £1 million and an income of £39,000. Grants totalled £38,000 and previously most of the funding was allocated to individuals, although the foundation can also make grants to youth groups and clubs.

Exclusions

The trustees are unlikely to fund applications for computers or other equipment that is for wider use.

Applications

Application forms and full guidelines are available on the website along with deadlines. The trustees meet four times a year to allocate grants; in February, May, August and November. For an application to be considered at a meeting a completed application form must have been received by the clerk by the end of the prior month.

The website notes that there is 'no limit to the number of times an eligible applicant may seek a grant but it would be most unusual for the trustees to make more than one in each year'.

Warwick Apprenticing Charities

£71,500 (64 grants)

Correspondent: C. E. R. Houghton, Clerk to the Trustees, Moore & Tibbits Solicitors, 34 High Street, Warwick CV34 4BE (01926 491181; email: choughton@moore-tibbits.co.uk; website: www. warwickapprenticingcharities.org.uk)

CC number: 528745

Eligibility

People under the age of 25 who live in Warwick.

Types of grants

Grants are given to support young people with educational pursuits aiming to 'broaden their life experiences and skill sets ahead of seeking employment', according to the charity's website.

The charity's main grants offer support to students who have left school and are in further or higher education, apprenticeships, college or university. Grants are given to pay for purposes such as equipment, work clothing, books, travel and other maintenance expenses.

Grants are also given to 15- to 19-year-olds towards an Outward Bound Skills for Life course or similar courses.

Annual grant total

In 2015 the charity had assets of £781,000 and an income of £36,000. Grants totalled £71,500 and consisted of 75 'advancement in life' awards totalling £68,500, as well as paying for outward bound places totalling £3,100.

Applications

Applications can be made using the forms provided on the charity's website, which should be sent by post. Requests for grants other than Outward Bound courses should be submitted with a letter giving further information about the applicant, their course of study/project and the costs involved.

Charity of Sir Thomas White, Warwick

£22,500

Correspondent: Belinda Shuttleworth, Clerk and Receiver, 12 High Street, Warwick CV34 4AP (01926 350555; email: connect@sirthomaswhite.org.uk; website: www.sirthomaswhite.org.uk)

CC number: 1073331

Eligibility

People between the ages of 18 and 35 who are ordinarily resident in the town of Warwick who are establishing a business or undertaking tertiary education.

Types of grants

Interest-free loans to young people wishing to establish themselves in business, or assist them to improve their existing business in the town of Warwick. These interest-free loans are available up to £10,000 (for five years). The charity also provides for making interest-free loans to young people who or whose parents are ordinarily resident in the town of Warwick, towards the cost to them of undertaking further education or vocational training. These interest-free loans are available up to £1,500 per year for each year of their course.

Annual grant total

In 2016 the charity held assets of £410,500 and had an income of £238,000. Interest-free loans during the year totalled £22,500.

Applications

Application forms are available from the correspondent or from the charity's website.

▹ Applications for educational loans should include details of the course to be undertaken and the applicant's financial requirements for the duration of the course. An interview with a small panel of trustees will be arranged and applications must be received by the charity at least three weeks prior to the interview date. Successful applicants are required to sign a Loan Agreement and two adults are required to guarantee repayment of the loan

▹ Applications for business loans should be submitted along with a business plan. An interview will be arranged with a small panel of trustees to discuss the business idea and applications must be received by the charity at least three weeks prior to the interview date. Successful applicants must sign a joint and several bond, as must their sureties. The number of sureties required ranges from 2 to 4, depending on the amount requested

West Midlands

The W. E. Dunn Trust

£1,200 (six grants)

Correspondent: Alan Smith, Secretary to the Trustees, 30 Bentley Heath Cottages, Tilehouse Green Lane, Knowle, Solihull B93 9EL (01564 773407; email: wedunn@tiscali.co.uk)

CC number: 219418

Eligibility

People who are in need and live in the West Midlands, particularly Wolverhampton, Wednesbury, North Staffordshire and the surrounding area.

Types of grants

One-off grants.

Annual grant total

In 2015/16 the trust held assets of £4.5 million and had an income of £177,000. During the year, six grants were made to individuals for educational purposes and totalled £1,200. A further £54,000 was awarded to individuals for welfare purposes and charitable organisations received £121,000.

Applications

Apply in writing to the correspondent.

Sir Josiah Mason's Relief in Need and Educational Charity

£12,000

Correspondent: The Trustees, Mason Court, Hillborough Road, Birmingham B27 6PF (0121 245 1001; email: enquiries@sjmt.org.uk; website: www.sjmt.org.uk)

CC number: 1073756

Eligibility

People under 25 who live or study in the West Midlands area and are in genuine financial hardship. There is a particular focus on 'looked after' young people.

Types of grants

The website states that the charity currently offers bursaries at the University of Birmingham through its Access to Birmingham scholarship programme. In 2015/16 the charity also provided tuition fee funding for 'looked after' young refugees to improve their English language skills.

Annual grant total

In 2015/16 the charity had assets of £4.4 million and an income of almost £100,000. Grants totalling £12,000 were made to support individuals for educational purposes (scholarships at the University of Birmingham and English tuition fees for young refugees). Grants were also made to organisations totalling £23,000.

Applications

Applications can be made on a form available from the correspondent, to be returned by email or post.

Other information

The charity also makes grants to the Sir Josiah Mason's Almshouse Charity (CC number: 209283) and the Sir Josiah Mason's Care Charity (CC number: 1073755) in support of apprenticeship training, as well as other purposes.

The James Frederick and Ethel Anne Measures Charity

£11,000

Correspondent: Craig Sisson, The Measures Trust, 33 Great Charles Street, Queensway, Birmingham B3 3JN

CC number: 266054

Eligibility

Applications are welcome from residents of Birmingham, Coventry, Dudley, Sandwell, Solihull, Walsall and Wolverhampton.

Types of grants

One-off and recurrent grants to assist with costs associated with education, for example to purchase uniforms and equipment.

Annual grant total

In 2015/16 the charity had assets of £1 million and an income of £36,500. We estimate that the charity awarded £11,000 in grants to individuals for education.

Applications

Applications should be made in writing to the correspondent.

Other information

The charity also makes awards to individuals for welfare purposes, and to organisations active in the local community.

The Newfield Charitable Trust

£2,400 (seven grants)

Correspondent: Mary Allanson, Littleworth House, Littleworth, Warwick CV35 8HD (024 7622 7331; email: m.allanson@rotherham-solicitors.co.uk)

CC number: 221440

Eligibility

Girls and women (under the age of 30) who are in need of care and assistance and live in Coventry or Leamington Spa.

Types of grants

Grants are given towards school uniforms and other school clothing, educational trips, college fees, textbooks and equipment. Most grants are of less than £500.

Annual grant total

In 2016/17 the trust had assets of £1.7 million and an income of £64,000. Educational grants to individuals totalled £2,400.

Exclusions

Grants are not made for postgraduate education.

Applications

Contact the correspondent to request an application form. Applications are accepted from individuals or third parties e.g. social services, Citizens Advice, school/college etc. A letter of support/reference from someone not a friend or relative of the applicant (i.e. school, social services etc.) is always required. Details of income/expenditure and personal circumstances should also be given. Applications are considered eight times a year.

The Norton Foundation

£2,200 (15 grants)

Correspondent: Richard Perkins, 50 Brookfield Close, Hunt End, Redditch B97 5LL (01527 544446; email: correspondent@nortonfoundation.org; website: www.nortonfoundation.org)

CC number: 702638

Eligibility

Young people aged under 25 who live in Birmingham, Solihull, Coventry and Warwickshire. Applicants must be 'in need through some aspect of disadvantage defined as: in care or in need of rehabilitation, lapsing into delinquency, suffering from maltreatment or neglect, or whose potential is not yet realised due to circumstances beyond their control'.

Types of grants

One-off grants are available to schoolchildren and further and higher education students for school clothing, books, equipment, instruments, fees, maintenance and living expenses and educational outings in the UK. Grants of up to £500 can be made, although they usually range between £50 and £250.

Annual grant total

In 2015/16 the foundation held assets of £4.5 million and had an income of £154,500. A total of 121 grants were made directly to individuals totalling £14,900, of which £2,200 was awarded in 15 grants to individuals for educational purposes. In addition, £30,500 was paid in block discretionary grants to eight 'sponsors' for redistribution to individuals. Sponsors included South Birmingham Young Homeless Project (£13,900), St Basil's Centre Ltd (£12,200), Citizens Advice (£1,300) and Spurgeons (£1,000).

Applications

Applications should be made through a sponsor who should consult the foundation's helpful website for guidance and deadlines. Applications should be made in writing and contain all the information described in the guidance notes. Applications must be submitted through a social worker, Citizens Advice, probation service, school or other welfare agency, and should be typed or printed, if possible. They are considered on a monthly basis and awarded on or about the 5th day of each month.

Other information

The foundation's website also lists helpful information on why applications fail:

- the trustees are not convinced by the case being presented
- too many assumptions and unrealistic aspirations
- the amount requested is outside the range for the grant being applied for
- the bid was to fund long-term commitments
- financial information was insufficient and inadequate
- the contact details were insufficient for the trustees to obtain further information

Birmingham

Birmingham Bodenham Trust

£15,000

Correspondent: Jackie Crowley, Finance, PO Box 16306, Birmingham B2 2XR (0121 464 3928; email: jackie.crowley@birmingham.gov.uk)

CC number: 528902

Eligibility

Young people under the age of 19 who have special educational needs. Preference may be given to people in Birmingham area.

Types of grants

Grants are given to provide equipment and facilities to enhance the learning and educational experience of people who have special educational needs.

Annual grant total

In 2015/16 the trust had an income of £23,000 and a total expenditure of £21,000. We estimate the amount awarded in grants was £15,000.

Applications

Apply in writing to the correspondent. Our research indicates that applications are considered at quarterly meetings.

Other information

The trust also awards grants to people with special educational needs for recreation, treatment, and care.

The George Fentham Birmingham Charity

£28,000 (29 grants)

Correspondent: Jaime Parkes, Correspondent, Veale Wasbrough Vizards LLP, Second Floor, 3 Brindley Place, Birmingham B1 2JB

CC number: 214487

Eligibility

Long-term residents of the city of Birmingham who are under the age of 25 and studying at college or university.

Types of grants

Small grants to individuals experiencing hardship, for the purpose of education.

Annual grant total

In 2016 the charity had assets of £6.5 million and an income of £200,500. Throughout the year the charity gave around £28,000 in grants to individuals.

The charity also gives grants to organisations.

Applications

Application forms can be downloaded from the website, once completed they must be returned by post or email. Students must supply evidence that they are in receipt/have applied for a student loan.

The King's Norton United Charities

£2,500

Correspondent: Revd Larry Wright, The Rectory, 273 Pershore Road, Kings Norton, Birmingham B30 8EX (0121 459 0560; email: parishoffice@kingsnorton.org.uk; website: www.knuc.org.uk)

CC number: 202225

Eligibility

The charity is able to assist only those who live within the boundary of the Ancient Parish of Kings Norton, formerly in Warwickshire and Worcestershire, now in Warwickshire and the West Midlands. This area includes the current Church of England parishes of Kings Norton, Cotteridge, Stirchley, parts of Bourneville, Balsall Heath, Kings Heath, Moseley (St Anne's and St Mary's), Brandwood, Hazelwell, Highters Heath, Wythall, West Heath, Longbridge, Rubery and Rednal.

Types of grants

One-off emergency grants between £50 and £350 are available to cover unforeseen expenditure such as equipment or fees.

Annual grant total

In 2016 the charity had an income of £9,000 and a total expenditure of £5,500. We estimate the charity awarded £2,500 in grants for education.

Exclusions

Organisations are not supported.

Applications

The trustees prefer to receive referrals from a doctor or other agency, however there is a form available on their website to refer yourself or a friend if necessary. The trustees will then contact you to discuss the situation. Applications are considered on an ongoing basis.

Other information

The charity also makes grants for welfare purposes.

The Mitchells & Butlers Charitable Trusts

£23,500 (27 grants)

Correspondent: Ms Burton, Mitchells & Butlers, 73–77 Euston Road, London NW1 2QS (0121 498 6514; email: charitable.trusts@mbplc.com; website: www.mbtrusts.org.uk)

CC number: 528922

Eligibility

Grants from the Welfare Fund are given to students resident in the UK who are over the age of 16 and who live in the city of Birmingham and Smethwick. Preference may be given to the employees and children of the employees of Mitchells & Butlers and 'successors in business' of the company. External applicants are also invited to apply, provided they can demonstrate financial hardship.

Grants are also given from a scholarship fund to students studying courses relating to brewing, catering, hotel management or hospitality management.

Types of grants

The Welfare Fund offers support to secondary schoolchildren and further/higher education students, including mature students and individuals with special educational needs. Financial assistance is available towards the course fees, living expenses, course-related necessities and expenses, such as books, equipment, clothing and uniforms, travel costs and so forth.

The trust's Scholarship Fund can assist students in courses relating to brewing industry, licenced retailing, catering and hotel management. Support can be given towards general educational expenses, including fees, books or the cost of equipment.

Annual grant total

In 2015/16 the trust had assets of £3.3 million and an income of £83,000. Grants to individuals for educational purposes totalled £23,500 altogether, which included 25 grants from the Welfare Fund totalling £21,500 and two grants from the Scholarship Fund totalling £2,000. A further two grants were given to individuals for welfare purposes from the Mitchell Fund. Grants awarded to organisations totalled £17,100.

Exclusions

Support is not given towards master's degree courses.

Applications

Application forms for the Welfare Fund can be found on the trust's website and should be submitted by the date given on the website, in advance of the trustees' meeting which is normally held in July.

Applications for the Scholarship Fund should be made using the form on the trust's website and should be submitted by the date given on the website.

Other information

There are four funds – The Welfare Fund; The Scholarship Fund; The Mitchell Fund; and The Common Investment Fund – which are all administered under the same Charity Commission number. The Mitchell Fund provides grants to employees and former employees for welfare purposes.

Joseph Scott's Educational Foundation

£3,000

Correspondent: The Trustees, 35 Medcroft Avenue, Birmingham B20 1NB (email: josephscott1901@gmail.com; website: www.josephscottseducationalfoundation.co.uk)

CC number: 528919

Eligibility

Young people who live and have been educated for at least two years at a school provided by the Birmingham education authority, or at an academy or free school in the city of Birmingham.

Types of grants

Grants are generally given towards a first degree course, but the website states that grants may also be awarded 'to obtain the standards necessary to achieve admission to a degree course' (e.g. access courses), or for obtaining a professional qualification after a degree (e.g. a PGCE or law qualification). Grants can be used for essential living expenses and course requirements, and a maximum of £500 is given for each year of a course.

Annual grant total

In 2016/17 the foundation had an income of £1,900 and a total expenditure of £3,600. We estimate that educational grants to individuals totalled £3,000.

Applications

Applications can be made on a form on the foundation's website. They are considered on at quarterly meetings, usually in March, July, September and November, and should be received by the 14th of the month preceding a meeting, to be considered within six weeks. References should be sent to the foundation's secretary as soon as possible.

Sutton Coldfield Municipal Charities

£25,500 (335 grants)

Correspondent: The Almshouse Manager, Lingard House, Fox Hollies Road, Sutton Coldfield, West Midlands B76 2RJ (0121 351 2262 (Tuesday to Thursday, 9am to 4pm); fax: 0121 313 0651; email: info@suttoncharitabletrust.org; website: www.suttoncoldfieldcharitabletrust.com)

CC number: 218627

Eligibility

Parents/guardians of children at primary and/or secondary school can apply if they are a permanent resident of Sutton Coldfield (New Hall, Vesey, Trinity or Four Oaks wards) and are in receipt of any one of the following support payments: income tax credit; child tax credit; working tax credit; job seekers allowance; guarantee element of state pension credit; employment and support allowance.

Types of grants

Almost all educational grants are given to assist with the costs of school uniforms. At the time of writing (November 2017) the value of the grant was £75 per child. A maximum of four children per family can be assisted. Payment is made in the form of vouchers for use at Clive Mark Schoolwear, Wylde Green.

Annual grant total

In 2015/16 the charity had assets of £52.9 million and an income of £1.6 million. Educational grants to individuals totalled £25,500.

Applications

Applications for school uniform grants can be made using a form, which is available to download from the website or directly from schools in Sutton Coldfield or the correspondent. They can be made from the start of the summer term and must be submitted by 30 November.

Contact the correspondent for information on how to apply for assistance with other educational needs.

Other information

The principal objective of the charity, which is also known as the Sutton Coldfield Charitable Trust, is the provision of almshouses, the distribution of funds and other measures for the alleviation of poverty and other needs for inhabitants and other organisations within the boundaries of the former borough of Sutton Coldfield.

Yardley Educational Foundation

£107,500

Correspondent: Derek Hackett, Clerk to the Trustees, Edzell House, 121 Chester Road, Castle Bromwich, Birmingham B36 0AE (01212463625; email: enquiries@yardleyeducationalfoundation. org; website: www. yardleyeducationalfoundation.org)

CC number: 528918

Eligibility

Children and young people in need between the ages of 11 and 19 who have lived in the ancient parish of Yardley for at least two years (a map of the eligible area is provided on the website). For specific geographical area covered by the foundation, see the map on the website. The applicant's family income must be below £16,000 per year (including maximum tax credits).

Types of grants

Grants are provided to secondary school pupils for school uniforms, sports equipment, as well as a range of other purposes which may be considered, such as Duke of Edinburgh Awards, overseas exchanges and adventure trips, musical instruments and the costs of attending university interviews. The foundation can also provide grants to 16- to 18-year-olds in training for a profession or on an apprenticeship. Awards are generally in the region of £80 per year.

The foundation also provides book vouchers of £25 to students at secondary school redeemable at Waterstones, for reading material of any kind.

Annual grant total

In 2015/16 the foundation had assets of £4.1 million and an income of almost £170,000. During the year the foundation received more than 1,232 applications for help. A total of around £94,000 was given in grants for clothing, sports equipment, school trips, apprenticeships and other support and a further £13,300 was given in book vouchers.

Applications

Application forms can be obtained from the individual's school or college and should be submitted through the school before the end of June. The foundation requires proof of parental income and proof of any course or employment being started.

Other information

The foundation states in its 2015/16 annual report that 'the clerk to the trustees has close liaison with the secondary schools throughout the parish and is in constant touch with them to ascertain their needs'.

According to its website, the foundation 'has its roots dating back to 1347 when the monks at Maxstoke Priory, which then had Yardley Parish as an appendage, ran the church school'.

Coventry

The Children's Boot Fund

£4,000

Correspondent: Janet McConkey, 123A Birmingham Road, Coventry CV5 9GR (024 7640 2837; email: martin_harban@ btconnect.com)

CC number: 214524

Eligibility

Schoolchildren in the city of Coventry between the ages of 4 and 16.

Types of grants

Grants for school footwear for children in need. No other type of award is given. Grants are made directly to footwear suppliers in the form of vouchers. Normally one child per family can be awarded within one year, but exceptions for families in difficult circumstances may be made. Twins are usually given an award each. People leaving school may receive a grant for shoes to attend interviews.

Annual grant total

In 2015/16 the fund had an income of £9,400 and a total expenditure of £15,000. We estimate that grants totalled around £4,000. Grants are only made for footwear.

Applications

Application forms are available from schools in the area. They should be made by the parents/guardians and supported by the headteacher of the child's school. Applications from social care services are also considered. Applicants are required to list their benefits and income. Requests are considered four times a year.

The John Feeney Charitable Bequest

£6,600 (two grants)

Correspondent: Amanda Cadman, 55 Wychall Lane, Birmingham B38 8TB

CC number: 214486

Eligibility

Birmingham-based arts practitioners who have a minimum of three years experience in their field.

Types of grants

Grants in the form of fellowships. The trustees award two grants at £3,000 each year to two individuals.

Annual grant total

In 2016 the charity had assets of £1.7 million and an income of £81,500. Throughout the year the charity awarded £6,600 in grants to individuals.

The charity also awards grants to organisations.

Applications

Applicants are required to submit a proposal in writing by email, showing how the award of a fellowship will be of benefit to them in their further career development. The proposal, together with a budget and an up-to-date CV and the names and addresses of two relevant referees, must be received by the secretary by email. The deadline is usually around September time.

Shortlisted applicants will interviewed by a panel of trustees, who will make awards based on their judgment of the likely value of the proposal to the individual and of its contribution to the development of the arts in Birmingham.

Other information

Grants to individuals were awarded through the charity's 'Feeney Fellowships' fund.

General Charity (Coventry)

£89,500 (140 grants)

Correspondent: Susan Hanrahan, General Charities Office, Old Bablake, Hill Street, Coventry CV1 4AN (024 7622 2769; email: cov.genchar@outlook. com)

CC number: 216235

Eligibility

Children and young people under the age of 25 who are in need and live in the city of Coventry. Preference may be given to children of the freemen of the city.

Types of grants

Grants are given towards school fees, books or specialised equipment, also to support music education.

Annual grant total

In 2016 the charity had assets of £10.4 million and an income of £1.5 million. Grants totalled £1.3 million and, of this amount, educational grants to individuals totalled £89,500. They were distributed as follows:

School fees	2	£18,400
Books and equipment	137	£16,300
Music Award	1	£5,000

Support totalling £50,000 was also given to four PhD students at the Department of Biological Sciences, University of Warwick.

Exclusions

Our research suggests that maintenance costs are not supported. Cash grants are not given.

Applications

Application forms can be requested from the correspondent, normally in late August/early September. They should be submitted for consideration in November. The outcome of the application is communicated in December.

Other information

The charity consists of the charities formerly known as The Relief in Need Charity, Sir Thomas White's Pension Fund and Sir Thomas White's Educational Foundation. The trustees are also responsible for the administration of Lady Herbert's Homes and Eventide Homes Ltd, providing accommodation for older people in the city of Coventry.

Grants are also made for welfare purposes and in pensions to people over the age of 60 in the city of Coventry. Most of the charity's assistance is given to organisations. An annual payment is made to the Coventry School Foundation.

The Andrew Robinson Young People's Trust

£7,500

Correspondent: Clive Robinson, Trustee, 31 Daventry Road, Coventry CV3 5DJ (024 7650 1579; email: arypt@ googlemail.com)

CC number: 1094029

Eligibility

Young people who live in Coventry, particularly those who are facing social or economic disadvantages, or suffer from ill health.

Types of grants

One-off and recurrent grants to advance the religious education of young people and their faith within the Catholic Church. The support is also given to assist individuals in their personal development through various leisure activities and trips related to the Catholic faith.

Annual grant total

In 2015/16 the trust had an income of £15,600 and a total expenditure of £16,600. We estimate that grants to individuals totalled around £7,500.

Applications

Apply in writing to the correspondent.

Other information

The trust also makes grants to organisations and provides support to relieve poverty.

Soothern and Craner Educational Foundation

£7,500

Correspondent: The Clerk, The Hollies, Priory Road, Wolston, Coventry CV8 3FX (024 7654 4255; email: admin@ soothernandcraner.org.uk; website: www. soothernandcraner.org.uk)

CC number: 528838

Eligibility

Girls and young women who live in Coventry or who are Quakers connected to Coventry Quaker Meeting. Studies may be undertaken away from Coventry but the connection with the city is crucial to eligibility.

Types of grants

Grants are mainly given to further education students and people in vocational training for general educational costs, including equipment/ instruments, outfits, books and so on. Our research indicates that support is intended to supplement existing grants or where no mandatory award is available. The website states that the trustees offer support to 'encourage those taking lower levels of education and only very rarely assist beyond first degree level'.

Annual grant total

In 2015/16 the foundation had an income of £12,800 and a total expenditure of £8,600. The website states that the foundation is able to distribute between £7,000 and £8,000 each year.

Exclusions

Support will rarely be given to people studying at or above first degree level.

Applications

The foundation's website provides two application forms – for those still in school and for school leavers. Applicants should have two references available. Applications can also be made on behalf of groups (by a teacher or group leader) for educational activities. The trustees request the applicants to use ordinary post rather than recorded delivery in order to avoid delays. The trustees meet in July each year with additional meetings held in October and January if funds are available.

Dudley

Baylies' Educational Foundation

£29,000 (Up to 100 grants)

Correspondent: David Hughes, 53 The Broadway, Dudley, West Midlands DY1 4AP (01384 259277; email: bayliesfoundation@hotmail.co.uk; website: www.dudleyrotary.org.uk/ baylies.html)

CC number: 527118

Eligibility

People under the age of 25 living in Dudley, West Midlands, who are in need. Candidates must demonstrate genuine financial need and show they have attempted to secure funding elsewhere.

Types of grants

Grants range in purpose, from assisting with the costs of university or college, travel expenses, educational trips both at home and abroad, school uniforms, and the encouragement of arts and sport. Grants are also made to help unemployed candidates retrain, and to others who face barriers in their access to education.

Annual grant total

In 2015/16 the foundation had assets of £601,000 and an income of £48,000. We estimate that the total amount awarded in grants to individuals was £35,000.

Applications

Application forms are available on the foundation's website or can be requested from the correspondent.

Other information

Local schools and organisations are also supported.

The Palmer and Seabright Charity

£7,000

Correspondent: Susannah Griffiths, Clerk to the Trustees, c/o Wall James Chappell, 15–23 Hagley Road, Stourbridge, West Midlands DY8 1QW (01384 371622; email: sgriffiths@wjclaw. co.uk)

CC number: 200692

Eligibility

People under the age of 25 who live in the borough of Stourbridge.

Types of grants

One-off and recurrent grants are made to college students and undergraduates for fees, books, equipment/instruments and maintenance/living expenses. Grants are also given to schoolchildren for fees.

Annual grant total

In 2016 the charity had assets of £313,500 and an income of £49,000. Grants were made totalling £16,400 (including £2,400 in Christmas grants). We estimate that educational grants to individuals amounted to £7,000.

Applications

Applications can be made on a form available from the correspondent. Applications can be submitted either directly by the individual or a family member, through a third party such as a social worker or teacher, or through an organisation such as Citizens Advice or a school.

Daniel Parsons Educational Charity

£8,000

Correspondent: David Hughes, Trustee, 53 The Broadway, Dudley, West Midlands DY1 4AP (01384 259277; email: parsonscharity@hotmail.com; website: www.dudleyrotary.org.uk/parsons.html)

CC number: 1068492

Eligibility

People under the age of 25 who (or whose parents) live in Dudley and its neighbourhood or who have attended school in that area.

Types of grants

One-off grants in the range of £200 to £500 towards education and training.

Annual grant total

In 2016 the charity had an income of £13,100 and a total expenditure of £8,600. We have estimated that grants to individuals totalled £8,000.

Exclusions

The charity does not provide long-term support.

Applications

Application forms can be requested from the correspondent or downloaded from the website. They can be submitted to the correspondent at any time.

Sandwell

The Chance Trust

£1,000

Correspondent: Revd Ian Shelton, Trustee, 192 Hanover Road, Rowley Regis B65 9EQ (0121 559 1251; email: ianshelton232@hotmail.co.uk; website: www.warleydeanery.co.uk)

CC number: 702647

Eligibility

People in need in the rural deaneries of Warley and West Bromwich (the area covered by the southern parts of Sandwell borough).

Types of grants

One-off grants, usually ranging from £50 to £400, can be given to help access the education. Our research suggests that support can occasionally be made to university students for up to three years.

Annual grant total

In 2016/17 the trust had an income of £2,600 and a total expenditure of £2,200. Grants are made to individuals for educational and social welfare purposes. We estimate that educational grants to individuals totalled £1,000.

Exclusions

Grants are not normally provided where statutory funding is available.

Applications

Apply in writing to the correspondent. Applications should specify the need and the amount required. They are usually considered in January and July.

The Mackmillan Educational Foundation

£1,200

Correspondent: Mr V. J. Westwood, 18 Westdean Close, Halesowen, West Midlands B62 8UA (0121 602 2484; email: vicwestw@blueyonder.co.uk)

CC number: 529043

Eligibility

People under 25 who live in the ancient parish of Rowley Regis.

Types of grants

Grants to people at school and college.

Annual grant total

In 2016/17 the foundation had an income of £1,400 and a total expenditure of £1,500. We estimate the amount of grants made to individuals for education totalled around £1,200.

Applications

Apply in writing to the correspondent.

The Oldbury Charity

£6,000

Correspondent: Ronald Kay, 43 Lee Crescent, Birmingham B15 2BJ (0121 440 7755; email: rolandkay@tiscali.co.uk)

CC number: 527468

Eligibility

Schoolchildren in the borough of Oldbury.

Types of grants

Small grants are available to help with general educational costs, including books, clothing, equipment/instruments and travel expenses.

Annual grant total

In 2015/16 the charity had an income of £7,400 and a total expenditure of £6,400. We have estimated that grants totalled £6,000.

Applications

Apply in writing to the correspondent.

Palmer Educational Charity (The Palmer Trust)

£3,500

Correspondent: David Flint, The Church of England, 1 Colmore Row, Birmingham B3 2BJ (0121 426 0400)

CC number: 508226

Eligibility

Children and young people under the age of 25 who live in the Warley Deanery.

Types of grants

Grants are available to schoolchildren and further/higher education students. Our research suggests that support can mainly be given towards the cost of books directly related to Christianity and religious education.

Annual grant total

In 2016 the charity had an income of £8,900 and a total expenditure of £4,100. We estimate that grants totalled around £3,500.

Applications

Apply in writing to the correspondent. According to our research, applications should be submitted through the PCC or clergy of Warley Deanery and are normally considered in March and October.

Other information

Primarily grants are made to the Church of England schools in the Warley Deanery. Local churches and organisations may also be supported.

George and Thomas Henry Salter Trust

£20,500

Correspondent: J. Styler, Lombard House, Cronehill Linkway, West Bromwich, West Midlands B70 7PL (0121 553 3286)

CC number: 216503

Eligibility

Students in further or higher education who are in need and resident in the borough of Sandwell.

Types of grants

Grants for individuals of any age, resident in the borough of Sandwell to pursue their education including general, professional, vocational and technical training, whether in the UK or abroad.

Annual grant total

In 2016 the trust had assets of £1.7 million and an income of £42,500. Educational grants paid to local trainees at colleges and universities amounted to £20,500.

Applications

Our research indicates that individuals should initially contact the correspondent by letter. Applicants must provide full written details of their circumstances and study courses. The trustees meet regularly and will occasionally interview applicants.

Walsall

The Fishley Educational and Apprenticing Foundation

£11,500

Correspondent: Neil Picken, Administrator, Constitutional Services, Walsall Council, The Civic Centre, Darwall Street, Walsall WS1 1TP (01922 654369; email: charities@walsall.gov.uk; website: cms.walsall.gov.uk/charities)

CC number: 529010

Eligibility

Young people in need who are under the age of 25 and live, work or study in Walsall.

Types of grants

Grants are available towards general educational needs, including tuition fees, specialist equipment, books, clothing, field trips, study of music and arts, study/travel overseas and so on. Pupils and further/higher education students are supported.

Annual grant total

In 2015/16 the foundation had an income of £20,000 and a total expenditure of £11,700. We estimate that the foundation gave around £11,500 in grants to individuals.

Applications

Application forms can be downloaded from the foundation's website or requested from the correspondent via phone. Grants are considered at least twice a year. Applications must be supported by a member of teaching staff.

Note that applications for grants towards educational trips should be made through the educational establishment.

C. C. Walker Charity

£7,500

Correspondent: Neil Picken, Clerk to the Trustees, Constitutional Services, Walsall Council, The Civic Centre, Darwall Street, Walsall WS1 1TP (01922 654369; email: charities@walsall.gov.uk; website: cms.walsall.gov.uk/charities)

CC number: 528898

Eligibility

People who are under the age of 25 and live or study in the borough of Walsall. Preference is given to those people whose one or both parents have died and who were born in Walsall and/or whose parents or surviving parent have lived there at any time since the birth of the applicant.

Types of grants

Grants according to need for any educational purpose. Grants have been given towards clothing for schoolchildren and books, fees, living expenses and equipment for students in further/higher education.

Annual grant total

In 2015/16 the charity had an income of £19,700 and a total expenditure of £8,200. We have estimated that grants to individuals totalled £7,500 during the year.

Applications

Application forms are available to download from the charity's website or can be requested from the correspondent. The trustees meet at least twice a year. Grants are normally considered in January, June and October.

Walsall Wood (Former Allotment) Charity

£5,000

Correspondent: Craig Goodall, Democratic Services, Walsall Council, Council House, Lichfield Street, Walsall WS1 1TW (01922 654765; email: goodallc@walsall.gov.uk; website: www.walsall.gov.uk/charities)

CC number: 510627

Eligibility

Residents of the borough of Walsall who are in need.

Types of grants

Grants for school uniforms and clothing, including footwear.

Annual grant total

In 2015/16 the charity had an income of £23,500 and a total expenditure of £11,200. We estimate that grants for social welfare purposes totalled around £5,000.

Applications

A form is available to download from the council website and can also be requested from the correspondent by telephone. It is helpful, but not essential, to submit supporting evidence along with an application. This could include proof of income, such as a wage slip, benefit letter or bank statement, or a supporting letter from a professional familiar with the applicant's case. The trustees meet around six times a year.

Other information

The charity is administered by the Walsall Council Democratic Services team, which also administers a number of other funds.

Wolverhampton

The Sedgley Educational Trust

£300

Correspondent: Chris Williams, Trustee, 12 Larkswood Drive, Dudley DY3 3UQ (01902 672880)

CC number: 1091563

Eligibility

People in need who live in the ecclesiastical parishes of All Saints Sedgley, St Chad Coseley and St Mary the Virgin Sedgley.

Types of grants

One-off and recurrent grants are given according to need are available to people in education, including religious education in accordance with the doctrines of the Church of England.

Annual grant total

In 2016 the trust had an income of £2,600 and a total expenditure of £550. We have estimated that grants totalled around £300.

Applications

Apply in writing to the correspondent.

Worcester-shire

Bromsgrove

Alvechurch Grammar School Endowment

£13,500 (30+ grants)

Correspondent: David Gardiner, 18 Tanglewood Close, Blackwell, Bromsgrove, Worcestershire B60 1BU (0121 445 3522; email: enquiries@ alvechurchgst.org.uk; website: www. alvechurchgst.org.uk)

CC number: 527440

Eligibility

Children and young people under the age of 25 who (or whose parents) live in the old parish of Alvechurch (Hopwood, Rowney Green, Bordesley and parts of Barnt Green) and who require financial assistance.

Types of grants

Funding is available for specific purposes such as buying school uniform, books, or IT equipment necessary to further education. The charity also funds recreational educational activity such as trips in the UK and abroad, sports and music. Funding is also available for help purchasing equipment for apprenticeships and travel in the pursuance of education. The charity is willing to sponsor a wide range of educational activities including personal development, training and language courses.

Annual grant total

In 2015/16 the charity had an income of £24,000 and a total expenditure of £17,500. We estimate the total amount awarded in grants was £13,500. The website states 'in the past 12 months the trust has made more than 30 awards'.

Exclusions

Assistance is only available where support cannot be received from the local authority.

Applications

An application form can be downloaded from the website or requested from the correspondent. Completed applications

should be returned by post. The deadlines for applications are 1 January, 1 May, and 1 September.

Other information

Grants are also given to local youth organisations.

Malvern Hills

Alfrick Educational Charity

£9,000

Correspondent: Andrew Duncan, Bewell, Alfrick, Worcestershire WR6 5EY (01905 731731; email: a.duncan@wwf.co. uk)

CC number: 517760

Eligibility

People who live in the parish of Alfrick, Lulsley and Suckley and are under the age of 25.

Types of grants

Grants are given to further and higher education students for books, maintenance/living expenses and educational outings in the UK.

Annual grant total

In 2015/16 the charity had an income of £9,400 and a total expenditure of £12,400. We estimate that the total amount given in grants was £9,000.

Applications

Applications can be made in writing to the correspondent at any time.

Other information

Support is also given to the Suckley primary school and other educational establishments serving Alfrick, Lulsley and Suckley.

The Ancient Parish of Ripple Trust

£3,000

Correspondent: John Willis, 7 Court Lea, Holly Green, Upton-upon-Severn, Worcestershire WR8 0PE (01684 594570; email: willis.courtlea@btopenworld.com)

CC number: 1055986

Eligibility

Students in higher education who live in the parishes of Ripple, Holdfast, Queenhill and Bushley.

Types of grants

Small cash grants are made.

Annual grant total

In 2015/16 the trust had an income of £13,700 and a total expenditure of £13,600. We estimate that grants given

to individuals for education purposes totalled around £3,000.

Applications

Applications may be made in writing to the correspondent. The trustees meet twice a year to consider appeals and the funds are advertised locally before these meetings.

Other information

The trust gives to both individuals and organisations and for educational and welfare purposes. The trust's record on the Charity Commission's website notes that 50% of the net income is paid to the trustees of the Ripple Ecclesiastical Charity (CC number: 1059002) for the repair of the St Mary's Church, Ripple.

Walwyn's Educational Foundation

£3,500

Correspondent: Charles Walker, Clerk to the Trustees, 29 Brookmill Close, Colwall, Malvern WR13 6HY (01684 541995; email: cdw1810@btinternet.com)

CC number: 527152

Eligibility

People under the age of 25 who live in the parishes of Colwall and Little Malvern and are pursuing approved courses in tertiary education up to first degree level or equivalent (including vocational training).

Types of grants

Small grants are available towards general educational expenses, including the cost of books, fees, equipment/ instruments and living expenses. There is an additional award, the John Pell Special Award, which can be given to applicants who can demonstrate that they have made a significant contribution to a community project, either locally or further afield.

Annual grant total

In 2016/17 the foundation had an income of £4,300 and a total expenditure of £3,900. We estimate that around £3,500 was given in grants.

Applications

Application forms can be requested from the correspondent. They are considered in September.

Redditch

The Feckenham Educational Foundation

£3,100

Correspondent: Judy Bate, Administrator, Wychway, Droitwich Road, Hanbury, Bromsgrove B60 4DB (01527 821285; email: judy.bate@ hotmail.co.uk)

CC number: 527565

Eligibility

People under the age of 25 who live in the ancient parish of Feckenham.

Types of grants

Schoolchildren and students can be supported towards general educational needs and people preparing to enter a trade or profession can be assisted towards the cost of outfits, clothing, tools or books.

Annual grant total

In 2015/16 the foundation had an income of £3,400 and a total expenditure of £3,300. We estimate that the foundation awarded around £3,100 in grants to individuals for educational purposes.

Applications

Apply in writing to the correspondent.

Worcester

Worcester Municipal Charities (CIO)

£1,500 (two grants)

Correspondent: Maggie Inglis, Office Manager, Kateryn Heywood House, Berkeley Court, The Foregate, Worcester WR1 3QG (01905 317117; email: admin@wmcharities.org.uk)

CC number: 1166931

Eligibility

People of any age living in Worcester, the parishes of Powick, Bransford and Rushwick, and the ancient parish of Leigh. People who live outside these areas but have attended school in the city of Worcester for at least two years are also eligible.

Types of grants

One-off grants for equipment and supplies or to help someone stay in or continue education.

Annual grant total

In 2016 the charity held assets of £15.8 million and had an income of £16.2 million, which largely came from the consolidation of several charities

assets. Grants to two individuals for educational purposes totalled £1,500, with a further £240,000 awarded to organisations and individuals in financial need.

Exclusions

Applications in respect of fee-paying institutions, for travel abroad, and awards beyond first degree level are normally excluded.

Applications

Application forms can be downloaded from the charity's website and returned via email – handwritten forms are no longer accepted. The grants committee meets monthly to discuss applications and the deadline for grant applications is 12pm on the Thursday before they meet. The charity's website lists all the meeting dates for the year.

Other information

This CIO consolidates Worcester's charitable trusts. All the assets and liabilities of the Worcester Municipal Exhibitions Foundation and the Worcester Consolidated Municipal Charity were transferred to this CIO on 30 June 2016. The charity provides accommodation for people in financial need and homeless people as well as making grants to individuals in need and charitable organisations. The charity's website provides detailed guidelines on how to apply and other sources of support.

Wychavon

John Martin's Charity

£267,500

Correspondent: John Daniels, The Clerk to the Trustees, 16 Queen's Road, Evesham, Worcester WR11 4JN (01386 765440; email: enquires@johnmartins. org.uk; website: www.johnmartins.org. uk)

CC number: 527473

Eligibility

People resident in Evesham, Worcestershire. To qualify for a grant, an applicant must have been permanently resident or (if living away from home during term term) have maintained a residential address in the town of Evesham for at least 12 months immediately prior to 1 September in the year of the application.

Types of grants

Individual students, between the ages of 16 and state retirement age, may apply for educational grants to support study in a wide variety of courses at local colleges in addition to universities and colleges throughout the country and the

Open University. Qualifying courses include Higher National Diplomas (HND) and degree, postgraduate and part-time vocational courses. Applicants must have been a permanent resident or (if living away from home during term time) have maintained a residential address in the town for a minimum of twelve months immediately prior to 1 September in the year of application.

The charity also makes grants for:

- School uniform costs – grants may be available to assist with the cost of school uniforms for children aged 4 to 18 who live with a parent/guardian in Evesham
- Educational visits and music, arts and sports activities (Miscellaneous Education Grant) – grants of up to £140 may be available to students aged 4 to 18 for activities including school trips, music lessons/instrument hire and sporting activities. Applications are assessed based on the number of children and adults in the household, and housing costs are also taken into consideration. There is an easy-to-use eligibility calculator on the website
- 'Standards of Excellence' awards – grants for students aged 4 to 18 for achieving a 'standard of excellence' in a sporting or arts/music area. Applications are not subject to a financial assessment; however, suitable evidence of the achievement must be provided

Annual grant total

In 2016/17 the charity had assets of £24 million and an income of £808,500. Grants were made to individuals totalling £396,000 and were distributed as follows:

Promotion of education	£267,500
Relief in need	£118,500
Health and other charitable purposes	£7,500
Religious support	£3,000

Exclusions

The charity does not currently provide grants for full-time courses below HND/ degree level.

Applications

Application forms are available from the correspondent or as a download from the website, where eligibility criteria is also posted, along with the grants on offer. Applications are usually accepted from July to September for further and higher education grants. Grants for part-time vocational courses are available throughout the year. Original documentation as proof of residency in Evesham must be provided and grants will not be considered without this evidence. Applications from those over 25 are financially assessed.

Application forms for Miscellaneous Education Grants and 'Standards of Excellence' Awards are available to download from the website, where eligibility criteria is also available. Application forms for school uniforms can be downloaded from the 'families and individuals' page on the website.

Other information
Grants are also made to organisations and to individuals for welfare purposes. The charity has an informative website.

Randolph Meakins Patty's Farm and the Widows Lyes Charity

£1,000

Correspondent: Lesley Houghton, Hollyhocks, Main Street, Cropthorne, Pershore, Worcestershire WR10 3LT (01386 860217)

CC number: 500624

Eligibility
People in need who live in the village of Cropthorne, Worcestershire.

Types of grants
One-off grants according to financial need for the provision of educational items.

Annual grant total
In 2016/17 the charity had an income of £26,000 and a total expenditure of £5,000. We estimate that the charity awarded £1,000 in educational grants.

Applications
Apply in writing to the correspondent.

Other information
The charity also makes awards to individuals for welfare and relief-in-need purposes.

Perkins's Educational Foundation
See entry on page 177

Wyre Forest

The Bewdley Old Grammar School Foundation

£7,000

Correspondent: Shana Kent, The Bewdley School, Stourport Road, Bewdley DY12 1BL (01299 403277; email: office@bewdley.worcs.sch.uk)

CC number: 527429

Eligibility
People under the age of 25 living in Bewdley, the parish of Rock and Ribbesford and Stourport-on-Severn.

Types of grants
Grants are available to anyone under the age of 25 in education, to cover the costs of general educational needs such as books, equipment, travel, and school trips. Provisions are also made for candidates to study music and art.

Annual grant total
In 2015/16 the foundation had an income of £9,000 and a total expenditure of £6,400. We estimate that the total amount awarded in grants was £6,000.

Applications
Apply in writing to the correspondent.

East of England

General

Nichol-Young Foundation

£250 (one grant)

Correspondent: The Trustees, PO Box 4757, Windsor SL4 9EE

CC number: 259994

Eligibility

Individuals in need who are in full-time education, with a possible preference for those who live in East Anglia. The trustees' report 2015/16 states that they 'have had a social concern to help those who perhaps feel marginalised by society or who wish to improve their life skills so that they in turn can then be of benefit to others'.

Types of grants

One-off and recurrent grants, generally of up to £500, are given for general educational needs, educational trips, medical electives and other such projects undertaken by individuals. Grants may also be given for computers, equipment and tools.

Annual grant total

In 2015/16 the foundation had an income of £33,000 and a total expenditure of £37,500. Grants totalled £31,500, almost all of which was distributed to organisations. One grant of £250 was awarded to an individual.

Applications

Apply in writing to the correspondent. Applications are normally considered on a quarterly basis. Unsuccessful applicants will only be contacted if an sae is provided. Where possible, payments are paid through an educational institution.

Note: The foundation has previously stated that telephone enquiries are not welcomed.

Cambridge-shire

The Henry Morris Memorial Trust

£5,500

Correspondent: Peter Hains, Trustee, 24 Barton Road, Haslingfield, Cambridge CB23 1LL (email: info@henrymorris.org; website: www.henrymorris.org)

CC number: 311419

Eligibility

Young people between the ages of 13 and 19 who live or attend/have attended school or college in Cambridge/Cambridgeshire, and who would like to travel abroad or in Britain, or run a project.

Types of grants

The trust is offering grants for short travel expeditions (abroad or in the UK) with specific purpose, or to help with the cost of materials and running expenses for a project not involving travel. Projects must be planned independently by the applicant (although an adult may accompany the applicant in a care/protection role). Applications may be made by individuals, with a friend or in a small group.

Some examples of previously supported activities include: making a video diary of the village shop, constructing a wildlife garden pond, investigating local wartime airfields, comparing two local windmills (home-based projects); a journey to learn about the Romans in Britain at Hadrian's Wall, a visit to a famous harpist in Dresden to listen and learn, a journey to investigate the history of the piano at the Paris Museum of Music, an enquiry into the story surrounding the fate of the 44 Jewish children of Izieu (travel awards). Further examples and ideas are given on the trust's website.

Grants are from £20 to £200. Candidates are encouraged to fundraise towards their goal themselves and should be able to demonstrate how they would raise any shortfall.

Annual grant total

In 2016 the trust had an income of £4,400 and a total expenditure of almost £6,000. We estimate that grants totalled around £5,500.

Exclusions

Grants will not normally be made towards the full cost of a gap year project, foreign exchange, school coursework, a holiday or a project planned and managed by a school/other organisation (for example, Raleigh International). The cost of permanent equipment is not usually covered. The website notes: 'In general, the trust is looking to help with expeditions or enterprises substantially planned by you.'

Applications

Application forms are available from the local schools or from the trust's website. They can be submitted directly by the individual by 31 January for consideration in February/March. Candidates under the age of 18 will need a full approval from a parent/guardian. Potential grant recipients are invited for an interview in Cambridge in March. Projects should take place between April and September, and grant recipients are expected to submit a report on their project to the trust by the end of September.

The website states: 'Applicants who can demonstrate the strength of their interest, and evidence of planning, stand the best chances.'

Other information

The trustees are looking for independently planned and managed projects and particularly seek to encourage 'individual candidates wishing to pursue topics of particular fascination to them'. All travel and accommodation arrangements have to be made by the applicants themselves.

The Charities of Nicholas Swallow and Others

£1,200

Correspondent: Nicholas Tufton, Clerk, 11 High Street, Barkway, Royston SG8 8EA (01763 848888; email: nicholas@ntufton.co.uk)

CC number: 203222

Eligibility
People in need who live in the parish of Whittlesford (near Cambridge) and the adjacent area.

Types of grants
One-off grants according to need.

Annual grant total
In 2016/17 the charity had assets of £846,000 and an income of £84,000. We estimate that educational grants to individuals totalled around £1,200.

Applications
Individuals can apply in writing directly to the correspondent.

Other information
The principal activity of this charity is as a housing association which manages bungalows and garages.

Elizabeth Wright's Charity

£2,000

Correspondent: Dr Iain Mason, Trustee, 13 Tavistock Road, Wisbech, Cambridgeshire PE13 2DY (01945 588646; email: i.h.mason60@gmail.com)

CC number: 203896

Eligibility
People who live in the parishes of St Peter and Paul and St Augustine, Cambridgeshire.

Types of grants
Grants for students of music and other arts and towards vocational education or training among other areas. Primary, secondary and further education students can receive grants for projects in the areas of RE, citizenship, arts, music and drama or Christian and youth work.

Annual grant total
In 2016 the charity had an income of £42,000 and a total expenditure of £31,500. We estimate that grants to individuals totalled £2,000.

Exclusions
Grants are not given for people starting work.

Applications
Apply in writing to the correspondent. Applications can be submitted directly by the individual at any time.

Other information
The charity also makes grants to schools and organisations and supports individuals for welfare purposes.

East Cambridgeshire

The Downham Feoffee Charity

£2,600

Correspondent: Jo Howard, 35 Fieldside, Ely, Cambridgeshire CB6 3AT (01353 665774; email: downhamfeoffees@hotmail.co.uk)

CC number: 237233

Eligibility
Residents of the ancient parish of Downham.

Types of grants
Grants for students attending higher education. Support to people in other education or training may also be given.

Annual grant total
In 2016/17 the charity had assets of £4.9 million and an income of £102,000. Higher education grants totalled £2,600.

Applications
Applications may be made in writing to the correspondent.

Other information
Awards are also made to individuals in need, schools and other public organisations, although its main focus is the provision of housing.

John Huntingdon's Charity

£8,400

Correspondent: Jill Hayden, Charity Manager, John Huntingdon House, Tannery Road, Sawston, Cambridge CB2 3UW (01223 830599; email: office@johnhuntingdon.org.uk; website: www.johnhuntingdon.org.uk)

CC number: 1118574

Eligibility
People who are in need and live in the parish of Sawston in Cambridgeshire.

Types of grants
One-off grants, usually ranging from £25 to £250, are given to help with the costs of school trips, school uniforms and, sometimes, with nursery or playgroup fees.

Annual grant total
In 2016 the charity had assets of £16.4 million and an income of £394,000. We estimate that educational grants to individuals totalled £8,400.

Applications
In the first instance, call the charity's office to arrange an appointment with one of its support workers.

Other information
The charity is proactive in supporting the community in Sawston and documents its activities in its informative annual report. Among its activities, the charity provides advice and housing services, sometimes in partnership with other local organisations. More details are available on the website or by contacting the charity's office.

Bishop Laney's Charity

£34,000

Correspondent: Richard Tyler, Secretary, George Court, Bartholomew's Walk, Ely, Cambridgeshire CB7 4JW (01353 662813; email: secretary@bishoplaneyscharity.org.uk or richard_j_tyler@hotmail.com; website: www.bishoplaneyscharity.org.uk/index.html)

CC number: 311306

Eligibility
People in need under the age 25 who live in the parishes of Soham and Ely. Consideration might be given to people under 25 who live in other parts of Cambridgeshire where funds permit.

Types of grants
Grants are given towards education and training, especially apprentices and people starting work. Where possible awards are recurrent and can be given towards uniforms/clothing, books and equipment/instruments, also study or travel abroad, excursions in the UK and maintenance/living expenses. Grants to individuals are of around £150 to £250.

Annual grant total
In 2015/16 the charity held assets of £3.2 million and had an income of £119,500. A total of £34,000 was awarded to individuals.

Applications
Application forms are available from the charity's website or can be requested from the correspondent. They can be submitted directly by the individual. Applications should include a copy of the applicant's birth certificate, proof of attendance at college/university/training and details of the items needed. Full

details are available from the charity's website.

Other information

The charity can also give grants to educational establishments (£15,300 in 2015/16).

Fenland

Town Lands Educational Foundation

£5,500

Correspondent: R. Gagen, 78 High Road, Gorefield, Wisbech, Cambridgeshire PE13 4NB (01945 870454; email: leveoffees@aol.com)

CC number: 311325

Eligibility

Schoolchildren and people in further/ higher education who live in Leverington, Parson Drove and Gorefield.

Types of grants

One-off grants according to need.

Annual grant total

In 2015/16 the foundation had an income of £13,700 and a total expenditure of £12,600. We estimate that around £5,500 was made in grants to individuals for education.

Applications

Applications can be made on a form available from the correspondent.

Other information

Grants are also made to local schools.

Huntingdonshire

Hilton Town Charity

£400

Correspondent: Phil Wood, 1 Sparrow Way, Hilton, Huntingdon, Cambridgeshire PE28 9NZ (01480 830866; email: phil.n.wood@btinternet.com)

CC number: 209423

Eligibility

People who live in the village of Hilton, Cambridgeshire.

Types of grants

Only a limited number of grants are given for educational purposes. Individuals at any stage or level of their education, undertaking study of any subject can be supported.

Annual grant total

In 2015 the charity had an income of £5,100 and a total expenditure of £1,900.

Grants are made to individuals and organisations for a wide range of purposes. We estimate that educational grants to individuals totalled £400.

Applications

Apply in writing to the correspondent.

Huntingdon Freemen's Trust

£153,500

Correspondent: Karen Clark, Grants Officer, 37 High Street, Huntingdon, Cambridgeshire PE29 3AQ (01480 414909; email: info@huntingdonfreemen. org.uk; website: www. huntingdonfreemen.org.uk)

CC number: 1044573

Eligibility

People in need resident in Huntingdon (normally for at least one year but exceptions are sometimes made depending on circumstances).

Types of grants

Students over 16 taking vocational courses in local colleges are assisted with course fees and some equipment costs. Students going away to university/college are helped with accommodation costs. Grants to students have now been capped at £1,000 per student per year.

Annual grant total

In 2015/16 the trust had assets of £15.8 million and an income of about £425,000. Student grants for accommodation totalled £103,000 and school grants totalled £50,500.

Applications

Applications can be made using the contact page on the trust's website. Applicants should send their name, contact details and a brief description of the type of help required. Most applications will require the visit of an officer who will assess your needs and financial circumstances. Applications are assessed at monthly meetings.

Other information

The trust's website notes that applications are only considered 'from individuals, groups and organisations who live or are based within the area covered by Huntingdon Town Council, including Oxmoor, Hartford, Sapley, Stukeley Meadows and Hinchingbrooke Park'.

South Cambridgeshire

The Samuel Franklin Fund Elsworth

£1,000

Correspondent: Serena Wyer, 5 Cowdell End, Elsworth, Cambridge CB23 4GB (01954 267156; email: serena.wyersff@gmail.com; website: www. samuelfranklinfund.co.uk)

CC number: 228775

Eligibility

People who live in the parish of Elsworth.

Types of grants

One-off and recurrent grants for clothing and equipment, to be paid to individuals entering a trade, occupation, or profession.

Annual grant total

In 2016 the fund had assets of £112,500 and an income of £30,000. We estimate that the amount awarded in grants for education was £1,000.

Applications

In the first instance, applicants should contact the trustees by email or telephone.

Other information

Grants are also made to individuals for welfare purposes and to local organisations providing services to the parish.

Girton Town Charity

£13,500 (59 grants)

Correspondent: Dr Charles Hiley, 1 Fairway, Girton, Cambridge CB3 0QF (01223 277296; email: gtc@girtontowncharity.co.uk; website: www. girtontowncharity.co.uk)

CC number: 1130272

Eligibility

College and university students resident in Girton.

Types of grants

Assistance with buying books and equipment for recent school leavers who have moved on to further and higher education.

Annual grant total

In 2015/16 the charity had assets of £30.7 million and an income of £962,000. Educational grants to individuals totalled £13,500.

Applications

Apply in writing to the correspondent.

Lincolnshire

The Alenson and Erskine Educational Foundation

£4,000

Correspondent: Edwina Arnold, Crooks Cottage, Wrangle Bank, Wrangle, Boston PE22 9DL (01205 270352; email: wranglepc@aol.com)

CC number: 527671

Eligibility

People under the age of 25 who live in the parishes of Old Leake, New Leake and Wrangle. Preference is given to people who have attended county or voluntary school for at least two years. Candidates should normally have been resident in the area of benefit for at least five years.

Types of grants

Grants can be given to further/higher education students towards educational necessities and fees, or to school leavers entering a trade/profession to help with the cost of books, equipment, clothing or travel.

Annual grant total

In 2016 the foundation had an income of £4,100 and a total expenditure of £4,500. We estimate that the total amount awarded in grants was £4,000.

Exclusions

Grants are not given for A-levels. According to our research, schoolchildren (other than those with special education needs) are only considered if family difficulties are serious.

Applications

Application forms can be requested from the correspondent. They can be submitted by individuals directly via post or email and are usually considered in October/November. Applicants can only claim for what they have bought and not what they would like to buy and must submit receipts with their application.

Cowell and Porrill

£3,500

Correspondent: Roger Hooton, Clerk, 33 Glen Drive, Boston, Lincolnshire PE21 7QB (01205 310088)

CC number: 240438

Eligibility

People under the age of 25 who live, or whose parents live, in the parishes of Benington and Leverton.

Types of grants

Awards are usually in the range of £250 and £600. Support is given for general educational needs to people at any level or stage of their education and undertaking the study of any subject.

Annual grant total

In 2016 the charity had an income of £17,200 and a total expenditure of £9,000. We estimate that the charity awarded around £3,500 in grants to individuals for educational purposes.

The charity also provides almshouses for the poor residents of Benington and Leverton and can support local schools, where assistance is not already provided by the local authorities.

Applications

Apply in writing to the correspondent.

Cowley and Brown Charity

£800

Correspondent: K. J. Watts, Clerk, 99 Hawthorn Bank, Spalding, Lincolnshire PE11 1JQ (01775 760911; email: kenwattsathome@hotmail.com)

CC number: 217099

Eligibility

People in education who live in the ancient parish of Quadring. Support is generally given to individuals under the age of 25.

Types of grants

Small grants can be given towards the cost of books, clothing and other educational essentials.

Annual grant total

In 2016 the charity had an income of £4,100 and a total expenditure of £3,300. We estimate that around £800 was given to individuals for educational purposes.

The charity also awards grants to organisations and individuals for welfare purposes.

Applications

Apply in writing to the correspondent. Applications are usually considered in July and November.

Other information

Support is also given to schools, organisations and for general relief-in-need purposes or in Christmas gifts to pensioners.

Deacon and Fairfax Educational Foundation

£3,400

Correspondent: Jill Harrington, Administrator, 11 West End, Holbeach, Spalding PE12 7LW (01406 426739)

CC number: 527639

Eligibility

People who live in the parish of Fleet (Lincolnshire), aged between 16 and 25 and attending further education.

Types of grants

Grants are given to further and higher education students.

Annual grant total

In 2015/16 the foundation had an income of £10,100 and a total expenditure of £7,000. We estimate that the foundation gave around £3,400 in grants to individuals for educational purposes.

Applications

The individual should apply directly to the correspondent in writing.

Other information

Grants are also made to schools in the area.

Farmer Educational Foundation

£11,500

Correspondent: Michael Griffin, Administrator, 39 Church Street, Warmington, Peterborough PE8 6TE (01832 281076; email: griffin325@btinternet.com)

CC number: 527636

Eligibility

Children and young people who live in the parish of Holbeach, South Lincolnshire.

Types of grants

Grants are given up to £150 to help schools in higher or further education and sometimes to assist schools serving Holbeach with projects.

Annual grant total

In 2015/16 the foundation had an income of £37,500 and a total expenditure of £56,000. Grants throughout the year totalled £22,500. We estimate that £11,500 of this amount went to individuals.

The charity also awards grants to organisations.

Applications

Application forms are available from Holbeach Library, to be submitted by the individual at the end of August. Applications are considered in September.

Frampton Educational Foundation

£2,400

Correspondent: Mark Hildred, Correspondent, Moore Thompson, Bank House, Broad Street, Spalding PE11 1TB (01775 711333)

CC number: 527784

Eligibility

People who have lived in the ancient parish of Frampton for at least five years (generally above elementary education).

Types of grants

One-off and recurrent grants are given according to need.

Annual grant total

In 2015/16 the foundation had an income of £5,800 and a total expenditure of £5,000. We estimate that they awarded around £2,400 to individuals for educational purposes.

Applications

Applications may be made in writing to the correspondent. Requests are considered in early October and students must re-apply each year.

Other information

Grants are also given to local schools.

Gainsborough Educational Charity

£7,800

Correspondent: Maria Bradley, Clerk to the Trustees, c/o Burton & Dyson Solicitors, 22 Market Place, Gainsborough DN21 2BZ (01427 610761; email: law@burtondyson.com; website: www.burtondyson.com/about-burton-and-dyson/corporate-social-responsibility/gainsborough-educational-charity)

CC number: 527299

Eligibility

Children and young people between the ages of 11 and 25 who live, or whose parents live, in Gainsborough, Lea, Morton or Thonock.

Types of grants

The charity provides grants, bursaries, allowances to help with the cost of uniforms and specialist clothing, fees, books, equipment/instruments and other necessities to schoolchildren, further/higher education students and people starting work. Travel costs in the UK

and abroad for educational purposes and music/arts studies are also supported.

Annual grant total

In 2015/16 the charity had an income of £6,400 and a total expenditure of £8,000. We estimate that around £7,800 was given to individuals for educational purposes.

Exclusions

Grants are not given towards the purchase of computers.

Applications

Application forms can be downloaded from Burton and Dyson Solicitor's website or requested from the correspondent. A completed application form, together with a reference from an academic tutor, can be submitted directly by the individual in advance to the trustees' meetings, which are held twice a year, normally in March and November.

The Hesslewood Children's Trust (Hull Seamen's and General Orphanage)
See entry on page 311

The Kesteven Children in Need

£3,000

Correspondent: Alexandra Howard, Trustee, Nocton Rise, Lincoln LN4 2AF (01522 791217; email: enquiries@kcin.org or kcin@kcin.org; website: www.kcin.org)

CC number: 700008

Eligibility

Children/young people who live in Kesteven.

Types of grants

Grants of up to £500 towards books, clothing and educational outings.

Annual grant total

In 2016 the charity had an income of £11,000 and a total expenditure of £23,500. The majority of grants are usually awarded for welfare purposes. We estimate that approximately £3,000 was awarded for educational purposes.

Applications

Generally through local social workers, health visitors, teachers and education officers. Information should include the family situation, the age of the child and his/her special needs. Applications are considered throughout the year.

Kirton-in-Lindsey Exhibition Foundation

£3,800

Correspondent: Julia Melling, 7 Darwin Street, Kirton Lindsey, Gainsborough, Lincolnshire DN21 4BZ (01652 649425; email: julia.melling@btinternet.com)

CC number: 529749

Eligibility

People who live in the parishes of Blyborough, Grayingham, Hibaldstow, Kirton-in-Lindsey, Manton, Northorpe, Redbourne, Scotter, Scotton or Waddingham and who have attended one of the following primary schools for at least two years: Hibaldstow; Kirton-in-Lindsey; Messingham; Scotter; or Waddingham.

Types of grants

The foundation's record on the Charity Commission's website notes that it offers the awards of Junior and Senior Exhibitions. The Junior awards are available to secondary school pupils and the Senior awards are given to higher education students. Awards are also available to students 'at any institution of technical, industrial or professional instruction'. Grants are given to higher education students towards the cost of books. Additional support given to children resident in the beneficial area to continue their education at evening schools, day or evening classes.

Annual grant total

In 2016/17 the foundation had an income of £4,200 and a total expenditure of £4,100. We have estimated that grants to individuals totalled around £3,800.

Applications

Application forms are available from the correspondent.

Other information

The foundation may also provide books or fittings for a school library in the parish of Kirton-in-Lindsey for the use of scholars.

Kitchings Educational Charity

£6,000

Correspondent: Kimberley Dove, 71 Silver Street, Bardney, Lincoln LN3 5XG (01526 399529)

CC number: 527707

Eligibility

Children and young people under the age of 25 who live in Bardney, Bucknall, Southrey or Tupholme and are in need of financial assistance.

Types of grants

Small grants to schoolchildren and further/higher education students to assist with the costs of books, equipment/instruments or other general educational necessities.

Annual grant total

In 2016/17 the charity had an income of £11,200 and a total expenditure of £12,400. We estimate that grants to individuals totalled about £6,000.

Applications

Apply in writing to the correspondent. Applications can be submitted directly by the individual or through the applicant's school, university/college, educational welfare agency, if applicable. Applications are normally considered in October and should be received by the end of September.

Other information

The charity also provides financial support to The Bardney Joint Church of England and Methodist Primary School or The Bucknall Primary School, where support is not already provided by the local authority.

The Kochan Trust

£24,500 (21 grants)

Correspondent: Revd Roger Massingberd-Mundy, Honorary Secretary, The Old Post Office, The Street, West Raynham, Fakenham, Norfolk NR21 7AD (01328 838611; email: roger_mundy@btconnect.com)

CC number: 1052976

Eligibility

People studying veterinary science or creative arts, music and performance who live in Lincolnshire and are in need of financial assistance.

Types of grants

One-off grants are given according to need. Support can be given for tuition fees, the purchase of an instrument, research of veterinary science or other educational expenses.

Annual grant total

In 2016/17 the trust had an income of £35,500 and a total expenditure of £29,500. Grants were awarded to nine veterinary students totalling £16,200 and a further 12 music and art students received £8,300 in total.

Applications

Apply in writing to the correspondent. The trustees meet four times a year, usually in January, April, July and November. Applications should give some details about the candidate and state what the grant is needed for. They can be made by individuals directly or through a third party, such as a school/college, educational welfare agency, if applicable.

Lincolnshire Community Foundation

£14,600

Correspondent: Sue Fortune, Grants Director, 4 Mill House, Moneys Yard, Carre Street, Sleaford, Lincolnshire NG34 7TW (01529 305825; email: lincolnshirecf@btconnect.com; website: www.lincolnshirecf.co.uk)

CC number: 1092328

Eligibility

Generally, residents of Lincolnshire who are in need; however, different funds have different eligibility criteria attached.

Types of grants

The type and amount of grant available depends on the fund being applied to. See the foundation's website for more information on open funds.

Annual grant total

In 2016/17 the foundation had assets of £5.64 million and an income of £945,000. Grants totalled £902,500 and we believe the vast majority were awarded to organisations. We estimate that educational grants to individuals totalled around £14,600 and were awarded through The Colin Batts Family Trust and the Make a Start (MAST) programme.

Exclusions

Grants cannot be awarded retrospectively.

Applications

See the foundation's website for more information on the funds it operates and how to apply for assistance.

The Joseph Nickerson Charitable Foundation

£14,400

Correspondent: Eric White, Villa Office, Rothwell, Market Rasen, Lincolnshire LN7 6BJ (01472 371216; email: j.n. farms@farmingline.com)

CC number: 276429

Eligibility

Young people, normally aged 18 or over, in further or higher education. Preference may be given to people from Lincolnshire.

Types of grants

Grants to assist with general educational expenses.

Annual grant total

In 2015/16 the foundation had an income of £45,500 and a charitable expenditure of £28,000. A total of £14,400 was given in grants to young people in education. A further £11,000 was given in grants to organisations.

Applications

Apply in writing to the correspondent. Our research suggests that applications for grants starting in September should be made by the end of June for consideration in July.

Other information

Grants can also be made to charitable organisations.

Dame Margaret Thorold's Apprenticing Charity

£2,500

Correspondent: Jackie Watts, Clerk to the Trustees, c/o Tallents Solicitors, 2 Westgate, Southwell NG25 0JJ (01636 813411)

CC number: 527628

Eligibility

People aged 18 to 25 living in the ancient parishes of Sedgebrook, Marston and Cranwell who are undertaking an apprenticeship or training to enter a profession or occupation, or further or higher education with the aim of entering a particular profession.

Types of grants

Grants of around £100 per year are available to assist students in their training or course.

Annual grant total

In 2016 the charity had an income of £1,300 and a total expenditure of £2,800. We estimate that grants to individuals totalled approximately £2,500.

Applications

Applications should be made in writing to the correspondent. The trustees meet in February to consider applications.

Boston

Sir Thomas Middlecott's Exhibition Foundation

£17,400

Correspondent: Frank Wilson, Clerk, 57A Bourne Road, Spalding PE11 1JR (01775 766117; email: info@ middlecotttrust.org.uk; website: www. middlecotttrust.org.uk)

CC number: 527283

Eligibility

Students who live/have lived in the parishes of Algarkirk, Fosdyke, Frampton, Kirton, Sutterton and Wyberton in Lincolnshire, who are in further/higher education and are aged under 25. Applicants must have attended a maintained primary school in the area for at least two years.

Types of grants

Grants are given to students in further/ higher education towards books, clothing and equipment/instruments.

Annual grant total

In 2015/16 the foundation had assets of £781,000 and an income of £41,000. Grants were made totalling £17,400.

Applications

Application forms are available to download from the foundation's website and should be submitted by post. The deadline for applications is 31 September each year.

The Sutterton Educational Foundation (Sutterton Education Trust)

£600

Correspondent: Deirdre McCumiskey, 6 Hillside Gardens, Wittering, Peterborough PE8 6DX (01780 782668; email: deirdre.mccumiskey@tesco.net)

CC number: 527771

Eligibility

Schoolchildren in the parish of Sutterton.

Types of grants

Small grants are given towards general educational costs, including books, clothing, educational outings and other necessities.

Annual grant total

In 2016/17 the foundation had an income of £1,300 and a total expenditure of £1,400. We estimate that grants to individuals totalled around £600.

Applications

Apply in writing to the correspondent.

Other information

Grants are also made to local schools.

East Lindsey

George Jobson's Trust

£2,000

Correspondent: Sarah Steel, Clerk, Chattertons Solicitors, 5 South Street, Horncastle LN9 6DS (01507 522456; email: sarah.webster@chattertons.com)

CC number: 213875

Eligibility

Children and young people in need who live or attend/have attended school in the parish of Horncastle.

Types of grants

Grants to people in education and training for general educational needs, including books, courses, equipment/ instruments and various projects. Most funding for individuals appears to be for students in college.

Annual grant total

In 2015/16 the trust had assets of £1.2 million and an income of £24,500. Grants totalled £14,800; at least £12,000 of this was to organisations. We estimate that grants given to individuals totalled around £2,000.

Applications

Application forms can be requested from the correspondent and submitted directly by the individual or through a social worker/welfare agency, if applicable.

Other information

Most of the trust's funding appears to go to schools and youth organisations.

Kitchings General Charity

£1,500

Correspondent: Mrs J. Smith, 42 Abbey Road, Bardney, Lincoln LN3 5XA (01526 398505)

CC number: 219957

Eligibility

People living in the parish of Bardney, Southrey, Tupholme and Bucknall. Our research suggests that support is particularly given to students, especially mature, part-time, and vocational students.

Types of grants

Grants may be given for playgroup fees, books, excursions, uniforms and sports equipment.

Annual grant total

In 2016 the charity had assets of £6,700 and an income of £42,500. Grants made for educational purposes totalled around £3,000 and we estimate that about £1,500 was given to individuals.

Applications

Applications may be made in writing to the correspondent and should include some background details, such as your age, the name of the educational establishment and course undertaken and a brief description of education to date. Our research indicates that applications are normally considered in May, October and January.

Other information

Grants are also given to local schools and organisations, and to individuals for welfare purposes.

Mapletoft Scholarship Foundation

£3,500

Correspondent: Patrick Purves, c/o Bridge McFarland Solicitors, 9 Cornmarket, Louth, Lincolnshire LN11 9PY (01507 605883; email: pmp@ bmcf.co.uk)

CC number: 527649

Eligibility

People between the ages of 16 and 25 who are engaged or about to engage in higher education or apprenticeship training. Applicants must have attended primary school in the parishes of North Thoresby, Grainsby and Waithe and have been resident there for at least five years.

Types of grants

Grants of up to about £150 to help with further/higher education costs, including books, fees, living expenses or to supplement existing grants. Travel grants are also available. Grants are generally recurrent.

Annual grant total

In 2016/17 the foundation had an income of £5,000 and a total expenditure of £3,800. We have estimated that about £3,500 was given in grants.

Applications

Apply in writing to the correspondent.

The Stickford Relief-in-Need Charity

£8,000

Correspondent: Katherine Bunting, 28 Wide Bargate, Boston, Lincolnshire PE21 6RT (01205 351114)

CC number: 247423

Eligibility

Schoolchildren in need who live in the parish of Stickford.

Types of grants

School clothing grants. Grants are also made for welfare purposes.

Annual grant total

In 2015 the charity had an income of £17,100 and an total expenditure of £17,600. We estimate that educational grants to individuals totalled around £8,000.

Applications

Applications can be made in writing to the correspondent. They should be submitted directly by the individual and are considered all year.

Lincoln

Leeke Church Schools and Educational Foundation

£29,000 (150 grants)

Correspondent: Anne Young, Administrator, Leeke Educational Foundation, PO Box 1294, Lincoln LN5 5RD (01522 526466; email: leekeclerk@gmail.com)

CC number: 527654

Eligibility

People under the age of 25 who live, or whose parents live, in the city of Lincoln. People studying in Lincoln with a home address elsewhere are ineligible.

Preference can be given to students from families on low income, minimum wage, state benefits, with a single parent or living independently.

Types of grants

One-off and recurrent grants, normally in the range of £150 to £500 each term. Grants are given to schoolchildren, further/higher education students and people entering a trade/profession. Support is aimed to help with the cost uniforms, outfits, books, equipment/instruments, fees, educational outings in the UK, educational leisure time activities, study or travel abroad and student exchanges.

Annual grant total

In 2015/16 the foundation held assets of £946,500 and had an income of £57,000. Grants to 150 individuals totalled £29,000. A further £500 was awarded to schools during the year.

Exclusions

Grants are not given for private education – there must be a financial need.

Applications

Apply in writing to the correspondent. Applications can be submitted by the individual for consideration at any time. Educational costs should be listed either giving the real amount or a fair estimate.

North East Lincolnshire

The Educational Foundation of Philip and Sarah Stanford

£5,000

Correspondent: Eleanor Hine, Clerk, 86 Brigsley Road, Waltham, Grimsby, South Humberside DN37 0LA (01472 827883; email: eleanor.hine@btinternet.com)

CC number: 529755

Eligibility

People under 25 who live in the ancient parishes of Aylesby, Barnoldby-le-Beck, Bradley, Irby-upon-Humber and Laceby.

Types of grants

Grants towards books, clothing or equipment/instruments for college students, undergraduates or apprentices.

Annual grant total

In 2016 the foundation had an income of £24,000 and a total expenditure of £11,300. We estimate that the total amount of grants awarded to individuals was approximately £5,000.

Exclusions

Grants are not given for subjects and courses available in schools, or for help with student fees, travel nor living expenses.

Applications

Applications can be made on a form available from the correspondent and should usually be submitted by 1 October each year. Forms must be completed in the applicant's own handwriting.

Other information

Grants are also made to organisations. The foundation's Charity Commission record also states that it provides a Bible or dictionary to those leaving primary school and also provides shopping vouchers for people in need at Christmas.

North Kesteven

Christ's Hospital Endowment at Potterhanworth

£6,300

Correspondent: Yvonne Woodcock, The Conifers, Barff Road, Potterhanworth, Lincoln LN4 2DU (01522 790942)

CC number: 527669

Eligibility

People under the age of 25 who live, or whose parents live, in the parish of Potterhanworth, Lincolnshire.

Types of grants

Grants are available to schoolchildren towards the cost of educational visits and extracurricular activities such as music, arts, sports and other social and physical training. Further education students and people in vocational training, including apprentices, can be supported for general educational needs. including tuition fee support.

Annual grant total

In 2016 the charity had an income of £154,000 and awarded £6,300 to individuals.

Applications

Apply in writing to the correspondent. Applications can be made either directly by individuals or through a third party, for example a parent/guardian or the individual's educational institution. Applications are normally considered once a year in November and should be received before 31 October. Where applicable, valid receipts for the items/services purchased must be included.

Other information

The charity also provides funding to local schools for purposes not normally covered by the local authority.

The Navenby Town's Farm Trust

£4,000

Correspondent: Leonard Coffey, 17 North Lane, Navenby, Lincoln LN5 0EH (01522 810273)

CC number: 245223

Eligibility

Individuals under the age of 25 who are in need and live in the village of Navenby.

Types of grants

Grants are given to support students in further education and training.

Annual grant total

In 2016/17 the trust had an income of £19,900 and a total expenditure of £16,400. Grants are made to individuals and organisations for both social welfare and educational purposes. We estimate that social welfare grants to individuals totalled £4,000.

Applications

Apply using a form available from the correspondent, the village post office, or the local newsagents. Applications are considered in September. Urgent applications may occasionally be considered at other times. Unsolicited applications are not responded to.

North Lincolnshire

The James Reginald Heslam Settlement

£800

Correspondent: Donald Johnson, Trustee, 2 Park Square, Laneham Street, Scunthorpe DN15 6JH (01724 281616; email: don.johnson@sbblaw.com)

CC number: 256464

Eligibility

People in need who are resident in, or originally from, Scunthorpe and immediate district.

Types of grants

One-off grants of up to £1,000 towards books, computers, laptops, other electronic equipment and fees for further education.

Annual grant total

In 2016/17 the charity had an income of £1,800 and a total expenditure of £900. We estimate that grants to individuals totalled around £800.

Applications

Applications should be made in writing to the correspondent by post or email. Our research suggests that applications should include a CV and details of the applicant's financial situation.

Henry Samman's Hull Chamber of Commerce Endowment Fund

See entry on page 310

Withington Education Trust

£3,000

Correspondent: Benjamin Lawrence, Trustee, Frederick Gough School, Grange Lane South, Bottesford, Scunthorpe DN16 3NG (01724 860151; email: admin@frederickgoughschool.co.uk)

CC number: 507975

Eligibility

People under the age of 21 who live in the area of the North Lincolnshire Council area (comprising Scunthorpe, Glanford and Boothferry).

Types of grants

Grants can be given for a wide range of educational needs, including non-formal educational pursuits, for example, music, artistic activities, dance, sports and international opportunities. Grants usually range from £50 to £300.

Annual grant total

In 2015/16 the trust had an income of £5,200 and a total expenditure of £3,400. We estimate that grants totalled around £3,000.

Exclusions

Grants towards fees for private schooling are not normally given. Our research suggests that general educational necessities, such as books or equipment, are not usually covered.

The Charity Commission record states that the area of benefit excludes 'the parishes of East Halton, North Killingholme and South Killingholme in the borough of Glanford and that part of the district of Boothferry which lies north of the river Ouse'.

Applications

Apply in writing to the correspondent. Applications can be made at any time and preferably should be supported by the applicant's school or college. Awards are considered each term.

Other information

The trust was set up in 1979 in memory of Peter Withington, headteacher of Frederick Gough Comprehensive School.

South Holland

Allen's Charity (Apprenticing Branch)

£4,500

Correspondent: Keith Savage, Correspondent, 94 Wignals Gate, Holbeach, Spalding PE12 7HR (01406 490157)

CC number: 213842–1

Eligibility

Children and young people in need who live in the parish of Long Sutton. Higher education students between the ages of 18 and 25 are also supported.

Types of grants

Grants towards apprenticeships and related costs. University students can be assisted towards general educational necessities.

Annual grant total

In the past the charity has made grants totalling £4,500.

Applications

Application forms can be requested from the correspondent. The scheme is normally advertised in the local press and promoted by local employers.

Other information

This charity is linked to Allen's Charity (registered charity number 213842).

The Moulton Harrox Educational Foundation

£10,000

Correspondent: Jane Mawer, 23 New Road, Spalding, Lincolnshire PE11 1DH (01775 722261; email: john.grimwood@oldershawgroup.com)

CC number: 527635

Eligibility

People up to 25 who live in the South Holland district council area.

Types of grants

Grants for school pupils and college students, including mature students, to help with books, equipment, fees, clothing, educational outings and study or travel abroad. Preference is given to schoolchildren with serious family difficulties so the child has to educated away from home, and to people with special education needs. One-off and recurrent grants are given according to need. Individuals must re-apply in order to receive the grant in the following year.

Annual grant total

In 2015/16 the foundation had an income of £42,000 and a total expenditure of £39,500. Grants were made to individuals for education totalling £10,000.

Applications

Application forms are available from the correspondent. Applications should be submitted before 31 August for consideration in September.

Other information

Financial assistance is also provided to schools.

The Moulton Poors' Lands Charity

£200

Correspondent: Richard Lewis, Maples & Son Solicitors, 23 New Road, Spalding, Lincolnshire PE11 1DH (01775 722261)

CC number: 216630

Eligibility
People in need who live in the civil parish of Moulton.

Types of grants
One-off grants for books and equipment.

Annual grant total
In 2016 the charity had assets of £935,000 and an income of £42,000. During the year £8,400 was awarded in grants, the majority of which we believe was to individuals for welfare purposes. We estimate that educational grants to individuals amounted to no more than £200.

Applications
Applications may be made in writing to the correspondent, usually through a trustee. Appeals are normally considered in April and December.

Other information
The charity also manages almshouses, the rent from which makes up a small part of its income.

Spalding Relief-in-Need Charity

£10,000

Correspondent: R. Knipe, Clerk and Solicitor, Dembleby House, 12 Broad Street, Spalding, Lincolnshire PE11 1ES (01775 768774; email: patrick.skells@chattertons.com)

CC number: 229268

Eligibility
People in need who live in the area covered by the district of South Holland. Preference is given to residents of the urban district of Spalding and the parishes of Cowbit, Deeping St Nicholas, Pinchbeck and Weston.

Types of grants
One-off grants.

Annual grant total
In 2016 the charity had an income of £51,000 and a total expenditure of £33,000. We estimate that grants given to individuals for educational purposes totalled £10,000.

Exclusions
Grants are not intended to be made where support can be obtained from statutory sources.

Applications
Application forms can be requested from the charity. They can be submitted directly by the individual or assisted by a social worker/Citizens Advice/other welfare agency, if applicable. Grants are considered fortnightly.

Other information
This charity is connected with the Spalding Almshouse Charity (registered charity number 220077) and share the same body of administration, the Spalding Town Husbands.

The Sutton St James' Foundation for Education and the Poor (Sutton St James United Charities)

£3,500

Correspondent: Keith Savage, 94 Wignals Gate, Holbeach, Spalding, Lincolnshire PE12 7HR (01406 490157)

CC number: 527757

Eligibility
People under the age of 25 who are in need and live in the parish of Sutton St James and the surrounding area. Applicants must have lived in the area for at least three years.

Types of grants
Small, one-off grants are made to residents of Sutton St James for the provision of general educational equipment such as books, clothing, and equipment. Grants are made to pupils of all levels of education, including university, and to people starting work or entering a trade.

Annual grant total
In 2016/17 the foundation had an income of £25,000 and a total expenditure of £11,000. We estimate that a total of £3,500 was awarded in grants for education.

Applications
Applications can be requested from the correspondent.

Other information
Grants are also made to schools and universities, and to individuals for general welfare purposes.

South Kesteven

Barkston Educational Foundation

£7,000

Correspondent: Malcolm Ellison, Correspondent, Tallents Solicitors, 2 Westgate, Southwell, Nottinghamshire NG25 0JJ (01636 813411; email: Malcolm.Ellison@tallents.co.uk)

CC number: 527724

Eligibility
People under the age of 25 who live or whose parents live in the parish of Barkston.

Types of grants
General educational grants are made to promote education, for example for books or school uniform.

Annual grant total
In 2015/16 the foundation had an income of £5,500 and a total expenditure of £11,000. We estimate the total amount given in grants was £7,000.

Applications
Applications may be made in writing to the correspondent.

Other information
The foundation provides special benefits for Barkston School for needs not met by the local authority.

Deeping St James United Charities

£8,500

Correspondent: Julie Banks, The Institute, 38 Church Street, Deeping St James, Peterborough PE6 8HD (01778 380367; email: dsjunitedcharities@btconnect.com; website: www.dsjunitedcharities.org.uk)

CC number: 248848

Eligibility
School pupils, college/university students and people in training under the age of 25 in the parish of Deeping St James (including Frognall).

Types of grants
Schoolchildren in the three local schools (Deeping St James Community Primary School; Linchfield Community School; and The Deepings School) can receive grants to assist with the costs of school uniforms and educational outings.

Further and higher education students are given an annual award for three years, to be used for books or equipment for study towards a degree or vocational qualification.

Annual grant total

In 2016 the trust had assets of £3 million and an income of £118,000. The amount awarded in educational grants totalled £8,500.

Applications

Applications for further and higher education students are available to download from the trust's website, and should be sent via post to the correspondent. If you are applying for a grant before your course starts, apply as soon as your qualifications and place on the course have been awarded.

Families should enquire directly with their child's school for school pupil grants.

Other information

The trust is an amalgamation of a number of small charities from the local area. This trust also gives grants to individuals for welfare purposes.

West Lindsey

Tyler Educational Foundation

£4,000

Correspondent: Mrs E. Bradley, Correspondent, 22 Market Place, Gainsborough, Lincolnshire DN21 2BZ (01427 010761; email: mb@burtondyson.com)

CC number: 527691

Eligibility

People under the age of 21 who live in parishes of Morton and Thornock and are in financial need. Preference may be given for causes and activities related to the Church of England.

Types of grants

Grants are available for general educational needs.

Annual grant total

In 2015/16 the foundation had an income of £7,000 and a total expenditure of £4,300. We have estimated that grants to individuals totalled around £4,000 during the year.

Applications

Apply in writing to the correspondent.

Norfolk

The Harold Moorhouse Charity

£9,000

Correspondent: Christine Harrison, Trustee, 30 Winmer Avenue, Winterton-on-Sea, Great Yarmouth NR29 4BA (01493 393975; email: haroldmoorhousecharity@yahoo.co.uk)

CC number: 287278

Eligibility

Individuals in need who live in Burnham Market in Norfolk only.

Types of grants

One-off grants are made ranging from £50 to £200 for educational equipment and school educational trips.

Annual grant total

In 2015/16 the charity had an income of £21,500 and a total expenditure of £19,000. We estimate that grants given to individuals totalled around £9,000.

Applications

Applications can be made in writing to the correspondent. They should be submitted directly by the individual in any month.

Norfolk Community Foundation

£58,500

Correspondent: Grants Team, St James Mill, Whitefriars, Norwich, Norfolk NR3 1SH (01603 623958; email: grants@norfolkfoundation.com; website: www.norfolkfoundation.com)

CC number: 1110817

Eligibility

Individuals living in Norfolk.

Types of grants

The foundation operates a several funds that support individuals up the age of 25. Grants are available for (volunteer) training, transport, equipment, sports coach development and support for elite athletes.

Annual grant total

In 2016 the foundation had assets of £21.9 million and an income of £5.2 million. The amount of grants given to individuals totalled £78,000. We estimate that around £58,500 was given for education.

Applications

Application forms are available to download from the foundation's website

and should be returned by email to the relevant grants officer.

The Charity of Sir John Picto and Others

£750

Correspondent: Stephen Pipe, Correspondent, Beam End, Mill Street, Buxton, Norwich NR10 5JE (01603 279823; email: stephenpipe@live.co.uk)

CC number: 208896

Eligibility

People in need who live in the parish of Buxton Lamas, Little Hautbois, Brampton and Oxmead.

Types of grants

One-off grants of £100 to £200 to schoolchildren for uniforms/clothing, books and excursions and to college students, undergraduates, vocational students, mature students and people starting work towards books.

Annual grant total

In 2015/16 the charity had an income of £34,500 and a total expenditure of £10,000. We estimate that grants given to individuals for educational purposes totalled £750.

Applications

Applications may be made in writing to the correspondent directly by the individual or a family member, or through a third party, such as a social worker or teacher. Applications are considered at any time.

Other information

Grants are also available for social welfare purposes and to organisations or groups within the parish boundary.

The Sir Philip Reckitt Educational Trust Fund
See entry on page 42

The Foundation of Joanna Scott and Others

£85,500

Correspondent: Sam Loombe, Clerk to the Trustees, Hansells, 13–14 The Close, Norwich NR1 4DS (01603 632225; email: secretary@foundationofjoannascott.org.uk; website: www.foundationofjoannascott.org.uk)

CC number: 311253

Eligibility

People under the age of 25 who are being educated or live within five miles of Norwich City Hall. Preference is given to families in financial need.

Types of grants

Grants are given towards the costs of uniforms/other school clothing, books, equipment/instruments, fees, maintenance/living expenses, childcare, educational outings in the UK, study or travel abroad and student exchanges. The trust also offers interest-free loans.

Annual grant total

In 2015/16 the foundation had assets of £2.4 million, an income of £76,500 and made grants to individuals totalling £85,500. There were also grants made to organisations totalling £6,100.

Applications

Application forms are available from the foundation's website and can be posted or sent via email.

Other information

Grants are also given to organisations and schools.

The Shelroy Charitable Trust

£4,000

Correspondent: Norfolk Community Foundation, St James Mill, Whitefriars, Norwich NR3 1TN (01603 623958; fax: 01603 230036; email: jennybevan@ norfolkfoundation.com)

CC number: 327776

Eligibility

Young people who live in Norfolk. Preference is given to those studying medicine or religion.

Types of grants

One-off grants to support costs associated with education.

Annual grant total

In 2015/16 the trust had an income of £3,000 and a total expenditure of £12,000. We estimate the amount awarded in grants to individuals for education was £4,000.

Applications

An online application process is available at www.norfolkfoundation.com/funds/ shelroy-charitable-trust-fund.

Applications can also be made in writing to the correspondent if preferred.

Other information

The charity also awards funds to individuals for welfare purposes, and to local organisations.

As of October 2014, the charity has been administered by Norfolk Community Foundation.

Breckland

The Garboldisham Parish Charities

£2,000

Correspondent: Mr P. Girling, Treasurer, Sandale, Smallworth Common, Garboldisham, Diss IP22 2QW (01953 681646; email: pandw6@btinternet.com)

CC number: 210250

Eligibility

People under 25 who have lived in Garboldisham for at least two years.

Types of grants

One-off and ongoing grants, including gifts in kind, are given to school leavers and those continuing their education. Grants given include those for uniforms/ clothing, study/travel abroad, books, equipment/instruments and maintenance/living expenses. Grants are usually in the range of £30 to £600.

Annual grant total

In 2016/17 the charity had an income of £8,900 and a total expenditure of £8,000 Grants are made to individuals and organisations for educational and social welfare purposes. We estimate that educational grants to individuals totalled £2,000.

Applications

Applications can be submitted directly by the individual including specific details of what the grant is required for. They are usually considered in July and December.

Swaffham Relief in Need Charity

£3,500

Correspondent: Richard Bishop, Town Clerk, The Town Hall, Swaffham, Norfolk PE37 7DQ (01760 722922; email: reliefinneed@ swaffhamtowncouncil.gov.uk; website: swaffhamtowncouncil.gov.uk)

CC number: 1072912

Eligibility

People in need who have lived in Swaffham for at least 12 months.

Types of grants

Grants are given for welfare purposes, including for school uniforms, clothing and other necessities for those returning to work and to people who are re-entering education and need help with the cost of books, for example.

Annual grant total

In 2015/16 the charity had an income of £6,000 and a total expenditure of £7,300. We estimate that around £3,500 was given in grants to individuals for educational purposes.

Applications

Application forms are available to download from the charity's website. The trustees meet six times a year to consider applications – in January, March, May, July, September and November.

Other information

Information on the charity is available from the Swaffham Town Council website. The charity supports both individuals and organisations for social welfare and educational needs.

Broadland

Educational Foundation of Alderman John Norman

£149,135 (364 grants)

Correspondent: Jo Chaney, Membership Secretary, The Atrium, St George's Street, Norwich NR3 1AB (01603 629871; email: grants@ normanfoundation.org; website: wp.normanfoundation.org.uk)

CC number: 313105

Eligibility

Young people descended from Alderman John Norman, who are residing in the parish of Old Catton or the city of Norwich and if funds permit, Norfolk. Children are supported from the age of seven through to the completion of higher education (at the normal school leaving age). Grants are also available for first level university degree courses.

Types of grants

Annual grants for children who hold a pedigree, see more about this in the Applications section.

Annual grant total

In 2015/16 the foundation held assets of £7.5 million and had an income of £278,500. Grants were made to 364 individuals descended from Alderman John Norman and totalled £110,000 with a further £39,500 awarded to residents of Old Catton. The foundation also makes grants to local educational organisations in the beneficial area (£114,500 in 2015/16).

Applications

Individuals must first prove that they are direct descendants from the beneficiaries listed in the First Schedule of the will.

Contact the Claimants Unity who will assist you with establishing a pedigree. The trustees meet at the start of the year to confirm grants for the forthcoming academic year starting in September and should be contacted before applying.

King's Lynn and West Norfolk

The Brancaster Educational and Almshouse Charity

£1,500

Correspondent: Jane Gould, Brette Cottage, Cross Lane, Brancaster, King's Lynn PE31 8AW (01485 210721; email: jjgould10@gmail.com)

CC number: 311128

Eligibility

People living in the ancient parishes of Brancaster, Titchwell, Thornham, and Burnham Deepdale only.

Types of grants

Small grants are made to schoolchildren for educational necessities, such as books and equipment.

Annual grant total

In 2016 the charity had an income of £11,000 and a total expenditure of £5,200. We estimate the total amount awarded in grants to individuals for educational purposes was £1,500.

Applications

Apply in writing to the correspondent.

Other information

The charity also awards grants to local schools for benefits not provided by the local authority. The charity also uses income for the running and maintenance of their owned almshouses, and the care of the residents there.

Richard Bunting's Educational Foundation (The Bunting's Fund)

£5,200

Correspondent: Christopher Padley, Hedges, Creake Road, Burnham Thorpe, King's Lynn, Norfolk PE31 8HW (01328 730258; email: padleychris@btinternet. com)

CC number: 311175

Eligibility

Children and young people in need who are under the age of 25 and live in the parish of Burnham Thorpe.

Types of grants

The foundation provides grants, scholarships, bursaries and maintenance allowances to individuals at school, university or any other educational establishment. Financial assistance is available towards the cost of clothing, school uniforms, books, equipment/ instruments, tools, educational outings, travel/study abroad, student exchange and other educational necessities or expenses. People entering a trade/ starting work and students of music or other arts are also supported. Our research shows that grants cover up to £400.

Annual grant total

In 2015/16 the foundation had an income of £4,400 and a total expenditure of £6,000. The amount awarded in grants for education was £5,200.

Applications

Apply in writing to the correspondent. Our research suggests that applications can be made either directly by the individual (if over 18) or by a parent/ guardian. Applications are normally considered in February and September, but emergencies can be dealt with on an ongoing basis.

Other information

The foundation can give financial assistance towards the provision of facilities for recreation, social or physical training for students in primary, secondary or further education, where these are not normally provided by the local authorities.

Hall's Exhibition Foundation

£68,500 (85+ grants)

Correspondent: Christopher Holt, Administrator, 4 Bewick Close, Snettisham, King's Lynn, Norfolk PE31 7PJ (01485 541534; email: mail@ chrisholtphotographic.co.uk; website: www.hallsfoundation.co.uk)

CC number: 325128

Eligibility

People between the ages of 11 and 25 (as of 1 September in the year of the course) who have been resident in the village of Snettisham for at least one year and are in need for financial assistance.

Types of grants

Grants are available to the following categories:

- Students over the age of 11 moving on to secondary education can be awarded grants of up to £200
- Young people over the age of 16 going on to further education/ undertaking A-levels or training

courses can be awarded grants of up to £200 per each year of the course
- Students over the age of 18 undertaking higher education at universities/colleges can be awarded grants of up to £1,600 per each year of the course (this payment will be awarded in two separate grants)
- Students on further degree or postgraduate courses can be awarded grants of up to £1,000

From the charity's website:

Grants are awarded to assist students in their secondary and further education courses. They are in addition to any local authority or state entitlement. Grants are not linked in any way to any national or local government education authority policy. It is up to the individual student, with input from parent/guardian as appropriate, to decide just how the money is spent be it on books, materials, uniform/dress, travel costs or, in the case of university students, accommodation costs.

Annual grant total

In 2015/16 the foundation held assets of almost £1.5 million and had an income of £71,500. Grants to over 85 individuals totalled £60,000. The grants were distributed in the following categories:

Students undertaking university/ HE courses	37	£50,500
Students undertaking sixth form/ FE education courses	36	£7,200
Pupils moving from primary to secondary school	12	£2,400
Other grants	-	£125

Exclusions

No additional grants are made for word processors, computers, normal travelling expenses or work experience costs. Grants must be returned if any year of the course is not completed.

Applications

Application forms are available on the foundation's website or can be requested from the correspondent. More application forms are also distributed in the local area. They can be submitted either directly by the individual or through a third party.

Hilgay United Charities (Non-Ecclesiastical Branch)

£1,500

Correspondent: Mr A. Hall, Windrush, Church Road, Ten Mile Bank, Downham Market, Norfolk PE38 0EJ (01366 377127; email: hilgay.feoffees@aol.com)

CC number: 208898

Eligibility

People starting an apprenticeship or work who live in the parish of Hilgay.

Types of grants

One-off and ongoing grants towards apprenticeships or training to help individuals enter employment.

Annual grant total

In 2015 the charity had an income of £23,000 and a total expenditure of £22,500. Research has found that grants to individuals have, in the past, totalled around £2,000 with 75% going to education, training and apprenticeships, and the remainder for general grants.

Applications

Individuals can apply to the correspondent in writing. Applications are considered in June each year.

Other information

The charity also supports the maintenance of two village halls.

The King's Lynn General Educational Foundation

£500

Correspondent: Andrew Cave, 27–29 Old Market, Wisbech, Cambridgeshire PE13 1NE (01945 582547; email: gina.borrmann@wheelers.co.uk)

CC number: 311104

Eligibility

People aged under 25 who have lived in the borough of King's Lynn for not less than two years, or those who have attended school in the borough for not less than two years, who are going on to further education.

Types of grants

One-off grants of £75 to £200 for people at school, college or university or any other further education institution towards the cost of books, equipment, fees and living expenses.

Annual grant total

In 2016 the foundation had an income of £2,200 and a total expenditure of £800. We estimate that educational grants to individuals totalled £500.

Applications

Application forms are available from R G Pannell, 21 Baldwin Road, King's Lynn, Norfolk PE30 4AL, to be submitted by 30 August each year. The application should be supported by the applicant's previous educational establishment.

Sir Edmund Moundeford Charity

£4,300

Correspondent: Barry Hawkins, The Estate Office, 15 Lynn Road, Downham Market, Norfolk PE38 9NL (01366 387180)

CC number: 1075097

Eligibility

Individuals in need who live in Feltwell.

Types of grants

One-off cash grants and grants in kind are made to university students who live in Feltwell (and who are former pupils of Feltwell School) to purchase books, as well as to assist school leavers.

Annual grant total

In 2015 the charity had assets of £6.3 million and an income of £128,00. Grants totalled £33,500. Individuals received grants totalling £13,800 for both social welfare and educational purposes. They were distributed as follows:

Fuel grants (Christmas)	£9,300
Student grants	£2,700
School leavers	£1,000
Almshouse tenants	£800

Applications

Applications can be made writing to the correspondent either directly by the individual or through an organisation such as Citizens Advice or a school. Applications are considered at meetings held quarterly.

Other information

The main purpose of this charity is the provision of almshouse accommodation.

South Creake Charities

£3,500

Correspondent: Susan Hart, 26 Front Street, South Creake, Fakenham NR21 9PE (01328 823515; email: sccharities@hotmail.co.uk)

CC number: 210090

Eligibility

People in further or higher education who are in need and live in South Creake, Norfolk. Help may also be available to younger children.

Types of grants

One-off grants range from £100 to £200 and are given to help further and higher education students with the cost of books, equipment/instruments, fees and educational outings in the UK. Younger children may be assisted with the cost of educational projects or field trips.

Individuals can apply for a grant in each year of their studies.

Annual grant total

In 2015/16 the charities had an income of £5,800 and a total expenditure of £8,000. We estimate that grants awarded to individuals for educational purposes totalled around £2,600.

Applications

Applications may be made in writing to the correspondent. They can be submitted directly by the individual and are considered in November (any requests should be received before the end of October).

Other information

Grants are given for both educational and social welfare purposes. Our research suggests that occasional awards may also be made to schools and playgroups.

Town Lands Educational Foundation (Outwell Town Lands Educational Foundation)

£3,000

Correspondent: Debbie Newton, 90 Wisbech Road, Outwell, Wisbech PE14 8PF (01945 774327; email: outwellpc@btinternet.com)

CC number: 311211

Eligibility

People who live in the ancient parish of Outwell.

Types of grants

Recurrent grants are usually made to: those staying at school beyond normal school-leaving age; those attending courses of further education at various colleges (e.g. agricultural, technical and teacher training) and universities; those taking an apprenticeship course or other work leading to a trade qualification. Grants are awarded for general educational purposes.

Annual grant total

In 2016 the foundation had an income of £7,600 and a total expenditure of £3,800. We estimate that about £3,000 was given in grants for educational purposes.

Applications

Applications can be made on a form available from the correspondent. Our research suggests that applications should be submitted directly by the individual in September for consideration in October. Proof of satisfactory attendance may be requested. Grants are paid at the end of January.

Other information

Some support is also given to older people in the local area at Christmas.

Walpole St Peter Poor's Estate

£1,800

Correspondent: Edward Otter, Correspondent, 1 Sutton Meadows, Leverington, Wisbech, Cambridgeshire PE13 5ED (01945 665018)

CC number: 233207

Eligibility

Full-time students in need aged 16 or over attending college or university who live in the old parishes of Walpole St Peter, Walpole Highway and Walpole Marsh.

Types of grants

One-off and recurrent grants are made for educational necessities.

Annual grant total

In 2015 the charity had an income of £4,900 and a total expenditure of £3,800. We estimate that grants for educational purposes totalled around £1,800.

Applications

Applications may be made in writing to the correspondent. They can be submitted directly by the individual and are generally considered in November.

Other information

Grants are also made to older people.

West Norfolk and King's Lynn Girls' School Trust

£22,500 (29 grants)

Correspondent: Miriam Aldous, Clerk, The Goodshed, Station Road, Little Dunham, King's Lynn PE32 2DJ (01760 720617; website: www.wnklgirlsschoolstrust.org.uk)

CC number: 311264

Eligibility

Girls and young women over the age of 11 who are at a secondary school or in their first years after leaving school or further education, who live in the borough of King's Lynn and West Norfolk. Awards to older candidates will be made in exceptional circumstances.

Types of grants

One-off and recurrent grants. Grants are provided for school uniforms, books, equipment/instruments, and educational outings in the UK and overseas.

Annual grant total

In 2015/16 the trust held assets of £297,500 and had an income of £27,000. Grants were made to 29 individuals totalling £22,500.

Applications

Apply on a form available on the trust's website. Application forms should be completed together with a supporting letter outlining the proposed venture or study course, and include two independent references, one of which must be a teacher or tutor who can vouch for the suitability of the course.

Other information

This trust also gives grants to secondary schools within the area.

North Norfolk

Saxlingham United Charities

£5,000

Correspondent: Julie Queen, Correspondent, 22 Henry Preston Road, Tasburgh, Norwich NR15 1NU (01508 470759; email: saxlingham.uc@gmail.com)

CC number: 244713

Eligibility

People who live in the parish of Saxlingham. Our research suggests that applicants for educational support must be under the age of 21 and have lived in the parish for at least five years.

Types of grants

Grants of £50 to £100 are made towards the cost of books, clothing or tools to young people starting work or in further or higher education.

Annual grant total

In 2015/16 the charity had an income of £7,300 and a total expenditure of £11,200. We estimate the amount of grants for educational purposes totalled around £5,000.

Applications

Applications may be made in writing to the correspondent. They can be submitted directly by the individual and are usually considered in October.

Other information

Grants are made for both welfare and educational purposes.

Norwich

Anguish's Educational Foundation

£433,500 (2,288 grants)

Correspondent: David Hynes, 1 Woolgate Court, St Benedicts Street, Norwich NR2 4AP (01603 621023; email: david.hynes@norwichcharitabletrusts.org.uk; website: www.anguishseducationalfoundation.org.uk)

CC number: 311288

Eligibility

Individuals under the age of 25 who have been residents of the city of Norwich and the parishes of Costessey, Hellesdon, Catton, Sprowston, Thorpe and Corpusty for at least two years.

Preference is given to individuals who have lost either one or both parents. Household income should not exceed £29,980 per year (£575 per week). A further allowance is made for young people in families of up to ten children in total.

Types of grants

Grants are mainly awarded to cover the cost of school uniforms. Residential school trips (minus a contribution from parents, depending on weekly income), university maintenance, personal tuition, and specialist glasses are also covered by grants from the trust.

Annual grant total

In 2015/16 the foundation held assets of £21 million and had an income of £886,500. Grants totalling £433,500 were made to 2,288 individuals, as follows:

School clothing	£161,000
University maintenance	£113,500
Further education (includes grants in lieu of Educational Maintenance Allowance)	£65,000
Educational travel	£64,000
College fees	£26,500
Books, equipment and trade tools	£1,900
Dyslexia, scotopic sensitivity and childminding	£800
Music and dance training	£500

Exclusions

Postgraduates are not supported.

Applications

There is no formal application form to complete. Applicants are required to write to the registered address, telephone the trust, or send an email. You will then be given an interview with a Grants Officer and will be required to detail your personal or family income. You must take copies of evidence of your income, e.g. letters, wage slips etc.

Other information

The foundation also made grant payments totalling £75,500 to 13 other organisations across Norwich.

Norwich French Church Charity

£16,500

Correspondent: Samantha Loombe, Clerk, Hansells Solicitors, 13–14 The Close, Norwich NR1 4DS (01603 275814; email: samanthaloombe@hansells.co.uk; website: www.norwichfrenchchurch charity.org.uk)

CC number: 212897

Eligibility

Children and young people up to the age of 25 who are resident in Norwich. Priority is given to those who are of Huguenot descent and then to those whose education or training is threatened by financial difficulty.

Types of grants

Grants, ranging from £250 to £500, for schoolchildren and college students for uniforms/other school clothing, books, equipment/instruments, maintenance/ living expenses, childcare, educational outings in the UK, study or travel abroad, etc.

Annual grant total

In 2015 the charity had an income of £14,000 and a total expenditure of £17,100. We estimate that grants given to individuals totalled around £16,500.

At the time of writing (November 2017) the latest financial information available was from 2015.

Applications

Applications can be submitted using the online form on the website or by downloading a printable application form. Applications should be accompanied by a covering letter about your circumstances as well as evidence of the education to be undertaken.

Norwich Town Close Estate Charity

£73,500

Correspondent: David Walker, Clerk to the Trustees, 1 Woolgate Court, St Benedicts Street, Norwich NR2 4AP (01603 621023; email: info@ norwichcharitabletrusts.org.uk; website: www.norwichcharitabletrusts.org.uk)

CC number: 235678

Eligibility

People under the age of 25 living in Norwich. Priority is given to freemen and their dependants.

Types of grants

Grants are given to schoolchildren, further and higher education students, including mature students and postgraduates. Support may cover school clothing and school trips, further education and apprenticeship costs, university maintenance/living expenses, travel costs, postgraduate studies or music, dance and sports tuition (provided applicants are likely to reach a professional standard).

Annual grant total

In 2015/16 the charity had assets of £24 million and an income of £924,500. Educational grants to individuals totalled £73,500.

Exclusions

Day outings are not assisted (only residential trips).

Applications

Applications may be made in writing to the correspondent. Our research suggests that they should be submitted by June/ early July each year for consideration in August.

Other information

This is one of the three grant-making charities under the Norwich Charitable Trusts (others are Norwich Consolidated Charities and Anguish Educational Foundation).

The annual report for 2015/16 states that 'no eligible applicant has been refused a grant for lack of available funds'.

Sir Peter Seaman's Charity

£12,000

Correspondent: Andrew Barnes, Great Hospital, Bishopgate, Norwich NR1 4EL (01603 622022; email: andrewbarnes@ greathospital.org; website: www. greathospital.org.uk/charities/peter- seaman-charity.htm)

CC number: 311101

Eligibility

People under the age of 21 who live in Norwich.

Types of grants

Grants can be given towards all kinds of educational purposes. There is no upper limit for the grant amount, but funding for more than £1,500 is unlikely.

Annual grant total

In 2015/16 the charity had an income of £21,000 and a total expenditure of £16,000. We estimate that grants given

to individuals totalled approximately £12,000.

Exclusions

Applications for salaries and/or general costs will not be considered.

Applications

Application forms can be accessed on the charity's web page. Applications can be submitted at any time, the trustees meet four times a year for consideration.

Applications towards a specific project are more likely to be supported by the trustees.

Applicants must wait one year before applying again.

Other information

Awards may also be made 'to charitable organisations which support the educational and other needs of young persons living in Norwich'.

South Norfolk

The Sir John Sedley Educational Foundation

£5,000

Correspondent: Elaine Everington, Clerk to the Trustees, 29 Mill Grove, Whissendine, Oakham, Leicestershire LE15 7EY (01664 474593; email: ellemai@btinternet.com)

CC number: 527884

Eligibility

People under the age of 25 in further and higher education living in the parish of Wymondham and peripheral areas. Young people in work are also eligible for support.

Types of grants

The foundation provides scholarships, bursaries, financial assistance towards the cost of books, clothing, equipment/ instruments and travel costs. Financial help is also available for people starting work/entering a trade.

Annual grant total

In 2015/16 the foundation had an income of £14,900 and a total expenditure of £10,700. We estimate that grants given to individuals totalled around £5,000.

Applications

Apply in writing to the correspondent, including a quotation for requested items where possible. For further information, contact the clerk.

Other information

The trustees have a discretionary power to allocate up to one quarter of the income towards the benefit of the local schools. The foundation also supports charitable organisations and maintains a hall for the benefit of the local area.

The Town Estate Educational Foundation (Hempnall)

£5,500

Correspondent: David Hook, Trustee, 1 Freemasons Cottage, Mill Road, Hempnall, Norwich NR15 2LP (01508 498187)

CC number: 311218

Eligibility
People under the age of 25 who live in Hempnall and have done so for a year.

Types of grants
Grants are made to help with:
- Costs of educational outings for schoolchildren
- Expenses incurred while at college or university such as books, help with fees and study or travel abroad
- Help with the cost of vocational courses
- Other activities, including athletic expenses and the study of the arts

Annual grant total
In 2016 the foundation had an income of £16,900 and a total expenditure of £12,000. We have estimated that educational grants to individuals totalled £5,500, with funding also awarded to the village primary school and other organisations.

Applications
Apply in writing to the correspondent, including evidence of the course being taken and relevant receipts.

Woodton United Charities

£900

Correspondent: Daphne Littleboy, 34 The Ridings, Poringland, Norwich NR14 7GE (01508 494318)

CC number: 207531

Eligibility
People in need who live in the parish of Woodton. The charity is particularly interested in supporting young people undertaking apprenticeships or going on to further/higher education.

Types of grants
One-off and recurrent grants can be given according to need, mainly for books and equipment. Previous grants have included tools for an apprentice and books for an A-level student.

Annual grant total
In 2015 the charity had an income of £4,200 and a total expenditure of £3,900. We estimate that educational support to individuals totalled around £900.

Applications
Applications may be made in writing to the correspondent. They can be submitted at any time directly by the individual, including full details and nature of the need.

Other information
Grants are also given for welfare causes.

Suffolk

The Annie Tranmer Charitable Trust

£17,000 (22 grants)

Correspondent: Anne-Marie Williams, 55 Dobbs Lane, Kesgrave, Ipswich IP5 2QA (07801556002; email: amwilliams7903@gmail.com)

CC number: 1044231

Eligibility
Young people who live in Suffolk who are keen to develop their physical, mental and spiritual capacities through their leisure time activities.

Types of grants
One-off and recurrent grants are given according to need, towards activities which seek to increase education attainment, for example educational outings, fees, equipment/instruments and travel overseas.

Annual grant total
In 2015/16 the trust held assets of £3.5 million, and an income of £120,500. A total of £17,000 was awarded in grants to individuals.

Applications
Apply in writing to the correspondent, including details of the specific need, finances and alternative funding sources.

Other information
Grants are also made to other local agencies for the benefit of individuals.

Ann Beaumont's Educational Foundation

£12,000

Correspondent: Rose Welham, Correspondent, 55 Castle Road, Hadleigh, Ipswich IP7 6JP (email: rosewelham55@aol.com)

CC number: 310397

Eligibility
Students under the age of 25 years who are in need of financial assistance and live in the parish of Hadleigh.

Types of grants
Grants to help with course books, equipment or educational trips for people at school, college, university or those starting work.

Annual grant total
In 2015/16 the foundation had assets of £1.6 million and an income of £41,500. The total amount awarded in grants to individuals was £12,000.

Applications
Applications are to be requested from the correspondent.

Other information
A further £11,000 was donated in grants to organisations.

Calthorpe and Edwards Educational Foundation

£8,500

Correspondent: R. Boswell, Chegwidden, Beauford Road, Ingham, Bury St Edmunds IP31 1NW (01284 728288; email: rgboswell@care4free.net)

CC number: 310464

Eligibility
People between the ages of 16 and 25, who are attending a further or higher educational institution, including NVQ study.

The applicant must live in one of the parishes of Ampton, Great Livermere, Little Livermere, Ingham, Timworth, Troston, Ixworth, Culford, Great Barton, West Stow, Wordwell, Fornham St Genevieve or Fornham St Martin.

Types of grants
A maximum of £360 per year per student supported, to assist with costs associated with books and equipment.

Annual grant total
In 2015/16 the foundation had an income of £9,500 and a total expenditure of £9,000. We estimate the total amount awarded in grants to individuals was £8,500.

Applications
Application forms can be requested form the correspondent or are available to download from the Thurston Community College website. The application deadline is 15 September.

The Mills Educational Foundation

£11,400

Correspondent: Bob Snell, PO BOX 1703, Framlingham, Woodbridge, Suffolk IP13 9WW (01728 685031; email: themillscharity@btconnect.com; website: www.themillscharity.co.uk)

CC number: 310475

Eligibility

Children and young people up to the age of 24 who live in Framlingham and the surrounding district, or attend a school there. Each application is based on merit, not all requests are agreed.

Types of grants

One-off grants ranging from £50 to £550. Schoolchildren and further/higher education students can be supported for uniforms, other school clothing, books, equipment, instruments, educational outings in the UK and study or travel abroad. People starting work can receive grants for uniforms, other clothing, equipment and instruments.

Annual grant total

In 2015/16 the foundation had an income of £56,800 and a total expenditure of £42,800. Grants given totalled £11,400.

Applications

Apply in writing to the correspondent, the trustees meet every two months.

Other information

Local schools are supported including: Thomas Mills High School, Framlingham Primary School, Meadow Brook Centre, Dennington Primary School, Framlingham Area Youth Action Partnership (FAYAP).

David Randall Foundation
See entry on page 223

Babergh

The Charity of Joseph Catt

£2,500

Correspondent: Keith Bales, Trustee, 34 Cattsfield, Stutton, Ipswich IP9 2SP (01473 328179)

CC number: 213013

Eligibility

People in need who live in the parish of Stutton.

Types of grants

One-off grants and loans are given according to need.

Annual grant total

In 2016 the charity had an income of £10,900 and a total expenditure of £5,000. Grants are made to individuals for a range of purposes. We estimate that educational grants totalled £2,500.

Applications

Applications can be submitted by the individual, or through a recognised referral agency (e.g. social worker, Citizens Advice or doctor).

Forest Heath

George Goward and John Evans

£21,300 (35 grants)

Correspondent: Laura Williams, 8 Woodcutters Way, Lakenheath, Brandon, Suffolk IP27 9JQ (07796 018816; email: laurawill@btinternet.com)

CC number: 253727

Eligibility

People under the age of 25 who live in the parish of Lakenheath, Suffolk.

Types of grants

Support can be given for people leaving school/starting work for equipment and other necessities and to further/higher education students to help with the maintenance/living expenses and books. Schoolchildren can also receive grants towards uniforms, clothing and educational outings.

Annual grant total

In 2015 the charity had assets of £1.7 million and an income of £37,000. Educational grants to 35 individuals totalled £21,300.

Applications

Applications can be made in writing to the correspondent. They can be submitted either directly by the individual or through a third party, such as a family member, social worker, teacher, or an organisation, such as Citizens Advice. Applications should generally be submitted by February and August for consideration in March and September, respectively. Candidates should provide brief details of their financial situation and include receipts for the items purchased.

Other information

One-eighth of the charity's income is allocated to Soham United Charities. Grants are also made to other organisations, local primary, secondary, nursery and Sunday schools, and to individuals for welfare purposes.

Ipswich

Hope House and Gippeswyk Educational Trust

£7,900

Correspondent: John Clements, Trustee, 4 Church Meadows, Henley, Ipswich IP6 0RP (email: clements4henley@aol.com)

CC number: 1068441

Eligibility

Children and young people in need who are under the age of 21 and live in Ipswich or the surrounding area.

Types of grants

One-off grants towards the costs of school uniforms/clothing, books, educational outings, travel, fees, maintenance/living expenses and other necessities.

Annual grant total

In 2016/17 the trust had an income of £12,300 and a total expenditure of £16,300. The trust also supports organisations, therefore we have estimated that grants to individuals totalled £7,900.

Applications

Apply in writing to the correspondent. Our research indicates that applications should be submitted through the individual's school/college or welfare agency, if applicable, for consideration throughout the year.

Other information

Financial assistance can be given to both individuals and organisations.

Mid Suffolk

Earl Stonham Trust

£1,000

Correspondent: Sam Wilson, Trustee, College Farm, Forward Green, Stowmarket, Suffolk IP14 5EH (01449 711497)

CC number: 213006

Eligibility

People with educational needs who live, or whose parents live, in the parish of Earl Stonham.

Types of grants

One-off grants are given up to a maximum of £200.

Annual grant total

In 2015/16 the trust had an income of £6,000 and a total expenditure of £5,000. We estimate that educational grants to individuals totalled around £1,000.

Applications

Individuals can apply in writing to the trust directly.

Gislingham United Charity

£18,000

Correspondent: Sheila Eade, Woodberry, High Street, Gislingham, Suffolk IP23 8JD (01379 783541; email: gislinghamunitedcharity@gmail.com; website: gislingham.onesuffolk.net/organisations/gislingham-united-charity)

CC number: 208340

Eligibility

People in need who live in Gislingham. A few years ago the trustees extended the eligibility for support from children under the age of 18 to 'any resident of Gislingham who genuinely needs help towards the cost of education'.

Types of grants

Grants are given to school excursions and necessities, college or university fees, vocational education, re-training and other educational needs.

Annual grant total

In 2016 the charity had an income of £17,100 and a total expenditure of £24,500. In previous years around 90% of grants were given for education. We therefore estimate that around £18,000 was given in educational grants.

Applications

Apply in writing to the correspondent.

Other information

The charity gives educational grants (Education Branch – the largest division), grants to individuals in need (Non-Ecclesiastical Branch) and supports ecclesiastical causes (Ecclesiastical Branch – the smallest division). Village organisations are also assisted.

The Non-Ecclesiastical Branch is divided into two 'moieties': 'for the relief of residents of Gislingham in need, hardship or distress' and 'for the provision and maintenance of facilities for recreation or other charitable purposes for the benefit of the inhabitants of the Parish of Gislingham'.

The Mendlesham Education Foundation

£13,000 (34 grants)

Correspondent: Shirley Furze, Clerk, Beggars Roost, Church Road, Mendlesham, Stowmarket IP14 5SF

CC number: 271762

Eligibility

People under 25 who live in the parish of Mendlesham.

Types of grants

It appears that grants are mainly given to further and higher education students.

Annual grant total

In 2015 the foundation had assets of £691,500 and an income of £26,000. Grants were awarded to 34 individuals and nine organisations, totalling £26,000 altogether. We estimate that grants given to individuals totalled around £13,000.

Exclusions

Grants are not given for school fees or maintenance. They are not normally available towards the cost of school educational outings or for special education needs.

Applications

Apply on a form available from the correspondent, including details of education to date, details of course to be taken, other grants applied for, estimated expenditure, parents' financial position and other dependent children in the family. Applications should be made by the individual or through a parent/guardian by mid-September.

Other information

Grants are also made to organisations and schools.

St Edmundsbury

Hundon Educational Foundation

£6,000

Correspondent: Bernard Beer, Beauford Lodge, Mill Road, Hundon, Sudbury CO10 8EG (01440 786942; email: beaufordlodge@hotmail.com)

CC number: 310379

Eligibility

Children and young people under the age of 25 living in the parish of Hundon.

Types of grants

Financial support is available to pre-schoolchildren, school pupils, further/higher education students, people in training and those starting work/entering a trade. Grants are given towards the costs of the course fees, educational outings/visits and for general educational purposes, including books, clothing, equipment/instruments.

Annual grant total

In 2016 the foundation had an income of £5,800 and had a total expenditure of £7,000. We have estimated that grants totalled £6,000 during the year.

Exclusions

The foundation is strictly limited to beneficiaries within the specified area.

Applications

Apply in writing to the correspondent. Applications can be submitted by individuals directly or by their parent/guardian. The trustees meet two or three times a year. Our research suggests that the trust is well advertised in the village. Applications are considered in March, July and November and should be received in the preceding month.

Pakenham Educational Trust

£2,500

Correspondent: Sally Smith, Clerk, 13 Manor Garth, Pakenham, Bury St Edmunds, Suffolk IP31 2LB (01359 239431)

CC number: 310364

Eligibility

Residents of the parish of Pakenham who are undertaking post-school education or training and require financial assistance.

Types of grants

Small grants (normally in the range of £50 to £300) are given to people attending university and college courses or vocational training, including apprenticeships. Support can be given for general educational needs, including books, equipment, tools, accommodation and fees. Grants may also be given towards activities such as Duke of Edinburgh Award Scheme, cathedral camps, sports scholarships and other purposes.

Annual grant total

In 2016 the trust had an income of £5,400 and a total expenditure of £5,500. We estimate that grants given to individuals for educational purposes totalled around £2,500.

Applications

Application forms can be obtained from the correspondent or the Pakenham post office. They can be submitted directly by individuals by mid-November. The trustees meet in early December to consider applications but if necessary, urgent meetings can also be held in mid-summer.

Other information

Grants are also given to local schools and organisations for educational causes.

The Risby Fuel Allotment

£500

Correspondent: Penelope Wallis, Trustee, 3 Woodland Close, Risby, Bury St Edmunds IP28 6QN (01284 81064)

CC number: 212260

Eligibility

People in need who live in the parish of Risby.

Types of grants

Grants are given to higher education students.

Annual grant total

In 2015/16 the charity had an income of £7,300 and a total expenditure of £8,200. Grants are made predominantly for relief-in-need purposes. They are also made to organisations. We estimate that educational grants to individuals totalled £500.

Applications

Apply in writing to the correspondent. Applications can be submitted by the individual.

Suffolk Coastal

The Dennington Consolidated Charities

£500

Correspondent: Peter Lamb, 2 The Coach House, The Square, Dennington, Woodbridge IP13 8AB (01728 638897; email: peterlamb54@googlemail.com)

CC number: 207451

Eligibility

Grants are awarded to those embarking on tertiary education and vocational training living in the village of Dennington.

Types of grants

One-off and ongoing grants.

Annual grant total

In 2016 the charity had an income of £17,000 and a total expenditure of £13,900. In previous years educational grants have totalled around £500.

Exclusions

The trust does not make loans, nor does it make grants where public funds are available unless they are considered inadequate.

Applications

Apply in writing to the correspondent. Applications are considered throughout the year and a simple means-test questionnaire must be completed by the applicant.

Other information

The charity also supports the maintenance of services in the parish church.

Waveney

Kirkley Poor's Land Estate

£4,900

Correspondent: Lucy Walker, Clerk to the Trustees, 4 Station Road, Lowestoft, Suffolk NR32 4QF (01502 514964; email: kirkleypoors@gmail.com; website: www.kirkleypoorslandestate.co.uk)

CC number: 210177

Eligibility

Students undertaking their first degree who live in the parish of Kirkley and are in need.

Types of grants

One-off grants of about £100 per term to help towards university degree expenses and can be for up to three years.

Annual grant total

In 2015/16 the charity had assets of £2.2 million and an income of £91,500. Educational grants to individuals totalled £4,900.

Applications

Applications can be made writing to the correspondent.

Other information

The boundaries of the parish are fully defined on the charity's website. The charity can support both individuals for welfare and educational purposes, and organisations.

Lowestoft Church and Town Educational Foundation

£18,200 (91 grants)

Correspondent: Matthew Breeze, Clerk, Lowestoft Charity Board, c/o Norton Peskett Solicitors, 148 London Road North, Lowestoft, Suffolk NR32 1HF (01493 849200; email: m-breeze@nortonpeskett.co.uk)

CC number: 310460

Eligibility

Children and young people between the ages of 5 and 25 who live (or whose parents live) in the parish of Lowestoft and have attended school in the area for at least three years.

Types of grants

Small, one-off grants are available to schoolchildren, higher or further education students or people entering a trade/starting work. Support is given towards the cost of uniforms/clothing, books, equipment/instruments, tools, travel expenses, educational outings, study/travel abroad in pursuance of education and other general educational needs.

Annual grant total

In 2016 the foundation had assets of £236,000 and an income of £25,500. Grants to 91 individuals for educational purposes totalled £18,200, mainly for higher education students.

Applications

Application forms can be requested from the correspondent and submitted directly by the individual. The trustees meet on a quarterly basis.

Other information

Lowestoft Church and Town Educational Foundation is administered jointly with the Lowestoft Church and Town Estate Charity (CC number: 1043557), The Lowestoft Church and Town Relief in Need Charity (CC number: 1015039) and the Eleemosynary Charity of John Wilde (CC number: 261239) by Lowestoft Charity Board.

Up to a third of the foundation's funding is directed to support local schools, for purposes where assistance is not already provided by the local authority.

London

General

The Aldgate and Allhallows Foundation

£46,500 (38 grants)

Correspondent: Richard Foley, Clerk, 31 Jewry Street, London EC3N 2EY (020 7488 2489; email: aldgateandallhallows@ sirjohncass.org; website: www. aldgateallhallows.org.uk)

CC number: 312500

Eligibility

Grants are made to individuals who meet the following criteria:

- Under the age of 30 on the day their course is due to begin
- Permanently reside in Tower Hamlets or the City of London and have done so for the last three years
- Are from a low-income background
- Studying full-time in further, higher or postgraduate education for at least one year, which will result in a recognised qualification

Individuals with refugee status are eligible to apply as long as they have been granted indefinite leave to remain, or full refugee status.

Types of grants

Most of the grants made are through undergraduate bursaries at Queen Mary University. However, grants for students are other universities are considered, and can be used for payment of tuition fees, living expenses, and educational costs.

Annual grant total

In 2015/16 the foundation had assets of £7.8 million, an income of £72,000 and a total expenditure of £260,500. The amount of grants given to individuals totalled £46,500.

Exclusions

Grants are not normally given for courses at private colleges, independent schools, or courses less than a year in length.

Grants are not given towards the cost of repeated years of study, a qualification that is lower than the individual already holds (even if the subject/s or module/s are different), medical electives, or fees for higher education courses, unless they relate to a second degree and a student loan is unavailable.

Individuals with limited leave to remain in the UK can not apply.

Applications

Applications can be made in writing to the correspondent, specifying the applicant's 'name, address, phone number, email address, age, course, how long they have lived in the city of London or Tower Hamlets, how they heard about the trust, and what they need a grant for'. Eligible candidates will then be sent an application form which should include full details of their financial circumstances.

Applications can be made throughout the year.

Other information

The foundation also makes grants to educational institutions within the area. Grants to 13 institutions totalling £126,500 were made in 2015/16, including £15,000 in scholarships to the Royal Drawing School.

Sir William Boreman's Foundation

£19,500 (16 grants)

Correspondent: Andrew Mellows, The Drapers' Company, Drapers' Hall, Throgmorton Avenue, London EC2N 2DQ (020 7588 5001; fax: 020 7628 1988; email: charities@thedrapers. co.uk; website: www.thedrapers.co.uk/ Charities/Grant-making-trusts/Sir-William-Boremans-Foundation.aspx)

CC number: 312796

Eligibility

Children and young people under the age of 25 with the household income of £30,000 or less who live in the London boroughs of Greenwich and Lewisham or in the area of Newham which was formerly in the Metropolitan Borough of Woolwich.

Preference is given to the borough of Greenwich, to practising members of the Church of England and to sons and daughters of seamen, watermen and fishermen, particularly those who have served in the armed forces. Boys and young men pursuing a career in seafaring are also favoured. Applicants should be a UK national or have 'Settled' status under the terms of the Immigration Act 1971.

Types of grants

One-off grants usually of up to £1,000 are given to higher or further education students and people starting work towards living expenses, travel costs, educational necessities, books, equipment/instruments, childcare costs. Schoolchildren are eligible to assistance with the cost of the school uniforms, sports kits, travel costs and educational outings/visits.

Annual grant total

In 2015/16 the foundation held assets of £3.7 million and an income of £128,500. A total of £19,500 was awarded in educational grants to 16 individuals

Exclusions

Grants are not made for:

- Students aged over 25 or pre-schoolchildren
- Non-UK citizens and asylum seekers (only those with full refugee status may apply)
- Postgraduate students who have attained a 2:2 or lower
- Overseas study/travel or exchange visits
- Retrospective grants
- Tuition fees
- Non-education related loans or debts
- Setting up business ventures
- Performing arts courses (acting, dance, drama)
- Private school fees

Applications

Application forms can be found on the foundation's website or can be requested form the correspondent. The trustees welcome unsolicited applications which should be submitted at least four weeks before the meetings held in November,

February and June each year. Further guidelines are available on the website.

Our research suggests that applicants are expected to have applied for a grant from their local authority and to have received a decision on this before applying to the foundation. Some applicants may be asked to attend a brief interview with the governors.

Other information

The foundation also supports organisations. In 2015/16 the foundation awarded £97,500 to organisations. Beneficiaries included Lewisham Education Service, Greenwich Education Service and Volunteer Centre Lewisham.

Sir John Cass's Foundation

£147,500

Correspondent: Richard Foley, Sir John Cass's Foundation, 31 Jewry Street, London EC3N 2EY (020 7480 5884; fax: 020 7480 4268; email: contactus@ sirjohncass.org; website: www. sirjohncassfoundation.com/grants-toindividuals)

CC number: 312425

Eligibility

Individuals must:

- Be under 25 years of age
- Be from a low-income background
- Be studying full-time or part-time on a course that is at least one year in length
- Permanently live in London, or have lived there for at least one year

The London boroughs supported are: Camden; Greenwich; Hackney; Hammersmith and Fulham; Islington; Kensington and Chelsea; Lambeth; Lewisham; Newham; Southwark; Tower Hamlets; Wandsworth; Westminster and the City of London.

Types of grants

Grants are for educational costs, such as books and equipment, travel costs, living costs, tuition fee payments, second qualifications at the same level, or repeated year of study. Many of the foundation's grants are for one year, but can cover activities lasting two or three years. There is no minimum or maximum grant size – the amount requested should be the amount you need.

Annual grant total

In 2015/16 the foundation held assets of £147.6 million and had an income of £5.5 million. The total amount awarded in educational grants for individuals was £147,500.

Exclusions

Funding is not available for:

- Projects that do not meet a priority area
- Holiday projects, school trips, journeys abroad, or exchange visits
- Supplementary schools
- Independent schools
- Youth/community groups, or projects taking place in these settings
- Pre-school or nursery education
- General campaigns or appeals
- Costs for equipment or salaries that are the responsibility of the local education authority
- Substitution costs due to statutory funding withdrawal or reduction
- Retrospective costs
- Costs already covered by core funding or other grants
- Capital costs

Applications

The application process is in two stages. Applicants should download an initial enquiry form from the foundation's website, to be completed and sent back with the requested supporting documents via post. The trustees will consider the application, and you will be notified of the outcome within three weeks.

Other information

The foundation also awards funding to organisations and institutes bearing the founder's name, for example the Sir John Cass Faculty of Art, Architecture, and Design at London Metropolitan University.

The Castle Baynard Educational Foundation

£4,000

Correspondent: Catherine McGuiness, 3 Northolme Road, London N5 2UZ

CC number: 312502

Eligibility

People in need under the age of 25 who are (or whose parents are) resident or employed in the Castle of Baynard Ward of the City of London or in the former county of Middlesex, or who are/have been in full-time education at any educational establishment closely connected with the corporation of London. Preference may be given to the City of London School and The City of London School for Girls or to people with special educational needs.

Types of grants

Grants range from £100 to £500 and are available to schoolchildren, further/ higher education students and people starting work. Financial assistance is given towards the cost of books,

equipment/instruments, tools, materials, events and educational outings, clothing/ outfits, also travel expenses and research.

Annual grant total

In 2015/16 the foundation had an income of £7,000 and a total expenditure of £8,000. We estimate that grants given to individuals totalled £4,000.

Exclusions

Support is not normally available for the course fees or general maintenance.

Applications

Apply in writing to the correspondent. Applicants should provide an sae and include the following details: the purpose of the grant; a CV; evidence of financial need; and a reference of support to confirm their current educational status and financial circumstances. Applications are normally considered in March, June, September and December.

Other information

The foundation also supports a Sunday school at St Andrew by the Wardrobe, as well as exhibitions at any secondary school, teacher training college, university, or other further education institute.

The City and Diocese of London Voluntary Schools Fund

£12,500 (292 grants)

Correspondent: Inigo Woolf, Administrator, 36 Causton Street, London SW1P 4AU (020 7932 1165; email: inigo.woolf@london.anglican.org; website: www.london.anglican.org/ schools)

CC number: 312259

Eligibility

Children who are attending Church of England voluntary aided schools in the diocese of London (i.e. north of the river) for at least two years.

Types of grants

The grant is named 'Grants for School Journeys' and is available to support expenses travelling to and from school, and to cover the costs of school trips.

Annual grant total

In 2016/17 the fund had assets of £2.5 million and an income of £873,500. The total amount awarded in grants was £12,500.

Exclusions

Retrospective applications are not considered.

Applications

Application forms and supporting guidelines are available on the fund's website.

Other information

The fund also accepts group applications for school journeys.

The City of London Corporation Combined Education Charity

£39,500 (16 grants)

Correspondent: Barbara Hamilton, Head of Adult Education, Community & Children's Services, City of London, PO Box 270 EC2P 2EJ (020 7332 1755; email: adulteducation@cityoflondon.gov. uk; website: www.cityoflondon.gov.uk/ about-the-city/community-work/Pages/ central-grants-programme.aspx)

CC number: 312836

Eligibility

Further the education of people attending secondary schools or higher educational institutions in the City of London or other London boroughs.

Types of grants

Grants range between £5,000 (which must be spent in one year) and £25,000 (which must be spent in two years).

Annual grant total

In 2015/16 the charity had assets of £1 million and an income of £38,000. A total of £39,500 was awarded in bursaries to 16 individuals.

Applications

Application forms and eligibility criteria are available to download from the charity's website. Ensure you use the correct application for individuals. Funding calls and deadlines are available on the website.

Other information

This fund was previously called the Higher Education Research and Special Expenses Fund (HERSEF), which received no applications in the year 2010/11. In 2011 a new scheme was approved whereby this fund merged with Archibald Dawnay Scholarships, Robert Blair Fellowships for Applied Science and Technology and Alan Partridge Smith Trust to form the City of London Corporation Combined Education Charity (retaining the charity registration number for HERSEF).

Francon Trust

£16,500 (12 grants)

Correspondent: Colonel Derek Ivy, Administrator, Smithtown, Kirkmahoe, Dumfries DG1 1TE (01387 740455)

CC number: 1003592

Eligibility

Students in tertiary education and vocational training who were born or brought up and live in London. Support is aimed at 'school examination high achievers' entering vocational training or proceeding to first degree courses, particularly in medicine, architecture, accountancy, insurance, banking, law or other professional business or trade fields, including science and engineering.

Types of grants

Our research suggests that grants range from £1,000 to £3,000 and are normally given in the form of interest-free loans which become gifts on completion of the course after six months of employment in a related occupation. Grants may be in the form of a single payment or a series of successive payments, depending upon circumstances.

Annual grant total

In 2015/16 the trust had assets of £1.2 million and an income of £31,500. The trust awarded £33,100 in grants to 12 individuals for educational and welfare purposes during 2015/16. Therefore we estimate that the amount awarded to individuals solely for educational purposes to be around £16,550.

Applications

Applicants should contact the correspondent by sending a brief letter. Application forms will then be provided.

The trust's annual report from 2015/16 states:

> The objectives are achieved based upon guidelines established during the early years of operation in accordance with the wishes of the original benefactors. Potential students for first degree courses are selected in accordance with the guidelines, based upon applications and recommendations from headteachers in support of bright students who have little or no financial means. After application potential students are selected for interview by the Trustees to decide those that should receive support.

Other information

The number of students supported is gradually increasing.

The Canon Holmes Memorial Trust

See entry on page 265

The Hornsey Parochial Charities

£25,000

Correspondent: Lorraine Fincham, PO Box 22985, London N10 3XB (020 8352 1601; email: hornseypc@ blueyonder.co.uk; website: www. hornseycharities.com)

CC number: 229410

Eligibility

People under the age of 25 who live in Hornsey, including the parish of Clerkenwell in Haringey.

Types of grants

Grants of £75 to £1,000 are available to cover the costs incurred through education and beginning work, and can be used towards books, equipment, clothing, fees, and transport. The average grant is £500.

Annual grant total

In 2016 the charity had assets of £1.6 million and an income of £70,000. We estimate the amount awarded in grants for education and entry to work was £25,000.

Applications

Application forms are available to download from the charities' websites, to be completed and returned to the trustees via post. There is also a useful eligibility checker on the website, including eligible postcode boundaries, and a timetable of upcoming trustee meetings.

Other information

The charity also awards grants for poverty and hardship relief purposes, and to organisations for education and welfare.

The London Youth Trust

£2,000

Correspondent: The Clerk, The Worshipful Company of Carpenters, Carpenters' Hall, 1 Throgmorton Avenue, London EC2N 2JJ (020 7588 7001; email: info@carpentersco.com)

CC number: 230990–1

Eligibility

People under the age of 25 who are resident in London and are studying at the Building Crafts College.

Types of grants

Three types of grants are available:

LYT Scholarships – a small number of student fee scholarships will be provided to support students enrolled on the high fee, flagship courses at the BCC (Fine

Woodwork, Stonemasonry and Historic Building Conservation). A scholarship for one student on each of the three courses at present will cost a total of £6,500.

LYT Bursaries – a number of hardship/welfare grants will support students in training and during transition from training to employment. These bursaries will be comparatively small (typically £15 to £20 for each student in need each week at the BCC).

LYT Prizes – two LYT Prizes, of £250 each, will be awarded at the annual Building Crafts College Prize Giving in Carpenters' Hall each November.

Annual grant total
The London Youth Trust is administered by the Norton Folgate Trust. In previous years, grants have been for around £2,000.

Applications
Applications should be made to the Norton Folgate Trust at:

The Bursar, Building Crafts College, Kennard Road, Stratford, London E15 1AH.

Other information
In September 2012 the funds of the trust were passed over to the Worshipful Company of Carpenters. It remains as a restricted fund administered by the company via the Norton Folgate Trust.

North London Welfare and Educational Foundation

£152,500

Correspondent: Benedict Chayim Joseph, Trustee, 44 Warwick Avenue, Edgware HA8 8UJ (020 8905 4766)
CC number: 1155103

Eligibility
Primarily, people who live in North London and are in need.

Types of grants
Grants for items, services and facilities that relieve financial hardship.

Annual grant total
In 2015/16 the foundation had assets of £13,600 and an income of £437,500. Grants totalled £426,500, of which £305,000 was awarded to individuals. We estimate that educational grants to individuals totalled around £152,500.

Applications
Apply in writing to the correspondent.

Philological Foundation

£15,000 (15 grants)

Correspondent: Helen Forde, Clerk, The Cardinal Hume Centre, 3–7 Arneway Street, London SW1P 2BG (email: thephilological@gmail.com or admin@philological.org.uk; website: www.philological.org.uk)
CC number: 312692

Eligibility
Individual recipients of grants must be under 26 years of age and be or have been pupils at a secondary school in the City of Westminster or London Borough of Camden.

Types of grants
Grants are offered towards tuition fees, study/travel costs, educational necessities, such as books, equipment/instruments, materials, clothing or other. Schoolchildren, further/higher education students and individuals in vocational training or people starting work/entering trade can be assisted. Awards are normally in the range from £150 to £2,000. Apprenticeships can also be considered.

Grants for education are considered at the following levels: GNVQ; A-level; Access Foundation; Diploma; First Degree and Postgraduate Taught Degrees. Awards are not normally made for Postgraduate Research Degrees. Apprenticeships will also be considered.

Annual grant total
In 2015/16 the foundation had assets of £1.12 million and an income of £43,000. A total of £24,500 was spent in grants to 15 individuals and 12 schools. We have estimated that grants to individuals totalled £15,000.

Exclusions
Support will not be given to individuals who could be assisted by a statutory loan or for postgraduate research degrees. Retrospective funding cannot be given.

Applications
Applicants are invited to email the correspondent to request further information and application forms. Request for information and application forms should be made via email to: thephilological@gmail.com. Trustees normally meet during the third week of September, December, February, April and June. Deadlines for applications are two months prior to a meeting, Further information is available on the website.

Other information
Grants are also given to state-funded primary and secondary schools in Westminster or Camden for the provision of recreation or leisure activities such as playground equipment and educational visits.

Scotscare

£30,000 (42+ grants)

Correspondent: Shona Fleming, 22 City Road, London EC1Y 2AJ (020 7240 3718; email: info@scotscare.com; website: www.scotscare.com)
CC number: 207326

Eligibility
Scottish people, their children and widows, who are in need and have lived within a 35-mile radius of Charing Cross for at least two years.

Types of grants
Grants are given for a variety of educational and training purposes including course fees, books and living expenses. Assistance is also given with school uniforms and trips.

Annual grant total
In 2015/16 the charity had assets of £46 million and an income of more than £2.3 million. The amount of grants given to individuals totalled £467,500. In previous years educational grants have totalled around £30,000.

Exclusions
The charity cannot fund postgraduate courses.

Applications
There is an online Scotscare application request form on the website. Alternatively, call the Freephone helpline on 0800 652 2989; the Scotscare team is there to give advice from Monday to Thursday 9 am to 5 pm and on Friday from 9 am to 4 pm.

Other information
In addition to making grants, Scotscare also offers a range of services for beneficiaries in the areas of advocacy, employment and training, families, health, housing, money management, mental health, socialising and substance misuse.

The Sheriffs' and Recorders' Fund
See entry on page 40

St Clement Danes Educational Foundation
See entry on page 220

Sir Walter St John's Educational Charity

£6,300 (three grants)

Correspondent: Susan Perry, Manager, Office 1A, Culvert House, Culvert Road, London SW11 5DH (020 7498 8878; email: manager@swsjcharity.org.uk; website: www.swsjcharity.org.uk)

CC number: 312690

Eligibility

People under the age of 25 (in practice, aged 16 to 24) who have been resident in the boroughs of Lambeth and Wandsworth for at least six months. Preference is given to the Battersea area. Grants can only be given to students who are following a validated, approved or recognised course and can demonstrate a good prospect of successfully completing it. Individual grants will only be given in exceptional circumstances and where the award would have a critical effect on the applicant's opportunity to study.

Types of grants

Support is available for core expenditure for attendance of the course – registration fees, travel expenses, books, equipment or instruments. The upper limit for grants is £500 to students aged 16 to 18 and £750 to students aged 19 to 24. Lone parents who are in receipt of benefit can receive grants of up to £1,500 towards childcare. Grants above £1,500 may be awarded in exceptional circumstances to students on foundation or access courses in arts, dance and drama who have good prospects of progressing to higher education afterwards. Students with disability are eligible for grants to meet additional education/training expenditure.

Annual grant total

In 2015/16 the charity held assets of £3.9 million and had an income of £156,000. Grants totalling £6,300 were made to three individual students undertaking further education.

A block grant totalling £6,000 was given to the South Thames College to be distributed to ten students, all of whom were either lone parents or potentially homeless young people. An additional grant of £1,000 to contribute to travel costs of students visiting colleges and universities.

Exclusions

Grants are not normally given to schoolchildren under the age of 16 or full-time university students. Maintenance expenses are not supported and the charity will not usually contribute towards the cost of a computer or laptop.

Applications

Applicants are invited to contact the correspondent for an initial discussion. Eligible applicants will be sent an application form which has to be returned together with the supporting information and evidence.

Students at South Thames College should contact the college's student services directly to find out specific criteria for applications.

Other information

Currently the charity is focusing its funding to support local organisations providing education and training opportunities for children and young people in the area of benefit. Only a small amount of money is allocated annually to support individual students. Block grants are also made to local colleges for distribution to their students.

Truro Fund

£8,500

Correspondent: Lt Col Richard Martin, Clerk to the Trustees, St Margaret's Church, Lothbury, London EC2R 7HH (email: lm800aat@hotmail.com)

CC number: 312288

Eligibility

Children and young people under the age of 21 living or attending an educational establishment in Greater London.

Types of grants

One-off bursaries, scholarships and maintenance allowances are available to schoolchildren, further/higher education students, people entering a trade/profession, people starting work/business or apprentices. Support is given towards the cost of outfits/clothing, books, equipment/instruments, materials, tools, travel/study abroad, also for music and arts studies.

Annual grant total

In 2016/17 the fund had an income of £10,100 and a total expenditure of £9,600. Normally around £8,500 is available to distribute in grants and around 12 to 15 small awards are given every six months.

Exclusions

Our previous research suggests that grants are not intended to cover fees.

Applications

Apply in writing to the correspondent. Applications should include three references (at least one of which should be from the applicant's educational establishment), evidence of the date of birth (either a photo page from a British passport or a birth certificate), full financial details and any information concerning the immigration status (if applicable).

The trustees meet twice a year in April and September to consider applications.

Other information

The fund is an amalgam of three small charities – The Rt Hon. the Dowager Baroness Truro's Fund (The Truro Fund), The East London Industrial School Fund and the Regent's Park Boy's Home Fund.

Sir Mark and Lady Turner Charitable Settlement

£8,500

Correspondent: The Trustees, c/o SG Kleinwort Hambros Trust Company (UK) Ltd, 5th Floor, 8 St James's Square, London SW1Y 4JU (020 3207 7041; email: katie.styles@kleinwortbenson.com)

CC number: 264994

Eligibility

University students in need living in North London, particularly Highgate.

Types of grants

One-off and recurrent grants between £100 and £500 are given for university tuition fees and necessities, including books or equipment/instruments.

Annual grant total

In 2015/16 the charity had an income of £8,200 and a total expenditure of £18,000. We estimate that educational grants to individuals totalled about £8,500.

Exclusions

The charity does not support PhD students.

Applications

An application form can be obtained from the trust's administrator. This needs to be sent back via email with two complete references and a CV. The trustees meet twice a year.

Other information

Both individuals and organisations can be supported.

Barnet

Elizabeth Allen Trust

£9,200 (13 grants)

Correspondent: Helen Rook, Clerk, PO BOX 1180, St Albans AL1 9XP (01727 823206; email: clerk@elizabethallentrust.org.uk; website: www.elizabethallentrust.org.uk)

CC number: 310968

Eligibility

People in need under the age of 25 who live, are employed, or in education in the borough of Barnet.

Types of grants

One-off grants are offered to those in education and people starting work/entering a trade. Financial assistance is given for general educational expenses, including books, fees, maintenance expenses, and travel for education. For apprentices or those preparing for entry into employment, funding can be provided for tools, clothing/outfits, uniforms, and other necessary equipment.

Annual grant total

In 2015/16 the trust held assets of £766,000, had an income of £27,000 and a total expenditure of £26,000. Of this, £9,200 was paid in grants to 13 successful applicants across the school years 2015/16 and 2016/17.

Exclusions

Grants are not given for private school fees, postgraduate studies, gap year activities or where funding can be received from the local authority.

Applications

Application forms can be requested by emailing the clerk. The trustees meet around four times per year to consider applications. Genuine financial hardship must be established.

Other information

The trust also supports local voluntary aided schools.

The Mayor of Barnet's Benevolent Fund

£2,000

Correspondent: Ken Argent, Grants Manager, The London Borough of Barnet, Building 4, North London Business Park, Oakleigh Road South, London N11 1NP (020 8359 2020; email: ken.argent@barnet.gov.uk; website: www.barnet.gov.uk/info/930094/grants_for_individuals/262/grants_for_individuals)

CC number: 1014273

Eligibility

Schoolchildren who have lived in the London borough of Barnet for at least a year and whose parents are in receipt of on an income-related statutory benefit (such as Income Support or Child Tax Credit).

Types of grants

Small, one-off grants of up to £60 per child can be given towards school uniforms to pupils transferring from primary to secondary school or starting a new secondary school. Up to two awards can be given to each applicant.

Annual grant total

In 2015/16 the fund had an income of £21,500 and a total expenditure of £10,500. Most support is given in relief-in-need grants; therefore we estimate that educational grants totalled around £2,000.

Exclusions

Children attending East Barnet School, Finchley Catholic High School and The Wren Academy, which operate their own schemes of financial assistance to parents in need.

Applications

Applications have to be made in writing to the correspondent via post or email. Applications can be submitted directly by the individual or through a third party, such as a social worker, health visitor or an advice agency. Candidates should provide full details of their name, address, contact number, confirmation and length of residence in the borough, number and ages of the family members, family income, a proof of entitlement to a benefit, a summary of the applicant's circumstances, details of support requested, a quotation for any items required and information on other sources of funding approached.

Other information

Grants are mainly made for welfare purposes.

The Hyde Foundation

£11,600 (17 grants)

Correspondent: Robin Marson, Clerk to the Trustees, 1 Hillside, Codicote, Hitchin SG4 8XZ (020 8449 3032; email: marson36@homecall.co.uk)

CC number: 302918

Eligibility

People in education up to first degree level in the ancient parishes of Chipping Barnet and Monken Hadley.

Types of grants

One-off grants in the range of £100 to £6,000. Grants are given to college students, undergraduates, vocational students, mature students, people with special educational needs and people starting work. Grants given include those for music lessons, fees, travel abroad, books, equipment and maintenance/living expenses.

Annual grant total

In 2016 the foundation held assets of £760,500 and had an income of £40,500. Grants made to 17 individuals totalled £11,600 and a further £4,800 was awarded to organisations and schools.

Applications

Apply in writing to the correspondent, who will forward an application form. The trustees meet quarterly in January, April, July and October to consider applications and applications should be received at the end of December, March, June and September respectively.

The Valentine Poole Charity

£21,000

Correspondent: Victor Russell, Ewen Hall, Wood Street, Barnet, Hertfordshire EN5 4BW (020 8441 6893; email: vpoole@btconnect.com; website: www.valentinepoole.org.uk)

CC number: 220856

Eligibility

People who are resident in Barnet, East Barnet, and Chipping Barnet.

Types of grants

One-off grants for general educational purposes.

Annual grant total

In 2016 the charity had assets of £662,000 and an income of £68,000. We estimate the amount awarded in grants for education was £21,000.

Applications

Applications should be made in writing to the correspondent.

Other information

The charity also makes awards for welfare purposes and Christmas gifts, and to organisations active in the local community.

Bromley

The Hayes (Kent) Trust

£6,300 (ten grants)

Correspondent: Andrew Naish, Trustee, 2 Warren Wood Close, Bromley BR2 7DU (020 8462 1915; email: hayes. kent.trust@gmail.com)

CC number: 221098

Eligibility

People who live in the parish of Hayes and can demonstrate that they are in need.

Types of grants

One-off grants, generally in the region of £75 to £1,500, are given according to need.

Annual grant total

In 2016/17 the trust had assets of £1.1 million and an income of £50,500. The amount of grants given to individuals totalled £18,200 and were broken down as follows:

Relief in need	45	£10,600
Advancement of education	10	£6,300
Relief in sickness	2	£1,300

Applications

Applications can be made in writing to the correspondent. They should include the full name of the applicant, postal address in Hayes (Kent), telephone number, email, date of birth and details of why support is required. Applications may include any supporting information and can be made at any time either directly by the individual or through a third party, such as the individual's college, school or educational welfare agency.

Other information

The trust is an amalgamation of the following charities: The Poors Land Cottage Charity; The Poors Land Eleemosynary Charity; The Hayes (Kent) Educational Foundation.

Camden

Bromfield's Educational Foundation

£21,000

Correspondent: Nicholas Hills, 5 St Andrew Street, London EC4A 3AB (020 7583 7394; email: info@ standrewholborn.org.uk; website: www. standrewholborn.org.uk)

CC number: 312795

Eligibility

People in need under 25 who live (or whose parents or guardians live) in the Holborn area of the London borough of Camden for at least two years.

Types of grants

One-off and termly grants for clothing, books, equipment/instruments, music lessons, computers and maintenance/ living expenses.

Annual grant total

In 2016 the foundation had assets of £2.1 million and an income of £79,500. A total of £21,000 was awarded to individuals.

Exclusions

No grants are given for school, college or university fees. Applications for postgraduate studies will not be considered.

Applications

Application forms are available from the website. Details of income, expenditure and personal information are required, supported by documentary evidence which will be treated in the strictest confidence. Applications can be submitted at any time, and will be considered within 21 days.

Other information

Priority is given to families of children with disabilities. Almost all of the families who receive termly grants are caring for a child with disabilities. Grants are also given to organisations.

Hampstead Wells and Campden Trust

£3,100 (11 grants)

Correspondent: Sheila Taylor, 62 Rosslyn Hill, London NW3 1ND (020 7435 1570; email: grant@hwct.co.uk; website: www.hwct.org.uk)

CC number: 1094611

Eligibility

Residents of the former Metropolitan Borough of Hampstead (the area of benefit, a map of which is available on the trust's website) who are in need.

Types of grants

Grants are given to people at any stage of their education, or who are entering a trade or profession, for uniforms and other clothing, books, equipment, instruments, maintenance, living expenses, childcare and educational outings in the UK.

Annual grant total

In 2015/16 the trust had assets of £17 million and an income of £479,000. The trust made 11 grants for educational purposes totalling £3,100.

Exclusions

The trustees are unable to offer assistance with course or school fees.

Applications

Applications are accepted on behalf of individuals from any local constituted group, departments/units of Camden Council or the health service, a housing association, advice agency or other voluntary agency where the individual is known. The applying organisation must be willing to receive and account for any grant offered. The trust prefers to receive applications via the appropriate form, which is available to download from the website; however, it also accepts applications in letter form. There is a list of essential information which must be included in any letter application on the website.

St Andrew Holborn Charities

£50,000

Correspondent: Nicholas Hills, 5 St Andrew Street, London EC4A 3AB (020 7583 7394; email: charity@ standrewholborn.org.uk; website: www. standrewholborn.org.uk)

CC number: 1095045

Eligibility

People who are under the age of 25 and live in the area of benefit (a defined area of Holborn; see the website or contact the charity for specific details).

Types of grants

Financial assistance can be provided in the form of grants for school uniform, books, travel expenses, materials for courses, training, equipment etc. Termly grants can be provided to children with disabilities.

Annual grant total

In 2016 the charity had assets of £11.8 million and an income of £347,500. We estimate that educational grants to individuals totalled around £50,000.

Exclusions

Grants will not be provided for private school fees.

Applications

Application forms are available to download from the website, where guidelines can also be found. Applicants must provide evidence that they are a 'bona fide' student on a 'recognised and accredited course'. All applicants are means-tested.

Other information

This charity is the result of an amalgamation of three trusts: The City

Foundation, The Isaac Duckett Charity and The William Williams Charity. Grants are also made to local organisations.

City of London

Lawrence Atwell's Charity (Skinners' Company)

£122,500 (145 grants)

Correspondent: The Trustees, The Skinners' Company, Skinners' Hall, 8 Dowgate Hill, London EC4R 2SP (020 7213 0561; email: atwell@skinners.org. uk; website: www.skinners.org.uk/grants-and-trusts/atwell)

CC number: 210773

Eligibility

From the 2015/16 annual report:

The Charity considers requests from young people between 16 and 26 who are focused on a particular vocational goal and who need help with the costs of vocational and pre-vocational training or to begin work. There is a particular interest in reaching those with additional barriers in life, employment and training (e.g. with no or few qualifications, caring responsibilities, family estrangement or separation through having to seek asylum, people affected by a disability, ex-offenders or those at risk of offending)

Applicants must be UK citizens, refugees, asylum seekers, or have lived in the UK for a minimum of three years.

Types of grants

Support towards:

- Vocational training below the level of a first undergraduate degree – for example, NVQ Level 3, BTEC National Diplomas, City and Guilds courses
- 'First step' qualifications to help people become qualified for work – such as NVQ Level 1/2, BTEC First Diplomas/Certificates and access and foundation courses
- Costs of finding a job – including the costs of attending an interview or buying tools to get someone started

Grants are given according to need, usually in the range of £100 to £1,500, and can be one-off or recurrent (re-application each year is required). The majority of grants are given towards tuition, enrolment, registration and examination fees, however help is also given towards general living expenses, travel costs, household bills, accommodation and specific items, tools, childcare costs, clothing.

Annual grant total

In 2015/16 the charity had assets of £15.7 million, £375,000 in income and £122,500 was available in grants from Lawrence Atwell's Charity. £117,000 was donated in grants through the main charity and a further £5,300 donated through subsidiary charities.

A further £147,500 in grants was made available to affiliated Skinner's Company schools and other educational institutes.

Exclusions

Funding is not provided for:

- Any course that is not vocational or accredited
- Secondary education (including GCSEs and A-levels, unless you are returning to education as an adult)
- University or postgraduate fees
- A course at a private dance/drama college

Applications

Applicants are asked to register online and complete an eligibility test. Successful completion of the test will then redirect the applicant to the online application form. Requests for assistance can only be processed through the use of the online application.

Applicants are requested to provide a personal reference (from a social worker, counsellor or family friend) and a tutor or professional reference. Applicants must provide details of full household income, in the form of pay slips or letters to detail this.

Applicants are recommended to apply at least eight weeks before the start date of their course. There is no deadline for applications as funding is ongoing on a first-come, first-served basis. The deciding committee meets at the end of every calendar month and aims to inform applicants of their outcome within three to five working days.

Grand payments are made termly, subject to satisfactory attendance and progress as confirmed by the educational provider.

Other information

The charity also provides grant support to Skinner's Company schools and other educational institutions. In 2015/16 grant support to other educational institutions totalled £147,500.

The Thomas Carpenter Educational and Apprenticing Foundation (Thomas Carpenter's Trust)

£37,000 (16 grants)

Correspondent: Lt Col. Richard Martin, St Margaret's Church, Lothbury, London EC2R 7HH (email: lm800aat@hotmail. com)

CC number: 312155

Eligibility

People under the age of 25 who have (or whose parents have) lived or worked for three years in Bread Street and adjoining wards in the City of London, or who attend educational establishment in that area.

Types of grants

Grants of around £500 to £3,000 towards general course-related costs, including outfits, fees, books, equipment/tools, study of music or other arts, travel/study abroad and so on. People in schools, universities/colleges or those starting work/entering trade can be supported.

Annual grant total

In 2015/16 the foundation held assets of £1 million and had an income of £37,000. A total of £37,000 was awarded in grants to 16 individuals.

Exclusions

Grants are not normally given towards electives or field trips which are not part of a full-time study course.

Applications

Application forms can be requested from the correspondent. They should normally be submitted before 31 July by the individual's parent or guardian, details of whose financial circumstances should be included.

Other information

Applications from local groups for recreational, social and physical training or equipment will also be considered.

The Mitchell City of London Educational Foundation

£70,000 (37 grants)

Correspondent: Lucy Jordan, Administrator, 24 Station Lane, Holme-on-Spalding Moor, York YO43 4AL (0845 600 1558; email: mitchellcityoflondon@gmail.com)

CC number: 312499

Eligibility

People aged 11 to 19 who are either attending school in the City of London or whose parents have lived or worked there for at least five years.

The 'city' is classified as the area of almost all postcodes EC3, EC4 and a small area of EC1, EC2.

Types of grants

Awards are given as sixth form bursaries for A-level or IB students within independent education, or in grants to children from single-parent families who are within independent education and have been at the school of choice for one year. Support is available towards general educational needs. Choral bursaries may also be provided.

The foundation grants Diploma Awards of £2,500 to students in need.

Annual grant total

In 2015/16 the foundation held assets of £2 million and had an income of £80,100. Grants to 37 individuals totalled £70,000. The awards consisted of:

Sixth form bursaries	29
Pupils from single-parent families	6
Diploma Awards	2
Choral bursaries	0

The Diploma Award of £2,500 was made to a needy student at Barts and The London Hospital. An award of £2,500 was also made to a needy student at the City University of London.

Applications

Apply in writing to the correspondent. Applications can be submitted either directly by the individual or through a third party, such as a parent or guardian, school or education welfare agency, if applicable. Grants are normally considered in March and September.

Other information

The annual report for 2015/16 notes the following: 'A further 89 (2014/2015: 84) applications and enquiries for awards did not meet the terms of reference of the charities.'

City of Westminster

Hyde Park Place Estate Charity

£7,200

Correspondent: Shirley Vaughan, St George's Hanover Square Church, The Vestry, 2A Mill Street, London W1S 1FX (020 7629 0874; website: www. stgeorgeshanoversquare.org)

CC number: 212439

Eligibility

Residents of the City of Westminster.

Types of grants

Grants are made for the advancement of education and can be used towards costs associated with study, for example to purchase equipment and clothing.

Annual grant total

In 2015/16 the charity had assets of £14 million and an income of £485,000. We estimate the charity awarded £7,200 in grants for educational purposes.

Applications

Applications should be made in writing to the correspondent. They are considered on an ongoing basis.

Other information

The charity also awards grants to organisations and individuals for education and welfare purposes. The charity also runs a programme awarding grants to churches.

The Sir Simon Milton Foundation

£38,000 (17 grants)

Correspondent: Matthew Sykes, Chief Executive, Westminster City Hall (6th Floor), 5 Strand, London WC2N 5HR (020 7641 8088; email: info@ sirsimonmiltonfoundation.com; website: www.sirsimonmiltonfoundation.com)

CC number: 1149166/1174405

Eligibility

Applicants must be under the age of 30 and former attendees of a school or college in Westminster; living or have lived in Westminster; come from a household with an income below £25,000. They must be in the first year of their first undergraduate degree in either engineering, construction, politics, history, or a combined course that includes one of these subjects.

In 2017 the foundation prioritised the following groups: young people with registered disabilities, young women, first generation attendees of university in a family and young people leaving care.

Types of grants

Scholarships of £10,000 over the course of the degree. The grant can cover accommodation and living costs or tuition fees.

Bursaries are available to students at Gonville and Caius College Cambridge and are to cover the living costs of students from low-income backgrounds.

Annual grant total

In 2015/16 the foundation held assets of almost £1.2 million and had an income of £854,000. Scholarships were awarded to 17 individuals during the year and totalled £38,000.

Applications

Application forms can be download and completed on the foundation's website, where deadlines, further guidance and the terms and conditions of the scholarship can also be found. The application period generally opens from July to September, in advance of the start of the course.

Other information

In September 2017, the foundation opened the Sir Simon Milton Westminster University Technical College for students studying science, technology, engineering and maths (STEM) subjects with a focus on transport engineering and construction and the built environment. The foundation also provides services and events for older people in the borough, to combat loneliness and isolation.

Paddington Charitable Estates Educational Fund

£26,500

Correspondent: Caroline Headley-Barton, Clerk to the Trustees, 15th Floor, City of Westminster, Westminster City Hall, 64 Victoria Street, London SW1E 6QP (020 7641 1859; email: cheadley@westminster.gov.uk; website: www.westminster.gov.uk/paddington-charities)

CC number: 312347

Eligibility

People under the age of 25 who are living in Paddington and who are in need of financial assistance to enable them to pursue their education, including primary, secondary and further education and vocational training.

Types of grants

Grants are given to help individuals pursue an educational course or training in a profession or trade, to study music or other arts, as well as for school uniforms and educational holidays or trips and other educational purposes. Grants are also given for school and course fees, particularly to children who excel in a particular area or who are in need of special tuition.

Annual grant total

In 2015 the fund had an income of £22,000 and a total expenditure of £104,000. Grants to seven children and young people for educational purposes totalled £26,500. There were also grants to schools totalling £60,000 and to other organisations totalling £14,900.

Applications

Potential applicants should contact the clerk for further information.

Other information

Grants are also made to voluntary-aided schools in Paddington for repairs or physical alterations and to organisations in the area of benefit.

The Paddington Charities consist of the Paddington Welfare Charities and the Paddington Charitable Estates Educational Fund. Further details on the charities can also be obtained from the clerk to the trustees (020 7641 1859; email: cheadly-barton@westminster.gov.uk).

Saint Marylebone Educational Foundation

£49,500 (seven grants)

Correspondent: The Trustees, Marylebone Station, 12 Melcombe Place, Marylebone, London NW1 6JJ (email: stmaryedf@gmail.com)

CC number: 312378

Eligibility

People aged between 8 and 18 who have lived or been educated in the former borough of St Marylebone and the City of Westminster for at least two years. Preference may be given to individuals experiencing unforeseen circumstances affecting their financial situation or for whom boarding school is a preferred option due to a parental illness or specific educational need.

Support is also given to postgraduate students at the Royal Academy of Music and the Royal College of Music.

Types of grants

Generally recurrent grants for school pupils to help with fees or other educational needs. Awards usually range from £500 to £5,500.

Annual grant total

In 2015/16 the foundation held assets of £816,500 and had an income of £178,500. Grants to seven pupils totalled £49,500 and a further £116,000 was awarded to schools and colleges.

Exclusions

Grants for further/higher education are not provided.

Applications

Apply in writing to the correspondent. Applications should be made by the applicant's parent/guardian or by the individual, if aged over 18. Applications can also be submitted through a third party such as a teacher, school or welfare

agency, if applicable. Applications are considered in January and July.

Postgraduate students should apply through one of the specified schools.

St Clement Danes Educational Foundation

£20,100 (37 grants)

Correspondent: Deb Starkey, Clerk to the Trustees, St Clement Danes School, Drury Lane, London WC2B 5SU (020 7641 6593; email: dstarkey@stcd.co.uk)

CC number: 312319

Eligibility

Grants are awarded to young people under the age of 25 in the following groups, in order of priority:
- Pupils or ex-pupils of St Clement Danes Church of England Primary School
- Individuals who normally live in the City of Westminster
- Individuals who normally live in the diocese of London

The guidance states that, in the case of students in further and higher education, 'normally live' refers to the home address of the parent or guardian where the students has lived for most of their primary/secondary education. It also states that preference is given to those who 'show planning and initiative, for example by taking a part-time or casual job to supplement their income to decrease reliance on outside sources'.

Types of grants

Grants are given to schoolchildren for items such as uniform, sports equipment, school trips or travel. Grants for further or higher education students or those entering a trade, profession or sporting career, can be given for fees, travel, living expenses, course materials and equipment, field trips or computing equipment. There are no restrictions on the subjects or professions supported. In the case of university fees, it is expected that other sources of funding should have been exhausted before applying.

Annual grant total

In 2016 the foundation had assets of £3.7 million and an income of £161,000. During the year, 37 grants were awarded to individuals, totalling £20,100. A further £43,000 was awarded to St Clement Danes Church of England Primary School.

Exclusions

Grants are not given to pupils attending independent schools out of parental choice, but pupils at an independent school due to a scholarship may be supported.

Applications

Application forms are available from the Clerk, and should be returned along with references and a letter confirming the place on a course/college, where possible. Applications for those under the age of 18 should be made by a parent or guardian. The Grants Committee meets in January, May, September and November and applications should be submitted in plenty of time ahead of when the funds are required, to allow time for obtaining references.

Croydon

The Church Tenements Charities – Educational and Church Branches

£13,000

Correspondent: Margot Rohan, Bernard Weatherill House, 7th Floor Zone C, 8 Mint Walk, Croydon CR0 1EA (020 8726 6000 ext. 62564; email: margot.rohan@croydon.gov.uk)

CC number: 312554

Eligibility

People under the age of 25 who are living or studying in the London borough of Croydon (including people from overseas studying in Croydon) who are experiencing financial hardship.

Preference is given to people requesting funding below £500 who have not received support from the local authorities or where the applicants have made some effort to raise funds themselves.

Types of grants

Small, one-off grants in the range of £50 to £500 mainly to people in primary, secondary and post-school education and training. Support is given towards books, stationery, uniforms, travelling to and from the place of education, music tuition and instruments, also educational outings, study/travel abroad or school fees. People entering a trade may also be supported.

Annual grant total

In 2015/16 the charity had an income of £21,000 and a total expenditure of £27,500. We estimate a total of £13,000 was awarded in grants.

Applications

Application forms can be requested from the correspondent. It is helpful to provide as much supporting information as possible.

Other information

The charity also gives grants to youth services, ecclesiastical organisations and supports Archbishop Tenison's School.

The Frank Denning Memorial Charity

£1,600

Correspondent: Angela Haynes-Ranger, Croydon Council, Chief Executive's Department, Zone 4G, Bernard Weatherhill House, 8 Mint Walk, Croydon CR0 1EA (020 8726 6000 Ext 60125; email: angela.haynesranger@ croydon.gov.uk; website: www.croydon. gov.uk/advice/grants/frankdenning)

CC number: 312813

Eligibility

Students between the ages of 19 and 25 (by 30 April in the year of their application) who are (or whose parents are) resident in the London borough of Croydon and who want to carry out an educational project overseas. The applicant's travel plans must commence between 1 May and 30 April of the year of application.

Types of grants

One-off travelling scholarships of up to £1,000 are available to full-time university or college students for undertaking a specific project abroad as a part of their course of study.

Annual grant total

In 2015/16 the charity had an income of £4,800 and a total expenditure of £1,800. We estimate that the charity gave around £1,600 in grants to individuals for educational purposes.

Exclusions

Support is not available for holidays and journeys that have been completed or have already started at the time of application.

Applications

Application forms can be requested from the correspondent. If the application is successful, candidates will be invited to an interview where they will discuss their proposals with the trustees, who will then make their final decision.

Ealing

Acton (Middlesex) Charities – Educational Charity

£10,300

Correspondent: Lorna Dodd, Clerk to the Trustees, c/o St Mary's Parish Office, 1 The Mount, Acton High Street, London W3 9NW (email: acton. charities@virgin.net; website: www. actoncharities.co.uk)

CC number: 312312

Eligibility

Students whose home residence is in the former ancient parish of Acton in West London (their term-time address does not have to be in Acton). Candidates must be over the age of 18 (and normally up to the age of 25) and have entered a full-time course in the UK, usually of at least three years, which will lead to a recognised qualification.

If there is a high demand, priority will be given to students who have spent some part of their education in an Acton school.

Types of grants

Grants of £300 per year to assist with books or equipment.

Annual grant total

In 2015 the charity had an income of £9,800 and a total expenditure of £8,200. The Acton (Middlesex) Charities' website notes that during the year a total of £10,300 was given 'to students in various stages of further education'.

Exclusions

Anyone outside the area of benefit (there is a helpful map on the charity's website). Grants are not given for courses in private schools or institutions.

Applications

Application forms are available online or can be obtained from the clerk. Applications must be accompanied by written proof of attendance from the applicant's educational institute.

Other information

This charity is one of four organisations that make up the Acton (Middlesex) Charities group. Also included are Relief in Need Charity, John Perryn Relief in Need Fund, and the Athawes Art Gallery. In 2015 the combined charities donated a total of £15,500 in grants.

Enfield

The Old Enfield Charitable Trust

£115,000

Correspondent: Personal Grants Administrator, 22 The Town, Enfield, Middlesex EN2 6LT (020 8367 8941; email: enquiries@thetrustenfield.org.uk; website: www.toect.org.uk)

CC number: 207840

Eligibility

People in need who live in the ancient parish of Enfield.

Types of grants

Grants are made to students and other residents who are undertaking education or training. Help is towards living costs, equipment, stationery, childcare costs, travel expenses and so on. People starting work/entering a trade are also supported.

Annual grant total

In 2016/17 the trust had assets of £6.6 million and an income of £679,500. The amount of grants given to individuals totalled £231,500. We estimate that educational grants totalled £115,000.

Exclusions

The trust will not provide support where local authority or central government should be assisting. Grants are not normally given for second degrees or master's degree courses.

Applications

Application forms are available to download from the trust's website. There is also an eligibility checker on the website.

Other information

Community grants are also made to organisations. The trust also administers Ann Crowe's and Wright's Almshouse Charity which owns ten almshouses that are let to needy people already resident in the Ancient Parish of Enfield.

Greenwich

Greenwich Blue Coat Foundation

£10,500 (40 grants)

Correspondent: M. Baker, Clerk to the Trustees, 136 Charlton Lane, London SE7 8AB (020 8858 7575; email: bluecoat@baker5.co.uk; website: www.bluecoathistory.co.uk/page829.html)

CC number: 312407

Eligibility

Young people up to 25 years of age who have lived or have been educated in the London borough of Greenwich for at least two years previous to their application. Preference is given to individuals with limited means.

Types of grants

One-off and recurrent grants, normally of around £500, are given to help individuals to further their education, develop life skills or enter a chosen career path. Financial assistance can be given for the course fees, equipment/instruments or other course-related expenses.

Annual grant total

In 2015/16 the foundation had assets of £1.7 million and an income of £34,000. A total £19,800 was awarded in 40 grants to individuals. Of these, one individual received a grant in excess of £1,000.

Exclusions

Maintenance or travel costs are not normally supported.

Applications

Application forms can be downloaded from the foundation's website or requested from the correspondent. Candidates are required to provide a name of a referee. The trustees usually meet four times a year to consider applications. The trustees may ask applicants to attend an interview to help determine their suitability for an award.

Other information

The website states that the foundation only has 'a relatively small sum of money available annually and does not therefore usually make large individual awards'.

Hackney

The Hackney Parochial Charities

£10,000

Correspondent: Sarah Bennett, Correspondent, c/o Trust Partnership, 6 Trull Farm Buildings, Trull, Tetbury, Gloucestershire GL8 8SQ (020 3397 7805; email: hackney@thetrustpartnership.com; website: www.hackneyparochialcharities.org.uk)

CC number: 219876

Eligibility

People in need who live in the former metropolitan borough of Hackney (as it was before 1970).

Types of grants

Help is given towards the cost of books, equipment, tools and examination fees for apprentices and young people at college or university who are not in receipt of a full grant. Grants are one-off, although applicants can re-apply annually.

Annual grant total

In 2015/16 the charity had assets of £6 million and an income of £291,000. Grants were made totalling £223,500, most of which appears to be given to organisations. We estimate that around £20,000 was given to individuals for both social welfare and educational needs.

Applications

Applications can be made via a form available on the charity's website.

Hammer-smith and Fulham

Dr Edwards and Bishop King's Fulham Charity

£8,300 (five grants)

Correspondent: Jonathan Martin, Clerk to the Trustees, Percy Barton House, 33–35 Dawes Road, London SW6 7DT (020 7385 9387; fax: 020 7610 2856; email: clerk@debk.org.uk; website: www.debk.org.uk)

CC number: 1113490

Eligibility

People in need who are undertaking education or training and live in the old metropolitan borough of Fulham. This constitutes all of the SW6 postal area and parts of W14 and W6. Educational support is given on a limited basis. The website gives a detailed list of geographical area eligible for support.

Types of grants

One-off grants are made to individuals for short accredited training courses which are likely to lead to employment; also support with childcare and other needs.

Annual grant total

In 2015/16 the charity had assets of £9.3 million and an income of £443,000. Grants to five individuals for education purposes totalled £8,300.

Exclusions

According to the website, the charity does not:

▶ Normally help those who are homeowners
▶ Help those out with the area of benefit
▶ Give cash grants (unless they are to be administered by an agency)
▶ Give grants retrospectively or pay arrears on utility bills
▶ Provide funds for funerals
▶ Provide wheelchairs or electric scooters
▶ Provide computer equipment of any sort, except to those who are housebound
▶ Provide dishwashers
▶ Provide laminate flooring
▶ Provide grants for equipment where government, or local government, or any other agency is required to provide that equipment by law
▶ Provide items (other than clothing or books) where the individual purchase value is less than £15
▶ Provide funding for postgraduate courses

The charity prefers not to satisfy repeat requests and is extremely unlikely to help requests for which funding may be available from other places.

Applications

Application forms are available to download from the charity's website and should be returned at least six weeks before the start of the course you want to be considered for. The charity's website states: 'We would suggest that anyone considering applying for an educational grant will benefit from ringing us, in advance of applying, to discuss the proposal.'

Other information

The charity gives money to both individuals and organisations, with its main responsibility being towards the relief of poverty rather than assisting students.

There are also 'Summer Schemes' whereby funding is given to help with 'organised activities and day trips for young local people from challenging backgrounds, over the July and August school holidays'. Assistance for longer trips – provided the destination venues are reputable, reasonably priced, and within the UK – may also be given under the scheme.

Haringey

The Tottenham Grammar School Foundation

£326,153

Correspondent: Graham Chappell, Clerk to the Foundation, PO Box 34098, London N13 5XU (020 8882 2999; email: info@tgsf.info or trustees@tgsf.org.uk; website: www.tgsf.org.uk)

CC number: 312634

Eligibility

Young people under the age of 25 who live/whose parents normally live in the borough of Haringey and who have attended a school in the borough.

Types of grants

The foundation has different types of awards and there are different eligibility criteria for each:

- The Somerset Award – generally one-off grant of up to £250 to students on full-time vocational courses at colleges of further education (or equivalent)
- The Somerset Undergraduate Award – recurrent payments (£750 payable in annual instalments of £250) to university students following a full-time degree or an equivalent higher education course of at least two years' duration
- The Somerset Special Award – a wide range of grants awarded to postgraduate students, young sportspeople at a county standard or higher, musicians at a conservatoire standard and individuals with special needs
- The foundation also makes a limited number of Somerset Scholarships and Sponsorships each year. Generally, these are made in partnership with Mountview Academy of Theatre Arts, the Harrington scheme, and The College of Haringey, Enfield and North East London

Further information on each type of award is given on the foundation's website.

Annual grant total

In 2015/16 the foundation had assets of £24.6 million and an income of £438,500. The amount of grants given to individuals totalled £326,000 and a further £543,000 was given in grants to organisations.

Exclusions

Grants are not made to young people who do not live in the London borough of Haringey (unless they attend/attended a school in the borough).

Somerset Awards/Undergraduate Awards are not given for:

- A or AS levels, GCSEs or any courses at a school or sixth form college
- Part-time courses
- Apprenticeships
- Students aged under 16 or over 25

Applications

Separate application forms for the Somerset Awards and the Somerset Undergraduate Awards can be downloaded from the foundation's website. Applications can also be made through a fast-track online system on the website. Candidates are invited to apply from 1 May each year (for the academic year commencing the following September). The closing date for applications for each academic year is 31 January.

Applications for special grants must be made in writing to the correspondent providing the date of birth, relevant documentation, letters of support and other information specific for different categories (see the website for details). For children with special needs, there is an application form for use by the parent, guardian or other appropriate person applying for assistance on their behalf (which can be downloaded from the website).

Other information

Grants are also made to charities, voluntary groups, schools and other organisations which work with young people in the borough of Haringey for the purposes such as trips, special educational needs, sports and art activities, etc.

Havering

David Randall Foundation

£2,100

Correspondent: Sue Randall, 7 Browning Road, Maldon, Essex CM9 6BU (01621 858449; email: info@davidrandallfoundation.org; www.davidrandallfoundation.org.uk)

CC number: 1151121

Eligibility

Applicants should:

- Be aged 12 to 25
- Reside in Essex, Suffolk or the London borough of Havering
- Demonstrate exceptional dedication to the interest they wish to pursue

Types of grants

Financial support from the foundation will be offered to those who demonstrate exceptional dedication and passion in pursuing their ambitions in music or sport but are held back by financial means. There will be a major annual award called The David Randall Scholarship. Applications open at the beginning of October and must be submitted by 31 December. A decision will be made by 23 February. In exceptional circumstances applications may be considered outside this time scale. Contact the foundation if you need to apply outside of the normal application time.

Annual grant total

In 2015/16 the foundation had assets of £77,500 and an income of £32,600. Educational grants to individuals totalled £2,100.

Applications

Application forms are available to download from the foundation's website. All applications should be supported by a referee, who knows the applicant well and can vouch for their dedication and passion in their chosen field.

Hillingdon

Uxbridge United Welfare Trusts

£7,300 (14 grants)

Correspondent: Mrs J. Duffy, Grants Officer, Woodbridge House, New Windsor Street, Uxbridge UB8 2TY (07912 270937; email: grants.officer@uuwt.org; website: www.uuwt.org)

CC number: 217066

Eligibility

People under the age of 25 who are in need and live in (or has a parent who lives in) or have a very strong connection with the Uxbridge area. The area of benefit covers Crowley, Harefield, Hillingdon, Ickenham and Uxbridge.

Types of grants

The trust's 2016 accounts state: 'Educational grants to individuals are primarily for school trips, clothing, books, course fees, and similar items.'

Annual grant total

In 2016 the trust had assets of £14 million and an income of £660,500. There were 14 educational grants made to individuals totalling £7,300.

Exclusions

Our research suggests that grants are not normally given for school fees. Funding is not intended to be provided where statutory support is available.

Applications

Application forms can be requested from the correspondent. They can be submitted directly by the individual or through a social worker, Citizens Advice or educational welfare agency, if applicable. Awards are considered each month.

Other information

Grants are also awarded for welfare purposes and may be given to support organisations. The trust also runs almshouses.

Islington

Worrall and Fuller Exhibition Fund

£7,500

Correspondent: Manar Sabri, Clerk, St Luke's Community Centre, 90 Central Street, London EC1V 8AJ (020 7549 8181; email: msabri@slpt.org.uk; website: www.worrallandfuller.org)

CC number: 312507

Eligibility

Children and young people between the ages of 5 and 25 who are resident in the old borough of Finsbury (now part of Islington). Preference is given to those who live in the parish of St Luke, Old Street, or whose parents have had their business or employment there in previous years.

Types of grants

The fund awards scholarships, bursaries, maintenance allowances, grants to schoolchildren, further/higher education students and people entering a trade/ starting work. Grants are typically between £250 and £750. Financial assistance is given towards the cost of books, clothing/outfits, uniforms, equipment/instruments, other necessities and organised school trips during term time. Arts and music studies can be supported.

Annual grant total

In 2015/16 the fund had an income of £19,800 and a total expenditure of £15,500. Support is given to both organisations and individuals. The

estimated grants to individuals for educational purposes totalled £7,500 during the year.

Applications

Apply in writing to the correspondent. The trustees meet three times a year to discuss new applications and make decisions. Further details can be found on the fund's website.

Kensington and Chelsea

The Campden Charities

£483,000

Correspondent: Christopher Stannard, Clerk, Studios 3&4, 27a Pembridge Villas, London W11 3EP (020 7243 0551 or 020 7313 3797; website: www. campdencharities.org.uk)

CC number: 1104616

Eligibility

Individuals applying for funding must: have been continuously living in Kensington for at least two years (there is a helpful area of benefit map on the website); be a British or European citizen or have indefinite leave to remain; live in rented accommodation and not be a homeowner; be in receipt of benefits, including housing benefits, or in low-paid work.

Types of grants

The charity divides its educational support into two main areas:

▷ To assist people of working age to obtain employment with grants for course fees, travel, childcare and equipment
▷ To support university students aged 24 and under

For more information on the 'Employment Routes' the charity may be able to help with, see its website.

Annual grant total

In 2016/17 the charity had assets of £152.2 million and an income of £3.6 million. Throughout the year the charity awarded £483,000 in grants to individuals for educational purposes.

The charity also gave £973,000 to individuals for welfare purposes and over £355,000 to organisations.

Exclusions

Previous research indicates that the charity will not give funding for: direct payment of council tax or rent; debt repayments; fines or court orders; foreign travel or holidays; career changes; personal development courses; postgraduate studies; computers;

individuals whose immediate goal is self-employment; goods and services catered for by central government.

Applications

The charity's website advises that eligible individuals living in the area of benefit should call 020 7243 0551 to apply.

Other information

The charity provides debt advice for all of its beneficiaries through its partnership with Nucleus (nucleus.org.uk).

The Pocklington Apprenticeship Trust (Kensington)

£10,500

Correspondent: Debra Cole, Grants and Funding Administrator, Malton Road Hub, 2–4 Malton Road, London W10 5UP (020 7598 4779; email: debra. cole@rbkc.gov.uk; website: www.rbkc. gov.uk)

CC number: 312943

Eligibility

Young people aged 21 years or younger (occasionally up to the age of 25) who were either born in the borough of Kensington and Chelsea or whose parent(s) has/have lived there for at least ten years, and who are in financial need. Those who are in care of the borough will also be considered.

Types of grants

Grants are made for a range of educational purposes. According to the website, this may include: fees and expenses for young people undertaking an apprenticeship; scholarships, bursaries and maintenance allowances for those studying at university or another educational institution; clothing, equipment or books for young people leaving school, university or other education to start in a profession or trade; scholarships and maintenance allowances to support young people to travel abroad for educational purposes; support for children and young people to study music or arts; other educational purposes.

Annual grant total

In 2015/16 the trust had an income of £6,200 and a total expenditure of £11,000. We estimate that grants given to individuals totalled £10,500.

Applications

Application forms are available to download from the trust's website.

Westway Trust

£18,300

Correspondent: Grants Team, 1 Thorpe Close, London W10 5XL (020 8962 5720; email: grants@westway.org; website: www.westway.org)

CC number: 1123127

Eligibility

Support is available to people who live in the borough of Kensington and Chelsea and are in need. Applicants who have disabilities or a long-term health condition are encouraged to apply.

Types of grants

The trust offers two grant programmes for people who are unable to afford sports and fitness activities or coaching;

- Sports bursaries – up to £500 for adults or children who want to take part in sports and fitness activities but find it difficult to pay the fees. There are three separate bursary schemes for training, coaching and NGB training courses (Levels 1 and 2)
- Tim Davis scholarships – annual awards of up to £5,000 to young people of outstanding sporting talent

Annual grant total

In 2015/16 the trust held assets of £46.4 million and had an income of almost £8.1 million. The amount of grants given to individuals totalled £18,300 and were awarded through the trust's sports bursaries and scholarship programmes.

Exclusions

The trust does not fund retrospective costs and cannot award grants for any accrued debts for activities.

Applications

Application forms and further details can be requested from the correspondent. Note that application criteria are subject to change. For the latest updates consult the website.

Other information

The trust offers education and training programmes, runs sports facilities, health and fitness services and provides facilities for arts, culture and other events. Grants are also made to local community groups and charities.

Lambeth

Walcot Educational Foundation

£64,000

Correspondent: Grants Team, 127 Kennington Road, London SE11 6SF (020 7735 1925; email: grants@ walcotfoundation.org.uk; website: www. walcotfoundation.org.uk)

CC number: 312800

Eligibility

People, normally under 30 years of age, who are on low income and live in the borough of Lambeth. Individuals currently living outside the area but who are still considered to be Lambeth residents will also qualify for assistance.

Types of grants

The foundation offers:

- Student grants – one-off or recurrent awards of up to £2,000 per academic year to help young people over the age of 18 with the costs of their first degree or vocational training, that has a strong likelihood of leading to work. Grants can be given for: course fees (not for private institutions), associated travel costs, books, special clothing, equipment, study/field trips and childcare.
- Moving into employment grants – one-off grants for vocational training and related activities are available to people who have been out of work for most of the previous five years and have not gained a degree or qualification in the past ten years. The support is intended to help to move back to work and can be given for costs associated with further education or vocational courses, work experience and necessities such as clothing and equipment/instruments.
- Talented young people awards – to children between the ages of 10 and 18 who have exceptional talents in sports, music, drama, dance or other areas can apply for a grant of £500 to help with tuition fees, equipment or summer schools.

Annual grant total

In 2015/16 the foundation had assets of £91.5 million and an income of £2.39 million. Grants awarded to individuals for educational purposes totalled £64,000.

Exclusions

Grants are not given for:

- Postgraduate studies
- Second degrees
- Personal development courses
- Studies at private institutions
- Repayment of debts
- Career changes
- Course fees in cases where it is not clear that the applicant will be able to raise the balance of funds to complete the entire course
- The cost of goods/services already purchased or those provided by the central/local government
- Council tax, rent or other taxes
- Household goods, furnishing, clothing, unless directly related to work or education progress
- Travel abroad and holidays
- Gifts or toys
- Funeral costs
- Court orders or fines

If the applicant already has significant work experience with a reasonable level of responsibility, or a vocational qualification (at NVQ-4 or equivalent), the trust will not fund further study.

Applications

Application forms are available on the foundation's website or from the correspondent. Applications can be made at any time and a referral may be required by a staff in educational institutions, social care officer or other professional. The trustees meet six times a year and it is aimed to respond to applications from individuals within six weeks.

Other information

The foundation is made up of four charities – The Cynthia Mosley Memorial Fund, Hayle's Charity, Walcot Educational Foundation and The Walcot Non-Educational Charity. The general financial information given above represents the funds of the four charities and the information on grants for educational purposes concerns the Walcot Educational Foundation only.

The foundation also provides additional services to beneficiaries including careers advice, debt and budgeting advice, capacity building and low-cost psychotherapy. Various projects, schools and organisations working for individuals can also be supported.

Lewisham

The Lee Education Charity of William Hatcliffe

£12,700 (21 grants)

Correspondent: Anne Wilson, Clerk, PO Box 7041, Bridgnorth WV16 9EL (07517 527849; email: annewilsontc@ hotmail.co.uk)

CC number: 312801

Eligibility

Young people under the age of 25 living in Lewisham, with some preference for those living in the ancient parish of Lee.

Types of grants

One-off support for education and training purposes.

Annual grant total

In 2015/16 the charity had assets of £201,000 an income of £40,500. Grants totalling £12,700 were awarded to individuals for educational purposes.

Applications

Applications should be made through a relevant local charity or other organisation. The 2015/16 accounts state:

In 2005 the Charity set up a 'partnership panel' of 10 charities operating in Lewisham across a wide spectrum of those with differing needs to act as sponsors for grant applications for individuals. Publicity of the Charity's activities continue to be circulated to not only panel members but to other agencies inviting applications to be made for individuals.

The trustees meet at least four times a year.

Other information

Grants may also made to local charities.

Merton

Alf and Hilda Leivers Charity Trust

£8,500

Correspondent: The Trustees, Rosewood End, Windsor Road, Chobham, Surrey GU24 8NA

CC number: 299267

Eligibility

Young people in need up to the age of 18 who live or attend school/college in the London borough of Merton. The trust particularly aims to assist in the fields of education, arts, drama, music or athletics.

Types of grants

One-off and recurrent grants to help with the cost of books, clothing, equipment/instruments, educational outings and other essentials for those at school.

Annual grant total

In 2015/16 the trust had an income of £11,900 and a total expenditure of £18,500. We estimate that around £8,500 was awarded in educational grants to individuals.

Applications

Apply in writing to the correspondent. Our previous research suggests that applications can be submitted by individuals, their headteacher or a social care worker, if applicable.

Other information

Grants are also made to organisations.

Richmond upon Thames

The Barnes Workhouse Fund

£18,800 (19 grants)

Correspondent: Miranda Ibbetson, Director, PO Box 665, Richmond, Surrey TW10 6YL (020 8241 3994; email: mibbetson@barnesworkhousefund.org. uk; website: www.barnesworkhousefund. org.uk)

CC number: 200103

Eligibility

Students and trainees of any age who have resided in the ancient parish of Barnes (broadly the SW13 postcode) for at least six months. The charity actively encourages applications from those returning to education or entering into further education, with a view to improving their chances of employment. Applications must be based on financial need; the parental income of applicants up to the age of 25 is taken into account and after this age, the trustees' discretion is used.

Types of grants

One-off grants are given where statutory assistance is not available, for costs such as fees, maintenance, educational equipment, travel costs and childcare. Families can also be supported with the costs of school trips.

Annual grant total

In 2016 the fund had assets of £11.3 million and an income of £721,000. Grants totalled £259,000, the majority of which (£223,000) was distributed to organisations. Of the £36,000 given to individuals, £18,800 was awarded for educational purposes.

Exclusions

The website states that trustees are unlikely to support applications to help with the costs of postgraduate study; however, such an application may be considered if it can be demonstrated that the applicant's employment prospects will improve 'to a measurable extent'.

Applications

Applications for educational grants can be made online via the fund's website. All applicants for educational grants are interviewed by a representative of the trustees.

Other information

The Barnes Workhouse Fund provides 33 units for sheltered accommodation at Walsingham Lodge and Berkeley Road Bungalows.

The fund has an informative website and annual report, which each provide in great detail information on the fund's activities and its history.

The Hampton Wick United Charity

£9,000

Correspondent: The Clerk, 258 Hanworth Road, Hounslow TW3 3TY (020 8737 0371; email: info@ hwuc.org.uk; website: hwuc.org.uk)

CC number: 1010147

Eligibility

Individuals who are under the age of 25 and have lived in the area of benefit (the parishes of St John the Baptist in Hampton Wick, St Mark in Teddington, and St Mary with St Alban in Teddington) for at least 12 months.

Types of grants

Grants have been given towards, for example: tutorial fees and accommodation costs at university; school uniforms; fares to and from school and college; academic books; school and field trips.

Annual grant total

In 2015/16 the charity had assets of £1 million and an income of £25,000. Educational grants to individuals totalled £9,000.

Applications

In the first instance, contact the Clerk.

Richmond Parish Lands Charity (RPLC)

£79,500 (67 grants)

Correspondent: Jonathan Monckton, The Vestry House, 21 Paradise Road, Richmond, Surrey TW9 1SA (020 8948 5701; email: grants@rplc.org.uk; website: www.rplc.org.uk)

CC number: 200069

Eligibility

People above school age who are in need and have lived in the TW9, TW10 or SW14 areas of Richmond, Ham, Sheen and Mortlake for at least six months prior to application and have no other possible sources of help.

The trustees will favour applicants who have been educated in the borough and/or can demonstrate community links. Occasionally applications from people who work in the benefit area but do not reside in it will be considered but applicants will have to show that the course is directly related to the efficacy of their role in the community and is of benefit to the residents.

Types of grants

One-off and recurrent support is given towards fees, equipment, childcare costs and/or other living expenses.

The charity states:

> We recognise that especially in today's competitive economy, people may need additional qualifications to find employment or improve their income potential. Some will be building on previous educational achievements, others could be rethinking their career path because of changed circumstances or limited opportunities in their field. We aim to enable entry to Further and Higher Education Programmes to help: increase job prospects; set up/expand one's own business; achieve independence and/or quality of life.

Annual grant total

In 2016/17 the charity had assets of £98.8 million and an income of £2.1 million. Educational grants to individuals totalled £79,500.

Exclusions

Schoolchildren are not supported, although the trustees will apply their discretion with regard to applications for assistance for help with uniform or school trips for children of families on low income. Gap year activities are not funded but contributions to trips directly relating to a course of study may be considered.

Applications

Applications can be made through the charity's website where application deadlines and grant guidelines are also available.

The Thomas Wilson Educational Trust

£59,500 (28 grants)

Correspondent: Marianne Malam, Secretary to the Trust, 94 Oldfield Road, Hampton TW12 2HR (email: marianne.malam.flp@gmail.com)

CC number: 1003771

Eligibility

People under 25 who live in Teddington and neighbourhood.

Types of grants

Grants are given to schoolchildren towards clothing, books, educational outings and fees (only in exceptional circumstances) and to students in further or higher education, including overseas students (depending on how long they have been a resident in Teddington), towards books, fees, living expenses and study or travel abroad. Help may also be given to mature students under 25.

Annual grant total

In 2016 the trust had an income of £97,000 and a total expenditure of £111,500. Grants totalling £59,500 were awarded to 28 students. Of the 28 grants, eight were awarded to help pupils attend school trips and other educational needs, and the rest were awarded to students attending university or higher education courses.

Applications

Application forms are available from the correspondent. Applications can be submitted directly by the individual, by a parent or guardian, or by a school or case worker. They are considered throughout the year.

Other information

The trust also makes grants towards the upkeep of a local school.

Southwark

Charity of Thomas Dickinson

£1,100

Correspondent: David Freeman, Trustee, Flat 99 Andrewes House, Barbican, London EC2Y 8AY (020 7628 6155)

CC number: 802473

Eligibility

Young people aged 25 or under and in financial need who are living in, studying in or have at least one parent working in the ancient parishes of: St Giles without Cripplegate; St Sepulchre, St George the Martyr or St Olave, Southwark; or St Mary Magdalene, Bermondsey.

Types of grants

One-off grants ranging from £100 to £500 are given to:

- Schoolchildren for uniforms and educational outings in the UK and overseas
- Students in further or higher education for books
- Vocational students for equipment and instruments
- Individuals with special educational needs for uniforms/clothing

Annual grant total

In 2016 the charity had an income of almost £2,400 and a total expenditure of £2,300. The charity had no accounts available to view. Therefore, we estimate that around £1,100 was awarded to individuals for educational purposes.

The charity also awards grants to organisations.

Applications

Apply in writing to the correspondent.

Newcomen Collett Foundation

£32,000

Correspondent: Catherine De Cintra, 66 Newcomen Street, London SE1 1YT (020 7407 2967; email: grantoffice@newcomencollett.org.uk; website: www.newcomencollett.org.uk/index.html)

CC number: 312804

Eligibility

People under the age of 25 who have lived in the London borough of Southwark for at least two years. Priority is given to natives of Southwark, and to those embarking on their first post-school qualification.

Types of grants

The majority of grants are awarded towards the living costs of those attending tertiary or higher education. Grants are also made for school uniform.

Annual grant total

In 2015/16 the foundation had assets of £3.3 million and an income of £182,500. We estimate that grants given to individuals totalled around £32,000.

Exclusions

Grants are not given for independent school fees, overseas travel, postgraduate degrees or for retrospective expenditure.

Applications

Applications can be made through the foundation's website.

Other information

Grants are also given to schools and organisations.

St Olave's and St Saviour's Schools Foundation

£20,500 (24 grants)

Correspondent: Cathy Matthews, Administration Manager, Europoint Centre, 5–11 Lavington Street, London SE1 0NZ (020 7401 2871; email: cathymatthews@stolavesfoundation.co.uk; website: www.stolavesfoundationfund.org.uk)

CC number: 312987

Eligibility

Students who are under the age of 25 (at the time of the course) and are undertaking higher, further or vocational education courses. They must have lived in the London borough of Southwark for at least two years prior to starting their course. Consideration will also be given to young people looking to pursue courses in drama, music, sport, dance, etc.

Types of grants

The following information was provided by the foundation:

Individuals may receive a maximum grant of £2,000 per academic year over 3 years; however, the normal level of funding is around £500 to £700 per application. Grants will be for specific items or to meet specific costs. More than 3 grants (regardless of value) will not be considered other than in the most exceptional of cases at the discretion of the Trustees.

Examples of grants that have been awarded in the past include: money towards the cost of a laptop, printer, books, educational materials, travel expenses, expenses associated with vocational training, musical instruments etc.

Grants can be split into termly payments depending on the award granted. The second payment will be dependent upon the Foundation receiving a copy of the receipt(s) for the agreed purchases made with the first payment as proof of purchase. The same happens with the third payment.

Annual grant total

In 2016/17 the foundation held assets of £30 million and had an income of £1.4 million. Grants to 24 individuals totalled £20,500. The foundation's primary aim is to support organisations, youth groups and schools based in the London borough of Southwark and awarded grants totalling £133,000 to a variety of projects across the area. A further £951,500 was given in grants to local schools.

Exclusions

Grants are not awarded for individual salaries, school fees, domestic bills, childcare, food or payment of debts. Grants are also not awarded for items that have already been purchased. Grants may only be considered for direct educational needs.

Applications

The following information was provided by the foundation:

Applications should include the following:
- an application grant form (which can be downloaded from the website)
- an official reference from your current (or most recent) course tutor and/or key/youth worker
- proof of enrolment for the current academic year (or, if not yet enrolled, official confirmation of acceptance onto a course showing proof of home address)
- a copy of your Government Student loan/grant award/refusal letter (if applicable)
- copies of your last 2 bank statements
- a short personal statement explaining the reasons why you feel you should be granted funding over and above other applicants and a short explanation as to why you need the items you have requested.

When considering applications from Individuals, the Trustees will bear in mind the following:
- age and residency
- how the grant will explicitly benefit the applicant's education
- whether a formal offer of a place at an educational establishment has been made and accepted
- whether the individual has demonstrated financial hardship
- previous grant awards from the Foundation to the individual
- evidence of items purchased with any previous grant, in the form of copy receipts
- evidence of other funding applications and their results, if known, e.g. bursaries, hardship funds, etc.
- official references received from previous educational establishment and others
- short personal statement demonstrating need for requested items
- whether the individual has made contact with the Foundation Office to discuss the application
- how much funding will make a real difference to the applicant
- whether the application was received before the deadline date for receiving applications

The Trustees meet four times a year and grant applications can be made at any time. The dates and application deadline dates of the meetings are on the website.

Tower Hamlets

Stepney Relief-in-Need Charity

£1,000

Correspondent: Mrs J. Partleton, Clerk to the Trustees, Rectory Cottage, 5 White Horse Lane, Stepney, London E1 3NE (020 7790 3598; email: jeanpartleton194@btinternet.com)

CC number: 250130

Eligibility

People in need who live within the old metropolitan borough of Stepney.

Types of grants

One-off grants, usually of £100 to £500, for uniforms/clothing, school trips, books and equipment, for example.

Annual grant total

In 2015/16 the charity had both an income and total expenditure of £17,500. We estimate that educational grants totalled around £1,000.

Applications

An application form is available from the correspondent and may be submitted either directly by the individual or through a relative, social worker or other welfare agency. The trustees usually meet four times a year, but some applications can be considered between meetings at the chair's discretion.

Waltham Forest

Henry Green Scholarships in Connection with Council Schools

£450

Correspondent: Debbie Callender-O'Neill, Correspondent, The Business Support Team – Charity Trust Fund, Room 001, Waltham Forest Town Hall, Forest Road, Walthamstow, London E17 4JF (email: debbie.callender-oneill@walthamforest.gov.uk; website: www.walthamforest.gov.uk/Pages/Services/wf-ect.aspx)

CC number: 310918

Eligibility

People under the age of 25 and who are residents or either Leyton or Leytonstone and are attending a full-time course at the universities of Oxford, Cambridge or London and have attended one or more of the following schools for at least two years:

Buxton All-through School Secondary Phase; Connaught School for Girls; George Mitchell Secondary Phase All-through School; Leyton Sixth Form College; Leytonstone School; Norlington School for Boys; or The Lammas School.

In making their decision, the trustees may give consideration to the results of any examinations passed by the applicants, their school record, the headteacher's report, financial needs and their ability to profit by further education.

Types of grants

Small annual grants for educational necessities, books, equipment/instruments or living expenses. Our research suggests that on average grants are from £50 to £200.

Annual grant total

In 2015/16 the charity had an income of £3,800 and a total expenditure of £500. We estimate that the charity awarded around £450 in grants to individuals.

Applications

Application forms can be requested from the correspondent or found on the charity's website. Completed applications should be returned to: Tammy Hanna, Business Support – Henry Green Charity Trust Fund, London Borough of Waltham Forest, Juniper House, 221 Hoe Street, Walthamstow, London E17 9PH.

Or email completed application forms to tammy.hanna@walthamforest.gov.uk.

Grants are paid in two parts, the second part subject to a satisfactory report from the course tutor/principal by 31 January 2018. It is the responsibility of the applicant to ensure this report is sent to the trustees. Each grant will be made for one year only.

Applications for grants for further years must be the subject of a separate application each year.

Sir George Monoux Exhibition Foundation

£4,000

Correspondent: Tammy Hanna, Clerk to the Trustees, Walthamstow Town Hall, Forest Road, Walthamstow, London E17 4JF (email: tammy.hanna@walthamforest.gov.uk)

CC number: 310903

Eligibility

Students who are undertaking a full-time course at a university or college of higher education, are in need of financial assistance, are under the age of 25, live in the London borough of Waltham Forest and are pupils or former pupils of the following schools: Frederick Bremer School; Leyton Sixth Form College; Walthamstow Academy; Connaught School For Girls; Leytonstone School; Buxton All-through School Secondary Phase; George Mitchell Secondary Phase All-through School; Norlington School For Boys; Walthamstow School For Girls; Highams Park School; Rushcroft Foundation School; Willowfield School; Holy Family Catholic School and Sixth Form; Sir George Monoux Sixth Form College; Waltham Forest College; Kelmscott School; The Lammas School; Chingford Foundation School; Heathcote School and Science College; Belmont Park School; Brookfield House School; Whitefield Academy; William Morris School.

In making their decision, the trustees may take into consideration results of any examinations taken by the applicants, their school record, the headteacher's report, their financial needs and their ability to profit by further education.

Types of grants

One-off awards ranging from £250 to £2,000 are available towards the costs associated with higher education.

Annual grant total

In 2015/16 the foundation had an income of £4,500 and a total expenditure of £4,100. We estimate that grants totalled around £4,000.

Applications

Application forms are available from the foundation's website or can be requested from the correspondent. The application must be accompanied with a supporting statement and signature of a referee from the applicant's school/college/university. Applications open in April and should be submitted before the end of May. Candidates who are successful in their initial application are invited for an interview which is normally held in September.

North East

General

Alderman Worsley Bursary

£3,000 (three grants)

Correspondent: Hugh McGouran, Tees Valley Community Foundation, Wallace House, Falcon Court, Preston Farm Industrial Estate, Stockton-On-Tees TS18 3TX (01642 260860; email: info@ teesvalleyfoundation.org; website: www. teesvalleyfoundation.org)

CC number: 1111222

Eligibility

Applicants must be between 17 and 60 years old, living in Thornaby-on-Tees (excluding Ingleby Barwick), and currently studying or about to study at university, evening classes, college, or other further education institute. Applicants may apply for the bursary more than once if they can demonstrate educational progression since their last application.

Types of grants

A bursary of £1,000 paid in two instalments (£700 in September and £300 in January).

Annual grant total

In 2015/16 three successful candidates received £1,000 each.

The bursary is administered by Tees Valley Community Foundation, which had an income of £1 million and a total expenditure (across all governed charities) of £1.2 million.

Exclusions

Residents from Ingleby Barwick.

Applications

Application forms are available on the Tees Valley Foundation website. The application process opens on 1 April each year and closes on 30 June.

S. Y. Killingley Memorial Trust

£10,000

Correspondent: Dermot Killingley, Chair, 9 Rectory Drive, Newcastle upon Tyne NE3 1XT (0191 285 8053; email: trust@grevatt.f9.co.uk; website: syktrust.org.uk)

CC number: 1111891

Eligibility

People aged 18 or over residing in the North-East of England (Northumberland, Tyne and Wear, County Durham and Teesside), or if the proposed course is based in the North-East of England

The proposed course must be wholly or at least mainly based in arts and humanities (e.g. history, philosophy, languages, creative and expressive arts)

Types of grants

Grants for course fees, books, equipment, materials, travel or childcare and similar expenses. Grants have been awarded for as little as £7 up to £1,300 for postgraduate students.

Annual grant total

In 2015/16 the trust had an income of £8,000 and a total expenditure of £10,800. We estimate that around £10,000 was awarded in grants.

Exclusions

No grants are given for living costs.

Applications

Contact the trust for an application form or download it from the website at syktrust.org.uk/apply-for-a-grant-2/. This should be submitted by post along with a letter of support from a referee such as a teacher. Applications sent by email will not be accepted. The selection panel meets about three times a year, usually in January, April and September. Applicants may be asked to attend an informal interview.

Other information

Successful applicants are assigned a mentor to provide them with informal support and advice during the course.

The Northern Counties Children's Benevolent Society

£128,500 (35 grants)

Correspondent: Glynis Mackie, Secretary, 29A Princes Road, Gosforth, Newcastle upon Tyne NE3 5TT (0191 236 5308; email: info@gmmlegal.co.uk)

CC number: 219696

Eligibility

Children in need through sickness, disability or other causes who live in the counties of Cheshire, Cleveland, Cumbria, Durham, Greater Manchester, Humberside, Lancashire, Merseyside, Northumberland, North Yorkshire, South Yorkshire, Tyne and Wear and West Yorkshire. Preference is given to individuals who have lost one or both of their parents.

Types of grants

One-off and recurrent grants are available mainly towards school fees and clothing. The society has previously stated that support is also given for necessities, equipment, computers, or, in a limited number of cases, the provision of special equipment of an educational or physical nature for children with disabilities. In almost every case, the need for assistance arises through the premature death of the major wage earner or the break up of the family unit. Applications are treated in strict confidence and the financial circumstances of each applicant are fully and carefully considered by the trustees before an award is made.

Annual grant total

In 2016 the society held assets of £1.6 million and had an income of £64,000. Grants totalling £128,500 were awarded to 35 individuals.

Applications

Application forms are available from the correspondent. Grants are normally considered in January, April, July or October. The trustees will usually undertake home visits and may ask a report from a third party, such as a medical professional or a teacher.

The Gus Robinson Foundation

£12,500

Correspondent: Jeanette Henderson, Gus Robinson Developments Ltd, Stranton House, West View Road, Hartlepool TS24 0BW (01429 234221; website: www.gusrobinson.com/foundation)

CC number: 1156290

Eligibility

Individuals in need under the age of 25 living in the Tees Valley.

Types of grants

Grants are available to support individuals with education, training, sport, music, art and entrepreneurship.

Annual grant total

In 2016 the foundation had assets of £29,000 and an income of £39,500. The amount of grants given to individuals totalled £12,500.

Applications

Apply in writing to the correspondent.

Tees Valley Community Foundation Bursaries

£19,500 (four grants)

Correspondent: Hugh McGouran, Wallace House, 23 Falcon Court, Preston Farm Industrial Estate, Stockton-on-Tees TS18 3TX (01642 260860; email: info@teesvalleyfoundation.org; website: www.teesvalleyfoundation.org)

CC number: 1111222

Eligibility

Students in local authority areas of Hartlepool, Stockton-on-Tees, Redcar and Cleveland, Middlesbrough and Teesside Wide – see separate funds for specific criteria as they will vary.

Types of grants

The John Bloom Law Bursary supports students intending to study for a full-time undergraduate degree in law at a UK university.

The Pursuit of Excellence scheme awards grants of up to £1,000 for young people aged 12 to 24 and who are excelling in their chosen speciality and who are in need of financial assistance to achieve their aims.

Annual grant total

In 2015/16 the organisation had assets of £12.8 million and an income of £1.1 million. Bursaries to four individuals totalled £19,500.

Applications

Application forms and guidelines for separate funds can be found on the Tees Valley Community Foundation website, once the application round begins.

Other information

Tees Valley Community Foundation administers a number of funds providing funding to organisations and individuals. See the website for the funds currently open for applications.

There is also the Teesside Emergency Relief Fund supporting people who face an unexpected crisis.

County Durham

County Durham Community Foundation

£747,000

Correspondent: Barbara Gubbins, Victoria House, Whitfield Court, St John's Road, Meadowfield Industrial Estate, Durham DH7 8XL (0191 378 6340; email: info@cdcf.org.uk; website: www.cdcf.org.uk)

CC number: 1047625

Eligibility

People in the County Durham and Darlington areas who are in, or wish to return to, education and training. Eligibility for education schemes are as follows:

- **Durham County Cricket Youth Trust Fund:** must be aged 12 to 23, live between the River Tyne and the River Tees, and a member of a cricket club affiliated with Durham Cricket Board
- **Durham Johnston Educational Fund:** past and present pupils, aged 24 or under, of selected secondary schools (Belmont Community School; Durham Community School; Durham Johnston Comprehensive School; Durham Sixth Form Centre; Durham Trinity School and Sports College; Framwellgate School; St Leonard's RC Comprehensive School). Must have lived in Durham for at least two years
- **Durham Works 6/12 Months:** unemployed individuals aged 16 to 24 enrolled on the Durham Works programme

- **Young PCVC Community Safety Fund:** young people aged 9 to 18 who wish to undertake a project on crime and offending in their area
- **Stanhope Castle School Charitable Trust Fund:** people under the age of 25 who are, or who were, in the care of or looked after under a Supervision Order to the local authority in the north east for a minimum of six months
- **Talent Individuals:** young people under the age of 21 who have potential to compete in international sport
- **Dover Prize Fund:** contemporary artists from across the UK. Applicants must meet a minimum of three of the following: work is regularly exhibited; the artist has received grants before; a degree in visual arts; work commissioned by public institution; work previously purchased by a public collection; work featured in a journal, newspaper or other curated platform; artist is represented by a gallery; or has taken part in a residency scheme

Types of grants

The wide range of funds on offer provide support for different educational purposes, including:

- Fees
- School uniform/clothes for a job interview/work clothes or uniform
- Sporting equipment
- Musical equipment
- Private tutoring
- Books, stationery, computers, and other learning aids
- Work tools
- Childcare
- Transport to and from school or work
- School trips
- Research, projects and exhibitions

Annual grant total

In 2016/17 the foundation had assets of £18.3 million and an income of £3.7 million. The amount awarded for educational purposes was £747,000.

Applications

All application forms and processes can be found on the foundation's website. At the time of writing (November 2017), there were eight grant-making programmes available to individuals for educational purposes. Each grant-making scheme has its own eligibility and deadlines, contact the foundation if you are unsure.

Other information

Grants are also made to organisations and to individuals for social welfare needs.

Lord Crewe's Charity
See entry on page 116

County Durham

Johnston Educational Foundation

Correspondent: David Watchman, Durham County Council Resources, County Hall, Durham DH1 5UL (email: david.watchman@durham.gov.uk)

CC number: 527394

Eligibility
People under the age of 25 who live, or whose parents live, in the city of Durham.

Types of grants
Support is available to further and higher education students, for travel, voluntary work, accommodation, fees, extracurricular coaching, and the arts.

Annual grant total
In 2015/16 the foundation had an income of £3,300 and no expenditure. Note, charitable expenditure is around £500 to £1,000 per year.

Applications
Application forms can be requested from the correspondent. Our research shows that applications are considered in February, June, October and can be submitted directly by the individual.

The Sedgefield District Relief in Need Charity (The Sedgefield Charities)

£430

Correspondent: John Hannon, East House, Mordon, Stockton-on-Tees, County Durham TS21 2EY (01740 622512; email: east.house@btinternet.com)

CC number: 230395

Eligibility
Students who live in the parishes of Bishop Middleham, Bradbury, Cornforth, Fishburn, Mordon, Sedgefield and Trimdon, in County Durham.

Types of grants
Modest, one-off grants are made to students of further, higher, and vocational education for fees, equipment, clothing, and other costs associated with education.

Annual grant total
In 2016 the charity had an income of £31,000 and a total expenditure of £16,500. The amount awarded for educational purposes was £430.

Applications
Application forms can be requested from the correspondent.

Other information
The charity also gives grants to local organisations, and to individuals for relief in need.

The Sedgefield Educational Foundation

£3,000

Correspondent: John Hannon, Clerk, East House, Mordon, Stockton-on-Tees TS21 2EY (01740 622512; email: east. house@btinternet.com)

CC number: 527317

Eligibility
People between the ages of 18 and 25 who or whose parents are resident in the parishes of Fishburn, Sedgefield, Bradbury and Morden.

Types of grants
Small grants to people in full-time further/higher education and training. Our research suggests that recurrent grants are available for the duration of the study. Support is given to help with the cost of books, equipment, fees and living expenses. The trustees normally only help with education higher than A-level and support those courses that are not available at schools. Grants can range from £140 to £300 (depending on the applicant's circumstances).

Annual grant total
In 2016 the foundation had an income of £3,000 and a total expenditure of £3,400. We estimate that grants to individuals totalled around £3,000.

Applications
Application forms are available from the correspondent. They should be submitted by 30 September for consideration in October.

Other information
Students seeking funds for study or travel abroad and students over 25 may be referred to the Sedgefield District Relief-in-Need Charities, to which welfare applications are also referred. Local schools may also be assisted.

Hartlepool

The Preston Simpson and Sterndale Young Musicians Trust

£6,500

Correspondent: Christine Lowson, Hartlepool Borough Council, Civic Centre, Victoria Road, Hartlepool TS24 8AY (01429 523754; email: christine.lowson@hartlepool.gov.uk; website: www.hartlepool.gov.uk/ youngmusicianstrust)

CC number: 512606

Eligibility
Young musicians between the ages of 15 and 25 who were born in the borough of Hartlepool or have a parent who has lived in the area for at least five years. The grant is designed to support those who have already achieved a good standard in their studies and wish to pursue a career in music. Applicants' achievements should be demonstrated by participation in concerts, membership in bands or orchestras, a minimum standard of Grade V in the Associated Board Examination or equivalent qualification from Trinity College London and genuine intentions to use musical abilities in their future career (such as commitment to GCSE Music).

Types of grants
Scholarships to musicians studying music at any school, college or university.

Annual grant total
In 2015/16 the trust had an income of £7,500 and a total expenditure of £7,000. We have estimated that grants totalled around £7,000.

Applications
Application forms and guidelines can be requested from the correspondent. Applicants should also provide two written references, one of which must be from music teacher or head of music. The deadlines for applications are usually in late autumn, but consult the website for the current deadline. Handwritten applications will not be accepted.

Northumber-land

Allendale Exhibition Endowment

£7,400

Correspondent: Joseph Robinson, Trustee, Amberlea, Catton, Hexham, Northumberland NE47 9QS (01434 683586)

CC number: 505515

Eligibility

People under the age of 25 who live, or whose parents live, in the parishes of East and West Allendale.

Types of grants

Funding is available for secondary school students, further education and university students, and people entering work. Grants are awarded to cover the cost of educational supplies such as books, and to help towards the cost of tools and uniforms for starting work. Grants can also be awarded as maintenance allowances or bursaries, and particular interest is given to those studying music or the arts.

Annual grant total

In 2015/16 the charity had an income of £8,300 and a total expenditure of £7,900. We estimate the total given in grants was around £7,400.

Applications

Application forms are available at the charity address and should be submitted directly to the correspondent. An advert is placed in the local paper, post office and library in mid-August and the deadline is usually the end of October.

Blyth Valley Trust for Youth

£4,000

Correspondent: Lee Paris, Blyth Sports Centre, Blyth NE24 5BT

CC number: 514145

Eligibility

Children and young people under the age of 21 who live or attend school in the borough of Blyth Valley. The trust will provide financial assistance to attend a centre of excellence or similar establishment and further their activities in a chosen field of arts, sciences or sport. Applicants should be of amateur status.

Types of grants

Grants are provided to support activities in the fields of arts, music, sciences or sport/physical recreation. Our research shows that the trust awards one-off grants, usually between £50 and £250. Support may only be given to those who are able to identify specific centres of excellence which they will be attending.

Annual grant total

In 2016/17 the trust had no income and a total expenditure of £4,600. The total amount awarded in grants to individuals was £4,000.

Applications

Application forms can be requested from the correspondent and can be submitted either directly by the individual or by a school/college. Applicants are requested to include full details of the activity and provide references. Our research indicates that applicants should apply early (preferably before February each year) in time for the trustees' meeting, usually held in April.

Coates Educational Foundation

£9,550

Correspondent: Andrew Morgan, Trustee, 14 Bell Villas, Ponteland, Newcastle upon Tyne NE20 9BE (01661 871012; email: amorgan@nicholsonmorgan.co.uk)

CC number: 505906

Eligibility

People under the age of 25 who live in the parishes of Ponteland, Stannington, Heddon-on-the-Wall, and the former district of Newburn or are current/former pupils of the Richard Coates Church of England Voluntary Aided Middle School.

Types of grants

One-off grants and bursaries to help with the cost of books, equipment/materials, clothing, educational outings, maintenance and fees. Support can be given to schoolchildren and students at college/university. People starting work/entering a trade can also be helped with the cost of books, equipment/instruments, clothing or travel.

Annual grant total

In 2016 the foundation had an income of £19,300 and a total expenditure of £19,300. The foundation had no accounts available to view. We estimate that they gave around £9,550 to individuals for educational purposes.

The foundation also awards grants to local organisations and schools.

Applications

Application forms are available from the correspondent.

Community Foundation Serving Tyne and Wear and Northumberland

See entry on page 235

The Eleemosynary Charity of Giles Heron

£4,000

Correspondent: George Benson, Trustee, Walwick Farmhouse, Humshaugh, Hexam NE46 4BJ (01434 681203; email: office@chestersestate.co.uk)

CC number: 224157

Eligibility

People in need who live in the parish of Wark and Simonburn.

Types of grants

One-off grants according to need towards the cost of education, training, apprenticeship and equipment for those starting work and for educational visits abroad.

Annual grant total

In 2015/16 the charity had an income of £17,700 and a total expenditure of £17,400. We estimate that educational grants to individuals totalled around £4,000.

Applications

The individual should apply directly to the correspondent in writing.

The Kirkwhelpington Educational Charity

£3,500

Correspondent: Helen Cowan, 11 Meadowlands, Kirkwhelpington, Newcastle upon Tyne NE19 2RX (01830 540374)

CC number: 506869

Eligibility

Young people under the age of 25 who live, or whose parents live, in the civil parish of Kirkwhelpington.

Types of grants

Usually one-off grants towards broad educational purposes. Our research suggests that assistance to help with the cost of equipment, books, transport and extra courses has been given to individuals going on to some form of training or further education after school. Schoolchildren have also received help with the cost of educational outings and special tuition.

Annual grant total

In 2016 the charity had an income of £5,300 and a total expenditure of £7,600. We estimate that about £3,500 was awarded in grants to individuals.

Exclusions

Grants are not provided where support is available from the local authority.

Applications

Apply in writing to the correspondent. Candidates should include details of how the money is to be spent, other possible sources of funding secured or applied to, and provide receipts of items/services purchased (where possible).

Other information

Grants are also given to schools and voluntary organisations in the parish providing educational and training facilities for people under the age of 25, where support is not given by the local authorities.

Prowde's Educational Foundation (Prowde's Charity)

£20,000

Correspondent: Richard Lytle, 39 Stanley Street, Southsea PO5 2DS (023 9279 9142; email: mbyrne@vwv.co.uk)

CC number: 310255

Eligibility

Boys and young men aged 9 to 25 who live in Somerset or the North or East Ridings of Yorkshire. Preference is given to those who are descendants of the named persons in the will of the founder, and boys with serious family difficulties and/or those with special educational needs.

Types of grants

One-off grants are given for a wide range of educational purposes, including postgraduates, uniforms, other school clothing, books and equipment.

Annual grant total

In 2015/16 the foundation had an income of £22,600, and spending of £21,000. We estimate that around £20,000 was spent on grants to individuals.

Exclusions

Females.

Applications

Application can be submitted directly by the individual, parents or sometimes social workers. The application should include the applicant's birth certificate

and evidence of acceptance for a course. Forms should be submitted by May/June for consideration in July.

Rothbury Educational Trust

£5,000

Correspondent: Susan Rogerson, 1 Gallow Law, Alwinton, Morpeth NE65 7BQ (01669 650390)

CC number: 505713

Eligibility

Higher education students between the ages of 18 and 25 who live or have attended school in the parishes of Cartington, Hepple, Hesleyhurst, Rothbury, Snitter, Thropton and Tosson and the parts of the parishes of Brinkburn, Hollinghill and Netherton that lie within the ancient parish of Rothbury.

Applicants must be pursuing a full-time further education course at a technical college, university or similar establishment approved by the trustees.

Types of grants

Small grants towards general educational expenses, including the cost of books, fees, equipment/instruments, clothing and so on.

Annual grant total

In 2015/16 the trust had an income of £6,500 and a total expenditure of £6,000. We estimate that grants totalled around £5,000.

Applications

Apply in writing to the correspondent. Our research shows that applications are normally considered in late August/early September and grants are usually advertised in the local newspapers.

Shaftoe Educational Foundation

£20,500 (59 grants)

Correspondent: Peter Fletcher, The Clark, Chesterwood Grange, Chesterwood, Hexham, Northumberland NE47 6HW (01434 688872; email: info@shaftoecharities.org.uk; website: www.shaftoecharities.org.uk)

CC number: 528101

Eligibility

People in further/higher education or vocational training who live, or whose parents live, in the parish of Haydon.

Types of grants

One-off and recurrent grants in the range of about £400 are available to further/higher education students

(including mature students) for all years of their course and to people in vocational training or undertaking apprenticeships. Support is available towards the cost of fees, equipment/instruments, tools, books, clothing or other necessities, also study/travel overseas for educational purposes.

Annual grant total

In 2016/17 the foundation had assets of £8.6 million, and an income of £300,000. There were 59 grants awarded, which amounted to £20,500.

Applications

Application forms can be downloaded from the foundation's website or requested from the correspondent. The trustees meet three times a year, normally in March, July and November.

Other information

The foundation own nine almshouses on Shaftoe Terrace, where the Almshouse Charity of John Shaftoe can assist people aged over 60 who are in need of housing.

Tyne and Wear

Community Foundation Serving Tyne and Wear and Northumberland

£32,000

Correspondent: The Trustees, Philanthropy House, Woodbine Road, Gosforth, Newcastle upon Tyne NE3 1DD (0191 222 0945; email: general@communityfoundation.org.uk; website: www.communityfoundation.org.uk)

CC number: 700510

Eligibility

See the specific fund for details of eligibility and exclusions.

Types of grants

The following information on the foundation's funds has been taken from its website:

The Brian Roycroft Fund helps young people who have been in local authority care, and are now entering adult life, to achieve their aspirations.

The Robert Wood Trust Fund provides grants of up to £500 to individuals aged 12–18 from Tyne & Wear or Northumberland who have been offered a life-enhancing opportunity that will contribute towards educational achievement.

The Watson Family Fund supports care leavers aged 16–25 to move into accommodation, enter further or higher education, find employment or achieve good health.

The Young Musicians Fund supports the musical skills of children and young people in Tyne & Wear, Northumberland and Durham under 18 through tuition fees or help to purchase an instrument.

The Emma Newton Fund supports young people in Tyne & Wear and Northumberland to support pursuits in the performing arts.

Annual grant total

In 2015/16 the foundation had assets of £70.4 million and an income of £8.9 million. Welfare grants to individuals totalled £32,000.

Applications

Applications can be made via the foundation's website.

Cullercoats Education Trust

£2,300

Correspondent: Helen Lawlan, Administrator, 66 Northfield Road, Gosforth, Newcastle upon Tyne NE3 3UN (email: helenlawlan@sky.com)

CC number: 506817

Eligibility

People who live in the ecclesiastical parishes of St Paul, Whitley Bay and St George, Cullercoats.

Types of grants

Grants are made towards religious instruction in accordance with the doctrines of the Church of England and to promote the education, including social and physical training, of beneficiaries.

Annual grant total

In 2015/16 the trust had an income of £5,000 and a total expenditure of £4,700. We estimate that the trust gave around £2,300 in grants to individuals for educational purposes.

Applications

Apply in writing to the correspondent.

Other information

The trust is also known as the Old Church of England School Fund.

Charity of John McKie Elliott Deceased (The John McKie Elliot Trust for the Blind)

£150

Correspondent: Robert Walker, Trustee, 6 Manor House Road, Newcastle Upon

Tyne NE2 2LU (0191 281 4657; email: bobwalker9@aol.com)

CC number: 235075

Eligibility

People who are blind or have a visual impairment and live in Gateshead or Newcastle upon Tyne.

Types of grants

One-off and ongoing grants are given according to need for items, equipment or activities.

Annual grant total

In 2015 the charity had an income of £1,000 and a total expenditure of £300. We estimate £150 was awarded in education grants.

Applications

Apply in writing to the correspondent.

Sunderland

The Sunderland Orphanage and Educational Foundation

£15,000

Correspondent: Peter Taylor, 19 John Street, Sunderland SR1 1JG (0191 567 4857; email: petertaylor@mckenzie-bell.co.uk)

CC number: 527202

Eligibility

Young people under the age of 25 who are resident in or around Sunderland and who have one or two parents who are deceased, separated, divorced, or who have a disability.

Types of grants

Grants are awarded for the following educational purposes:

- Provision of tools, equipment, books, and other physical necessities for education
- Purchasing school uniforms or job-related clothing
- Scholarships, bursaries, and maintenance allowances tenable at any place of learning approved by the trustees
- Financial assistance for people leaving school and about to enter employment or trade
- Provision and tutoring of musical instruments
- Travelling abroad for study
- Coaching and training in sports and athletics
- Financial assistance to study music and the arts

Annual grant total

In 2015/16 the foundation had an income of £23,000 and a total

expenditure of £25,500. We estimate that the amount awarded for educational purposes was £15,000.

Applications

Applications can be made in writing to the correspondent.

Other information

The foundation also provides grants in the form of boarding and 'pocket money' to young people in financial need.

North West

General

Crabtree North West Charitable Trust

£50

Correspondent: Ian Currie, Trustee, 3 Ralli Courts, New Bailey Street, Salford M3 5FT (0161 831 1512)

CC number: 1086405

Eligibility

Children and young people up to the age of 18 who are in education in the North West.

Types of grants

One-off grants are given according to need towards general educational purposes and sports causes.

Annual grant total

In 2015/16 the trust had an income of £2,500 and a total expenditure of £300. We estimate that the trust awarded around £50 in grants to individuals for educational purposes.

The trust also awards grants to organisations.

Applications

Apply in writing to the correspondent.

The Northern Counties Children's Benevolent Society

See entry on page 231

The Pinecone Trust

£11,000

Correspondent: The Pinecone Trust, Brabners LLP, Horton House, Exchange Flags, Liverpool, c/o Charities Department L2 3YL (0151 600 3079; email: pineconetrust@btinternet.com)

CC number: 1158563

Eligibility

Young people between the ages of 16 and 25 who live in Merseyside, Lancashire, and Cumbria.

Types of grants

One-off grants are available to assist with education and training expenditure, for example course fees or equipment, to help the applicant gain employment after education.

Annual grant total

In 2015/16 the trust had an income of £19,500 and a total expenditure of £12,000. We estimate the trust awarded a total of £11,000 towards education and training grants.

Applications

Applications should be made in writing to the correspondent, detailing financial need, what the grant will be used for, and how it may lead to employment.

Other information

The trust was established in 2015.

The Winwick Educational Foundation

£4,000

Correspondent: Ian Sydenham, Forshaws Davies Ridgway LLP, 17–21 Palmyra Square South, Warrington, Cheshire WA1 1BW (01925 230000)

CC number: 526499

Eligibility

Further education students who live in the parishes of Winwick, Emmanuel Wargrave, Lowton St Luke's, Lowton St Mary's, Newton All Saints, Newton St Peter's and St John's Earlestown.

Types of grants

Small, one-off and recurrent grants are available to further education students towards general educational needs, including books, equipment/instruments and fees.

Annual grant total

In 2015/16 the foundation had an income of £2,600 and a total expenditure of £9,000. We estimate that grants to individuals totalled around £4,000.

Applications

Apply in writing to the correspondent. Applications should normally be submitted in February and March for consideration in April. They can be made directly by the individual or through a third party, such as the individual's school, college or educational welfare agency, if applicable.

Other information

The foundation also supports four specific Church of England primary schools in north Warrington.

Cheshire

Cheshire East

Alsager Educational Foundation

£11,000

Correspondent: Catherine Lovatt, 6 Pikemere Road, Alsager, Stoke-on-Trent ST7 2SB (01270 873680; email: colovatt@hotmail.com)

CC number: 525834

Eligibility

Children and young people who live in the parish of Alsager.

Types of grants

Financial assistance is given to individuals in scholarships, bursaries, and maintenance allowance to enable them to travel abroad and improve educational recreation. Preference is given to those who choose to study music or religious education within the doctrines of the Church of England.

Annual grant total

In 2015/16 the foundation had an income of £25,400 and a total expenditure of £15,600. We estimate the total amount given in grants was £11,000.

Applications

Apply in writing to the correspondent. Applications are considered four times per year.

Other information

Both individuals and organisations can be supported. Special benefits are provided to the Alsager Church of England Junior School.

Audlem Educational Foundation

£6,500

Correspondent: Judy Evans, 1 Shropshire Street, Audlem, Crewe, Cheshire CW30AE (01270 686193; website: www.audlem.org/directories/groups/audlem-education-foundation.html)

CC number: 525810

Eligibility

Children and young people under the age of 25 resident in the ancient parish of Audlem, including Buerton and Hankelow and part of Dodcott-cum-Wilkesley and Newhall.

Types of grants

Financial assistance in the form of grants and bursaries for children and young people in Audlem, to pay for educational enhancement, such as student exchanges, field trips or vocational courses.

Annual grant total

In 2015/16 the foundation had a total income of £16,300 and a total expenditure of £10,700. Two-thirds of the total expenditure were awarded as educational grants for individuals, estimated at around £6,500. The remaining third of available funds was used in local schools.

Applications

Application forms can be found on the foundation's website or requested from the correspondent. The trustees meet three times a year, usually in November, February and July. Applications should be made in advance to these dates. Candidates are also required to provide a confirmation of attendance and receipts for the items purchased or other financial details of the course/trip taken.

Other information

The foundation allocates a third of its income and interest from the investments to support schools in the area of benefit. The remainder is used to award grants to individuals.

The Congleton Town Trust

£6,000

Correspondent: Jo Money, Clerk, Congleton Town Hall, High Street, Congleton, Cheshire CW12 1BN (01260 270908; email: info@congletontowntrust.co.uk; website: www.congletontowntrust.co.uk)

CC number: 1051122

Eligibility

People in need who live in the town of Congleton (this refers only to the area administered by Congleton Town Council).

Types of grants

The principal aim of the trust is to give grants to individuals in need or to organisations which provide relief, services or facilities to those in need. The trustees will, however, consider a grant towards education or training if the applicant is in need. Support can be given in the form of books, tools or in cash towards tuition fees or maintenance.

Annual grant total

In 2016 the trust had an income of £25,000 and a total expenditure of £26,500. We estimate that educational grants to individuals totalled around £6,000.

Applications

We would advise potential applicants to, in the first instance, contact the correspondent for more information. This can be done using the online form on the website.

Lindow Workhouse Charity

£5,000

Correspondent: John Fallows, Correspondent, 1 Thornfield Hey, Wilmslow, Cheshire SK9 5JY (01625 533950; email: lwt@jfallows.org.uk)

CC number: 226023

Eligibility

Our research suggests that children with special educational needs who live in the ancient parish of Wilmslow can be supported. The charity only serves people in the parish but any cases of real need can be considered, so other educational needs may potentially be assisted.

Types of grants

One-off grants of up to £500.

Annual grant total

In 2015/16 the charity had an income of £10,500 and a total expenditure of £10,700. We estimate that around £5,000 was awarded to individuals for educational purposes.

Applications

Application may be made in writing to the correspondent at any time. They can be submitted directly by the individual or a family member, through a third party (such as a social worker or teacher), or through an organisation (such as Citizens Advice or a school).

Other information

Awards are made for welfare needs as well.

Cheshire West and Chester

Chester Municipal Charities

£63,500

Correspondent: Peter Catherall, The Bluecoat, Upper Northgate Street, Chester CH1 4EE (01244 403277; email: administration@chestermc.org.uk; website: www.thebluecoat-chester.org.uk/about)

CC number: 1077806

Eligibility

Young people under the age of 25 who are attending or have attended a school in Chester and who are resident in the city.

Types of grants

Grants may come in the form of bursaries/grants paid directly to schools/colleges/universities. Grants are made for education to help with the costs of equipment, educational trips and other expenses. The charity also provides a limited number of bursaries and a programme of funding support in Early Years education.

Annual grant total

In 2015 the charity had assets of £14.6 million and an income of £554,000. We estimate that grants given to individuals totalled around £63,500.

Applications

An application form is available from the correspondent.

Other information

The charity also manages almshouses.

The Sir Thomas Moulson Trust

£6,000

Correspondent: Julie Turner, Clerk to the Trustees, Meadow Barn, Cow Lane, Hargrave, Chester CH3 7RU

CC number: 214342

Eligibility
Students under the age of 25 who live in the villages of Huxley and Tarvin.

Types of grants
One-off grants to students in further/higher education towards books, fees/living expenses and study or travel abroad.

Annual grant total
In 2016 the trust had an income of £23,000 and a total expenditure of £39,000. We have estimated that around £6,000 was given in grants to individuals for educational purposes, with the rest of the expenditure awarded to the parish church of St Peter in Hargrave.

Applications
Apply in writing to the correspondent.

Other information
Support is also given to the parish church of St Peter, Hargrave and associated buildings/land provided for community use.

The Thornton-Le-Moors Education Foundation

£1,400

Correspondent: Roy Edwards, Trustee, 4 School Lane, Elton, Chester CH2 4LN (01928 725188)

CC number: 525829

Eligibility
People under 25 in full-time education who live in the ancient parish of Thornton-Le-Moors which includes the following villages: Dunham Hill, Elton, Hapsford, Ince and Thornton-Le-Moors.

Types of grants
The foundation gives grants mostly to students leaving school to train for a profession or going to university, and are given for purposes such as books, equipment and outfits.

Annual grant total
In 2016 the foundation had an income of £2,800 and a total expenditure of £1,700. We estimate that around £1,400 was awarded to individuals.

Applications
Apply in writing to the correspondent. The trustees meet twice a year, usually in April and November.

Other information
Grants also to the local youth groups and other educational organisations.

Cumbria

Cartmel Old Grammar School Foundation

£6,000

Correspondent: Colin Milner, Cartmel Old Grammar School Foundation, Quintaine, Cardonara Road, Grange-over-Sands, Cumbria LA11 7EW (01539 535043; email: mrcolinmilner@gmail.com)

CC number: 526467

Eligibility
Children and young people between the ages of 18 and 25 who live in the parishes of Cartmel Fell, Broughton East, Grange-over-Sands, Lower Holker, Staveley, Lower Allithwaite, Upper Allithwaite and that part of the parish of Haverthwaite east of the River Leven.

Types of grants
Small, one-off and recurrent (up to three years) grants of about £90 are awarded to further/higher education students to help with the costs of books, fees/living expenses or study/travel abroad and in the UK. Support is also given for music and arts studies.

Annual grant total
In 2016/17 the foundation had an income of £13,000 and a total expenditure of £11,000. We estimate the amount awarded in grants to individuals was around £6,000.

Applications
Application forms are available from the correspondent and are also distributed in local churches and educational establishments. Applications are to be sent by email; if sending by post, include an sae. The trustees meet in November and applications should be submitted by the end of September at the latest.

Other information
The foundation also makes payments to the Cartmel Poor Charity and Brow Edge Foundation. Local schools are also supported to meet expenditure not covered by the local authority.

Edmond Castle Educational Trust

£15,000

Correspondent: Andrew Beeforth, c/o Cumbria Community Foundation, Dovenby Hall, Dovenby, Cockermouth CA13 0PN (01900 825760; fax: 01900 826527; email: enquiries@cumbriafoundation.org; website: www.cumbriafoundation.org)

CC number: 1075120–4

Eligibility
Disadvantaged children and young people under the age of 21, who live in Cumbria.

Types of grants
Grants of up to £500 per year to assist with activities or equipment to further education. Supported projects in the past have included funding for computer equipment and a sensory room.

Annual grant total
In 2015/16 the trust held assets of £291,000 and awarded £15,000 in grants to individuals.

Exclusions
Activities which are the statutory duty of the government are not funded; people over the age of 21.

Applications
Application forms can be requested from the Cumbria Community Foundation in writing, by telephone, or by email. Applications should be supported by a third party, such as a social worker or health visitor.

Other information
The trust supports both individuals and organisations. The trust is administered and managed by the Cumbria Community Foundation.

Cumbria Community Foundation

£61,000 (64 grants)

Correspondent: The Grants Team, Cumbria Community Foundation, Dovenby Hall, Cockermouth, Cumbria CA13 0PN (01900 825760; fax: 01900 826527; email: enquiries@cumbriafoundation.org; website: www.cumbriafoundation.org)

CC number: 1075120

Eligibility
The restrictions of each grant are as follows:

Beck Burn Wind Farm: applicants must be aged 16 or over, studying full-time for a vocational qualification, and must live within a 5km radius of the wind farm. There is a preference to support STEM and environmental students.

Cultural Fund: applicants can reside in any part of Cumbria, but must show talent in any area of the arts.

Cumberland Educational Foundation: applicants must be under the age of 25, and live in the Copeland, Allerdale,

239

Carlisle, or North Eden areas. This fund is for further and higher education students.

Cumbria Young People's Fund: applicants must be between the ages of 14 and 22. Preference is given to those in Barrow and Carlisle, or those studying sports or arts. Household income will be factored into this application.

Dora Beeforth Memorial: applicants must be aged 11 to 21 and have a household income of less than £539 per week.

Edmond Castle Fund: see the separate entry in this book.

Gibb Charitable Trust Fund: applications are open to people over the age of 16, who are employed or resident in Copeland, Allerdale, or Alston Moor and have been for at least two years.

Hunter Davies Fund: applicants must attend either Trinity School or Cockermouth School.

Johnson Fund: applicants applying for sport or music training must be under 30 years old.

Lawrence Fund: applications are only open to musicians or horticulture students.

Live The Dream Fund: open to applicants aged 11 to 25, who live in Allerdale or Copeland. This fund is for vocational, higher, and further education students.

Swales Trust Fund: applicants must be studying farming, forestry, or land agriculture.

Types of grants

There are 12 grant-making schemes offering one-off and recurrent grants, in the range of £300 to £2,000. Support is available for tuition fees, books, equipment, instruments, course/exam fees, study and travel abroad, and job- or school-related clothing. There are funds that have a preference for supporting sport, the arts, horticulture, and STEM subjects. The majority of grants available are for students studying for a vocational qualification, or those in further and higher education.

Annual grant total

In 2015/16 the foundation had assets of £18 million and an income of £12.3 million. A total of £61,000 was awarded in educational grants to 64 individuals.

Applications

There are currently 12 educational funds available through the foundation. All application forms are available to download from the website, however they are all very similar and often the foundation may decide which fund is best for your needs.

The Hunter Davies Fund only accepts applications from the headteacher of a school on behalf of an individual.

Other information

The foundation also administers grants to individuals for welfare purposes, and to local organisations working within the community.

The Mary Grave Trust

£29,500 (46 grants)

Correspondent: Administrator, Cumbria Community Foundation, Dovenby Hall, Dovenby, Cockermouth CA13 0PN (01900 825760; email: enquiries@ cumbriafoundation.org; website: www. cumbriafoundation.org/archives/301)

CC number: 526869

Eligibility

Young people in need aged between 11 and 21 who were born in the former county of Cumberland (excluding those whose parents were resident in Carlisle). Applicants must live, study or have studied (for at least two years, in secondary/further education) within the area of benefit, with priority being given to the areas of Workington, Maryport and Whitehaven.

Students in sixth forms, further education colleges, universities and higher education colleges or in the gaps between these stages can all be considered as well as those at work, in training or involved in youth organisation activities.

Types of grants

Grants of around £1,000 to fund travel overseas in furtherance of education. The full cost of trips up to a set maximum can be provided and additional assistance for clothing and pocket money may also be given. Support is aimed at activities organised by a school/college or other trips, such as field-work expeditions, work-experience visits, specialist study bursaries for art and music schools, gap year activities and outward bound courses such as Raleigh International.

Annual grant total

In 2015/16 the trust had assets of £1.7 million. Throughout the year the trust awarded a total of 46 grants to individuals totalling £29,500.

Exclusions

The trust will not fund:

- Individuals born outside the old county of Cumberland
- Individuals born in Carlisle (unless mother resident outside Carlisle at the time of birth)

- Trips in the UK of less than three nights' duration
- Family holidays

Applications

Application forms and guidelines are available from the Cumbria Community Foundation's website. Applications can be submitted by the individual directly or through a school/college. Applicants are required to submit a full copy of their birth certificate and provide information about their financial circumstances.

Other information

The fund is administered by the Cumbria Community Foundation but is treated as a separate entity.

Kelsick's Educational Foundation

£66,500 (39 grants)

Correspondent: Peter Frost, Clerk, The Kelsick Centre, St Mary's Lane, Ambleside LA22 9DG (01539 431289; email: john@kelsick.plus.com; website: www.kelsick.org.uk)

CC number: 526956

Eligibility

Apprentices, further and higher education students under the age of 25 who have been resident in the Lake parishes (Ambleside, Grasmere, Langdale and as far south as the river at Troutbeck Bridge) for at least four years.

Types of grants

The foundation offers grants for additional teaching support, extra assistance for pupils with special needs, music, drama lessons, hire of instruments, travel costs for certain educational trips, for undertaking performing arts or sport activities, books for A-levels, books for college and university courses and any other activity which the trustees consider to be of educational benefit. Apprentices can be supported towards the cost of tools, equipment and extra training. First year higher education students are eligible for a purchase of computer and all eligible students attending universities or colleges of further education can apply for subsistence grants. Awards will be given to address essential needs and can be one-off or recurrent, ranging from £25 to £3,000.

Annual grant total

In 2015/16 the foundation held assets of £7.2 million and had an income of £394,000. The amount of grants given to individuals totalled £66,500.

Exclusions

Tuition fees and residency expenses cannot be paid by the trust.

Applications

Application forms can be found on the foundation's website. Grants are considered at quarterly meetings in February, May, August and November. The deadlines for applications are 31 January, 30 April, 31 July and 31 October respectively. Candidates must list detailed costs (with receipts) of the items required. Forms should be submitted directly by the individual or by a parent/guardian, if the applicant is under the age of 18.

Other information

Grants totalling £141,500 were awarded to schools and organisations in the area of benefit (2015/16).

Carlisle

Carlisle Educational Charity

£7,500

Correspondent: Alison Taylor, Carlisle City Council, Civic Centre, Rickergate, Carlisle CA3 8QG (01228 817290; email: alison.taylor@carlisle.gov.uk; website: www.carlisle.gov.uk/Council/More-about-the-Council/Carlisle-Educational-Charity)

CC number: 509357

Eligibility

Students in further/higher education under the age of 25 who or whose parents live within the Carlisle district. Financial circumstances of the individual's parents and the extent to which they can support the applicant can be taken into account. Generally, preference is given to students with joint family income below £21,000.

Types of grants

Grants are available to students in higher or further education and young graduates undertaking higher studies or professional qualification. Support is given for general educational costs or for students travelling in the UK or abroad for educational purposes associated with their course of study.

Annual grant total

In 2016/17 the charity had an income of £10,000 and a total expenditure of £8,000. We estimate the total amount awarded in grants was £7,500.

Applications

Application forms are available on the charity's website or can be requested from the correspondent. Applications should be submitted by September for consideration in the following month.

Copeland

Silecroft School Educational Charity

£2,500

Correspondent: Catherine Jopson, Hestham Hall Farm, Millom LA18 5LJ (01229 772525)

CC number: 509580

Eligibility

People under 25 who were born in the parishes of Whicham, Millom, Millom Without and Ulpha.

Types of grants

Recurrent grants are given for a wide range of educational needs for people at university or college. From books, clothing, equipment and other supplementary awards to foreign travel and other educational visits. However, the trust does not give grants for travel to and from the applicant's place of residence.

Annual grant total

In 2016 the charity had an income of £2,600 and a total expenditure of £2,800. We estimate that educational grants to individuals totalled around £2,500.

Exclusions

Grants are not given for schoolchildren, people starting work or to students who have not moved away from home to continue their education.

Applications

Application forms are available from the correspondent and can be submitted in September for consideration in November. Applications can be made either directly by the individual, or through their school, college or educational welfare agency.

Eden

Crosby Ravensworth Relief in Need Charities

£1,000

Correspondent: George Bowness, Ravenseat, Crosby Ravensworth, Penrith, Cumbria CA10 3JB (01931 715382; email: gordonbowness@aol.com)

CC number: 232598

Eligibility

People in need who have lived in the ancient parish of Crosby Ravensworth for at least 12 months.

Types of grants

One-off grants are available for general educational needs such as equipment or uniform.

Annual grant total

In 2016 the charity had an income of £14,000 and a total expenditure of £7,000. The amount awarded in educational grants was £1,000.

Applications

Applications may be made in writing to the correspondent, submitted directly by the individual. They should include details of the applicant's financial situation.

Other information

Grants are also made by the trust to individuals in need, and to other organisations.

South Lakeland

Brow Edge Foundation

£2,000

Correspondent: Gordon Egglestone, Bethany, Brow Edge Road, Backbarrow, Ulverston LA12 8PS (01539 531507; email: gordon@421.co.uk)

CC number: 526716

Eligibility

People in need who live in the area of Haverthwaite and Backbarrow, aged between 16 and 25. Preference is given to young people from disadvantaged backgrounds.

Types of grants

Small grants to assist pupils attending schools, institutions or classes for post-16 education.

Annual grant total

In 2016 the foundation had an income of £2,500 and a total expenditure of £2,500. We estimate the amount awarded in grants to individuals was £2,000.

Applications

Apply in writing to the correspondent, the application must be made directly by the individual. Applicants must state the type of course of study or apprenticeship they are about to undertake, and include an acceptance letter from the institution. Applications must be received by the correspondent by 21 October each year.

Burton-in-Kendal Educational Foundation

£2,900

Correspondent: Marion Robinson, 45 Pear Tree Park, Holme, Carnforth LA6 1SD (01524 784918; email: mvrob23@gmail.com)

CC number: 526953

Eligibility

People under the age of 25 who are in sixth form education or university/college and living in the parishes of Arnside, Beetham and Burton-in-Kendal, in Cumbria. Applicants must have attended a county or voluntary primary school for no less than two years.

Types of grants

Scholarships, bursaries and maintenance allowances are available as well as financial assistance towards study/travel abroad, books, equipment/instruments, maintenance/living expenses or facilities for social and physical training. Our research suggests that average grants range between £10 and £60 and that support can also be made to people with special educational needs.

Annual grant total

In 2015/16 the foundation had an income of £3,600 and a total expenditure of £3,100. We estimate that grants given to individuals totalled £2,900.

Applications

Applications may be made in writing to the correspondent. They are considered twice a year.

Robinson's Educational Foundation

£5,000

Correspondent: Ian Jenkinson, Milne Moser Solicitors, 100 Highgate, Kendal, Cumbria LA9 4HE (01539 729786; email: solicitors@milnemoser.co.uk)

CC number: 529897

Eligibility

Children and young people under the age of 25 who live in the parish of Sedbergh, with a preference for people who live in Howgill.

Types of grants

Scholarships, bursaries and maintenance allowances are available to schoolchildren and further/higher education students. One-off grants, in the range of £15 to £1,000 are given towards general educational necessities, including books, fees, equipment, travel costs, study/travel abroad, and music lessons.

Annual grant total

In 2016/17 the foundation had an income of £14,100 and a total expenditure of £11,200. It supports both individuals and organisations, therefore we estimate that grants to individuals totalled around £5,000.

Applications

Apply in writing to the correspondent. Applications can be submitted either directly by individuals or through a social worker/Citizens Advice/welfare agency, if applicable. Applications are normally considered in September.

Other information

The foundation also supports local schools, where assistance is not already provided by the local authority.

Greater Manchester

The Community Foundation Greater Manchester (Forever Manchester)

£5,500

Correspondent: The Grants and Awards Officer, 2nd Floor, 8 Hewitt Street, Manchester M15 4GB (0161 214 0940; email: info@forevermanchester.com; website: forevermanchester.com)

CC number: 1017504

Eligibility

People in need who live in Greater Manchester.

Types of grants

Grants are usually one-off.

Annual grant total

In 2015/16 the foundation had assets of £9.5 million and an income of £3.2 million. Throughout the year the foundation awarded a total of £1.6 million in grants to both organisations and individuals. Of this amount, £10,900 was given to individuals.

We estimate that the amount awarded to individuals for educational purposes to be around £5,500.

Applications

Visit the foundation's website and contact the foundation for details of grant funds that are currently appropriate for individuals to apply for. The website states:

> Please contact our awards team on 0161 214 0940 to discuss deadline dates,

eligibility and criteria and to receive guidelines and an application pack.

Other information

The Community Foundation for Greater Manchester manages a portfolio of grants for a variety of purposes which are mostly for organisations, but there also are a select few aimed at individuals. Funds tend to open and close throughout the year as well as new ones being added – check the website for up-to-date information on currently operating schemes.

The foundation's working name is now 'Forever Manchester'.

Manchester Publicity Association Educational Trust

£1,000

Correspondent: Gillian Cosser, Trustee, 7 Heigham Gardens, St Helens, Merseyside WA9 5WB (email: theeducationaltrust@btinternet.com; website: www.theeducationaltrust.org.uk)

CC number: 1001134

Eligibility

People over the age of 16 living in Greater Manchester and the surrounding area who either are studying for a recognised qualification in marketing communications, or already work in or aim to enter marketing, advertising and related occupations.

Types of grants

Our research suggests that grants range between £200 and £500 and are given towards the cost of books or fees for education/training, usually to cover the second half of the year.

Annual grant total

In 2015/16 the trust had an income of £100 and a total expenditure of £1,500. We estimate that grants totalled about £1,000. Both the income and the total expenditure vary each year.

Exclusions

Bursaries are not intended to replace student loans, and funding is not available for international students who require a Tier 4 (General) study visa to remain in the UK.

Applications

Application forms are available from the correspondent. They must be supported by a statement from the tutor and are considered on demand. Applicants must also provide their CV, without it the application will not be considered.

Grants are not intended to fully fund a course, applicants must provide information on their intended method of overall funding.

Mynshull's Educational Foundation

£6,500

Correspondent: Trust Administration, Gaddum Centre, Gaddum House, 6 Great Jackson Street, Manchester M15 4AX (0161 834 6069; email: info@gaddumcentre.co.uk)

CC number: 532334

Eligibility
Children and young people aged 25 and under who are at school, university or college, on an apprenticeship or attending another educational/training course. Applicants must be resident or have been born in the city of Manchester or adjoining districts.

Types of grants
Grants towards the costs of education, training and apprenticeships, for items such as books, equipment, clothing, uniforms and travel costs.

Annual grant total
In 2015/16 the foundation had an income of £14,000 and a total expenditure of £6,900. We estimate that grants totalled £6,500.

Exclusions
Funding is not given for course fees, ongoing expenditure or postgraduate studies.

Applications
Application forms and guidance notes can be requested from the correspondent and must be submitted by a professional such as a teacher or social worker. Potential applicants should also contact the correspondent to check deadlines for applications.

Other information
The foundation is administered by the Gaddum Centre (CC number: 507162).

Rochdale Ancient Parish Educational Trust

£12,700

Correspondent: The Trustees, Wyatt Morris Golland & Co., 200 Drake Street, Rochdale, Lancashire OL16 1PJ (01706 864707 or 01706 655117; email: info@e-wmg.co.uk; website: www.rochdaleonline.co.uk/sites/rochdale-ancient-parish-educational-trust)

CC number: 526318

Eligibility
People who live or attend/have attended school in the ancient parish of Rochdale (which includes: Rochdale, Littleborough, Milnrow, Wardle, Whitworth, Todmorden, Saddleworth, Newhey and Bacup) or attend a school in the area, or have attended a school in the area.

There is no age limit for applicants, but preference will be given to those under the age of 25.

Types of grants
Grants are given for a range of purposes – according to the website, 'any purpose which promotes the education of the applicant (including social and physical training)'. This may include: scholarships, bursaries and maintenance grants for those at school, university, college or other educational institution; travel grants, for educational initiatives in the UK or abroad; assistance towards costs such as clothing, tools, equipment or books to assist with training or entry into a profession or to pursue a vocation. Grants usually range between around £100 to £1,000.

Annual grant total
In 2015/16 the trust had assets of £694,500 and an income of £27,500. The amount of grants given to individuals totalled £12,700.

Exclusions
Grants are not given to those who have received an award in the previous year.

Applications
Application forms can be requested from the correspondent or found on the trust's website together with guidelines. Applicants are required to submit evidence of enrolment on a particular course and specify the required support with approximate costs. The trustees meet three times a year and applications should be received by 20 February, 20 May or 31 August for consideration at a meeting.

Bolton

James Eden's Foundation

£11,400

Correspondent: The Trustees, R. P. Smith and Co., 71 Chorley Old Road, Bolton, Lancashire BL1 3AJ (01204 534421; email: info@rpsmithbolton.co.uk; website: www.rpsmithbolton.co.uk)

CC number: 526265

Eligibility
Young people resident in the metropolitan borough of Bolton who are in need of financial assistance, particularly for individuals in further education. Preference is given to people who have lost either or both parents, or whose parents are separated or divorced.

Types of grants
Cash grants of between £400 and £1,500 are given to assist college students and undergraduates with fees, books, equipment/instruments, maintenance/living expenses, educational outings in the UK and study or travel overseas. Parental income is taken into account in awarding grants.

Annual grant total
In 2015/16 the foundation had an income of £19,000 and a total expenditure of £23,000. We estimate that they gave around £11,400 in grants to individuals for educational purposes.

The charity also awards grants to organisations.

Applications
Application forms are available from the correspondent.

Provincial/Walsh Trust for Bolton

£3,000

Correspondent: Joan Bohan, Secretary, 237 Ainsworth Lane, Bolton BL2 2QQ (email: joan.bohan@ntlworld.com; website: www.pwtb.org.uk)

CC number: 222819

Eligibility
Young people, usually under the age of 25, who live or work within the Bolton Metropolitan Borough.

Types of grants
Grants are mainly one-off and generally range between £500 and £1,500, although higher amounts may be awarded. Applicants will be expected to have raised some money through other sources.

Grants are given with the aim of assisting people to achieve their personal goals or small projects (particularly helping others) rather than to provide relief in need. Character development activities, such as voluntary activities or exchanges abroad or outward bound courses, can be supported. Previously grants have been awarded for specialist equipment, tuition costs, sports activities, volunteering expenses and educational travel.

Annual grant total
In 2015/16 the trust had assets of £1 million and an income of £36,500. A

total of £4,400 was awarded in grants to individuals. A further £42,000 was given in grants to organisations.

Exclusions

Grants are not awarded for building projects, commercial ventures or for personal loans.

Applications

Application forms are available on the trust's website or can be requested from the correspondent. Supporting information may be provided but the candidates are requested to limit this to three A4 sheets. The trustees usually meet in April and October, but urgent requests can also be considered.

Other information

This charity is the result of a merger of The Provincial Insurance Trust for Bolton and David Walsh Trust.

It also makes grants to charitable organisations.

Rochdale

Middleton Educational Trust (The Emerson Educational Trust for Middleton)

£3,500

Correspondent: The Trustees, c/o 94 Whalley Road, Clayton-le-Moors, Accrington BB5 5DY (07833249318; email: middletonemersontrust@hotmail. com; website: www.rochdale.gov.uk/the_ council/more_about_the_council/ charitable_trusts.aspx)

CC number: 510495

Eligibility

People who live or attend/have attended school in the area of the former borough of Middleton. There is no age limit.

Types of grants

The Rochdale Borough Council website states:

'We can provide assistance for any purpose that promotes the education, training and development of the applicant. Or, helps ease financial barriers to achieve the required education, training or development.'

Our research suggests that support is given to a wide range of purposes, including schoolchildren, further/higher education students and people starting work, with grants towards the cost of books, equipment/instruments, uniforms/clothing, educational outings in the UK, study/travel abroad and student exchanges, apprenticeships, fees and maintenance expenses.

Annual grant total

In 2015/16 the trust had an income of £7,100 and a total charitable expenditure of £3,900. We have estimated that grants totalled around £3,500.

Exclusions

The website states that grants are not provided for 'the full cost of fees or expenses, unless exceptional hardship is shown on the application'.

Applications

Application forms can be downloaded from the Rochdale Borough Council website or requested from the correspondent. The guidance states:

'Please note that funds are very limited and not all applications for funding are approved for support – so please try to be clear on your need and reasons why you are seeking support, to help the trustees in their consideration of your application.'

The Middleton United Foundation Trust

£3,000

Correspondent: Mrs E. Foulkes, Horse Shoes, Crowberry Lane, Middleton, Tamworth B78 2AJ (0121 308 3107; email: elainehorseshoes44@talktalk.net)

CC number: 528699

Eligibility

Young people under the age of 25 who are in need and live, or whose parents live, in the parish of Middleton or the immediate vicinity.

Types of grants

One-off and recurrent grants usually of up to £300 each. Schoolchildren, further and higher education students and postgraduates can be supported for books, equipment/instruments, educational outings in the UK and study or travel abroad. In addition, schoolchildren can be helped with uniforms/other school clothing and students in further and higher education can be supported with maintenance and living expenses. People starting work can be helped with books and equipment/ instruments. Grants can also be made towards the costs of developing a hobby.

Annual grant total

In 2015/16 the foundation had an income of £3,600 and a total expenditure of £3,600. We estimate that grants totalled around £3,000.

Applications

Apply in writing to the correspondent, giving as many details as possible, for example, the purpose and size of grant requested, the cost of books/equipment,

the age of the applicant and a description of the course.

Other information

Grants are occasionally made to organisations.

Salford

The Salford Foundation Trust

£9,800 (34 grants)

Correspondent: Peter Collins, Administrator, Foundation House, 3 Jo Street, Salford M5 4BD (0161 787 8170; email: mail@salfordfoundationtrust.org. uk; website: www.salfordfoundationtrust. org.uk)

CC number: 1105303

Eligibility

Young people between the ages of 5 and 25 who are resident in Salford. Preference is given to applicants who have lived in Salford for a minimum of three years.

Types of grants

Grants of up to £500 to fund opportunities that will enable a young person to learn, develop or gain new skills, take part in a character building experience and so on.

Annual grant total

In 2015/16 the trust held assets of £32,500 and had an income of £31,000. The trust supported 32 applications under its Hobbies, Interests, Talents and Skills programme totalling £6,000 and an additional two grants were awarded totalling £3,800 through the Business Start-Up programme.

Exclusions

Funding will not be considered for the following:

▶ Driving lessons
▶ Childcare costs
▶ Higher education course fees and living expenses
▶ Membership fees
▶ Remedial intervention (speech/ language/occupational therapies)
▶ Retrospective funding
▶ Standard school/college and sports trips or residential excursions
▶ Activities with political or religious focus
▶ Needs that should be financed by statutory services

Group applications, organised group activities and so forth are not supported.

Applications

Application forms are available from the trust's website or can be requested from the correspondent and can be submitted directly by the individual or a third party (but this should not be someone who will directly benefit from the grant). Applications are decided in four rounds per year, details of which are posted on the website. Note that applications can only be submitted by post and have to include two references.

Other information
The trust has recently entered into a partnership with the Charles Camilleri Foundation to joint fund a part-time post to develop and manage the Business Start-Up programme and increase the number of applications.

Stockport
The Barrack Hill Educational Charity (Barrack Hill Trust)

£4,000
Correspondent: Julie Green, 7 Henbury Drive, Woodley SK6 1PY

CC number: 525836

Eligibility
Children and young people under the age of 21 who live or whose parents live in Bredbury and Romiley.

Types of grants
One-off grants to assist with general educational expenses. Schoolchildren can be supported towards the cost of uniforms, other school clothing, books and equipment/instruments. Students in full/part-time education can be assisted towards books, study or travel abroad and equipment. People in vocational training may also be helped with the costs of tools, uniforms, equipment and similar needs.

Annual grant total
In 2016 the charity had an income of £9,300 and a total expenditure of £8,000. We estimate a total of £4,000 was awarded in grants to individuals.

Applications
Application forms can be requested from the correspondent. They are usually made available from the local libraries towards the end of the school year as well. Awards are normally considered in September and October.

Other information
The charity also makes grants to organisations and schools in the local area.

The Ephraim Hallam Charity

£6,000
Correspondent: Stephen Tattersall, 3 Highfield Road, Poynton, Stockport, Cheshire SK12 1DU (01625 874445; email: smt@lacywatson.co.uk)

CC number: 525975

Eligibility
People under the age of 25 who are resident in the Metropolitan Borough of Stockport.

Types of grants
Grants to support people at any institution of further or higher education, including the study of music and arts, travel costs, vocational training and people starting work.

Annual grant total
In 2016 the charity had an income of £13,800 and a total expenditure of £13,300. We estimate that grants given to individuals totalled about £6,000.

Applications
Applications may be made in writing to the correspondent.

Sir Ralph Pendlebury's Charity for Orphans

£900
Correspondent: Stephen Tattersall, Correspondent, Lacy Watson & Co., Carlyle House, 107–109 Wellington Road South, Stockport SK1 3TL

CC number: 213927

Eligibility
Orphans who have lived, or whose parents have lived, in the borough of Stockport for at least two years and who are in need.

Types of grants
General educational needs of schoolchildren.

Annual grant total
In 2015 the charity had an income of £13,500 and a total expenditure of £6,500. We estimate that around £900 was awarded in grants for educational purposes.

Applications
Applications can be made in writing to the correspondent. They should be made by a parent/guardian.

Other information
Grants are also made for social welfare purposes.

Tameside
The Believe and Achieve Trust

£4,600
Correspondent: Gillian Taylor, Secretary, Active Copley, Huddersfield Road, Stalybridge SK15 3ET (0161 330 2501; email: hello@believeandachieve. org.uk; website: www.believeandachieve. org.uk)

CC number: 1157173

Eligibility
Young people who live in Tameside and have been affected by meningitis or need help to achieve in sport.

Types of grants
Grants of up to a maximum of £2,000 are given for items and services which allow children to take part in sports, such as specialist equipment and kit.

Annual grant total
In 2016/17 the charity had assets of £14,000 and an income of £30,000. Grants totalled almost £9,400. We estimate that grants for purposes relating to sports totalled around £4,600.

Exclusions
Grants cannot be given for: domestic bills (e.g. telephone, gas, electricity); arrears (e.g. mortgage payments); general clothing, bedding, furniture and domestic appliances; holidays; building or garden adaptations in rented premises; or the purchase or maintenance of minibuses and private transport.

Applications
Application forms are available to download from the website, where full eligibility criteria and guidance can also be found. Applications for assistance with sports must be supported by a letter from a professional involved with the sport/activity (e.g. a sports coach, club chair, Active Tameside employee or teacher). Applications from individuals who have a disability or additional needs must be supported by a letter from a professional involved with their care (e.g. a GP, health visitor or social worker). The charity may favour applicants who can provide match funding from another source.

Other information

The charity was established in 2014 in honour of Alex Williams, who was a dedicate meningitis campaigner. It is funded by voluntary donations and through the fundraising efforts of its supporters. More information is available from its very informative website.

Trafford

Sale Educational Foundation

£4,000

Correspondent: Barry Brotherton, 3 Highfield Avenue, Sale M33 3DW (0161 912 2637; email: barry. brotherton@trafford.gov.uk; website: saleeducationalfoundation.weebly.com)

CC number: 532317

Eligibility

Young people residing in the borough of Sale. Applicants must have lived there at least a year prior to when the application was submitted.

Types of grants

One-off grants of up to £1,000 for students take any course in higher education at a university, college or another recognised educational institution. Postgraduate study will only be considered in the most exceptional circumstances.

Annual grant total

In 2015/16 the foundation had an income of £6,400, and a total expenditure of £5,000. Grants towards education for individuals are estimated to have totalled £4,000.

Applications

Application forms can be downloaded from the foundation's website. Completed forms should be returned no later than late November, and should be sent to Councillor Barry Brotherton.

Wigan

The Golborne Charities – Charity of William Leadbetter

Correspondent: Paul Gleave, 56 Nook Lane, Golborne, Warrington WA3 3JQ (01942 727627)

CC number: 221088

Eligibility

People in need who live in the parish of Golborne as it was in 1892.

Types of grants

One-off grants usually between £70 and £100, although larger sums may be given. Grants are usually cash payments, but are occasionally in-kind, for equipment such as books, school uniforms and instruments, or for excursions.

Annual grant total

In 2015/16 the charity had an income of £6,800 and a total expenditure of £6,400. Grants are made to individuals for both social welfare and educational purposes. We estimate that educational grants totalled £1,500.

Applications

Apply in writing to the correspondent through a third party such as a social worker or a teacher, or via a trustee. Applications are considered at three-monthly intervals. Grant recipients tend to be known by at least one trustee.

The Leigh Educational Endowment

£14,000

Correspondent: The Trustees, Fairhouse Farm, Pocket Nook Lane, Lowton, Warrington WA3 1AL (01942 244991; walter.glen@hotmail.com)

CC number: 526469

Eligibility

Children and young people under the age of 25 who live in the former borough of Leigh and are attending any institution of education approved by the trustees. In practice, further/higher education students who have achieved high A-level results are normally supported.

Types of grants

Grants of between £250 and £500 are available to assist with the course fees, living expenses, books, equipment and other necessities.

Annual grant total

In 2015/16 the trust had an income of £14,800 and a total expenditure of £15,300. We estimate that grants totalled around £14,000.

Applications

Normally, applications should be submitted through the individual's college as a part of a list of suitable applicants for the trustees to choose from. Applications should be made in September after A-level results are released. Grants are considered in October.

The Lowton United Charity

£2,000

Correspondent: John Naughton, Secretary, 51 Kenilworth Road, Lowton, Warrington WA3 2AZ (01942 741583)

CC number: 226469

Eligibility

People in need who live in the parishes of St Luke's and St Mary's in Lowton.

Types of grants

Help can be given towards the cost of books, clothing and other essentials for schoolchildren. Support is also available for those at college or university.

Annual grant total

In 2015/16 the charity had an income of £7,400 and a total expenditure of £7,300. Our research suggests that grants for individuals total about £4,000 each year. About half of the grants are given at Christmas for relief-in-need purposes and the rest are given throughout the year. We estimate that grants given to individuals for educational purposes totalled about £2,000.

Exclusions

Grants are not given to postgraduates.

Applications

Applications are usually accepted through the rectors of the parishes or other trustees.

Other information

Some assistance may also be given to organisations.

Spencer's Educational Foundation Trust

£3,000

Correspondent: Linda Orchard, Bustomley Farm, Middleton Green, Leigh, Stoke-on-Trent ST10 4PQ (01889 502278; email: lindaorchard89@icloud. com)

CC number: 528442

Eligibility

People under the age of 25 who live in the village of Leigh.

Types of grants

Grants of around £150 are given to people in secondary, further or higher education towards educational necessities, maintenance costs, fees or travel in pursuit of education. Individuals starting work/entering a trade can be assisted with the cost of books, clothing and equipment/ instruments.

Annual grant total

In 2016 the trust had an income of £8,100 and a total expenditure of £3,300. We estimate that grants given to individuals totalled around £3,000.

Exclusions

Applications from people outside the area of benefit will not be considered.

Applications

Application forms can be requested from the correspondent. They are normally considered in September and should be received by August. Our research suggests that grants are paid in arrears after a reference from the educational body is received.

Other information

Some support may be given to local schools where help is not already provided by the local authorities.

Isle of Man

The Manx Marine Society

£5,000

Correspondent: Capt. R. Cringle, 10 Carrick Bay View, Ballagawne Road, Colby, Isle of Man IM9 4DD (01624 838233)

Eligibility

Young Manx people under the age of 18 who wish to attend sea school or become a cadet.

Types of grants

One-off grants are made to people who are about to start a career at sea to help with the costs of uniforms, books, equipment/instruments and fees.

Annual grant total

Our research indicates that around £5,000 a year is awarded to individuals for educational purposes.

Applications

Applications can be made in writing to the correspondent. They are considered at any time and can be submitted by the individual or through a school/college or educational welfare agency.

Other information

The trustees also award grants for social welfare purposes.

Lancashire

Baines's Charity

£3,500

Correspondent: Duncan Waddilove, Correspondent, 2 The Chase, Normoss Road, Blackpool, Lancashire FY3 0BF (01253 893459; email: duncanwaddilove@hotmail.com)

CC number: 224135

Eligibility

Young people in further education or training and those entering a trade who are in need and live in the area of Blackpool, Fylde and Wyre.

Types of grants

One-off grants ranging from £100 to £250. Requests are considered on their merits.

Annual grant total

In 2016 the charity had an income of £19,000 and a total expenditure of £16,100. We estimate that the amount paid in grants to individuals for educational purposes was about £3,500.

Applications

Application forms are available from the correspondent. They can be submitted either directly by the individual or through a social worker, Citizens Advice or other welfare agency. Applications are considered upon receipt.

Other information

Grants can be made to individuals and organisations for both welfare and educational purposes, including support to schools. The charity works in conjunction with John Sykes Dewhurst Bequest (CC number: 224133).

The charity's charitable objects include the ancient townships of Carleton, Hardhorn-with-Newton, Marton, Poulton and Thornton.

The Harris Charity

£850

Correspondent: David Ingram, Secretary, c/o Moore and Smalley, Richard House, 9 Winckley Square, Preston PR1 3HP (01772 821021; email: harrischarity@mooreandsmalley.co.uk; website: theharrischarity.co.uk)

CC number: 526206

Eligibility

People in need under 25 who live in Lancashire, with a preference for the Preston district, who are in further or higher education.

Types of grants

One-off grants, usually of £250 to £1,000, for equipment/instruments, tools and books, for example.

Annual grant total

In 2015/16 the charity had an income of £127,000 and a total expenditure of £90,500. We estimate that grants given to individuals totalled around £850.

Applications

Application forms are available to download from the charity's website. Applications made by individuals must be accompanied by supporting references from responsible referees.

The half-yearly dates by which the applications must be submitted are 31 March and 30 September. Successful applicants are notified in July and January respectively following the closing date each year.

Other information

The original charity known as the Harris Orphanage Charity dates back to 1883. A new charitable scheme was established in 1985 following the sale of the Harris Orphanage premises in Garstang Road, Preston. The charity also supports charitable organisations that benefit individuals, recreation and leisure, as well as the training and education of individuals.

Swallowdale Children's Trust

£15,000

Correspondent: Alexa Alderson, PO Box 1301, Blackpool FY1 9HD (01253 767112; email: secswallowdale@hotmail.co.uk; website: www.swallowdaletrust.co.uk)

CC number: 526205

Eligibility

People living in the Blackpool area who are under the age of 25.

Types of grants

One-off payments are made for general educational purposes, including fees, instruments, trips, equipment and clothing.

Annual grant total

In 2016/17 the trust had assets of £1 million and an income of £42,500. We estimate the amount awarded in grants for education was £15,000.

Applications

Application forms can be downloaded from the trust's website and must be supported by a social or professional worker. Once the form has been completed by the relevant parties, return it to the correspondent's PO box. The trustees meet bimonthly to review applications.

Other information

The trust mainly awards grants to individuals to relieve hardship.

Blackburn with Darwen

It's Your Wish – The John Bury Trust

£11,000

Correspondent: Pamela Rodgers, Trustee, 2 Eckersley Close, Blackburn, Lancashire BB2 4FA (079834 738356; email: info@thejohnburytrust.co.uk; website: www.johnburytrust.co.uk)

CC number: 1108181

Eligibility

Young people between the ages of 10 and 25 who reside within the boundaries of Blackburn with Darwen borough council.

Types of grants

Grants are given to 'promote the mental, spiritual, moral and physical development and improvement' of the individuals, according to the website. Support can be for a wide range of causes, including purchase of equipment, other necessities, short-term projects, study/travel overseas, expeditions, personal development opportunities, gaining new skills, travel costs and extracurricular activities. Examples of grants previously awarded are given on the trust's website.

Annual grant total

In 2015/16 the trust had an income of £10,500 and a total expenditure of £12,500. We estimate that grants to individuals totalled around £11,000.

Applications

Application forms can be downloaded from the trust's website together with full terms and conditions. Applicants who are successful in the initial consideration are invited for an interview.

Other information

All grants are expected to be spent within a 12-month period of receiving the award.

The W. M. and B. W. Lloyd Trust

£30,000

Correspondent: John Jacklin, Gorse Barn, Rock Lane, Tockholes, Darwen, Lancashire BB3 0LX (01254 771367; email: johnjacklin@homecall.co.uk)

CC number: 503384

Eligibility

People in need who live or have been/are being educated in the borough of Blackburn with Darwen, Lancashire.

Types of grants

One-off and recurrent grants to individuals in need to cover the costs of educational necessities.

Annual grant total

In 2016/17 the charity had an income of £82,000 and a total expenditure of £93,000. The charity awarded £30,000 in grants for education.

Applications

Applications should be made in writing to the correspondent. Our research suggests applications are considered quarterly – in March, June, September and December.

Other information

Grants are made to both individuals and organisations (grants are usually restricted to hospices and hospitals) for educational and social welfare purposes.

The trustees also administer the following funds:

- **The Peter Pan Fund** – for the benefit of people with mental disabilities
- **The Darwen War Memorial and Sick Poor Fund** – originally to help war widows and dependants after the First World War and people of Darwen who are sick and/or poor
- **The Darwen Disabled Fund** – originally designed to assist with the social welfare of people with physical disabilities in Darwen
- **The Ernest Aspin Donation** - to support sporting activities and in particular training and educating young people in sports
- **The T P Davies Fund** – for the benefit of the residents of Darwen
- **Darwen Probation Volunteers Fund** – supporting people in Darwen who have come under the probation and after care service, and their families

The Peel Foundation Scholarship Fund

£2,000

Correspondent: Anthony Hedley, Trustee, Burwood, Pleasington Lane, Pleasington, Blackburn BB2 5JH (01254 202251)

CC number: 526101

Eligibility

Students under the age of 25 resident in or in the neighbourhood of Blackburn who are entering higher education course to obtain a degree. The trustees choose successful applicants based on academic excellence, career ambitions and financial need.

Types of grants

Grants are for general student expenses. The fund may also support people entering a professional trade.

Annual grant total

In 2015/16 the fund had an income of £3,000 and a total expenditure of £2,200. We have estimated that grants to individuals totalled £2,000 during the year.

Applications

Application forms can be requested from the correspondent. Candidates must be nominated by the headteacher or principal of their school or college. Our research shows that applicants may be called for an interview. Candidates must begin their course in the term following the award of scholarships (usually in September), unless excused by the trustees for sufficient cause. Applications are normally considered in July and August and should be submitted in advance.

Blackpool

Blackpool Children's Clothing Fund

£3,500

Correspondent: Alan Rydeheard, 96 West Park Drive, Blackpool FY3 9HU (01253 736812)

CC number: 215133

Eligibility

Schoolchildren aged 4 to 16 who live in and attend an educational establishment in the borough of Blackpool.

Types of grants

Clothing, footwear and equipment for disadvantaged children in Blackpool. The trust awards funds in the form of vouchers which can be redeemed in participating local retailers and school shop suppliers.

Annual grant total

In 2015/16 the charity had an income of £1,100 and a total expenditure of £4,000. The amount awarded in grants was £3,500.

Applications

Apply in writing to the correspondent. If applicable, applications should be made by a third party, such as education or social work service, on behalf of the applicant. Individuals in need identified by the local education authority are also considered. Applications are administered by members of the student support team.

Superintendent Gerald Richardson Memorial Youth Trust

£7,000

Correspondent: David Williamson, Trustee, Northdene, Stoney Lane, Hambleton, Poulton-Le-Fylde FY6 9AF (01253 590510; email: david@davidwilliamsonaccountants.co.uk)

CC number: 504413

Eligibility

Children and young people under the age of 25 who live or work within 15 miles of Blackpool Town Hall. There is a preference for people with disabilities.

Types of grants

Our research suggests that the trust can provide small, one-off and recurrent grants. Awards are aimed to encourage children and young people to attend courses and activities of an educational, cultural, sporting, adventuresome or character-building nature. Assistance towards the cost of equipment, instruments, special educational needs, projects, study or travel overseas can also be provided.

Annual grant total

In 2016/17 the trust had an income of £15,300 and a total expenditure of £15,600. The trust also supports organisations, therefore we estimate that grants totalled around £7,000.

Applications

Apply in writing to the correspondent, giving details of the individual's age and the cost of the course. Applications should be submitted at least two months before the amount being requested is required. Our research suggests that they are considered bimonthly from September and can be submitted either directly by the individual, or via a third party such as a school/college welfare agency or carer.

Other information

The trust provides funds to youth organisations and schools. Generally, requests for help with major capital projects or where aid from the trust would be insignificant are rejected.

Burnley

Edward Stocks Massey Bequest Fund

£8,300

Correspondent: Chris Gay, Burnley Borough Council, Town Hall, Manchester Road, Burnley, Lancashire BB11 9SA (01282 425011; email: cgay@burnley.gov.uk)

CC number: 526516

Eligibility

People who live in the borough of Burnley and higher education students who have been previously educated in the borough.

Types of grants

The primary purpose of the fund is to assist local individuals and voluntary organisations in the fields of education, science, music and arts. Two higher education student support scholarships are considered each year to support students in higher education who have been previously educated in the borough of Burnley.

Annual grant total

In 2016/17 the fund had assets of £1 million and an income of £35,500. Total charitable expenditure was around £46,000, of which grants to individuals and student scholarships totalled £8,300.

Exclusions

Our research suggests that support is not given to people already in receipt of funding from the local authority. It is required that other sources of funding are explored before applying to the trust.

Applications

Application forms can be requested from the Democracy Unit at Burnley Council, or from the charity. Applications are considered in April/May with a decision made by July.

Scholarship applications: students must be nominated by their previous school/college, have demonstrated academic achievement, contribution to school/college life, or have difficulty in financing their higher education.

Other information

Support is mostly given to organisations and groups.

Lancaster

Tunstall Educational Trust

£2,500

Correspondent: Malcolm Robinson, Trustee, Cant Beck House, Church Lane, Tunstall, Carnforth, Lancashire LA6 2RQ (01524 274206; email: malc.r.robinson@gmail.com)

CC number: 526250

Eligibility

Schoolchildren above elementary education level living in Burrow, Cansfield and Tunstall.

Types of grants

One-off and recurrent grants are given according to need and are available to schoolchildren 'to encourage them to continue at school'. Our research suggests that the charity mainly makes travel grants.

Annual grant total

In 2016 the charity had an income of £6,200 and a total expenditure of £5,800. We estimate that grants to individuals totalled around £2,500.

Applications

Applications may be made in writing to the correspondent. The trustees normally meet in June and November to consider applications.

Other information

Schools in the area may also be supported.

Thomas Wither's Charity

£3,000

Correspondent: David Mills, Clerk to the Trustees, 51 Greenways, Over Kellet, Carnforth, Lancashire LA6 1DE (01524 732194)

CC number: 526079

Eligibility

People under the age of 25 who live in the parish of Over Kellet, in Lancashire.

Types of grants

Originally grants were given to people starting work/entering a trade and people undertaking apprenticeships. Currently the funds are also available to support general educational needs. Support can be given for various educational necessities, including clothing, outfits, equipment, tools, and towards courses, workshops and other training helping to get into employment.

Annual grant total

In 2016 the charity had an income of £5,000 and a total expenditure of £3,400. We estimate that grants to individuals totalled around £3,000.

Applications

Application forms can be requested from the correspondent.

Pendle

The Fort Foundation

£14,400

Correspondent: Edward Fort, Trustee, Fort Vale Engineering Ltd, Calder Vale Park, Simonstone Lane, Simonstone, Burnley BB12 7ND (01282 440000; email: info@fortvale.com)

CC number: 1028639

Eligibility

According to the trustees' annual report, the foundation operates throughout England and Wales and gives grants to individuals and organisations for general charitable purposes. Our research indicates that there may be a preference for young people in Pendle borough and district, especially those undertaking courses in engineering.

Types of grants

Our research suggests that one-off grants of £50 to £1,000 are available to schoolchildren, college students, undergraduates and vocational students for uniforms/clothing, study/travel overseas, books and equipment/instruments and excursions.

Annual grant total

In 2016/17 the foundation had assets of £905,500 and an income of £338,000. Grants were made totalling £219,500, the vast majority (£201,000) of which was awarded to organisations. Of the £18,900 distributed to individuals, we have calculated that £14,400 was given for purposes relating to education and amateur sport.

Exclusions

Our research indicates that awards are not made for fees.

Applications

Apply in writing to the correspondent. Appeals are considered at any time.

Preston

John Parkinson (Goosnargh and Whittingham United Charity)

£1,300

Correspondent: John Bretherton, Clerk to the Trustees, Lower Stanlea Farm, Stanlea Lane, Goosnargh, Preston PR3 2EQ (01995 640224)

CC number: 526060

Eligibility

People under the age of 25 who live in the parishes of Goosnargh, Whittingham and part of Barton.

Types of grants

One-off grants are available to people starting work, entering a trade or preparing for a profession/occupation. Support can be given for tools, books, outfits, payment of fees towards training and courses, also travel expenses or maintenance costs. Our research suggests that students in further or higher education may be given help towards the cost of books.

Annual grant total

In 2016 the charity had an income of £4,500 and a total expenditure of £1,500. We estimate that grants given to individuals totalled around £1,300.

Applications

Apply in writing to the correspondent. Our research suggests that applications are normally considered in May and November.

West Lancashire

Peter Lathom's Charity

£5,400

Correspondent: Christine Aitken, 13 Mallard Close, Aughton, Ormskirk L39 5QJ (0151 520 2717; email: c.aitken@brighouse-wolff.co.uk)

CC number: 228828

Eligibility

People under 25 who live in West Lancashire.

Types of grants

Cash grants according to need for education and training.

Annual grant total

In 2016 the charity had assets of £1.6 million and an income of £53,500. Educational grants to students totalled £5,400.

Applications

Applications can be made using a form available from the correspondent. Our research suggests that they should be submitted by 30 September. Awards in all cases are based on financial need as applications always exceed distributable income. Grants are awarded in November/December of each year.

Merseyside

The Girls' Welfare Fund

£3,500

Correspondent: Mrs S. O'Leary, Trustee, West Hey, Dawstone Road, Heswall, Wirral CH60 4RP (email: gwf_charity@hotmail.co.uk)

CC number: 220347

Eligibility

Girls and young women, usually those aged between 15 and 25 years, who were born in Merseyside. Applications from outside this area will not be acknowledged.

Types of grants

One-off and ongoing grants, usually of £100 to £1,000. According to the fund's Charity Commission record at the time of writing (November 2017) support is given 'to assist young women, of non-vocational education, in buying equipment or materials to help gain a qualification and achieve independence'.

Annual grant total

In 2016 the fund had an income of £8,200 and a total expenditure of £7,100. We estimate that grants given to individuals for educational purposes totalled around £3,500, with funding also awarded to organisations.

Exclusions

Grants are not made to charities that request funds to pass on and give to individuals.

Applications

Apply in writing to the correspondent or by email. Applications can be submitted directly by the individual or through a social worker, Citizens Advice, other welfare agency or college/educational establishment. Applications are considered quarterly in March, June, September and December, and should include full information about the college, course and particular circumstances.

The Sheila Kay Fund

£8,500

Correspondent: David Bingham, Trustee, c/o LCVS, 151 Dale Street, Liverpool L2 2AH (0151 237 2689; email: enquiries@skfund.org.uk)

CC number: 1021378

Eligibility

People in need living in Merseyside (Liverpool, Knowsley, Sefton, St Helens, Wirral) who have a can demonstrate a commitment to their community (paid or volunteering) and are pursuing education (often having missed out on earlier opportunities for formal education) but lack the necessary financial means.

Individuals should be aged 18 and over, be able to demonstrate a need for financial support and have permanent residency/indefinite leave to remain.

Types of grants

Grants of up to £200 can be used for expenses allowing an individual to access learning or development opportunities, working towards a career relating to community work and social welfare.

Learning opportunities up to Level 4 standard can be supported. The trust helps people at a range of educational stages, including higher education, access courses, vocational qualifications, introductory courses to Maths, English and IT, and community courses.

Annual grant total

In 2015/16 the fund had assets of £141,000 and an income of £143,500. Charitable expenditure totalled £40,000. Educational grant awards totalled £8,500. A further £16,700 was spent on 'enabling adults to access education and employment opportunities'.

Applications

The fund welcomes individuals to contact them on the telephone number provided.

Other information

The fund also provides a range of other services and support including: advice sessions; workshops; events and drop-in support; a project for young people who have been in care; a project to help individuals overcome barriers to employment.

The 2015/16 annual report states that the fund's principle is to: 'Try to make sure that those applicants who have clear financial need but do not qualify for our direct support, are directed to resources which may help them.'

Community Foundations for Lancashire and Merseyside

£75,500

Correspondent: Sarah Mitchell, Community Foundation for Merseyside, 43 Hanover Street, Liverpool, Merseyside L1 3DN (0151 232 2420; email: info@cfmerseyside.org.uk; website: www.cfmerseyside.org.uk)

CC number: 1068887

Eligibility

Each grant-maker currently available for educational funding has their own eligibility criteria. They are as follows:

- **Sefton Education and Learning Fund**: individuals under the age of 25 who live in Sefton
- **Joseph Harley Bequest Fund**: individuals under the age of 25 who live in Formby
- **23 Foundation for Individuals**: individuals under the age of 25 who live in the wider Merseyside area, but with a preference for applicants from Sefton
- **John Gore Fund**: individuals of any age who live in the Lydiate area

Types of grants

The foundation administers a number of funds for individuals and organisations. At the time of writing (November 2017), the following schemes were available to provide educational grants:

- **Sefton Education and Learning Fund**: up to £250 per applicant to assist with purchasing learning materials, such as books, computers, and musical equipment
- **Joseph Harley Bequest Fund**: up to £250 per applicant to assist young people who are undertaking an educational project or learning activity
- **23 Foundation for Individuals**: up to £1,000 per applicant to promote sporting education and training, and prepare young people for a career in sport
- **John Gore Fund**: up to £1,000 per applicant to help students in higher education, students on vocational courses, or adults retraining after a period of unemployment

Annual grant total

In 2015/16 the foundation had assets of £12.4 million and an income of £2.9 million. From the funds available to individuals, £75,500 was awarded in grants for education.

Applications

All applications can be made online. As the foundation manages various sources of funding, application details for each grant-maker are available on the website. Each grant-maker has different deadlines and requirements, if you are unsure contact the foundation.

Other information

The foundation administers a number of funds for various purposes. Most of the funding is given to organisations, however there are also funding schemes for individuals in need. The funds tend to open and close regularly, therefore potential applicants should check the foundation's website for the most up-to-date information.

John James Rowe's Foundation for Girls

£11,000

Correspondent: Gill Gargan, 18–28 Seel Street, Liverpool L1 4BE (0151 702 5555)

CC number: 526166

Eligibility

Girls between the ages of 10 and 22 who live in Merseyside and whose parents are separated/divorced, or whose home conditions are especially difficult, or who have lost one or both of their parents.

Types of grants

Assistance is given for girls at secondary school, further/higher education students and those entering a profession/trade or undertaking apprenticeships. One-off grants are made for equipment/instruments, clothing, tools, books, boarding expenses and the cost of holidays.

Annual grant total

In 2015/16 the foundation had an income of £15,200 and a total expenditure of £11,900. We estimate that grants given to individuals totalled around £11,000.

Applications

Application forms can be requested from the correspondent.

The Rushworth Trust

£2,000

Correspondent: The Administrator, Liverpool Charity and Voluntary Services, 151 Dale Street, Liverpool L2 2AH (0151 227 5177; email: grants@lcvs.org.uk)

CC number: 1076702

Eligibility

Music students living within a 60-mile radius of Liverpool Town Hall. Grants can be awarded to a wide range of musicians, including composers, young conductors, young performers, student singers and instrumentalists, and choirs.

Types of grants

One-off grants to help with the cost of the study of music and to develop the taste and appreciation of music. Financial assistance is available for publishing music, promotion, training, equipment/instruments, music tours and concerts. Our research suggests that grants can only be made if the individual is not eligible for grants from any other source and awards are not usually repeated.

Annual grant total

At the time of writing (November 2017) only the 2014/15 accounts had been submitted to the Charity Commission. In 2014/15 the trust had an income of £4,700 and a total expenditure of £2,400. We have estimated that grants totalled £2,000.

Exclusions

Grants are not available for course fees and maintenance.

Applications

Application forms can be requested from the correspondent and should be submitted in advance to the trustee meetings which are normally held in March, June, September and December.

Other information

The trust has been formed by the merging of The William Rushworth Trust, The Thew Bequest and The A K Holland Memorial Award.

Liverpool

The Liverpool Council of Education (Incorporated)

£12,000

Correspondent: Roger Morris, Trustee, 4 St Anne's Road, Aigburth, Liverpool L17 6BW (0151 417 1766)

CC number: 526714

Eligibility

Pupils, students and teachers in Liverpool.

Types of grants

Grants are given according to need.

Annual grant total

In 2015/16 the charity had an income of £23,000 and a total expenditure of £27,500. We have estimated that grants to individuals totalled around £12,000 during the year.

Applications

Apply in writing to the correspondent. Our research suggests that the charity

shares its details with the schools in Liverpool at the beginning of each school year.

Other information

The charity acts as a trustee to various charitable funds providing educational support to schools, pupils and teachers in Liverpool.

The Bishop Sheppard Tenth Anniversary Trust

£10,500

Correspondent: Margaret Sadler, Administrator, c/o St James House, 20 St James Road, Liverpool L1 7BY (07506 233922; email: margaret.sadler@hotmail.co.uk)

CC number: 517368

Eligibility

People between the ages of 21 and 49 who live in the Anglican diocese of Liverpool (which includes Southport, Kirkby, Ormskirk, Skelmersdale, Wigan, St Helens, Warrington and Widnes) and who are doing second-chance learning at a college or training centre.

Types of grants

Grants are provided for books and equipment needed to complete courses or training programmes.

Annual grant total

In 2015 the charity had an income of £10,500 and a total expenditure of £11,200. We have estimated that grants to individuals totalled £10,500.

Exclusions

No grants are given to students who have had no break from their education (or schoolchildren), to people with good vocational qualifications or on degree courses, or to organisations.

Applications

Application forms are available from the administrator to be submitted directly by the individual at any time.

World Friendship

See entry on page 32

St Helens

The Rainford Trust

£1,000 (one grant)

Correspondent: William Simm, c/o Pilkington Group Ltd, Prescot Road, St Helens, Merseyside WA10 3TT (01744 20574; email: rainfordtrust@btconnect.com)

CC number: 266157

Eligibility

People in need who are normally resident in the borough of St Helens.

Types of grants

One-off and recurrent grants are usually paid directly to the college or other third party organisation. Grants can be for schoolchildren for equipment/instruments, fees, maintenance/living expenses and educational outings in the UK. Further and higher education students and mature students can receive grants for books, equipment/instruments, fees, childcare and educational outings in the UK.

Annual grant total

In 2015/16 the trust had assets of £10.1 million and an income of £282,000. There were two grants made to individuals for educational purposes, which totalled £2,000. A further £143,500 was given in grants to organisations.

Applications

Apply in writing to the correspondent, for consideration throughout the year. Applications can be made directly by the individual, or through his or her school, college or educational welfare agency. The trust sends out a questionnaire, if appropriate, after the application has been made.

Other information

Grants are mostly made to organisations.

Wirral

Lower Bebington School Lands Foundation

£2,500

Correspondent: S. R. Lancelyn Green, Trustee, Poulton Hall, Poulton Road, Bebington, Wirral, Cheshire CH63 9LN (0151 334 3000)

CC number: 525849

Eligibility

Higher or further education students residing in the area of the parish of St Andrew, Lower Bebington, as it was in 1924.

Types of grants

Small grants of up to £300 are available towards general educational costs, including books, equipment/instruments, necessities, fees and living expenses. Some assistance may also be available towards facilities not normally provided by the local authorities for public school pupils.

Annual grant total

In 2015/16 the trust had an income of £3,200 and a total expenditure of £2,800. We have estimated that grants totalled around £2,500.

Applications

Application forms can be obtained from the correspondent. Our research has suggested that applications should be submitted by August each year but may be considered at other times if funds are available.

Other information

The trustees have previously informed us that 'owing to poor drafting when state education was introduced [the beneficial area] cannot be adjusted to suit current boundary' and further suggest that applicants should refer to the Poulton Lancelyn Lands Foundation (CC number: 1071450) which covers omitted areas.

South East

General

The Chownes Foundation

£17,000

Correspondent: Sylvia Spencer, Secretary, The Courtyard, Shoreham Road, Upper Beeding, Steyning, West Sussex BN44 3TN (01903 816699; email: sylvia@russellnew.com)

CC number: 327451

Eligibility

Individuals living in Sussex, particularly mid-Sussex.

Types of grants

One-off and ongoing grants.

Annual grant total

In 2016/17 the foundation had an income of £7,200 and a total expenditure of £68,000. Due to its low income, the charity was not required to submit accounts. We estimate that around £17,000 was awarded to individuals for educational purposes.

The charity also awards grants to organisations and individuals for welfare purposes.

Applications

Apply in writing to the correspondent.

Other information

Our previous research indicates that the majority of the foundation's funds are committed to long-term support for poor and vulnerable beneficiaries, so only very few applications are successful.

The Ewelme Exhibition Foundation (Ewelme Exhibition Endowment)

£144,500

Correspondent: James Oliver, Clerk and Trust Manager, 126 High Street, Oxford OX1 4DG (01865 244661; fax: 01865 721263; email: clerk@ewelme-education-awards.info; website: www.ewelme-education-awards.info)

CC number: 309240

Eligibility

Young people (both in state and independent education) aged between 11 and 21 who live in Berkshire, Buckinghamshire, Conock in Wiltshire, Oxfordshire or Ramridge in Hampshire and demonstrate exceptional talent or need.

Types of grants

Grant awards for educational purposes:

- Scholarships or maintenance allowances at school, university or place of learning approved by the Governors
- Financial assistance to beneficiaries on leaving school, university or other place of learning to prepare for, or to assist their entry into a trade, profession or calling
- Travel bursaries
- Providing facilities of any kind not normally provided by the local education authorities for recreation and social and physical training
- Financial assistance for the study of music or other arts

In the state sector the foundation provides funds for additional tuition, educational visits, sports, music and arts, also books and equipment for skills training. The trustees note that a large proportion of the endowment income is currently used to support young people in independent education and mostly at secondary education level. Beneficiaries are young people aged under 21 who, in the opinion of the Governors, are in need of financial assistance and who have residential qualification in Ewelme and Marsh Gibbon, the other estate areas and the counties of Oxfordshire, Buckinghamshire and former Berkshire.

Annual grant total

In 2015/16 the foundation had assets of £106,000 and an income of £157,500. Throughout the year the foundation awarded around £144,500 to individuals.

Applications

Application forms can be requested from the correspondent via email. Applications are advertised in the regional press in late September/October and the closing date for submissions is the end of November. Candidates are invited to an interview in February. The foundation requires details of the parental income and a testimonial from the school's headteacher.

Other information

The annual report (2016) states:

> 67 bursary and scholarship awards were funded at independent schools and a further 13 young people in both state and independent education benefited from individual awards and grants during the year and grants were awarded to one Church of England primary school within the endowed estate areas to fund facilities and projects for which State funding was unavailable in order to benefit the pupils from financially disadvantaged families.

Paradigm Foundation

£6,800

Correspondent: The Trustees, Paradigm Housing Group, Glory Park Avenue, Wooburn Green, High Wycombe, Buckinghamshire HP10 0DF (01628 811784; email: enquiries@ paradigmfoundation.org.uk; website: www.paradigmfoundation.org.uk)

CC number: 1156204

Eligibility

Paradigm residents who are in need.

Types of grants

Grants of up to £1,500 are available to support Paradigm residents and members of their immediate family into further education, work and training.

Annual grant total

In 2015/16 the foundation had assets of £111,500 and an income of £418,000. We estimate that educational grants to individuals totalled around £6,800.

Applications

Applications are available to download from the charity's website.

Sarum St Michael Educational Charity
See entry on page 290

Bedfordshire

Chew's Foundation at Dunstable

£5,300

Correspondent: Yvonne Beaumont, Administrator, Grove House, 76 High Street North, Dunstable, Bedfordshire LU6 1NF (01582 660008; email: dunstablecharity@yahoo.com)

CC number: 307500

Eligibility
Children and young people, normally under the age of 25, living within the boroughs of Dunstable and Luton and parish of Edlesbrough who are (or whose parent(s) is/are) 'in sympathy' with the Church of England and other Christian churches. Our research suggests that a certificate of baptism is required.

Types of grants
The trust provides scholarships to individuals in education and can assist people undertaking apprenticeships. Support is given towards general educational costs including books, school uniforms, educational outings, equipment/instruments and so forth.

Annual grant total
In 2016/17 the foundation had an income of £16,300 and a total expenditure of £10,800. Throughout the year we estimate that the charity awarded around £5,300 in grants to individuals for educational purposes.

The trust also maintains the Chew's House and the old library (now the Little Theatre).

Applications
Apply in writing to the correspondent.

Bedford
The Harpur Trust

£117,000 (29 grants)

Correspondent: Grants Team, Princeton Court, The Pilgrim Centre, Brickhill Drive, Bedford MK41 7PZ (01234 369500; email: grants@harpurtrust.org.uk; website: www.harpurtrust.org.uk)

CC number: 1066861

Eligibility
Adults who are returning to work or study or planning a career change, who left formal education at least five years ago, are permanently resident in the borough of Bedford and are on a low income.

Students aged 19 or under who are looking to study an undergraduate or foundation degree course and have been resident in the borough of Bedford for at least two years. To be eligible, students must attend one of the colleges or schools listed on the trust's website and must meet two or more of the following criteria: from the first generation of their family to attend university; come from a low-income family; are living independently; have financial difficulties due to family or personal circumstances.

Types of grants
Grants to individuals programme
Grants are given to contribute towards the costs of study for adults to access education which will improve their quality of life by leading to a return to work or a career change. The trust's website states that 'competition for individuals' grants is considerable and, even if an application is successful, it is likely that only a modest contribution towards the costs of study can be made'.

University bursary programme
Grants are awarded to 16 students at listed schools (see the website) wishing to undertake a degree course. Bursaries of £1,200 a year are provided for up to three years.

Other partnership programmes
The trust works in partnership with local organisations and institutions to administer other funds, which are dealt with within the relevant organisations, rather than being open to application. This includes the trust's school uniform grants scheme for children who are eligible for free school meals and are undergoing the transition from middle/primary school to upper/secondary school. The trust also offers means-tested bursaries at the schools it runs.

Annual grant total
In 2015/16 the trust had assets of £159.3 million and an income of £53.2 million. Grants to 29 individuals for educational purposes totalled £117,000 and were broken down as follows:

University bursary programme	£57,500
School uniform grants	£24,000
College bursary programme	£20,000
Grants to individuals	£15,700

Grants were also made to 61 organisations totalling £770,000.

Exclusions
Grants are not given for: PGCE courses and certificates of education; recreational courses, including academic courses taken for recreational purposes only. The trust cannot provide emergency funding.

Applications
Grants to individuals
Adults returning to education may use the form available on the trust's website, where guidelines are also available to download. Forms should be submitted by the end of May for courses beginning in September/October. Successful candidates are invited for an interview. Applicants must determine their entitlement to statutory funding before making an application.

University bursaries
Application forms can be downloaded from the trust's website and should be submitted by May (refer to the website for the exact deadline).

Other information
Most grants are given to registered charities, voluntary organisations and other groups. The trust also runs four independent schools (Bedford School, Bedford Modern School, Bedford Girls' School, Pilgrims Pre-Preparatory School), sponsors Bedford Academy, and provides almshouse accommodation in Bedford.

Oakley Educational Foundation

£1,400

Correspondent: Louise Tunley, c/o Steve Monico Ltd, 19 Goldington Road, Bedford MK40 3JY (01234 402040; email: louise.tunley@monico.co.uk)

CC number: 307464

Eligibility
Young people between the ages of 16 and 25 who live in the parish of Oakley.

Types of grants
Small grants are available to people leaving school, individuals starting work, further and higher education students (including mature students and postgraduates). Support can be given for general educational costs, including books, equipment/instruments, tools, educational outings in the UK and study/travel abroad.

Annual grant total
In 2015/16 the foundation had an income of £8,000 and a total expenditure of £1,700. We estimate that grants given to individuals totalled around £1,400.

Exclusions
According to our research, grants are not normally provided for travel fares.

Applications
Application forms are available upon request from the correspondent.

Ursula Taylor Charity

£1,400

Correspondent: Mavis Nicholson, Secretary to the Trustees, 39 George Street, Clapham, Bedford MK41 6AZ (01234 405141; email: mavis. nicholson1@ntlworld.com)

CC number: 307520

Eligibility

Children and young people between the ages 11 and 25 who live in the parish of Clapham and are in full-time education or training.

Types of grants

Grants are made to schoolchildren, people starting work, individuals undertaking apprenticeships and students in further/higher education. Support can be given for books, course fees, equipment/instruments, tools, clothing and other educational needs.

Annual grant total

In 2016 the charity had an income of £2,200 and a total expenditure of £1,600. We estimate that educational grants to individuals totalled £1,400.

Exclusions

Our research suggests that grants are not given for bus passes or school uniforms.

Applications

Application forms together with further guidance are available from the correspondent. According to our research, submissions can be made either directly by the individual or through the charity's trustees. Applications are considered four times a year in February, April, June and November. Candidates should provide receipts for the items purchased.

Central Bedfordshire

Ashton Schools Foundation

£23,000

Correspondent: Yvonne Beaumont, Administrator, Grove House, 76 High Street North, Dunstable, Bedfordshire LU6 1NF (01582 660008; email: dunstablecharity@yahoo.com; website: www.associationofdunstablecharities.co. uk)

CC number: 307526

Eligibility

Children and young people under the age of 25 living within the Dunstable area. Proof of receipt of housing benefit is required, however if you do not receive housing benefit contact the clerk for a finance form.

Types of grants

One-off and recurrent grants (up to four per child), in the form of scholarships and bursaries towards general educational needs, including books; equipment/instruments; clothing; study/ travel overseas; educational outings; and the study of music or other arts. Schoolchildren, further/higher education students or people entering work can be supported.

Annual grant total

During 2015/16, the trust had an income of £22,500 and a total expenditure of £34,000. We estimate the total amount given in grants to individuals was £23,000.

Exclusions

Those who have applied for a Chew's Foundation Grant are ineligible.

Applications

Application forms are available to download from the trust's website and should be signed by the applicant and the applicant's school or college. Applications are to be sent back via post.

Other information

The trust also provides annual grants to Manshead, Ashton Middle and Ashton Lower schools in Dunstable.

Clophill United Charities

£2,500

Correspondent: Gillian Hill, 10 The Causeway, Clophill, Bedford MK45 4BA (01525 860539)

CC number: 200034

Eligibility

People who live in the parish of Clophill and are in need.

Types of grants

One-off and recurrent grants can be given 'in times of need'. Support can be provided towards various school activities and trips in the UK or abroad. Assistance can be given to people preparing for employment.

Annual grant total

In 2016 the charity had an income of £10,000 and a total expenditure of £7,500. We estimate the amount awarded in grants for education was £2,500.

Exclusions

Grants are not given where statutory funds are available, for example, towards school fees.

Applications

Application forms can be obtained from the correspondent.

Other information

Grants are also made to organisations operating in Clophill, and to individuals for welfare causes.

Flitwick Combined Charities

£5,000

Correspondent: David Empson, Trustee, 28 Orchard Way, Flitwick, Bedford MK45 1LF (01525 718145; email: deflitwick8145@aol.com; website: www. flitwickcombinedcharities.org.uk)

CC number: 233258

Eligibility

Students who have completed their first year at university and are about to start the second, and whose home is the parish of Flitwick.

Types of grants

Grants are of around £100 to £250. As a general rule, educational grants are awarded to students at the start of their second year of study in higher education. In exceptional circumstances, one-off grants may be given for other reasons, such as providing sports equipment to a youth group.

Annual grant total

In 2015/16 the charity had an income of £11,400 and a total expenditure of £10,350. We estimate that grants for education purposes totalled around £5,000.

Applications

Application forms are available from the charity's website or the correspondent. The charity's website states: 'Anything not covered by these forms should be sent to us as a short paragraph outlining the reasons for the request and how any money will be spent, **using the contact us form**, following which we will then be in touch for extra information.'

The trustees' meetings are held three times a year and the dates are publicised on the website. Applications need to be submitted a month in advance to the meeting.

Other information

There are three charities (The Deacon's Dole, The Poor's Moor and The Town Lands Charity) collectively known as Flitwick Combined Charities. The objectives of the trustees are to provide both educational and relief-in-need help.

Potton Consolidated Charity

Correspondent: Dean Howard, Clerk, 69 Stotfold Road, Arlesey, Bedfordshire SG15 6XR (01462 735220; email: clerk@potton-consolidated-charity.co.uk; website: www.potton-consolidated-charity.co.uk)

CC number: 201073

Eligibility

People between the ages of 16 and 25 who live in the parish of Potton.

Types of grants

Students aged between 16 and 18 can apply for assistance with the costs of transport to school and college. Students who are aged between 18 and 25 and are in full-time education can apply for higher education grants.

Annual grant total

In 2015/16 the charity had assets of £4.1 million and an income of £152,500. Educational grants to individuals totalled £38,500.

Applications

Applications can be submitted using the online form or, alternatively, using the appropriate form, which is available to download from the website. Guidelines can be found on the website.

The Sandy Charities

£5,000

Correspondent: Charlotte Benjamin, 6 Bedford Road, Sandy, Bedfordshire SG19 1EN (01767 680251; email: cbenjamin@woodfines.co.uk)

CC number: 237145

Eligibility

People who live in Sandy and Beeston and are in need.

Types of grants

One-off grants towards costs such as school uniforms, equipment, school trips and other educational expenses.

Annual grant total

In 2015/16 the charity had an income of £9,500 and a total expenditure of £12,500. We estimate the amount awarded in grants for education was £5,000.

Applications

Applications should be made in writing to the correspondent.

Other information

The charity also awards grants to individuals for welfare purposes.

Town Lands

£1,800

Correspondent: Julian Barrett, Trustee, South Cottage, 18 Broughton Road, Salford, Milton Keynes MK17 8BH (01908 583494)

CC number: 256465

Eligibility

People in need who live in the parish of Hulcote and Salford.

Types of grants

Grants are one-off and range from £100 to £200. They can be awarded for the cost of school uniforms and other school clothing, books, educational outings and maintenance for schoolchildren; books and help with fees/living expenses for students in further/higher education; books, travel expenses and fees for mature students; and books, equipment/instruments, clothing and travel for people starting work.

Annual grant total

In 2015 the charity had an income of £7,900 and a total expenditure of £7,700. We estimate that educational support to individuals totalled around £1,800.

Applications

Applications may be made in writing to the correspondent. They can be submitted directly by the individual or through any other parishioner.

Other information

Grants are also made to organisations supporting the community. Welfare support can also be given.

Berkshire

The Earley Charity

£500

Correspondent: Jane Wittig, Clerk to the Trustees, Liberty of Earley House, Strand Way, Earley, Reading RG6 4EA (0118 975 5663; fax: 0118 975 2263; email: enquiries@earleycharity.org.uk; website: www.earleycharity.org.uk)

CC number: 244823

Eligibility

People in post-school education who live in Earley, the northern part of Shinfield, Winnersh, central, east and south Reading, and the immediate neighbourhood, including Sonning and lower Caversham. Applicants must have lived in the area for at least six months.

In order to check whether you live within the area of benefit, see the map available on the website. If in doubt, get in touch with the correspondent to confirm.

Types of grants

Grants to individuals are generally one-off with the majority being relatively small. Assistance is given towards general educational necessities, such as books, tools, equipment, materials or clothing.

Annual grant total

In 2016 the charity had assets of £12.5 million and an income of £1.1 million. The amount of grants given to individuals totalled £6,400. We estimate that educational grants totalled around £500.

Exclusions

The charity does not make grants to:

▷ Pay for general living costs
▷ Pay off debts
▷ Buy floor coverings
▷ Buy non-essential items

Applications

Application forms can be requested from the correspondent. They can be submitted either directly by the individual or through a social worker, Citizens Advice or other welfare agency. Applications for grants under £500 and applications for grants over £500 are considered at separate meetings which take place about five times each year. The dates of these meetings, along with application submission deadlines, are published on the website.

Other information

Support is given to individuals and organisations for welfare purposes.

John Sykes Foundation

£3,500

Correspondent: Koichi Nicholas, 23/24 Market Place, Reading RG1 2DE (0118 903 5909; email: mail@johnsykesfoundation.org; website: johnsykesfoundation.org)

CC number: 1156623

Eligibility

Individuals who live in and around Reading who are in need of help and support. A map showing the area of benefit can be found on the website.

Types of grants

Grants are given to individuals for a wide range of needs, including for the following purposes stated on the website:

▷ Education – 'The Foundation wants to give people the opportunity to improve their lives through education and training. The opportunity to develop, grow and learn new skills will enable people to fulfil future hopes, dreams and aspirations'

- Arts and culture – 'Through heritage, culture and arts so much can be learnt and kept for future generations. The charity wants to support individuals that have a talent or special project that they want to create. A project can be a work of art, a musical talent, or may be a restoration project'
- Science – 'The foundation will support the advancement of science and technology. If an individual has a new idea to develop and needs a helping hand the John Sykes Foundation will consider an application for support'
- Sport – 'Amateur sport brings great opportunities for a healthy lifestyle, sporting career and achieving a personal goal. The foundation offers support and encouragement to individuals who live in and around the Reading area that have aspirations or dreams to reach milestones in the world of sport'

The foundation has four grant programmes and states on its website: 'Each grant is not currently time-specific. The individual grants are structured with a grant total therefore it's important to apply to the correct grant programme.' The four grant programmes are: Minster – grants of £500 or less; Abbey – grants of £2,500 or less; Forbury – grants of £5,000 or less; and Maiwand – grants of £10,000 or less. It is important that applicants apply to the application appropriate for the amount needed.

Annual grant total

In 2016 the charity held assets of £14,700 and an income of £17,000. Educational grants to individuals totalled £3,500.

Applications

Application forms can be downloaded from the website and should be completed and returned to the foundation's office by post or email.

Note: As the foundation is a newly registered grant-maker and is in the early stages of its development, we would advise potential applicants to consider the information on the website thoroughly before beginning an application.

Other information

The foundation's informative website presents the following information:

The foundation established by John Sykes in 2014 aims to help, support, and transform the lives of people living in and around the Reading area. John not only has a passion for business but his hometown of Reading too. It's from where over the last 15 years he has built his successful companies. He now wants to give something back for the people of Reading and his foundation is set to do just that.

Wellington Crowthorne Charitable Trust

£10,000

Correspondent: Paul Thompson, Trustee, Wellington College, Crowthorne, Berkshire RG45 7PU (email: pft@wellingtoncollege.org.uk)

CC number: 277491

Eligibility

People who live in the parishes of Crowthorne, Finchampstead, Sandhurst and Wokingham Without. Preference is given to applicants under the age of 25.

Types of grants

Grants are given to 'promote spiritual, moral, mental and physical capacities of individuals', according to the trust's Charity Commission record. Previously grants have been awarded for a wide range of overseas gap year projects, outward bound expeditions, school trips and international sports events.

Annual grant total

In 2015 the trust had an income of £12,800 and a total expenditure of £15,100. We estimate that grants given to individuals totalled around £7,000.

Applications

Applications may be made in writing to the correspondent.

Other information

Grants may also be made to organisations. The trust is maintained and mainly supported by Wellington College.

Windsor and Maidenhead

The Prince Philip Trust Fund

£3,400 (four grants)

Correspondent: Kevin McGarry, Secretary, 10 Cadogan Close, Holyport, Maidenhead, Berkshire SL6 2JS (01628 639577; email: kmmcgarry@talktalk.net; website: www3.rbwm.gov.uk/info/200156/community_grants/727/the_prince_philip_trust_fund)

CC number: 272927

Eligibility

Young people from the royal borough of Windsor and Maidenhead undertaking voluntary work or training schemes. Support is also given to individual pupils selected to represent their district, county or country in an activity considered worthy of the fund's support.

Types of grants

One-off grants of around £200 towards educational opportunities and travel, particularly to undertake voluntary service. Loans may also be provided.

Annual grant total

In 2015/16 the fund had assets of £1.8 million and an income of £107,000. Grants to four individuals totalled £3,400.

Exclusions

Grants are not made for tuition fees.

Applications

Apply in writing to the correspondent. Application letter should include full details of the project, the amount of grant required, sources of other funding secured or applied to, the amount of funds in hand, budget projection, the names of two referees and a letter of acceptance on a course (if applicable). The trustees meet twice a year, usually in April and November.

Other information

Grants are mainly made to organisations and various projects. In 2015/16 grants to 35 organisations totalled £35,000.

The Spoore Merry and Rixman Foundation

£122,000 (114 grants)

Correspondent: Clerk to the Trustees, PO Box 4787, Maidenhead SL60 1JA (020 3286 8300; email: clerk@smrfmaidenhead.org; website: www.smrfmaidenhead.org.uk)

CC number: 309040

Eligibility

People under the age of 25 who are in need and live in the former (pre-1974) borough of Maidenhead or the ancient parish of Bray, including Holyport and Woodlands Park.

Types of grants

Grants can be given for a range of general educational needs, such as: school uniforms; musical or arts tuition; books; musical instruments and sporting equipment; school trips; residential courses; recreational activities such as swimming lessons; special educational needs and aids, such as laptops for children with dyslexia.

Support is also given to those in further or higher education, which may include funding the cost of a university course for students from low-income families.

Grants are available for young people under 25 on low incomes who have been accepted on an apprenticeship – up to £1,500 for those living independently and up to £1,000 for those living with parents/guardians.

Annual grant total

In 2015 the foundation had assets of £11.2 million and an income of £363,500. A total of almost £122,000 was awarded in grants to 114 individuals during the year. A further £304,500 was given in grants to 61 organisations.

Applications

Application forms can be found on the foundation's website. They can be submitted by post or online by the individual or through a educational institution. Applications for school uniforms should be submitted by a parent or guardian with a supporting statement from a social worker/teacher/Citizens Advice worker/health professional. Parents are also required to provide a statement of their income.

Applications should not be sent via recorded or registered delivery, as the foundation uses with a PO Box address so is unable to sign receipts. The trustees meet four times each year and the dates of upcoming meetings are posted on the foundation's website. Applications must be received two weeks prior to a meeting, or they will be considered at the next meeting instead.

Other information

Grants are also given to schools for educational facilities not funded by school budgets (e.g. development of school grounds or specialist equipment), as well as to youth clubs and other organisations for wider educational facilities.

Every child leaving a local authority maintained primary school in Maidenhead and Bray receives a dictionary from the trust.

Wokingham

The Polehampton Charity

£1,500

Correspondent: Miss E. Treadwell, Assistant Clerk to the Charity, 65 The Hawthorns, Charvil, Reading RG10 9TS (0118 934 0852; email: polehampton.applications@gmail.com; website: www.thepolehamptoncharity.co.uk)

CC number: 1072631

Eligibility

People in need who are under the age of 25 and live in the former ecclesiastical parishes of St Mary the Virgin – Twyford and St. James the Great – Ruscombe.

Types of grants

The website notes:

> Educational grants cover assistance with the purchase of books and tools which are essential for the completion of

courses of training at university, college, or other recognised educational establishments, including apprenticeships.

Annual grant total

In 2016 the charity had assets of £3.4 million and an income of £106,500. Educational grants to individuals totalled £1,500.

Applications

Applications should be made in writing to the correspondent, including full details of the applicant and his need, as well as giving full costings.

The Wokingham United Charities Trust

£4,000

Correspondent: P. Robinson, Clerk, 66 Upper Broadmoor Road, Crowthorne, Berkshire RG45 7DF (01344 351207; email: peter.westende@btinternet.com; website: www.westende.org.uk)

CC number: 1107171

Eligibility

Schoolchildren in need who live in the civil parishes of Wokingham, Wokingham Without, St Nicholas, Hurst, Ruscombe and the part of Finchampstead known as Finchampstead North.

Types of grants

One-off grants, usually between £25 and £150. Grants have been given towards school uniforms and educational visits.

Annual grant total

In 2015/16 the trust had assets of £1 million and an income of £171,500. The amount of grants given to individuals totalled £16,000. We estimate that educational grants totalled around £4,000.

Applications

Apply using a form available from the correspondent or to download from the website. Applications must be supported by a letter from a supporting professional agency.

Buckingham-shire

Norman Hawes Memorial Trust

£3,000

Correspondent: Sara Butler, Milton Keynes Council, Education Department, 502 Avebury Boulevard, Milton Keynes

MK9 3HS (01908 253614; email: sara.butler@milton-keynes.gov.uk)

CC number: 310620

Eligibility

Young people between the ages of 15 and 18 who are in full-time education in Milton Keynes and North Buckinghamshire.

Types of grants

Financial assistance to students travelling abroad for educational purposes. Grants range between £50 and £200.

Annual grant total

In 2015/16 the trust had an income of £4,200 and a total expenditure of £6,800. We have estimated that grants totalled around £3,000.

Applications

Application forms are available from the correspondent. They can be submitted either by individuals or through their school/college/educational welfare agency, if applicable. Considerations take place in November and February/March, therefore applications should be made in September/October and January/February respectively.

Other information

Grants may also be made to schools and colleges in the area.

The Stoke Mandeville and Other Parishes Charity

£16,000

Correspondent: Caroline Dobson, 17 Elham Way, Aylesbury HP21 9XN (01296 431859; email: smandopc@gmail.com; website: smandopc.org)

CC number: 296174

Eligibility

The educational grant is open to residents of Great and Little Hampden, and Stoke Mandeville parishes.

The school trips grant is open to Stoke Mandeville parish residents only.

Types of grants

Educational Grant: this grant is intended to assist those continuing in higher education at college or university, to assist with the costs of books, equipment, and any clothing needed.

School Trips: this grant is open to students in compulsory education to help meet the costs of school trips or equipment.

Annual grant total

In 2016 the charity had assets of £1.8 million and an income of £103,000. We estimate the amount awarded in grants for education was £16,000.

Exclusions

Students undertaking A-levels or GCSEs cannot apply for an educational grant.

Applications

Application forms can be found on the charity's website.

Other information

The charity also makes awards to residents of Stoke Mandeville, Great and Little Hampden, and Great Missenden for welfare purposes.

Aylesbury Vale

William Harding's Charity

£340,500

Correspondent: John Leggett, Clerk to the Trustees, 14 Bourbon Street, Aylesbury, Buckinghamshire HP20 2RS (01296 318501; email: doudjag@pandcllp.co.uk)

CC number: 310619

Eligibility

People under the age of 25 who live in the town of Aylesbury.

Types of grants

One-off grants are made to schoolchildren towards uniforms, clothing, fees, study/travel overseas, books, educational outings, equipment/instruments, maintenance/living expenses or for special educational needs. Further/higher education students and people in vocational training can also be supported. Facilities for recreation, social or physical training may be provided to people in primary, secondary or further education.

Annual grant total

In 2016 the charity held assets of £34.35 million and had an income of over £1 million. During the year grants to individual pupils totalled £340,500 and a further £688,500 was awarded to organisations and schools in Aylesbury.

Applications

Apply in writing to the correspondent. Application forms are available on request from the charity either by collection or by sending an sae and can be submitted at any time.

Other information

The charity also owns almshouses, provides relief in need and supports local educational institutions, youth groups and organisations.

Thomas Hickman's Charity

£15,000 (135 grants)

Correspondent: John Leggett, Clerk, Parrott & Coales, 14–16 Bourbon Street, Aylesbury, Buckinghamshire HP20 2RS (01296 318500; email: doudjag@pandcllp.co.uk)

CC number: 202973

Eligibility

People who live in Aylesbury town and are in need, hardship or distress.

Types of grants

Grants for school uniforms, books and similar items.

Annual grant total

In 2016 the charity had an income of £696,000 and a total expenditure of £665,000. A total of 135 grants were made to individuals, amounting to £59,000. We estimate that educational grants to individuals totalled around £15,000.

Applications

Application forms can be requested from the correspondent. They should be submitted either directly by the individual or through a third party, such as a family member, social worker, school or Citizens Advice. The trustees meet on a regular basis and applications are considered as they arise.

Other information

The charity provides almshouses to older people, supports the welfare needs of individuals and makes grants to organisations.

The Saye and Sele Foundation

£3,500

Correspondent: Richard Friedlander, Clerk, Parrot & Coales LLP, 14–16 Bourbon Street, Aylesbury, Buckinghamshire HP20 2RS (01296 318500)

CC number: 310554

Eligibility

People under the age of 25 who live in the parishes of Grendon Underwood and Quainton.

Types of grants

One-off and recurrent grants to help schoolchildren, college or university students and people entering a trade/profession. Awards are made to help with the cost of books, equipment/instruments, tools, clothing, training expenses, sport activities. Previously grants have been made towards computers for people from low-income families and equipment for people with disabilities.

Annual grant total

In 2016 the foundation had an income of £14,900 and a total expenditure of £7,800. We estimate that grants given to individuals totalled around £3,500.

Applications

Apply in writing to the correspondent.

Other information

The foundation also provides building space in the community and can support local schools.

Town Lands Charity

£3,300

Correspondent: Derek Berra, 9 Church Hill, Cheddington, Leighton Buzzard, Bedfordshire LU7 0SX (email: berraassociates@aol.com)

CC number: 235076

Eligibility

People in need who live in the parish of Cheddington.

Types of grants

One-off and recurrent grants are given according to need.

Annual grant total

In 2016/17 the charity had an income of £22,500 and a total expenditure of £19,500. We estimate the trust awarded £3,300 in grants for education.

Applications

Applications can be made in writing to the correspondent, directly by the individual or a family member.

Other information

One-third of the charity's income goes to the maintenance of the parish church. The remainder is split between village organisations, students, volunteer hospital drivers, and individuals suffering from hardship.

Chiltern

Amersham United Charities (Amersham and Coleshill Almshouse Charity)

Correspondent: R. Atkinson, Clerk to the Trustees, 84 Bois Lane, Chesham Bois, Amersham, Buckinghamshire HP7 0HX (01494 726445)

CC number: 205033

Eligibility

People under the age of 21 who live in the parishes of Amersham and Coleshill, Buckinghamshire.

Types of grants

One-off grants for those at school, college or university, or about to start work, to help with the cost of fees (students only), books, equipment, clothing and travel.

Annual grant total

In 2016 the charity had assets of £2.27 million and an income of £379,500. The latest accounts state:

The accounts of the Young Persons and Poor Endowment Fund (from which grants are made), are now amalgamated into the main accounts of the United Charities.

The correspondent has previously informed us that, although no grants have been made in recent years, the charity is open to applications from individuals for relief in need and education.

Applications

Applications should be made in writing to the correspondent.

Other information

The main work of the charity is the administration and management of 13 almshouses. Grants can be made through the Young Persons and Poor Endowment Fund. Welfare support can also be given.

Milton Keynes

The Ancell Trust

£2,500

Correspondent: Karen Phillips, Secretary, 78 London Road, Stony Stratford, Milton Keynes MK11 1JH (01908 563350; email: karen.phillips30@ hotmail.co.uk)

CC number: 233824

Eligibility

People in need in the town of Stony Stratford.

Types of grants

Grants are made for general educational and welfare purposes. Grants may also be given for travel expenses and other training needs, including apprenticeships.

Annual grant total

In 2015/16 the trust had an income of £14,000 and a total expenditure of £10,200. We estimate that grants given to individuals totalled around £2,500.

Applications

Applications may be made in writing to the correspondent at any time.

Other information

The trust owns the sports ground in Stony Stratford, which provides cricket, football, bowls, croquet and tennis facilities. Grants are also made to organisations or groups.

Emberton United Charity

£950

Correspondent: Warwick Clarke, Trustee, Old Pits, West Lane, Emberton, Olney, Buckinghamshire MK46 5DA (01234 713174)

CC number: 204221

Eligibility

People under the age of 25 who are in higher education and live in the parish of Emberton.

Types of grants

One-off and recurrent grants, usually of up to £350, towards books and equipment/instruments.

Annual grant total

In 2016 the charity had an income of £42,000 and a total expenditure of £34,500. Educational grants totalled £950.

Applications

Individuals can apply in writing to the correspondent directly.

Other information

Grants are also given to older people living in the parish for welfare purposes.

Wolverton Science and Art Institution Fund

£2,000

Correspondent: Karen Phillips, 78 London Road, Stony Stratford, Milton Keynes MK11 1JH (01908 563350; email: karen.phillips30@hotmail. co.uk)

CC number: 310652

Eligibility

People who live, study or work in the parishes of Wolverton or Stantonbury.

Types of grants

The fund awards scholarships, bursaries and grants to schoolchildren, people starting work, further and higher education students, mature students and postgraduates. Particular preference is given to the arts, science and related subjects. Our research suggests that grants can range between £100 and £500

and are given towards the cost of school uniforms, other clothing, books, equipment/instruments, fees and educational outings in the UK.

Annual grant total

In 2016/17 the fund had an income of £5,800 and a total expenditure of £3,700. We have estimated that grants to individuals totalled about £2,000.

Applications

Application forms are available from the correspondent and can be submitted either directly by the individual or through a school/college/educational welfare agency, if applicable.

Other information

The fund allocates up to a third of the income to provide benefits to educational organisations not normally provided by the local authorities.

South Buckinghamshire

Stoke Poges Hastings Community Fund

£4,000

Correspondent: Mary Crocker, 129 Rogers Lane, Stoke Poges, Slough SL2 4LP (01753 646323; email: SPHCF11@outlook.com; website: www. stokepogescharities.com)

CC number: 206915

Eligibility

Individuals in need resident in the parish of Stoke Poges.

Types of grants

Grants are available for a range of educational support including non-university courses and school uniforms.

Annual grant total

In 2016 the fund had an income of £19,500 and a total expenditure of £12,500. We estimate that educational grants totalled around £4,000.

Applications

Application forms can either be downloaded from the fund's website and returned by post or completed online.

Wycombe

The Marlow Educational Foundation

£2,500

Correspondent: Debra Cooper, The Marlow Educational Foundation, 4 Chiltern Road, Marlow SL7 2PP (01628 472119)

CC number: 310650

Eligibility

People under the age of 25 who live or were born in the parish of Great Marlow or the urban districts of Marlow, and are attending, or for not less than one year have attended, any school in that parish or urban district.

Types of grants

Grants are given for tools, clothing and the like for individuals starting work, training or apprenticeships, and for assistance to study music or the arts.

Annual grant total

In 2016 the foundation had an income of £5,900 and a total expenditure of £2,700. We have estimated that grants to individuals totalled about £2,500.

Applications

Application forms are available from the correspondent. They can be submitted directly by the individual, by a parent/guardian, a teacher, or through an organisation, such as a school or educational welfare agency.

Stokenchurch Educational Charity

£38,500

Correspondent: Martin Sheehy, Administrator, The Fish Partnership LLP, The Mill House, Boundary Road, Loudwater, High Wycombe HP10 9QN (01628 527956; email: martins@fishpartnership.co.uk)

CC number: 297846

Eligibility

People under the age of 25 who live in the parish of Stokenchurch.

Types of grants

Grants are available for educational expenses and training, including awards for clothing, tools, books, equipment/instruments and study of music and other arts. Schoolchildren, further/higher education students and people entering a trade/starting work or undertaking apprentices can be supported.

Annual grant total

In 2015/16 the charity held assets of £2.3 million and had an income of £65,500. Grants to individuals for educational purposes totalled £38,500, with a further £8,600 awarded to community organisations.

Exclusions

Grants are not normally made for private tuition and where statutory grants are available. Applications from outside the parish cannot be considered.

Applications

Application forms can be requested from the correspondent. Ordinarily the trustees place an advertisement in the local press and two public places in Stokenchurch in August to invite applications. They should be returned by 30 November each year. Grants are paid in or around April. Applications from outside the parish cannot be considered and will not receive a response.

East Sussex

The Bedgebury Foundation
See entry on page 274

The Blatchington Court Trust (BCT)

£60,500 (250 grants)

Correspondent: Anthony Schofield, 6A Hove Park Villas, Hove, East Sussex BN3 6HW (01273 727222; fax: 01273 722244; email: info@blatchingtoncourt.org.uk; website: www.blatchingtoncourt.org.uk)

CC number: 306350

Eligibility

People under the age of 30 who live in the Sussex area and are visually impaired.

Types of grants

One-off and recurrent support to people at any school, university, college or other institution of further education and training, approved by the trustees. The trust provides equipment, mobility aids, books and other study necessities (including those for the study of music and other arts) which will assist in the pursuit of education, training and employment or business development. Assistance will also be given in connection with preparation to enter a school, profession, trade, occupation or service. Most grants awarded are under £3,000.

Annual grant total

In 2016/17 the trust held assets of £14 million and had an income of £527,000. A total of £60,500 was awarded in grants to individuals.

Exclusions

The trust does not give cash grants or bursaries and will not normally provide funding for wheelchairs, school fees, holidays or travel costs.

Applications

Apply in writing to the correspondent. Include a costed proposal which fits the trust's objectives. Applications should normally be made by September.

Other information

The trust also puts on social activities for beneficiaries and their families so people can get together and get to know each other. There is also an outreach service, providing one-to-one support for socially isolated clients. The trust also runs various support and advice lines, including life coaching; IT training and support; employment advice; benefits advice; advocacy and information; and counselling.

Catherine Martin Trust

£12,000

Correspondent: The Trustees, Hove Vicarage, Wilbury Road, Hove, East Sussex BN3 3PB (email: marion197@btinternet.com)

CC number: 258346

Eligibility

Children and young people under the age of 21 who are in full-time education, British-born and have lived in the old borough of Hove and Portslade for at least one year. Support is intended to help individuals whose parents cannot work due to ill health or are deceased. It is necessary to demonstrate that an applicants' next of kin or another person/people acting as guardian(s) do not have sufficient means to support the child.

Types of grants

Recurrent grants are available to schoolchildren and further/higher education students for educational expenses, including books, equipment/instruments, clothing, fees, travel and maintenance costs.

Annual grant total

In 2015/16 the trust had an income of £13,800 and a total expenditure of £12,700. We estimate that grants to individuals totalled around £12,000.

Applications

Apply in writing to the correspondent. Applications can be made by the individual directly or through a third party, such as a relative, solicitor, school/college or educational welfare agency or a social/health worker, if applicable.

The Mrs A. Lacy Tate Trust

£8,700

Correspondent: The Trustees, Heringtons Solicitors, 39 Gildredge Road, Eastbourne, East Sussex BN21 4RY (01323 411020)

CC number: 803596

Eligibility
Schoolchildren who are in need and live in East Sussex.

Types of grants
One-off and recurrent grants are given according to need.

Annual grant total
In 2015/16 the trust had assets of £697,500 and an income of £56,000. There were 69 grants made to individuals totalling £17,400. We therefore estimate that grants educational grants totalled around £8,700.

Applications
Applications can be made in writing to the correspondent.

Other information
Grants are also made to individuals in need for relief-in-need purposes and to organisations.

Hastings
The Isabel Blackman Foundation

£46,500 (31 grants)

Correspondent: The Trustees, Stonehenge, 13 Laton Road, Hastings, East Sussex TN34 2ES (01424 431756; email: ibfoundation@uwclub.net)

CC number: 313577

Eligibility
People in education who live in Hastings and St Leonards district and require financial assistance.

Types of grants
Scholarships are available to schoolchildren for educational outings and further/higher education students (including mature students and postgraduates) for books, equipment/ instruments, fees, maintenance/living expenses or childcare costs.

Annual grant total
In 2016/17 the foundation had assets of £6.3 million and an income of £303,000.

A total of £46,500 was awarded in educational grants to individuals.

Applications
Apply in writing to the correspondent. Applications can be made directly by individuals.

Other information
The foundation also supports the prevention and relief of sickness and poverty, care for older people, and the advancement of Christianity. The foundation mainly supports these areas through grants to organisations.

Magdalen and Lasher Educational Foundation

£37,000

Correspondent: Marcia Woolf, Administrator, 132 High Street, Hastings, East Sussex TN34 3ET (01424 452646; email: mlc@oldhastingshouse.co. uk; website: www.magdalenandlasher.co. uk)

CC number: 306969

Eligibility
People under 25 who live in the borough of Hastings or who have attended schools in the borough for more than two years.

Types of grants
Scholarships, bursaries or maintenance allowances at any education institutions for any profession, trade or calling; scholarships and maintenance allowances for education abroad; financial assistance to study music or other arts.

Annual grant total
In 2015/16 the foundation held assets of £4.76 million and had an income of £175,500. Bursaries totalled £23,500 and grants to individuals totalled £13,500. A further £86,000 was awarded to schools, colleges and charitable organisations.

Applications
Application forms are available from the correspondent. The trustees meet every three months. Applications by individuals will normally be subjected to some form of means-testing and should be supported by a third party who is familiar with the individual's circumstances, such as a social worker, Citizens Advice, a headteacher or a key worker from Hastings Advice and Representation Centre.

Lewes
The Lady Vernon (Newick) Educational Foundation

£3,000

Correspondent: Colin Andrews, Trustee, 91 Katherine Way, Seaford, East Sussex BN25 2XF (01323 351561)

CC number: 306410

Eligibility
People under 25 living in and/or attending school in Newick only.

Types of grants
Scholarships, bursaries, maintenance grants and educational equipment.

Annual grant total
In 2015/16 the foundation had an income of £3,500 and a total expenditure of £3,800. We estimate the amount of grants totalled around £3,000.

Applications
Apply in writing to the correspondent, either directly by the individual if aged 18 or over, or by the parent/guardian or through an organisation such as a school or educational welfare agency. Details of the purpose of the grant and the amount anticipated to be spent should be included in the application. The trustees meet twice each year, in April and autumn.

Essex
Chelmsford Educational Foundation (CEF)

£17,000 (19 grants)

Correspondent: Richard Emsden, Administrator, 19 Rushleydale, Chelmsford CM1 6JX (07941 958652; email: remsden@gmail.com)

CC number: 310815

Eligibility
People who live or have been educated in the borough and former rural district of Chelmsford.

Types of grants
Grants are given to people in education and training towards general needs, such as books, fees, tools, equipment, instruments, also travel/study abroad, study of music, and for any other activities that will help the applicant to achieve employment or qualifications. In 2016 awards of up to £1,000 were awarded.

Annual grant total

In 2016 the foundation had assets of £758,500 and an income of £25,000. The foundation had a total charitable expenditure of £18,700. Of this amount, 19 grants were awarded to individuals for educational purposes totalling £17,000.

The foundation also gave grants to two organisations.

Applications

Apply in writing to the correspondent.

Earls Colne and Halstead Educational Charity

£9,700 (50 grants)

Correspondent: Martyn Woodward, Clerk to the Trustees, St Andrew's House, 2 Mallows Field, Halstead, Essex C09 2LN (01787 479960; email: earlscolnehalstead.edcharity@yahoo.co.uk; website: www.echec.org.uk)

CC number: 310859

Eligibility

Children and young people between the ages of 5 and 25 who have lived for at least one year or attended school in the charity's catchment area in North Essex.

The following parishes are eligible: Alphamstone, Ashen, Belchamp Otten, Belchamp St Paul, Belchamp Walter, Birdbrook, Borley, Bulmer, Bures Hamlet, Castle Hedingham, Coggeshall, Colne Engaine, Earls Colne, Foxearth, Gestingthorpe, Gosfield, Great Henny, Great Maplestead, Great Yeldham, Greenstead Green and Halstead Rural, Helions Bumpstead, Lamarsh, Liston, Little Henny, Little Maplestead, Little Yeldham, Middleton, Ovington, Pebmarsh, Pentlow, Ridgewell, Sible Hedingham, Stambourne, Steeple Bumpstead, Stisted, Sturmer, Tilbury Juxta Clare, Toppesfield, Twinstead, White Colne and Wickham St Paul, the town of Halstead (all in the district of Braintree) and Chappel, Mount Bures and Wakes Colne (all in the district of Colchester).

Types of grants

The charity offers Book Grants for books, equipment/instruments, tools, outfits usually to further/higher education students; and Projects Grants for various educational projects and educational outings to schoolchildren. Priority is given to people studying for a recognised higher education qualification or who are already performing to a high level in the arts or sports.

Annual grant total

In 2016/17 the charity had assets of £1.4 million and an income of £42,500.

Throughout the year the charity made 50 grants to individuals totalling £9,700. A total of £32,800 was given to organisations.

Exclusions

Tuition fees are not normally supported.

Applications

Application forms can be found online or requested from the correspondent. Applications for book grants may be made at any time. Book Grants may cover the costs of further education, including: books, specialist clothing, tools or equipment but usually excluding costs of tuition. All Project Grant applications are considered at meetings of the board of trustees. The trustees normally meet to consider grant applications during February, July and November. The cut-off date for Project Grant applications to be considered at meetings of the trustees is three weeks prior to the date of the meeting. After this, all applications will be closed. See the charity's website for details.

Other information

The charity also gives grants to local schools for educational travel or other purposes and supports voluntary bodies working for the benefit of young people in the charity's beneficial area.

Great Bursthead Exhibition Foundation (Billericay Educational Trust)

£13,400

Correspondent: Jennifer Moore, Clerk to the Trustees, The Billericay School, School Road, Billericay, Essex CM12 9LH (01277 655191; email: info@billericayeducationaltrust.co.uk; website: www.billericayeducationaltrust.co.uk)

CC number: 310836

Eligibility

Young people under the age of 25 who live within a six-mile radius of Billericay (including Noak Bridge, Ramsden Bellhouse, Ramsden Heath and Stock) and are in need.

Types of grants

One-off or recurring grants may be given for up to three years to further/higher education students and people in vocational training or those starting work. Help is given towards general educational necessities, including clothing, tools, instruments and equipment, books, also tuition fees, travel for educational purposes in the UK or abroad, study of music or other arts, recreational activities or physical training.

The trustees can make awards for:

▶ University or college education
▶ Vocational Grants for help to enter a trade or profession
▶ Travel grants in furtherance of education
▶ Recreational grants for recreation and social and physical training not provided by a local educational authority
▶ Cultural Grants to enable beneficiaries to study music or other arts

Annual grant total

In 2015/16 the foundation had an income of £14,800 and a total expenditure of £13,700. We estimate that the foundation awarded around £13,400 in grants to individuals for welfare purposes.

Applications

Application forms can be downloaded from the foundation's website and should be submitted by May and returned via post or email.

Other information

Previously grants have also been given to schools to help with specific educational projects.

The Canon Holmes Memorial Trust

£14,000

Correspondent: John Brown, Trustee, 556 Galleywood Road, Chelmsford CM2 8BX (01245 358185; email: canonjbrown@mac.com; website: www.canonholmes.org.uk)

CC number: 801964

Eligibility

Children between the ages of 7 and 13 who live or have recently lived in the Roman Catholic diocese of Brentwood or the Anglican diocese of Chelmsford – roughly the historic county of Essex, as well as the London boroughs of Barking and Dagenham, Havering, Newham, Redbridge and Waltham Forest. Support is given to those in independent schools who cannot continue their education because their parents/guardians are experiencing financial difficulties as a result of circumstances such as employment problems, marital breakdown, illness or death.

Types of grants

Grants can be awarded for short-term scholarships and bursaries to continue school education in the moment of crisis. Grants are given for private school fees, for one year at a time.

Annual grant total

In 2015/16 the trust had an income of £15,500 and a total expenditure of

265

£14,700. We estimate that grants to individuals totalled around £14,000.

Exclusions
The trust is not able to provide grants to cover school fee arrears.

Applications
Applications should be made by a parent or guardian, using the form available to download from the trust's website. The trust welcomes contact from anyone who is considering making an application. Gants will be made directly to the school.

David Randall Foundation
See entry on page 223

Braintree

Sir Robert Hitcham's Exhibition Foundation

£5,500

Correspondent: Nicholas Johnson, Trustee, 75 Queen Street, Coggeshall, Colchester CO6 1UE (01376 562915; email: nicjo@btinternet.com)

CC number: 1095014

Eligibility
People under the age of 25 who live in Coggeshall and have left school and are moving on to higher education or training.

Types of grants
Small grants are given towards books, equipment/instruments, clothing/uniforms/outfits, tools and living costs to students and people starting work/entering a trade.

Annual grant total
In 2015/16 the foundation had an income of £7,000 and a total expenditure of £6,100. We have estimated that grants to individuals totalled £5,500.

Applications
Application forms can be requested from the correspondent. Our research suggests that applications are normally considered in early September and should be submitted by the end of August.

City of Chelmsford

The Butler Educational Foundation

£5,000

Correspondent: Nicholas Welch, Duffield Stunt, 71 Duke Street, Chelmsford, Essex CM1 1JU (01245 262351)

CC number: 310731

Eligibility
Children and young people living in the parishes of Boreham and Little Baddow who have attended a public primary school in the area for at least two years.

Types of grants
Grants are available for general educational expenses, including clothing/uniforms, books, tools, equipment/instruments, maintenance costs, educational visits, fees, equipment for special projects and so on. Financial assistance is available to secondary school pupils, further/higher education students, people entering a trade/starting work or individuals undertaking apprenticeships.

Annual grant total
In 2015/16 the foundation had an income of £9,000 and a total expenditure of £9,500. We estimate the total amount awarded in grants to individuals was £5,000.

Exclusions
Primary schoolchildren are not supported.

Applications
Apply in writing the correspondent. The trustees meet three times a year, usually in January, April and October.

Other information
The foundation may also assist school libraries in provision of books and fittings.

Ann Johnson's Educational Foundation

£15,100 (13 grants)

Correspondent: Jonathan Douglas, 58 New London Road, Chelmsford, Essex CM2 0PA (01245 493939; fax: 01245 493940; email: douglas-hughesj@gepp.co.uk)

CC number: 310799

Eligibility
People living or educated in Chelmsford and the surrounding parishes, who are under 25.

Types of grants
Help with the cost of books, clothing and other essentials for schoolchildren, including school fees. Grants are also available for those at college or university and towards the cost of books, equipment and instruments, clothing and travel for people starting work.

Annual grant total
In 2015/16 the trust had assets of £37,000 and an income of £29,500. Grants were awarded to 13 individuals totalling £15,100.

| Boys | £11,000 |
| Girls | £5,100 |

Applications
Applications for grants are invited through advertisement in schools and colleges in qualifying districts. Applications are considered by two subcommittees who then make recommendation to the governors when they meet quarterly.

Other information
The trust also gives funding to local schools.

Epping Forest

Joseph King Trust

£32,000 (60 grants)

Correspondent: Catherine Kenny, Secretary, 36 Coopers Hill, Ongar, Essex CM5 9EF (01277 366167; email: JKT1678@btinternet.com)

CC number: 810177

Eligibility
People between the ages of 16 and 25 who live in the civil parish of Chipping Ongar, Marden Ash, Greensted and Shelley.

Types of grants
Help with the cost of books, clothing and other essentials for schoolchildren. Help may also be available for students at college or university. Preference is given to the advancement of the Christian religion.

Annual grant total
In 2016 the charity held assets of £1.8 million and had an income of £79,000. Educational grants to 60 students totalled £32,000.

Applications
Apply in writing to the correspondent.

Rochford

The Canewdon Educational Foundation

£2,500 (25 grants)

Correspondent: Alan Lane, Trust House, Anchor Lane, Canewdon, Rochford, Essex SS4 3PA (email: alanrlane@ hotmail.co.uk)

CC number: 310718

Eligibility
People under the age of 25 living in the parish of Canewdon.

Types of grants
Grants are made to assist with general expenses associated with education, for anyone under the age of 25 who lives in Canewdon, at any level of education or if the applicant is entering a trade. In previous years, awards have been made for singing and swimming lessons, tuition fees, and school trips.

Annual grant total
In 2015 the foundation had assets of £778,500 and an income of £43,000. A total of £2,500 was awarded in educational grants to individuals.

Exclusions
Individuals from outside the parish of Canewdon will not be supported.

Applications
Applications may be made in writing to the correspondent. Information sheets are normally delivered to each household in the parish giving details of how, and to whom, applications should be made. The trustees meet monthly.

Other information
The trustees use a proportion of the income to maintain Canewdon Endowed Primary School and 20% of the unrestricted fund income (after the deduction of the trustees' expenses) is paid to the Canewdon Poor's Charity (CC number: 210406).

Grants are also made to organisations – in 2015, this included the local Horticultural Society and a pre-school group.

Hampshire

The Robert Higham Apprenticing Charity

£9,500

Correspondent: Roy Forth, PO Box 7721, Kingsclere RG20 5WQ (07796 423108; email: kclerecharities@aol.co.uk)

CC number: 307083

Eligibility
People aged between 16 and 25 attending sixth forms, colleges and universities who live in the parishes of Kingsclere, Ashford Hill and Headley.

Types of grants
Grants towards books, specialist equipment and clothing or travelling expenses (for those preparing for or engaged in any profession, trade, occupation, service) or towards books, study or travel abroad for those studying for A-levels. Grants can be one-off or recurrent and are given according to need.

Annual grant total
In 2015 the charity had an annual income of £7,000 and a total charitable expenditure of £10,100

We estimate that grants made totalled around £9,500.

Applications
Application forms are available from the correspondent. Applications must include a letter outlining the applicant's further education plans. Applications are not accepted from parents. The trustees meet five times a year.

Basingstoke and Dean

Aldworth's Educational Trust (Aldworth Trust Foundation)

£26,000

Correspondent: Debbie Reavell, Clerk to the Trustees, 25 Cromwell Road, Basingstoke RG21 5NR (01256 473390; email: reavell@btinternet.com)

CC number: 307259

Eligibility
Children and young people who are either resident or were educated/are attending school in the borough of Basingstoke and Deane.

Types of grants
Grants can be awarded for travel, books, equipment and clothing.

Annual grant total
In 2015/16 the trust had an income of £9,700 and a total expenditure of £28,000. Total amount given in grants was £26,000.

Applications
Apply in writing to the correspondent. Applications are considered in February, June and October.

Other information
Grants may also be paid to the school which the individual attends.

The Ashford Hill Educational Trust

£3,900

Correspondent: Caroline Hellings, Minnesota, Ashford Hill Road, Headley, Thatcham RG19 8AB (01635 269596)

CC number: 1040559

Eligibility
People who live in the parish of Ashford Hill with Headley or the surrounding area. There are no age restrictions on these grants.

Types of grants
Grants are generally given to promote social and physical education. They are given towards the cost of formal education, enhancement of employment prospects, group activities, music, adult education and sporting and recreational activities.

Annual grant total
During 2015/16, the trust had an income of £6,500 and a total expenditure of £4,300. We estimate the total amount in grants awarded was £3,900.

Applications
Application forms are available from the correspondent. Applications are considered in January, March, July and October.

The Cliddesden and Farleigh Wallop Educational Trust

£15,000

Correspondent: Alison Mosson, 11 Southlea, Cliddesden, Basingstoke RG25 2JN

CC number: 307150

Eligibility
People under 25 who are in need of financial assistance and live within the original boundaries of the parishes of Cliddesden and Farleigh Wallop only.

Types of grants
One-off and recurrent grants to assist with academic, physical, and musical education.

Annual grant total
In 2016 the charity had an income of £11,000 and a total expenditure of £17,000. We estimate the amount awarded in grants for education was £15,000.

Applications

Apply in writing to the correspondent. Applications should be submitted through a school or directly by the individual or their guardian to reach the secretary by the end of April, August or December.

East Hampshire

Bramshott Educational Trust

£5,500

Correspondent: Richard Weighell, 107 Haslemere Road, Liphook GU30 7BU (01428 724289; email: clerk.bramshott.trust@hotmail.co.uk; website: www.bramshotteducationaltrust.org.uk)

CC number: 277421

Eligibility

Children and young people under the age of 25 who live, or have a parent/guardian who lives, in the ancient parish of Bramshott, which includes Liphook, Bramshott, Passfield, Conford and the parts of Hammer Vale located in Hampshire.

Types of grants

Grants of up to £250 are awarded for general educational needs which in the past have included equipment/instruments, tools, school uniforms/clothing, books, educational trips/visits, specialist courses and tuition, attendance at educational events, also extracurricular activities, such as music or ballet lessons.

Annual grant total

In 2015/16 the trust had an income of £7,500 and a total expenditure of £7,500. We estimate a total of £5,500 was awarded in grants to individuals.

Exclusions

The trust's eligibility guidelines remind that 'in order to support as many applicants as possible, the trustees do not fund the whole amount required and do not award grants for expenditure which would reasonably be provided by the local authority'.

The trustees will not consider late, incomplete or retrospective applications.

Applications

Application forms can be found on the trust's website or requested from the correspondent. The deadlines for submission are 15 March for consideration in April and 15 September for consideration in October.

Other information

Up to one-third of the yearly income can be allocated to help local schools.

Wield Educational Charity

£5,000

Correspondent: Robert Grande, Trustee, Wield Manor Cottage, Upper Wield, Alresford SO24 9RS (01420 562876; email: bertie.grande@gmail.com)

CC number: 288944

Eligibility

Schoolchildren under the age of 18 living in the parish of Wield.

Types of grants

Grants are provided towards educational activities which are not available within the school curriculum. Our previous research suggests that people with special educational needs are given preference.

Annual grant total

In 2015/16 the charity had an income of £7,200 and a total expenditure of £10,600. We estimate that grants given to individuals totalled around £5,000.

Exclusions

School fees or maintenance costs are not normally supported.

Applications

Apply in writing to the correspondent.

Other information

The charity also provides support to the local schools where assistance is not already given by the local authority.

Fareham

The William Price Charitable Trust

£16,900 (73 grants)

Correspondent: Dr Christopher Thomas, Clerk, 24 Cuckoo Lane, Fareham, Hampshire PO14 3PF (01329 663685; email: mazchris@tiscali.co.uk; website: www.pricestrust.org.uk)

CC number: 307319

Eligibility

Children and young people under the age of 25 who live in the parishes of St Peter and St Paul, Holy Trinity with St Columba and St John the Evangelist (the same area as the original Fareham town parish but not the whole area of the Fareham borough).

Types of grants

Grants are given to individuals to support activities which the trustees feel 'do not command adequate priority in education', according to the website. In particular, these may include activities which 'enrich the quality of life and widen horizons, encourage participation and appreciation of the arts, develop good citizenship and encourage help in the community and local environment'. The trust can help children in school, students at college, university or those undertaking an apprenticeship, as well as trips abroad.

Support can equally be given towards fees, travel costs, school uniforms, books, equipment or other necessities. Grants are also given to enable pupils to take part in educational trips. Major grants for educational benefits are normally in the range of £1,000 while smaller 'hardship' grants for urgent needs are generally less than £300 (in 2016/17 the average grant was £127).

Annual grant total

In 2016/17 the trust had assets of £7.8 million and an income of £219,000. Grants to individuals amounted to £16,900, which included 66 'hardship' grants, totalling £8,400, and seven other grants for college, university or other bursaries, totalling £8,500. A further £156,000 was given in grants to organisations (local schools, colleges and churches).

Applications

Where possible applications should be made through a school/college; however individual applications will be considered, particularly from people in further/higher education. Application forms can be downloaded from the trust's website or requested from the correspondent. Bursaries and college/university grants are considered twice a year, normally in March and September, and applications should be received by the first day of these months. Applications for smaller 'hardship grants' can be made at any time and will be paid through a school/college.

Other information

Grants are also made to churches and schools/colleges and there is an annual grant to the Fareham Welfare Trust.

The Earl of Southampton Trust

£1,400

Correspondent: Sue Boden, 24 The Square, Titchfield PO14 4RU (01329 513294; email: earlstrust@yahoo.co.uk; website: eost.org.uk)

CC number: 238549

Eligibility

People in need who live in the ancient parish of Titchfield (now subdivided into the parishes of Titchfield, Sarisbury, Locks Heath, Warsash, Stubbington and Lee-on-the-Solent).

Types of grants

One-off grants, usually ranging from £25 and £1,000, are given to schoolchildren, college students, mature students and to people with special educational need towards tuition fees, uniforms and books.

Annual grant total

In 2015/16 the trust had assets of £1.65 million and an income of £94,000. Grants to individuals are mainly made for welfare purposes. Educational grants to individuals totalled £1,400.

Applications

Application forms can be downloaded from the trust's website and must be submitted through a recognised agency (social services, a health visitor etc.). Applications must include details of medical/financial status and are usually means-tested. They are normally considered on the last Tuesday of every month, although in the event of extreme urgency requests can be fast tracked between meetings.

Other information

The trust runs almshouses and a day centre for older people.

Gosport

Thorngate Relief-in-Need and General Charity

£1,800

Correspondent: Kay Brent, 6 Hartspiece Road, Redhill RH1 6RS (01737 479729; email: kay.brent@btinternet.com)

CC number: 210946

Eligibility

People in need who live in Gosport.

Types of grants

One-off grants usually of between £100 and £500.

Annual grant total

In 2015/16 the charity had an income of £10,700 and a total expenditure of £7,500. Grants are made to individuals and organisations for a wide range of purposes. We estimate that educational grants to individuals totalled £1,800.

Exclusions

No grants are made towards legal expenses.

Applications

Apply using a form available from the correspondent. Applications can be made either directly by the individual or through a social worker, Citizens Advice, Probation Service or other welfare agency.

New Forest

Dibden Allotments Fund

£10,200 (271 grants)

Correspondent: Valerie Stewart, Dibden Allotments Charity, 7 Drummond Court, Prospect Place, Hythe, Southampton SO45 6HD (023 8084 1305; email: dibdenallotments@btconnect.com; website: daf-hythe.org.uk)

CC number: 255778

Eligibility

People in need who live in the parishes of Hythe, Dibden, Marshwood and Fawley in Hampshire.

Types of grants

One-off and recurrent grants are given according to need. In previous years, grants have been awarded for books, equipment, fees and living expenses for students in further and higher education, educational outings for schoolchildren and childcare for mature students.

The charity also runs a shoe vouchers scheme in participation with local shoe retailers, to provide school shoes to children whose families are in financial need.

Annual grant total

In 2015/16 the charity had assets of £9.5 million and an income of £394,500. The charity awarded two educational grants totalling £2,200, as well as grants to 269 pupils for school shoes totalling £8,000.

Applications

Application forms are available on the fund's website, where the fund's criteria, guidelines and application process are also posted. It is helpful to supply a supporting statement from a 'professional' such as a health or social worker, midwife or teacher.

Applicants for the shoe vouchers scheme should speak directly to their child's school.

Other information

Grants are also made to individuals for welfare purposes, and to local organisations and groups.

Portsmouth

The Bentley Young Person's Trust

£2,000

Correspondent: John Turner, Trustee, Highfield Barn, Lewdown, Okehampton, Devon EX20 4DS (01566 783194; email:

john@bypt.org.uk; website: www.bypt.org.uk)

CC number: 1069727

Eligibility

People under the age of 25 who were born in, or who now live in, Portsmouth or the surrounding area. Applicants must have also been educated in Portsmouth and have a genuine financial need.

Types of grants

Grants are awarded to help finance general educational costs such as books, tools, equipment, instruments, travel, school trips etc.

Annual grant total

In 2015/16 the trust had an income of £3,500 and a total expenditure of £3,000. We estimate the amount awarded to individuals was £2,000.

Exclusions

Direct educational fees are not provided.

Applications

Application forms are available to fill out on the website to be directly submitted to the trust.

Other information

Grants are also made to local organisations to help young people experience new activities, and a bursary is also available to final-year Portsmouth university students to help them complete their education.

Test Valley

Miss Gale's Educational Foundation (The Gale Trust)

£7,400

Correspondent: John Butcher, Trustee, 58 Wolversdene Road, Andover, Hampshire SP10 2BA (01264 355445; email: gales.trust@yahoo.co.uk)

CC number: 307145

Eligibility

Children and young people in need who are under the age of 25, live in or near Andover and are attending/have attended any school in the area. Preference is given to girls and applicants from families with serious difficulties.

Types of grants

The foundation provides small, one-off grants to schoolchildren, higher or further education students and people starting work/entering a profession. Financial assistance is available towards general educational expenses, including the cost of uniforms/clothing, books, equipment/instruments, tools, educational outings and study/travel abroad.

Annual grant total

In 2016 the foundation had an income of £16,200 and a total expenditure of £15,000. We estimate that the charity awarded around £7,400 in grants to individuals for educational purposes.

The charity also gives grants to organisations.

Exclusions

Our research suggests that grants are not normally given towards the cost of school or college fees or living expenses.

Applications

Apply in writing to the correspondent. Applications can be made by individuals directly or through their educational establishment or welfare agency, if applicable. According to our research, it is required to specify the individual's date of birth, give reasons why the family are not able to provide themselves and explain what the grants is required for.

Sarah Rolle's Foundation

£4,500

Correspondent: Gregory McCann, Secretary, Mount View, East Dean Road, Lockerley, Romsey SO51 0JQ (01794 340698)

CC number: 307157

Eligibility

Schoolchildren, people starting work and further and higher education students under the age of 25 who live, or whose parents live, in the parishes of East Tytherley and Lockerley.

Types of grants

Grants from £50 to £250 may be given for uniforms/other school clothing, books, equipment/instruments, educational outings in the UK and study or travel abroad.

Annual grant total

In 2016 the foundation had an income of £9,000 and a total expenditure of £10,600. We estimate that around £4,500 was given in grants to individuals.

Exclusions

Grants are not given for school or college fees or living expenses.

Applications

Application forms are available from the correspondent. The trustees meet in March and October, and applications should be submitted at least three weeks in advance.

Other information

Local schools are also supported.

Hertfordshire

Fawbert and Barnard's School Foundation

£4,500

Correspondent: Pamela Rider, Trustee, 22 South Brook, Sawbridgeworth, Hertfordshire CM21 9NS (01279 724670)

CC number: 310965

Eligibility

People between the ages of 16 and 25 years of age who live within a three-mile radius of Great St Mary's Church in Sawbridgeworth or who attend/have attended school in that area for at least three years.

Types of grants

One-off grants, scholarships and bursaries to assist further/higher education students. Awards are made to help with the cost of books or materials associated with the course. Grants are usually in the range of £100 to £200.

Annual grant total

In 2016 the foundation had an income of £10,200 and a total expenditure of £9,000. As the foundation had no accounts available to view, we estimate that the foundation awarded around £4,500 to individuals for educational purposes.

The foundation also awards grants to organisations.

Applications

Application forms can be requested form the correspondent.

Other information

As the grant is awarded once only, students who do not apply during their first year can apply at any time during their period of study.

The Hertfordshire Educational Foundation

£15,000

Correspondent: The Trustees, c/o County Hall, Post Point CHO 126, Pegs Lane, Hertford, Hertfordshire SG13 8DF (01992 556340; email: hertfordshireeducationalfoundation@ hertfordshire.gov.uk; website: www. hertfordshire.gov.uk/services/schools-and-education/at-school/financial-help/ hertfordshire-educational-foundation. aspx)

CC number: 311025

Eligibility

Pupils and students up to 21 years who have a home address in Hertfordshire.

Types of grants

The foundation administers a number of different grant schemes, which are detailed on the website.

Travel scholarships

Grants of between £100 and £500 to individuals aged 12 to 21 to undertake approved courses of study, expeditions, voluntary work and other projects in overseas countries. The usual duration is for a minimum of one month and individuals should be able to demonstrate how their project will benefit the local community they are visiting.

School visits

Grants of up to £75 each for primary school pupils taking part in educational visits arranged by their school whose parents, due to exceptional circumstances other than financial, are unable to pay for all or part of the board and lodging element of the visit.

The Sir George Burns Fund

Grants of between £50 and £500 to enable young people aged 16 to 21 who have a disability or are disadvantaged to purchase special equipment, take part in recreational or educational activities or to participate in expeditions, educational visits, short courses or conferences

Donald Mackean Trust

Grants of between £50 and £1,000 to enable young people aged 14 to 25 to participate in learning or careers in the areas of science, technology, engineering, maths or health and environment-related subjects. Grants can be used for purposes such as equipment, personal development, additional support or other costs. This funding particularly targets those who are disadvantaged – for example, looked-after children, care-leavers, people who have offended, refugees, young parents, people with mental health problems or other circumstances.

Annual grant total

In 2016 the foundation had an income of £16,900 and a total expenditure of £34,000. We estimate that educational grants to individuals totalled around £15,000.

Applications

Application forms are available to download from the foundation's website. Applications should be submitted at least eight weeks before the activities (for which the grant is required) take place – the foundation will not consider any applications that are received less than six weeks in advance. The closing dates for applications and guidance notes for each fund are provided on the website.

Other information

The foundation may also provide grants to organisations.

Kentish's Educational Foundation

£12,000

Correspondent: Margery Roberts, 7 Nunnery Stables, St Albans, Hertfordshire AL1 2AS (01727 856626)

CC number: 313098

Eligibility

Young people in need between the ages of 11 and 35, particularly (but not exclusively) those who are permanently resident in Hertfordshire or Bedfordshire. Preference can be given to people with the family name Kentish or people related to the founder Thomas Kentish.

Types of grants

Grants towards costs arising from education at any secondary school, University, further education college or other educational establishment approved for the purpose by the trustees or for the purpose of enabling beneficiaries to study music or other arts or to undertake travel in furtherance of their education. Grants towards the cost of outfits, clothing, tools, instruments or books to help them on leaving secondary school, university or other educational establishment to prepare for, or to enter, a profession, trade or calling.

Grants towards postgraduate education are awarded in exceptional cases.

Annual grant total

In 2016/17 the foundation had assets of £1.1 million and an income of £28,000. The amount of grants given to individuals totalled £12,000.

The following table shows a breakdown of the charitable expenditure of the foundation:

Grants for Secondary education	£1,500
Grants for Higher education/Further education	£7,500
Grants for travel	£3,000

Exclusions

Support is normally available up to first degree level.

Applications

Application forms can be requested from the correspondent and can be submitted by individuals directly or through their parents/guardians. Applicants should also provide a copy of their school/tutor report and copies of birth or marriage certificates (for applicants claiming kinship). Grants are normally considered

in October/November, therefore applications should be received by the end of August.

Broxbourne

Robert Dewhurst's School Foundation

£6,300

Correspondent: Jill Hempleman, 215 Northbrooks, Harlow, Essex CM19 4DH (01279 425251; email: jillhempleman@yahoo.co.uk)

CC number: 310972

Eligibility

Children and young people under the age of 25 who live within the ancient parish of Cheshunt. Preference is given to people who have attended Dewhurst St Mary's Church of England Primary School for at least two years.

Types of grants

One-off grants to secondary schoolchildren, further/higher education students and people starting work to help with general educational costs, including books, equipment/instruments, tools, materials, clothing, travel, fees and educational outings in the UK.

Annual grant total

In 2015/16 the foundation had an income of £13,000 and a total expenditure of £12,600. We estimate that the foundation gave around £6,300 in grants to individuals for educational purposes.

The foundation had no accounts available to view due to their low income.

Applications

Apply in writing to the correspondent.

Other information

The foundation also provides support to Dewhurst St Mary's Church of England Primary School.

The Wormley Parochial Charity

£1,600

Correspondent: Carol Proctor, Trustee, 5 Lammasmead, Broxbourne, Hertfordshire EN10 6PF

CC number: 218463

Eligibility

Students who are over the age of 18 and live in the parish of Wormley as it was defined before 31 March 1935.

Types of grants

Grants are made to people over the age of 18 towards essential clothing, equipment, instruments or books.

Annual grant total

In 2016 the charity had an income of £13,300 and a total expenditure of £6,800. Grants are made to individuals and organisations for a range of purposes. We estimate that educational grants to individuals totalled around £1,600.

Applications

Applications can be made in writing to the charity, either directly by the individual, or through a social worker, Citizens Advice, welfare agency or a third party such as a friend who is aware of the situation. Applications are considered in April and October.

East Hertfordshire

Newton Exhibition Foundation

£13,500

Correspondent: Anne Haworth, Clerk to the Trustees, 117 Ladywood Road, Hertford SG14 2TA (01992 550121; email: clerk@ newtonexhibitionfoundation.co.uk)

CC number: 311021

Eligibility

Young people under the age of 25 who are attending/have attended school in the town of Hertford. Preference is given to members of the Church of England. Our research also suggests that grants may be awarded to otherwise eligible applicants who, because of special learning difficulties or disabilities, are attending/have attended schools outside the town.

Types of grants

According to our research, grants between can be awarded to schoolchildren and further/higher education students (including postgraduates). Financial support is available for general educational purposes, such as uniforms/clothing, books, equipment/instruments, fees, educational outings in the UK and study or travel overseas.

Annual grant total

In 2016/17 the foundation had an income of £14,800 and a total expenditure of £14,500. We have estimated that grants totalled around £13,500.

Applications

Apply in writing to the correspondent. Our research indicates that the application should include the name(s) of schools attended, full details and costs of the support required, also information about any other grants obtained or applied for. Applications can be submitted either directly by individuals or through their school, welfare agency/ social worker, if applicable.

The Ware Charities

£12,500 (17 grants)

Correspondent: Susan Newman, Correspondent, 3 Scotts Road, Ware, Hertfordshire SG12 9JG (01920 461629; email: suedogs@hotmail.com)

CC number: 225443

Eligibility

Schoolchildren, college students and people starting work who live in the area of Ware Town Council, the parish of Wareside and the parish of Thundridge.

Types of grants

Grants are given to schoolchildren, college students, people with special educational needs, people starting work and overseas students, including those for uniforms/clothing, fees, study/travel abroad, books, equipment/instruments and excursions. Grants are also made to undergraduates and vocational students for uniforms/clothing. Awards are not paid to individuals directly, rather through a third party.

Annual grant total

In 2016/17 the charity had assets of £1.6 million and income of £72,000. The amount of grants given to individuals totalled £25,000 and we estimate that around £12,500 was given for educational purposes.

Applications

Applications may be made in writing to the correspondent at any time. They should be submitted directly by the individual or a family member. Applications must include brief details of the applicant's income and savings and be supported and signed by a headteacher, GP, nurse, member of clergy or social worker.

Other information

Grants are also made to local organisations and individuals for general welfare needs.

Hertsmere
The Platt Subsidiary Foundation

£2,500

Correspondent: Alan Taylor, Secretary, 57A Loom Lane, Radlett, Hertfordshire WD7 8NX (01923 855197)

CC number: 272591

Eligibility

People under the age of 25 who live in the parishes of Christ Church – Radlett, St John the Baptist – Aldenham or St Martin's – Shenley, and are in need.

Types of grants

Grants can be given to people planning expeditions away from home, such as gap year schemes, volunteering opportunities and adventure trips. Community projects are particularly favoured. Applicants are expected to raise a proportion of money themselves.

Annual grant total

In 2016 the foundation had an income of £8,200 and a total expenditure of £5,400. We have estimated that grants to individuals totalled around £2,500.

Applications

Application forms can be requested from the correspondent. Our previous research has suggested that the deadline for applications is normally by the end of March, and that applicants are required to attend an interview in April.

Other information

Grants may also be made to organisations.

North Hertfordshire
Hitchin Educational Foundation

£24,500

Correspondent: Brian Frederick, Clerk to the Governors, 33 Birch Close, Broom, Biggleswade SG18 9NR (01767 313892; email: brian.frederick@hotmail.co.uk)

CC number: 311024

Eligibility

People who live in the former urban district of Hitchin and surrounding villages, aged under 25.

Types of grants

One-off grants are given towards the costs of uniforms, books, scholarships and any other educational facilities. Grants are means-tested, so income and size of family are taken into account.

Annual grant total

In 2015/16 the foundation held assets of over £1.1 million and had an income of £98,500. The amount of grants given to individuals totalled £24,500 and a further £53,500 was awarded to educational establishments in the area.

Exclusions

Grants are not available for books, fees, travel, living expenses or mature students.

Applications

Application forms are available from the correspondent, and can be completed by the individual, or through the individual's school, college, educational welfare agency or any third party. They are considered monthly.

The Leete Charity

£1,400

Correspondent: Susan Thornton-Bjork, Royston Town Council, Town Hall, Melbourn Street, Royston, Hertfordshire SG8 7DA (01763 245484; email: enquires@roystontowncouncil.gov.uk; website: www.roystontowncouncil.gov.uk)

CC number: 311084

Eligibility

People under the age of 25 going into further education who are either resident in Royston or attending school there.

Types of grants

Small grants to help with the costs of books, travel expenses, equipment/ instruments and other educational necessities.

Annual grant total

In 2016/17 the charity had an income of £2,400 and a total expenditure of £1,600. We estimate that grants totalled around £1,400.

Exclusions

According to our research, grants are not normally available to people starting work or mature students.

Applications

Application forms are available from the Royston Town Council offices at the town hall or can be downloaded from the council's website. Applicants are requested to submit all the relevant information about their financial situation and their general background to speed up the consideration. For the items the funding is requested for, the estimated costs would also be helpful.

The Letchworth Civic Trust

£41,500

Correspondent: Sally Jenkins, Broadway Chambers, Letchworth Garden City, Hertfordshire SG6 3AD (01462 686919; email: letchworthct@gmail.com; website: letchworthct.org.uk)

CC number: 273336

Eligibility

Schoolchildren and students attending college or university who are in need and have lived in Letchworth Garden City for two years or more. University students can be studying at any institution but must have a home address in Letchworth.

Types of grants

Apprentices, college pupils, and university students who have lived in Letchworth for at least two years will usually receive a grant of £300 towards the costs of books and learning materials. They may apply for a 'top-up' grant of £100 upon reaching their third year of study.

Schoolchildren whose families have great difficulty supporting a school activity (in particular a residential field visit or camp), which the headteacher believes would benefit the pupil, can receive a grant of up to £60 towards the costs.

Bursaries are occasionally available to exceptionally talented musicians, athletes, swimmers etc.

Annual grant total

In 2015/16 the trust had assets of £820,000 and an income of £79,000. The trust awarded £43,500 in grants for education, broken down as follows:

Purpose	No. of applicants	Average award	Total awarded
University students, for educational materials	166	£236	£39,200
Schoolchildren from disadvantaged backgrounds	57	£58	£3,200
Education and sport support	3	£550	£1,100

Applications

Application forms are available to download from the website. Be aware there are separate forms for further education and school students. Applications should be received by the beginning of February, May, August, September, November, or December for consideration at the next trustee meeting – applications are not normally acknowledged before the next meeting.

Prospective university students must not apply until they have received their A-level results in August.

Other information

The trust also provides grants to individuals for welfare purposes, usually for mobility and medical support, or if they have particular social needs. Around 200 individuals are supported each year, particularly young people.

The trust also makes awards to around 20 local organisations per year.

St Albans

The 948 Sports Foundation

£16,000

Correspondent: Alexander Bell, Old Albanian Sports Club, Woollam Playing Fields, 160 Harpenden Road, St Albans AL3 6BB (01727 864476; website: www.the948sportsfoundation.org)

CC number: 1088273

Eligibility

Applications must be for the benefit of residents in St Albans and the immediate surrounding areas.

Types of grants

Grants of up to £1,000 will be made for planned expenditure.

Annual grant total

For 2015/16, the foundation has an income of £24,000 and a total expenditure of £22,000. No accounts have been published for 2015/16, however based on previous trends, grant awards are estimated at a total of £16,000.

Exclusions

Grants will not be available for the reimbursement of already incurred expenditure. General grants, running costs (including salaries), capital costs and holidays are not covered either.

Applications

Application forms can be downloaded from the foundation's website and must be submitted at least ten days before the committee meeting. Applicants must demonstrate they have attempted to secure funding from other sources, whether successful or not. Applicants must also attach copies of their sport association's accreditation, and where applicable, attach quotations or invoices along with a copy of recent accounts.

Other information

Grants are also made to St Albans school and organisations towards projects, equipment and facilities.

The Harpenden Trust

£8,500 (92 grants)

Correspondent: Dennis Andrews, Secretary, The Trust Centre, 90 Southdown Road, Harpenden AL5 1PS (01582 460457; email: admin@theharpendentrust.org.uk; website: www.theharpendentrust.org.uk)

CC number: 1118870

Eligibility

Children in need who live in the 'AL5' postal district of Harpenden.

Types of grants

One-off grants are given to assist pupils with the cost of essential school trips.

Annual grant total

In 2016/17 the trust had assets of £5.1 million and had an income of £626,000. The amount of grants given to individuals totalled £52,900, of which £8,500 was given in 59 grants to young people for what we consider to be educational purposes. They were distributed as follows:

General grants	402	£23,500
Utilities grants	82	£19,500
Youth grants	59	£8,500
Christmas parcels	125	£1,400

Applications

Apply in writing to the correspondent.

Other information

The Harpenden Trust was founded in 1948 by Dr Charles Hill. The trust organises outings, coffee morning, befriending and home visits for older people in the community.

The James Marshall Foundation

£173,500 (325 grants)

Correspondent: Lynne Machin, Clerk to the Trustees, Unit 6, 17 Leyton Road, Harpenden, Hertfordshire AL5 2HY (01582 760735; email: jmfoundation@btconnect.com; website: www.wheathampstead.net/jmf)

CC number: 312127

Eligibility

People under the age of 25 who live in Harpenden and Wheathampstead and are in financial need. Priority is given to individuals over the age of 16.

Types of grants

Grants are awarded to pay for or contribute to educational purposes such as: apprenticeships; work tools, clothing and training; career development; books and study materials; laptops; university-related (including postgraduate study) costs such as accommodation, travel and books or equipment; school trips; school uniforms; travel for work or study; extracurricular sport, music or dance tuition; course or examination fees. The website states that this is not an exhaustive list and that potential applicants can contact the foundation to see if their cause may be eligible.

Annual grant total

In 2015/16 the foundation had assets of £5.8 million and an income of £257,000. The foundation made 325 grants (of which 257 were new and 68 were continued from the previous year) totalling £173,500. Of this, £106,000 (in 173 grants) was given in Harpendnen and £67,500 (in 152 grants) was given in Wheathampstead.

The grants were made in the following categories:

Degree	63
School trips	57
School uniform	50
Computers	30
Diploma	19
Postgraduate degree	11
Work-related	10
Educational equipment	8
Sport	7
Music	2

Exclusions

Grants are given for up to one academic year only, although repeat applications will be considered.

Applications

Application forms and further guidance can be requested from the correspondent. Applications can be submitted directly by the individual at any time and are considered every six weeks – dates of trustee meetings are posted on the website. Applicants should provide details of their parental or other income and state the purpose for the requested grant.

Welwyn Hatfield

Wellfield Trust

£500

Correspondent: The Trust Manager, Birchwood Leisure Centre, Longmead, Hatfield, Hertfordshire AL10 0AN (01707 251018 (Monday to Friday, 9.30 am to 3 pm); email: wellfieldtrust@aol. com; website: www.wellfieldtrust.co.uk)

CC number: 296205

Eligibility

People in need who are on a low income, who live in the parish of Hatfield and are undertaking vocational courses, such as computer training or hairdressing. Schoolchildren in the parish may also be supported.

Applicants usually have to be a resident in Hatfield for six months at least.

Types of grants

One-off grants of £100 to £500 to schoolchildren, college students, mature students, people with special educational needs and people starting work. Grants are made to help with examples such as course equipment, school uniforms and school trips.

Annual grant total

In 2015/16 the trust had assets of £968,500 and an income of £66,000. We estimate educational grants to individuals totalled £500.

Exclusions

If an applicant has had a grant within the last two years, they are not usually considered for another grant (unless there are special circumstances).

Applications

There is an application form available to download from the website, which must be completed by the individual or a member of the household in need and a sponsor. The sponsor should be somebody from an organisation who is familiar with the applicant's personal circumstances such as a social worker or school. Applicants who cannot think of an appropriate sponsor should contact the trust for advice.

The trust's committee meets on the second Tuesday of every month to consider applications which, to be considered at the next meeting, must be submitted by the first Monday of every month.

Other information

The trust also gives to organisations, has a room at a local leisure centre (which can be hired free of charge to charitable organisations) and a scooter loan scheme. It has a helpful and informative website.

Isle of Wight

The Broadlands Fund (Broadlands Home Trust)

£4,000

Correspondent: Mrs M. Groves, 2 Winchester Close, Newport, Isle of Wight PO30 1DR (01983 525630; email: broadlandstrust@btinternet.com)

CC number: 201433

Eligibility

Girls and young single women (under the age of 22) in need who live on the Isle of Wight.

Types of grants

One-off grants of £100 to schoolchildren, vocational students, people with special needs and people starting work, including those for uniforms/clothing, books, fees, equipment/instruments, travel expenses and educational trips.

Annual grant total

In 2015/16 the trust had an income of £11,100 and a total expenditure of £8,300. We estimate that educational grants to individuals totalled around £4,000.

Exclusions

Grants are not made for married women or graduates.

Applications

Application forms are available from the correspondent and should be submitted either directly by the individual or a family member. They should include the applicant's name, date of birth, address, financial details (family income and expenditure), details of course undertaken, reference and confirmation of attendance, and specify the support needed. Requests are considered quarterly in January, April, July and October. If you are applying by post, enclose an sae.

Other information

Support to single women or widows who are over the age of 40 is also provided through pensions.

Kent

The Bedgebury Foundation

£62,000 (61 grants)

Correspondent: Jane Angell-Payne, Priory Cottage, Romford Road, Pembury, Tunbridge Wells TN2 4JD (07872464195; email: clerk@ bedgeburyfoundation.org.uk; website: www.thebedgeburyfoundation.org.uk)

CC number: 306306

Eligibility

Due to high demand, awards are only available to those who live, or who had secondary education, in the counties or Kent or East Sussex. This geographical restriction does not apply to former Bedgebury School pupils, or their dependants.

Types of grants

One-off and recurrent grants not to exceed a total of £10,000 over three years.

Annual grant total

In 2015/16 the foundation had assets of £4.4 million and an income of £142,000. A total of £62,000 was awarded in educational grants to individuals.

Applications

Applications can be made through the portal on the foundation's website. Applications must include relevant background information about yourself; how a grant award has the potential to benefit you; referees and assessment details; and household information such as income.

See the website for open funding calls.

Other information

The foundation also provides grants to schools and organisations to undertake relevant projects (£19,000 was awarded to organisations in 2015/16).

Dunk's and Springett's Educational Foundation

£4,200

Correspondent: Andrew Davis, Clerk to the Trustees, Fothersby, Rye Road, Hawkhurst, Kent TN18 5DB (01580 388973; email: dunksclerk@outlook.com; website: www.dunkscharities.com)

CC number: 307664

Eligibility

Children and young people under the age of 25 who live in the ancient parish of Hawkhurst and are in need.

Types of grants

The website notes that grants are made to support local young people 'in various ways, especially those of school-leaving age contemplating apprenticeships or further training'.

Annual grant total

In 2016 the foundation had an income of £12,800 and a total expenditure of £8,600. The charity had no accounts available to view, therefore we estimate that they gave around £4,200 to individuals for educational purposes.

The charity also awards grants to organisations.

Applications

Apply in writing to the correspondent.

Other information

The clerk to the trustees is responsible for both Dunk's charities. Should you need to contact the correspondent, it is helpful to specify that the query is for the educational foundation not the almshouses charity.

The foundation's record on the Charity Commission's website indicates that organisations may also be assisted.

Educational Foundation of James Morris

£2,000

Correspondent: Maria Wells, Trustee, 4 Bybrook Field, Sandgate, Folkestone CT20 3BQ (01303 248092; email: robjhudson@ntlworld.com)

CC number: 307559

Eligibility

Young people who live within the boundaries of Sandgate on a permanent basis.

Types of grants

Our previous research suggests that one-off and recurrent grants can range from £75 to £275 and are awarded to help further and higher education students with fees, books, equipment/instruments and maintenance/living expenses. Support is also offered towards the cost of school uniforms, books and equipment/instruments for schoolchildren and towards books and fees for people starting work. Mature students can receive help towards books, fees and maintenance/living expenses and vocational students can receive help towards fees.

Annual grant total

In 2015/16 the foundation had an income of £2,800 and a total expenditure of £2,200. We estimate that the charity gave around £2,000 in grants to individuals throughout the year.

Applications

Apply in writing to the correspondent.

The Gibbon and Buckland Charity

£13,900

Correspondent: David Harmsworth, Trustee, Hemsted Oaks, Cranbrook Road, Benenden, Cranbrook TN17 4ES (01580 240683; email: daharmsworth@ hotmail.com; website: www. benendenparishcouncil.org/content/ grants-young-persons-aged-16-25)

CC number: 307682

Eligibility

People between the ages of 16 and 25 who have lived in Benenden for at least three years.

Types of grants

Grants are given to students entering further/higher education, also people starting work and apprenticeships. Awards are of around £150 to £300 and can be given for general educational needs or gap years and similar projects.

Annual grant total

In 2016 the charity had an income of £25,000 and a total expenditure of £28,000. We estimate that the charity awarded around £13,900 in grants to individuals for educational purposes.

The charity also awards grants to organisations.

Applications

Application forms can be requested from the correspondent, downloaded from the Benenden parish council's website and are also placed in the village shop. The trustees meet twice a year with additional meetings being called as the need arises. Applications should be made by 30 September.

Other information

The charity also supports a Benenden Primary School and provides bibles to year six pupils in the school.

The Hugh and Montague Leney Travelling Awards Trust

£6,000

Correspondent: Lyn Edwards, Awards Group, Education and Libraries, Bishops Terrace, Bishops Way, Maidstone, Kent ME14 1AF (01622 605111; email: leneytrust@hotmail.co.uk; website: www. leneytrust.org)

CC number: 307950

Eligibility

Children and young people between the ages of 16 and 19 who are attending/ have attended within the previous 12 months a school in the county of Kent. The trustees will give preference to individuals in their final year of school showing qualities of leadership.

Types of grants

Grants of between £750 and £2,500 are awarded towards charitable trips abroad (generally at least four weeks long, although shorter applications will be considered) with a humanitarian/ philanthropic focus, aiming to help those who are less fortunate and benefit a local community. Preference is given to those whose venture is likely to help in their future life and career. Grants are not intended to cover the whole cost of a trip and individuals are expected to show initiative in raising funds from other sources.

Annual grant total

In 2015/16 the trust had an income of £6,000 and a total expenditure of £6,600. We estimate that grants totalled around £6,000.

Exclusions

The trust supports trips with a philanthropic/humanitarian focus, rather than holidays, structured school visits or periods of paid employment.

Applications

Applications can be made using a form available to download from the trust's website, which may also be provided through a local school. The closing date for applications is 31 January each year.

Anne Peirson Charitable Trust

£4,000

Correspondent: Ina Tomkinson, Trustee, Tyrol House, Cannongate Road, Hythe, Kent CT21 5PX (01303 260779; fax: 01303 238660)

CC number: 800093

Eligibility

People in need who live in the parish of Hythe and are at any level of their education. Our research suggests that in practice, it is mainly children who are assisted.

Types of grants

One-off grants ranging between £50 and £600 given mainly to early years children and schoolchildren for books, educational outings, fees and equipment. Extracurricular activities are also supported.

Annual grant total

In 2016 the trust had an income of £15,000 and a total expenditure of £17,300. We estimate the amount given to individuals for educational purposes was around £4,000.

Exclusions

Grants are not made where statutory support is available.

Applications

Applications should be made in writing to the correspondent via either Citizens Advice, a social worker, health visitor, school headteacher or other appropriate third party. Grants are considered at quarterly meetings of the trustees, but emergency applications can be considered in the interim.

Other information

Grants are awarded to individuals and organisations for both educational and social welfare purposes.

Ashford

Godmersham Relief in Need Charity

£1,500

Correspondent: David Swan, Fele Berge, Canterbury Road, Bilting, Ashford TN25 4HE (01233 812125)

CC number: 206278

Eligibility

Students who live in the ancient parish of Godmersham in Kent.

Types of grants

One-off and recurrent grants to help with the costs of equipment, instruments, books, study or travel overseas and extracurricular activities, such as music lessons and sports coaching.

Annual grant total

In 2015 the charity had an income of £7,000 and a total expenditure of £6,000. Grants are made to individuals and organisations for a wide range of purposes. We estimate that educational grants to individuals totalled £1,500.

Applications

The individual or a third party can apply to the correspondent in writing.

Headley-Pitt Charitable Trust

£21,500

Correspondent: Thelma Pitt, Old Mill Cottage, Ulley Road, Kennington, Ashford, Kent TN24 9HX (01233 626189; email: thelma.pitt@headley.co. uk)

CC number: 252023

Eligibility

Individuals in need who live in Kent, with a preference for those residing in Ashford.

Types of grants

One-off grants, usually in the range of £100 and £300. Recent grants have been given for various educational purposes to schoolchildren, college students, undergraduates, vocational students, mature students, people with special educational needs, people starting work and overseas students.

Annual grant total

In 2015/16 the trust had assets of £2.4 million and an income of £76,000. A total of 122 grants were made to individuals, for both social welfare and educational purposes, totalling £43,500. We estimate that educational grants to individuals amounted to £21,500.

An additional £35,000 was awarded in 165 grants to organisations.

Applications

Apply in writing to the correspondent, either directly by the individual or through a third party.

Hothfield Educational Foundation

£18,600 (19 grants)

Correspondent: Pater Patten, Trustee, The Paddocks, Hothfield, Ashford TN26 1EN (01233 620880; email: marianne.highwood@btinternet.com)

CC number: 307670

Eligibility

Adults or children of any age who live in the parish of Hothfield. The trustees are particularly keen 'to identify adults who need financial assistance to retrain or extend their employability skills as they seek employment', according to the 2015/16 annual report.

Types of grants

Grants are given for a wide range of educational purposes. Examples include: support for university students; educational trips abroad; support for children to go on school trips or residential adventure camps; music lessons; support for adults retraining for a new career or to gain skills for employment.

Annual grant total

In 2015/16 the foundation had an income of £27,000 and a total expenditure of £23,500. It made 19 grants to individuals during the year, totalling £18,600. Grants totalling £4,700 were also made to organisations.

Applications

Apply in writing to the correspondent. Applications are considered on an ongoing basis.

Other information

Grants are also made to local organisations.

City of Canterbury

The Canterbury United Municipal Charities

£4,500

Correspondent: Aaron Spencer, Furley Page Solicitors, 39 St Margaret's Street, Canterbury, Kent CT1 2TX (01227 863140; email: aas@furleypage.co.uk)

CC number: 210992

Eligibility
People who are in need and have lived within the boundaries of what was the old city of Canterbury for at least two years.

Types of grants
Small, one-off and ongoing grants are made to further and higher education students for books and equipment/ instruments.

Annual grant total
In 2016 the charity has an income of £8,500 and a total expenditure of £9,900. We estimate that educational grants to individuals totalled around £4,500.

Applications
Applications can be made in writing to the correspondent through the individual's school/college/educational welfare agency or directly by the individual. They are considered on an ongoing basis and should include a brief statement of circumstances and proof of residence in the area.

Fordwich United Charities

£4,000

Correspondent: Dr Roger Green, Trustee, 15 Water Meadows, Fordwich, Canterbury, Kent CT2 0BF (01227 713661 or 07981 491654; email: rogergreen@fordwich.net)

CC number: 208258

Eligibility
People under the age of 25 who live in the parish of Fordwich.

Types of grants
One-off Student Grants of about £150 are given towards books to assist people with their training and education after leaving school.

Annual grant total
In 2016 the charity had an income of £20,500 and a total expenditure of £19,400. We estimate that grants awarded to individuals for educational purposes totalled around £4,000.

Applications
Applications may be made in writing to the correspondent. The deadline for applications is normally 1 September and a decision should be made within a month.

Other information
The charity gives to individuals and organisations for both educational and social welfare purposes (mostly towards household bills and 'coal grants'). It also maintains its properties, particularly the Town Hall.

Streynsham's Charity

£3,300

Correspondent: The Clerk to the Trustees, PO Box 970, Canterbury, Kent CT1 9DJ (0845 094 4769)

CC number: 214436

Eligibility
Young people who live or attend school in the ancient parish of St Dunstan's, Canterbury, and are under the age of 21.

Types of grants
Maintenance allowances; financial assistance for books, clothing, tools or for travel etc.; assistance to students with higher or further education fees; support for schoolchildren to enable them to take part in educational activities which otherwise, on account of cost, they could not have taken part in.

Annual grant total
In 2015 the charity had assets of £94,000 and an income of £75,500. Educational grants to individuals totalled £3,300.

Applications
Apply in writing to the correspondent. Applications can be made directly by the individual, through the individual's school/college/educational welfare agency or through another third party on behalf of the individual. They are usually considered in March and October but can be made at any time and should include an sae and telephone number if applicable.

Dartford

Wilmington Parochial Charity

£750

Correspondent: Regina Skinner, Correspondent, 101 Birchwood Road, Dartford DA2 7HQ (01322 662342)

CC number: 1011708

Eligibility
People in need who live in the parish of Wilmington.

Types of grants
One-off grants are available according to need.

Annual grant total
In 2015/16 the charity had an income of £13,100 and a total expenditure of £9,600. The charity's record on the Charity Commission's website states that about 15%-17% of the expenditure is given for educational purposes. We estimate that around £750 could be given in educational grants to individuals.

Exclusions
Educational support is offered where funding is not provided by the local authorities.

Applications
Applications should be submitted by the individual or through a social worker, Citizens Advice or other welfare agency. The trustees meet in February and November. Urgent applications can be considered between the meetings in exceptional circumstances.

Other information
Grants are also given to local schools at Christmas and to individuals for welfare purposes.

Maidstone

The Mike Collingwood Memorial Fund

£4,300

Correspondent: Peter Green, Trustee, Acorn House, 12 The Platt, Sutton Valence, Maidstone, Kent ME17 3BQ (01622 843230; email: peter@ acornshouse.plus.com; website: www. wealdofkentrotary.org.uk/MCMF.html)

CC number: 288806

Eligibility
Young people who live within a 20-mile radius of the Who'd A Thought It pub in Grafty Green, Kent, where the Rotary Club of the Weald of Kent holds its weekly meetings.

Types of grants
Support can be given to undertake projects, trips and challenges in the UK and abroad, practice towards excellence in a chosen sport or vocation, and similar activities. The fund aims to give learning opportunities which may not be essential for a course, but are a good learning experience and will contribute to the applicant's future career.

Grants and loans are available. Due to the limited amount available, support is only supplementary and the applicants are expected to raise the balance by other means, ideally, with an entrepreneurial spirit and personal effort.

Annual grant total

In 2015/16 the fund had an income of £7,100 and a total expenditure of £4,500. We estimate that the fund awarded around £4,300 in grants to individuals for educational purposes.

Exclusions

The fund is not able to help with recurring costs such as university fees.

Applications

Application forms can be found on the Rotary Club of The Weald of Kent website or requested from the correspondent. Awards are normally made in February and October and applications should reach the trustees a month in advance.

Applications can be submitted by email at: mcmf@wealdofkentrotary.org.uk, or by post to: Derek Lamb, 68 Oak Lane, Headcorn TN27 9TB.

Yalding Educational Foundation

£3,500

Correspondent: Jenny Scott, Hollies, Benover Road, Yalding, Maidstone ME18 6EL (01622 298221; email: jscott@cfsbroadband.co.uk)

CC number: 307646

Eligibility

Children and young people who have attended a primary school in the parishes of Collier Street, Laddingford and Yalding for at least two years.

Types of grants

The foundation provides grants, awards and prizes of around £200. It can support schoolchildren and people in further or higher education to assist with general educational costs, including fees, books, clothing, equipment/instruments and other necessities.

Annual grant total

In 2015/16 the foundation had an income of £7,800 and a total expenditure of £7,700. We estimate that grants to individuals totalled about £3,500.

Applications

Applications can be made in writing to the correspondent. Our research suggests that applicants should provide details of the school attended in the parish, the college or university to be attended, the course to be taken and the length of the course. The trustees meet several times a year.

Other information

The foundation also sponsors a spoken English competition in local primary schools and provides financial assistance to local schools.

Medway

Cliffe and Cliffe Woods Community Trust (formerly known as Cliffe-at-Hoo Parochial Charity)

£2,000

Correspondent: Paul Kingman, 52 Reed Street, Cliffe, Rochester ME3 7UL (01634 220422; email: paul.kingman@ btopenworld.com)

CC number: 220855

Eligibility

People in need who live in the ancient parish of Cliffe-at-Hoo.

Types of grants

One-off grants according to need for any educational purpose.

Annual grant total

In 2016/17 the trust had an income of £9,000 and a total expenditure of £5,000. We estimate the total amount awarded to individuals for education was £2,000.

Applications

Apply in writing to the correspondent. Applications can be submitted directly by the individual or a family member, or through a third party such as a social worker or teacher.

Other information

The trust also awards grants to individuals for welfare purposes.

Arthur Ingram Trust

£91,000 (53 grants)

Correspondent: Margaret Taylor, Medway Council, Gun Wharf, Dock Road, Chatham, Kent ME4 4TR (01634 332144; email: margaret.taylor@medway.gov.uk)

CC number: 212868

Eligibility

Young people in need between the ages of 14 and 20 who are in full-time education, live in the Medway council area and are on a low income/from a low-income family.

Types of grants

The 2015/16 annual report states that grants are provided for the following purposes:

- 'To families with young persons in further education (or to independent students where they have no family)'
- 'For the purchase of school uniforms'
- 'For specialist equipment needed for training in a profession'
- 'To school voluntary funds to meet special hardship cases'
- 'Towards school trips which are identified as being linked to exam-related studies.'

Annual grant total

In 2015/16 the trust had assets of almost £2.2 million and an income of £72,000. It made 53 grants to individuals totalling £91,350, in the following categories:

Bursary grants	29	£84,000
Continuing education	16	£6,400
Uniforms	8	£950

Grants totalling £11,300 were also made to organisations for the following purposes:

School field trips	11	£11,000
School equipment/books	6	£300

Applications

Application forms can be requested from the correspondent. Applications can be made by the individual or through a third party, such as a teacher, school/college or educational welfare agency, if applicable.

Richard Watts and The City of Rochester Almshouse Charities

£9,200

Correspondent: Jane Rose, Clerk and Chief Officer, Administrative Offices, Watts Almshouses, Maidstone Road, Rochester, Kent ME1 1SE (01634 842194; fax: 01634 409348; email: admin@richardwatts.org.uk; website: www.richardwatts.org.uk)

CC number: 212828

Eligibility

People in need who live in the city of Rochester and urban Strood.

Apprenticeship grants are available for trade apprentices aged up to 25 years of age who live in ME1 and ME2 and who have successfully completed their first year apprenticeship (at least) and wish to continue for a subsequent year.

Types of grants

Grants are available to support education and training, purchase school uniforms and to support apprenticeships.

Annual grant total

In 2016 the charity had assets of £25.5 million and an income of £1.3 million. We estimate that educational grants totalled around £9,200.

Applications

Education and training: applications must be made by a body or organisation supporting the person, a simple letter of application outlining the request is usually sufficient.

Apprenticeships: application forms are available to download from the charity's website. Applications must be endorsed by the applicant's employer(s).

School uniforms: application forms are available to download from the charity's website. A letter of support from the school, social services, GP or other care organisation is normally required.

Other information

This charity was founded in 1579 and, aside from making grants, also runs almshouses. There are four main sites: Maidstone Road; Reeves House in Watts Avenue; St Catherine's at the top of Star Hill; and Hayward House in Corporation Street.

Sevenoaks
Kate Drummond Trust

£1,500

Correspondent: Robin Lochhead, Trustee, 25 Bankside, Dunton Green, Sevenoaks, Kent TN13 2UA (077 13412333; email: kdtrustees@gmail.com)

CC number: 246830

Eligibility

Young people, especially girls, living in Sevenoaks urban district and neighbourhood.

Types of grants

One-off grants are given towards education, recreation or training, including vocational training or people entering a trade.

Annual grant total

In 2015/16 the trust had an income of £8,800 and a total expenditure of £6,500. We estimate that grants given to individuals for educational purposes totalled around £1,500.

Applications

Applications may be made in writing to the correspondent. Include an sae if a reply is required.

Other information

The trust owns and operates a residential house offering either rent-free or subsidised accommodation. Grant-

making is available when there is surplus money. It can also give grants to organisations and for social welfare purposes.

Shepway
The Reverend Tatton Brockman

£5,500

Correspondent: Janet Salt, Greatfield House, Ivychurch Road, Brenzett, Romney Marsh, Kent TN29 0EE (01797 344364; email: bracken@ciarrai364.plus.com)

CC number: 307681

Eligibility

People under the age of 25 who are in full-time education and live in the ancient parishes of Brenzett, Cheriton, and Newington-next-Hythe in the county of Kent.

Types of grants

One-off grants in the range of £100 to £500 to help with the cost of fees, study or travel abroad, books, equipment and instruments for schoolchildren, students in further/higher education, vocational students and people with special educational needs.

Annual grant total

In 2015/16 the charity had an income of £24,000 and a total expenditure of £18,500. The total amount awarded in educational grants to individuals was £5,500.

Applications

The individual should apply directly in writing to the correspondent. Applications are normally considered in May and November.

Other information

The charity also awards payments to voluntary schools in the area to cover costs not provided by the local authority.

Southland's Educational Charity

£3,000

Correspondent: Mrs U. Wooding, c/o Town Hall, High Street, New Romney, Kent TN28 8BT (01797 362348; email: sacclerk@gmail.com)

CC number: 307783

Eligibility

Children under the age of 25 who are continuing into further education, live in the parish of New Romney and are in need.

Types of grants

Grants are given towards the cost of books, equipment, instruments, fees, maintenance/living expenses, educational outings in the UK and study or travel overseas.

Annual grant total

In 2015/16 the charity had an income of £3,900 and a total expenditure of £3,300. We estimate that about £3,000 was given in grants to individuals.

Applications

Application forms are available from the correspondent.

Swale
The William Barrow's Charity

£12,500 (42 grants)

Correspondent: Stuart Mair, Clerk, 43 Park Road, Sittingbourne, Kent ME10 1DY (01795 470556; email: stuart@georgewebbfinn.com)

CC number: 307574

Eligibility

Grants for education for those who are under 25 and who live, or whose parents live, in Borden. Preference is given to candidates in further and higher education.

Types of grants

Grants are available on a one-off or recurrent basis to assist with the costs of school uniforms, books, equipment, instruments, school trips etc.

Annual grant total

In 2015/16 the trust had £7.7 million in assets and an income of £245,500. The total amount awarded as grants to individuals was £12,500.

Applications

Application forms are available from the charity's website. Candidates are required to submit completed applications between 1 June and 30 September for consideration in October.

Other information

Grants were made to Borden C.E. Primary School towards the cost of expenses, including coach hire for swimming lessons and educational visits. Grants were also made to Borden Grammar School.

Thanet

The Gibbons Family Trust

See entry on page 293

Oxfordshire

Bartholomew Educational Foundation

£3,000

Correspondent: Robin Mitchell, Clerk to the Trustees, 20 High Street, Eynsham, Witney, Oxfordshire OX29 4HB (01865 880665; website: eynsham-pc.gov.uk/org.aspx?n=Bartholomew-Educational-Foundation)

CC number: 309278

Eligibility

People under the age of 25 who live in the parish of Eynsham.

Types of grants

A maximum amount of £3,000 is available towards educational travel abroad; study of music and other arts; the cost of tools, equipment/instruments, books and clothing to students, apprentices and trainees; to schoolchildren and university/college students for general educational needs.

Annual grant total

In 2015/16 the foundation had an annual income of £3,500 and a total expenditure of £3,000. The amount donated in grants was £3,000.

Applications

Applications should be made in writing to the correspondents. The trustees meet four times per year in February, May, August/September, and November. To be considered, applications must be received the month before the next meeting.

Other information

Local educational bodies can also be supported, after the needs of individuals have been met.

Culham St Gabriel's Trust (The Culham Institute)

£22,500 (seven grants)

Correspondent: Mark Chater, Director, Culham St Gabriel's, 60–62 Banbury Road, Oxford OX2 6PN (01865 612035; email: enquiries@cstg.org.uk; website: www.cstg.org.uk)

CC number: 309671

Eligibility

People who are, or intend to become, teachers in religious education or are otherwise involved in work, development, research and studies of the Church of England.

Types of grants

Grants are aimed to help further/higher education students and to promote life-long learning of teachers. Financial support is available towards books, equipment, necessities and the costs of classes, lectures or various development opportunities.

Annual grant total

In 2015/16 the trust had assets of £16.7 million and an income of £783,500. Throughout the year the trust awarded £22,500 in grants to seven individuals towards the advancement of religious education.

Organisations are also supported.

Exclusions

Grants are not given for work outside the UK, for general running costs, deficit reduction or religious instruction (as distinct from education).

Applications

Application forms can be obtained from the trust's website and should be submitted by January, May and September (specified dates may be subject to change; see the trust's website for further information).

Other information

The trust awarded eight grants to organisations totalling £253,000.

Ducklington and Hardwick with Yelford Charity

£750

Correspondent: Gillian Caton, 10 Lovell Close, Ducklington, Witney OX29 7YQ (01993 702261)

CC number: 237343

Eligibility

People in need or hardship who live in the villages of Ducklington and Hardwick with Yelford.

Types of grants

Grants of up to £200 can be awarded to people 'embarking on courses'. University/college students can be assisted with the cost of books, also travel/study overseas. Individuals undertaking apprenticeships/starting work are given help for equipment, clothing and similar necessities.

Annual grant total

In 2016 the charity had a total income of £3,600 and a total expenditure of £3,100. We estimate that educational support to individuals totalled around £750.

Applications

Applications may be made in writing to the correspondent. The trustees normally meet in March and November but applications can be submitted at any time.

Other information

Grants are also made to organisations, clubs, schools and so on. Support is also given for welfare needs.

The Exuberant Trust

£2,800

Correspondent: Megan Boyes, Trust Administrator, 11 St Margaret's Road, Oxford, Oxfordshire OX2 6RU (01865 751056; email: admin@exuberant-trust.org.uk; website: www.exuberant-trust.org.uk)

CC number: 1095911

Eligibility

People up to the age of 30 who are from Oxfordshire and are developing their interest in the arts (music, drama, dance, arts and crafts, jewellery, multimedia and so on). Preference is given for first-time applicants.

Types of grants

One-off grants of up to a maximum of £500 for a specific project or activity. These awards can be made for tools, training, music lessons, general costs, instruments and so on.

Previous grant recipients include: musicians, designers, jewellers, theatre directors, dancers, performing artists, composers, conductors, DJs, film makers, singers, art promoters, concert organisers, instrumentalists, bands and chamber groups.

Annual grant total

In 2016 the trust had an income of £4,200 and a total expenditure of £3,000. We estimate that the trust awarded around £2,800 in grants to individuals for educational purposes.

Applications

The application form and guidelines can be downloaded from the website. Applicants should give convincing reasons for applying and should include appropriate references and a budget proposal. When fully completed, applications must be sent by post and email to the correspondent.

Full details are available on the website.

Other information

The trust's website states that it 'raises funds by organising concerts throughout the year and from donations received from its supporters' and notes that 'successful applicants are encouraged to take part in concerts and other activities in support of the trust'.

The Faringdon United Charities

£2,500

Correspondent: Vivienne Checkley, Bunting & Co., Faringdon Business Centre, Brunel House, Volunteer Way, Faringdon, Oxfordshire SN7 7YR (01367 243789; email: vivienne.checkley@ buntingaccountants.co.uk)

CC number: 237040

Eligibility

People who are in need and live in the parishes of Great Faringdon, Littleworth or Little Coxwell, all in Oxfordshire.

Types of grants

One-off grants to: schoolchildren for study/travel abroad, equipment/ instruments and excursions; mature students for books; people with special educational needs for equipment/ instruments; and people starting work for equipment/instruments.

Annual grant total

In 2015/16 the charity had an income of £16,300 and a total expenditure of £10,000. We estimate that educational grants to individuals totalled £2,500.

Applications

Applications can be made in writing to the correspondent throughout the year. They can be submitted either through Citizens Advice, a social worker or other third party, directly by the individual or by a third party on their behalf for example a neighbour, parent or child.

The Kathryn Turner Trust (Whitton's Wishes)

£10,000

Correspondent: Kathryn Turner, Founder and Trustee, Unit 3, Suffolk Way, Abingdon, Oxfordshire OX14 5JX (01235 527310; email: kathrynturnertrust@hotmail.co.uk)

CC number: 1111250

Eligibility

Children and young people, individuals with disabilities or special needs in Oxfordshire. Members of the Royal Navy, Army and Royal Air Force, and their dependants are also supported.

Types of grants

Grants towards various educational needs, including equipment and necessities.

Annual grant total

In 2015 the trust held assets of £7,500 and had an income of £178,500. Grants totalled £40,000 of which we have estimated that £10,000 was awarded to individuals for educational purposes.

Applications

Apply in writing to the correspondent. The trustees meet every three months.

Other information

Organisations and individuals are supported for both educational and welfare purposes.

Cherwell

Bakehouse or Shepherd's Charity

£1,400

Correspondent: Carole Coppin, Trustee, Barn Elms, The Green, Barford St Michael, Banbury OX15 0RN (01869 338937; email: carole.coppin@hotmail. co.uk)

CC number: 309173

Eligibility

Young people under the age of 25 who (or whose parents) have lived in the parish of Barford St John or Barford St Michael for at least three years.

Types of grants

Financial assistance for undertaking apprenticeships; clothes for employment; fees and expenses for advancement of education; and scholarships, grants and maintenance allowances tenable at any secondary school, further education college or university

Annual grant total

In 2015/16 the charity had an income of £5,000 and a total expenditure of £1,600. We estimate that around £1,400 was awarded in grants.

Exclusions

Provisions are not made for primary schoolchildren.

Applications

Applications may be made in writing to the correspondent.

The Banbury Charities

£37,000

Correspondent: Nigel Yeadon, Clerk, 36 West Bar, Banbury OX16 9RU (01295 251234)

CC number: 201418

Eligibility

People under the age of 25 who live in the former borough of Banbury.

Types of grants

Grants are given to assist people who are preparing for or entering a profession or trade and students who are in higher and further education. Grants are also given to assist young people under the age of 25 who are studying the arts, literature or science.

Annual grant total

In 2016 the charity had assets of £5.9 million and an income of £414,500. During the year there were 236 grants made to individuals totalling £74,000. We estimate that grants given to individuals for education totalled around £37,000.

Applications

Apply in writing to the correspondent. Applicants are encouraged to obtain a letter of support from their social worker, carer or other person in authority to give credence to their application.

Other information

Banbury Charities is a group of eight registered charities. These are as follows: Bridge Estate Charity; Countess of Arran's Charity; Banbury Arts and Educational Charity; Banbury Almshouses Charity; Banbury Sick Poor Fund; Banbury Welfare Trust; Banbury Poor Trust; and Banbury Recreation Charity.

The Bletchington Charity

£2,500

Correspondent: Sue Green, Bletchingon Village Hall, Whitemarsh Way, Bletchington, Kidlington OX5 3FD (01869 350895; email: sue@sueg.co.uk)

CC number: 201584

Eligibility

People in need who live in the parish of Bletchington.

Types of grants

Grants to students and apprentices to help with the purchase of books, instruments or tools necessary for their course.

Annual grant total

In 2016 the charity had an income of £11,000 and a total expenditure of £17,300. Grants are made to individuals and organisations for both educational and social welfare purposes. We estimate that educational grants to individuals totalled £2,500.

Applications

Applications can be made in writing to the correspondent by the individual.

Other information

The charity seeks to support any medical and social needs that will benefit the village community as a whole.

City of Oxford

The Charity of Thomas Dawson

Correspondent: K. Lacey, Clerk and Receiver, 56 Poplar Close, Garsington, Oxford OX44 9BP (01865 368259)

CC number: 203258

Eligibility

Children and young people in need who have lived in the city of Oxford (postcodes OX1 to OX4) for three years, with a preference for those resident in the parish of St Clements.

Types of grants

Help is given with the cost of books, clothing, fees and other essentials for schoolchildren and for people at college or university. Grants are also made to people preparing for entering or engaging in a profession, trade, occupation or service. Awards generally range from £40 to £1,500.

Annual grant total

In 2015/16 the charity had assets of £14.1 million and an income of £433,000. Grants totalled £104,500. No grants were made to individuals during the year.

Exclusions

Grants are not normally given for medical sponsorships or electives, or towards accommodation, travel or living expenses.

Applications

Applications may be made in writing to the correspondent, with evidence regarding course fees.

Note: Applicants can only apply for one degree course.

Other information

Grants may also be made to schools and young people, family and volunteer organisations. One-half of the income is applied for the upkeep and repair of the parish church St Clement and one

quarter to The Parochial Charities of St Clements, Oxford.

The City of Oxford Charity

£16,200 (31 grants)

Correspondent: David Wright, The Office, Stones Court, St Clements, Oxford OX14 1AP (01865 553043; email: enquiries@oxfordcitycharities.fsnet.co.uk; website: www.oxfordcitycharities.org)

CC number: 239151

Eligibility

Children and young people under the age of 25 who have lived in the city of Oxford for at least three years.

Types of grants

One-off grants are given to schoolchildren and college or university students. Assistance can be given with school uniforms, books, materials and also special educational needs.

Annual grant total

In 2016 the charity had assets of £6.2 million and an income of £418,000. Educational grants to individuals totalled £16,200.

Applications

Application forms can be downloaded from the charity's website or requested from the correspondent. Grants are considered quarterly in March, June, September and December. Applications from pupils must be accompanied by a letter of support from an educational social worker/health visitor/welfare worker/similar professional.

Other information

The charity is an amalgamation of a number of charities working for the benefit of the people of Oxford city. It also accepts applications from schools to help with 35% of the full costs of educational trips for children from low-income families, supports the social welfare of individuals and maintains almshouses in the local area.

South Oxfordshire

Henley Educational Trust

£11,400 (55 grants)

Correspondent: Claire Brown, Clerk, Syringa Cottage, Horsepond Road, Gallowstree Common, Reading, Oxfordshire RG4 9BP (0118 972 4575; email: henleyeducationaltrust@hotmail.co.uk; website: www.henleyeducationaltrust.com)

CC number: 309237

Eligibility

People under the age of 25 who live in the parishes of Henley North, Henley South, Bix, Remenham or Rotherfield Greys. Those who currently attend, or have attended for a minimum of two year at the following qualifying schools or colleges are also eligible: Nettlebed Primary, Trinity Primary, Valley Road Primary, Sacred Heart RC Primary, Badgemore Primary, Crazies Hill Primary, Henley College or Gillotts School.

Types of grants

Grants are given for a wide range of educational purposes, such as: school trips; music lessons and instruments; playgroup fees; after school clubs; sports activities and equipment; school uniforms (up to £75 for primary school and £120 for secondary school); study/travel overseas; support for people starting an apprenticeship or work.

Annual grant total

In 2015/16 the trust had assets of £3.4 million and an income of £148,500. During the year, the trust awarded 55 grants to individuals for educational purposes, totalling £11,400. A further £114,500 was given in grants to local schools and other organisations.

Exclusions

Funding for pre-school fees is only provided where the extra sessions can be supported by an educational or healthcare professional and are essential to the child's development. The trust will not help merely to allow the parent/guardian to engage in employment.

Applications

Application forms can be obtained from the trust's website. The trustees meet six times a year – dates are usually published on the website. Note that email applications are not accepted. Candidates are required to provide evidence of their financial circumstances and a letter of support from an educational or healthcare professional.

Other information

A third of the trust's income is awarded in grants to individuals for educational purposes. The other two-thirds are distributed to local schools and colleges and to other educational and youth organisations.

The Stevens Hart and Municipal Educational Charity (Henley Municipal Charities)

£400

Correspondent: Jean Pickett, Henley Municipal Charities, Rear, 24 Hart Street, Henley-on-Thames, Oxfordshire RG9 2AU (01491 412360; email: henleymcharities@aol.com)

CC number: 292857

Eligibility
Children and young people in need of financial assistance who live in the parishes of Bix and Rotherfield Greys or the town of Henley-on-Thames.

Types of grants
Our research shows that grants are awarded up to a maximum of £300 and can be given towards the cost of books, clothing and other educational necessities. Support is mainly for schoolchildren but students at college or university may also be assisted.

Annual grant total
In 2015/16 the charity had an income of £5,400 and a total expenditure of £750. We estimate that grants to individuals totalled around £400.

Applications
Apply in writing to the correspondent.

Other information
The charity also supports local schools with maintenance and special benefits not normally provided by the local authorities.

Thame Charities (The Thame Welfare Trust)

£10,000

Correspondent: John Gadd, 2 Cromwell Avenue, Thame, Oxfordshire OX9 3TD (01844 212564; email: johngadd4@gmail.com)

CC number: 241914

Eligibility
People in need who live in Thame and the immediately adjoining villages.

Types of grants
One-off grants of up to £1,000 are given to help towards a wide variety of needs to schoolchildren, college students, undergraduates, vocational students, mature students, people with special educational needs and people starting work.

Annual grant total
In 2016/17 the charity had an income of £15,000 and a total expenditure of £20,000. The amount awarded in educational grants was £10,000.

Applications
Apply in writing to the correspondent.

Other information
The charity also provides grants for welfare purposes.

Wallingford Relief in Need Charity

£2,500

Correspondent: Jamie Baskeyfield, Correspondent, Wallingford Town Council, 9 St Martin's Street, Wallingford, Oxfordshire OX10 0AL (01491 835373; email: queries@ wallingfordtc.co.uk)

CC number: 292000

Eligibility
People in need who live in Wallingford and the neighbourhood (including the former parish of Clapcot).

Types of grants
Help is given towards the cost of bills, clothing and other essentials. The charity gives one-off grants only.

Annual grant total
In 2015/16 the charity had an income of £8,700 and a total expenditure of £10,300. We estimate that grants for educational purposes totalled about £2,500.

Applications
Application forms are form available from the correspondent. They should be submitted either directly by the individual or through a local organisation. The trustees meet about every three months, although emergency cases can be considered in between the meetings. Urgent cases may require a visit by a trustee.

Other information
The majority of grants are given for welfare needs.

The Wheatley Charities

£3,500

Correspondent: R. F. Minty, Trustee, 24 Old London Road, Wheatley, Oxford OX33 1YW (01865 874676)

CC number: 203535

Eligibility
People who are under the age of 25 and live in the parish of Wheatley.

Types of grants
Grants are given to help young people prepare for any trade or occupation or to promote their education.

Annual grant total
In 2016 the charity had an income of £4,300 and a total expenditure of £7,000. Grants are made to individuals and organisations for social welfare and educational purposes. We estimate that educational grants to individuals totalled £3,500.

Applications
Apply in writing to the correspondent.

Vale of White Horse

The Hope Ffennell Trust

£5,500

Correspondent: Louis Letourneau, Trustee, Church End, Wytham Abbey, Wytham, Oxfordshire OX2 8QE (01865 203475)

CC number: 309212

Eligibility
People under the age of 25 years who live in the parishes of Wytham and North Hinksey.

Types of grants
Help towards outings and educational visits, books and equipment.

Annual grant total
In 2016 the trust had an income of £6,800 and a total expenditure of £5,900. We have estimated that grants to individuals totalled £5,500.

Applications
Apply in writing to the correspondent.

The Steventon Allotments and Relief-in-Need Charity

£13,300 (28 grants)

Correspondent: Patricia Effer, 19 Lime Grove, Southmoor, Abingdon, Oxfordshire OX13 5DN (01865 821055; email: info@sarinc.org.uk)

CC number: 203331

Eligibility
People who are in full-time education in Steventon who are eligible for a student loan. Applications are considered from anyone living in the parish or with a significant connection to the parish.

Types of grants
One-off grants of up to £500 are given according to need for costs associated with higher education.

SOUTH EAST – OXFORDSHIRE / SURREY

Annual grant total

In 2016 the charity had assets of £3 million and an income of £127,000. Educational grants to individuals totalled £13,300.

Applications

Apply in writing to the correspondent. The charity advertises regularly in the local parish magazine. Applications should include full details of income and expenditure, and will be treated in strictest confidence.

West Oxfordshire

The Bampton Exhibition Foundation

£4,000

Correspondent: Nigel Wallis, Trustee, 2 Castle Mews, Bridge Street, Bampton OX18 2HA

CC number: 309238

Eligibility

People under 25 who live in Bampton, Aston, Cote, Weald or Lew and are in need. Primary, secondary, college/further education, undergraduate and postgraduate students are all welcome to apply.

Types of grants

Grants are given to for projects/courses which would be otherwise beyond the means of applicants. Support that can be given includes books, equipment/instruments, fees, maintenance/living expenses, educational outings in the UK, study or travel abroad and so on.

Annual grant total

In 2015/16 the foundation had an income of £10,000 and a total expenditure of £6,300. We estimate that the total amount given in grants was £4,000.

Applications

Apply in writing to the correspondent, including details regarding the proposed project/course, any expenses involved and relevant references. Applications can be submitted either directly by the individual, through the individual's school or college, or by a teacher or parent. Applications have no deadline.

Other information

The foundation also spends some of its income on a listed building used as a community library and historical archive.

The Burford Relief-in-Need Charity

£25,000

Correspondent: Anne Burgess Youngson, Whitehill Farm, Burford, Oxfordshire OX18 4DT (01993 822894)

CC number: 1036378

Eligibility

People who are in need and live within seven miles of the Tolsey, Burford.

Types of grants

Grants are given to assist recipients to earn a living.

Annual grant total

In 2016 the charity had an income of £13,300 and a total expenditure of £55,000. We estimate that educational grants to individuals totalled £25,000 with funding also awarded to individuals for social welfare purposes.

Applications

Apply in writing to the correspondent either directly by the individual or, where applicable, through a social worker, Citizens Advice or other third party. Applications should include the individual's full name, address, age, and the number of years they have lived in Burford or their connection with Burford.

Charlbury Exhibition Foundation

£13,000

Correspondent: Kathryn Jones, Took House, Sheep Street, Charlbury, Chipping Norton, Oxfordshire OX7 3RR (01608810793)

CC number: 309236

Eligibility

People under the age of 25 who live in the ancient township of Charlbury and are going into further or higher education, including vocational courses and apprenticeships.

Types of grants

Recurrent grants for up to three years. Our research shows that grants are of about £100 a year per individual but depend on the foundation's income. Support is given towards general educational costs, necessities and maintenance expenses.

Annual grant total

In 2015/16 the foundation had an income of £14,000 and a total expenditure of £14,500. We estimate that the amount awarded in grants to individuals was £13,000.

Applications

Apply in writing to the correspondent. Applications should be submitted by October and include the individual's age, school, details of course, university/college and so on. People attending short training courses sponsored by Charlbury Youth Organisations can also apply.

Other information

The foundation owns a property and a field in Charlbury, Oxfordshire and uses the rental income from these assets to award grants.

Surrey

The Archbishop Abbot's Exhibition Foundation

£4,500

Correspondent: Richard Middlehurst, Clerk, 17 Ashdale, Great Bookham, Surrey KT23 4QP (01483 302345; email: grants@aaef.org.uk; website: aaef.org.uk)

CC number: 311890

Eligibility

People aged between 11 and 28 who live in, or attend school, in the boroughs of Guildford or Waverley in Surrey.

Types of grants

Grants of £50 to £1,250 are available and can be made on a single or recurrent instance (recurrent grants must be re-applied for)

Annual grant total

In 2015 the foundation had an income of £6,400 and a total expenditure of £4,900. We estimate that grants totalled £4,500.

Applications

First-time applicants or applications on behalf of another individual must first complete the quick application form available on the website. The quick application will be assessed, and if the applicant is successful in the first instance they will be required to complete the full application and provide a parent/guardian form, both available on the website.

Chobham Poor Allotment Charity

£500

Correspondent: Elizabeth Thody, 46 Chertsey Road, Windlesham GU20 6EP

CC number: 200154

Eligibility

People in need who live in the ancient parish of Chobham, which includes the civil parishes of Chobham and West End.

Types of grants

Grants usually ranging between £100 and £500, are made typically towards the cost of school uniforms and educational outings, trips and visits.

Annual grant total

In 2016/17 the charity had assets of £435,500 and an income of £49,700. Grants to four individuals amounted to £1,000, of which we estimate £500 was given for educational purposes.

Applications

Apply in writing to the correspondent.

Other information

The main activities of the charity are the provision and maintenance of allotments, almshouses and relief in need. The charity is also involved in provision/maintenance of recreational and educational facilities. The trustees can support both individuals and organisations, nevertheless only a small amount each year is awarded in educational grants.

The Humphrey Richardson Taylor Charitable Trust

£36,000

Correspondent: B. M. Bennett, 28 Chipstead Station Parade, Chipstead, Surrey CR5 3TF (01737 557546; email: hrtaylortrust@btconnect.com; website: www.hrtaylortrust.org.uk)

CC number: 1062836

Eligibility

Children and young adults living in or with a strong link to Surrey with exceptional musical talent.

Types of grants

Grants for the purchase of musical equipment or part-funding of tuition.

Annual grant total

In 2016 the trust had assets of £14.6 million and an income of £518,000. Grants to individuals totalled £36,000.

Exclusions

UK citizens only. The trust will not fund courses at foreign universities.

Applications

Applications can be made by email and should be no longer than four to six A4 pages when printed. Full details of what should be included can be found on the trust's website.

The Seckford Foundation

£15,000 (25 grants)

Correspondent: Graham Watson, Seckford Springboard, Marryott House, Burkitt Road, Woodbridge IP12 4JJ (01394 615173; email: enquiries@ seckford-foundation.org.uk; website: www.seckford-foundation.org.uk)

CC number: 1110964

Eligibility

Individuals who are aged 25 and under or 65 and over, who live in Surrey.

Types of grants

Through its Seckford Springboard initiative, the foundation offers grants (usually up to £500) for purposes which support access to education, training and employment, or which improve quality of life. The guidance notes state that the foundation will support: 'Interventions that will raise self-esteem and self-confidence to enable participation in education, employment or training, or activities aimed at promoting independence and social inclusion'.

Examples include: books; equipment; childcare; interview clothing; course costs (where the course is required for employment); assistance is also given to help access volunteering opportunities; transport for activities which encourage life-long learning and independent living; activities which engage younger and older people and help them face challenges.

School trips are only funded in cases which the foundation 'deems to have the most need'.

Annual grant total

In 2015/16 the foundation had assets of almost £45 million and an income of £20.15 million. Grants were made to 25 individuals totalling £15,000. A further seven grants were made to organisations, totalling £21,000.

Exclusions

The foundation will not support:

- Overseas projects or gap years
- Retrospective funding
- Activities which should be funded by statutory bodies

- Building projects or refurbishments/ adaptations
- Loan or debt repayments, or budget shortfalls
- Medical treatment
- Postgraduate study
- Those who have received a grant in the last 12 months
- Individuals living outside Suffolk

The foundation is unlikely to provide funding if their grant only forms a small contribution to the funding required.

Applications

Applications should be made in a letter, stating: the age of the individual; where they live; what the funding is required for; and why they are unable to provide the funds themselves. Potential applicants are welcome to contact the foundation by telephone to ascertain their eligibility. Guidance notes are provided on the website and should be read before applying. In most cases, the foundation can make a decision within three weeks of receiving an application. Larger applications may take longer, in which case the foundation will notify applicants of a likely timescale.

Other information

Seckford Springboard is part of the Seckford Foundation, and also provides apprenticeships and mentoring opportunities, as well as making grants to organisations. The Seckford Foundation runs Woodbridge School and two free schools, as well as almshouses.

Epsom and Ewell

Chessington Charities

£2,000

Correspondent: Revd Scott Edwards, The Vicarage, Garrison Lane, Chessington KT9 2LB (020 8397 3016; email: stmaryschessington@hotmail.co. uk)

CC number: 209241

Eligibility

People in need who live in the parish of St Mary the Virgin, Chessington. Applicants must have lived in the parish for at least one year.

Types of grants

One-off grants are made for general educational and training needs.

Annual grant total

In 2016 the charity had an income of £4,500 and a total expenditure of £4,000. The charity awarded £2,000 in grants for education.

Exclusions

Grants are not given to pay debts. The area of benefit is only the parish of St Mary the Virgin and excludes the rest of the Chessington postal area.

Applications

Application forms are available from the correspondent and can be submitted by the individual or through a social agency such as Citizens Advice.

Other information

Grants are also given to those in financial hardship, and in the form of Christmas gifts to older people.

Epsom Parochial Charities (Epsom Almshouse Charity)

£1,900

Correspondent: John Steward, Trustee, 26 Woodcote Hurst, Epsom, Surrey KT18 7DT (email: vanstonewalker@ntlworld.com)

CC number: 200571

Eligibility

People in need who are under the age of 25, live in the ancient parish of Epsom and are in need of financial assistance in connection with their education.

Types of grants

One-off and recurrent grants are given according to need to schoolchildren, college students, undergraduates, vocational students, mature students, people starting work and people with special educational needs, including awards towards clothing/uniforms, fees, books, equipment/instruments maintenance/living expenses and excursions.

Annual grant total

In 2015 the charity had assets of £1.7 million and an income of £86,500. Grants to individuals for educational purposes totalled £1,900.

Applications

Application forms are available from the correspondent and can be submitted directly by the individual.

Other information

Grants are also made for social welfare purposes. The charity also provides residential accommodation through its three almshouses.

Mole Valley

John Bristow and Thomas Mason Trust

£3,000 (three grants)

Correspondent: Sam Longhurst, Trust Secretary, Beech Hay, Ifield Road, Charlwood, Surrey RH6 0DR (01293 862734; email: trust.secretary@jbtmt.org.uk; website: www.jbtmt.org.uk)

CC number: 1075971

Eligibility

People who live in the ancient parish of Charlwood.

Types of grants

Grants are given to schoolchildren, college students, undergraduates, vocational students, mature students, people with special educational needs and to people starting work. Help is given for the cost of uniforms/other school clothing, books, equipment/instruments, fees, maintenance/living expenses, childcare, education outings in the UK, study or travel abroad and student exchanges.

Annual grant total

In 2015/16 the trust had assets of £2.7 million representing mainly endowment funds with only £104,500 being unrestricted. The trust had an income of £102,000 and made grants totalling almost £56,000, of which £3,000 went to individuals for educational purposes and almost £11,500 to individuals for social welfare purposes. The remainder was awarded to organisations.

Applications

Application forms are available from the correspondent or to download from the website. Applications can be submitted directly by the individual or through a third party. They will normally be considered within two weeks but can be dealt with more quickly in urgent cases.

Other information

The trust also supports schools, churches, and the overall improvement of the area of benefit.

Leatherhead United Charities

£4,000

Correspondent: David Matanle, Clerk to the Trustees, Homefield, Forty Foot Road, Leatherhead, Surrey KT22 8RP (01372 370073; email: luchar@btinternet.com)

CC number: 200183

Eligibility

People in need who live in the area of the former Leatherhead urban district council (Ashtead, Bookhams, Fetcham and Leatherhead). Preference is given to residents of the parish of Leatherhead as constituted on 27 September 1912.

Types of grants

Support is available for general educational expenses.

Annual grant total

In 2016 the charity had assets of £6.4 million and an income of £313,500. During the year 31 grants were made to individuals. We estimate that education grants to individuals totalled £4,000.

Applications

Application forms can be requested from the correspondent. Our research suggests that they can be submitted by the individual directly or by a family member. Awards are considered throughout the year.

Other information

The charity also provides residents of Mole Valley District Council with sheltered housing and associated services.

Reigate and Banstead

The Pilgrim Band Trust

£9,000

Correspondent: Roger Key, Trustee, 10 Carlton Road, Redhill RH1 2BX (01737 216514; email: principal@pilgrimband.org)

CC number: 1140954

Eligibility

Children and young people between the ages of 8 and 18 living in Reigate and surrounding areas who want to learn to play an instrument. Young musicians are also supported. Preference may be given to individuals or families with limited means or children with disabilities.

Types of grants

The trust gives an opportunity to children and young people to learn music by loaning the instruments and providing one-to-one or group tuition sessions for acoustic and electric guitars, piano, singing, drums and steel pans. Grants can also be provided for tuition fees to young musicians.

Annual grant total

In 2015/16 the trust held assets of £4.7 million and had an income of £138,500. Grants to individuals totalled £9,000 with a further £17,500 awarded to local schools.

Applications

Apply in writing to the correspondent.

Other information

The trust also supports local schools, with priority given to state schools, and local music festivals. Most of its charitable expenditure supports the activities of the band.

Mary Stephens Foundation

£4,500

Correspondent: John Stephenson, Trustee, Doghurst Cottage, Doghurst Lane, Chipstead, Surrey CR5 3PL (01737 556548; email: john.stephenson24@ gmail.com or marystephensfoundation@talktalk.net)

CC number: 311999

Eligibility

People under the age of 25 who live, or whose parents live, in the ancient parish of Chipstead, which includes Hooley and Netherene.

Types of grants

One-off and recurrent grants of up to a maximum of £1,200 a year. Assistance can be given towards purposes such as books, equipment, uniforms and school trips. Three-year scholarships may also be awarded to those in higher education, towards costs of accommodation, study materials and field trips.

Annual grant total

In 2015/16 the foundation had an income of £6,300 and a total expenditure of £4,800. We estimate that grants totalled around £4,500.

Exclusions

The foundation does not issue grants to pre-school children or provide loans.

Applications

Application forms can be requested from the correspondent. They are considered at quarterly meetings and should be made directly by the individual, or by the individual's head of school or church leader.

Runnymede

The Chertsey Combined Charity

£2,800

Correspondent: M. R. O'Sullivan, Secretary, PO Box 89, Weybridge, Surrey KT13 8HY (email: info@charity.me.uk)

CC number: 200186

Eligibility

People in need who live in the electoral divisions of the former urban district of Chertsey.

Types of grants

Grants are often given to help towards the cost of books, clothing and other essentials for those at school. Grants may also be given to people at college or university.

Annual grant total

In 2016/17 the charity had an income of £64,500 and a total expenditure of £42,000. Throughout the year the charity awarded almost £5,600 in grants to individuals. We estimate that £2,800 of this amount was given for educational purposes.

Grants to organisations totalled £7,200.

Applications

Application forms are available from the correspondent.

The Egham Education Trust

£4,500

Correspondent: Max Walker, Correspondent, 33 Runnemede Road, Egham TW20 9BE (01784 472742; email: eghamunicharity@aol.com; website: www.eghamunitedcharity.org)

CC number: 311941

Eligibility

People in need who are between the ages of 16 and 25 and have lived in the electoral wards of Egham, which is now Egham, Engerfield Green, Virginia Water and Hythe, ideally for at least five years.

Types of grants

One-off and recurrent grants in the range of £100 to £500 are made towards further and vocational education. Awards may be made to students in secondary school, training college, university or other institution of further (including technical and professional) education. Students undertaking second degree courses may also be assisted.

Grants can be given towards:

- initial expenses when a student first leaves home to take up a course
- the costs of outgoings and equipment for Outward Bound, Duke of Edinburgh's Award and similar character and experience-building schemes
- those studies that involve exceptionally costly items, such as musical instruments and specialist project work
- vocational and professional training course costs and equipment
- exceptional travel costs

Annual grant total

In 2016 the trust had an income of £9,600 and a total expenditure of £4,700. We estimate that the trust gave around £4,500 in grants to individuals for educational purposes.

Applications

Application forms are available from trust's website or the correspondent (there are separate forms for different types of applicants/requests). Applications should include details of other grants and loans secured or applied for. The trustees meet regularly at six-weekly intervals to consider applications.

The website states: 'The application is usually followed by a meeting between the applicant and two Trustees, who subsequently present the case to a full meeting of the Trustees.'

Other information

The website states:

> For undergraduates, the student's entitlement to assistance with fees and student loans from the Student Loan Company will be the principal guide for the Trustees in assessing each application. Likewise, for 16–19 year olds at Sixth Form and FE Colleges, the student's eligibility for help via EMA, free school meals or the Student Bursary fund will be taken into account.

> For those seeking help with vocational or post-graduate courses, the Trustees will make an appraisal of the applicant's financial position and the total costs to be incurred.

> For Duke of Edinburgh applicants there is a standard scale of payments regardless of parental income.

Waverley

The Witley Charitable Trust

£900

Correspondent: Daphne O'Hanlon, Trustee, Triados, Waggoners Way, Grayshott, Hindhead, Surrey GU26 6DX (01428 604679)

CC number: 200338

Eligibility

Children and young people (normally under the age of 20) who are in need and live in the parishes of Witley, Milford and a small part of Brook.

Types of grants

One-off, modest grants ranging from £25 to £300 can be given for educational needs. In the past the trust has supported a pupil to attend a local pre-school.

Annual grant total

In 2016 the trust had an income of £3,700 and a total expenditure of £1,900. We estimate that grants for educational purposes totalled around £900.

Exclusions

The trust does not give loans or support for items which should be provided by statutory services.

Applications

Applications can be made in writing to the correspondent. Applications should be submitted through nurses, doctors, social workers, clergy, Citizens Advice, etc., but not directly by the individual. Awards are usually considered in early February and September, although emergency applications can be considered throughout the year.

Other information

Grants are also given for welfare purposes.

West Sussex

The Blatchington Court Trust (BCT)
See entry on page 263

The Bassil Shippam and Alsford Trust

£5,000

Correspondent: The Trustees, The Corn Exchange, Baffins Lane, Chichester, West Sussex PO19 1GE (01243 786111; email: shippam@thomaseggar.com)

CC number: 256996

Eligibility

Students in need living in West Sussex.

Types of grants

One-off grants ranging from £100 to £1,000 for gap year activities and other educational or personal development projects.

Annual grant total

In 2015/16 the trust had assets of £4.4 million and an income of £157,000. Grants to both individuals and organisations totalled £113,000; it appears that around £5,000 of this was given in grants to individuals.

Exclusions

According to our research, funding cannot be provided towards academic courses.

Applications

Apply in writing to the correspondent. Applications can be submitted at any time directly by the individual and should include a summary of their proposal.

Other information

The trust mainly supports organisations.

Arun

William Older's School Charity

£4,000

Correspondent: The Honorary Secretary, Parish Office, Church House, Arundel Road, Angmering, Littlehampton BN16 4JS

CC number: 306424

Eligibility

Children and young people aged 25 or under who live in the ecclesiastical parish of Angmering. Our research suggests that the applicant's parents must reside in the parish.

Types of grants

One-off and recurrent grants of up to £500. Grants are given to schoolchildren towards the cost of equipment/instruments and fees, and to students in further or higher education towards books, equipment/instruments, childcare and educational outings in the UK. Gap year opportunities, volunteering, musical or sports activities or field trips can all be supported.

Annual grant total

In 2016 the charity had an income of £17,100 and a total expenditure of £8,300. We estimate that grants given to individuals totalled about £4,000.

Applications

Applications should be made in writing to the correspondent, giving details about the applicant's income and expenditure, the course being studied and residence in Angmering. Applications are usually considered in January, May and September.

Other information

Grants can also be made to organisations.

Chichester

Betty Martin Charity

£7,000

Correspondent: Madeleine Crisp, 46 Guillards Oak, Midhurst, West Sussex GU29 9JZ (01730 813769)

CC number: 1029337

Eligibility

People who live in Sussex, with a preference for those who live within a 15-mile radius of the parish church in Midhurst, West Sussex

Types of grants

According to the trustees' report for 2015/16, the charity provides 'financial help to young people to enable them to acquire marketable skills.' Support is mainly given in the form of top-up grants to pay fees, travel expenses, maintenance for those in apprenticeships and for the purchase of books, tools, etc.

Annual grant total

In 2015/16 the charity held assets of £730,000 and had an income of £27,500. Grants given to individuals totalled £7,000.

Applications

An application form is available from the correspondent which is then submitted directly by the individual along with a reference.

South West

General

Viscount Amory's Charitable Trust

£2,900

Correspondent: Secretary to the Trustees, The Island, Lowman Green, Tiverton, Devon EX16 4LA (01884 254899; email: office@vact.org.uk; website: www.vact.org.uk)

CC number: 204958

Eligibility

People in need in the south west of England. Grants are mainly made to organisations.

Types of grants

One-off and recurrent grants are given according to need.

Annual grant total

In 2015/16 the trust had assets of almost £13 million and an income of £469,500. The trust awarded £3,600 to individuals, of which £2,900 was awarded for educational purposes. A further £400,000 was given to organisations.

Applications

Apply in writing to the correspondent, for consideration every month.

M. R. Cannon 1998 Charitable Trust

Correspondent: Chris Mitchell, 53 Stoke Lane, Westbury-on-Trym, Bristol BS9 3DW (0117 377 6540; email: chris@twocannons.co.uk)

CC number: 1072769

Eligibility

Preference is given to individuals from Bristol, County Durham, Dorset, North Devon and North Yorkshire.

Types of grants

One-off and recurrent grants are given for general educational purposes, according to need.

Annual grant total

In 2015/16 the trust held assets of £3.9 million and had an income of £192,000. No grants were awarded to individuals in this financial year.

Applications

Apply in writing to the correspondent.

Other information

Support is given to individuals and organisations for general charitable purposes. In 2016 the trust committed a grant of £40,000 to be paid over the next four years to the Royal Yacht Squadron.

Devon and Cornwall Aid for Girls Trust

£8,000

Correspondent: Ria Knight, 48 Charles Darwin Road, Plymouth PL1 4GU (01752 930915; email: j30vrk@gmail.com)

CC number: 202493

Eligibility

Girls aged 16 to 23 whose normal place of residence is within the counties of Devon and Cornwall. This trust was set up in the 1840s to help orphaned girls, and while this provision still exists, it has changed to help any girls in need.

Types of grants

Grants are made towards the cost of care, maintenance or other needs, particularly for those entering university, college or a training apprenticeship. Assistance is given with the provision of tools, books, computers, special fees, travelling expenses, or other items as may help them advance in their chosen work.

Annual grant total

In 2015/16 the trust had an income of £13,000 and a total expenditure of £8,200. We estimate that grants for educational purposes totalled around £8,000.

Exclusions

Grants are not normally awarded for postgraduate and mature students, second qualifications or part-time studies.

Applications

Apply in writing to the correspondent.

Dyke Exhibition Foundation

£3,300

Correspondent: Maddy Harrison-Hall, Staddon Farm, Winsford, Minehead TA24 7HY (07834 312315; email: clerkdef@gmail.com)

CC number: 306610

Eligibility

Further and higher education students (between the ages of 16 and 25) who are resident in Somerset, Devon or Cornwall. Applicants must either have been born in the area, have been resident there for at least three years, or have been attending school in the area of benefit for at least two years prior to application.

Preference is given to individuals who are in most need and those who are, or are about to become, undergraduates of Oxford University or another university.

Types of grants

Grants are given towards fees, accommodation, books and equipment, travel costs or 'any other expense incurred by the student'. Awards usually range between £100 and £300 a year for up to three years.

Annual grant total

In 2015/16 the foundation had an income of £3,500 and a total expenditure of £3,500. We estimate that the foundation awarded around £3,300 in grants to individuals for educational purposes.

Applications

Application forms can be obtained by sending an sae to the correspondent.

The Elmgrant Trust

£2,900

Correspondent: Amanda Horning, Secretary, Elmhirst Centre, Dartington Hall, Totnes, Devon TQ9 6EL (01803 863160; email: info@elmgrant.org.uk; website: www.elmgrant.org.uk)

CC number: 313398

Eligibility

People living in the south west of England (Cornwall, Devon, Dorset, Gloucestershire, Somerset and Wiltshire).

Types of grants

The trust offers one-off grants to help schoolchildren with the cost of books, equipment/instruments, fees, educational outings/visits. Further/higher education students are also assisted with the cost of books, equipment/instruments, fees, maintenance/living expenses, educational outings in the UK and childcare. People who are furthering their training to improve work prospects are also assisted.

Average grants are in the region of £450 or £150 for individuals.

Annual grant total

In 2015/16 the trust had assets of £2.2 million and an income of £70,500. Throughout the year the trust awarded around £2,900 in grants to 12 individuals.

Exclusions

The trustees will not provide support towards the following:

- Postgraduate study or related expenses
- Second and subsequent degrees
- Overseas student grants
- Expeditions, travel and study projects overseas
- Training in counselling courses

Grants will not be given to organisations or individuals who have already received a grant from the trust within the previous two years. Research is rarely funded and support cannot be given retrospectively.

Applications

Applications can be made in writing to the correspondent.

Applications should provide the following details:

- Full contact details (name, address, email address, phone number, etc.)
- For students – evidence of your attendance or course place
- Full list of items required, including costs
- Evidence of your financial status and why you need funding – receipt of benefits, low income etc. (all information is confidential)
- Letters of support from a professional person who knows you, for example a tutor, GP, employer or social worker
- If a medical condition is part of the application – evidence from the medical professional

The website states: 'We aim to respond to every application we receive with a decision of being short-listed or not within six weeks. The Trustees decision is final and we do not usually enter into further correspondence.'

Our research suggests that the trustees meet three times a year on the last Saturday of February, June and October. It is crucial to submit the application at least one month prior to the meeting. Any applications received two weeks before the deadline with not enough information will be automatically rejected.

Other information

The trust also supports organisations, groups and educational establishments throughout the UK, with strong preference for those in the South West.

In 2015/16 the trust awarded £37,000 in grants to 77 organisations.

Sarum St Michael Educational Charity

£50,500 (51 grants)

Correspondent: Clerk to the Governors, First Floor, 27A Castle Street, Salisbury SP1 1TT (01722 422296 (Monday to Thursday mornings); email: clerk@sarumstmichael.org; website: www.sarumstmichael.org)

CC number: 309456

Eligibility

People over the age of 16 who live or study in the diocese of Salisbury or adjoining dioceses, including Bath and Wells, Exeter, Oxford and Winchester (for exact geographical area see the map on the website). The charity provides teaching bursaries for students who are intending to specialise in religious education and to people in need of financial assistance to enable them to pursue higher or further education.

Types of grants

Grants are available to those studying for first degrees (including mature students), diplomas, access courses, Open University courses, vocational courses, postgraduate degrees, gap year activities and projects. Support can be given towards general educational expenses, including fees, necessities, books, equipment, travel, dissertation expenses and so on. Clergy can also apply for grants to attend conferences and travel.

Annual grant total

In 2016 the charity held assets of £5.77 million and had an income of £215,000. Grants to individuals totalled £50,500.

Exclusions

The charity will not:

- Make retrospective grants
- Contribute towards maintenance (unless an integral part of a residential course)
- Pay money for buildings, fixtures or fittings

Grants for people attending educational establishments are continued only if the applicant remains at that establishment.

Applications

Application forms can be obtained from the charity's website. Grants are considered four to five times a year, normally in January, March, June, August and October. Exact dates of the meetings are available online. Applications can be submitted directly by individuals, preferably by email.

City of Bristol

R. W. Barnes Educational Fund

£10,000

Correspondent: D. Kent, Quartet Community Foundation, Royal Oak House, Royal Oak Avenue, Bristol BS1 4GB (0117 989 7700; fax: 0117 989 7701; email: info@quartetcf.org.uk; website: www.quartetcf.org.uk)

CC number: 1080418

Eligibility

Before going to university, applicants must live in Bristol, Bath, West Somerset or Dartford, or in the SP3/7/8 postcodes of Salisbury, SN10/12/13/14/15 postcodes in Swindon, or G19 in Gloucester.

Candidates must be studying an undergraduate degree programme in which at least 60% of course material is in maths, physics, engineering, astronomy or oceanography.

Candidates must be UK nationals by birth and UK citizens at the time of applying.

Priority is given to those attending Bath University, Cambridge University, or Imperial College London. This is followed by preference for Russell Group universities, and other top 40 universities.

Priority is given to those with no family history of higher education.

Types of grants

One-off or recurrent grants of up to £2,500, subject to satisfactory A-level or university results.

Annual grant total

A specific breakdown of grants from the fund was not available, however grants in previous years have totalled around £10,000.

Exclusions

Grants are not awarded to those studying biosciences, chemistry, civil engineering, or chemical engineering. Postgraduate and second degree studies are not funded.

Applications

Application forms can be downloaded from the Quartet Community Foundation's website or requested from the correspondent and should be returned via post by the end of July for consideration in September. Applicants must show that their family income is less than £45,000.

Other information

This fund is managed by Quartet Community Foundation.

The Christ Church Exhibition Fund

£10,000

Correspondent: Ian Millsted, 1 All Saints Court, Bristol BS1 1JN (0117 929 2709; email: ccl.charity@btconnect.com)

CC number: 325124

Eligibility

- Boys and girls over the age of 11 who live in the city of Bristol and are attending fee-paying schools
- Students in higher education up to the age of 25 who have received at least two years' secondary education in Bristol or who have long residential connections with the city

Types of grants

Grants are awarded for fee-paying secondary education, the cost of school uniforms, other school clothing, books, and educational outings. Occasional support is given to talented pupils at state schools who need help to pay for music lessons.

Grants of between £100 and £300 a year are awarded to students unable to obtain discretionary awards or for higher education courses not qualifying for grants. Grants are awarded only for courses in the UK and can be given to help with the cost of books or towards fees and living expenses.

Annual grant total

In 2015 the charity had an income of £17,000 and a total expenditure of £13,500. We estimate that the amount awarded in educational grants to individuals was £10,000.

Exclusions

Grants are not given for trips abroad, for courses outside the UK or for postgraduate study.

Applications

Apply in writing to the correspondent.

Other information

The charity also provides funding for the running of a Sunday school in St Ewen and funding for the education of choristers of St Ewen.

Edmonds and Coles Scholarships (Edmonds and Coles Charity)

£8,800

Correspondent: Jo McNab, Administrator, The Society of Merchant Venturers, Merchants' Hall, The Promenade, Clifton Down, Bristol BS8 3NH (0117 973 8058; email: treasurer@merchantventurers.com; website: merchantventurers.com/charitable-activities/edmonds-and-coles-scholarships)

CC number: 311751

Eligibility

People in need who are under the age of 25 and live in the area of benefit, which includes: Aust, Avonmouth, Bishopston, Brentry, Charlton Mead, Coombe Dingle, Cotham, Durdham Down, Hallen, Henbury, Henleaze, Horfield, Kingsweston, Kingsdown, Lawrence Weston, New Passage, Northwick, Pilning, Redland, Redwick, Sea Mills, Severn Beach, Shirehampton, Southmead, Stoke Bishop, Tyndalls Park, Westbury-on-Trym, Westbury Park and Woolcott Park.

Types of grants

Our previous research indicates that the charity awards small grants, usually in the range of £100 to £1,000, which are available towards general educational expenses, including the cost of books, equipment/instruments or travel. Support can be given to people at school, college/university, or those undertaking vocational training. Awards are not normally made to enable a child to enter private education. Help may, however, be given in respect of pupils already in private education when there has been a change in financial circumstances through, for example, death of a parent, divorce or

unemployment, and there are good reasons for avoiding disruption of a child's education.

Annual grant total

In 2015/16 the charity had an income of £11,200 and a total expenditure of £9,000. We estimate that the charity gave around £8,800 in grants to individuals.

Exclusions

At primary and secondary school level, grants are not normally given to enable children to enter private education when parents cannot afford the cost. Help may, however, be given in respect of children already in private education – see 'Types of grants' for details.

Applications

Application forms are available from the charity's website or the correspondent. They can be submitted by the individual or, if the applicant is under 16, a third party. Grants are usually considered in February, July and September.

Other information

Our research shows that this charity consults and co-operates with Bristol Municipal Charities in some cases.

Anthony Edmonds Charity

£3,200

Correspondent: Fran Greenfield, Clerk, 43 Meadowland Road, Bristol BS10 7PW (0117 909 8308; email: fran.greenfield@blueyonder.co.uk; website: www.edmondscharity.org.uk)

CC number: 286709

Eligibility

Young people up to the age of 25 who live in any of the ancient parishes of Henbury, Westbury and Horfield.

Types of grants

Grants to help with activities of a broadly educational nature including apprenticeships, courses and less formal projects that can be academic, artistic, technical, social or sporting.

Annual grant total

In 2015/16 the charity had an income of £58,500 and a total expenditure of £47,500. Throughout the year the charity awarded almost £6,400 in educational grants. We estimate that £3,200 of this amount went directly to individuals.

The charity also gives grants to organisations.

Applications

Application forms are available from the correspondent, to be submitted directly by the individual. You can download an application form online or contact the clerk for a hard copy. The trustees meet to consider applications in March and September.

The Gane Charitable Trust

See entry on page 147

The Redcliffe Parish Charity

£1,500

Correspondent: Paul Tracey, Trustee, 18 Kingston Road, Nailsea, Bristol, North Somerset BS48 4RD (email: redcliffeparishclerk@mail.com)

CC number: 203916

Eligibility

Schoolchildren in need who live in the city of Bristol, with preference for those who live in the ecclesiastical parish of St Mary Redcliffe with Temple – Bristol, and St John the Baptist – Bedminster.

Types of grants

One-off grants, usually of £25 to £50. The trustees generally limit grants to families or individuals who can usually manage, but who are overwhelmed by circumstances and are in particular financial stress, rather than those in continual need. Our research suggests that grants can be for children's school trips and school uniforms.

Annual grant total

In 2015/16 the charity had an income of £8,300 and a total expenditure of £6,200. We estimate that educational grants to individuals totalled £1,500.

Applications

Awards are made through a third party, for example, social services, housing associations, a doctor or health visitor, Citizens Advice or other appropriate body. Applications need to be made in writing on behalf of an individual for consideration each month.

Other information

Grants to schoolchildren occur as part of the charity's wider welfare work.

The Stokes Croft Educational Foundation

£11,000

Correspondent: Frances Webster, Secretary, 120 Badger Road, Thornbury, Bristol BS35 1AD (email: scefbristol@live.com)

CC number: 311672

Eligibility

People of any age who reside in Bristol.

Types of grants

Grants are given for maintenance allowances, overseas travel, books, clothing, and equipment/instruments for beneficiaries looking to enter a particular profession, trade or calling.

Annual grant total

In 2016 the foundation held assets of £393,500 and had an income of £62,500. Grants to individuals for educational purposes totalled £11,000.

Applications

Apply in writing to the correspondent.

Cornwall

Blanchminster Trust

£250,500 (283 grants)

Correspondent: Jane Bunning, Blanchminster Building, 38 Lansdown Road, Bude, Cornwall EX23 8EE (01288 352851; email: office@blanchminster.plus.com; website: www.blanchminster.org.uk)

CC number: 202118

Eligibility

Past pupils of Budehaven Community School.

Types of grants

One-off and recurrent grants to former pupils of Budehaven School who are entering further education. Grants can be used for the provision of books, equipment, instruments, clothing, travel or other associated study cost.

Annual grant total

In 2016 the trust had assets of £11.1 million and an income of £501,000. The trust awarded 283 educational grants totalling £250,500.

Exclusions

Grants are not given to foreign students studying in Britain.

Applications

The trust has no standard application form, therefore applicants should send a letter stating what assistance is needed and why. Following receipt of this, the trust will send the applicant a Financial Enquiry Form for completion.

All applications must include weekly income and expenditure, and what efforts have been made to seek help elsewhere.

If you are applying for the first time, contact the clerk in October after you have started your course.

If you are applying for a second or subsequent grant, download the 'Repeat SSG Form' on the trust's website and return it via email or post.

Other information

Grants are also made to individuals for social welfare purposes and for community projects.

The Heathcoat Trust

See entry on page 294

Trevilson Educational Foundation

£13,000

Correspondent: David Laud, Trustee, 5 Churchtown, St Newlyn East, Newquay TR8 5LQ (01872 519270; email: info@chy-an-eglos-bb.co.uk)

CC number: 306555

Eligibility

People under the age of 25 who live in the parish of St Newlyn East and are in need.

Types of grants

Grants are available to schoolchildren, further/higher education students and people starting work or undertaking apprenticeships. Help is given towards books, equipment/necessities, educational outings and other essentials. Awards usually range from £50 to £500.

Annual grant total

In 2016 the foundation had an income of £17,800 and a total expenditure of £31,000. We estimate that grants given to individuals totalled around £13,000.

Note that both the income and expenditure vary annually. Over the past five years the charitable expenditure fluctuated between £2,700 and £31,000.

Applications

Apply in writing to the correspondent.

Other information

Some support may be given to local schools and organisations helping people under the age of 25.

Devon

Adventure Trust for Girls

£6,700

Correspondent: Allison Ferrero, 28 Richmond Road, Exmouth EX8 2NB (01395 265391; email: info@adventuretrustforgirls.org.uk; website: www.adventuretrustforgirls.org.uk)

CC number: 800999

Eligibility

Girls and young women between the ages of 10 and 20 who live or attend school within eight miles of Exmouth Town Hall, south of the M5 and east of the Exe. The website includes a map which shows eligible areas.

Types of grants

One-off grants to help towards payment for travel, accommodation, living expenses and insurance. A wide range of trips can be supported, including summer schools, camps, school exchange programmes and any other adventure that would develop the individual's personality, self-confidence, physical abilities, leadership and team working skills.

Assistance can also be given to girls from low-income households to participate in school trips and educational outings.

Annual grant total

In 2015/16 the trust had an income of £8,300 and expenditure of £7,100. We estimate that the total amount given in grants was £6,700.

Exclusions

Areas to the west of the river Exe are excluded. Our research suggests that grants are not given towards organised school ski trips.

Applications

Applications can be downloaded from the trust's website. Applicants must detail how much funding they need and what it is for (e.g. travel, accommodation etc.), and must also explain any other fundraising they have done to finance the trip.

Cranbrook Charity

£2,500

Correspondent: Stephen Purser, Venn Farm, Bridford, Exeter EX6 7LF (01647 252328; email: purseratvenn@hotmail.com)

CC number: 249074

Eligibility

People under the age of 25 who are in need and live in the parishes of Dunsford, Doddiscombsleigh and 'that part of the parish of Holcombe Burnel as in 1982 constituted part of the parish of Dunsford'.

Types of grants

One-off and recurrent grants to those in need.

Annual grant total

In 2015/16 the charity had an income of £11,000 and a total expenditure of £5,000. We estimate that the amount awarded in educational grants was £2,500.

Applications

Applications may be made in writing to the correspondent.

Other information

Grants are also made to individuals for poverty relief and social welfare purposes.

The Devon Educational Trust

£25,500

Correspondent: The Clerk to the Trustees, PO Box 86, Teignmouth TQ14 8ZT (email: devonedtrust@talktalk.net; website: devoneducationaltrust.co.uk)

CC number: 1157674

Eligibility

Pupils and students under the age of 25 who live, or whose parents' normal place of residence is, in Devon. Preference is given to applicants from low-income families. Applicants or their parents must be living in Devon on a permanent basis for at least 12 months.

Types of grants

One-off grants of between £100 and £500 to:

- Schoolchildren for uniforms/clothing and equipment/instruments
- College students and undergraduates for special clothing, study/travel costs, books, equipment/instruments and maintenance/living expenses
- Vocational students and people starting work for uniforms/clothing, books, equipment/instruments and maintenance/living expenses
- Young people with specific learning difficulties for assistance with the cost of one-to-one specialist tuition and, for those who are visually impaired, by the provision of computer equipment and software

Annual grant total

In 2016 the charity had assets of £1.2 million and an income of £37,000. A total of 93 grants were made to individuals totalling £25,500 for educational purposes.

The charity also awarded £5,700 to six organisations.

Exclusions

Assistance is not normally given to those embarking on a second or higher degree course. In some cases, however, the trustees may make a small grant to assist with living costs or the purchase of books, equipment, etc. No assistance is available for the payment of university fees and only in exceptional cases will the trustees consider paying school or boarding fees.

Applications

Apply on a form available from the correspondent or to download from the website. Applications must include details of two referees. The completed application form must be returned by post or email, contact details are available on the website. Application deadlines fall on 1 February, 1 June and 1 October each year.

Other information

The charity also provides assistance to any voluntary charitable organisation for the promotion of education or improvement in conditions of life.

The Gibbons Family Trust

£10,500 (23 grants)

Correspondent: Roger Dawe, Trustee, 14 Fore Street, Budleigh Salterton, Devon EX9 6NG (01395 445259; email: web.enquiry@gibbonstrusts.org; website: www.gibbonstrusts.org)

CC number: 290884

Eligibility

People up to 25 in Devon and the Isle of Thanet area of Kent with a preference for those from East Devon.

Types of grants

Grants towards the maintenance and educational advancement, training and recreation of children and young people.

Annual grant total

In 2015/16 the trust had assets of £2.2 million and an income of £91,500. Grants to 23 individuals totalled £10,500.

Exclusions

No grants are given for private school fees, gap year projects or other types of overseas trips.

Applications

Application forms are available to download from the website with a short covering letter and a supporting statement from a third party such as a school, club, doctor or social worker. Applications must be posted and are not accepted by email.

Other information

Grants were also made to organisations.

The Heathcoat Trust

£167,000

Correspondent: Mrs C. J. Twose, Secretary, The Factory, Tiverton, Devon EX16 5LL (email: heathcoattrust@ heathcoat.co.uk)

CC number: 203367

Eligibility

Applicants must reside in Cornwall or Devon. Previous research indicates applicants are mainly students in secondary and further education.

Types of grants

One-off and recurrent grants towards costs associated with education.

Annual grant total

In 2015/16 the trust had assets of £21.6 million and an income of £773,000. The charity awarded a total of £167,000 in educational grants.

Applications

Apply in writing to the correspondent. For A-level applicants who attend East Devon College, application forms are available and should be submitted between April and June each year.

Other information

The trust also awards grants to individuals for a variety of welfare purposes, and to organisations.

Dulce Haigh Marshall Trust

£3,500

Correspondent: The Secretary, Rosemary Cottage, 38 Fore Street, Otterton, Budleigh Salterton, Devon EX9 7HB (01395 568802; email: nicholas.marshall21@btinternet.com; website: www.dulcehaighmarshalltrust. com)

CC number: 286273

Eligibility

Individuals under the age of 25 who live in Devon, are studying a stringed instrument (violin, viola, cello, double bass), and are in need of financial assistance.

Types of grants

Grants ranging between £200 and £500 towards tuition fees or the purchase of instruments. Only in exceptional circumstances will the trust consider funding the costs of courses or travelling expenses.

Annual grant total

In 2015/16 the trust had an income of £330 and a total expenditure of £3,600. We have estimated that grants totalled around £3,500.

Exclusions

Grants are not given to people who or whose parents have sufficient income to meet their needs.

Applications

Application forms are available from the trust's website or can be requested from the correspondent. They should be returned before 1 May. Grants are usually distributed in August each year. Applications can be made directly by the individual and should include a teacher's report. Students may be asked to attend an audition. The website states that the trustees look for evidence of the need for financial assistance, as well as 'sufficient ability and dedication to justify an award'.

City of Exeter

The Exeter Advancement in Life Charity

£9,800

Correspondent: Steven Sitch, Chichester Mews, Exeter Municipal Charities, 6 Southernhay West, Exeter, Devon EX1 1JG (01392 421162; fax: 01392 201551; email: info@ exetermunicipalcharity.org.uk)

CC number: 1002151

Eligibility

Children and young people under the age of 25 who are in need and live in the city of Exeter or within 15 miles of the city centre. Preference may be given to schoolchildren with serious family difficulties so that the child has to be educated away from home.

Types of grants

One-off and recurrent grants of up to £500 a year. Support can be given to schoolchildren towards clothing and uniforms, books, equipment/ instruments, fees or educational outings in the UK. Further/higher education students (including mature and postgraduate) can be assisted with the cost of books, equipment/instruments, course fees and related necessities, as well as study or travel overseas. People in vocational training/starting work can receive help with equipment/ instruments, travel costs, outfits and materials. Grants towards study/travel overseas are subject to a minimum study period of six months (unless it is an obligatory part of an approved course).

Annual grant total

In 2016 the charity had an income of £8,200 and a total expenditure of £10,100. We estimate that the charity

gave around £9,800 in grants to individuals for educational purposes.

Applications

Application forms are available from the correspondent. They can be submitted directly by the individual or through a third party, such as a parent/guardian or educational welfare agency, if applicable. Candidates should provide an academic reference and outline their financial circumstances. Prospective grant recipients are usually interviewed in February, May, August and November.

Note: This charity is comprised of two educational trusts: John Dinam School Endowment and Lady Ann Clifford Trust. These two charities have the same criteria, described above, with the exception that the John Dinam School Endowment can make grants outside Exeter – up to 15 miles from the city centre. Applicants can only receive a grant from one of these charities. Those living outside the city should apply to John Dinam School Endowment.

Other information

This charity is part of Exeter Municipal Charities. Support for welfare needs is available through The Exeter Relief in Need Charity.

City of Plymouth

Albert Casanova Ballard Deceased (A. C. Ballard Deceased Trust)

£26,000 (132 grants)

Correspondent: Lynn Smith, Trustee, Claremont, Dousland, Yelverton PL20 6NN (01822 854457; email: ballardplymouth@outlook.com)

CC number: 201759

Eligibility

Boys aged between 11 and 16 (years 7 to 11) who are attending, or about to attend, secondary education in Plymouth city and live within the boundary of Plymouth.

Types of grants

One-off grants are offered towards general educational expenses, including school uniforms, books and equipment or instruments.

Annual grant total

During 2015/16, the trust had £1.1 million in assets and an income of £54,000. The total amount given in grants was £24,000 to 132 individuals.

Applications

Application forms can be requested from the correspondent. Written requests must be sent with a self-addressed A5 envelope and large stamp. The closing date for applications is early May, for consideration in June.

Other information

Grants are also awarded to organisations and clubs in Plymouth.

The Maudlyn Lands Charity

£2,000

Correspondent: Anthony Golding, Blue Haze, Down Road, Tavistock, Devon PL19 9AG (01822 612983; email: avda10@dsl.pipex.com)

CC number: 202577

Eligibility

People in need who live in Plympton St Mary and Sparkwell.

Types of grants

One-off grants to help with general educational costs.

Annual grant total

In 2015/16 the charity had an income of £7,400 and a total expenditure of around £8,100. We estimate that about £2,000 was awarded to individuals for educational purposes.

Applications

Applications may be made in writing to the correspondent. They are considered in November.

Other information

This charity also gives grants to individuals for welfare purposes, and to organisations.

The Olford Bequest

£3,500 (five grants)

Correspondent: John Coates, Clerk to the Trustees, 24 Dolphin House, Sutton Wharf, Plymouth PL4 0BL (01752 225724; email: johnbcoates@btinternet.com; website: olfordbequest.weebly.com)

CC number: 306936

Eligibility

Young people from Plymouth who are going to university. To be eligible, students must have completed their A-levels at a school or college in Plymouth.

Types of grants

Allowances are available to five students each year who are going to university. Two grants are reserved for students from Devonport School for Boys. The charity provides £250 a year for three years to be spent on anything which will allow the student to 'more fully enjoy their stay at university'. The website states that 'ability to pass exams or buy books is therefore not a criterion which the Trustees will consider'.

Annual grant total

In 2016/17 the charity had an income of £4,600 and a total expenditure of £4,000. We estimate that grants totalled about £3,500.

Applications

Applications can be made on a form available to download from the charity's website, which should be submitted the end of June. Interviews take place in August.

Orphan's Aid Educational Foundation (Plymouth)

£1,800

Correspondent: Vanessa Steer, Clerk and Treasurer, 184 Mannamead Road, Plymouth PL3 5RE (01752 703280; email: v_steer@yahoo.co.uk)

CC number: 306770

Eligibility

Children who live in the city and county borough of Plymouth who are of school age and are in need, particularly those from single-parent families.

Types of grants

One-off grants of up to £250 for items such as school uniforms and shoes and other essential items.

Annual grant total

In 2016 this charity had an income of £2,500 and a total expenditure of £2,100. We estimate that grants totalled £1,800.

Exclusions

No grants are given for school fees or maintenance, for people starting work or for mature students.

Applications

Applications can be made on a form available from the correspondent by email or post, including information about income, expenditure and dependants. Applicants are usually interviewed.

East Devon

The Colyton Parish Lands Charity

£1,300

Correspondent: Sarah Charman, Administrator, Fermain House, Dolphin Street, Colyton, Devon EX24 6LU (01297 553148; website: www.colytonfeoffees-townhall.org.uk)

CC number: 243224

Eligibility

Young people in need in the ancient parish of Colyton.

Types of grants

One-off and recurrent grants in support of education and training.

Annual grant total

In 2015/16 the charity had an income of £61,500 and a total expenditure of £67,000. The charity awarded £2,500 to ten individuals throughout the year. We estimate that £1,300 was given to individuals for educational purposes.

Applications

Apply in writing to the correspondent. Applications should be submitted either directly by the individual or a family member, through a third party such as a social worker or teacher, or through a welfare agency such as Citizens Advice. Applications are considered monthly.

Other information

The charity also awards grants for social welfare purposes and for the maintenance of the town hall and other properties owned by the charity.

Sidmouth Consolidated Charities

£1,700

Correspondent: Ruth Rose, 22 Alexandria Road, Sidmouth, Devon EX10 9HB (01395 513079; email: ruth.rose@eclipse.co.uk)

CC number: 207081

Eligibility

People in need who live in Sidmouth, Sidford, Sidbury or Salcombe Regis.

Types of grants

Our research suggests that one-off grants are available for educational needs, such as computers and books for university students.

Annual grant total

In 2015 the charity had assets £1.4 million and an income of £39,000. We estimate that grants given to individuals totalled around £1,700.

Applications

Applications may be made in writing to the correspondent, either directly by the individual or through a social worker, Citizens Advice or welfare agency. Applications are considered at monthly meetings.

Other information

The charity supports both organisations and individuals for social welfare and educational needs.

Mid Devon

Fuel Allotment Charity (formerly known as Culmstock Fuel Allotment Charity)

£1,000

Correspondent: Rosalyn Channon, 24 The Brendons, Sampford Peverell, Tiverton EX16 7BQ (01884 820495)

CC number: 205327

Eligibility

Students in need who live in the ancient parish of Culmstock.

Types of grants

Recurrent grants according to need. Books and equipment for college courses.

Annual grant total

In 2015/16 the charity had both an income and a total expenditure of £4,600. We estimate that grants for educational purposes totalled around £1,000.

Applications

Apply in writing to the correspondent.

Other information

Grants are also given for welfare purposes.

The Richards Educational Charity

£36,500 (84 grants)

Correspondent: Dr John Thomas, Treasurer, 5 Tuns Lane, Silverton, Exeter EX5 4HY (01392 860464; email: jmthomas1951@yahoo.co.uk)

CC number: 306787

Eligibility

Young people under 25 who live in the parish of Silverton.

Types of grants

Recurrent grants in the range of £5 to £750 are given to schoolchildren and college students for study/travel abroad, books, equipment/instruments, maintenance/living expenses and excursions. Grants are also given to undergraduates, vocational students, mature students, and people starting work for fees, study/travel abroad, books, equipment/instruments, maintenance/living expenses and excursions.

The trustees consider the level of family income when deciding how much to give.

Annual grant total

In 2016 the charity held assets of £1.35 million and had an income of £284,500. Educational grants to individuals totalled £36,500 and were distributed as follows:

University students	25	£23,000
Schoolchildren	51	£8,200
Vocational training	6	£4,600
Pre-school	2	£600

A further £4,200 was awarded in three grants to groups.

Applications

Application forms are available at the village post office, school or health centre. They should be submitted directly by the individual or a parent. They are considered regularly.

Silverton Parochial Charity

£2,500

Correspondent: The Revd Preb Sue Sheppard, Secretary to the Trustees, Lamb Cottage, 49 Fore Street, Silverton, Devon EX5 4HZ (01392 860408; email: suesheppard59@gmail.com; website: www.silvertonparochialtrust.co.uk)

CC number: 201255

Eligibility

People in need who live in the parish of Silverton only.

Types of grants

One-off grants, with no minimum or maximum limit, to 'parishioners who are in a condition of need, hardship or distress'.

Annual grant total

In 2016 the charity had an income of £24,000 and a total expenditure of £21,000. We estimate that educational grants totalled around £2,500.

Applications

Application forms are available to download from the website and should be returned to the correspondent. The trustees meet eight times per year.

Other information

Grants are also made to people in need who live in the parish and to organisations providing assistance for them. The charity has an informative website.

North Devon

The George Ley Educational Trust

£4,000

Correspondent: David Richards, Trustee, Springside, Rews Close, Combe Martin, Ilfracombe EX34 0DW

CC number: 306788

Eligibility

People who live in Combe Martin.

Types of grants

Grants of up to £200 can be made for books and equipment to higher or further education students or schoolchildren.

Annual grant total

In 2016 the trust had an income of £5,000 and a total expenditure of £4,800. We estimate that the total of grants awarded to individuals was approximately £4,000.

Exclusions

Our previous research suggests that grants are not given for core expenses, such as fees or living costs.

Applications

Applications can be made in writing to the correspondent. Our previous research has suggested that the committee meets to consider applications in May and September. Individuals who have previously received support from the trust are able to re-apply.

The Vivian Moon Foundation

£12,000

Correspondent: The Trustees, c/o Simpkins Edwards, Millennium House, Brannam Crescent, Roundswell Business Park, Barnstaple EX31 3TD (email: info@vivianmoonfoundation.co.uk; website: www.vivianmoonfoundation.co.uk)

CC number: 298942

Eligibility

People over the age of 18 who have links with North Devon and have an offer of a place on a course of further educational, professional or vocational training which will lead to employment or improve individuals' skills and their career opportunities. Preference is given to people who intend to return to North Devon to work and, ideally, have an employment secured there at the end of their training.

Types of grants

One-off and recurrent grants, usually ranging between around £100 and £300 (rarely more than £500), are available to people in further education and training, including college students, vocational students, mature students, people starting work, unemployed people seeking to get into employment or working people who wish to develop their skills. Both full-time, part-time and distance-learning courses can be supported, as well as those including a placement year. Most applicants are funded partially and on a course or annual basis.

Annual grant total

In 2015/16 the foundation had an income of £14,100 and a total expenditure of £41,500. We estimate that grants totalled around £12,000.

Exclusions

First degree applicants are unlikely to be supported, unless in extraordinary circumstances.

Applications

The foundation prefers to receive applications online through its website in order to speed up the process. Applicants who are unable to apply in such way can book computer time at a Pathfinder centre (contact details on the foundation's website) or request an application from the correspondent. Applicants should provide an email address of one referee. Grants are considered in January, May and September.

Other information

North Devon comprises the area administered by either Torridge or North Devon District Council.

South Hams

Parish Lands (South Brent Feoffees)

£11,300

Correspondent: J. Blackler, Luscombe Maye, 6 Fore Street, South Brent TQ10 9BQ (01364 646180; website: www.sbrentfeoffees.btck.co.uk)

CC number: 255283

Eligibility

Grants are available to support post-18 The charity's website states: 'Grants are not income-related but reflect whether the student is studying away from home or living locally and in what year of study the application is made. Each individual can apply once a year for 3 years whether it is a university course or vocational training.'

Types of grants

Grants can be given for general educational needs. Our research suggests that support is mainly given to further education students.

Annual grant total

In 2015 the charity had assets of around £60,500 and an income of £53,500. A total of £32,500 was given in grants. We estimate that educational support to individuals totalled around £11,300.

Applications

Application forms can be requested from the correspondent. Applications need to be supported by a letter of authority from the student's college or university. The charity's website notes: 'Please note that this is not the offer from a place of higher education, but a confirmation of attendance.' Check the charity's website for details of application deadlines.

Other information

Grants are also given to organisations and for welfare purposes. The trustees' annual report from 2015 further specifies that one-third of the income of the charity is to be applied for upkeep of the parish church, one-third for the benefit of deserving people in need living in the parish and one-third to form the endowment of the Parish Lands Educational Foundation (to support the education and advancement in life of the parish children).

Reverend Duke Yonge Charity

£3,800

Correspondent: Janet Milligan, 8 Chipple Park, Lutton, Nr Cornwood, Ivybridge PL21 9TA

CC number: 202835

Eligibility

People in need who live in the parish of Cornwood.

Types of grants

One-off grants according to need.

Annual grant total

In 2016 the charity had an income of £14,500 and a total expenditure of £16,300. Grants are made to individuals and organisations for both educational and social welfare purposes. We estimate that educational grants to individuals totalled £3,800.

Applications

Apply in writing to the correspondent via the trustees, who are expected to make themselves aware of any need. Applications are considered at trustees' meetings.

Torridge

The Bridge Trust (Bideford Bridge Trust)

£113,500 (38 grants)

Correspondent: P. R. Sims, Steward, 24 Bridgeland Street, Bideford, Devon EX39 2QB (01237 473122)

CC number: 204536

Eligibility

Each type of grant has different eligibility criteria:
- Book grants and bursaries – applicants must live within the parish of Bideford or to the north of the parish (but south of the Link Road)
- Hardship grants – students who do not live within the parish of Bideford, but who live within the area of benefit set out by the trust
- Discretionary grants – applicants must live within the parish of Bideford
- Business start-up scheme – applicants must be unemployed or recently unemployed

Types of grants

One-off grants, usually of £150 to £500, are awarded in the following categories:
- Book grants and bursaries for post-A-level education
- Hardship grants for post-A-level education
- Discretionary grants for students attending vocational or apprenticeship schemes
- Business start-up grants for people who are unemployed

Annual grant total

In 2015/16 the charity had assets of £15.9 million and an income of £788,000. The total amount awarded in educational grants was £113,500.

Exclusions

Applications from individuals in Barnstaple, Torrington and the areas beyond this are not accepted. Grants are not given to postgraduates or for computers for personal use.

Applications

Application forms are available from the correspondent, to be submitted at any time during the year by the individual. A sponsor is usually required. Applications are considered monthly.

Other information

The charity also awards welfare grants to individuals and support grants to organisations.

Great Torrington Town and Lands Charity

£16,000

Correspondent: Ian Newman, Steward, 25 South Street, Great Torrington, Devon EX38 8AA (01805 623517; email: greattorringtoncharities@btconnect.com)

CC number: 202801

Eligibility

People in need who live in Great Torrington.

Types of grants

Our research suggests that grants are usually made to students towards a year out (voluntary work). Requests are also considered for school uniform costs for schoolchildren and for other costs for mature students. Individual grants are generally up to £250 but may reach up to £500 in extreme cases.

Annual grant total

In 2015/16 the charity had assets £6.4 million and an income of £268,000. We estimate that educational grants to individuals totalled £16,000.

Exclusions

Needs that should be addressed by statutory sources are not funded. The charity cannot make recurrent grants.

Applications

Applications should be made in writing to the correspondent, providing all relevant personal information.

Other information

The charity is concerned with the provision of almshouse accommodation and affordable rented housing. Grants are provided for organisations with various purposes, local churches, pensioners and other people in need.

Dorset

Ashley Churchill and Thorner Educational Trust

£4,700

Correspondent: Sara Wood, Clerk to the Trustees, Whetstones, West Walks, Dorchester DT1 1AW (01305 262662; email: info@actet.org.uk; website: www.actet.org.uk)

CC number: 306229

Eligibility

Children and young people under 25 years of age who live within five miles of County Hall Dorchester and in the civil parish of Crossways. Household income must not exceed £30,000 per year.

Types of grants

One-off grants of up to the value of £500 for young people under 25, to assist with purchasing educational equipment or trade tools, clothing, books, stationery, or to cover travel expenses, fees or maintenance expenses.

Annual grant total

During 2015/16, the trust had an income of £6,700 and a total expenditure of £5,400. The total amount awarded in grants was £4,700.

Applications

Applications are available on the trust's website – applicants should complete the 'student form' and parents, or the applicant if they are self-supported, should complete the 'parents form'. Applications must also include a reference from the headteacher or tutor of the applicant.

The trustees meet to discuss applications in mid-September, January and May and request all completed applications be returned at least three weeks before the next meeting.

Clingan's Trust

£43,500

Correspondent: David Richardson, 4 Bournewood Drive, Bournemouth, Dorset BH4 9JP (01202 766838; email: davidrichardson652@gmail.com; website: www.clinganstrust.co.uk)

CC number: 307085

Eligibility

Applicants must be under 25 with the family home and in education at some time in the trust area, which is broadly speaking Christchurch, Highcliffe, parts of Bournemouth to the east of the town centre and other outlying areas to the north and east of Christchurch.

Types of grants

One-off grants of between £100 and £1,000 for any educational need for people under 25. Our previous research indicates that preference is given to schoolchildren with serious family difficulties where the child has to be educated away from home and people with special educational needs.

Annual grant total

In 2016 the trust had an income of £74,000 and a total expenditure of £69,300. Throughout the year the charity awarded £43,500 in grants to individuals for educational purposes.

Funding is occasionally awarded to organisations.

Exclusions

The trust is normally unable to consider applicants who have applied for a grant within six weeks of the next meeting.

Applications

Application forms are available from the correspondent or to download from the website.

Dorchester Relief in Need Charity

£5,000

Correspondent: Robert Potter, 8 Mithras Close, Dorchester, Dorset DT1 2RF (01305 262041; email: robjoy1@talktalk.net)

CC number: 286570

Eligibility

People in need who live in the ecclesiastical parish of Dorchester.

Types of grants

One-off grants to those in need. In the past, grants have been given for school uniforms and excursions, and to people starting work for books and equipment.

Annual grant total

In 2016/17 the charity had an income of £3,300 and a total expenditure of £1,500. We estimate that a total of £500 was awarded in grants for education.

Applications

Application forms are available from the correspondent and can be submitted by the individual, or through a school/teacher, social worker, etc.

Other information

This charity also gives grants for relief-in-need purposes.

Dorset Community Foundation

£19,000

Correspondent: Jon Yates, Dorset Community Foundation, The Spire, High Street, Poole BH15 1DF (01202 670815; email: philanthropy@dorsetcf.org; website: www.dorsetcommunityfoundation.org)

CC number: 1122113

Eligibility

Each fund has different eligibility guidelines. They are:

Dorset Community Fund Bursary Scheme
- Ages 16 to 21
- Vocational courses only
- Family income less than £21,000 per year

- Must live in Dorset, and have done for at least three years
- Preference for those with caring responsibilities, people with disabilities, or those with special educational needs
- Must attend one of the following colleges: Bournemouth and Poole College; Kingston Maurward College; Brockenhurst College; Weymouth College; Yeovil College; or Wiltshire College (Salisbury Campus)

Superior STEM Bursary Fund
- Ages 16 to 21
- Planning to attend a course at Brockenhurst or Bournemouth and Poole Colleges
- Enrolling on a science, technology, engineering or maths course
- Family income less than £21,000 per year

Lord Lieutenant's Fund for Young and Talented
- Ages 14 to 21
- Must live in Dorset
- Must have exceptional sporting talent which has been recognised or acknowledged by an appropriate national governing body
- Applicants must be unable to achieve their ambitions without help due to financial or personal circumstances

Types of grants

The Dorset Community Fund Bursary Scheme provides grants of up to £1,000 to applicants who are studying for a vocational qualification, to assist with the costs of tools and clothing etc.

The Superior STEM Bursary Fund provides grants of up to £1,500 to young people studying science, technology, engineering or maths, to pay for course fees, IT equipment and travel.

The Lord Lieutenant's Fund for Young and Talented gives grants of up to £1,000 to assist young people to develop their ability and ambition for sports.

Annual grant total

In 2015/16 the foundation had assets of £1.9 million and an income of £970,500. The amount awarded to individuals in education was £19,000.

Applications

There are three educational bursaries available from the foundation with differing application processes. They are as follows:

Dorset Community Fund Bursary Scheme – application forms are available to download from the website, to be returned via email. While there are deadline dates, the application process usually reopens the following month.

Superior STEM Bursary Fund – application forms are available from the website or from your college. Grants are awarded throughout the year.

The Lord Lieutenant's Fund for Young and Talented – applicants must complete the application form (available from the website) and return it along with two letters of endorsement, one of which should be completed by a representative of a national governing body. Applicants may be required to attend an interview.

Other information

Dorset Community Foundation also manages funds which give grants to local community organisations.

Gordon Charitable Trust

£14,900 (14 grants)

Correspondent: Gerry Aiken, Trustee, 45 Dunkeld Road, Bournemouth BH3 7EW (01202 768337; email: gerry_aitken@hotmail.com)

CC number: 200668

Eligibility

Young people between the ages of 15 and 25 living in the county of Dorset who are in further/higher education or undertaking apprenticeships. Preference is given to individuals who have lived, or whose parents have lived, in the borough council areas of Bournemouth, Poole and Christchurch.

Types of grants

The trust provides scholarships, bursaries and other financial help 'to a very limited extent'. Grants are one-off or recurrent for three or four years (depending on the course) of up to £1,000 per year per individual. Support is given towards the cost of books, clothing, equipment/instruments, maintenance/living expenses. People starting work and music/arts students are also supported.

Annual grant total

In 2015/16 the trust had an income of £30,400 and a total expenditure of £14,900. The trust's entire expenditure was awarded in grants to individuals for educational purposes.

Applications

Apply in writing to the correspondent.

Other information

Our research indicates that the trust is reliant upon donations from other sources, therefore its income is limited and variable.

The annual report for 2015/16 states that the trust's financial assistance was aimed towards young people with no family financial support and mainly from single-parent households.

Bournemouth
Cole Anderson Charitable Foundation

£800

Correspondent: Martin Davies, Rawlins Davy, Rowlands House, Hinton Road, Bournemouth BH1 2EG (01202 558844)

CC number: 1107619

Eligibility

Individuals studying medicine, architecture or music who live in Bournemouth and Poole.

Types of grants

Grants are awarded for general educational purposes.

Annual grant total

In 2015/16 the foundation had an income of £5,000 and a total expenditure of £2,000. We estimate that the amount awarded in educational grants was £800.

Applications

Applications should be sent in writing to the correspondent.

Other information

The charity also awards welfare grants to individuals facing financial hardship.

North Dorset
The William Williams Charity

£110,500

Correspondent: Ian Winsor, Steward, Stafford House, 10 Prince of Wales Road, Dorchester, Dorset DT1 1PW (01305 264573; email: enquires@williamwilliams.org.uk; website: www.williamwilliams.org.uk)

CC number: 202188

Eligibility

People who live in the ancient parishes of Blandford Forum, Shaftesbury or Sturminster Newton.

Types of grants

One-off grants to students, mature students or apprentices embarking on higher education or recognised training schemes.

Annual grant total

In 2016 the charity had assets of £9.1 million and an income of £460,500. Grants to individuals amounted to £160,000 with £110,500 of this awarded for educational purposes.

Exclusions

The website states:

> Due to the increased number of applications from the three towns and the finite nature of the funds available to the Charity, the Trustees found it necessary, from 2008, to require parental income to be taken into account. Therefore those students whose parental/household annual income exceeds £35,000 net per annum will not generally be considered eligible in the future.

Applications

Application forms are available to download from the website (form 'A' should be completed by the student and form 'B' by the student's parent or guardian). They should be submitted along with a covering letter describing more about the applicant, their education and background, preferably to a trustee from the town in which the student lives (there is a list of trustees' names and contact details on the website), or to the charity's office. There is an annual cut-off date for applications in September, which is stated on the application forms; however, in cases of need, trustees may consider applications outside this timeframe. Following the receipt of both forms before the deadline, a trustee from the town in which the student lives will arrange a meeting to discuss the application.

Purbeck

The Cecil Charity

£22,000

Correspondent: Lord Rockley, Lytchett Heath House, Lytchett Heath, Poole BH16 6AE (email: charity@lytchettheath.co.uk)

CC number: 306248

Eligibility

Young people under the age of 25 who live within a ten-mile radius of the parish church at Lytchett Matravers.

Types of grants

Grants, scholarships and bursaries at any secondary school, university, college or other place of education. The provision of clothing, books and equipment and studying abroad, and financial assistance to study music or the arts.

Annual grant total

In 2016/17 the charity had an income of £21,000 and a total expenditure of £23,500. We estimate that the amount awarded in grants to individuals was £22,000.

Applications

An application form is available from the correspondent and can be submitted directly by the individual. Applications

are considered in March, August and November.

Corfe Castle Charity

£31,500 (21 grants)

Correspondent: Amanda Meaker, 2 Battlemead, Corfe Castle, Wareham BH20 5ER (01929 480873; email: cccharity1602@outlook.com)

CC number: 1055846

Eligibility

People in need who live in the parish of Corfe Castle.

Types of grants

One-off grants for students in higher education for necessities and learning aids such as books and educational trips. The charity also provides six half-termly grants to the Corfe Castle Community Pre-School for provision of clubs before and after school, as well as during the holidays.

Annual grant total

In 2015/16 the charity had assets of £3.2 million and an income of £206,500. The amount awarded to individuals for education was £31,500.

Applications

Application forms are available from the correspondent and should be sent back by post. Emergency applications are accepted.

Other information

The charity also makes grants to individuals for welfare purposes, and to organisations within the local area.

West Dorset

The Bridge Educational Trust (1996)

£40,000 (38 grants)

Correspondent: The Administrator, c/o Piddle Valley First, Piddletrenthide, Dorchester, Dorset DT2 7QL (07775961370; email: bridgeeducationaltrust@outlook.com; website: www.bridgeeducationaltrust.org.uk)

CC number: 1068720

Eligibility

People in need who were born in or are resident in the county of Dorset, primarily from the parishes of Alton Pancras, Piddlehinton, Piddletrenthide and Plush. The trust provides grants for people in the following circumstances:

- Students undertaking a first degree or other qualification in order to further their career who are experiencing financial difficulty
- Mature students retraining
- Students, whether studying or on a gap year, who wish to undertake an educational expedition
- Individuals working with support agencies looking to improve their life chances
- Students with special educational needs that cannot be met by the local authority
- Single parents, or those with a partner who has a disability, undertaking training to support their children or family members
- Individuals in probation services where education can help rehabilitation

Types of grants

One-off and recurrent grants (for a maximum of three years) are offered to people in education at school, college or other educational establishment. Grants are not normally paid to individuals directly. Average grants range from £500 to around £2,000 and are awarded towards fees, study/travel abroad, books, equipment/instruments, excursions and visits, childcare and other expenses.

Annual grant total

In 2016/17 the trust held assets of £2.2 million and had an income of £69,500. During this year, the trust awarded a total of £40,000 to 38 individuals. The majority of grants were for less than £500.

Exclusions

The trust does not:

- Make loans
- Provide grants for fees which can be covered by student loans
- Give retrospective grants
- Support postgraduate degrees
- Assist people living in temporary student accommodation while studying at an educational establishment in Dorset, unless their permanent home is also in Dorset

Applications

Applications should preferably be submitted about three to four weeks before one of the regular meetings of the trustees which are normally held in February, May and September.

For a course of study over twelve months, a fresh application is required for the second and subsequent years. Three years is normally the maximum period for a grant to any one person.

An application form is available on request to be completed by the applicant in person (or by a parent in the case of a child under the age of 18). This may be completed and returned either electronically or in paper form.

Completed applications can be sent by post to: Piddle Valley First School, Piddletrenthide, Dorset DT2 7QL or by email to: admin@bridgeeducationaltrust. org.uk.

The Litton Cheney Relief in Need Trust

£1,700

Correspondent: Brian Prentice, Trustee, Steddings, Chalk Pit Lane, Litton Cheney, Dorchester DT2 9AN (01308 482535; email: fandspicer@gmail.com)

CC number: 231388

Eligibility

University students and people starting work or undertaking apprenticeships who live in the parish of Litton Cheney.

Types of grants

Grants are made towards those leaving school and about to start a career, undertake an apprenticeship or embark on a university course. Grants are given towards books and equipment.

Annual grant total

In 2016 the trust had an income of £6,200 and a total expenditure of £3,800. We estimate that about £1,700 was given in educational grants to individuals.

Exclusions

Grants are not given for people taking A-levels or for schoolchildren.

Applications

Applications may be made in writing to the correspondent.

Other information

Organisations are also supported, including schools, churches and community associations.

Weymouth and Portland

Sir Samuel Mico's Charities

£27,500

Correspondent: Howard Jones, Administrator, c/o Edwards & Keeping Unity Chambers, 34 High East Street, Dorchester, Dorset DT1 1HA (01305 251333; email: howardjones@ edwardsandkeeping.co.uk; website: www. weymouthtowncharities.org.uk)

CC number: 202629

Eligibility

Young people between the ages of 16 and 24 who reside in the borough of Weymouth and Portland and have been born in the borough, or have resided there for at least ten years. The charity particularly welcomes applications for

those on apprenticeships and those wishing to take up professional careers.

Types of grants

One-off and recurrent grants are made to students in further or higher education or those undertaking apprenticeships. Grants are given towards educational course fees, living costs for those on educational courses, equipment, books and assisted places on the Tall Ships Youth Trust ships.

Annual grant total

In 2016 the charity held assets of £869,500 and had an income of £46,000. It made grants to individuals totalling £27,500.

Applications

Apply on a form available to download from the website or from the correspondent. Applicants must be able to show that they are in difficult financial circumstances and have a desire to extend their education.

Gloucester-shire

Barnwood Trust

£122,000 (116 grants)

Correspondent: Barnwood Trust Chief Executive, Ullenwood Manor Farm, Ullenwood, Cheltenham, Gloucestershire GL53 9QT (01452 614429; fax: 01452 634011; email: sally.byng@ barnwoodtrust.org; website: www. barnwoodtrust.org)

CC number: 1162855

Eligibility

People who are aged 18 or over and live in Gloucestershire, with a long-term disability or mental health problem. Applicants must have a specific need that cannot be provided for by the state, and must not be able to afford the costs themselves.

Types of grants

Opportunities Award

Awards of up to £2,000 are available to fund training, equipment and clothing that may help the recipient towards a job, volunteering, or setting up their own business. It can also be used on materials or equipment for a hobby or sport.

Annual grant total

In 2016 the trust had assets of £92.5 million and an income of £3.7 million. A total of £122,000 was awarded in educational grants to 116 individuals.

Exclusions

Grants are not usually made to:

⟩ People living outside Gloucestershire
⟩ Those under the age of 18
⟩ People with problems relating to drugs and alcohol, unless they also have physical disabilities or a diagnosed mental illness
⟩ Fund anything normally considered by the Individual Wellbeing Fund such as daily living equipment, computers or holidays
⟩ Fund university fees or associated costs for which statutory grants or student loans are available
⟩ Help retrospectively, or when an item has been ordered prior to the grant application

Applications

Application forms are available to download from the trust's website, or can be requested from the correspondent. All applications must be made through, or endorsed by, a social or healthcare professional. Applicants must show they have sought state help they may be entitled to before applying.

Requests for grants over £500 will require an informal interview with the trust (applicants are welcome to bring someone with them to the interview and reasonable travel expenses will be repaid).

Other information

Small grants of up to £1,000 are also awarded to local organisations with the same aims as the trust. In 2016 £171,000 was awarded in grants to 204 organisations.

The trust also makes grants to individuals for independent living and well-being purposes.

John Edmonds' Charity

£6,800

Correspondent: Richard Mullings, Administrator, 7 Dollar Street, Cirencester, Gloucestershire GL7 2AS (01285 650000; email: rrm@sml-law.co. uk)

CC number: 311495

Eligibility

People under the age of 25 who were born in Cirencester. Our research indicates that people who currently live or were educated in Cirencester are also eligible for support.

Types of grants

Help is given to people entering a trade/ starting work. Assistance is given towards the cost of education, training or apprenticeships, including fees, equipment/tools, clothing/outfits, travel costs or maintenance expenses. Grants could be made to schoolchildren and students as well. Awards can range from £100 to £500 and are one-off.

Annual grant total

In 2016 the charity had an income of £6,800 and a total expenditure of £7,100. We estimate that the charity gave around £6,800 in grants to individuals.

Applications

Application forms can be requested from the correspondent.

Higgs and Cooper's Educational Charity

£7,500

Correspondent: Martin Fry, 7 Branch Hill Rise, Charlton Kings, Cheltenham GL53 9HN (01242 239903; email: martyn.fry@dsl.pipex.com; website: www.higgsandcooper.org)

CC number: 311570

Eligibility

People under the age of 25 who were born or live in the former Charlton Kings civil parish. Preference is given to people from single-parent families.

Types of grants

Grants are awarded to people in secondary education, further/higher education students and people starting work/entering a trade. Support is mainly given towards educational outings and study/travel overseas, but also for general educational expenditure, including books, equipment/instruments, fees and so on. Grants can also be given for postgraduate degrees and training.

Annual grant total

In 2015/16 the charity had an income of £21,000 and a total expenditure of £14,200. We estimate that grants to individuals totalled around £7,500.

Applications

Application forms can be found on the website and must be forwarded to the clerk by post or hand two weeks before the meeting at which they are to be considered. Two reference letters must be submitted along with the application: one professional reference (school, institution for which the applicant needs support), and one personal reference from someone who has known the applicant for a number of years (family is not allowed). A stamped addressed envelope should accompany the application.

The trustees meet four times a year normally in March, June, September and December.

Other information

The charity also supports local schools and youth organisations in their educational development and pursuits.

Lumb's Educational Foundation

£11,500

Correspondent: Neville Capper, Trustee, 54 Collum End Rise, Leckhampton, Cheltenham GL53 0PB (01242 515673; email: lumbsfoundation@virginmedia.com)

CC number: 311683

Eligibility

People between the ages of 16 and 25 who live in the borough of Cheltenham and the surrounding parishes. Students whose home address is in Gloucestershire can be considered.

Types of grants

One-off grants towards general education and training. Support can be given for the course fees, books, clothing, equipment/instruments and educational visits in the UK or study/travel abroad. People starting work can be helped with the cost of uniforms/outfits, books and equipment/instruments. Gap year and similar official travel projects are supported.

Annual grant total

In 2015 the foundation had an income of £11,600 and a total expenditure of £12,100. We estimate that grants to individuals totalled around £11,500.

Exclusions

People who are permanently resident outside the area of benefit are ineligible. Grants are not made towards trips that are not of an educational nature. Living expenses or school fees are not supported.

Applications

Application forms can be requested from the correspondent. Once completed they should be returned with a supporting letter, including details of income, expenditure, the applicant's parents' financial situation and the purpose of the grant. Candidates are interviewed. Each application is assessed according to need and funds available at the time.

Cotswold

Weston-sub-Edge Educational Charity

£7,000

Correspondent: Rachel Hurley, Longclose Cottage, Weston-sub-Edge, Chipping Campden, Gloucestershire GL55 6QX (01386 841808; email: hurleyrac@gmail.com; website: www.westonsubedge.com/?page_id=143)

CC number: 297226

Eligibility

Children and young people under the age of 25 who or whose parents live in Weston-sub-Edge, or who have at any time attended (or whose parents have attended) Weston-sub-Edge Church of England Primary School.

Types of grants

Grants of between £10 and £500 can be given for purposes such as: books; equipment; fees; educational outings in the UK; study or travel abroad; maintenance allowances/living expenses for further or higher education students; uniforms or other clothing for schoolchildren; nursery fees; music, dance, drama and sports lessons; after school clubs; residential trips; clubs such as Scouts or Guides; extra tuition.

Annual grant total

In 2015/16 the charity had an income of £9,800 and a total expenditure of £7,900. We estimate that grants given to individuals totalled around £7,000.

Exclusions

Retrospective applications are unlikely to be considered.

Applications

Application forms can be obtained from the correspondent and should be submitted directly by the individual in question, unless they are under 16, in which case a parent or guardian can apply. The trustees meet on the fourth Monday in January, March, May, July, September and November, and applications must be received at least ten days in advance of a meeting. Only one application per student per term will be considered.

South Gloucestershire

Almondsbury Charity

£700 (two grants)

Correspondent: Peter Orford, Secretary, Shepperdine Road, Wayside, Oldbury Naite, Oldbury-on-Severn, Bristol BS35 1RJ (01454 415346; email: peter.orford@gmail.com; website: www.almondsburycharity.org.uk)

CC number: 202263

Eligibility
Young people who are in further or higher education and have lived in Almondsbury, Bradley Stoke North, Easter Compton, Patchway or parts of Pilning for at least one year.

Types of grants
One-off grants are made, usually for buying books.

Annual grant total
In 2015/16 the charity had assets of £2.5 million and an income of £72,000. Grants totalled £29,000 and were mainly made to organisations. Grants to four individuals from the Education and Relief Fund amounted to £1,400 although we were unable to determine how they were distributed between education and social welfare. We have estimated at £700 each.

Exclusions
No grants are made for school or course fees.

Applications
Applications can be made using the appropriate form. Forms are available to download from the charity's website and should be completed and returned to the correspondent along with any other relevant information. The charity does not make cash awards.

The Chipping Sodbury Town Lands

£17,900 (39 grants)

Correspondent: Nicola Gideon, Town Hall, 57–59 Broad Street, Chipping Sodbury, Bristol BS37 6AD (01454 852223; email: nicola.gideon@chippingsodburytownhall.co.uk; website: www.chippingsodburytownhall.co.uk)

CC number: 236364

Eligibility
People in need who are aged up to 25 years and live in the parish of Sodbury.

Types of grants
One-off and recurrent grants to aid the promotion of education, including further education courses.

Annual grant total
In 2016 the charity had assets of £9.9 million and an income of £309,000. Educational grants to individuals totalled £17,900. There were 39 educational grants made, 13 of which were to support further education courses.

Applications
Apply in writing to the correspondent. Grant aid is advertised locally in schools, clubs, associations, churches and other religious orders, in the local press, and the Town Hall.

Somerset

Blackford Educational Charity

£2,500

Correspondent: Simon Kraeter, Hugh Sexey Middle School, Blackford, Wedmore, Somerset BS28 4ND (01934 710041; email: simon.kraeter@blomasa.com)

CC number: 277339

Eligibility
Children and young people under the age of 25 who live in the parish of Blackford. Our research suggests that primary and secondary schoolchildren and higher or further education students can be supported.

Types of grants
Small grants are available for general educational expenses, including books, equipment/instruments or educational outings/visits.

Annual grant total
In 2015/16 the charity had an income of £5,200 and a total expenditure of £5,200. We estimate that the total amount awarded in grants was £2,500.

Applications
Application forms can be requested from the correspondent. Our research shows that applications can be submitted directly by the individual in January, May or September for consideration in the following month and must be accompanied by receipts for the expenses incurred.

Other information
The charity also assists primary and secondary schools in the parish of Blackford where these are not already supported by the local authority. Grants can also be provided for recreational development.

Doris Southcott Bursary

£3,200

Correspondent: The Trustees of Doris Southcott Bursary, c/o Carol Gaskell, Ashfords LLP, Ashford House, Grenadier Road, Exeter EX1 3LH (01392 334070; email: dorissouthcottbursary@gmail.com)

CC number: 1157091

Eligibility
Young people aged between 16 and 25 who are working to advance their education in fashion design and fabric technology. Recipients are usually resident in the administrative county of Somerset (including North Somerset, Bath and North East Somerset).

Types of grants
Bursaries, scholarships and grants.

Annual grant total
In 2015/16 the charity had an income of £14,100 and a total expenditure of £6,600. We estimate that grants given to individuals totalled around £3,200, with funding also awarded to educational organisations.

Applications
It would appear that applications are usually made through select educational establishments.

Taunton Maids Bursary

£3,600

Correspondent: The Trustees of Taunton Maids Bursary, c/o Carol Gaskell, Ashfords LLP, Ashford House, Grenadier Road, Exeter EX1 3LH (01392 334070; email: tauntonmaidsbursary@gmail.com)

CC number: 1157092

Eligibility
Young people aged between 16 and 25 who are working to advance their education in music. Recipients are usually resident in the administrative county of Somerset (including North Somerset, Bath and North East Somerset).

Types of grants
Scholarships, grants and bursaries.

Annual grant total
In 2015/16 the charity had an income of £14,100 and a total expenditure of £7,500. We estimate that grants given to individuals totalled around £3,600, with

funding also awarded to educational organisations.

Applications

It would appear that applications are usually made through select educational establishments.

Bath and North East Somerset

Richard Jones Charity (Richard Jones Foundation)

£2,500

Correspondent: Peter Godfrey, 24D Tyning Road, Saltford, Bristol BS31 3HL (01225 341085; email: peter.h.godfrey@ googlemail.com)

CC number: 310057

Eligibility

People under the age of 30 who live in the parishes of Chew Magna, Lawrence Stanton Prior, Newton St Loe, Stanton Drew, Stowey-Sutton (all in the area of Bath and North East Somerset).

Types of grants

Small educational grants are available to schoolchildren, college/university students, people starting work or entering a trade, and mature and postgraduate students. One-off and recurrent grants, usually from £30 to £400, are given for course books, equipment, instruments and tools.

The correspondent has previously stated that the majority of beneficiaries are students in higher and further education, and that they encourage more applications from those in vocational training. Grants are occasionally given towards musical instruments or music tuition, for school trips, and very occasionally towards school uniforms. Grants may also be made towards initiatives such as Outward Bound courses, exchanges and expeditions.

Annual grant total

In 2015/16 the charity had an income of £11,000 and a total expenditure of £3,200. We estimate that grants awarded to individuals totalled around £2,500.

Exclusions

Individuals attending private schools are not supported.

Applications

Application forms are available from the correspondent and can be submitted directly by the individual. Grants are normally considered in April and October and applications should be submitted in March and September, respectively. Specific dates of the trustees' meetings and application deadlines are normally advertised in parish magazines and on parish noticeboards. Candidates may be invited for an interview.

Other information

Small awards are also made to older people in need at Christmas time. Schools, clubs and other organisations supporting young people in the area of benefit may also receive grants towards equipment.

Ralph and Irma Sperring Charity

£19,000

Correspondent: E. W. L. Hallam, Company Secretary, Thatcher & Hallam Solicitors, Island House, Midsomer Norton, Bath BA3 2HJ (01761 414646; email: sperringcharity@gmail.com)

CC number: 1048101

Eligibility

People in need who live within a five-mile radius of the church of St John the Baptist in Midsomer Norton, Bath.

Types of grants

One-off and recurrent grants are given according to need.

Annual grant total

In 2015/16 the charity had assets of £6.1 million and an income of £220,000. We estimate that grants given to individuals for educational purposes totalled £19,000.

Applications

Apply in writing to the correspondent. Applications are considered quarterly.

North Somerset

Marchioness of Northampton (Wraxall Parochial Charities)

£400

Correspondent: Mrs A. Sissons, Clerk and Treasurer, 2 Short Way, Failand, Bristol BS8 3UF (01275 392691)

CC number: 230410

Eligibility

Residents of the parish of Wraxall and Failand, Bristol who are at any level of their education, in any subject, and are in need.

Types of grants

One-off grants in the range of £50 to £100.

Annual grant total

In 2016 the charity had an income of £21,000 and a total expenditure £21,500. Accounts were not available to view on the Charity Commission website but in previous years educational grants have totalled around £400.

Applications

Applications may be made in writing to the correspondent, directly by the individual. They are considered in February, June, September and November.

Nailsea Community Trust Ltd

£2,500

Correspondent: Ann Tonkin, 1st Nailsea Scouts Training and Activity Centre, Clevedon Road, Nailsea, North Somerset BS48 1EH (email: info@ nailseacommunitytrust.co.uk; website: www.nailseacommunitytrust.co.uk)

CC number: 900031

Eligibility

Young people under the age of 25 who live in Nailsea, Backwell, Chelvey, Tickenham or Wraxall.

Types of grants

One-off grants usually up to £500. Grants are made to assist with education particularly in the areas of the arts, science, religion, commerce and health care.

Annual grant total

In 2015/16 the trust had an income of £3,000 and a total expenditure of £12,000. Grants are made to individuals and organisations for social welfare and educational purposes. We estimate that educational grants to individuals totalled £2,500.

Exclusions

Applications from outside the area of benefit will not be considered.

Applications

The trust's website states that eligible individuals, or somebody who knows of an individual who may be eligible, should contact the trust by email or in writing. Applicants may be asked for a short interview with a couple of the trustees so that a fuller understanding of their situation can be established. All applications are dealt with in confidence.

Charles Graham Stone's Relief-in-Need Charity

£1,200

Correspondent: Philip Baird, The Boardroom, Cottage Homes, Front Street, Churchill, Winscombe BS25 5NE (07861 802085; email: clerkhillarmshouses@gmx.co.uk)

CC number: 260044

Eligibility
Vocational students who live in the parishes of Churchill and Langford, North Somerset.

Types of grants
One-off grants, typically of £50 to £150, towards fees, books, equipment and instruments.

Annual grant total
In 2015 the charity had an income of £3,900 and a total expenditure of £4,900. We estimate that educational grants to individuals totalled around £1,200.

Applications
Applications may be made in writing to the correspondent, providing a full explanation of the applicant's personal circumstances. Our research suggests that requests should be submitted by the end of February or August for consideration in the following month. Note that the charity does not welcome initial telephone calls.

Other information
The charity's record on the Charity Commission's website notes that financial help is provided 'to people or charitable organisations in need' in the area of benefit.

South Somerset

The Ilchester Relief-in-Need and Educational Charity (IRINEC)

£8,800

Correspondent: Kaye Elston, 15 Chilton Grove, Yeovil, Somerset BA21 4AN (01935 421208; website: www.ilchesterparishcouncil.gov.uk)

CC number: 235578

Eligibility
Students in financial need who live in the parish of Ilchester.

Types of grants
Travel grants are available for college students.

University students may be able to receive help with tuition fees and living costs.

Annual grant total
In 2016 the charity had assets of £457,500 and an income of £37,000. The total amount awarded in educational grants was £8,800.

Exclusions
Grants are not available where support should be received from statutory sources.

Applications
Applications are available from the correspondent. The clerk welcomes initial telephone calls to discuss needs and eligibility.

Other information
Grants are also given for relief-in-need purposes.

The Ilminster Educational Foundation

£18,300 (61 grants)

Correspondent: Edward Wells, 20 Station Road, Ilminster, Somerset TA19 9BD (01460 53029; email: e.wells125@btinternet.com)

CC number: 310265

Eligibility
People under the age of 25 who live or have attended an educational institution for at least two years in the parish of Ilminster.

Types of grants
Grants of up to 400 are available to schoolchildren for educational outings in the UK/overseas and to students at Ilminster-based universities or colleges for general educational expenses.

Annual grant total
In 2015/16 the foundation held assets of £106,700 and had an income of £51,000. A total of £12,700 was awarded in grants to 32 individuals, as well as a further £5,600 in special grants to 29 individuals.

The foundation also makes grants to five local schools, special grants to individuals and an annual grant for the general benefit of the parish of Ilminster (totalling £12,900 in 2015/16).

Exclusions
According to our research, grants are not made for A-level courses.

Applications
Apply in writing to the correspondent. Our research suggests that applications are normally considered in October and November. They should be submitted in advance to those dates.

John Nowes Exhibition Foundation

£5,000

Correspondent: Amanda Goddard, Clerk to the Trustees, Battens Solicitors, Mansion House, 54–58 Princes Street, Yeovil, Somerset BA20 1EP (01935 846000; email: amanda.goddard@battens.co.uk; website: www.battens.co.uk)

CC number: 309984

Eligibility
Children and young people between the ages of 16 and 25 living in the borough of Yeovil and surrounding parishes (including Alvington, Barwick, Brympton, Chilthorne Domer, East Coker, Limington, Mudford, Preston Plucknett, Yeovil Without or West Coker), who have a household income of less than £33,000 per annum.

Types of grants
Scholarships, bursaries and maintenance allowances are provided to those in school, university or college. Small grants are awarded towards clothing, equipment or books for those preparing to enter work. There are also grants available towards travel abroad for educational purposes, as well as support for those pursuing music, arts or sports, for those in primary, secondary or further education, where this is not provided by the local authority.

Annual grant total
In 2015/16 the foundation had an income of £7,000 and a total expenditure of £5,600. We estimate that grants totalled about £5,000.

Applications
An application form can be downloaded from the website or requested from the correspondent. It should be submitted along with a parental declaration, evidence of household income and a reference from the head of the student's current educational establishment, usually by the end of October (see the website for the exact date).

Taunton Deane

Taunton Heritage Trust

£13,700 (73 grants)

Correspondent: Karen White, Huish Homes, Magdalene Street, Taunton, Somerset TA1 1SG (01823 335348 (Mon-Fri, 9am-12pm); email: clerk@tauntonheritagetrust.org.uk; website: www.tauntonheritagetrust.org.uk)

CC number: 202120

Eligibility

People living in the borough of Taunton Deane that are of school age (generally up to the age of 16). Our research suggests that requests from colleges of further education on behalf of individuals may also be considered depending on circumstances and need.

Types of grants

Grants to schoolchildren are made according to need, towards school uniforms, educational visits and, in exceptional circumstances, computers.

Annual grant total

In 2016 the trust had assets of £7.3 million and an income of £700,000. Educational grants to individuals totalled £13,700.

Exclusions

The trust will not fund stationery, lunch boxes, book bags, water bottles, name labels, optional school wear items, school socks (PE socks will be considered) and any other non-clothing school items.

Applications

Applications can be downloaded from the trust's website. They must be completed and typed (not handwritten) by a recognised referral agency such as social services or Citizens Advice, for example. Applicants must not complete the forms themselves. Four copies of the completed form must be returned to the trust. The trust asks that, if possible, all information be included on one side of A4 (an accompanying letter should only be sent if absolutely necessary). The referral agency must check and provide details of the type and amount of benefits and/or other income that the applicant is receiving. The applicant's individual/family circumstances must also be described and the need for the grant fully explained. Specific items must be itemised and costed (more information on details to include is listed on the website).

The referral agency officer responsible for submitting the application, and for monitoring the use of any grant, must ensure that they have signed the form. Applications submitted by schools must be signed by the headteacher. If the applicant has moved home in the last 12 months, their previous address should be included. It is also essential (in order to arrange delivery of white goods) to include the applicant's correct telephone number.

Note that the trust cannot accept applications via email.

Other information

The primary role of the charity is to provide sheltered accommodation for people over the age of 60.

West Somerset

Arthur Allen Educational Trust

£4,900

Correspondent: Allison Dowding, Secretary, Park House, High Street, Evercreech, Shepton Mallet, Somerset BA4 6HZ (01749 830087; email: tom_stearn@btinternet.com; website: www.evercreech.org.uk/arthur-allen-education-trust.html)

CC number: 310256

Eligibility

Further and higher education students between the ages of 16 and 25 who were born or live in the parish of Evercreech.

Types of grants

One-off and recurrent grants are available to students attending college/sixth form and university, also vocational students or people starting work. Support is given towards travel expenses, books, equipment/instruments, study/travel abroad, clothing, maintenance/living expenses and fees.

Annual grant total

In 2016 the trust had an income of £6,200 and a total expenditure of £5,200. We estimate that a total of £4,900 was awarded in grants.

Applications

Application forms can either be downloaded from the Evercreech village and district website, requested from the correspondent, or collected from the Evercreech Pharmacy. The closing date for applications is 1 October each year and the awards are made in late October/early November. Two references are required to be sent with the application.

Wiltshire

Chippenham Borough Lands Charity

£14,000

Correspondent: Philip Tansley, 32 Market Place, Chippenham, Wiltshire SN15 3HP (01249 658180; fax: 01249 446048; email: sarah@cblc.org.uk; website: www.cblc.org.uk)

CC number: 270062

Eligibility

People in need who are living within the parish of Chippenham at the date of application, and have been for a

minimum of two years immediately prior to applying.

Types of grants

Usually one-off grants according to need, for things such as help towards travel costs, the provision of equipment to undertake a course or help towards actual course fees, depending on the nature of the course and the individual's personal circumstances.

Annual grant total

In 2015/16 the charity had assets of £13.8 million and an income of £457,500. We estimate that £14,000 was in educational awards during the year.

Exclusions

The charity is unable to help towards:

- Funding of individual sportspeople
- Direct funding of the local authorities
- Religious organisations (except projects with an entire community benefit)
- First degrees
- The provision of carpets or Council Tax arrears

The charity will not consider an application if a grant has been received within the past two years (or one year for mobility aids) unless the circumstances are exceptional.

Applications

In the first instance, applicants should contact the charity via email or telephone to discuss their needs and eligibility. The correspondent will then provide an application form. Previous research has indicated applications are welcome on an ongoing basis.

Other information

The charity also makes awards to individuals for welfare purposes, and to organisations supporting similar causes to the charity's objectives.

Note that after the changes to the parish boundary both the Cepen Park North and Cepen Park South estates are included.

The Community Foundation for Wiltshire and Swindon

£77,000

Correspondent: The Grants Team, Ground Floor, Sandcliff House, 21 Northgate Street, Devizes, Wiltshire SN10 1JT (01380 729284; email: info@wscf.org.uk; website: www.wscf.org.uk)

CC number: 1123126

Eligibility

Individuals who have been residents in Wiltshire or Swindon for at least two years. Visit the foundation's website for additional criteria specific to each grant.

Types of grants
The foundation provides three types of educational grants through its One Degree More programme:

University bursaries support young people who want to gain an undergraduate university degree. Scholarships are offered to talented individuals to help them overcome difficult financial circumstances and achieve their potential.

Bursaries of up to £1,500 are available plus the possibility of an extra £500 for certain situations and courses. Applicants must live in Swindon or Wiltshire, be aged between 17 and 24 at the time of application and either they or their parents/carers must be in receipt of means-tested benefits. Bursaries are awarded for each year of the course.

Vocational grants are open to individuals aged between 14 and 25 to support course costs – especially vocational courses – as well as young people on apprenticeships or looking to start a business. Applicants must live in Swindon or Wiltshire and either they or their parents/carers must be in receipt of means-tested benefits. Grants are up to £1,000.

Education support grants are open to individuals up to the age of 25 who have a disability or additional learning need, or have been in the care of the local authority. Applicants must live in Swindon or Wiltshire or be in education funded by one of these Councils and either they or their parents/carers are in receipt of means-tested benefits. Grants are up to £1,000.

Annual grant total
In 2015/16 the foundation had assets of £18.8 million and an income of £1.5 million. Grants to 212 individuals totalled £154,500. We estimate that around £77,000 was given to individuals in educational grants.

Exclusions
The following are not funded:
- School fees
- Money that has already been spent
- The promotion of party political or religious purposes
- Equipment or expenses which should be provided by someone else
- Activities or equipment that is not education-related
- Postgraduate (master's/PhD courses)

Applications
Application packs can be requested from the foundation's website.

The grants officer responsible for educational grants is Jonathan Whitehead-Whiting (email: jonathan.ww@wiltshirecf.org.uk).

As with any community foundation funds are likely to open and close – for the most up-to-date information on grant schemes currently operating consult the website.

Educational Foundation of Alice Coombe and Others (Alice Coombe's Education Charity)

£900

Correspondent: Kathleen Wright, Administrator, Court Street Farm Cottage, Court Street, Tisbury, Salisbury, Wiltshire SP3 6LN (01747 871774; email: kmmwright@hotmail.com)

CC number: 309359

Eligibility
Children and young people under the age of 25 who live in the ancient parish of Tisbury and West Tisbury.

Types of grants
One-off grants, usually in the range of £20 to £250, are available to secondary schoolchildren, higher or further education students, people in teacher training college or undertaking vocational training. Awards are given towards school uniforms, clothing, books, educational visits, and study or travel abroad for those in further/higher education. People starting work can be given help towards books, equipment/instruments, clothing and travel to interviews.

Annual grant total
In 2016 the foundation had an income of £3,100 and a total expenditure of £1,900. We estimate that the foundation gave around £900 to individuals for educational purposes.

The foundation also awards grants to organisations.

Exclusions
Applications from outside the area of benefit are not considered.

Applications
Apply in writing to the correspondent. Applications can be made directly by the individual or through their school/college, vicar, health visitor, educational welfare agency, if applicable, or other third parties. Applications are considered throughout the year.

Other information
Local schools may also be supported.

The Ewelme Exhibition Foundation (Ewelme Exhibition Endowment)
See entry on page 255

Wiltshire
The Rose Charity

£1,000

Correspondent: Charles Goodbody, Trustee, 94 East Street, Warminster, Wiltshire BA12 9BG (01985 214444; email: cgoodbody@mulaw.co.uk)

CC number: 900590

Eligibility
Schoolchildren in need who live in Warminster and the surrounding villages.

Types of grants
One-off grants towards general educational costs such as books, necessities, uniforms and other clothing, educational outings, etc. According to our research, music lessons can also be supported.

Annual grant total
In 2015/16 the charity had an income of £2,000 and a total expenditure of £2,100. We estimate that grants totalled around £1,000.

Applications
Apply in writing to the correspondent. Our research suggests that applications are considered throughout the year and should be supported by the social services/welfare agency or school/college.

Other information
Grants may also be made to organisations.

Salisbury City Educational and Apprenticing Charity

£970 (six grants)

Correspondent: Clerk to the Trustees, Trinity Hospital, Trinity Street, Salisbury, Wiltshire SP1 2BD (01722 325640; fax: 01722 325640; email: clerk@almshouses.demon.co.uk; website: www.salisburyalmshouses.co.uk)

CC number: 309523

Eligibility
Young people under the age of 25 who live in the district of Salisbury.

Types of grants
One-off educational and apprenticing grants are available for young people. Awards are given for education 'in the

SOUTH WEST – WILTSHIRE

broadest sense', for example, for courses, trips, books, equipment and tools, vocational training and professional qualifications, as well as school trips, play schemes, adventure activities, expeditions and voluntary work abroad.

Annual grant total

In 2016 the charity had an income of £2,100 and a total expenditure of £2,000. The Charity Commission record states that the trustees approved six grants, totalling £970.

Exclusions

Grants are not given for postgraduate study or for daily subsistence expenses (e.g. while at university). Regular payments towards fees or expenses are rarely made.

Applications

Application forms and full guidelines, stating what should be included, are available on the charity's website. Requests are considered on a monthly basis.

Other information

The charity shares the trustees with Salisbury City Almshouse and Welfare Charities (CC number: 202110), which maintains almshouses and may also provide emergency welfare support.

Yorkshire

General

The Northern Counties Children's Benevolent Society

See entry on page 231

Yorkshire Training Fund for Women

£3,000

Correspondent: Hon. Secretary, 5 Bede Court, College Grove Road, Wakefield, West Yorkshire WF1 3RW (website: ytfund.wordpress.com)

CC number: 529586

Eligibility

British women over the age of 16 and over who live in, or have connections to, Yorkshire.

Types of grants

One-off grants in the range of £100 to £300 are available to women undertaking training courses leading to qualifications for employment that will enable them to become self-sufficient financially. Grants are given towards general necessities, such as books, equipment and instruments.

Annual grant total

In 2016 the fund had an income of £2,900 and a total expenditure of £3,300. We estimate that grants to individuals totalled around £3,000.

Exclusions

Grants are not given to cover fees or to people on access courses.

Applications

Application forms can be accessed from the fund's website or requested from the correspondent. They should be completed by the individual. Applicants should provide details of two referees and detailed information of their financial position. Completed forms should be returned by 1 May or by 1 December, providing an sae.

Application forms should be returned to the correspondent.

Other information

Support may also be given to the Yorkshire Ladies' Council of Education and organisations, especially those working for the benefit of older people.

East Riding of Yorkshire

The Joseph and Annie Cattle Trust

£162,000

Correspondent: Roger Waudby, PO Box 23, Patrington, Hull HU12 0WF (01964 671742; email: rogerwaudby@hotmail.co.uk; website: www.jacattletrust.co.uk)

CC number: 262011

Eligibility

Children with dyslexia, children with disabilities, and children from low-income families who live in the Hull and East Riding area.

Types of grants

One-off grants are available to assist children with disabilities, children with dyslexia, and children from low-income families in education. Grants can be used for the purchase or installation of specialist learning equipment, books, uniforms, school trips etc.

Annual grant total

In 2016/17 the trust had assets of £10.2 million and an income of £384,500. We estimate that the charity awarded £162,000 in grants for education during the year.

Exclusions

Individuals cannot apply directly.

Applications

Applications must be made through a charitable organisation or statutory body. Application forms are available to download from the website and should

be returned via post to the correspondent's address.

Other information

The trust also makes awards for welfare purposes, and to charitable organisations and statutory bodies working with disadvantaged families.

The Leonard Chamberlain Trust

£11,000

Correspondent: Alison Nicholson, 6 Chamberlain Court, Chamberlain Street, Sutton-on-Hull, Hull HU7 4UF (email: alinicholson4@googlemail.com)

CC number: 1091018

Eligibility

People under the age of 25 who live in East Riding of Yorkshire, particularly Kingston upon Hull and Selby, who are in financial need which is creating a barrier to education.

Types of grants

One-off and recurrent grants are available to cover the costs associated with education, for example the purchase of books or computers.

Annual grant total

In 2016 the trust had assets of £8.1 million and an income of £209,000. The amount awarded in educational grants was £11,000.

Applications

Application forms can be obtained from the correspondent.

Other information

The trust's main purpose is the provision of housing for residents in the area of benefit who are in financial need and it also makes a small number of grants for religious purposes.

Christopher Eden Educational Foundation

£5,200

Correspondent: Judy Dickinson, Trustee, 85 East Street, Leven, Beverley HU17 5NG (01964 542593; email: judydickinson@mac.com)

CC number: 529794

Eligibility

Young people under the age of 25 who live in the town of Beverley and the surrounding area or have attended school there. People with special educational needs are given preference.

Types of grants

One-off and recurrent grants in the range of £50 to £400 are available to further/higher education students and people undertaking apprenticeships. Financial support is given towards any kind of educational needs, including fees, necessities, books, equipment/instruments, clothing, travel expenses, and sports or arts studies.

Annual grant total

In 2015/16 the foundation had an income of £11,400 and a total expenditure of £10,600. We estimate that the charity gave around £5,200 in grants to individuals for educational purposes.

The foundation also awards grants to organisations.

Applications

Apply in writing to the correspondent.

Alderman Ferries Charity (Hull United Charities)

£17,200

Correspondent: Janine Lambert, Secretary, Hull United Charities, The Office, Northumberland Court, Northumberland Avenue, Hull HU2 0LR (01482 323965; email: office@hulluc.karoo.co.uk; website: www.hullunitedcharities.org.uk/alderman-ferries.html)

CC number: 529821

Eligibility

People under the age of 25 who are entering secondary, further/higher education or apprenticeships and who have attended school or lived within Kingston upon Hull city boundary for at least two years prior to applying.

Types of grants

Grants are given for fees, books, equipment/instruments, clothing, travel costs and maintenance expenses.

Annual grant total

In 2015/16 the charity had an income of £18,400 and a total expenditure of £17,400. We estimate that the charity gave around £17,200 in grants to individuals for educational purposes.

Applications

Application forms and detailed guidelines are available on the trust's website or can be requested from the correspondent. The trustees consider grants every December and applications should be submitted by the middle of November.

Prowde's Educational Foundation (Prowde's Charity)
See entry on page 235

The Sir Philip Reckitt Educational Trust Fund
See entry on page 42

Henry Samman's Hull Chamber of Commerce Endowment Fund

£9,000

Correspondent: The Secretary, Hull & Humber, Chamber of Commerce, Industry & Shipping, 34–38 Beverley Road, Hull HU3 1YE (01482 324976; email: i.kelly@hull-humber-chamber.co.uk; website: www.hull-humber-chamber.co.uk/pages/henry-samman-fund)

CC number: 228837

Eligibility

British citizens who are over the age of 18 and can demonstrate some academic skills in either business methods or a foreign language. Preference is given to young people from Hull and East Riding or Northern Lincolnshire. Candidates should be studying or planning to study at degree level, although consideration will be given to those slightly under this age limit.

Types of grants

Bursaries to enable individuals to spend a period of 3 to 12 months abroad in connection to their studies of business methods and/or foreign languages. The award is generally of around £100 a month. Longer periods of travel may be funded at the trustees' discretion.

Annual grant total

In 2015 the fund had an income of £7,800 and a total expenditure of £9,700. We estimate that grants totalled around £9,000.

Applications

Apply in writing to the correspondent. Applicants should include a covering letter, a CV and outline how the award would benefit their education and training. Candidates may be required to attend an interview. The trustees meet once a year to consider applications, normally in summer.

Other information

The fund was set up in 1917 originally to encourage the study of Russian, in a commercial context, but has since been extended.

Ann Watson's Trust

£51,500

Correspondent: Karen Palmer, Flat 4 The College, 14 College Street, Sutton-on-Hull, Hull HU7 4UP (01482 709626; email: awatson@awatson.karoo.co.uk)

CC number: 226675

Eligibility

People under the age of 25 who live in East Riding, Yorkshire or who attend school in that area.

Types of grants

One-off and recurrent grants according to educational need.

Annual grant total

In 2015/16 the trust had assets of £20.1 million and an income of £469,000. Grants to individuals for educational purposes totalled £51,500. A further £94,000 was given to organisations.

Applications

Apply in writing to the correspondent. The trustees meet quarterly.

Other information

Grants are also given to local organisations, churches and to individuals for welfare purposes.

East Riding of Yorkshire

Heron Educational Foundation (Heron Trust)

£6,500

Correspondent: Brenda Frear, Trustee, 2 The Bungalows, Humbleton Road, Lelley HU12 8SP (01964 670788; email: mrscrawforth@btinternet.com)

CC number: 529841

Eligibility

People under the age of 25 living in the parish of Humbleton and the nearby villages of Flinton and Fitling.

Types of grants

Grants are available to pupils entering primary/secondary school and further/higher education students. People entering a trade/profession may also be assisted. Support can be given towards general educational needs, mainly clothing and books, and other necessities.

Annual grant total

In 2015/16 the foundation had an income of £14,300 and a total expenditure of £7,200. We estimate that grants given to individuals totalled around £6,500.

Applications

Apply in writing to the correspondent.

The Hesslewood Children's Trust (Hull Seamen's and General Orphanage)

£6,000

Correspondent: Lynne Bullock, 62 The Meadows, Cherry Burton, East Yorkshire HU17 7RQ (01964 550882; email: misslynneb@aol.com)

CC number: 529804

Eligibility

People under the age of 25 who live, or whose parent(s) live, in the county of Humberside, or the districts of Gainsborough or Caistor in Lincolnshire.

Types of grants

One-off grants are given towards general educational costs, such as books, school uniforms, educational outings and maintenance for schoolchildren, books for students in higher and further education, and equipment/instruments and clothing for people starting work.

Annual grant total

In 2016/17 the trust had assets of £3.1 million and an income of £108,500. The charity awarded £6,000 in grants for education.

Applications

Applications should be made in writing to the correspondent. Previous research has indicated that where possible, applications should be supported by the individual's school or college. Details of family income and what the grant will be used for are required in the application.

Other information

The trust also makes awards to individuals to relieve financial need, and to local organisations active in the community.

The Hook and Goole Charity

£14,000

Correspondent: Diane Taylor, Secretary, The Courtyard, Boothferry Road, Goole DN14 6AW (07539269813; email: hookandgoole@gmail.com)

CC number: 513948

Eligibility

Students and apprentices aged between 16 and 25 who have lived or attended school in the former borough of Goole or the parish of Hook for at least two years.

Types of grants

The charity generally supports students in higher education and apprenticeships. According to the website, grants can be given 'to help with almost any aspect of your education', including purposes such as equipment, clothing or special needs.

Annual grant total

In 2016 the charity had an income of £13,800 and a total expenditure of £15,400. We estimate that grants totalled around £14,000.

Applications

Application forms can be downloaded from the charity's website or requested from the correspondent, and should be submitted by post. Applications are accepted between July and September (refer to the website for specific dates).

The Nafferton Feoffees Charities Trust

£15,000

Correspondent: Margaret Buckton, South Cattleholmes, Wansford, Driffield, North Humberside, East Yorkshire YO25 8NW (01377 254293; email: secretary@feoffeetrust.co.uk; website: www.feoffeetrust.co.uk)

CC number: 232796

Eligibility

People in need who live in the parish of All Saints Nafferton with St Mary's Wansford.

Types of grants

Bursaries are available to local students going to a college or university for things such as educational overseas trips, course materials, laptops, books, etc. Grants are also made to primary and secondary school students for study trips, projects, etc.

Annual grant total

In 2016 the trust had assets of £2 million and an income of £52,000. Educational grants to individuals totalled £15,000.

Applications

Application forms for scholarships can be downloaded from the trust's website. Contact the secretary about other educational grants (books, equipment etc.).

Other information

Grants are also made to local organisations and to individuals for welfare purposes.

According to the 2016 trustees' report, the trust is 'made up of three charities known as the Poors Trust, the Town Trust, and the John Baron Trust covering the ecclesiastical parish of Nafferton, Wansford and Pockthorpe and was started in 1890'.

The Peter Nevill Charity

£1,700

Correspondent: Julie Rhodes, Trustee, Marleigh, Arnold Lane West, Arnold, Hull HU11 5HP (01964 562872)

CC number: 506325

Eligibility

Young people under 25 who live, or who have a parent/parents who live, in the parish of Long Riston and Arnold.

Types of grants

Grants are given towards books, clothing and other essentials for school leavers taking up employment and for students in further or higher education.

Annual grant total

In 2016/17 the charity had an income of £2,800 and a total expenditure of £2,900. We estimate that educational grants to individuals totalled around £1,700.

Applications

Apply in writing to the correspondent.

Other information

Grants are made to Riston Church of England Primary School and village organisations serving young people.

Newton on Derwent Charity

£3,000

Correspondent: The Trustees, Grays Solicitors, Duncombe Place, York YO1 7DY (01904 634771)

CC number: 529830

Eligibility

People who live in the parish of Newton upon Derwent. Our research suggests that grants are mainly available to higher education students.

Types of grants
One-off grants towards fees. Payments are usually paid directly to the relevant institution.

Annual grant total
In 2016 the charity had an income of £11,100 and a total expenditure of £13,000. Grants are made to individuals and organisations for both social welfare and educational purposes. We estimate that educational grants to individuals totalled around £3,000.

Applications
Apply in writing to the correspondent.

The Ottringham Church Lands Charity

£1,000

Correspondent: Mary Fairweather, Trustee, South Field, Chapel Lane, Ottringham, Hull, East Yorkshire HU12 0AA (01964 626908; email: maryfairweather@hotmail.com)

CC number: 237183

Eligibility
People in need who live in the parish of Ottringham.

Types of grants
Grants are made according to need.

Annual grant total
In 2016 the charity had an income of £10,900 and a total expenditure of £4,500. We estimate that educational grants to individuals totalled £1,000.

Applications
Apply in writing to the correspondent at any time. Applications can be submitted either directly by the individual, through a third party such as a social worker or teacher, or through an organisation such as Citizens Advice or a school.

The Rawcliffe Educational Charity

£11,000

Correspondent: Julie Parrott, 26 Station Road, Rawcliffe, Goole, North Humberside DN14 8QR (01405 839637)

CC number: 509656

Eligibility
People under the age of 25 in education who (or whose parents) live in the parish of Rawcliffe and who have attended one of the local schools, particularly those over 18 who are starting university.

Types of grants
Individuals finishing school are encouraged to apply for grants to help upon entering higher education. Assistance can be given towards the cost of books, equipment/instruments, outfits and clothing, fees, maintenance/living costs and travel expenses. Apprentices and people starting work are also eligible to apply for help with books, equipment, clothing and travel. The study of music and other arts may also be supported.

Annual grant total
In 2015/16 the charity had an income of £10,500 and a total expenditure of £11,900. We estimate that grants to individuals totalled around £11,000.

Exclusions
School fees or study/travel overseas are not normally covered.

Applications
Apply in writing to the correspondent. Applications should include the type and duration of the course to be studied. Candidates must confirm that they are not in receipt of any salary. The awards are normally considered in September.

Other information
Children in the parish who are leaving primary schools and going into secondary education are also provided with scientific calculators, according to the Charity Commission record.

Nancie Reckitt Charity

£6,000

Correspondent: Maureen Stansfield, 19 Northside, Patrington, Hull HU12 0PA (01964 630960; email: maureenstansfield838@btinternet.com)

CC number: 509380

Eligibility
People under the age of 25 who (or whose parents) have been resident in the parishes of Patrington, Rimswell and Winestead for at least five years.

Types of grants
Our research suggests that recurrent grants are available to students in further/higher education for general education expenses, including equipment/instruments, books and fees. Support is also given to people starting work for clothing and equipment/instruments and tools.

Annual grant total
In 2015/16 the charity had an income of almost £6,700 and a total expenditure of £6,600. We estimate that grants totalled around £6,000.

Applications
Application forms can be requested from the correspondent and submitted directly by the individual. Our research suggests that receipts for items such as books, materials and tools should be included.

Robert Towrie's Charity

£1,000

Correspondent: Debbie Ulliot, Correspondent, The Cottage, Carlton Lane, Aldbrough, Hull HU11 4RA (01964 527255; email: roberttowerytrust@googlemail.com)

CC number: 222568

Eligibility
People under the age of 25 who live in the parishes of Aldbrough and Burton Constable or who have parents living in the area.

Types of grants
One-off grants for educational or training needs.

Annual grant total
In 2015/16 the charity had an income of £10,200 and a total expenditure of £4,400. We estimate the total of grants awarded to individuals for educational purposes to be around £1,000.

Applications
Applications may be made in writing to the correspondent, directly by the individual.

Other information
The charity makes grants and organisations for both educational and social welfare purposes.

Wray Trust

£3,500

Correspondent: Judy Dickinson, Trustee, 85 East Street, Leven, Beverley HU17 5NG (01964 542593; email: judydickinson@mac.com)

CC number: 508468

Eligibility
People under the age of 25 who (or whose parents) have lived in the parish of Leven for at least three years.

Types of grants
One-off grants are given to schoolchildren, students in further or higher education and people starting work. Support is available towards general educational costs, including books, equipment/instruments, fees, educational outings, study or travel abroad and musical or sports activities.

Annual grant total

In 2015/16 the trust had an income of £7,300 and a total expenditure of £7,400. We have estimated that grants to individuals totalled £3,500. Grants are also given to local organisations working for the benefit of young people.

Applications

Application forms are available from the correspondent and should be submitted by the beginning of January, April, July and October for consideration during that month.

Hull

Dr A. E. Hart Trust

£18,000 (61 grants)

Correspondent: Secretary to the Trustees, Williamsons Solicitors, 45 Lowgate, Hull HU1 1EN (01482 323697; fax: 01482 328132; email: jfc@williamsons-solicitors.co.uk; website: www.williamsons-solicitors.co.uk/dr-hart-trust)

CC number: 529780

Eligibility

Prospective Candidates must: be at least 18 years old; be studying for their first degree, PGCE, Legal Practice Course (LPC) or Bar Professional Training Course (BPTC); reside within the boundary of the city and county of Kingston upon Hull; agree to permit the trustees to verify information provided in any manner they wish

Types of grants

Grants available are modest and unlikely to have a significant impact on the applicant's decision to embark on a given course. The trustees decide on the amount of the award and the method by which it should be applied based on the following considerations:

- The proposed programme of study
- Income and any forms of support available to the individual
- Costs of the programme
- Any special circumstances

Annual grant total

In 2015/16 the trust had an income of £33,000 and a total expenditure of £31,500. Grants were awarded to 61 individuals totalling £18,000.

Exclusions

Surrounding villages are not included (e.g. Willerby, Hessle, Anlaby, Hedon)

Applications from students who are resident in Hull only because they are attending an educational institution there will not be considered.

Applications

Application forms are available to download online. Applications must be filled out in block capitals and black ink. Applications cannot be considered unless all supporting documentation is attached. Eight copies of the application must be submitted before December. Applications received after the deadline will not be considered unless exceptional circumstances are outlined in the application.

The JVenn Foundation

£25,000

Correspondent: John Cliff, Trustee, Rockstones, March Road, Weybridge KT13 8XA (0785 675 1176; email: info@jvennfoundation.org; website: www.jvennfoundation.org)

CC number: 1160632

Eligibility

Young people (under 23) who are currently resident in the city of Hull, and are going to begin studying for a first degree at a British university or for an alternative tertiary qualification. According to the website, applicants must fall into one or more of the following categories of eligibility:

- Financial – a combined parent/guardian income of less than £20,000
- Disability – the student has a disability and is in receipt of appropriate disability benefit
- In care – students currently in care, care-leavers or those who have been in care for more than six months over the last three years
- Carers and parents – students who are carers or parents
- Ethnic minority – including refugees and those from traveller families

Types of grants

The foundation provides bursaries of £5,000 per year for students studying for a first degree at a British university, or for another tertiary educational qualification.

Annual grant total

In 2016/17 the foundation had assets of £222,000 and an income of £126,500. Bursaries were made to six students, totalling £25,000, with a further £250 awarded to unsuccessful applicants. The 2016/17 annual report states that there were 50 new student applications during the year, of which 11 were shortlisted, and three were successful. A further £2,400 was given in grants to organisations.

Applications

Application forms are available to download from the foundation's website and should be submitted either by post

(The JVenn Foundation, c/o HEY Smile Foundation, The Loft, Dock Street, Hull HU1 3AE), by email (info@jvennfoundation.org) or through the head of the applicant's school or college. A statement from a sponsor (a lecturer or teacher) should also be included – further guidance is given on the website. The deadline for applications is stated on the website – they are usually shortlisted in May and interviews are arranged afterwards.

Other information

The foundation also awards grants to secondary schools in Hull to support extracurricular activities.

Kingston upon Hull Education Foundation

£7,000

Correspondent: Brice McDermid, Administrator, Corporate Finance, City Treasury, Hull City Council, Guildhall Road, Hull HU1 2AB (01482 615010; email: corpfinanceplanning@hullcc.gov.uk)

CC number: 514427

Eligibility

People over 13 who live, or whose parents live, in the city of Kingston upon Hull and either attend, or have attended, a school in the city.

Types of grants

Awards of £80 to £250 are available as scholarships, bursaries or grants tenable at any school, university or other educational establishment approved by the trustees, and towards the cost of outfits, clothing, tools, instruments or books to assist the beneficiaries in pursuance of their education or to prepare them for entering a profession, trade, occupation or service on leaving school, university or other educational establishment.

Annual grant total

In 2015/16 the foundation had an income of £4,600 and a total expenditure of £7,500. We have estimated that grants totalled about £7,000.

Applications

Apply in writing to the correspondent. Applications are usually considered in November (closing date mid-October) and February (closing date mid-January). A letter of support from the applicant's class or course tutor, plus evidence of their progress and attendance on the course is needed before a grant is made.

North Yorkshire

The Beckwith Bequest

£9,000

Correspondent: Joy Richardson, Correspondent, 2 Station Court, Tollerton, York YO61 1RH (07929372352; email: beckwithbequest@outlook.com)

CC number: 532360

Eligibility

People resident or educated in the parishes of Easingwold and Husthwaite who are in need of financial assistance.

Types of grants

Grants are available to help with general educational costs, including books, equipment/instruments, clothing, travel etc.

Annual grant total

In 2015/16 the charity had an income of £11,000 and a total expenditure of £12,000. The total amount awarded in grants to individuals was £9,000.

Applications

Applications can be made in writing to the correspondent. Applications are considered at the trustees' quarterly meetings.

Bedale Educational and Bedale 750 Charity (The Rector and Four and Twenty of Bedale)

Correspondent: John Winkle, 25 Burrill Road, Bedale DL8 1ET (01677 424306; email: johnwinkle@awinkle.freeserve.co.uk)

CC number: 529517

Eligibility

People under the age of 25 who (or whose parents) live in the parishes of Aiskew, Bedale, Burrill, Cowling, Crakehall, Firby, Leeming Bar, Longthorne and Rand Grange in North Yorkshire. Preference is given to people with special educational needs or disabilities.

Types of grants

One-off grants are given to schoolchildren, college students and people in training. Support can be provided towards books, fees, maintenance/living expenses and excursions.

Annual grant total

In 2015/16 the charity had an income of £600 and no expenditure.

Applications

Application forms are available from the correspondent. They can be submitted at any time either directly by the individual or their parent.

Other information

Grants may also be made to organisations, such as local schools or clubs.

The Gargrave Poor's Land Charity

£22,000

Correspondent: The Trustees, Kirk Syke, High Street, Gargrave, Skipton, North Yorkshire BD23 3RA

CC number: 225067

Eligibility

People who are in need and are permanently resident in Gargrave, Banknewton, Coniston Cold, Flasby, Eshton or Winterburn.

Types of grants

One-off and recurrent grants and loans are given to: schoolchildren for uniforms, clothing and outings; and students in further or higher education towards maintenance, fees and textbooks. Help is also available to students taking vocational further education courses and other vocational training.

Annual grant total

In 2016/17 the charity had assets of £420,500 and an income of £29,000. Grants totalled £56,500 and were distributed as follows:

Hardship relief	£29,000
Educational assistance	£22,000
Christmas distribution	£5,300

Applications

Applications can be made on a form, which is available from the correspondent, and can be submitted at any time.

Reverend Matthew Hutchinson Trust (Gilling and Richmond)

£6,000

Correspondent: Christine Bellas, Oak Tree View, Hutton Magna, Richmond DL11 7HQ (01833 627997; email: cbellas4516@gmail.com)

CC number: 220870/220779

Eligibility

People who live in the parishes of Gilling and Richmond in North Yorkshire.

Types of grants

One-off and recurrent grants are available to cover costs for educational equipment, travel, and books.

Annual grant total

This charity has branches in both Gilling and Richmond, which are administered jointly, but have separate funding. In 2016 the combined income of the charities was £22,000 and their combined total expenditure was £12,000.

The combined grant total for education was £6,000.

Applications

Applications should be made in writing to the correspondent.

Other information

Grants are also made to organisations and to individuals in the area of benefit for relief-in-need purposes.

Muker Educational Trust

£5,000

Correspondent: Michael McGarry, 21 Galgate, Barnard Castle DL12 8EQ (01388 603073; email: office@mbmcgarry.co.uk)

CC number: 1002488

Eligibility

People who live in the ecclesiastical parish of Swaledale with Arkengarthdale.

Types of grants

The trust offers one-off and recurrent grants to schoolchildren, further/higher education students and people in training. Our research suggests that support can be given towards books, equipment/instruments, fees, study/travel overseas and other educational needs.

Annual grant total

In 2016/17 the trust had an income of £8,500 and a total expenditure of £11,100. We estimate that grants to individuals totalled around £5,000.

Exclusions

Grants are not usually given for maintenance, clothing or living expenses.

Applications

Application forms can be requested from the correspondent. All communications should be accompanied with an sae. Applications should be submitted by 1 November either directly by the individual or through an organisation such as school or educational welfare agency, if applicable.

Madeleine Mary Walker Foundation

£4,000

Correspondent: Paul Benfield, Trustee, 1 Levington Wynd, Nunthorpe, Middlesbrough TS7 0QD (email: m100pfb@yahoo.co.uk)

CC number: 1062657

Eligibility

People in need of support towards their education up to first degree or equivalent. Priority is given to those living within a 30-mile radius of Stokesley, North Yorkshire.

Types of grants

Assistance can be given towards various educational needs, including the cost of books, equipment/tools, musical instruments, fees, study/travel abroad, field trips and so forth. Grants usually range from £250 to £750.

Annual grant total

In 2015/16 the foundation had assets of £21,000 and an income of £28,000. A total of £4,000 was awarded in grants.

Applications

Apply in writing to the correspondent, providing an sae and a contact telephone number. The trustees usually meet three/four times per year. Applicants may be interviewed.

Yorebridge Educational Foundation

£5,000

Correspondent: Robert Tunstall, Treasurer, Kiln Hill, Hawes, North Yorkshire DL8 3RA (01969 667428; email: bobtunstall@hotmail.co.uk)

CC number: 518826

Eligibility

Students under 25 years of age undertaking full-time courses of further education. Students or parents must live in Wensleydale, North Yorkshire. Preference is given to those with parents resident in the parishes of Askrigg, Bainbridge, Hawes, High Abbotside or Low Abbotside.

Types of grants

One-off grants, towards purposes such as books, fees and living expenses.

Annual grant total

In 2015/16 the foundation had an income of £18,100 and a total expenditure of £11,700. We estimate that educational grants to individuals totalled £5,000.

Applications

Apply in writing to the correspondent.

Other information

Grants may also be made to organisations.

Craven

Raygill Trust

£2,500

Correspondent: John Brown, 6 The Fold, Lothersdale, Keighley BD20 8HD (01535 636682; email: stephen.z.brown@btinternet.com)

CC number: 249199

Eligibility

Full-time students on a first degree or equivalent course at a university or college who live in the ecclesiastical parish of Lothersdale.

Types of grants

Grants are made to students who are in the first three years of their further education.

Annual grant total

In 2015/16 the trust had an income of £11,600 and a total expenditure of £10,800. We estimate that grants given to individuals for educational purposes totalled around £2,500.

Applications

Apply in writing to the correspondent. Applicants who do not send thank you letters will not be considered for future grants.

Ryedale

Poad's Educational Foundation

£2,900

Correspondent: Mr P. J. Lawrence, 23 Larchfield, Stockton Lane, York YO31 1JS (01904 415526; email: peter@pjllaw.co.uk)

CC number: 529639

Eligibility

People under the age of 25 who are from a low-income background and live in the ancient town of Newton upon Rawcliffe.

Types of grants

Grants towards course fees, travel, books, incidental expenses and maintenance costs. Grants are also given for a broad range of educational needs, including support for non-formal education and extracurricular activities.

Annual grant total

In 2015/16 the foundation had an income of £3,100 and a total expenditure of £3,200. We estimate that grants totalled around £2,900.

Applications

Application forms are available from the correspondent.

Scarborough

The Scarborough Municipal Charity

£1,300

Correspondent: Fiona Mainprize, Halmar, Pickering Road West, Snainton, Scarborough YO13 9PL (01723 859534; email: scar.municipalcharity@yahoo.co.uk)

CC number: 217793

Eligibility

People who have lived in the borough of Scarborough for at least five years.

Types of grants

Small grants can be given towards general education or training needs and the purchase of necessities, including books, fees, uniforms, travel, equipment, maintenance/living expenses and excursions. Support is available for students of further, higher, and vocational education.

Annual grant total

In 2016 the charity had assets of £2.5 million and an income of £191,000. We estimate that the amount awarded in educational grants was £1,300.

Applications

Application forms can be requested from the correspondent.

Other information

The charity is mainly responsible for the provision and upkeep of almshouses in the community, and also gives grants to individuals for welfare purposes, and to local organisations.

Scarborough United Scholarships Foundation

£6,000

Correspondent: Anne Morley, Clerk to the Trustees, 169 Scalby Road, Scarborough YO12 6TB (01723 375908; fax: 01723 506382; email: anne.morley169@btinternet.com)

CC number: 529678

Eligibility

People under the age of 25 who live in the former borough of Scarborough and have attended school in the area for at least three years, and whose parent(s) are normally resident in the area. The geographical area of benefit stretches from Ravenscar in the north, to Gristhorpe in the south and inland to Ebberston.

The John Kendall Trust supports young people up to the age of 25, who are resident in the area of benefit who either live in a single-parent family or whose parents are in receipt of income support. Consideration can also be given to children or young people from abroad who may not be receiving state benefits but otherwise are eligible.

Types of grants

The foundation prefers to give grants towards specific items for educational benefit, such as computers, travel expenses, projects or equipment. The foundation has stated that it supports 'promoting education in its widest sense' – including, for example: music and the arts; vocational studies; educational visits; work experience opportunities; support for children with special needs.

Annual grant total

In 2015/16 the foundation had an income of £8,200 and a total expenditure of £9,400. We estimate that grants totalled around £6,000.

Applications

Application forms are available from the clerk. The foundation's information leaflet states the following information:

All applications are considered individually with full knowledge of the individual's financial circumstances as supplied on the form. We realise that grants from other funding bodies vary greatly.

Funding in schools and colleges for educational visits, work experience etc. varies too so each application is considered on its merits, based on need, for individuals, schools and organisations.

Other information

The foundation also administers a linked charity, the John Kendall Trust, which may also support organisations with similar aims, although the focus appears to be on supporting individuals.

York

The Company of Merchant Taylors of the City of York (Merchant Taylors – York)

£7,500

Correspondent: Nevil Pearce, Clerk, U. H. Y. Calvert Smith, 31 St Saviourgate, York YO1 8NQ (01904 557570; fax: 01904 557571; email: clerk@merchant-taylors-york.org; website: www.merchant-taylors-york.org)

CC number: 229067

Eligibility

Young people in education or training in the fields of arts, music and craftsmanship who live in York and the surrounding area.

Types of grants

Bursaries, prizes and other grants of up to £1,000 are available for a wide range of activities under the headings of arts, music and craftsmanship to develop applicants' skills and enhance their career prospects.

Annual grant total

In 2015/16 the charity had assets of £524,500 and an income of £94,000. Throughout the year the charity's charitable expenditure totalled £69,500. Of this amount, £7,500 was given to individuals for purposes relating to art, craftsmanship and music.

Applications

Application forms can be downloaded from the charity's website or requested from the correspondent. Applications can be submitted at any time and should be sent by email to the clerk at clerk@merchant-taylors-york.org.

Other information

The charity also maintains the company's hall and premises, almshouses, documents, runs the guild, pays pensions to tailors in the area of benefit and supports individuals and organisations for welfare causes.

The amount awarded to individuals for educational purposes includes the annual David Cramb Memorial Prizes for the best performing students on the York College BA Fashion Design Programme, bursaries awarded to students in the fashion, music, drama and craft departments at York College.

York Children's Trust

£3,700

Correspondent: Margaret Brien, 29 Whinney Lane, Harrogate HG2 9LS (01423 504765; email: yorkchildrenstrust@hotmail.co.uk)

CC number: 222279

Eligibility

Children and young people under 25 who live within 20 miles of the centre of York.

Types of grants

One-off grants, usually of between £100 to £300, are awarded to:

- Schoolchildren for uniforms/clothing, equipment/instruments and excursions
- College students for study/travel overseas, equipment/instruments, maintenance/living expenses and childcare
- Undergraduates for study/travel overseas, excursions and childcare
- Vocational students for uniforms/clothing, fees, study/travel overseas, excursions and childcare
- Mature students for childcare
- People starting work
- People with special educational needs for uniforms/clothing

Our research suggests that preference is given to schoolchildren with serious family difficulties so that the child has to be educated away from home and to people with special educational needs who have been referred by a paediatrician or educational psychiatrist.

Annual grant total

In 2016 the trust had an income of £100,000 and a total expenditure of £100,500. The charity awarded 102 grants totalling around £60,000, the majority of which was awarded to organisations, and to individuals for social welfare and medical needs. During the year, £800 was awarded to individuals for education, with a further £2,900 awarded for purposes relating to travel and 'fostering talents'.

Exclusions

Grants are not available for private education or postgraduate studies.

Applications

Application forms are available from the correspondent and can be submitted directly by the individual or by the individual's school, college or educational welfare agency, or a third party such as a health visitor or social worker. Applications are considered quarterly, normally in January, April, July and October, and should be received by the trust one month beforehand.

South Yorkshire

Armthorpe Poors Estate Charity

£1,400

Correspondent: Tracey Ellis, 6 The Lings, Armthorpe, Doncaster, South Yorkshire DN3 3RH (01302 355180; email: apecharity@gmail.com)

CC number: 226123

Eligibility
People who are in need and live in Armthorpe.

Types of grants
One-off and recurrent grants of a minimum of £50 are given to schoolchildren who are in need for educational outings and to undergraduates for books.

Annual grant total
In 2015/16 the charity had an income of almost £11,000 and a total expenditure of £5,900. Grants are made to individuals and organisations for a wide range of purposes. We estimate that educational grants to individuals totalled £1,400.

Exclusions
Applications from individuals outside Armthorpe will be declined.

Applications
Contact the clerk by telephone who will advise if a letter of application is needed. Undergraduates are required to complete an application form, available from the correspondent, and return it by 31 August.

Barnsley

The Shaw Lands Trust

£7,300 (15 grants)

Correspondent: Jill Leece, Clerk, 35 Church Street, Barnsley, South Yorkshire S70 2AP (01226 213434; email: jill.leece@newmanandbond.co.uk)

CC number: 224590

Eligibility
Children and young people under the age of 25 who live within the Barnsley metropolitan borough or have attended school there for at least two years. Preference is given to individuals from households with low income.

Types of grants
Grants in the range of £200 to £750. Support can be given to schoolchildren, further/higher education students or people starting work/entering a trade for various educational needs, including books, necessities, equipment/instruments, tools, outfits/clothing, uniforms, travel in the UK or abroad in pursuance of education and study of music or other arts.

Annual grant total
In 2015/16 the trust had assets of £1.46 million and an income of £50,000. Educational grants were made to 15 individuals and totalled £7,300. A further £24,000 was given in grants to organisations.

Applications
Apply in writing to the correspondent. The trustees meet to consider applications in April and October.

Other information
At least two-thirds of the charity's income is spent supporting local charitable organisations working for young people, with the remainder being allocated to assist individual students.

Sheffield

Beighton Relief in Need Charity

£4,000

Correspondent: Diane Rodgers, 41 Collingbourne Avenue, Sothall, Sheffield S20 2QR (email: beigtonrelief@hotmail.co.uk)

CC number: 225416

Eligibility
Students who live in the former parish of Beighton and are in need.

Types of grants
One-off grants according to need.

Annual grant total
In 2016 the charity had an income of £16,000 and a total expenditure of £8,500. We estimate that the amount awarded in grants for education was £4,000.

Applications
Apply in writing to the correspondent.

Other information
The charity also supports individuals for welfare purposes.

Bolsterstone Educational Charity

£4,000

Correspondent: Cliff North, 5 Pennine View, Stocksbridge, Sheffield S36 1ER (0114 288 2757; email: cliff.north39@icloud.com)

CC number: 529371

Eligibility
Children and young people under the age of 25 who live in the parishes of St Mary, Bolsterstone and St Matthias, Stocksbridge.

Types of grants
Grants are awarded for general educational items not normally provided by the local authority, such as books, equipment, and school uniform.

Annual grant total
In 2016/17 the charity had an income of £10,000 and a total expenditure of £9,000. We estimate that the total amount awarded in educational grants to individuals was £4,000.

Exclusions
No grants are given to mature students or people starting work.

Applications
Apply in writing to the correspondent. Our research suggests that the applications can be submitted directly by the individual normally for consideration at the beginning of March, July or November.

Other information
The charity also supports a number of local schools.

Church Burgesses Educational Foundation

£50,500

Correspondent: G. J. Smallman, 3rd Floor Fountain Precinct, Balm Green, Sheffield S1 2JA (0114 267 5594; fax: 0114 267 3176; website: www.sheffieldchurchburgesses.org.uk)

CC number: 529357

Eligibility
People under the age of 25 who (or whose parents) have lived in Sheffield for at least three years. Generally, grants are not given for university level or higher education.

Types of grants
Grants are available for general educational causes, such as school trips, gap year activities, equipment for sports and the arts, vocational training, and for additional educational needs.

Annual grant total

In 2016 the foundation had assets of £142,000 and an income of £153,000. A total of £50,500 was awarded in grants.

Exclusions

Individuals based in Sheffield on a temporary basis to attend an educational establishment are not eligible. As a general rule higher education courses are not supported.

Applications

Application forms are available from the foundation's website or can be requested from the correspondent. The trustees usually meet four times a year, in January, April, August (emergency cases) and October, but grants could be made outside these times as well. Applications will need to include confirmation of attendance at an educational institution, and any other supporting evidence.

Other information

Grants are also made for church-based youth work, to educational institutions, and for supporting music in the local area.

Hollowford Trust

£5,000

Correspondent: Lucy Nunn, Administrator, Sheffield Diocesan Church House, 95–99 Effingham Street, Rotherham, South Yorkshire S65 1BL (01709 309135; fax: 01709 512550; email: lucy.nunn@sheffield.anglican.org; website: www.sheffield.anglican.org/hollowford-trust)

CC number: 523918

Eligibility

Young people between the ages of 10 and 25 residing in, or near, the diocese of Sheffield.

Types of grants

Awards of up to £300 aim to help 'develop [the applicants'] physical, mental and spiritual capabilities, so that they may grow to full maturity as individuals and members of society and so that their conditions of life may be improved'. Grants of up to £300 each can be given towards experiences such as voluntary work – up to ten individuals for overseas activities and to up to ten individuals for UK-based activities. Grants of up to £75 can be given towards short trips in the UK (no more than 50% of the total cost of the trip).

Annual grant total

In 2016 the trust had an income of £9,000 and a total expenditure of £11,000. We estimate that about £5,000 was given in grants to individuals for educational purposes.

Exclusions

Funding is not given for:

- Repeat applications from an individual or the same group of young people for the same purpose
- Musical instruments
- Costs towards formal qualifications/education (including fees for course trips)
- Activities where evangelism is the primary purpose
- Employment of youth or children's workers
- Retrospective grants or those submitted after the closing dates
- Other grant-makers

Applications

Application forms are available on the trust's website and should be returned to the correspondent at least two weeks in advance to the trustees' meetings. There are four deadlines each year – exact dates are given in the guidance on the website.

Other information

Grants of up to £400 are also available to groups as start-up grants or for UK trips. Funding may also be given for events, concerts or outreach activities.

Sir Samuel Osborn's Deed of Gift Relief Fund

£3,500

Correspondent: Grants Team, South Yorkshire Community Foundation, Unit 3 – G1 Building, 6 Leeds Road, Attercliffe, Sheffield S9 3TY (0114 242 4294; email: grants@sycf.org.uk; website: www.sycf.org.uk)

CC number: 1140947

Eligibility

Residents of Sheffield, with some preference for former employees of the Samuel Osborn Company (or one if its subsidiaries) and their dependants.

Types of grants

Grants of between £250 and £1,000 are given for costs associated with undertaking any training or education, for example, books, equipment and living costs

Annual grant total

In 2013/14 the fund had an investment income of £5,800 and made grants totalling £7,000. We estimate that educational grants to individuals totalled around £3,500. Grants are also made to individuals for welfare purposes.

Exclusions

Individuals with large personal reserves of money will not be funded.

Applications

Apply using the form, which is available to download along with guidelines, from the South Yorkshire Community Foundation's website. The foundation welcomes informal approaches about applications prior to submitting. Applicants with a connection to the Osborn company should include written evidence. The foundation aims to assess cases within 12 weeks of receiving the completed application form with all enclosures.

Other information

The fund is administered by the South Yorkshire Community Foundation.

The Sheffield Bluecoat and Mount Pleasant Educational Foundation

£15,900 (27 grants)

Correspondent: Susan Greaves, Wrigleys Solicitors, Fountain Precinct, Balm Green, Sheffield S1 2JA (0114 267 5588; email: sue.greaves@wrigleys.co.uk)

CC number: 529351

Eligibility

People under the age of 25 who have lived within a 20-mile radius of Sheffield Town Hall for at least three years and are in need.

Types of grants

Grants of can be made for a range of general educational purposes, including necessities, clothing and outfits, equipment/instruments, maintenance expenses, fees, gap year opportunities, study/travel overseas and the study of music, arts, sports or physical education. Support is given to schoolchildren, further/higher education students or people in training and people starting work/entering a trade. In special cases private schooling costs could be assisted.

Annual grant total

In 2015/16 the foundation had assets of £1.6 million and an income of £67,500. During the year it awarded 18 grants to individuals totalling £15,900. A further £7,100 was awarded in grants to nine organisations.

Applications

Apply in writing to the correspondent. Applications should also include all the supporting documents and evidence of financial need. The trustees meet twice a year to award grants.

Other information

The foundation also supports local organisations.

Sheffield Grammar School Exhibition Foundation

£27,000 (62 grants)

Correspondent: Godfrey Smallman, Clerk, c/o Wrigleys Solicitors LLP, 3rd Floor, Fountain Precinct, Balm Green, Sheffield S1 2JA (0114 267 5594; fax: 0114 267 5630; email: godfrey. smallman@wrigleys.co.uk)

CC number: 529372

Eligibility

People who have lived within the city of Sheffield boundary for at least three years (excluding residency for educational purposes). There is a preference for people who are attending/ have attended King Edward VII School for at least two years.

Types of grants

Grants are awarded for general educational purposes, including course costs, study/travel overseas, training and retraining courses, medical electives, childcare costs, field trips, gap year and character building opportunities, and sports or musical training. Support can be given to schoolchildren, further/ higher education students and people entering a trade/occupation towards outfits, clothing, tools, books, equipment and instruments.

Annual grant total

In 2015/16 the foundation held assets of £3.2 million and had an income of £165,500. Grants to individuals totalled £27,000 and a further £18,500 was awarded to educational organisations.

Applications

The trustees' 2015/16 annual report notes that:

Applications are accepted from a wide range of individuals and organisations. Some of the grant programmes have application forms and financial eligibility documentation which requires completion, other applications are taken by letter with supporting documentation

All applications are reviewed by trustees at their quarterly meetings.

Details of how to apply for grants are available from the Law Clerk and his office, both in hard copy and by email.

The Sheffield West Riding Charitable Society Trust

£3,000

Correspondent: Heidi Adcock, Diocese of Sheffield, Diocesan Church House, 95–99 Effingham Street, Rotherham,

South Yorkshire S65 1BL (01709 309100; email: reception@sheffield.anglican.org; website: www.sheffield.anglican.org)

CC number: 1002026

Eligibility

Children of the clergy, deaconesses, and lay people in Sheffield.

Types of grants

Small grants of up to £300 per applicant for general costs associated with education.

Annual grant total

In 2016 the trust had an income of £12,000 and a total expenditure of £8,000. We estimate that the amount awarded in educational grants was £3,000.

Applications

The trust distributes grants from various funds. General application forms can be requested from the correspondent, who will match the need to the most suitable fund.

Other information

The charity also makes welfare grants to individuals, and manages a number of funds which provide for local organisations supporting religious work in the community.

West Yorkshire

Bowcocks Trust Fund for Keighley

£2,000

Correspondent: Alistair Docherty, 17 Farndale Road, Wilsden, Bradford BD15 0LW (01535 272657; email: wendy. docherty4@btinternet.com)

CC number: 223290

Eligibility

People in need who live in the municipal borough of Keighley as constituted on 31 March 1974.

Types of grants

One-off grants of no more than £350 are given according to need.

Annual grant total

In 2015/16 the charity had an income of £9,600 and a total expenditure of £7,700. Grants are made to individuals and organisations for both educational and social welfare purposes. We estimate that educational grants to individuals totalled £2,000.

Applications

Initial telephone calls are welcomed. Applications should be made in writing to the correspondent by a third party.

Lady Elizabeth Hastings' Educational Foundation

£129,000 (188 grants)

Correspondent: Andrew Fallows, Clerk, Carter Jonas, 82 Micklegate, York YO1 6LF (01904 558212; email: leh. clerk@carterjonas.co.uk; website: www. ladyelizabethhastingscharities.co.uk/ grants/education)

CC number: 224098–1

Eligibility

Individuals in education who are in need and live in the parishes of Bardsey with East Keswick, Burton Salmon, Collingham with Harewood, Ledsham with Fairburn, Shadwell and Thorp Arch in the North of England.

Grants can also be made to people who have at any time attended one of the Lady Elizabeth Hastings schools in Collingham, Ledston or Thorp Arch, irrespective of whether they are still resident in the area of benefit.

Types of grants

One-off and recurrent grants are given according to need can be given to college and university students, schoolchildren or people in vocational training, apprenticeships. Support can be given towards school uniforms, educational outings, sports equipment and musical instruments, university/college fees and associated necessities, tools, books and so on.

Annual grant total

In 2015/16 the foundation held assets of £15.8 million and had an income of £554,500. Grants were awarded to 188 individuals for educational purposes totalling £129,000.

Exclusions

Grants to purchase computers are only given in exceptional circumstances, however college and university grants are generally made without conditions and may be used towards buying computer equipment.

Applications

Application forms can be found on the foundation's website or requested from the correspondent. Applications can be completed by the individual directly or by a parent/guardian and must be submitted by post at any time a month in advance to the trustees' meeting. The meetings are held four times a year, in early March, June, October and December.

Other information

The foundation is managed by and derives its income from Lady Elizabeth Hasting's Estate Charity. The foundation also gives yearly payments to designated local schools, organisations and clergy to be applied for the benefit of people in the area of benefit.

W. W. Spooner Charitable Trust

£15,000

Correspondent: Michael Broughton, Trustees, 2 Elliot Road, Watford, Hertfordshire WD17 4DF

CC number: 313653

Eligibility

Preference is given for those living in Yorkshire (especially West Yorkshire) and former employees of the Spooner Industries Ltd or their dependants. Scholarships can also be awarded 'for the encouragement of young employees', according to the trust's Charity Commission record.

Types of grants

One-off and recurrent grants are available. Our research suggests that young people who are taking part in voluntary overseas projects and expeditions can be supported.

Annual grant total

In 2016/17 the trust had assets of £2 million and an income of £72,500. The accounts state that grants to both organisations and individuals totalled £50,500; we estimate that around £15,000 was given in grants to individuals.

Applications

Apply in writing to the correspondent.

Other information

The trust mainly supports charitable and community organisations, clubs and groups.

Calderdale

Bearder Charity

£26,500

Correspondent: Richard Smithies, Trustee and Secretary, 5 King Street, Brighouse, West Yorkshire HD6 1NX (01484 710571; email: bearders@ btinternet.com; website: www.bearder-charity.org.uk)

CC number: 1010529

Eligibility

People in need who are resident in Calderdale.

Types of grants

Grants for general educational needs, such as equipment/instruments, tools, travel costs, books, fees, clothing and uniforms, educational outings and so forth.

Annual grant total

In 2015/16 the charity held assets of £3.5 million and had an income of £130,000. Grants to individuals for educational purposes totalled £26,500 with a further £111,000 awarded to individuals for welfare purposes. Grants made to local charities and organisations totalled £55,500 during the year.

Applications

Apply in writing to the correspondent. Applications should outline details of required assistance and anticipated expenses (e.g. a project timetable, cost of items required, travel costs, etc.). Applications can also be made through organisations, such as Citizens Advice or social services, if applicable.

Community Foundation for Calderdale

£22,500 (154 grants)

Correspondent: Community Foundation for Calderdale, The 1855 Building (first floor), Discovery Road, Halifax, West Yorkshire HX1 2NG (01422 349700; fax: 01422 350017; email: grants@cffc.co.uk; website: www.cffc.co.uk)

CC number: 1002722

Eligibility

People in need who live in Calderdale and attend Calderdale College.

Types of grants

Grants of up to £1,000.

Annual grant total

In 2015/16 the foundation held assets of £11.4 million and had an income of £3.7 million. A total of £22,500 was awarded in educational grants to individuals.

Applications

Application forms are available from the College Learner Services and can either be filled out by the student or by a college employee on behalf of the student. Applications must include an endorsement from learner support in the college. Deadline dates are available online.

Other information

The foundation also gives to organisations and to individuals for relief-in-need purposes.

Kirklees

Mirfield Educational Charity

£9,200 (13 grants)

Correspondent: Malcolm Parkinson, Clerk, 6 Rectory View, Thornhill, Dewsbury, West Yorkshire WF12 0NN (01924 456780; email: parkinson922@ btinternet.com)

CC number: 529334

Eligibility

People under the age of 25 who or whose parents live in the former urban district of Mirfield.

Types of grants

One-off grants, usually ranging from £300 to £1,000 are awarded towards educational costs and opportunities, including tuition fees, travel/study overseas, expeditions, projects, living expenses or necessities.

In 2015/16 grants were awarded for purposes including course or tuition fees, travel expenses and expeditions, a student exchange programme, living expenses and accommodation.

Annual grant total

In 2015/16 the charity had assets of £1.5 million and an income of £48,500. Grants to 13 individuals totalled £9,200.

Applications

Applications may be made in writing to the correspondent. The trustees meet at least twice a year.

Other information

The charity also supports schools, groups and other organisations.

Leeds

The Bramley Poor's Allotment Trust

£1,200

Correspondent: Marian Houseman, 9 Horton Rise, Rodley, Leeds LS13 1PH (0113 236 0115)

CC number: 224522

Eligibility

People in need who live in the ancient township of Bramley, especially people who are older, poor and sick.

Types of grants

One-off grants between £40 and £120.

Annual grant total

In 2016 the charity had an income of £3,200 and a total expenditure of £2,400. We estimate that grants given to individuals for educational purposes totalled around £1,200.

Applications

Apply in writing to the correspondent. The trust likes applications to be submitted through a recognised referral agency (social worker, Citizens Advice, doctor, headmaster or minister). They are considered monthly.

The Community Shop Trust (also known as The Leeds Community Trust)

Correspondent: Lynn Higo, Administrator, McCarthy's Business Centre, Suite 23, Enterprise House, Leeds LS7 2AH (0113 237 9685; fax: 0113 278 3184; email: info@ leedscommunitytrust.org; website: www. leedscommunitytrust.org)

CC number: 701375

Eligibility

Children and young people who are in need and live in Leeds.

Types of grants

Small, one-off grants towards the costs associated with education, music and sports.

Annual grant total

In 2016 the trust had assets of £19,200 and a total expenditure of £14,500. Throughout the year the trust awarded a total of £14,500 to individuals for welfare purposes. During the year the foundation did not award any grants for educational purposes, but has in the past.

Applications

Applications can only be submitted by a social worker or care agency on behalf of the individual.

Other information

The trust runs two shops and distributes the profits to local charities, groups and individuals in need, particularly people who are in vulnerable situations.

Kirke's Charity

£1,800

Correspondent: Bruce Buchan, Trustee, 8 St Helens Croft, Leeds LS16 8JY (01924 465860)

CC number: 246102

Eligibility

People in need who live in the ancient parishes of Adel, Arthington or Cookridge.

Types of grants

One-off grants, usually of around £100.

Annual grant total

In 2015/16 the charity had an income of £13,000 and a total expenditure of £7,300. Grants are made to individuals and organisations for both educational and social welfare purposes. We estimate that educational grants to individuals totalled £1,800.

Applications

Applications can be submitted directly by the individual or through a social worker, Citizens Advice or other welfare agency.

Wakefield

Lady Bolles Foundation

£8,300

Correspondent: Stephen Skellern, 6 Lynwood Drive, Wakefield WF2 7EF (01924 250473; email: neil.holland@ wakefield-cathedral.org.uk)

CC number: 529344

Eligibility

People under the age of 21 who live in the county borough of Wakefield and are in full-time education. At the trustees' discretion support may be continued up to the age of 24.

Types of grants

Grants are given towards uniforms, clothing, fees, educational outings, books, travel and maintenance expenses. Apprentices and people starting work are also supported.

Annual grant total

In 2016 the foundation had an income of £9,500 and a total expenditure of £9,000. We estimate that the amount awarded in educational grants to individuals was £8,300.

Applications

Apply in writing to the correspondent. Grants are normally considered in February and October.

The Daniel Gaskell and John Wray Foundation

£9,100

Correspondent: Martin Milner, Clerk, Meadow View, Haigh Moor Road, Tingley, Wakefield WF3 1EJ (07947 611100)

CC number: 529262

Eligibility

People under 25 in full-time education who are living or who have a parent living in the former urban district council of Horbury.

Types of grants

Grants towards the cost of essential clothing, books, tools, instruments and travel required in the pursuance of educational or vocational training in preparation for entry to a profession or trade occupation on leaving school, university or other educational establishment (excluding sixth form college).

Annual grant total

In 2015 the foundation had an income of £23,000 and a total expenditure of £18,400. We estimate that the foundation awarded around £9,100 to individuals for educational purposes throughout the year.

The foundation also gives grants organisations.

Applications

Application forms may be collected from Handyman Supplies, Black Olive Delicatessen, Rickaro Books, Mr K's Newsagents, the Post Office or you can download a form from: www. horburyacademy.com/News/Daniel-Gaskell-Foundation-Form/. Completed forms must be returned directly to the correspondent.

Statutory grants and student support

A complete overview of benefits is beyond the scope of this book. There are a number of organisations which provide comprehensive guides, information and advice to students wishing to study in the UK and overseas. Contact details for these organisations can be found in the 'Contacts and sources of further information' section on page 339.

Statutory provision of both educational and welfare support is extremely complex and continuously changing. The following is intended to act as a signpost to helpful sources of information.

This chapter includes information on:
- Schoolchildren (aged 16 and under)
- Further education
- Student support

Schoolchildren (aged 16 and under)

The following benefits are all administered separately by individual local education authorities (LEAs) which set their own rules of eligibility and set the level of grants. The following information covers the basic general criteria for benefits, but you should contact your LEA directly for further information and advice.

Free school meals

At the time of writing (January 2018) all children in households that have been switched to universal credit also qualify for free school meals. However, under new government proposals households will stop being eligible when their income is more than £7,400 per year (excluding benefits). We are currently awaiting the outcome of the government's consultation on the matter. More information regarding eligibility for free school meals is available from www.gov.uk/apply-free-school-meals.

School clothing grants

In England and Wales, children who attend maintained schools, further education colleges and sixth form colleges may be able to receive help with the costs of their school clothing, including PE kits. However, this is at the discretion of their LEA and the policies (on who can receive help and what items help can be given for) vary widely from area to area. Check with your LEA to find out what the policy is in your area.

As it is not a legal requirement for schoolchildren to wear a uniform, some local authorities do not provide financial assistance to help with the purchase of school clothing. Citizens Advice is campaigning to encourage more parents to challenge local authorities that have policies of not providing financial assistance with school uniforms. More information on this is available from www.citizensadvice.org.uk.

More information on school clothing grants across the UK is available from:
- **England and Wales**: www.gov.uk/help-school-clothing-costs
- (contains a local authority postcode search)
- **Northern Ireland**: www.nidirect.gov.uk/articles/school-uniform-and-uniform-grants
- **Scotland**: www.citizensadvice.org.uk/scotland/family/education/school-and-pre-school-educations/help-with-school-costs-s
- **Wales**: www.gov.wales/topics/educationandskills/schoolshome/parents/uniform

School transport

Generally, children who are between 5 and 16 years old qualify for free school transport if they go to their nearest suitable school and live at least two miles from the school, if they are under eight years old, and three miles from the school, if they are over eight years old. Children who have no safe walking route to school are entitled to free transport, however far from the school they live. There are different requirements for families on low incomes and some LEAs may provide free transport for other reasons. Check with your local LEA for more information.

People who are over 16 years old and in further education may qualify for help with transport costs, although this varies for each LEA.

Local authorities also have to consider any disability or special educational needs when deciding whether transport is necessary for a child. If a child has a statement of special educational needs and disability (known as a SEND) and has transport requirements written into their statement, the local authorities must meet them. Discretionary grants may also be available from LEAs to cover travel expenses for parents visiting children at special schools.

Pupils living in London can also qualify for free transport on London buses and trams if they are in full-time education or work-based learning. For more information, a helpline is available on 0343 222 1234, or information can be found online at www.tfl.gov.uk.

Further education

Depending on their circumstances and the subject being studied, individuals who are in further education may qualify to receive help with the costs of their course, day-to-day living expenses and childcare. More information on the types of funding available can be found at www.gov.uk/further-education-courses/overview.

Student support

Information on financial support available for students can be found at www.gov.uk/browse/education/student-finance.

Advice is also available from your LEA. However, note that the busiest time for LEAs is the period between mid-August (when A-level results come out) and about mid-November (by which time most awards have been given). It is probably best not to contact your LEA for detailed advice at this time, unless absolutely necessary. Students should also check with their university or college for other funds that may be available within the institution.

Supplementary grants

Some students are entitled to extra statutory help; this is currently available through the following forms of support:
- Childcare Grant
- Parents' Learning Allowance
- Adult Dependants' Grant

- Disabled Students' Allowance (DSA)
- 16 to 19 Bursary Fund

Refer to the Gov.uk site referenced at the beginning of the 'Student support' section on this page, for current information on the types of grants available.

Further useful contacts include:
- **Student Finance England**: PO Box 210, Darlington DL1 9HJ (tel: 0300 100 0607; website: www.gov.uk/student-finance)
- **Student Finance Wales**: PO Box 211, Llandudno Junction LL30 9FU (tel: 0300 200 4050; website: www.studentfinancewales.co.uk)
- **Student Finance Northern Ireland**: tel: 0300 100 0077; website: www.studentfinanceni.co.uk)
- **Student Awards Agency for Scotland**: Saughton House, Broomhouse Drive, Edinburgh EH11 3UT (tel: 0300 555 0505; website: www.saas.gov.uk)
- **For students from other EU countries**: Student Finance Services Non UK Team, PO Box 89, Darlington DL1 9AZ (tel: 0141 243 3570; website: www.gov.uk/student-finance)

NHS bursaries

Subject to certain criteria, full-time or part-time NHS students can apply for a bursary from the NHS. Students starting on or after 1 August 2017 should be enrolled on a course that will lead to registering as a:
- Doctor or dentist (you can apply for an NHS bursary from the fifth year of a five or six-year undergraduate course, or from the second year of a four-year accelerated graduate course)
- Dental hygienist or dental therapist

Please visit www.gov.uk/nhs-bursaries for further current information.

NHS Learning Support Fund

Healthcare students starting a course on or after 1 August 2017 may be entitled to support under the Learning Support Fund. Students should be registered on one of the following courses:
- Dietetics
- Midwifery

- Nursing (adult, child, mental health, learning disability, joint nursing/social work)
- Occupational therapy
- Operating department practice
- Orthoptics
- Orthotics and prosthetics
- Physiotherapy
- Podiatry/chiropody
- Radiography (diagnostic and therapeutic)
- Speech and language therapy

Social Work Bursaries

Social Work Bursaries can help with living costs and tuition fees.

For students in England: Social Work Bursaries, PO Box 141, Hesketh House, 200–220 Broadway, Fleetwood FY7 9AS (tel: 0300 330 1342; website: www.nhsbsa.nhs.uk/social-work-students)

For students in Wales: Social Care Wales, South Gate House, Wood Street, Cardiff CF10 1EW (tel: 0300 30 33 444; email: info@socialcare.wales; website: www.socialcare.wales)

For students in Scotland: Scottish Social Services Council, Compass House, 11 Riverside Drive, Dundee DD1 4NY (tel: 0345 60 30 891; website: www.sssc.uk.com)

For students in Northern Ireland: Office of Social Services, Department of Health, Room C4.22, Castle Buildings, Stormont, Belfast BT4 3SQ (tel: 028 9052 0517; email: oss@health-ni.gov.uk; website: www.health-ni.gov.uk)

Teacher training funding

Funding is available for full-time or part-time students on Initial Teacher Training (ITT), Postgraduate Certificate in Education (PGCE) and School-Centred Initial Teacher Training (SCITT) courses through the main student finance avenue. For more details, visit: www.gov.uk/teacher-training-funding.

Department for Education: (tel: 0800 389 2500; website: http://getintoteaching.education.gov.uk)

Professional and career development loans

A professional and career development loan (PCDL) can be a useful means of helping to finance vocational courses for periods of up to two years, particularly if the course offers the prospect of obtaining a steady, reasonably well-paid job at the end.

Loans of between £300 and £10,000 are given to assist individuals who are aged 18 and over who have lived in the UK for at least three years before the start of the course, and who plan to work in the UK, EU or European Economic Area when the course ends.

They are commercial bank loans which must be paid back after the course has finished. Interest is not paid by the individual for the period of study but is instead covered by the government while the student is learning and for one more month after the course is completed (after that the repayment of the loan and the interest is the responsibility of the student).

Full information, including eligibility criteria and how to apply, is available at www.gov.uk/career-development-loans.

Types of schools in the UK and their funding

This section contains information about and details of the types of schools that exist in the UK, how they are funded and how funding can be obtained to attend them.

Local authority-maintained schools

These schools are funded by the local education authority and include foundation schools, community schools, voluntary-controlled schools, voluntary-aided schools, nursery schools and some special schools. They all follow the national curriculum and are inspected by Ofsted.

The Gov.uk website supplies some information about the different types of schools, how to find one and apply for a place. See www.gov.uk/types-of-school for more information.

Academies

Academies are independently-managed schools which are funded directly by the Education Funding Agency and operate outside the control of the local authority. They are set up by sponsors from business, faith or voluntary groups in partnership with the Department for Education and the local authority. In 2016 over 60% of secondary schools were academies. Many factors have caused academies to be a controversial current issue – because of this, there exists a wide range of information available about academies from all perspectives. The Department for Education supplies some details (see www.gov.uk/government/policies/academies-and-free-schools).

Free schools

These schools are non-profit, independent, state-funded schools which are not controlled by the local authority. They are similar to academies but are usually new schools, set up as a response to a demand that is not being met by existing schools.

The New Schools Network provides advice about free schools, including how to set one up. See www.newschoolsnetwork.org or call 020 7537 9208 for more information.

Independent schools

Independent schools are independent in their finances and governance, and are funded by charging parents fees (on average £13,000 a year, or £30,000 for boarders). They set their own curriculum and admission policies and are inspected by Ofsted or other approved inspectorates. According to the Independent Schools Council, around 7% of schoolchildren in the UK are educated in independent schools, with the figure rising to 18% of pupils for those over the age of 16.

Most independent schools offer scholarships and bursaries to some applicants, ranging from 10% of fees to (very occasionally) the full amount of fees being paid. They are subject to fierce competition and are usually awarded on the basis of academic merit, as well as individual need.

A number of independent schools also offer music scholarships, varying from 10% of fees to the full amount of fees being paid (including free musical tuition). Candidates are usually expected to offer two instruments at grades 6 to 8 at least. Contact the director of music at the school you are interested in for more details.

The Independent Schools Directory

The searchable directory lists all the UK independent schools, has an interactive map and offers further details on each school.

Tel: 020 8906 0911

Website: www.indschools.co.uk

The Independent Schools Council

The Independent Schools Council is the main source of information on independent schools. It has a website containing detailed information to help families select the right school and find possible sources of funding.

Website: www.isc.co.uk

The Independent Schools Yearbook

The Independent Schools Yearbook contains details of schools with a membership of one or more of the Constituent Associations of the Independent Schools Council. It is published by A&C Black and can be bought online.

Email: isyb@acblack.com

Website: www.isyb.co.uk

The Independent Association of Prep Schools

The Independent Association of Prep Schools is the professional association for headteachers of the leading 600 independent prep schools in the UK and worldwide.

Tel: 01926 887833

Email: iaps@iaps.uk

Website: http://iaps.uk

The Council of British International Schools

The Council of British International Schools is a membership organisation of British schools of quality, providing British education in Europe and worldwide.

Tel: 020 3826 7190

Website: www.cobis.org.uk

Boarding schools

Boarding Schools' Association

The Boarding Schools' Association serves and represents boarding schools and promotes boarding education in the UK, including both state and private boarding schools.

Very occasionally the local authority may pay for a child's boarding fees, if they have a particularly difficult home situation.

Contact the Director of Education or the Chief Education Officer for the area in which you live (if you live outside the UK approach the area with which you have the closest connection).

Tel: 020 7798 1580

Website: www.boarding.org.uk

Maintained boarding schools

These are state schools that take boarders as well as day pupils; they only charge for the cost of boarding, not for tuition. Boarding costs are generally between £8,000 and £13,000 a year. According to the State Boarding Schools' Association, there are 37 state boarding schools in England. They are a mix of all-ability comprehensive schools, academies and grammar schools. They all follow the national curriculum and take the same examinations as pupils in day state schools.

State Boarding Schools' Association

Tel: 020 7798 1580

Email: info@sbsa.org.uk

Website: www.sbsa.org.uk

Music, dance and stage schools

Choir schools

Choir Schools' Association

The Choir Schools' Association is a group of 44 schools which are attached to cathedrals, churches and college chapels around the country. The majority are fee-paying, with nine out of ten choristers qualifying for financial help with fees through the schools.

Tel: 01359 221333

Email: info@choirschools.org.uk

Website: www.choirschools.org.uk

Music schools

There are various specialist music schools in the UK, with no single umbrella body. Contact the school directly for information about fees and funding.

MMA

MMA is the national association for music teaching professionals. It annually publishes the *MMA Music Directory*, a comprehensive guide to music departments and music scholarships in the UK, which can be purchased on its website.

Tel: 01223 312655

Email: membership@mma-online.org.uk

Website: www.mma-online.org.uk

Music and dance

Music and Dance Scheme

This government scheme is designed to help exceptionally talented young musicians between the ages of 8 and 19, and dancers between the ages of 11 and 19. Means-tested fee support and grants are distributed through specialist centres of education and training and conservatoires. Applications should be made directly to the school or centre you wish to attend. A full list of schools is available on the scheme's website.

Website: www.gov.uk/music-dance-scheme

Foundations for Excellence
The Foundations for Excellence website provides information, guidance and signposting in the areas of health and well-being for young musicians and dancers.

Website: www.foundations-for-excellence.org

Dance schools

Council for Dance and Education Training
Information on dance education and training can be obtained from the Council for Dance and Education Training. It is a quality-assurance body of the dance and musical theatre industries and provides information on its recognised schools and teachers.

Tel: 020 7240 5703

Email: info@cdet.org.uk

Website: www.cdet.org.uk

Dance Schools UK
Dance Schools UK provides a directory of dance schools and teachers across the UK and Ireland.

Website: www.danceschools-uk.co.uk

Stage schools

Federation of Drama Schools
The Federation of Drama Schools was established in 2017 following the closure of Drama UK. It is a group of organisations that provide conservatoire-style vocational training for people who want to be professional performers, theatre makers and technical theatre practitioners.

Email: info@federationofdramaschools.co.uk

Website: www.federationofdramaschools.co.uk

FreeIndex
Using the FreeIndex directory you can browse a list of stage schools in the UK.

Website: www.freeindex.co.uk

Other possible sources of help with fees

Allowances for Crown servants
The Foreign and Commonwealth Office gives grants to enable children of diplomats and other government servants working abroad to attend boarding schools in the UK.

Tel: 020 7008 1500

Allowances for armed forces personnel
The Children's Education Advisory Service (CEAS) provides expert and impartial advice about the education of children of the armed forces personnel.

Children whose parents are members of Her Majesty's Forces are eligible for an allowance towards boarding education, whether their parent is (or whose parents are) serving at home or abroad. This is the Continuity of Education Allowance which is available for children who are eight years old and older. Families are expected to contribute a minimum of 10% towards the fees. Further information on the support available can be found at www.gov.uk/guidance/childrens-education-advisory-service.

Multinational companies
Some multinational companies and organisations help with school fees if parents have to work overseas. A few firms make grants, run scholarship schemes or provide low-interest loans for employees who reside in the UK. Consult your employer for further information.

Alternative routes to employment: apprenticeships

In this section, you will find information on apprenticeships and how to apply for one.

What is an apprenticeship?

Briefly, an apprenticeship is a job that also provides rigorous skills training in order to equip a school leaver with enough experience to work in their chosen field, and improve their career prospects. At the end of an apprenticeship, the apprentice is awarded a nationally recognised qualification.

Types of apprenticeship

Apprenticeship sectors include: agriculture, horticulture and animal care; higher education institutions; arts, media and publishing; business, administration and law; construction, planning and the built environment; education and training; engineering and manufacturing; health, public services and care; information and communication technology; leisure, travel and tourism; postgraduate teaching; financial services; public relations; retail and commercial enterprise; and traffic office.

Training duration

Generally, an apprenticeship takes between one and four years to complete. The duration varies depending on the level of existing skills of the apprentice, the qualification being obtained and the chosen industry sector.

Main benefits

The main benefits of becoming an apprentice are the following:

- You earn a wage during your entire apprenticeship
- There is a guaranteed, nationally recognised qualification awarded to you as you complete each stage of your training
- You gain skills and knowledge which can be used across a range of jobs and industries
- Once the apprenticeship has finished there is an opportunity to carry on working, maybe get promoted or go on to higher education in a college or university
- You can learn at your own pace and get support as and when you need it

Entry requirements

Different apprenticeships have different entry requirements depending on the type of work you will do. However, the most important requirements are the following:

- You must be living in England and not taking part in full-time education
- You must be aged 16 or over
- If you took your GCSEs more than five years ago and did not gain a top grade (A or A*), or you do not have good GCSE grades in maths and English, you will need to take a literacy and numeracy test

Are there any costs involved?

The National Apprenticeship Service supports, funds and co-ordinates the delivery of apprenticeships throughout England. It will pay the costs of your training depending on your age, with any remaining costs met by the employer if you are aged 23 or under.

How to apply

To apply for an apprenticeship or a traineeship, visit the apprenticeship vacancies' website (www. findapprenticeship.service.gov.uk/ apprenticeshipsearch).

Application support

If you would like some help on registering, searching and applying for your chosen apprenticeship, please read the 'How to write a winning apprenticeship application' guide at: www.gov.uk/government/ publications/how-to-write-a-winning-apprenticeship-application.

Company sponsorships

Company sponsorships particularly apply to people in their last year at school who are intending to study a business-related, engineering, or science-based subject at university.

Sponsorship of degree courses

A number of companies sponsor students who are taking degree courses at universities, usually in business, engineering, technology or other science subjects. Such sponsorships are generally for students who are UK residents and are taking their first degree course (or a comparable course).

Sponsorship generally takes the form of cash support (such as a bursary or scholarship) while at university, with a salary being paid during pre-university and holiday employment, or during periods of industrial training at the company concerned. If, for example, the sponsorship is for a sandwich course, the placements will be for longer than the holiday period and will form an integral part of the course. Sponsorships are highly competitive but can be of great value to students who, for any reason, do not receive the full grant. They may also help students avoid having to take out a loan.

Each company has its own sponsorship policy. Some sponsorships are tied to a particular course or institution, whereas others are only given for specific subjects. It is worth noting that the value of the sponsorship also varies. Additional help can be available in the form of discretionary educational gifts or degree prizes.

Sponsorships do not necessarily offer a permanent job at the end of the course (unless the student is classed as an employee). Equally, the student does not usually have to take up a job if offered by the company, although there may be at least a moral obligation to consider the offer.

Students should not decide on a course simply because there may be sponsorship available, they should choose the course first and seek sponsorship afterwards if appropriate.

In most sponsorships it is the student, not the company, who has to make arrangements to get on the course. Indeed some companies will only sponsor students who have already been accepted on a course. However, most university departments have well-established links with the industry and actively encourage students who are seeking sponsorship.

Students should apply for sponsorships as early as possible in the autumn term of their final year at school or college before moving to university.

Further information

Individuals are advised to identify major institutions working in the industry they intend to follow and see what schemes are available. An example of such an institution is The Engineering Development Trust (www.etrust.org.uk), which runs a number of schemes for individuals who wish to pursue a career in STEM (Science, Technology, Engineering, Mathematics) subjects.

Funding for gap years and overseas voluntary work

Gap years have traditionally been a popular choice with school leavers looking to travel, volunteer, work or broaden their horizons in some other way before embarking on university life. With increasingly high costs of education, many feel the need to be extra careful in choosing a career path. A short pause between leaving school and continuing education may be a smart rather than just an adventurous decision. A 'mini-gap', for example, during the summer holidays can equally add valuable experience and skills to a CV and is seen by many universities and potential employers as an advantage in what is a very competitive job market.

There are some opportunities to participate in voluntary work, expeditions and other activities which can be funded or partly funded through charities, bursaries and schemes. For further information on support available in this area see 'Study, work and voluntary work overseas' on page 41. The charities in this section include:

1   Charities that can provide funding towards study or work overseas
2   Grant-makers that can offer support towards volunteering opportunities

Generally, most grant-making charities have quite specific criteria which will not apply to all eligible applicants; it is important to keep this in mind and not assume that you can apply just because you wish to travel to a particular area or place. Likewise, some grant-makers have a particular preference for a certain type of project, for example conservation or one that involves working for the benefit of the local community. They may also give within a specific catchment area, so it can be useful to look at local grant-makers first. Many of the local charities in this guide will give grants under terms such as 'travel overseas' or 'personal development activities'. This allows them to give broadly to a number of different activities which may fall into these categories, such as gap year projects and voluntary work overseas.

It cannot be over-emphasised enough that it is your responsibility to check your eligibility for funding from any charity to which you intend to apply. Please do not apply if you are in doubt of your eligibility. Where appropriate, contact the organisation for further clarification.

If you succeed in gaining financial support, remember that it is always good practice to keep charities informed of the progress of your project and what you have achieved with the funding. This might even be a requirement of accepting the funding. You may also be asked to act as an ambassador to the charity back in the UK by giving talks or presentations on your experiences. This might be something to think about when making your application, particularly if the organisation is keen to involve past participants in promoting its scheme.

It may help your cause if you raise some of the funds yourself. By doing this, it might give you an edge over other applicants and prove how dedicated and determined you are to succeed. You may also find it useful to break down the total costs of your project and apply to several different grant-makers for smaller amounts of money, as this could increase your chances of securing the right amount of funding.

There are other alternatives to funding gap year projects and voluntary work overseas. Many large volunteer organisations provide funded or partly funded volunteering and exchange schemes that will allow you to take part in voluntary work at a minimum cost. Some can offer bursaries to cover specific costs, such as the project fee or flight fare, and others may ask you to fundraise a block amount of money but will pay for all your necessary costs in return.

Below are a few fully or partly funded voluntary schemes available to young people living in the UK.

The European Voluntary Service (EVS)

EVS is a fully funded youth volunteering scheme run by the British Council, the UK's national agency for the Erasmus+ programmes. EVS provides opportunities for young people to volunteer in another European country for two weeks to twelve months.

The scheme is open to all young people aged 17 to 30 who are resident in the UK or one of the other participating programme countries.

EVS placements can be in all member countries of the European Union, the European Economic Area, pre-accession countries and countries neighbouring the EU (Eastern Europe and Caucasus, the Western Balkans and Southern Mediterranean countries).

Most placements last from six to twelve months and priority is usually given to longer-term placements, short-term placements are however also available. Placements can be organised in variety of sectors (including the social, cultural, environmental and sports sectors) and are chosen by the volunteers themselves.

All EVS projects are fully funded by European Commission grants, which are applied for by the applicant's sending organisation. The grant covers the costs of travel, food and accommodation, insurance, training and living expenses and provides volunteers with a modest living allowance.

In order to take part in an EVS project, volunteers have to find a suitable host organisation to volunteer with and a sending organisation from their own country to sponsor them.

More information on programme countries, sending organisations, host organisations, projects and other information regarding EVS can be found on the European Youth Portal website (www.europa.eu/youth/eu_en).

Note that applicants are advised to plan their projects, preferably six months in advance (as the process can take this long to complete).

In addition to applying for a volunteer placement with EVS directly, it is also possible to organise a placement through certain volunteering organisations that are linked to the EVS programme. The Inter-Cultural Youth Exchange (www.icye.org.uk) and International Voluntary Service (www.ivsgb.org) will help volunteers through the application process and will sometimes carry out administrative work on their behalf. If you are interested in volunteering with EVS, it may be worthwhile contacting one of these organisations for help.

Students from the UK will be able to apply for Erasmus funding until 2020. Applications received after the point that the UK leaves the European Union will still be eligible for approval. Updates on the UK's Erasmus membership can be found at www.erasmusplus.org.uk/brexit-update.

Lattitude Global Volunteering

Lattitude Global Volunteering is a UK-based volunteering organisation and registered charity (Charity Commission no. 272761) that organises volunteer placements in developing countries for young people aged 17 to 25, as well as offering bursaries and funded projects for applicants in need of financial help. Volunteers can take part in a number of different projects, such as camps and outdoor education, as well as environmental, medical and community projects. More information about the opportunities that Lattitude Global Volunteering can offer is available from the charity's website (www.lattitude.org.uk).

The Jack Petchey Foundation

The foundation supports young people aged 11 to 25 who live in Essex or London who are raising money in order to be involved in a voluntary project or participate in events that will benefit others in society. Grants are given to cover up to 50% of the cost of the project (but no more than £300 per person). Full details of eligibility criteria and how to apply can be found on the foundation's website (www.jackpetcheyfoundation.org.uk).

Project Trust

Project Trust is an educational charity which specialises in overseas volunteering placements for school-leavers. Young people aged between 17 and 19 are given training and support to undertake voluntary teaching and social care projects abroad lasting around eight to twelve months. Living allowances are provided by the trust or by the overseas host. More details on the opportunities available can be found on the trust's website (www.projecttrust.org.uk).

Other helpful contacts

www.igapyear.com
iGapyear.com provides advice on how to put together a proposal for a funding application as well as offering other information on gap year and volunteering opportunities.

www.gapyear.com
An online community where backpackers and gap year travellers can meet, chat and share experiences.

www.idealist.org

Idealist.org is an independent online network of non-profit and voluntary organisations that provide information on voluntary opportunities worldwide.

www.eurodesk.eu/edesk

The website holds information on European policies and opportunities for young people.

www.yearoutgroup.org

Year Out Group is an association of organisations running gap year and volunteering projects. The website provides general information for people planning to take a year out and offers the details of member organisations.

Volunteer organisations

www.vsointernational.org

www.frontier.ac.uk

www.raleighinternational.org

Contacts and sources of further information

Many people in education and training need financial advice and help from time to time. It is usually best to contact somebody at one of the following organisations as a starting point:

- The educational institution you are studying at
- Your local education authority
- Your local Citizens Advice or other welfare agencies

These organisations will be in the best position to point you in the right direction for further or more specialist advice if necessary. For resources that offer information and advice in specific areas, readers should also see the details listed in the preceding sections:

- Statutory grants and student support (page 323)
- Types of schools in the UK and their funding (page 327)
- Alternative routes to employment: apprenticeships (page 331)
- Company sponsorships (page 333)
- Funding for gap years and overseas voluntary work (page 335)

We have put together the following list of organisations that provide information and guidance on a broad range of issues.

General

Citizens Advice
Provides free, independent, confidential and impartial advice to everyone on their rights and responsibilities. Find your local bureau or get advice online at www.citizensadvice.org.uk.

England: 03444 111 444

Wales: 03444 77 20 20

Scotland: 0808 800 9060

Northern Ireland: contact your local bureau (find your local bureau online at www.citizensadvice.co.uk/get-advice)

Department for Education
Piccadilly Gate, Store Street, Manchester M1 2WD (tel: 03700 002288; website: www.gov.uk/dfe).

Department of Education for Northern Ireland
Rathgael House, Balloo Road, Rathgill, Bangor, County Down BT19 7PR (tel: 028 9127 9279; email: de.dewebmail@education-ni.gov.uk; website: www.education-ni.gov.uk).

Education Scotland
Denholm House, Almondvale Business Park, Almondvale Way, Livingston EH54 6GA (tel: 0131 244 4330; email: enquiries@ educationscotland.gsi.gov.uk; website: www.education.gov.scot).

Gov.uk
General advice and information on government services.

Website: www.gov.uk

The Money Advice Service
The Money Advice Service helps people to manage their money, providing a free and impartial advice service. It also works in partnership with other organisations to help people to make the most of their money. It is an independent service set up by the government.

Holborn Centre, 120 Holborn, London EC1N 2TD (tel: 0800 138 7777 (English), 0800 138 0555 (Welsh); Typetalk: 18001 0800 915 4622 (Mon to Fri 8 am to 8 pm, Sat 9 am to 1 pm); email: enquiries@ moneyadviceservice.org.uk; website: www.moneyadviceservice.org.uk; and an online chat facility is also available).

The Prince's Trust

The Prince's Trust helps people aged 13 to 30 who are unemployed or struggling at school to transform their lives.

Prince's Trust House, 9 Eldon Street, London EC2M 7SL (tel: 0800 842842; website: www.princes-trust.org.uk).

Welsh Assembly Education and Skills

Cathays Park, Cardiff CF10 3NQ (tel: 03000 604400 (English and Welsh); email: customerhelp@gov.wales; website: www.gov.wales).

Children

Child Poverty Action Group (CPAG)

CPAG publishes a number of guides which include information on state benefits and entitlements for both schoolchildren and students.

Child Poverty Action Group, 30 Micawber Street, London N1 7TB (tel: 020 7837 7979; email: info@cpag.org.uk; website: www.cpag.org.uk).

CPAG in Scotland, Unit 9, Ladywell, 94 Duke Street, Glasgow G4 0UW (tel: 0141 552 3303; email: staff@cpagscotland.org.uk).

National Youth Advocacy Service

Tower House, 1 Tower Road, Birkenhead, Wirral CH41 1FF (tel: 0151 649 8700; helpline: 0808 808 1001 (Mon to Fri 8 am to 8 pm, Sat 10 am to 4 pm); email: main@nyas.net or help@nyas.net; website: www.nyas.net).

Youth Access

1–2 Taylors Yard, 67 Alderbrook Road, London SW12 8AD (tel: 020 8772 9900; email: admin@youthaccess.org.uk; website: www.youthaccess.org.uk – an online directory of information, advice and support services for young people).

Further and continuing education

City and Guilds

City and Guilds provides support to learners and training providers.

1 Giltspur Street, London EC1A 9DD (tel: 0844 543 0033; email: learnersupport@cityandguilds.com; website: www.cityandguilds.com).

Learning and Work Institute

National Learning and Work Institute, Chetwynd House, 21 De Montfort Street, Leicester LE1 7GE (tel: 0116 204 4200; email: enquiries@learningandwork.org.uk; website: www.learningandwork.org.uk).

Higher Education

The National Union of Students (NUS)

NUS UK, Macadam House, 275 Gray's Inn Road, London WC1X 8QB (tel: 0845 521 0262; email: please use online contact form; website: www.nus.org.uk).

NUS Scotland

1 Papermill Wynd, McDonald Road, Edinburgh EH7 4QL (tel: 0131 556 6598; email: mail@nus-scotland.org.uk; website: www.nus-scotland.org.uk).

NUS-USI

42 Dublin Road, Belfast BT2 7HN (tel: 028 9024 4641; email: info@nistudents.org; website: www.nus-usi.org).

NUS Wales

2nd Floor, Cambrian Buildings, Mount Stuart Square, Cardiff CF10 5FL (tel: 029 2043 5390 email: office@nus-wales.org.uk).

The Open University (OU)

The Open University, PO Box 197, Milton Keynes MK7 6BJ (tel: 0300 303 5303; email: please use online contact form; website: www.open.ac.uk).

Scholarship Search

Search scholarships in the UK for pre-university, undergraduate and postgraduate learning.

Website: www.scholarship-search.org.uk

Student Awards Agency for Scotland (SAAS)

Saughton House, Broomhouse Drive, Edinburgh EH11 3UT (tel: 0300 555 0505; email: please use online contact form; website: www.saas.gov.uk).

Student Cashpoint

Information on student grants, loans, bursaries, scholarships and awards.

Website: www.studentcashpoint.co.uk

University and Colleges Admissions Service (UCAS)

Rosehill, New Barn Lane, Gloucestershire GL5 3LZ (tel: 0371 468 0468; website: www.ucas.com).

UCAS can also be contacted via social media.

Applications for full-time university degree courses must be made through UCAS (part-time degree courses and the Open University are not covered by UCAS – apply directly to the university).

Careers

National Careers Service

The National Careers Service provides information, advice and guidance to help people make decisions on learning, training and work opportunities. The service offers confidential and impartial advice, supported by qualified careers advisers.

National Careers Service, PO Box 1331, Newcastle upon Tyne NE99 5EB (tel: 0800 100900; website: www.nationalcareersservice.direct.gov.uk; an online chat service is also available).

Not Going to Uni

Opportunities for people leaving school or college that are outside the traditional university route, including apprenticeships, sponsored degrees, diplomas, gap years, distance learning and jobs.

Mountcharm House, Ground Floor 102–104, Queen's Road, Buckhurst Hill IG9 5BS (tel: 020 3691 2800; email: info@notgoingtouni.co.uk; website: www.notgoingtouni.co.uk).

Prospects

Graduate careers website for jobs, postgraduate courses, work experience and careers advice.

Prospects, Booth Street East, Manchester M13 9EP (tel: 0161 277 5200; website: www.prospects.ac.uk).

Students with disabilities

Disability Rights UK

National pan-disability organisation led by people with disabilities that provides advice to students with disabilities.

Plexal, 14 East Bay Lane, Here East, Queen Elizabeth Olympic Park, Stratford, London E20 3BS (tel: 0330 995 0400; email: enquiries@ disabilityrightsuk.org; website: www. disabilityrightsuk.org).

Lead Scotland

Set up to widen access to learning for young people and adults with disabilities and carers across Scotland.

Room B05, Edinburgh Napier University, Merchiston Campus, 14 Colinton Road, Edinburgh EH10 5DT (tel: 0131 228 9441; email: enquiries@lead.org.uk; website: www. lead.org.uk).

Study overseas

The British Council

Advice and publications on educational trips overseas.

British Council Customer Service UK, Bridgewater House, 58 Whitworth Street, Manchester M1 6BB (tel: 0161 957 7755; email: please use online contact form; website: www. britishcouncil.org).

Erasmus

Erasmus enables higher education students, teachers and institutions in 32 European countries to study for part of their degree in another country.

Tel: 029 2092 4311; email: erasmus@ britishcouncil.org; website: www. erasmusplus.org.uk.

Overseas students

Refugee Women's Association

Provides advice and guidance on education, training, employment, health and social care for refugee women throughout London.

Print House, 18 Ashwin Street, London E8 3DL (tel: 020 7923 2412; email: info@refugeewomen.org.uk; website: www.refugeewomen.org.uk).

United Kingdom Council for International Students' Affairs (UKCISA)

UKCISA provides information for overseas students on entering the UK, as well as general advice.

9–17 St Alban's Place, London N1 0NX (advice line: 020 7288 4330; website: www.ukcisa.org.uk).

Other funding or sources of help

Community Foundations

These local organisations sometimes have a pot of money available for individuals to apply for. Use the website to identify your local community foundation.

Unit 1.04 Piano House, 9 Brighton Terrace, London SW9 8DJ (tel: 020 7713 9326; website: www. ukcommunityfoundations.org).

Money Saving Expert

A British consumer finance information and discussion website providing information and journalistic articles to help people save money.

Website: www.moneysavingexpert. com

Prisoners' Education Trust

Access to a grants programme to enable prisoners in England and Wales to study through distance learning. The trust also provides advice and support, influences policy and advocates best practice.

The Foundry, 17 Oval Way, London SE11 5RR (tel: 020 3752 5680; website: www.prisonerseducation.org. uk).

Index

What else can DSC do for you?

Let us help you to be the best you possibly can be. DSC equips individuals and organisations with expert skills and information to help them provide better services and outcomes for their beneficiaries. With the latest techniques, best practice and funding resources all brought to you by our team of experts, you will not only boost your income but also exceed your expectations.

Publications

We produce fundraising directories and research reports, as well as accessible 'how to' guides and best practice handbooks, all to help you help others.

Training

The voluntary sector's best-selling training, with courses covering every type of voluntary sector training.

In-house training

All DSC courses are available on your premises, delivered by expert trainers and facilitators. We also offer coaching, consultancy, mentoring and support.

Conferences and fairs

DSC conferences are a fantastic way to network with voluntary sector professionals while taking part in intensive, practical training workshops.

Funding websites

DSC's funding websites provide access to thousands of charities, grants, statutory funds and corporate donations. You won't get more funders, commentary and analysis anywhere else. Demo our sites free today.

www.dsc.org.uk/**fundingwebsites**

@DSC_Charity
For top tips and special offers

Visit our website today and see what we can do for you:

www.**dsc**.org.uk

Or contact us directly:
publications@dsc.org.uk